THE BIRDWATCHER'S YEARBOOK 2021

Edited by Neil Gartshore

Calluna Books

Published in 2020 by
Calluna Books
Moor Edge, 2 Bere Road, Wareham
Dorset BH20 4DD
United Kingdom

phone: 01929 552 560 ~ 07986 434 375
e-mail: enquiries@callunabooks.co.uk
website: www.callunabooks.co.uk

ISBN 978-0-9933477-6-4
ISSN 2048-7258

Cover photograph: by Neil Gartshore
In a family of its own (*Panuridae*), the Bearded Tit *Panurus biarmicus* is a popular resident species associated with reedbeds, with about 630 pairs breeding in the UK. They are a sociable bird and usually noisy - their distinctive 'ping' calls are often heard first, alerting the observer to their presence. The late summer and early autumn is a particularly good time to look for them as post-breeding groups move around the reedbeds.

Black & white illustrations: by Dan Powell
phone: 01329 668 465
e-mail: danpowell11@btinternet.com
website: www.powellwildlifeart.com

Printed and bound in Great Britain by
Ashford Colour Press Ltd
Gosport, Hampshire

CONTENTS

CONTENTS

PREFACE

COVID19 & *The Yearbook*

After a brief consideration as to whether there should be a *Yearbook* for 2021, the decision was made to go ahead and work began as the country was coming out of lock-down. It is obviously impossible to say when things are going to be 'back to normal' as the situation is changing on an almost daily basis.

In preparing this edition, the assumption has been made that we will be back to normal in 2021. The information in the 'County Directory' assumes that Bird Club/RSPB Local Group indoor meetings will resume; in the 'Reserves Directory' that reserves and their facilities be open and that transport will be operating as normal; and that any other activities listed elsewhere will be running.

However, due to the uncertainty for the foreseeable future, **IT IS ADVISABLE** to contact the groups, the reserves or the event organisers to check to see if any restrictions are still in place.

2020 is going to be a year to remember for all of us. From a birding point of view, it will be about a trip cancelled or put off; 'lock-down birding' in our own gardens and local patches; and frustrations of missing out on our annual rituals - about the regular birds we missed, not just what we saw. Nature itself has had mixed fortunes. With less disturbance (and good weather) in the spring many species had a good breeding season - bird song was more noticeable... a cuckoo was recorded from my road in Wareham (heard early one morning by my daughter, who didn't think to wake me ...a few brownie points lost there!)

Unfortunately there were inevitably downsides. Once lock-down began to lift, the countryside attracted large numbers of people and a big increase in disturbance - images of parked cars blocking roads in Snowdonia spring to mind. Locally to me, we lost a huge chunk of Wareham Forest (mainly internationally important heathland) to a fire - it took a week to finally extinguish the hot-spots. An indeterminable number of reptiles were killed; Nightjar and Dartford Warbler territories disappeared with nests (eggs or chicks) gone; and other wildlife/important habitats were burnt to a cinder. The likely cause: disposable barbecues!

On a positive note Hen Harriers have had a good breeding season in England - with 60 young raised from 19 nests across the northern Pennines (giving a total of 141 chicks over the last three years) and, after breeding for the first time in 2015, ten pairs bred on Lewis (Outer Hebrides). In both cases a good 'vole year' has been a factor. Unfortunately there has also been evidence of an increase in raptor persecution (including harriers) around the country - with no one out there to try and stop this barbaric activity, those involved have almost had free range to do what they like.

As I write this we are all still subject to restrictions and the next few months (even years!) will be affected by the events of covid19. Many of the conservation organisations have furloughed staff and in some cases have made redundancies. I would urge everyone to continue supporting these organisations through these times to help them continue the valuable work that they do... become a member/renew your membership; make a donation; or, where practical, offer your time.

From early 2020 all clubs and RSPB groups cancelled their programmes of indoor talks (and outdoor walks) and speakers were rearranged... with bookings running into 2022. A number of groups took the opportunity to embrace modern technology with 'zoom' meetings (or other packages) being used to deliver talks. The annual Bird Fair in Rutland was also cancelled early on, leaving a big gap in birdwatching's social calendar. In its place though came the 'Virtual Bird Fair' where many exhibitors had a virtual stand and a programme of events and lectures were delivered online - it was good to have access to them for three months after the event, may be this will be repeated next year.

••••••••••

As usual I would like to thank everyone who has responded to my queries over information contained in the *Yearbook* to ensure that it is as up to date and as accurate as possible. If you come across any errors, omissions or changes before the next edition please let me know (contact details below).

Best wishes, and lets hope for a better 2021.
Neil Gartshore
Wareham, September 2020

CONTACT US

The information contained in *The Yearbook* is sourced/checked in a number of ways ...websites, magazines, personal contacts, e-mails, phone calls, and so on. Once *The Yearbook* has been published there will inevitably be changes to some of the information that will not be amended until the next edition.

If someone has stepped down from a role you should be redirected to the new contact.

If you have any comments on this edition of *The Yearbook*, corrections to advise us of or suggestions for future editions, we would be pleased to hear from you.

*****

Neil Gartshore, Moor Edge, 2 Bere Road, Wareham, Dorset BH20 4DD
phone: 01929 552 560
e-mail: enquiries@callunabooks.co.uk

From the results of the 2019 Breeding Bird Survey,
the Wren *(Troglodytes troglodytes)* remains the UK's commonest bird.
(Illustration: Dan Powell)

FEATURES

RECORDING, DOCUMENTING & ARCHIVING OUR COUNTY BIRDS

Every birdwatcher has, no doubt, at least one avifauna, bird atlas or bird report on their bookshelves - usually covering their own county or may be a part of the country they visit regularly or have a connection to. These publications hold a wealth of information and are important historical documents - where else can we find records of species that are declining or increasing around the UK today to see where they were once common or scarce?

After a scattering of early titles, avifaunas for most counties began appearing during the latter part of the Victorian era. Atlases have become more frequent since *The Atlas of Breeding Birds in Britain and Ireland* was published in 1976, first covering the country as a whole and more recently down to a county level. Bird reports or reports of birds were becoming common place by the mid-1900's (usually in the 'transactions' of a local natural history society, before stand alone reports began to appear).

Current technology, and the number of observers in the field, has moved bird recording on in leaps and bounds. With available (and developing) software, millions of records can be stored electronically and extracted at will to study some aspect of a species population and distribution in a regional, national or global context.

The three articles in this feature look what we already have: at the history and the people behind the early avifaunas and atlases; the experience of actually writing a modern-day avifauna; and a personal perspective on county bird reports.

"AVIFAUNAS, ATLASES & AUTHORS"

David Ballance is an authority on County birds, writing a number of books on the subject. His latest is a personal view of the development of local ornithology including biographical details of authors, a discussion on atlases and an updated bibliography.

This title ***(see page 327)***, published by Calluna Books in February 2020, is a successor to my *Birds in Counties*, published in 2001 by Imperial College Press and followed by three *Supplements* from 2002 to 2015. These works are the fruit of a lifelong interest in the local ornithology of the United Kingdom, including the Isle of Man and the Channel Islands; the Irish Republic was also involved from 2008, but is excluded from the present work. Since 1959, I have collected relevant books and pamphlets, and by the 1990s, I felt the need of an updated bibliography, since the standard works by W.H.Mullens and his collaborators took the record no further than 1918. On my retirement from teaching in 1996, I was free to complete the research for *Birds in Counties*. This included detailed citations of all works with annotated species lists for areas from a garden up to a county, including papers in journals and annual reports. It was based on the 1900 boundaries, but included maps that showed changes in these up to 1998. The county sections were preceded by a brief history of local recording in the UK. Although the work was in general well received, and it has come to be seen as a standard reference book on its subject, its price was somewhat forbidding to all except the dedicated enthusiast.

I had originally hoped to include more critical discussion of the main works, and more personal and biographical detail on their authors, but space did not allow this. In the last twenty years, my collection of avifaunas has expanded to over a thousand titles, and I have managed to acquire photocopies of many of the rarest works: some of these are sections of well-known county histories; others are typescripts of surveys or early atlas attempts deposited in public libraries. So, before I started the present work, in 2018, I already owned most of the material that I needed, and it proved possible to complete "*AAA*" in just over a year, with the assistance of many helpful correspondents.

"AVIFAUNAS, ATLASES & AUTHORS"

The county boundaries & the text format

It was first necessary to re-organize the county arrangement into the current Recording Areas. In England, only four of the new creations of 1974 have been sustained as these: Avon and Greater Manchester are now entirely separate units, though the latter has ceased to produce an annual report; Cleveland, though responsible for its own verifications, is also reported on by Durham and Yorkshire; and West Midlands shares its report with its three parent-counties. Much of the mediaeval county system still survives. Wales has sensibly adopted a slightly modified version of the Watsonian Vice-counties; and Scottish recording has been roughly aligned with the 1974 "Regions", but with "Clyde Islands" and Caithness as separate Areas.

All Recording Areas, except some Scottish islands, are given separate sections which are subdivided into five parts: a short note on ***Boundary Changes***; the major section, ***The County/ Area and Its Literature***, where a brief topographical word-picture is followed by details of the development of its ornithology, including the major figures and their works, which may be illustrated; and some ***Facts*** on area and population. Then comes the bibliography of ***Principal Works***: first those on the whole Area, and then the more local ones.This section is a shortened and updated version of the listings in *Birds in Counties*, including almost all books and pamphlets, and many survey reports, but only the most important papers in journals, the selection of which may depend on the existence of a recent avifauna for the Area. If none exists, as in a number of Scottish Areas, a wider selection of papers will be given. Some very small (and often privately published) pamphlets are omitted. Apart from one or two atlases, no on-line material is included. The Area entry ends with a summary of local ***Journals***, which is in general confined to those that appeared in at least four years; on-line reports are not mentioned, unless they are continuations of a series that began in hard copy.

The authors

Readers who have access to *Birds in Counties* and its *Supplements* (none of which are available on-line) will probably find the greatest interest here lies in two subjects. The first is the biographical background to authors, especially those who died before 1920. Most of these came from the learned professions or the landed gentry, but increasingly also from prosperous industry or commerce; some were rich enough to devote their lives to collecting eggs and skins. By 1890, almost all the rail network existed, and its reach could be extended by the bicycle. The car was at first something of a rich man's toy; until the 1920s, it did not bring into the countryside many of the newly-termed "bird-watchers" (and many "oologists" with them). Some late-Victorian and Edwardian avifaunists were figures of astounding and prodigious energy, parallels to Dickens or Trollope in literature, or to Stephenson and Brunel in engineering: Lord Lilford and Harvie-Brown are well-known (and they were rich men, with no need to practise a profession), but George Bolam and Churchill Babington and Hugh Macpherson are in their way just as extraordinary, and they all had careers to make outside natural history. It is true that they were supported by their wives and housekeepers, and by domestic service, so that they never had to boil an egg, or lay a fire, or make a bed, but they did not waste their leisure staring passively at screens, and they later maintained huge circles of correspondence and waited for hours on freezing railway platforms.

George Bolam, Northumberland

"AVIFAUNAS, ATLASES & AUTHORS"

The atlases

A second feature of "*AAA*" is the history and nature of local atlases. Experimental work on these was first attempted over a century ago, and some early maps have here been reprinted, though the modern era of atlasing began with the national work (including Ireland) published in 1976 and followed by four county atlases. A further 30 of these followed up to 1999, and 45 counties or Areas have been covered since. These totals include second and third attempts as separate works. I was not aware that any overall discussion has appeared on these as a group. They obviously have much in common: all show distribution for summer or winter or both, over a period of at least three seasons, and by tetrad (apart from some islands, which use a square kilometre), most follow the triage system of breeding categories established for the first National Atlas, and many attempt the more difficult task of showing abundance. In order to produce an effective comparison between 28 of the more recent works, I compiled species-richness maps of identical iconography, of which nine are reproduced. Two-thirds of all these surveys were derivatives of the two most recent National BTO Atlases; the remainder were locally controlled. My own maps help to illustrate features discussed in the text, some to do with habitat (such as altitude, river valleys and coast) and others relating to the organisation, timing and competence of observers, and to such issues as access and residence.

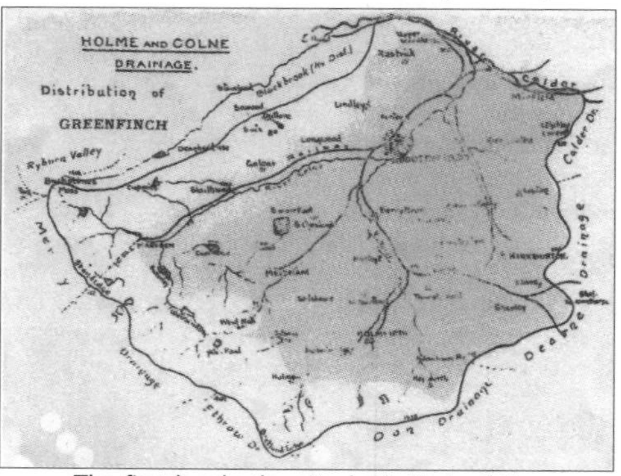

The first local atlas: Mosley's Birds of the Huddersfield District (1912-15) [Greenfinch]

The book ends with a farewell to School Natural History Societies. Only a few survive, but in my generation (and indeed for the previous century), they fired the enthusiasm of many boys who later became famous in local ornithology,and in the wider world.

I should perhaps add that down the years I have been an outsider to the world of ornithology, an amateur at heart, with no scientific or mathematical training. However, in the past 20 years I have continued my membership of the Editorial Committee of our local report, *Somerset Birds*, which I joined in 1963. I was involved, from 2009 to 2014, in the production of our first County Atlas, an interesting experience; for this, I wrote much of the species-text, and covered about 45 tetrads, as well as organising the work of local co-ordinators.

On Exmoor: Stanley Lewis collecting (1930s),
The author (DB) surveying (2007)

DIARY OF A COUNTY AVIFAUNA

Jason Reece is one of the principle authors of the latest county avifauna to hit the book shelves and shares his experience of getting the publication to press.

Why would anyone want to write a county avifauna?

This was a question which went through my mind on a number of occasions when I was helping to correct the seventh draft of *The Birds of Nottinghamshire* in the autumn of 2019. I was one of a team of five authors, including four members of Nottinghamshire Birdwatchers, who had seen the project through from the first optimistic meeting in The Nelson public house in Winthorpe in East Nottinghamshire to the point where, with the final corrections sorted out, Liverpool University Press could publish a new book on the birds of the county. The journey from conception to publication had taken eight years. In that time, we had all learnt a great deal about the challenges of producing an avifauna. This article is intended to review that experience and to give some helpful guidance to others who are contemplating taking on the same task.

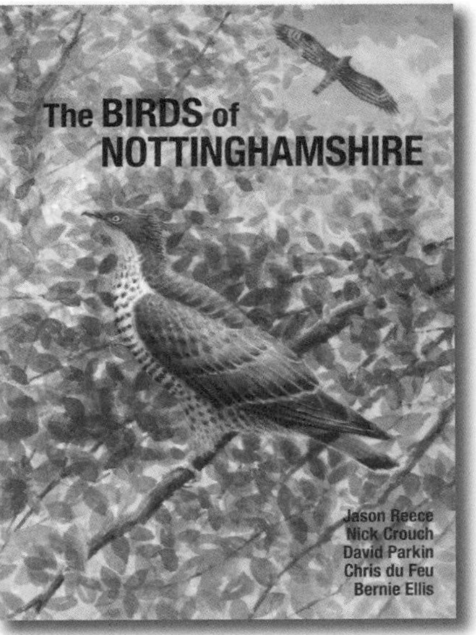

In the beginning...

The first issue to get sorted out is what you want to cover and, perhaps more importantly, what it is possible to produce.

At our first meeting, we had decided that we wanted to produce a full account of the birdlife of the county rather than an atlas or a work covering a narrow time frame but we had not got much further than that. We didn't have a very clear idea about how long things would take, who might publish the work and what we needed to include beyond an account for each species. Nor had we decided what the cut off date for records would be or how we would deal with issues such as copyright, funding, sourcing of photographs or the checking historical records. We were, in short, high on motivation and enthusiasm but less well geared up in terms of the practical requirements of writing and publishing a full account of the birdlife of the county. This meant that we were storing up some problems which would need to be addressed as the project evolved.

Out in the middle of the stream

Having set off with enthusiasm, the actual writing of the avifauna is bound to be a long haul and there is a need to maintain the momentum of the project.

In the case of *The Birds of Nottinghamshire*, three things worked in our favour from the outset. Firstly, Nottinghamshire Birdwatchers had received a significant financial legacy which put an end to the worries we had about the funding of the avifauna - otherwise it would have been necessary to have a small team working on fundraising. Secondly, we were lucky with regard to some of our local resources and contacts. We were able to draw upon the services of an internationally recognised artist, Michael Warren, who volunteered to produce a sketch of every species on the county list. We were also fortunate to have good links with the BTO, the RSPB, local ringing groups and the Nottinghamshire Wildlife Trust, all of whom provided us with key data.

Thirdly, we were fortunate to have the services of individuals with the knowledge and commitment to drive the project to completion. David Parkin played a key role in pushing the avifauna forward. He had the knowledge, drive and energy to cajole accounts of various species from tardy authors or, if that failed, to sit down and write these accounts himself drawing upon data from a wide variety of sources.

We also made some important decisions about the shape and design of our book as it became clearer that there were limits to what we were capable of producing ourselves. We soon realised that we would not be able to publish the avifauna without help and linked up with a suitable publisher with the specialist knowledge and experience of producing other county avifuanas to assist us through the project. The use of Liverpool University Press proved to be an inspired choice as they were receptive to a number of significant changes to the layout of pages and alterations to the draft text in the months leading up to publication.

We also reached a broad consensus position about what we wanted to include in the accounts of each species and how we wanted to present each account. The key aim was to produce a detailed and informative account of the status of each species to aid future researchers. We decided that the text for each species should therefore include a mix of the objective research material and more local information such as peak counts or early and late dates for migrants. By using this information, we hoped to be able to go beyond a simple narrative account for each regularly occurring species and to produce an analysis of the status of a given species in the county and population trends over time. For the rarer species, we wanted to move away from a bare listing of the records of rarities to include comparative information about national and regional patterns of occurrence. With these decisions in mind, we opted for a basic layout of one page for the rarer species and two pages for the more frequently occurring birds. This worked reasonably well as the draft accounts, sketches, maps and photographs were brought together and we were able to edit and adjust the account for each bird around this basic framework.

Not everything was plain sailing at this stage. There were inevitable compromises in terms of what we able to cover within the resources that we had. Over-ambitious plans to consider museum specimens and to conduct an extensive review of old paper records fell by the wayside. We also struggled to find authors for a number of species until quite late in the day and spent a good deal of time standardising the accounts which came in, partly as a result of our failure to produce clear guidelines for authors at the outset. We also expended quite a lot of time sourcing a county map and good local photographs for individual species, with some regularly occurring species (such as Common Redshank and Barnacle Goose) proving surprisingly difficult. There were also some subtle errors with the interpretation of the species data which took a significant amount of time to resolve. All of these things were eventually sorted out but used up plenty of energy.

Crossing the finish line

The last phase of the project was, by turns, the most frustrating and the most rewarding stage. For a long time, it seemed that we had a text which was almost ready to be published but which, as it was checked and rechecked, seemed not to be quite the finished product. This was an anxious phase in the process as there always seemed to be a danger that, in striving for perfection, the point of publication would never be reached and the passage of time would erode the validity of what had been written.

The key point to keep in mind is that the checking phase doesn't last for ever and that most errors will be chased down in the end. I remember experiencing a huge sense of relief when the last draft was finally sent off to the publishers. I have spotted one or two errors since then but I am keeping these to myself!

DIARY OF A COUNTY AVIFAUNA

A view from the armchair

The new *Birds of Nottinghamshire*, the first new account of the birdlife of the county in over forty years, was eventually published at the end of 2019. The county has therefore become the 36th of the 42 English recording areas to have published a full avifauna since 1980 and the 26th to have done so in the new millennium. This total includes Shropshire who published their avifauna at the same time, plugging another gap in the local ornithological record for England.

At 594 pages, our book has taken its place amongst other heavyweight works in what David Ballance, the eminent authority on local bird recording in Britain, has described as '*An Age of Great Volumes*'. As Ballance has detailed, there can be few other parts of the world with such a long history of local ornithological recording. This is a valuable inheritance. In Nottinghamshire the pioneering work of William Sterland, Joseph Whitaker and Austen Dobbs provided a strong foundation for the new county avifauna and a baseline against which the rise and fall of individual species could be measured. It is hoped that we have now extended that narrative and I would certainly encourage others to continue to work to fill in the local gaps which remain across the British Isles.

The project has inevitably come with a cost, most notably in the time spent on drafting and redrafting the text by a small team of volunteer authors. As a result of the attention given to the avifauna, the regular publication of the annual report has also been set back by a couple of years or so and we are having to work hard to try to catch up. However, that cost has to be measured against the fact that there is now a detailed point of reference for anyone keen to understand the birdlife of the county.

For me, the key reward of the project has been to read the fresh insights of my fellow authors about individual species which are scattered throughout the work. Examples which caught my eye ranged from an analysis of the impact of pollution upon a population of Grey Herons nesting in the east of the county and a detailed study of breeding Nightjars in west Nottinghamshire.

Want to write your own county avifauna?

My ten key recommendations for future authors would be to:

- Identify who is to publish the work at an early stage. An experienced publisher may be able to guide you through some of the issues (such as copyright and funding) which are likely to arise.
- Identify a core editorial team as soon as possible. Try to include a good blend of experience in the team and identify people with the time and energy (and literary skill) to see the project through.
- Decide the scope of the work and the cut-off date for the avifauna as soon as possible and try to keep to it as the project evolves.
- Draw up some clear guidelines about standard information you want to include about each species. The aim ought to be to produce as comprehensive and authoritative an account for each species as possible to serve as a point of reference for future analysis.
- Work out what else you want to include and exclude. Sections which are likely to compliment the main body of the work are likely to include chapters on methods, habitats and a section upon the history of local recording.
- Identify other sources of relevant material at an early stage and try to establish strong links to those organisations which will hold key records (i.e. local bird clubs, the BTO, ringing groups and the county wildlife trust).
- Try to allocate key tasks to named individuals from the outset. It is likely to be helpful to have small teams working on fundraising, artwork and photography and mapping and data analysis.
- Set a provisional date for publication and try to stick to it. Beware of setting an overambitious target date.
- Draw up a programme of future meetings to maintain oversight of the work. However, meetings are no substitute for getting on with the job!
- Be prepared to devote a great deal of effort to the checking stage. This is a necessary final hurdle.

Albert Spinks (L), slew an Egyptian Nightjar in 1883 - Joseph Whitaker (R), his master, rescued it from a rubbish heap.

BIRD REPORTS - the past, the present & the future

Steve Holliday offers an outlet to buy & sell bird reports (& other selected items). He shares his thoughts here on the subject.

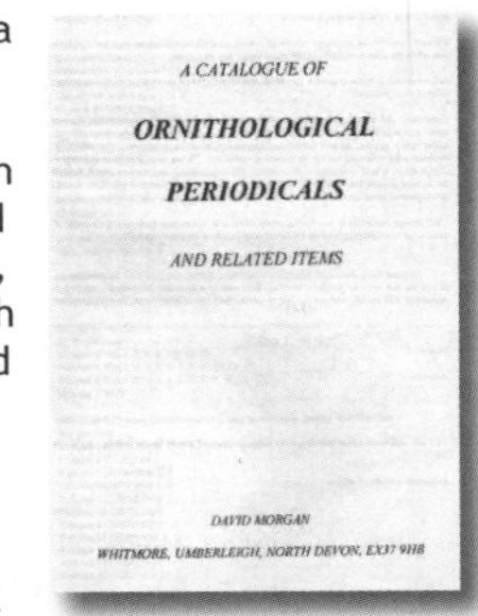

A CATALOGUE OF
ORNITHOLOGICAL
PERIODICALS
AND RELATED ITEMS
DAVID MORGAN
WHITMORE, UMBERLEIGH, NORTH DEVON, EX37 9HB

I've been collecting books and local bird reports ever since I was a teenager in the late 1970s. In the early 1980s I came across David Morgan's adverts in *British Birds* and subsequently added to my run of *British Birds* journals, which I have since been lucky enough to complete. The periodic catalogues issued by David, were pored over in detail immediately after they came through the letterbox, as these small catalogues were really the only way to acquire such journals, short of visiting numerous second-hand bookshops. David had started the business in 1976, but when he moved abroad in 1996 it was Doreen, his mother, who had kept things going.

Several events took place in 2012 which started my alarm bells ringing. Not one of us are getting any younger and I've found that the older one gets the less keen we can be when it comes to keeping 'clutter'. In a short space of time I heard about a large stock of county bird reports going into a skip following the death of a long-standing county stalwart and this was followed by a friend of mine passing to me a black bin bag of reports which were literally going into the dustbin later that day (this bag also contained a really rare Hancock Museum publication which I have since had bound). In September 2012 I attended the York Book Fair and picked up a presentation copy of Nethersole-Thompson's book *The Snow Bunting*, complete with signed presentation certificate pasted inside; I later found out that the original owner had passed away and his widow had very quickly disposed of his lifelong collection via a school, charity shops and the like - actually referring to her late husband's collection as 'Jim's rubbish'! By now, I was having serious concerns about just how many bird reports and other journals were fast disappearing from existence.

In November 2012, I heard that Doreen Morgan had sadly passed away and that David was looking for a buyer. I mulled the idea over but the day job made things difficult. In early 2013 an old friend, Derek Clayton, commented that it was a shame there was no-one around to fill the gap left by Doreen (ebay and AbeBooks don't meet everyone's needs) so, despite the day job, a few emails later I found myself agreeing a deal to purchase all the bird reports from David, whilst a second visit saw me collect a range of other birding journals. My first catalogue followed soon after in April 2013.

Having been a collector for many years myself, I know how difficult (even impossible) it is to find specific reports; I had been trying to complete my own run of Yorkshire bird reports for around 35 years and still needed the offprint for 1942 (since obtained thanks to a kindly donation). I could be wrong but I suspect that print runs in the past would have been much larger than some of today's. I am aware of some current print runs being as low as 100 e.g. a well-known bird observatory, or even lower. My own county of Northumberland used to print over 1,000 copies of the annual bird report in the 1970s but this has now reduced to 350-450 in recent years. Some southern counties have a much larger membership than we have locally and I suspect that print runs are in the order of 1,500 or more. The problem is, the print run (50, 100 or 1,500 etc) for a specific report, is merely a starting position. Over time, and for various reasons, the number of copies in existence then only goes in one direction i.e. downwards. And, once that number reaches zero, a report has been lost forever. My notes show that the BTO Library is missing over 50 pre-WWII county bird reports, perhaps extinct already? Every county bird club should have an archivist and archive (!) to ensure this doesn't happen.

BIRD REPORTS - THE PAST, THE PRESENT & THE FUTURE

The Biodiversity Heritage Library currently includes only a small number of bird reports e.g. Scottish, Welsh and Yorkshire, on its website and as a consequence we are very fortunate that we have the BTO Library, managed by Carole Showell, which is accessible to researchers on request. Carole's aim is to archive copies of <u>every</u> county's bird reports (plus ringing groups, nature reserves etc) and a great job Is being done in this respect (details of missing reports can be found at https://www.bto.org/about-bto/library/new-bird-reports). I'd like to think I'm helping in some small way and have added quite a number of reports to the Library over recent years.

My main role is one of a 'go-between', someone who happily accepts or pays for collections when a birder/collector decides they want to 'downsize' and move their journals on to equally 'good homes'. I have a great working relationship with the Scottish Ornithologists Club, who regularly receive their own donations and then 're-cycle' material to me and through me to others. I have a database of collectors where I have many hundreds of 'wants' logged on their behalf.

HASLEMERE EDUCATIONAL MUSEUM
SURREY BIRD REPORT
— FOR —
1954
Obtainable from the
HASLEMERE EDUCATIONAL MUSEUM, HASLEMERE, SURREY
Price - - Two Shillings and Sixpence

Collectors include people who seek reports for say their own county or favourite site, or perhaps all the bird observatories, or maybe a range of coastal sites due to an interest in seabirds, or even any of the older bird reports reflecting an interest in the history of ornithology. Many bird reports hold significant amounts of sought-after artwork, with artists like James Alder, Robert Gillmor, Dennis Harle (see Sandwich Bay example), Richard Richardson and Charles Tunnicliffe (see Surrey example), all providing their work over many decades.

For anyone wishing to learn more about what and when has been published in the UK, Isle of Man, Ireland and Channel Islands, then look no further than David Ballance's superb works 'Birds in Counties' (2000), its three Supplements (2002, 2009 and 2015) and his recently published 'Avifaunas, Atlases & Authors' (2020).

I have seen the value and purpose of county bird reports being questioned in a number of quarters (letters in *British Birds*, debates at local level and so on) and it's fair to ask the question given the resource hours and cost of production. For many years, recognition in the annual *British Birds* best bird report competition (last run in 2001) was something valued very highly and this certainly inspired report authors/editors to up their game. Many of the reports published in recent years are of an incredibly high standard; the B5 sized reports for example, for Bardsey and Spurn Bird Observatories, Hampshire, Isles of Scilly and Yorkshire, to name but a few, are magnificent productions. Digital photography, superb artwork and colour production, combine to produce publications and important records for, hopefully, many years to come.

Achieving total accuracy should be the paramount aim and it is also important of course not to overlook the (currently) common species; I think it is probably quite rare to see a list of 'other species also recorded' listed at the end of a report these days. The use of graphs, tables, comparisons with the recent past and so on, all help to portray a picture and place current year data into context. I guess the key is having a willing team and the finances in order to keep producing such reports.

BIRD REPORTS - THE PAST, THE PRESENT & THE FUTURE

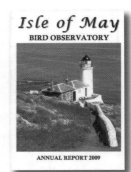

There are other approaches worthy of consideration. For example, since 2009 the Isle of May Bird Observatory, and possibly others, have taken the step to produce two versions of their annual report. The printed paper version is a slim 64 or 68 page output which includes mainly the systematic list, summary ringing report and colour photographs only on the cover pages, whereas the accompanying CD includes an all-colour extended bird report, full ringing and other reports plus several colour photo galleries and additional articles.

Other options inevitably involve an Internet-based version, usually in pdf form. In addition to the hardcopy version, some counties have also digitised many of their annual reports which can be found freely available on Club websites, for example the London Natural History Society and the Lundy Field Society. Additionally, some reports are now found only online in pdf form, for example, Cape Clear and Skokholm Bird Observatories, and Scarborough. However, I may be of the 'old school' as a big part of me would still like to experience the feel and enjoyment one gets from holding the original production. Are websites ever permanent? Having a run of bird reports bound up makes them both great to look at on the bookshelf and as permanent as can be.

In my view, the annual bird report is the pride and joy of the local or county birding community. It provides an opportunity for every birder to make their mark in history, and for upcoming researcher/writers to develop their skills, for local artists to either cut their teeth or demonstrate artistic ability and for local photographers to show off their skills. More importantly, the report becomes a readily available record of the important birding events that took place that year, whilst showing what the status of birds was at a local level at that point in time. Many reports include important research papers with for example, the Kent bird report for 1996 containing the full, 138 page, 1988-94 breeding bird atlas for the county. Other areas e.g. Kent and Northumberland, have also helpfully produced an online bibliography of articles published in their county bird reports.

In its own way, one of the first natural history books and indeed most successful books of all time, namely, 'The Natural History of Selborne' first published in 1789, was a form of bird report, detailing as it did, the species seen and phenological matters, albeit in a very different style to today's publications. I wonder what would Gilbert White think of today's crop of bird reports? I think he'd be delighted and would say 'long may they continue'!

If you are interested in bird reports and are looking for specific copies you can find Steve's current catalogue on the Calluna Books website or contact Steve directly.
See page 326 for details

Two iconic bird report cover designs from the 1960s...

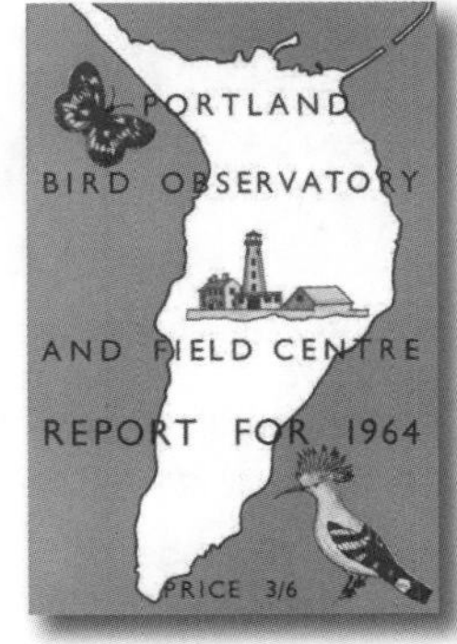

HELPING KENYA'S DAKACHA FOREST

Ann Scott provides an update on a project in East Africa helping to save an important area of coastal forest and its special wildlife.

Photos: Large Spotted Genet (A Rocha/camera trap); Sokoke Scops Owl (Mustafa Adamjee)

In 2014, a plea from A Rocha (The Christian Conservation Society) for help to save some of the wonderful forest in Kenya, resulted in the purchase of 219 acres of the Kenyan Coastal Forest in the Dakacha area, with funds from the Bob Scott Memorial Appeal (BSMA).

The area is now known as the Kirosa Scott Reserve and is watched over and maintained by A Rocha Kenya. Knowing of its importance for many African, Inter African, Eastern European and Asian species, as well as the endemic species found there, we have together now increased ownership of the forest to 1,128 acres and are still raising funds to purchase further land. Whilst continuing to survey the surrounding undamaged forest, which may be available for purchase, the A Rocha team have set camera traps. Some exciting and unexpected animals have been captured on film making it even more essential for us to extend the landholding.

Community Involvement

The BSMA is also helping 13 villages, who have formed themselves into the "Tujipange Community Based Organisation (TCBO)", to replant forest in the Gedi area, spreading northwards, including the hillsides around Lake Jilore. This lake is a wonderful area which holds many species of water birds at certain times of the year. The TCBO, under the guidance of Albert Baya, have successfully planted over 6,900 trees in the last three years - losing just 14 of them despite the lack of rainfall at times! These trees are mainly indigenous species and their presence has already seen the return into the area of many of the once abundant local species that have been missing for a number of years - one such bird that recently returned is the African Cuckoo Hawk. We CAN achieve success if we work with local people and that it what the BSMA is increasingly doing whilst trying to ensure the continued expansion of the ownership of Dakacha Forest by A Rocha.

TO LEARN MORE about the project or TO MAKE A DONATION, visit: www.whyTSbirds.org

Ann has a number of talks available about the project/the area.
For more information/contact details see her lecturer's listing on page 213.

NEWS FROM THE WORLD OF BIRDS

James Lowen offers a selection of the past year's interesting stories about wild birds from across the UK.

Illustrations: Dan Powell

Rare breeders

'Long legs' (long-legged waterbirds) seem to be continually in the news. **Cattle Egret** continues its colonisation, breeding for the first time in Norfolk (four pairs) and West Sussex (five pairs) during 2020, after nesting in three new counties during 2019. A controversial project seeking to establish **White Stork** as a UK breeder claimed success. Three pairs bred in West Sussex during 2020, with one of the males considered wild rather than feral. More than 100 storks have so far been released at three sites in the county.

Eurasian Bittern goes from strength to strength, with 198 'booming' males at 89 sites in 2019 (2018: 188 at 82). In 2019, a record 56 pairs of **Common Crane** bred countrywide, up two on 2018 and included the first in Lincolnshire for 400 years. The result of intensive conservation action, the total population is estimated to be 200. **Eurasian Spoonbill** has recolonised Britain entirely naturally, and a new UK Spoonbill Working Group has been established to collate and monitor their fortunes. Since 2010, more than 300 youngsters have fledged from the principal colony at Holkham, Norfolk. A pair of Black-winged Stilts bred successfully in Somerset, raising two chicks.

Among shorter-legged rare breeders, **Savi's Warbler** nested in Wales for the first time in 2019. Concern that Scotland's dwindling population of **Capercaillie** faces a 'genetic bottleneck' has prompted a DNA-based project to determine relatedness and estimate true numbers. Part of the growing phenomenon of 'biodiversity offsets', a housing-estate developer in Devon has been obligated to pay £430,000 to create new habitat suitable for five pairs of **Cirl Bunting**. In 2019, just 870 territorial male **Corncrakes** were counted across Scotland – a decline of more than 30% since 2014. Irish Corncrakes have declined by 85% since the 1970s, but hopes have been raised by the European Union's €4.3 million grant to fund four years of conservation action, which aims to deliver a 20% increase in the population by 2024.

The reintroduction of **White-tailed Eagles** on the Isle of Wight has had mixed fortunes. By October 2019, of six birds released two months previously, one had died with another missing. A third soon relocated to Oxfordshire/Buckinghamshire, then it and the three remaining birds went 'fly-about' across the country during spring 2020 – when their movements coincided with a notable influx of wild, continental eagles.

Finally, May and June 2020 saw an unprecedented influx of **Blyth's Reed Warblers** to Britain, with at least 35 singing males noted countrywide, several establishing multi-day territories. It surely cannot be long before this species becomes a UK breeding species...

NEWS FROM THE WORLD OF BIRDS

Seabird hope... and concern

Britain's sole regular colony of **Roseate Tern**, on Coquet Island (Northumberland), reached 122 pairs in 2019 - breaking the previous year's record by four pairs. The species also bred in Scotland during 2019, albeit by dint of hybridising with a **Common Tern** on the Isle of May (Fife). **Arctic Tern** was less fortunate. The UK's largest colony (2,814 pairs in 2019) normally breeds on The Skerries (Anglesey), but deserted the site during 2020. Because of the COVID-19 pandemic, no summer wardens were able to guard the colony, leading to disturbance from **Peregrines**.

Meanwhile, the RSPB has used satellite-tracking data to identify the location of marine hot-spots for **Kittiwake**, **Common Guillemot**, **Razorbill** and **European Shag**. For the first three species, mapping reveals particularly important feeding areas off Scotland's east coast, Yorkshire and Pembrokeshire, as well as around Rathlin Island (Northern Ireland). The RSPB hopes that the maps will inform spatial marine planning to protect wide-ranging seabirds in the context of constructing fossil-free energy-generation infrastructure in UK waters.

A Scottish Natural Heritage report suggests that the decline in **Scotland's breeding seabirds** may be slowing. Although overall numbers have dropped by a third on average since 1986, populations seem to have remained broadly stable since 2011. The removal of rodents and American Mink may partly explain the resurgence - a theory that may have inspired the RSPB to subsequently deploy a sniffer dog on 41 protected seabird islands.

Annual surveys suggest mixed picture

The BTO's **2019 Breeding Bird Survey** revealed contrasting fortunes. **Greenfinch** numbers have fallen by nearly two-thirds in 23 years, largely due to a parasite that causes the disease trichomonosis, first noted in UK finches in 2006. The same malady also affects **Chaffinch**, whose numbers have dropped by 18% since 1994, but not **Goldfinch**, whose populations have more than doubled over the same period. **Eurasian Wren** remains the UK's commonest bird, and its 30% increase in 23 years suggests an estimated population of 11 million individuals.

Another BTO publication, the 2018/19 Wetland Bird Survey (WeBS) report, demonstrated that **Greater Scaup**, **Common Goldeneye**, **Common Pochard** and **Purple Sandpiper** are becoming increasingly dependent on protected areas. Indeed, in Northern Ireland, virtually no Pochard occur outside reserves. The UK's wintering population of **Ruddy Turnstone** reached its lowest-ever total, being down a quarter on the 10-year trend. **Eurasian Curlew** was up slightly on the previous winter, although the overall long-term trend remains for this globally Near Threatened species remains firmly downward. **Whooper Swan** and **Bewick's Swan** wintering populations are going in opposite directions: the former is at its highest-ever value, the latter at historically low levels. A separate study suggests that, across half-a-century, Bewick's Swan wintering grounds have shifted east by 13 km/year - a phenomenon known as 'short-stopping'.

NEWS FROM THE WORLD OF BIRDS

Scientific insights

Two particular ecological studies caught the eye this year. The first revealed how the absence of urban invertebrates adversely impacts bird populations. Urban insect populations would need to increase by a factor of 2.5 for 'townie' **Great Tits** to have the same breeding success as conspecifics breeding in forests. The second publication demonstrated that the ear of the **Great Cormorant** is specially adapted to hear underwater - something not previously demonstrated for any waterbird. The revelation sits in the context of oceans being increasingly affected by noisy human activities such as ship traffic and wind-turbine construction.

Hen Harriers

Never out of the news, **the much-loved raptor** suffered another tricky year. Natural England's roundly criticised solution to the species's parlous status in England - the 'headstarting' of captive-bred youngsters - fell at the first hurdle. All five youngsters raised during 2019's 'brood management' scheme went missing (presumed dead) by June 2020. Four of the birds disappeared in northern England's uplands - a region that has become notorious for raptor persecution. Conservationists continue to argue that better regulation within the shooting industry is a better way forward than relocating young birds. Natural England nevertheless licensed brood management in 2020. There was some modest good news, however. In Northumberland, Hen Harrier bred for the fifth successive year in 2019, with six pairs producing nine young from three successful nests. In 2020, a dozen pairs bred successfully on moorland estates in Lancashire (six), Cumbria (four) and Yorkshire (two).

Wildlife crime

Even without accounting for Hen Harriers, **wildlife crime** provided disturbingly recurrent headlines. Raptors proved the main subject of illicit attention, with the RSPB's *Birdcrime* 2018 report revealing 87 confirmed incidents of persecution, up 19 from 2017. Victims included 31 **Common Buzzards**, 27 **Red Kites** and six **Peregrines**. The true scale of activities is undoubtedly greater: satellite-tagging data and other intelligence suggest that many more birds have been killed but remain unfound. Two-thirds of incidents occurred in England, with 'black-spots' identified in the Peak District and North Yorkshire and a continued association apparent between raptor persecution and grouse-moor management.

In December 2019, the Scottish Government's **Independent Grouse Moor Review Group** issued its long-awaited report. It recommended the introduction of a shooting licensing scheme if breeding populations of raptors show no marked improvement over the next five years, as well as new or enhanced regulation of grouse-moor management practices. At the time of writing, the Scottish Government has yet to respond.

Figures for raptor killing during 2019 and 2020 are not yet in, although the RSPB announced a surge in illegal killing during the COVID-19 lock-down - from three or four per week to the same number per day - presumably due to reduced detection risk.

Raptors were not the only victims of wildlife crime, of course. The past year has seen numerous instances of birds killed illegally. An illegal bird trader was found guilty of selling wild-caught **Barn Owls**, while an illicit trap targeting **finches** was seized by Essex police, and an unlawful bird-trading ring was uncovered in east London.

NEWS FROM THE WORLD OF BIRDS

Falcon controversies

Two Government decisions on falcons sparked uproar among birders. In May 2019, Scottish Natural Heritage issued a licence for up to 150 **Gyr Falcons** to be temporarily released in Moray between June and September. Releases (which apparently include hybrids as well as pure Gyrs) are for the purposes of 'hacking' and must be satellite-tagged. Concerns have been raised about the impact on predation of native birds.

In April 2020, Natural England issued licences for three falconers to take two chicks each from the nests of wild **Peregrines**, in an attempt to establish a stud book of British-born Peregrines for falconers to keep. Natural England stipulated that only the smallest chick could be taken from a brood of at least three, arguing that only two chicks normally survive to adulthood so this would have negligible effect on the wild population.

Gamebird releases

In June 2020, Wild Justice - established by Mark Avery, Chris Packham and Ruth Tingay - announced that the High Court had approved the campaigning organisation's application for a judicial review of the impacts of vast releases of non-native gamebirds, namely **Common Pheasant** and **Red-legged Partridge** on sites of high nature-conservation importance. The judicial review is due to take place by end October 2020. Were the crowdfunded review successful, it would likely have big impacts on gamebird shooting.

Places... bad news and good

After the 2019 **fire** that destroyed Fair Isle bird observatory, the element ravaged a number of important nature sites during 2020's hot, dry spring. Four heathlands important for European Nightjar among other rare species - Dorset's Wareham Forest, Surrey's Thursley and Chobham Commons and South Yorkshire's Hatfield Moors - went up in flames, as did Britain's largest reedbed, Tay Reedbeds (Tayside). Meanwhile, the high-speed train development known as HS2 has prompted outrage, with a report by the Wildlife Trusts setting out the vast scale of destruction to nature that it will cause.

In better news: a new 'super' National Nature Reserve has been created on the Purbeck heaths of Dorset; the sensitive dunes at Coul Links (Highland) have been spared conversion into a golf course; Askham Bog (North Yorkshire) has escaped development; the National Trust is to transform a golf course on the Lincolnshire coast into a 3,500-hectare nature reserve; and intriguing new wetlands are taking shape in Lincolnshire and Norfolk.

British list

Finally, the British list has grown by one species to 621 (**White-rumped Swift** from East Yorkshire in 2018). Three new subspecies have also been added: **'Taiga' Merlin** (nominate *columbarius*), **'North American' Horned Lark** (of the subspecies group *alpestris/praticola/hoyti*) and **'Mandt's' Black Guillemot** (*mandtii*).

BEST BIRD BOOKS OF THE YEAR

Despite recent restrictions, Gordon Hamlett has gathered together a wide selection of some of the year's new titles.

We all know that it has been a dreadful year, and it is fair to say that the bird book industry has had its share of problems too. There were several books that I wanted to include in this article, but have been unable to obtain a copy. Some titles, I have only seen as PDFs, not ideal, but better than nothing. I would like to take this opportunity to thank all the various PR people who have gone above and beyond the call of duty in helping me write this article.

Nevertheless, there is still a wonderful selection of books to peruse. You can do your bit to help this sector of the economy by asking for, and giving bird books as presents. And if you can source them through your local bookshop, so much the better.

Field Guides etc.

The most discussed book this year is the second edition of **Britain's Birds** (Hume et al, Wild Guides, £19.99). Totally updated, there are 800 new photos out of a total of 3,500. It is bang up to date with taxonomy too, and is particularly strong on subspecies. Every last inch of space is cram packed with information, including plenty of tables comparing the key features of similar species. The downside is that it is too heavy to be carried in your pocket, so one for the car maybe.

There are a few minor niggles. There is no mention of Coues's Arctic Redpoll, a term used in many of today's magazines. The maps need some updating too. For example, there are no longer any Golden Eagles in the Lake District and Ravens are now spreading into East Anglia and Essex.

I don't normally mention a book's cover; it is what it is. But I think that the publishers have made a serious error here. Both editions feature Robins and I can see a lot of people walking past a display and assuming that they already have the book. You really need a new species to separate the two editions.

That said, this is a stunning achievement and even those normally allergic to photographic guides will find more than enough new information to justify your outlay. At £20, you can't get more bangs for your buck. And I've already seen it for sale at £15... Undoubtedly the bargain of the year. If you like this format, then I can also recommend **Europe's Dragonflies** (Smallshire & Swash) and **Britain's Ferns** (Merryweather) in the same series.

It is almost a given that the best new foreign field guide is published by Helm. **Birds of Mongolia** (Gombobaatar Sundev & Leahy, £29.99) features over 500 species in the now traditional format of text and maps on one page, with the plates opposite. A mandatory choice for visitors.

Whether it is their colourful plumage or their amazing courtship displays, surely there can't be a more fascinating family of birds than Birds of Paradise. As well as the hundreds of photos, the latest identification guide from Helm, **Birds of Paradise and Bowerbirds**, (Gregory, £54.99) also covers their biology, taxonomy and relationship with humans. It is guaranteed to get your juices flowing, and with two more books featuring New Guinea (see below), visitors to this part of the world will have used up most of their luggage allowance already. Self recommending.

For those not planning to travel quite so far, two European field guides are likely to appeal to those planning a holiday to the Mediterranean next year. **Birds of Cyprus** (Richardson & Porter, Helm, £29.99) follows the traditional map and text on one page, with the plates - there are 95 - opposite. There is also a guide to the best birding hot-spots on the island, as well as information on what to do if you see any illegal shooting going on. An excellent one-volume guide for visitors.

Birds of Greece (Nason, Bloomsbury, £9.99) is aimed at the more casual birder, someone on holiday with their family perhaps. Slim enough to fit in your pocket, this is a photo guide to the country's commoner species.

Crime

Jeffrey Lendrum turned from a promising birder into an egg collector, before he started stealing Peregrine eggs to hatch and sell on to collectors in the Middle East. **The Falcon Thief** (Hammer, Simon & Schuster, £16.99) tells his story, and the attempts of a British policeman to bring him to justice. A few Americanisms aside, it reads like a true-life whodunnit.

By a strange quirk of fate, I came across **Scourge of the Birdman** (Tarvie, £14.99 from Amazon), the story of a convicted egg collector. The same police officer features prominently here too (albeit under a pseudonym), and suffice to say, the two books differ wildly in how that character is portrayed. As there may be libel cases pending in the future, I am saying no more, except to say that is worthwhile reading both books side by side.

Fans of Steve Burrows' Birder Murder series will need no encouragement to seek out the latest title in the series, **A Dance of Cranes** (Point Blank, £8.99), which again sets DCI Jejeune against his nemesis in Norfolk while simultaneously trying to solve a crime involving Whooping Crane migration in North America.

Sky Dance (Burns, Vertebrate Publishing, £9.99)is a strange book to categorise. To start with, it is a novel, set on an imagined Scottish island, and tells the story of the conflict between a landowner and environmental protesters over how the moors should be managed, illegal Hen Harrier persecution and so on. As the author says though, just because the names and settings are fictional, doesn't mean that the book isn't true...

Coffee-table books

If you have ever dreamed of seeing birds-of-paradise, are planning a trip to the country, or simply an armchair traveller, then **New Guinea** (Beehler, Princeton, £24.99) is the book for you. Sumptuously illustrated, it tells you all you need to know about New Guinea's wildlife, history and culture.

I missed out on leading a trip to the Scottish Highlands this year due to Covid, but fortunately, I had a copy of **The Secret Life of the Cairngorms** (Howard, Sandstone Press, £24.99) to fill the void. The breathtaking pictures of the wildlife and landscape remind me why I got rid of my camera; I was never going to compete at that level. If the Highland Tourist Board doesn't make good use of theses images, then someone needs to be looking for a new job.

Half of me wishes that **Red Sixty Seven** (ed Jewitt, BTO, £19.99) had never been published. Easily my favourite art book of the year, it features our 67 most vulnerable species, each painted by a different artist. Some styles you will like, some you won't. I have to confess that the dead Wood Warbler doesn't do it for me, though I have bought one of the other paintings.

BEST BIRD BOOKS OF THE YEAR

What makes this different though is that accompanying each picture is an essay, written by a top birder, celebrity or whoever, explaining why each individual species matters to them. Here's Simon Barnes (see On the Marsh below) writing about Savi's Warblers. '...like some great singer with the perfect tour schedule: Carnegie Hall, Royal Albert Hall and my back garden.'

One of the items on every birder's bucket list must be the high tide roost at Snettisham, with many tens of thousands of waders swirling around your head. Surely, you think to yourself, there must be more of these spectaculars elsewhere in the world. **Pacific Highway** (Benedict et al, Sasquatch Books, £24.99) will blow your mind. Covering wildfowl and wader migration from Arctic Russia down to Tierra del Fuego, the photos are jaw-droppingly stunning, ranging from huge flocks of waders and individual portraits to one of my personal favourites, a family of six Snowy Owls perched on a bit of driftwood.

Personal accounts

Who wouldn't want to own a bit of marshland in Norfolk? In **On the Marsh** (Simon & Schuster, £16.99), Simon Barnes has just moved house, and here he is exploring his new back garden, accompanied by his Down's Syndrome son Eddie. As you might imagine, his garden list is pretty spectacular. This is Barnes' most personal books, and one of his best.

It would have been easy to include **Diary of a Young Naturalist** (McAnulty, Little Toller, £16) in the children's section, forget about it and move on, but it so much more than that. Already featured as Book of the Week on Radio 4, Dara uses nature as a way of coping with his autism. His ability to write though is hugely uplifting, and you wonder if he can do this as a teenager, what is he going to do next?

Alan Stewart is a former wildlife detective and his books have featured regularly in these articles. **Walking with Wildlife** (Thirsty Books, £15) looks at how nature changes over the course of a year on a 13,000 acre Perthshire Estate. This is a huge patch to explore, set in a part of Scotland little visited by tourists.

Somewhat further afield, **Owls of the Eastern Ice** (Slaght, Allen Lane, £20) is part travelogue, part research project as the author tracks Blakiston's Fish Owls in the Primorye region of eastern of Russia, with a view to putting long term conservation plans into place to protect the future of the world's largest owl. A great story of a little-known bird and an even less well known region of the world.

Getting the army to pay for your travel is a great way of birding round the world. In **More Birds than Bullets** (https://morebirdsthanbullets.yolasite.com/ £14.99), Geoffrey McMullan details his birding adventures and conservation projects across several continents. Like many self-published books, it is a bit rough round the edges, but the anecdotes are all fresh and the book is an entertaining read.

In **Wintering** (Rutt, Elliott & Thompson, £12.99), the author takes delight in the huge flocks of geese that visit our shores every winter, following them through a variety of landscapes and weather. A nice, easy read, this is the ideal book to tuck yourself up with on a cold, dark winter's night, when the Pinkfeet have long since gone to roost.

How do you sum up a country's avifauna? There are many different approaches but the one taken by Conor O'Brien works perfectly well; take twelve iconic species that have somehow evaded you and go off in search of them. **Ireland through Birds** (Merrion Press, £14.99) sees the author seeking out such species as Hen Harriers, Corncrakes, Ring Ouzels, Great Skuas and Jack Snipe.

BEST BIRD BOOKS OF THE YEAR

In **Native** (Birlinn, £14.99), Patrick Laurie embarks on a new career - cattle farming in Galloway. As he struggles to preserve some of the old methods, he also gets tied up in Curlew conservation, a bird whose numbers have declined dramatically, due in part to afforestation on a massive scale. This will appeal to those who like to remember the countryside as it once was, rather than how it is now.

Fans of Guardian columnist Paul Evans will be delighted to read a selection of his musings about the countryside and all its quirks in **How to See Nature** (Batsford, £8.99). As well as essays on different habitats, there is a chapter on re-introduced species both in the immediate past such as Red Kites, and potentially in the future such as examining the benefits wolves could bring to the Scottish Highlands.

Scientific books

County avifaunas are a strange beast. Of immense interest if you happen to live in the area covered, they have a much reduced appeal if you live elsewhere. One thing that has improved beyond all recognition over recent years are the extremely high production values that we now see, with high quality computer mapping illustrating at a glance, regional abundances, and gains and losses over recent years.

Liverpool University Press has published a series of superbly produced titles over recent years. **Birds of Shropshire** (ed Smith, £44.99) is the latest and covers over 200 species, all accompanied by colour photographs. A must have if you go birding in the county regularly.

Two books look at different aspects of bird behaviour. There's not as much food as normal. Daylight hours are much reduced and marauding raptors want nothing more than to make a meal of you. **Birds in Winter** (Pasquier, Princeton UP, £24.99) examines just what strategies birds need to adopt in order to survive this most challenging of seasons. Illustrated with some delightful black and white drawings, this book expands our knowledge considerably, putting a lot of flesh onto what was previously a meagre set of bones.

Just as important as surviving from day to day is the need to pass on your genes to the next generation. **Bird Love** (Tong, Ivy Press, £24.99) looks at everything concerned with the mating process: nest building, display, monogamy and its alternatives and so on. Well illustrated, this book presents its ideas in bite-sized chunks and is ideal to dip into.

Buzzards are our commonest bird of prey; on a recent trip to the Scottish Highlands, I stopped counting after 180 sightings. **The Common Buzzard** (Walls & Kenward, Poyser £59.99 hb, £34.99 pb) is the 100th monograph from the Poyser stable, covering everything from the bird's biology, its hunting techniques to its relations with man. Whether you are simply interested in raptors, or a collector of the series, this is a must have addition to your library.

The first edition of the **Moult and Ageing of European Passerines** was the bible for bird ringers. It was also very hard to come by, with second hand prices commanding a hefty premium. Now, the second edition has just been published (Jenni & Winkler, Helm £94.99) and has been completely revised and updated. It is already disappearing quickly. Over 600 photos illustrate the various moult strategies of 74 species, and there is a plethora of diagrams, charts and graphs. Despite the hefty price tag, every ringer and serious ornithologist across the country will want - and should get - a copy. This is one one of the most significant books of the year.

BEST BIRD BOOKS OF THE YEAR

Children's books

Birds (Krestovnikoff & Harding, Bloomsbury, £12.99) is just the sort of book I would have loved to unwrap on Christmas Day when I was 7 or 8. Little bits of trivia are coupled with spectacular prints. I did have a Twitter spat with Angela Harding, the artist though. 'Why hadn't she included white wing bars and rump on the Redshank?' I asked. 'Artistic licence' she replied. 'You wouldn't have left the stripes off a tiger' I retorted.

By the same publishers, **Nature Guide: Birds** (Brereton & McLelland,£8.99) would make an ideal field guide for someone showing a first interest in birdwatching. Big, bold pictures of 135 species, the books sits well in the hand and looks a treat.

Eagle Warrior (Lewis, Barrington Stoke, £6.99) tells the story of a little girl who finds an eagle near her family farm. Not everyone is pleased to see it though... What sets this book apart is that it is specially designed for children (8+) with dyslexia or other reading difficulties. The book is printed on coloured paper, with well spaced-out text. Anything that encourages children to read has got to be welcome.

Miscellaneous

It might be minimalist in both size and title, but **Bird** (Anderson, Bloomsbury, £9.99) punches well above its weight. A series of short, idiosyncratic essays on bird themes range far and wide. For example, the piece on the Lesser Snow Goose touches on Macbeth, why brides wear white, racism and forced copulation etc., all in less that two small pages! Definitely one for the birding philosopher.

Penguin-lovers are being spoilt this year, with three titles to look out for. George Levick, the physician on Scott's ill-fated expedition, was the first person to study penguins, though his discoveries about their sex lives offended Edwardian sensibilities and were soon forgotten. Lloyd Spencer Davis is a modern day Antarctic scientist who rediscovered the original findings. **A Polar Affair** (Pegasus Books, £19.99) examines the study of penguins from that first expedition to the modern day.

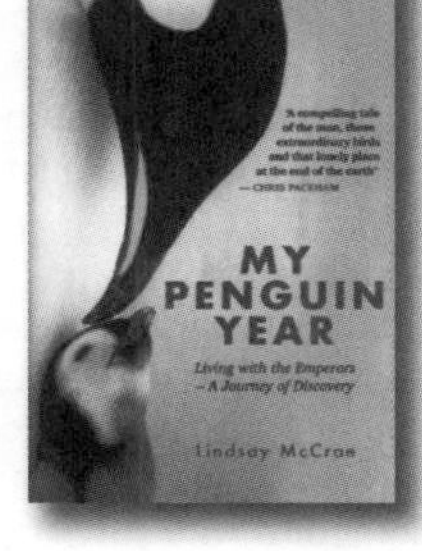

Every Penguin in the World (Bergman, Sasquatch Books, £19.99) follows the author's travels through South America, the Galapagos and Antarctica as he attempts to see and photograph all 18 species of penguin. An interesting mix of adventure and conservation. Lavishly illustrated. **My Penguin Year** (McCrae, Hodder & Stoughton, £20) follows a colony of Emperor Penguins, as seen through the eyes of a wildlife cameraman. If you are one of the eight million who watched the series on TV, you'll know that you can expect some stunning photographs too.

More tales from a wildlife cameraman come in **Untangling the Knot, Belugas and Bears** (Potts, Whittles Publishing, £20.95). Someone who has filmed Birds of Paradise with Sir David Attenborough is obviously at the top of his game and there are plenty of excellent photos to illustrate his tales from around the world.

Stephen Moss's books are always highly readable, and this year, he has two more out for your delectation. In **The Accidental Countryside** (Guardian Faber, £16.99), he looks at how mankind has had an effect on our wildlife. Starting with Storm Petrels on Mousa, nesting in prehistoric brochs and finishing with Peregrines using urban skyscrapers as artificial cliffs, he covers everything from road building to artificial reservoirs. Highly recommended.

BEST BIRD BOOKS OF THE YEAR

The Twelve Birds of Christmas (Square Peg, £12.99) looks at the birds associated with the well-known Christmas song. You need to stretch your imagination sometimes - sandpipers for eleven pipers piping for example, but this is great fun and would make an ideal and obvious stocking filler for someone. I disagree violently with Stephen though when he claims that 'five gold rings' is probably a corruption of 'yoldring', a folk name for Yellowhammer. It is far more likely to be a corruption of 'goldspink', an old name for Goldfinches, birds which were regularly kept as cage birds and given as presents.

There are two more titles in the ongoing Animal Series from Reaktion Books: **Kingfisher** (Szabo, £12.99) and **Pelican** (Allen, £12.99). If you haven't seen these books before, they offer a mix of natural history, folklore and culture, illustrated with artworks and quotations from assorted literary works. Having said that, I can't believe that the Pelican volume missed the opportunity to include the doggerel by Dixon Merritt that starts 'A wonderful bird is the Pelican, Its beak can hold more than its belly can...'. These enjoyable books form part of a highly collectable series.

Iolo Williams has selected 40 of his favourite sites to see wildlife, ranging from great sites such as Mull, the Dee Estuary and Arne RSPB, to places I had never come across before such as Whittington Farm Lodge near Cheltenham. **Wild Places UK** (Seren, £19.99) is profusely illustrated and would serve as a great starting point for someone new to the hobby who wants to know the best places to look for wildlife around Britain, though some maps and/or directions would have been nice.

How to See Birds (Stadlen, Papadakis, £20) comes with plenty of celebrity endorsements on the cover, but none from serious birders. It is a selection of fairly bog standard bird portraits, not always sharp in my copy, of mostly British birds. Much as I love bird books, I just couldn't get excited over this one.

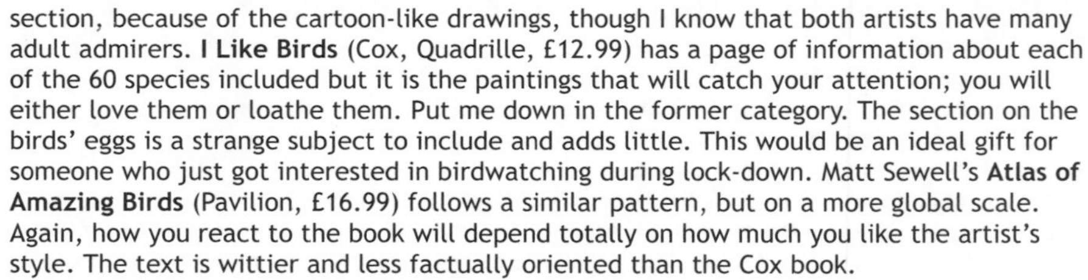

I could well have included these two books in the children's section, because of the cartoon-like drawings, though I know that both artists have many adult admirers. **I Like Birds** (Cox, Quadrille, £12.99) has a page of information about each of the 60 species included but it is the paintings that will catch your attention; you will either love them or loathe them. Put me down in the former category. The section on the birds' eggs is a strange subject to include and adds little. This would be an ideal gift for someone who just got interested in birdwatching during lock-down. Matt Sewell's **Atlas of Amazing Birds** (Pavilion, £16.99) follows a similar pattern, but on a more global scale. Again, how you react to the book will depend totally on how much you like the artist's style. The text is wittier and less factually oriented than the Cox book.

Finally, a couple of books that are ideal for anyone looking for a late stocking filler. **The Robin Book** (Russ, Graffeg, £9.99) starts with a series of pictures and facts about everyone's favourite garden bird, before finishing with an interesting section on the Robin in myth and legend.

Everything You Know About Animals is Wrong (Brown, Batsford, £9.99) is a trivia book exploding some of the common myths about assorted creatures. The bird section includes Ostriches burying their heads in the sand, ducks' quacks not echoing and Jimi Hendrix being responsible for releasing Ring-necked Parakeets in London.

Gordon's choice for one of the year's most significant books...

Neil Gartshore

One of the most spectacular winter gatherings of birds, & an experience not to be missed, is a murmuration of Starlings *(Sturnus vulgaris)*. As dusk draws close, the birds come in to roost in their 1,000's, 10,000's or 100,000's. Check out this website for a location near you: https://www.starlingsintheuk.co.uk/

BIRDWATCHER'S DIARY 2021

EVENTS DIARY for 2021

With the Covid19 situation taking hold from early 2020 many events around the world were cancelled (or were delivered online). Some of the international conferences have been already been rescheduled for 2021, whilst the regular annual UK events should be planned for 2021. However, due to the uncertainty (as of Sept 2020), many of the listings here are undated ***(tbc)*** but are listed under the months when they are usually held (they may or may not run).
It is always advisable to check the relevant website/contact the organiser to check date/venues.

JANUARY

4 Jan-19 Feb: Big Schools Birdwatch (RSPB)
UK-wide event to get children interested in wild birds (first half of Spring Term). For events in your area - W: www.rspb.org.uk/fun-and-learning/for-teachers/schools-birdwatch/

30-31: Big Garden Birdwatch (RSPB)
UK-wide survey of garden birds.
W: www.rspb.org.uk/get-involved/activities/birdwatch

FEBRUARY

2: World Wetlands Day
Theme: Wetlands and Water.
Various events around the globe celebrating the importance of wetland environments.
W: www.ramsar.org

23-27: Pacific Seabird Group
49th annual meeting. VIRTUAL event.
W: www.pacificseabirdgroup.org/annual-meeting/

14-21: National Nest Box Week
A BTO initiative to encourage more people to erect nestboxes. Various events - see website for details.
W: www.bto.org/how-you-can-help/nnbw
W: www.nestboxweek.com

MARCH

***tbc:* SOC/BTO**
Scottish Birdwatchers' Spring Conference
W: www.the-soc.org.uk/support-us/events

30-1 April: BOU Annual Conference
Restoring bird populations: scaling from species to ecosystems.
Nottingham University, UK.
W: www.bou.org.uk/bou-conferences

APRIL

***tbc:* African Bird Club**
AGM plus full programme of talks on research & conservation work in Africa.
E: info@africanbirdclub.org
W: www.africanbirdclub.org

MAY

JUNE

***tbc:* OSME (Ornithological Society of the Middle East, Caucasus & Central Asia)**
Summer Meeting & AGM.
BTO, The Nunnery, Thetford, Norfolk.
E: secretary@osme.org; W: www.osme.org

JULY

***tbc:* BirdsCaribbean 23rd International Conference**
Port-of-Spain, Trinidad.
W: www.birdscaribbean.org/our-work/international-conference/

AUGUST

***tbc:* BBC Countryfile Live**
2020 events were cancelled - 2021 events tbc.
Castle Howard, Yorks & Great Windsor Park, Berks.
W: www.countryfilelive.com

20-22: British Birdwatching Fair
Rutland Water Nature Reserve, Egleton, Rutland.
[Was held online in 2020]
E: nbrown@birdfair.org.uk; W: www.birdfair.org.uk

22-29: North American Ornithological Conference
London, Ontario, Canada. American Ornithological Society & Society of Canadian Ornithologists.
W: www.americanornithology.org;
W: www.sco-soc.ca; W: www.naocbirds.org

SEPTEMBER

***tbc:* Spurn Migration Festival**
W: www.spurnmigfest.com

***tbc:* Oriental Bird Club Autumn Meeting & AGM**
E: mail@orientalbirdclub.org
W: www.orientalbirdclub.org

6-10: 13th Congress of the European Ornithologists' Union.
University of Giessen, Germany.
W: https://eounion.org/

11-12: Festival of Bird Art incl. National Bird Carving Championships. The Agricultural Business Centre, Agricultural Way, Bakewell, Derbys DE45 1AH.
W: www.bdwca.org.uk

EVENTS DIARY for 2021

SEPTEMBER ctd

20-24: World Owl Conference
Stoney Creek Inn, La Crosse - Onalaska, Wisconsin USA.
W: www.WorldOwlConference.com

21-24: 35th International Union of Game Biologists (IUGB) Congress
Budapest, Hungary.

OCTOBER

***tbc:* RSPB Members' Day & AGM**
[Was held online in 2020]
W: www.rspb.org.uk/reserves-and-events/events-dates-and-inspiration/events/agm/

***tbc:* Society of Wildlife Artists**
The Natural Eye, 58th Annual Exhibition
Mall Galleries, Pall Mall, London SW1Y 5BD.
W: www.swla.co.uk

tbc: Neotropical Bird Club
W: www.neotropicalbirdclub.org/events/

4-8 Oct: 3rd World Seabird Conference
Hobart, Tasmania, Australia.
W: www.worldseabirdconference.com

8-11 Oct: International Wader Study Group Annual Conference Sylt, Germany.
W: www.waderstudygroup.org

9-12 Oct: Raptor Research Foundation and Neotropical Raptor Network
Boise, Idaho, USA.
W: www.raptorresearchfoundation.org/conferences/upcoming-conferences/

18-22: 4th International Bird Observatory Conference
Veracruz, Mexico.
W: www.iboc2021.org

NOVEMBER

tbc: Welsh **Ornithological Society National Conference**
W: www.birdsin.wales

***tbc:* 44th Annual Meeting of The Waterbird Society**
W: www.waterbirds.org

***tbc:* North West Bird Watching Festival**
WWT Martin Mere, Fish Lane, Burscough, Lancashire L40 0TA. T: 01704 895 181
W: www.wwt.org.uk/wetland-centres/martin-mere

***tbc:* Scottish Ornithologists' Club AGM & Annual Conference**
W: www.the-soc.org.uk/support-us/events

NOVEMBER ctd

15-19 Nov: 15th Pan-African Ornithological Conference (PAOC15)
Elephant Hills Conference Centre, Victoria Falls, Zimbabwe. E: info@paoc15.org; W: www.paoc15.org

DECEMBER

4-5: BTO Annual Conference
Hayes Conference Centre, Swanwick, Derbyshire DE55 1AU. E: info@bto.org; W: www.bto.org

~~~~~~~~~~

VARIOUS DATES THROUGH THE YEAR (BTO)

BTO Garden BirdWatch talks: these are given by a number of speakers to a wide variety of groups across the country.

BTO Training Courses: one day courses/residential courses - subjects include identifying birds; bird survey techniques; breeding bird survey; & bird identification/wetland bird survey.

Local Bird Club Conferences: the BTO encourage & support local bird clubs through their 'Bird Club Partnership'.

Regional Bird Ringer's Conferences: usually one-day conferences held in the different regions of the UK.

Check out the BTO's website: www.bto.org or phone: 01842 750 050 for more information on BTO-related talks, courses or conferences in 2021.

NOTE:
Due to the printing deadline of *The Yearbook* it is not always possible to confirm dates or if conferences, fairs etc will be running during the following year.

If you have, or know of, any events for 2022 & would like them mentioned in this section of *The Yearbook* then please contact us by the end of August 2021.

[See our contact details on P6.]
~~~~~~~~~~

DIARY – JANUARY 2021

(Inc. Bank Holidays for E&W = England & Wales; NI = Northern Ireland; S = Scotland and BST/time changes]

1	Fri	New Year's Day E&W, NI, S
2	Sat	Bank Holiday S
3	Sun	
4	Mon	Substitute Day for 2nd S
5	Tues	
6	Wed	
7	Thurs	
8	Fri	
9	Sat	
10	Sun	
11	Mon	
12	Tues	
13	Wed	
14	Thurs	
15	Fri	
16	Sat	
17	Sun	
18	Mon	
19	Tues	
20	Wed	
21	Thurs	
22	Fri	
23	Sat	
24	Sun	
25	Mon	
26	Tues	
27	Wed	
28	Thurs	
29	Fri	
30	Sat	
31	Sun	

DIARY – FEBRUARY 2021

1	Mon	
2	Tues	
3	Wed	
4	Thurs	
5	Fri	
6	Sat	
7	Sun	
8	Mon	
9	Tues	
10	Wed	
11	Thurs	
12	Fri	
13	Sat	
14	Sun	
15	Mon	
16	Tues	
17	Wed	
18	Thurs	
19	Fri	
20	Sat	
21	Sun	
22	Mon	
23	Tues	
24	Wed	
25	Thurs	
26	Fri	
27	Sat	
28	Sun	

DIARY – MARCH 2021

1	Mon	
2	Tues	
3	Wed	
4	Thurs	
5	Fri	
6	Sat	
7	Sun	
8	Mon	
9	Tues	
10	Wed	
11	Thurs	
12	Fri	
13	Sat	
14	Sun	
15	Mon	
16	Tues	
17	Wed	St Patrick's Day NI
18	Thurs	
19	Fri	
20	Sat	
21	Sun	
22	Mon	
23	Tues	
24	Wed	
25	Thurs	
26	Fri	
27	Sat	
28	Sun	British Summertime Begins (1 hour Forwards)
29	Mon	
30	Tues	
31	Wed	

DIARY – APRIL 2021

1	Thurs	
2	Fri	Good Friday E&W, NI, S
3	Sat	
4	Sun	
5	Mon	Easter Monday E&W, NI
6	Tues	
7	Wed	
8	Thurs	
9	Fri	
10	Sat	
11	Sun	
12	Mon	
13	Tues	
14	Wed	
15	Thurs	
16	Fri	
17	Sat	
18	Sun	
19	Mon	
20	Tues	
21	Wed	
22	Thurs	
23	Fri	
24	Sat	
25	Sun	
26	Mon	
27	Tues	
28	Wed	
29	Thurs	
30	Fri	

DIARY – MAY 2021

1	Sat	
2	Sun	
3	Mon	Early May Bank Holiday E&W, NI, S
4	Tues	
5	Wed	
6	Thurs	
7	Fri	
8	Sat	
9	Sun	
10	Mon	
11	Tues	
12	Wed	
13	Thurs	
14	Fri	
15	Sat	
16	Sun	
17	Mon	
18	Tues	
19	Wed	
20	Thurs	
21	Fri	
22	Sat	
23	Sun	
24	Mon	
25	Tues	
26	Wed	
27	Thurs	
28	Fri	
29	Sat	
30	Sun	
31	Mon	Spring Bank Holiday E&W, NI, S

DIARY – JUNE 2021

1	Tues	
2	Wed	
3	Thurs	
4	Fri	
5	Sat	
6	Sun	
7	Mon	
8	Tues	
9	Wed	
10	Thurs	
11	Fri	
12	Sat	
13	Sun	
14	Mon	
15	Tues	
16	Wed	
17	Thurs	
18	Fri	
19	Sat	
20	Sun	
21	Mon	
22	Tues	
23	Wed	
24	Thurs	
25	Fri	
26	Sat	
27	Sun	
28	Mon	
29	Tues	
30	Wed	

DIARY – JULY 2021

1	Thurs	
2	Fri	
3	Sat	
4	Sun	
5	Mon	
6	Tues	
7	Wed	
8	Thurs	
9	Fri	
10	Sat	
11	Sun	
12	Mon	Orangemen's Day NI
13	Tues	
14	Wed	
15	Thurs	
16	Fri	
17	Sat	
18	Sun	
19	Mon	
20	Tues	
21	Wed	
22	Thurs	
23	Fri	
24	Sat	
25	Sun	
26	Mon	
27	Tues	
28	Wed	
29	Thurs	
30	Fri	
31	Sat	

DIARY – AUGUST 2021

1	Sun	
2	Mon	Summer Bank Holiday S
3	Tues	
4	Wed	
5	Thurs	
6	Fri	
7	Sat	
8	Sun	
9	Mon	
10	Tues	
11	Wed	
12	Thurs	
13	Fri	
14	Sat	
15	Sun	
16	Mon	
17	Tues	
18	Wed	
19	Thurs	
20	Fri	
21	Sat	
22	Sun	
23	Mon	
24	Tues	
25	Wed	
26	Thurs	
27	Fri	
28	Sat	
29	Sun	
30	Mon	Summer Bank Holiday E&W, NI
31	Tues	

DIARY – SEPTEMBER 2021

1	Wed	
2	Thurs	
3	Fri	
4	Sat	
5	Sun	
6	Mon	
7	Tues	
8	Wed	
9	Thurs	
10	Fri	
11	Sat	
12	Sun	
13	Mon	
14	Tues	
15	Wed	
16	Thurs	
17	Fri	
18	Sat	
19	Sun	
20	Mon	
21	Tues	
22	Wed	
23	Thurs	
24	Fri	
25	Sat	
26	Sun	
27	Mon	
28	Tues	
29	Wed	
30	Thurs	

DIARY – OCTOBER 2021

1	Fri	
2	Sat	
3	Sun	
4	Mon	
5	Tues	
6	Wed	
7	Thurs	
8	Fri	
9	Sat	
10	Sun	
11	Mon	
12	Tues	
13	Wed	
14	Thurs	
15	Fri	
16	Sat	
17	Sun	
18	Mon	
19	Tues	
20	Wed	
21	Thurs	
22	Fri	
23	Sat	
24	Sun	
25	Mon	
26	Tues	
27	Wed	
28	Thurs	
29	Fri	
30	Sat	
31	Sun	British Summertime Ends (1 hour backwards)

DIARY – NOVEMBER 2021

1	Mon	
2	Tues	
3	Wed	
4	Thurs	
5	Fri	
6	Sat	
7	Sun	
8	Mon	
9	Tues	
10	Wed	
11	Thurs	
12	Fri	
13	Sat	
14	Sun	
15	Mon	
16	Tues	
17	Wed	
18	Thurs	
19	Fri	
20	Sat	
21	Sun	
22	Mon	
23	Tues	
24	Wed	
25	Thurs	
26	Fri	
27	Sat	
28	Sun	
29	Mon	
30	Tues	St Andrew's Day S

DIARY – DECEMBER 2021

1	Wed	
2	Thurs	
3	Fri	
4	Sat	
5	Sun	
6	Mon	
7	Tues	
8	Wed	
9	Thurs	
10	Fri	
11	Sat	
12	Sun	
13	Mon	
14	Tues	
15	Wed	
16	Thurs	
17	Fri	
18	Sat	
19	Sun	
20	Mon	
21	Tues	
22	Wed	
23	Thurs	
24	Fri	
25	Sat	Christmas Day E&W, NI, S
26	Sun	Boxing Day E&W, NI, S
27	Mon	Substitute Day for 25th E&W, NI, S
28	Tues	Substitute Day for 26th E&W, NI, S
29	Wed	
30	Thurs	
31	Fri	

YEAR PLANNER 2022

JANUARY
FEBRUARY
MARCH
APRIL
MAY
JUNE
JULY
AUGUST
SEPTEMBER
OCTOBER
NOVEMBER
DECEMBER

Neil Gartshore

Waders make up the largest group of non-passerines and are a favourite of many birders. They often provide an identification challenge - the larger male Ruff *(Calidris pugnax)* sports a range of finery amongst individuals in the breeding season & plumage variations in winter. The smaller females are more uniform.

CHECKLISTS

CHECKLIST OF BRITISH BIRDS

Based on the British List formulated by the British Ornithologists' Union

The official 'British List' is maintained by The British Ornithologists' Union (BOU) which sits in judgement on which birds you can count on your list, and which you can't. The official list can change from year to year in one of two ways:

1) If someone claims to have seen a species never recorded in Britain, a panel of experts sitting on the BOU Records Committee (BOURC) assesses the record, making sure that the identification of the bird was proved beyond all possible doubt. Then the bird's credentials are assessed, to determine whether it was a genuine vagrant, rather than one that had just hopped over the fence from the nearest zoo or aviary.

Only if the bird passes every single strenuous test does it get accepted onto the British List... a process that may take many years. Similarly, historical records may be reassessed in the light of advances in identification skills and could result in species being added to or removed from the list.

2) The BOU uses the International Ornithological Union's (IOU) IOC World Bird List (version 10.1) as its authority on the naming of full species and sub-species. Any changes on this list, for example a sub-species British List being amended accordingly.

The '9th edition' of the British List was published in December 2017 and the official British List stands (as of 24th January 2020) at 621 species. These are made up of 603 species in Category A, eight species in Category B and ten species in Category C. In addition there are two other catconsidered to be a full species or a full species considered only to be a sub-species, will result in the egories (D and E) - see below for a description of the five categories. *Note:* IOC version 10.2 released July 2020 has split Subalpine Warbler into two species... Eastern & Western.

For further information about the British List visit the BOU website: www.bou.org.uk/british-list/

SPECIES, CATEGORIES, CODES - YOUR GUIDE TO GETTING THE BEST USE FROM THE CHECKLIST

Species Categories (column 1)

The following categories are those assigned by the British Ornithologists' Union.

A - Species recorded in an apparently natural state at least once since 1st January 1950.

B - Species recorded in an apparently natural state at least once between 1st January 1800 and 31st December 1949, but not subsequently.

C - Species that, though introduced, now derive from the resulting self-sustaining populations:

C1 (***Naturalised introduced species)*** Species that have occurred only as a result of introduction, e.g. Egyptian Goose;

C2 (***Naturalised established species)***
Species resulting from introduction by man, but which also occur in an apparently natural state, e.g. Greylag Goose;

C3 (***Naturalised re-established species***)
Species successfully re-established by man in areas of former occurrence, e.g. Red Kite;

C4 (***Naturalised feral species***)
Domesticated species established in the wild, e.g. Rock Pigeon (Dove)/Feral Pigeon;

C5 (***Vagrant naturalised species)***
Species from established naturalised populations abroad. Currently no species in category C5;

C6 (***Former naturalised species)***
Species formerly in C1 whose naturalised populations are either no longer self-sustaining or are considered extinct, e.g. Lady Amherst's Pheasant.

D - This is for species that would otherwise appear in Category A but there is reasonable doubt that the species have ever occurred in a natural state. Species held here are regularly reviewed with a view to assigning them to either Category A or E. Species placed solely in Category D form no part of the British List, and are not included in the species totals.

E - Species that have been recorded as introductions, human-assisted transportees or escapees from captivity, and whose breeding populations (if any) are thought not to be self-sustaining. Species in Category E that have bred in the wild in Britain are designated as E*. Category E species form no part of the British List (unless already included within Categories A, B or C).

Although the majority of species usually only fall into one category, a few are placed in multiple categories, for example, those species occurring in Category A which now have naturalised populations (e.g. Red Kite).

The British List comprises only of those species placed in Categories A, B or C.

CHECKLISTS

Species List (column 2)

The *Yearbook* Checklist includes all species from categories A, B and C on the British List, based on the latest BOU listing.

Vagrants which are not on the British List, but which may have occurred in other parts of the British Isles, are not included. Readers who wish to record such species may use the extra rows provided. In this connection it should be noted that separate lists exist for Northern Ireland (kept by the Northern Ireland Birdwatchers' Association) and the Isle of Man (kept by the Manx Ornithological Society), and that Irish records are assessed by the Irish Rare Birds Committee.

The species names are those most widely used in the current field guides and each is followed by its scientific name, printed in italics.

Columns 3 to 22

These columns are for personal use and include a Life List, a 2021 list, and monthly lists from Jan to Dec. There are six columns (A-F) which could be used for a variety of reasons such as a local patch, birds in the garden, a bird race or holidays.

Generally a tick suffices in each of the columns to record a bird seen. However, added benefit can be obtained by replacing ticks with specific dates.

How you fill in these columns is a matter of personal choice. *For example:* you may want to keep your Life List up to date with the first year you saw a species - if you see your first Corncrake (a lifer) on 10th June 2021, it could be logged as '6/21' in the Life List column (as well as being recorded in the 2021 column as '10/6' and the June column as '10th'). As Life List entries are carried forward annually, in years to come it would be a simple matter to relocate the original dates first seen into subsequent *Yearbooks*.

As space within the columns is limited, it is recommended to use a thin pointed pen or pencil.

ADDITIONAL COLUMNS, make your own list	
A	
B	
C	
D	
E	
F	

BTO species codes (column 23)

The British Trust for Ornithology two-letter species codes are shown in the fourth column from the right. Readers should refer to the BTO if more codes are needed (the other species have been allocated 5-digit codes).

Rare breeding birds (column 24)

The species monitored by the Rare Breeding Birds Panel (see National Directory) comprise of those with a sustained population of fewer than 2000 breeding pairs and rarer non-native species with fewer than 300 breeding pairs. For full details, visit: www.rbbp.org.uk

The following annotations in the charts (third column from the right) reflect the panel's categories:

A) Rare Breeding Birds in UK (Regular);
B) Rare Breeding Birds in UK (Occasional);
C) Rare Breeding Birds in UK (Potential);
D) Rare Non-native Breeding Birds in UK (Regular);
E) Rare Non-native Breeding Birds in UK (Occasional);
F) Rare Non-native Breeding Birds in UK (Potential).

Rarities (column 25)

Rarities are indicated by a capital letter 'R' (and subspecies rarities by an asterisk *) in the column headed BBRC (British Birds Rarities Committee). For full details, visit: www.bbrc.org.uk

EURING species numbers (column 26)

EURING databanks collect copies of recovery records from ringing schemes throughout Europe and the official species numbers are given in the last column. As they are taken from the full Holarctic bird list there are many apparent gaps. It is important that these are not filled arbitrarily by observers wishing to record species not listed in the charts, as this would compromise the integrity of the scheme.

Similarly, the addition of a further digit to indicate sub-species is to be avoided, since EURING has already assigned numbers for this purpose. The numbering follows the Voous order of species so some species are now out of sequence following the re-ordering of the British List. For full details, visit: www.euring.org

Butterflies & Dragonflies

As most birdwatchers have an interest in other areas of natural history, checklists have been included for two of the most popular groups with a column for a Life List and another for 2021 records.

	GAMEBIRDS, GEESE, SWANS		Life	2021	Jan	Feb	Mar	Apr	May	Jun	Jul	Aug	Sep	Oct	Nov	Dec	A	B	C	D	E	F	BTO	RBBP	BBRC	EU
C3E*	**Capercaillie**	*Tetrao urogallus*																					CP	A		0335
AE	**Black Grouse**	*Lyrurus tetrix*																					BK			0332
A	**Ptarmigan**	*Lagopus muta*																					PM			0330
A	**Red Grouse**	*Lagopus lagopus*																					RG			0329
C1E*	**Red-legged Partridge**	*Alectoris rufa*																					RL			0358
AC2E*	**Grey Partridge**	*Perdix perdix*																					P.			0367
AE*	**Quail**	*Coturnix coturnix*																					Q.	A		0370
C1E*	**Pheasant**	*Phasianus colchicus*																					PH			0394
C1E*	**Golden Pheasant**	*Chrysolophus pictus*																					GF	D		0396
C6E*	**Lady Amherst's Pheasant**	*Chrysolophus amherstiae*																					LM	D		0397
AE	**Brent Goose**	*Branta bernicla*																					BG			0168
AE*	**Red-breasted Goose**	*Branta ruficollis*																					EB	E	R	0169
AC2E*	**Canada Goose**	*Branta canadensis*																					CG		*	0166
AC2E*	**Barnacle Goose**	*Branta leucopsis*																					BY			0167
AE	**Cackling Goose**	*Branta hutchinsii*																							R	
AC2E*	**Snow Goose**	*Anser caerulescens*																					SJ	D		0163
AC2C4E*	**Greylag Goose**	*Anser anser*																					GJ			0161
AE*	**Taiga Bean Goose**	*Anser fabalis*																					XF	E		0157
AE*	**Pink-footed Goose**	*Anser brachyrhynchus*																					PG	E		0158
AE	**Tundra Bean Goose**	*Anser serrirostris*																					XR	E		
AE*	**White-fronted Goose**	*Anser albifrons*																					WG	E		0159
AE*	**Lesser White-fronted Goose**	*Anser erythropus*																					LC	F	R	0160
AC2	**Mute Swan**	*Cygnus olor*																					MS			0152
AE	**Bewick's Swan**	*Cygnus columbianus*																					BS	C	*	0153
	Sub total																									

	SWANS, DUCKS		Life	2021	Jan	Feb	Mar	Apr	May	Jun	Jul	Aug	Sep	Oct	Nov	Dec	A	B	C	D	E	F	BTO	RBBP	BBRC	EU
AE*	**Whooper Swan**	*Cygnus cygnus*																					WS	A		0154
C1C5E*	**Egyptian Goose**	*Alopochen aegyptiaca*																					EG			0170
A	**Shelduck**	*Tadorna tadorna*																					SU			0173
BDE*	**Ruddy Shelduck**	*Tadorna ferruginea*																					UD	D	R	0171
C1E*	**Mandarin Duck**	*Aix galericulata*																					MN			0178
AE	**Baikal Teal**	*Sibirionetta formosa*																					IK		R	1830
A	**Garganey**	*Spatula querquedula*																					GY	A		0191
AE*	**Blue-winged Teal**	*Spatula discors*																					TB	E	R	0192
A	**Shoveler**	*Spatula clypeata*																					SV	A		0194
AC2E*	**Gadwall**	*Mareca strepera*																					GA			0182
AE	**Falcated Duck**	*Mareca falcata*																							R	
AE*	**Wigeon**	*Mareca penelope*																					WN	A		0179
AE	**American Wigeon**	*Mareca americana*																					AW			0180
AC2C4E*	**Mallard**	*Anas platyrhynchos*																					MA			0186
A	**Black Duck**	*Anas rubripes*																					BD	B	R	0187
AE	**Pintail**	*Anas acuta*																					PT	A		0189
A	**Teal**	*Anas crecca*																					T.			0184
A	**Green-winged Teal**	*Anas carolinensis*																					TA	C		1842
AC2E*	**Red-crested Pochard**	*Netta rufina*																					RQ	D		0196
AE	**Canvasback**	*Aythya valisineria*																							R	0197
AE	**Redhead**	*Aythya americana*																					AZ		R	0199
AE*	**Pochard**	*Aythya ferina*																					PO	A		0198
AE	**Ferruginous Duck**	*Aythya nyroca*																					FD	B	R	0202
AE	**Ring-necked Duck**	*Aythya collaris*																					NG	B		0200
	Sub total																									

	DUCKS, NIGHTJARS		Life	2021	Jan	Feb	Mar	Apr	May	Jun	Jul	Aug	Sep	Oct	Nov	Dec	A	B	C	D	E	F	BTO	RBBP	BBRC	EU
A	**Tufted Duck**	*Aythya fuligula*																					TU			0203
A	**Scaup**	*Aythya marila*																					SP	B		0204
A	**Lesser Scaup**	*Aythya affinis*																					AY	C		0205
A	**Steller's Eider**	*Polysticta stelleri*																					ES		R	0209
A	**King Eider**	*Somateria spectabilis*																					KE	C	R	0207
A	**Eider**	*Somateria mollissima*																					E.			0206
A	**Harlequin Duck**	*Histrionicus histrionicus*																					HQ		R	0211
A	**Surf Scoter**	*Melanitta perspicillata*																					FS			0214
A	**Velvet Scoter**	*Melanitta fusca*																					VS	C		0215
A	**White-winged Scoter**	*Melanitta deglandi*																							R	
A	**Common Scoter**	*Melanitta nigra*																					CX	A		0213
A	**Black Scoter**	*Melanitta americana*																							R	2132
A	**Long-tailed Duck**	*Clangula hyemalis*																					LN	C		0212
AE	**Bufflehead**	*Bucephala albeola*																					VH		R	0216
AE*	**Goldeneye**	*Bucephala clangula*																					GN	A		0218
AE	**Barrow's Goldeneye**	*Bucephala islandica*																							R	0217
A	**Smew**	*Mergellus albellus*																					SY	C		0220
AE	**Hooded Merganser**	*Lophodytes cucullatus*																					HO		R	2190
A	**Goosander**	*Mergus merganser*																					GD			0223
A	**Red-breasted Merganser**	*Mergus serrator*																					RM			0221
C1E*	**Ruddy Duck**	*Oxyura jamaicensis*																					RY	D		0225
A	**Common Nighthawk**	*Chordeiles minor*																							R	0786
B	**Red-necked Nightjar**	*Caprimulgus ruficollis*																							R	0779
A	**Nightjar**	*Caprimulgus europaeus*																					NJ			0778
	Sub total																									

	NIGHTJARS, SWIFTS, BUSTARDS, CUCKOOS, PIGEONS, DOVES		Life	2021	Jan	Feb	Mar	Apr	May	Jun	Jul	Aug	Sep	Oct	Nov	Dec	A	B	C	D	E	F	BTO	RBBP	BBRC	EU
A	**Egyptian Nightjar**	*Caprimulgus aegyptius*																							R	0781
A	**White-throated Needletail**	*Hirundapus caudacutus*																					NI		R	0792
A	**Chimney Swift**	*Chaetura pelagica*																							R	0790
A	**Alpine Swift**	*Tachymarptis melba*																					AI			0798
A	**Swift**	*Apus apus*																					SI			0795
A	**Pallid Swift**	*Apus pallidus*																						C	R	0796
A	**Pacific Swift**	*Apus pacificus*																							R	0797
A	**Little Swift**	*Apus affinis*																							R	0800
A	**White-rumped Swift**	*Apus caffer*																							R	0799
AE*	**Great Bustard**	*Otis tarda*																					US	A	R	0446
A	**Macqueen's Bustard**	*Chlamydotis macqueenii*																							R	0444
A	**Little Bustard**	*Tetrax tetrax*																							R	0442
A	**Great Spotted Cuckoo**	*Clamator glandarius*																					UK		R	0716
A	**Yellow-billed Cuckoo**	*Coccyzus americanus*																							R	0728
A	**Black-billed Cuckoo**	*Coccyzus erythropthalmus*																							R	0727
A	**Cuckoo**	*Cuculus canorus*																					CK			0724
A	**Pallas's Sandgrouse**	*Syrrhaptes paradoxus*																							R	0663
AC4E*	**Rock Dove / Feral Pigeon**	*Columba livia*																					DV			0665
A	**Stock Dove**	*Columba oenas*																					SD			0668
A	**Woodpigeon**	*Columba palumbus*																					WP			0670
A	**Turtle Dove**	*Streptopelia turtur*																					TD	A		0687
A	**Oriental Turtle Dove**	*Streptopelia orientalis*																							R	0689
A	**Collared Dove**	*Streptopelia decaocto*																					CD			0684
A	**Mourning Dove**	*Zenaida macroura*																							R	0695
	Sub total																									

	RAILS, CRAKES, GALLINULES, CRANES, GREBES, WADERS		Life	2021	Jan	Feb	Mar	Apr	May	Jun	Jul	Aug	Sep	Oct	Nov	Dec	A	B	C	D	E	F	BTO	RBBP	BBRC	EU
A	**Water Rail**	*Rallus aquaticus*																					WA	A		0407
AE*	**Corncrake**	*Crex crex*																					CE	A		0421
A	**Little Crake**	*Porzana parva*																					JC		R	0410
A	**Baillon's Crake**	*Porzana pusilla*																					VC	B	R	0411
A	**Spotted Crake**	*Porzana porzana*																					AK	A		0408
A	**Sora Rail**	*Porzana carolina*																							R	0409
AE	**Western Swamphen**	*Porphyrio porphyrio*																							R	
A	**Allen's Gallinule**	*Porphyrio alleni*																							R	0425
A	**American Purple Gallinule**	*Porphyrio martinica*																							R	0426
A	**Moorhen**	*Gallinula chloropus*																					MH			0424
A	**Coot**	*Fulica atra*																					CO			0429
A	**American Coot**	*Fulica americana*																							R	0430
A	**Sandhill Crane**	*Antigone canadensis*																							R	0436
AE*	**Crane**	*Grus grus*																					AN	A		0433
A	**Little Grebe**	*Tachybaptus ruficollis*																					LG			0007
A	**Pied-billed Grebe**	*Podilymbus podiceps*																					PJ	B	R	0006
A	**Red-necked Grebe**	*Podiceps grisegena*																					RX	B	*	0010
A	**Great Crested Grebe**	*Podiceps cristatus*																					GG			0009
A	**Slavonian Grebe**	*Podiceps auritus*																					SZ	A		0011
A	**Black-necked Grebe**	*Podiceps nigricollis*																					BN	A		0012
	Stone-curlew	*Burhinus oedicnemus*																					TN	A		0459
A	**Oystercatcher**	*Haematopus ostralegus*																					OC			0450
A	**Black-winged Stilt**	*Himantopus himantopus*																					IT	B		0455
AE	**Avocet**	*Recurvirostra avosetta*																					AV	A		0456
	Sub total																									

	WADERS		Life	2021	Jan	Feb	Mar	Apr	May	Jun	Jul	Aug	Sep	Oct	Nov	Dec	A	B	C	D	E	F	BTO	RBBP	BBRC	EU
A	**Lapwing**	*Vanellus vanellus*																					L.			0493
A	**Sociable Plover**	*Vanellus gregarius*																					IP		R	0491
A	**White-tailed Plover**	*Vanellus leucurus*																							R	0492
A	**Golden Plover**	*Pluvialis apricaria*																					GP			0485
A	**Pacific Golden Plover**	*Pluvialis fulva*																					IF		R	0484
A	**American Golden Plover**	*Pluvialis dominica*																					ID			0484
A	**Grey Plover**	*Pluvialis squatarola*																					GV			0486
A	**Ringed Plover**	*Charadrius hiaticula*																					RP			0470
A	**Semipalmated Plover**	*Charadrius semipalmatus*																					TV		R	0471
A	**Little Ringed Plover**	*Charadrius dubius*																					LP	A		0469
A	**Killdeer**	*Charadrius vociferus*																					KL	C	R	0474
A	**Kentish Plover**	*Charadrius alexandrinus*																					KP	B	R	0477
A	**Lesser Sand Plover**	*Charadrius mongolus*																							R	0478
A	**Greater Sand Plover**	*Charadrius leschenaultii*																					DP		R	0479
A	**Caspian Plover**	*Charadrius asiaticus*																							R	0480
A	**Dotterel**	*Charadrius morinellus*																					DO	A		0482
A	**Upland Sandpiper**	*Bartramia longicauda*																					UP		R	0544
A	**Whimbrel**	*Numenius phaeopus*																					WM	A	*	0538
A	**Hudsonian Whimbrel**	*Numenius hudsonicus*																							R	
A	**Little Whimbrel**	*Numenius minutus*																							R	0536
B	**Eskimo Curlew**	*Numenius borealis*																							R	0537
A	**Curlew**	*Numenius arquata*																					CU			0541
A	**Bar-tailed Godwit**	*Limosa lapponica*																					BA	C		0534
A	**Black-tailed Godwit**	*Limosa limosa*																					BW	A		0532
	Sub total																									

	WADERS		Life	2021	Jan	Feb	Mar	Apr	May	Jun	Jul	Aug	Sep	Oct	Nov	Dec	A	B	C	D	E	F	BTO	RBBP	BBRC	EU
A	**Hudsonian Godwit**	*Limosa haemastica*																					HU		R	0533
A	**Turnstone**	*Arenaria interpres*																					TT	C		0561
A	**Great Knot**	*Calidris tenuirostris*																					KO		R	0495
A	**Knot**	*Calidris canutus*																					KN			0496
A	**Ruff**	*Calidris pugnax*																					RU	A		0517
A	**Broad-billed Sandpiper**	*Calidris falcinellus*																					OA	C	R	0514
A	**Sharp-tailed Sandpiper**	*Calidris acuminata*																					VV		R	0508
A	**Stilt Sandpiper**	*Calidris himantopus*																					MI		R	5150
A	**Curlew Sandpiper**	*Calidris ferruginea*																					CV			0509
A	**Temminck's Stint**	*Calidris temminckii*																					TK	B		0502
A	**Long-toed Stint**	*Calidris subminuta*																							R	0503
A	**Red-necked Stint**	*Calidris ruficollis*																							R	0500
A	**Sanderling**	*Calidris alba*																					SS	C		0497
A	**Dunlin**	*Calidris alpina*																					DN			0512
A	**Purple Sandpiper**	*Calidris maritima*																					PS	A		0510
A	**Baird's Sandpiper**	*Calidris bairdii*																					BP		R	0506
A	**Little Stint**	*Calidris minuta*																					LX			0501
A	**Least Sandpiper**	*Calidris minutilla*																					EP		R	0504
A	**White-rumped Sandpiper**	*Calidris fuscicollis*																					WU			0505
A	**Buff-breasted Sandpiper**	*Calidris subruficollis*																					BQ	C		0516
A	**Pectoral Sandpiper**	*Calidris melanotos*																					PP	C		0507
A	**Semipalmated Sandpiper**	*Calidris pusilla*																					PZ		R	0498
A	**Western Sandpiper**	*Calidris mauri*																					ER		R	0499
A	**Long-billed Dowitcher**	*Limnodromus scolopaceus*																					LD		R	0527
	Sub total																									

	WADERS		Life	2021	Jan	Feb	Mar	Apr	May	Jun	Jul	Aug	Sep	Oct	Nov	Dec	A	B	C	D	E	F	BTO	RBBP	BBRC	EU
A	**Short-billed Dowitcher**	*Limnodromus griseus*																							R	0526
A	**Woodcock**	*Scolopax rusticola*																					WK			0529
A	**Jack Snipe**	*Lymnocryptes minimus*																					JS	C		0518
A	**Great Snipe**	*Gallinago media*																					DS	C	R	0520
A	**Snipe**	*Gallinago gallinago*																					SN			0519
A	**Wilson's Snipe**	*Gallinago delicata*																							R	5192
A	**Terek Sandpiper**	*Xenus cinereus*																					TR		R	0555
A	**Wilson's Phalarope**	*Phalaropus tricolor*																					WF		R	0563
A	**Red-necked Phalarope**	*Phalaropus lobatus*																					NK	A		0564
A	**Grey Phalarope**	*Phalaropus fulicarius*																					PL			0565
A	**Common Sandpiper**	*Actitis hypoleucos*																					CS			0556
A	**Spotted Sandpiper**	*Actitis macularius*																					PQ	B	R	0557
A	**Green Sandpiper**	*Tringa ochropus*																					GE	A		0553
A	**Solitary Sandpiper**	*Tringa solitaria*																					I.		R	0552
A	**Grey-tailed Tattler**	*Tringa brevipes*																					YT		R	0558
A	**Lesser Yellowlegs**	*Tringa flavipes*																					LY			0551
A	**Redshank**	*Tringa totanus*																					RK			0546
A	**Marsh Sandpiper**	*Tringa stagnatilis*																					MD		R	0547
A	**Wood Sandpiper**	*Tringa glareola*																					OD	A		0554
A	**Spotted Redshank**	*Tringa erythropus*																					DR			0545
A	**Greenshank**	*Tringa nebularia*																					GK	A		0548
A	**Greater Yellowlegs**	*Tringa melanoleuca*																					LZ		R	0550
A	**Cream-coloured Courser**	*Cursorius cursor*																							R	0464
A	**Collared Pratincole**	*Glareola pratincola*																							R	0465
	Sub total																									

	PRATINCOLES, GULLS		Life	2021	Jan	Feb	Mar	Apr	May	Jun	Jul	Aug	Sep	Oct	Nov	Dec	A	B	C	D	E	F	BTO	RBBP	BBRC	EU
A	**Oriental Pratincole**	*Glareola maldivarum*																					GM		R	0466
A	**Black-winged Pratincole**	*Glareola nordmanni*																					KW		R	0467
A	**Kittiwake**	*Rissa tridactyla*																					KI			0602
A	**Ivory Gull**	*Pagophila eburnea*																					IV		R	0604
A	**Sabine's Gull**	*Xema sabini*																					AB			0579
A	**Slender-billed Gull**	*Chroicocephalus genei*																					EI	C	R	0585
A	**Bonaparte's Gull**	*Chroicocephalus philadelphia*																					ON		R	0581
A	**Black-headed Gull**	*Chroicocephalus ridibundus*																					BH			0582
A	**Little Gull**	*Hydrocoloeus minutus*																					LU	B		0578
A	**Ross's Gull**	*Rhodostethia rosea*																					QG		R	0601
A	**Laughing Gull**	*Leucophaeus atricilla*																					LF		R	0576
A	**Franklin's Gull**	*Leucophaeus pipixcan*																					FG		R	0577
A	**Audouin's Gull**	*Ichthyaetus audouinii*																							R	0589
A	**Mediterranean Gull**	*Ichthyaetus melanocephalus*																					MU	A		0575
B	**Great Black-headed Gull**	*Ichthyaetus ichthyaetus*																							R	0573
A	**Common Gull**	*Larus canus*																					CM			0590
A	**Ring-billed Gull**	*Larus delawarensis*																					IN	B		0588
A	**Great Black-backed Gull**	*Larus marinus*																					GB			0600
A	**Glaucous-winged Gull**	*Larus glaucescens*																							R	5960
A	**Glaucous Gull**	*Larus hyperboreus*																					GZ	B		0599
A	**Iceland Gull**	*Larus glaucoides*																					IG		*	0598
A	**Herring Gull**	*Larus argentatus*																					HG			0592
A	**American Herring Gull**	*Larus smithsonianus*																							R	26632
A	**Caspian Gull**	*Larus cachinnans*																								5927
	Sub total																									

	GULLS, TERNS, SKUAS		Life	2021	Jan	Feb	Mar	Apr	May	Jun	Jul	Aug	Sep	Oct	Nov	Dec	A	B	C	D	E	F	BTO	RBBP	BBRC	EU
A	**Yellow-legged Gull**	*Larus michahellis*																					YG	A	*	5927
A	**Slaty-backed Gull**	*Larus schistisagus*																							R	
A	**Lesser Black-backed Gull**	*Larus fuscus*																					LB		*	0591
A	**Gull-billed Tern**	*Gelochelidon nilotica*																					TG	B	R	0605
A	**Caspian Tern**	*Hydroprogne caspia*																					CJ		R	0606
A	**Royal Tern**	*Thalasseus maximus*																					QT		R	0607
A	**Lesser Crested Tern**	*Thalasseus bengalensis*																					TF	B	R	0609
A	**Sandwich Tern**	*Thalasseus sandvicensis*																					TE			0611
A	**Cabot's Tern**	*Thalasseus acuflavida*																							R	
A	**Elegant Tern**	*Thalasseus elegans*																							R	
A	**Little Tern**	*Sternula albifrons*																					AF	A		0624
A	**Least Tern**	*Sternula antillarum*																							R	
A	**Aleutian Tern**	*Onychoprion aleuticus*																							R	0617
A	**Bridled Tern**	*Onychoprion anaethetus*																							R	0622
A	**Sooty Tern**	*Onychoprion fuscatus*																							R	0623
A	**Roseate Tern**	*Sterna dougallii*																					RS	A		0614
A	**Common Tern**	*Sterna hirundo*																					CN			0615
A	**Arctic Tern**	*Sterna paradisaea*																					AE			0616
A	**Forster's Tern**	*Sterna forsteri*																					FO		R	0618
A	**Whiskered Tern**	*Chlidonias hybrida*																					WD		R	0626
A	**White-winged Black Tern**	*Chlidonias leucopterus*																					WJ			0628
A	**Black Tern**	*Chlidonias niger*																					BJ	B	*	0627
A	**Great Skua**	*Stercorarius skua*																					NX			0569
A	**Pomarine Skua**	*Stercorarius pomarinus*																					PK			0566
	Sub total																									

	SKUAS, AUKS, TROPICBIRD, DIVERS, ALBATROSSES, PETRELS		Life	2021	Jan	Feb	Mar	Apr	May	Jun	Jul	Aug	Sep	Oct	Nov	Dec	A	B	C	D	E	F	BTO	RBBP	BBRC	EU
A	**Arctic Skua**	*Stercorarius parasiticus*																					AC	A		0567
A	**Long-tailed Skua**	*Stercorarius longicaudus*																					OG	B		0568
A	**Little Auk**	*Alle alle*																					LK			0647
A	**Brunnich's Guillemot**	*Uria lomvia*																					TZ		R	0635
A	**Common Guillemot**	*Uria aalge*																					GU			0634
A	**Razorbill**	*Alca torda*																					RA			0636
B	**Great Auk (extinct)**	*Pinguinus impennis*																								
A	**Black Guillemot**	*Cepphus grylle*																					TY			0638
A	**Long-billed Murrelet**	*Brachyramphus perdix*																							R	6412
A	**Ancient Murrelet**	*Synthliboramphus antiquus*																							R	0645
A	**Puffin**	*Fratercula arctica*																					PU			0654
A	**Tufted Puffin**	*Fratercula cirrhata*																							R	3565
AE	**Red-billed Tropicbird**	*Phaethon aethereus*																							R	0064
A	**Red-throated Diver**	*Gavia stellata*																					RH	A		0002
A	**Black-throated Diver**	*Gavia arctica*																					BV	A		0003
A	**Pacific Diver**	*Gavia pacifica*																							R	0033
A	**Great Northern Diver**	*Gavia immer*																					ND	C		0004
A	**White-billed Diver**	*Gavia adamsii*																					VW	C		0005
A	**Wilson's Petrel**	*Oceanites oceanicus*																								0050
B	**White-faced Storm Petrel**	*Pelagodroma marina*																							R	0051
A	**Black-browed Albatross**	*Thalassarche melanophris*																					AA	C	R	0014
A	**Atlantic Yellow-nosed Albatross**	*Thalassarche chlororhynchos*																							R	0150
A	**Storm Petrel**	*Hydrobates pelagicus*																					TM			0052
A	**Swinhoe's Petrel**	*Oceanodroma monorhis*																							R	0056
	Sub total																									

	PETRELS, SHEARWATERS, STORKS, CORMORANTS		Life	2021	Jan	Feb	Mar	Apr	May	Jun	Jul	Aug	Sep	Oct	Nov	Dec	A	B	C	D	E	F	BTO	RBBP	BBRC	EU
A	**Leach's Petrel**	*Oceanodroma leucorhoa*																					TL			0055
A	**Fulmar**	*Fulmarus glacialis*																					F.			0020
A	**Black-capped Petrel**	*Pterodroma hasitata*																							R	0029
A	**Scopoli's Shearwater**	*Calonectris diomedea*																							R	
A	**Cory's Shearwater**	*Calonectris borealis*																					CQ			0036
A	**Sooty Shearwater**	*Ardenna griseus*																					OT			0043
A	**Great Shearwater**	*Ardenna gravis*																					GQ			0040
A	**Manx Shearwater**	*Puffinus puffinus*																					MX			0046
A	**Yelkouan Shearwater**	*Puffinus yelkouan*																							R	
A	**Balearic Shearwater**	*Puffinus mauretanicus*																								0046
A	**Barolo Shearwater**	*Puffinus baroli*																						C	R	0048
AE	**Black Stork**	*Ciconia nigra*																					OS		R	0131
AE	**White Stork**	*Ciconia ciconia*																					OR	C		0134
A	**Ascension Frigatebird**	*Fregata aquila*																							R	
A	**Magnificent Frigatebird**	*Fregata magnificens*																							R	0093
A	**Gannet**	*Morus bassanus*																					GX			0071
A	**Red-footed Booby**	*Sula sula*																							R	
AE	**Double-crested Cormorant**	*Phalacrocorax auritus*																							R	0078
A	**Shag**	*Phalacrocorax aristotelis*																					SA			0080
A	**Cormorant**	*Phalacrocorax carbo*																					CA			0072
AE	**Glossy Ibis**	*Plegadis falcinellus*																					IB	C		0136
AE	**Spoonbill**	*Platalea leucorodia*																					NB	A		0144
A	**Bittern**	*Botaurus stellaris*																					BI	A		0095
A	**American Bittern**	*Botaurus lentiginosus*																					AM		R	0096
	Sub total																									

	BITTERNS/HERONS/EGRETS, PELICAN, RAPTORS		Life	2021	Jan	Feb	Mar	Apr	May	Jun	Jul	Aug	Sep	Oct	Nov	Dec	A	B	C	D	E	F	BTO	RBBP	BBRC	EU
A	Little Bittern	*Ixobrychus minutus*																					LL	B	R	0098
AE*	Night-heron	*Nycticorax nycticorax*																					NT	E		0104
A	Green Heron	*Butorides virescens*																					HR		R	0107
A	Squacco Heron	*Ardeola ralloides*																					QH		R	0108
A	Chinese Pond Heron	*Ardeola bacchus*																							R	
AE	Cattle Egret	*Bubulcus ibis*																					EC	B		0111
A	Grey Heron	*Ardea cinerea*																					H.			0122
A	Great Blue Heron	*Ardea herodias*																							R	1230
A	Purple Heron	*Ardea purpurea*																					UR	B		0124
A	Great White Egret	*Ardea alba*																					HW	C		0121
A	Snowy Egret	*Egretta thula*																							R	0115
A	Little Egret	*Egretta garzetta*																					ET	A		0119
A	Dalmatian Pelican	*Pelecanus crispus*																							R	
AE*	Osprey	*Pandion haliaetus*																					OP	A		0301
BDE	Egyptian Vulture	*Neophron percnopterus*																							R	0247
A	Honey-buzzard	*Pernis apivorus*																					HZ	A		0231
A	Short-toed Eagle	*Circaetus gallicus*																							R	0256
B	Spotted Eagle	*Clanga clanga*																							R	0293
AE	Golden Eagle	*Aquila chrysaetos*																					EA	A		0296
A	Sparrowhawk	*Accipiter nisus*																					SH			0269
AC3E*	Goshawk	*Accipiter gentilis*																					GI	A		0267
A	Marsh Harrier	*Circus aeruginosus*																					MR	A		0260
A	Hen Harrier	*Circus cyaneus*																					HH	A		0261
A	Northern Harrier	*Circus hudsonius*																							R	
	Sub total																									

	RAPTORS, OWLS, KINGFISHERS, WOODPECKERS		Life	2021	Jan	Feb	Mar	Apr	May	Jun	Jul	Aug	Sep	Oct	Nov	Dec	A	B	C	D	E	F	BTO	RBBP	BBRC	EU
A	Pallid Harrier	*Circus macrourus*																						C	R	0262
A	Montagu's Harrier	*Circus pygargus*																					MO	A		0263
AC3E*	Red Kite	*Milvus milvus*																					KT			0239
AE	Black Kite	*Milvus migrans*																					KB	B		0238
AC3E*	White-tailed Eagle	*Haliaeetus albicilla*																					WE	A		0243
AE	Rough-legged Buzzard	*Buteo lagopus*																					RF	C		0290
AE*	Buzzard	*Buteo buteo*																					BZ			0287
AE*	Barn Owl	*Tyto alba*																					BO		*	0735
A	Scops Owl	*Otus scops*																						C	R	0739
AE	Snowy Owl	*Bubo scandiacus*																					SO	B	R	0749
A	Tawny Owl	*Strix aluco*																					TO			0761
A	Hawk Owl	*Surnia ulula*																							R	0750
C1E*	Little Owl	*Athene noctua*																					LO			0757
A	Tengmalm's Owl	*Aegolius funereus*																							R	0770
A	Long-eared Owl	*Asio otus*																					LE	A		0767
A	Short-eared Owl	*Asio flammeus*																					SE	A		0768
AE	Hoopoe	*Upupa epops*																					HP	B		0846
A	Roller	*Coracias garrulus*																							R	0841
A	Kingfisher	*Alcedo atthis*																					KF			0831
A	Belted Kingfisher	*Megaceryle alcyon*																							R	0834
A	Blue-cheeked Bee-eater	*Merops persicus*																							R	0839
A	Bee-eater	*Merops apiaster*																					MZ	B		0840
A	Wryneck	*Jynx torquilla*																					WY	A		0848
A	Yellow-bellied Sapsucker	*Sphyrapicus varius*																							R	0872
	Sub total																									

	WOODPECKERS, FALCONS, USA FLYCATCHERS, SHRIKES		Life	2021	Jan	Feb	Mar	Apr	May	Jun	Jul	Aug	Sep	Oct	Nov	Dec	A	B	C	D	E	F	BTO	RBBP	BBRC	EU
A	Lesser Spotted Woodpecker	*Dryobates minor*																					LS	A		0887
A	Great Spotted Woodpecker	*Dendrocopos major*																					GS			0876
A	Green Woodpecker	*Picus viridis*																					G.			0856
A	Lesser Kestrel	*Falco naumanni*																							R	0303
A	Kestrel	*Falco tinnunculus*																					K.			0304
AE	American Kestrel	*Falco sparverius*																							R	0305
A	Red-footed Falcon	*Falco vespertinus*																					FV			0307
AE	Amur Falcon	*Falco amurensis*																							R	3080
A	Eleonora's Falcon	*Falco eleonorae*																							R	0311
A	Merlin	*Falco columbarius*																					ML	A		0309
A	Hobby	*Falco subbuteo*																					HY	A		0310
AE	Gyr Falcon	*Falco rusticolus*																					YF	C	R	0318
AE	Peregrine	*Falco peregrinus*																					PE	A		0320
C1E*	Ring-necked Parakeet	*Psittacula krameri*																					RI			0712
A	Eastern Phoebe	*Sayornis phoebe*																							R	0909
A	Acadian Flycatcher	*Empidonax virescens*																							R	
A	Alder Flycatcher	*Empidonax alnorum*																							R	9023
A	Eastern Kingbird	*Tyrannus tyrannus*																							R	
A	Brown Shrike	*Lanius cristatus*																							R	1513
A	Red-backed Shrike	*Lanius collurio*																					ED	A		1515
A	Daurian Shrike	*Lanius isabellinus*																					IL		R	1514
A	Turkestan Shrike	*Lanius phoenicuroides*																							R	
A	Long-tailed Shrike	*Lanius schach*																							R	1517
A	Lesser Grey Shrike	*Lanius minor*																							R	1519
	Sub total																									

	SHRIKES, VIREOS, ORIOLE, CORVIDS, WAXWINGS, TITS		Life	2021	Jan	Feb	Mar	Apr	May	Jun	Jul	Aug	Sep	Oct	Nov	Dec	A	B	C	D	E	F	BTO	RBBP	BBRC	EU
A	**Great Grey Shrike**	*Lanius excubitor*																					SR	C		1520
A	**Woodchat Shrike**	*Lanius senator*																					OO		*	1523
A	**Masked Shrike**	*Lanius nubicus*																							R	1524
A	**Yellow-throated Vireo**	*Vireo flavifrons*																							R	1628
A	**Philadelphia Vireo**	*Vireo philadelphicus*																							R	1631
A	**Red-eyed Vireo**	*Vireo olivaceus*																					EV		R	1633
A	**Golden Oriole**	*Oriolus oriolus*																					OL	A		1508
A	**Jay**	*Garrulus glandarius*																					J.			1539
A	**Magpie**	*Pica pica*																					MG			1549
A	**Nutcracker**	*Nucifraga caryocatactes*																					NC		R	1557
AE*	**Chough**	*Pyrrhocorax pyrrhocorax*																					CF	A		1559
A	**Jackdaw**	*Coloeus monedula*																					JD			1560
A	**Rook**	*Corvus frugilegus*																					RO			1563
A	**Carrion Crow**	*Corvus corone*																					C.			1567
A	**Hooded Crow**	*Corvus cornix*																					HC			1567
A	**Raven**	*Corvus corax*																					RN			1572
AE	**Waxwing**	*Bombycilla garrulus*																					WX	C		1048
AE	**Cedar Waxwing**	*Bombycilla cedrorum*																							R	1046
A	**Coal Tit**	*Periparus ater*																					CT			1461
A	**Crested Tit**	*Lophophanes cristatus*																					CI		*	1454
A	**Marsh Tit**	*Poecile palustris*																					MT			1440
A	**Willow Tit**	*Poecile montana*																					WT	A	*	1442
A	**Blue Tit**	*Cyanistes caeruleus*																					BT			1462
A	**Great Tit**	*Parus major*																					GT			1464
	Sub total																									

	PENDULINE TIT, LARKS, MARTINS, SWALLOWS, WARBLERS		Life	2021	Jan	Feb	Mar	Apr	May	Jun	Jul	Aug	Sep	Oct	Nov	Dec	A	B	C	D	E	F	BTO	RBBP	BBRC	EU
A	Penduline Tit	*Remiz pendulinus*																					DT	B		1490
A	Bearded Tit	*Panurus biarmicus*																					BR	A		1364
A	Woodlark	*Lullula arborea*																					WL			0974
A	White-winged Lark	*Alauda leucoptera*																							R	0965
A	Skylark	*Alauda arvensis*																					S.			0976
AE	Crested Lark	*Galerida cristata*																							R	0972
A	Shore Lark	*Eremophila alpestris*																					SX	B		0978
A	Short-toed Lark	*Calandrella brachydactyla*																					VL	C		0968
A	Bimaculated Lark	*Melanocorypha bimaculata*																							R	0962
A	Calandra Lark	*Melanocorypha calandra*																							R	0961
A	Black Lark	*Melanocorypha yeltoniensis*																							R	0966
A	Lesser Short-toed Lark	*Alaudala rufescens*																							R	0970
A	Sand Martin	*Riparia riparia*																					SM			0981
A	Tree Swallow	*Tachycineta bicolor*																							R	0983
A	Purple Martin	*Progne subis*																							R	0989
AE	Swallow	*Hirundo rustica*																					SL			0992
A	Crag Martin	*Ptyonoprogne rupestris*																							R	0991
A	House Martin	*Delichon urbicum*																					HM			1001
A	Red-rumped Swallow	*Cecropis daurica*																					VR	C	*	0995
A	American Cliff Swallow	*Petrochelidon pyrrhonota*																							R	0998
A	Cetti's Warbler	*Cettia cetti*																					CW			1220
A	Long-tailed Tit	*Aegithalos caudatus*																					LT		*	1437
A	Wood Warbler	*Phylloscopus sibilatrix*																					WO			1308
A	Western Bonelli's Warbler	*Phylloscopus bonelli*																					IW	C	R	1307
	Sub total																									

	WARBLERS		Life	2021	Jan	Feb	Mar	Apr	May	Jun	Jul	Aug	Sep	Oct	Nov	Dec	A	B	C	D	E	F	BTO	RBBP	BBRC	EU
A	**Eastern Bonelli's Warbler**	*Phylloscopus orientalis*																							R	1307
A	**Hume's Warbler**	*Phylloscopus humei*																							R	1300
A	**Yellow-browed Warbler**	*Phylloscopus inornatus*																					YB			1300
A	**Pallas's Warbler**	*Phylloscopus proregulus*																					PA	C		1298
A	**Radde's Warbler**	*Phylloscopus schwarzi*																								1301
A	**Dusky Warbler**	*Phylloscopus fuscatus*																					UY			1303
A	**Willow Warbler**	*Phylloscopus trochilus*																					WW			1312
A	**Chiffchaff**	*Phylloscopus collybita*																					CC			1311
A	**Iberian Chiffchaff**	*Phylloscopus ibericus*																						C	R	1311
A	**Eastern Crowned Warbler**	*Phylloscopus coronatus*																							R	12860
A	**Green Warbler**	*Phylloscopus nitidus*																							R	12910
A	**Two-barred Greenish Warbler**	*Phylloscopus plumbeitarsus*																							R	
A	**Greenish Warbler**	*Phylloscopus trochiloides*																					NP	C	R	1293
A	**Pale-legged Leaf Warbler**	*Phylloscopus tenellipes*																							R	
A	**Arctic Warbler**	*Phylloscopus borealis*																					AP			1295
A	**Great Reed Warbler**	*Acrocephalus arundinaceus*																					QW	C	R	1253
A	**Aquatic Warbler**	*Acrocephalus paludicola*																					AQ		R	1242
A	**Sedge Warbler**	*Acrocephalus schoenobaenus*																					SW			1243
A	**Paddyfield Warbler**	*Acrocephalus agricola*																					PY		R	1247
A	**Blyth's Reed Warbler**	*Acrocephalus dumetorum*																						C		1248
A	**Reed Warbler**	*Acrocephalus scirpaceus*																					RW			1251
A	**Marsh Warbler**	*Acrocephalus palustris*																					MW	A		1250
A	**Thick-billed Warbler**	*Iduna aedon*																							R	1254
A	**Booted Warbler**	*Iduna caligata*																						C	R	1256
	Sub total																									

	WARBLERS		Life	2021	Jan	Feb	Mar	Apr	May	Jun	Jul	Aug	Sep	Oct	Nov	Dec	A	B	C	D	E	F	BTO	RBBP	BBRC	EU
A	**Sykes's Warbler**	*Iduna rama*																							R	12562
A	**Eastern Olivaceous Warbler**	*Iduna pallida*																							R	1255
A	**Olive-tree Warbler**	*Hippolais olivetorum*																							R	12580
A	**Melodious Warbler**	*Hippolais polyglotta*																					ME	C		1260
A	**Icterine Warbler**	*Hippolais icterina*																					IC	B		1259
A	**Pallas's Grasshopper Warbler**	*Helopsaltes certhiola*																							R	1233
A	**Lanceolated Warbler**	*Locustella lanceolata*																							R	1235
A	**Grasshopper Warbler**	*Locustella naevia*																					GH		*	1236
A	**River Warbler**	*Locustella fluviatilis*																					VW	C	R	1237
A	**Savi's Warbler**	*Locustella luscinioides*																					VI	A	R	1238
A	**Fan-tailed Warbler**	*Cisticola juncidis*																							R	1226
A	**Blackcap**	*Sylvia atricapilla*																					BC			1277
A	**Garden Warbler**	*Sylvia borin*																					GW			1276
A	**Barred Warbler**	*Sylvia nisoria*																					RR			1273
A	**Lesser Whitethroat**	*Sylvia curruca*																					LW			1274
A	**Western Orphean Warbler**	*Sylvia hortensis*																							R	1272
A	**Eastern Orphean Warbler**	*Sylvia crassirostris*																							R	
A	**Asian Desert Warbler**	*Sylvia nana*																						C	R	1270
A	**Whitethroat**	*Sylvia communis*																					WH			1275
A	**Dartford Warbler**	*Sylvia undata*																					DW	A		1262
A	**Marmora's Warbler**	*Sylvia sarda*																						C	R	1261
A	**Spectacled Warbler**	*Sylvia conspicillata*																						C	R	1264
A	**Eastern Subalpine Warbler**	*Sylvia cantillans*																						C	*	1265
A	**Western Subalpine Warbler**	*Sylvia iberiae*																						C	*	
	Sub total																									

	WARBLERS, CRESTS, NUTHATCH, STARLINGS, THRUSHES		Life	2021	Jan	Feb	Mar	Apr	May	Jun	Jul	Aug	Sep	Oct	Nov	Dec	A	B	C	D	E	F	BTO	RBBP	BBRC	EU
A	**Moltoni's Subalpine Warbler**	*Sylvia subalpina*																							R	
A	**Sardinian Warbler**	*Sylvia melanocephala*																						C	R	1267
A	**Rüppell's Warbler**	*Sylvia ruppeli*																							R	1269
A	**Firecrest**	*Regulus ignicapilla*																					FC	A		1315
A	**Goldcrest**	*Regulus regulus*																					GC			1314
A	**Wren**	*Troglodytes troglodytes*																					WR			1066
A	**Nuthatch**	*Sitta europaea*																					NH			1479
A	**Red-breasted Nuthatch**	*Sitta canadensis*																							R	1472
A	**Wallcreeper**	*Tichodroma muraria*																							R	1482
A	**Treecreeper**	*Certhia familiaris*																					TC		*	1486
A	**Short-toed Treecreeper**	*Certhia brachydactyla*																					TH	A	R	1487
A	**Grey Catbird**	*Dumetella carolinensis*																							R	1080
AE	**Northern Mockingbird**	*Mimus polyglottos*																							R	1067
A	**Brown Thrasher**	*Toxostoma rufum*																							R	1069
AE	**Rose-coloured Starling**	*Pastor roseus*																					OE			1594
A	**Starling**	*Sturnus vulgaris*																					SG			1582
AE	**Siberian Thrush**	*Geokichla sibirica*																							R	1171
A	**White's Thrush**	*Zoothera aurea*																							R	1170
A	**Varied Thrush**	*Ixoreus naevius*																					VT		R	1172
A	**Veery**	*Catharus fuscescens*																							R	1179
A	**Grey-cheeked Thrush**	*Catharus minimus*																							R	1178
A	**Swainson's Thrush**	*Catharus ustulatus*																							R	1177
A	**Hermit Thrush**	*Catharus guttatus*																							R	1176
A	**Wood Thrush**	*Hylocichla mustelina*																							R	1175
	Sub total																									

	THRUSHES, FLYCATCHERS		Life	2021	Jan	Feb	Mar	Apr	May	Jun	Jul	Aug	Sep	Oct	Nov	Dec	A	B	C	D	E	F	BTO	RBBP	BBRC	EU
A	**Ring Ouzel**	*Turdus torquatus*																					RZ			1186
A	**Blackbird**	*Turdus merula*																					B.			1187
A	**Eyebrowed Thrush**	*Turdus obscurus*																							R	1195
A	**Black-throated Thrush**	*Turdus atrogularis*																							R	1197
A	**Red-throated Thrush**	*Turdus ruficollis*																							R	11970
A	**Naumann's Thrush**	*Turdus naumanni*																							R	11960
A	**Dusky Thrush**	*Turdus eunomus*																							R	1196
A	**Fieldfare**	*Turdus pilaris*																					FF	A		1198
A	**Redwing**	*Turdus iliacus*																					RE	A		1201
A	**Song Thrush**	*Turdus philomelos*																					ST			1200
A	**Mistle Thrush**	*Turdus viscivorus*																					M.			1202
AE	**American Robin**	*Turdus migratorius*																					AR		R	1203
A	**Rufous-tailed Scrub Robin**	*Cercotrichas galactotes*																							R	1095
A	**Spotted Flycatcher**	*Muscicapa striata*																					SF			1335
A	**Asian Brown Flycatcher**	*Muscicapa dauurica*																							R	
A	**Robin**	*Erithacus rubecula*																					R.			1099
A	**Siberian Blue Robin**	*Larvivora cyane*																							R	1112
A	**Rufous-tailed Robin**	*Larvivora sibilans*																							R	1102
A	**Bluethroat**	*Luscinia svecica*																					BU	B		1106
A	**Thrush Nightingale**	*Luscinia luscinia*																					FN	C	R	1103
A	**Nightingale**	*Luscinia megarhynchos*																					N.		*	1104
A	**White-throated Robin**	*Irania gutturalis*																							R	1117
A	**Siberian Rubythroat**	*Calliope calliope*																							R	1105
AE	**Red-flanked Bluetail**	*Tarsiger cyanurus*																								1113
	Sub total																									

	FLYCATCHERS, CHATS, WHEATEARS, DIPPER, SPARROWS		Life	2021	Jan	Feb	Mar	Apr	May	Jun	Jul	Aug	Sep	Oct	Nov	Dec	A	B	C	D	E	F	BTO	RBBP	BBRC	EU
A	**Pied Flycatcher**	*Ficedula hypoleuca*																					PF		*	1349
A	**Collared Flycatcher**	*Ficedula albicollis*																							R	1348
A	**Red-breasted Flycatcher**	*Ficedula parva*																					FY			1343
A	**Taiga Flycatcher**	*Ficedula albicilla*																							R	1343
A	**Black Redstart**	*Phoenicurus ochruros*																					BX	A	*	1121
A	**Redstart**	*Phoenicurus phoenicurus*																					RT			1122
A	**Moussier's Redstart**	*Phoenicurus moussieri*																							R	1127
A	**Rock Thrush**	*Monticola saxatilis*																					OH		R	1162
AE	**Blue Rock Thrush**	*Monticola solitarius*																							R	1166
A	**Whinchat**	*Saxicola rubetra*																					WC			1137
A	**Stonechat**	*Saxicola rubicola*																					SC			1139
A	**Siberian Stonechat**	*Saxicola maurus*																							R	
A	**Stejneger's Stonechat**	*Saxicola stejnegeri*																							R	
A	**Wheatear**	*Oenanthe oenanthe*																					W.			1146
A	**Isabelline Wheatear**	*Oenanthe isabellina*																							R	1144
A	**Desert Wheatear**	*Oenanthe deserti*																							R	1149
A	**Western Black-eared Wheatear**	*Oenanthe hispanica*																							R	1148
A	**Eastern Black-eared Wheatear**	*Oenanthe melanoleuca*																							R	
A	**Pied Wheatear**	*Oenanthe pleschanka*																					PI		R	1147
A	**White-crowned Black Wheatear**	*Oenanthe leucopyga*																							R	1157
A	**Dipper**	*Cinclus cinclus*																					DI		*	1050
A	**House Sparrow**	*Passer domesticus*																					HS			1591
A	**Spanish Sparrow**	*Passer hispaniolensis*																							R	1592
A	**Tree Sparrow**	*Passer montanus*																					TS			1598
	Sub total																									

	SPARROWS, ACCENTORS, WAGTAILS, PIPITS, FINCHES		Life	2021	Jan	Feb	Mar	Apr	May	Jun	Jul	Aug	Sep	Oct	Nov	Dec	A	B	C	D	E	F	BTO	RBBP	BBRC	EU
A	**Rock Sparrow**	*Petronia petronia*																							R	1604
A	**Alpine Accentor**	*Prunella collaris*																							R	1094
A	**Siberian Accentor**	*Prunella montanella*																							R	
A	**Dunnock**	*Prunella modularis*																					D.			1084
A	**Yellow Wagtail**	*Motacilla flava*																					YW		*	1017
A	**Eastern Yellow Wagtail**	*Motacilla tschutschensis*																							R	
A	**Citrine Wagtail**	*Motacilla citreola*																						C		1018
A	**Grey Wagtail**	*Motacilla cinerea*																					GL			1019
A	**Pied Wagtail**	*Motacilla alba*																					PW		*	1020
A	**Richard's Pipit**	*Anthus richardi*																					PR			1002
A	**Blyth's Pipit**	*Anthus godlewskii*																							R	1004
A	**Tawny Pipit**	*Anthus campestris*																					TI		R	1005
A	**Meadow Pipit**	*Anthus pratensis*																					MP			1011
A	**Tree Pipit**	*Anthus trivialis*																					TP			1009
A	**Olive-backed Pipit**	*Anthus hodgsoni*																					OV			1008
A	**Pechora Pipit**	*Anthus gustavi*																							R	1010
A	**Red-throated Pipit**	*Anthus cervinus*																					VP		R	1012
A	**Buff-bellied Pipit**	*Anthus rubescens*																							R	1014
A	**Water Pipit**	*Anthus spinoletta*																					WI			1014
A	**Rock Pipit**	*Anthus petrosus*																					RC			1014
AE	**Chaffinch**	*Fringilla coelebs*																					CH			1636
A	**Brambling**	*Fringilla montifringilla*																					BL	B		1638
A	**Evening Grosbeak**	*Hesperiphona vespertina*																							R	1718
A	**Hawfinch**	*Coccothraustes coccothraustes*																					HF	A		1717
	Sub total																									

	FINCHES, BUNTINGS		Life	2021	Jan	Feb	Mar	Apr	May	Jun	Jul	Aug	Sep	Oct	Nov	Dec	A	B	C	D	E	F	BTO	RBBP	BBRC	EU
AE	**Pine Grosbeak**	*Pinicola enucleator*																							R	1699
A	**Bullfinch**	*Pyrrhula pyrrhula*																					BF			1710
AE	**Trumpeter Finch**	*Bucanetes githagineus*																							R	1676
A	**Common Rosefinch**	*Carpodacus erythrinus*																					SQ	B		1679
AE	**Greenfinch**	*Chloris chloris*																					GR			1649
A	**Twite**	*Linaria flavirostris*																					TW			1662
A	**Linnet**	*Linaria cannabina*																					LI			1660
A	**Common Redpoll**	*Acanthis flammea*																					FR	A		1663
A	**Lesser Redpoll**	*Acanthis cabaret*																					LR			1663
A	**Arctic Redpoll**	*Acanthis hornemanni*																					AL		R	1664
A	**Parrot Crossbill**	*Loxia pytyopsittacus*																					PC	A		1668
A	**Scottish Crossbill**	*Loxia scotica*																					CY			1667
A	**Crossbill**	*Loxia curvirostra*																					CR			1666
A	**Two-barred Crossbill**	*Loxia leucoptera*																					PD		R	1665
A	**Goldfinch**	*Carduelis carduelis*																					GO			1653
A	**Citril Finch**	*Carduelis citrinella*																							R	1644
A	**Serin**	*Serinus serinus*																					NS	B		1640
A	**Siskin**	*Spinus spinus*																					SK			1654
A	**Lapland Bunting**	*Calcarius lapponicus*																					LA	B		1847
A	**Snow Bunting**	*Plectrophenax nivalis*																					SB	A		1850
A	**Corn Bunting**	*Emberiza calandra*																					CB			1882
A	**Yellowhammer**	*Emberiza citrinella*																					Y.			1857
A	**Pine Bunting**	*Emberiza leucocephalos*																					EL		R	1856
A	**Rock Bunting**	*Emberiza cia*																							R	1860
	Sub total																									

	BUNTINGS, NEW WORLD SPARROWS~WARBLERS etc		Life	2021	Jan	Feb	Mar	Apr	May	Jun	Jul	Aug	Sep	Oct	Nov	Dec	A	B	C	D	E	F	BTO	RBBP	BBRC	EU
AE	**Ortolan Bunting**	*Emberiza hortulana*																					OB			1866
A	**Cretzschmar's Bunting**	*Emberiza caesia*																							R	1868
A	**Cirl Bunting**	*Emberiza cirlus*																					CL	A		1958
A	**Chestnut-eared Bunting**	*Emberiza fucata*																							R	1869
A	**Little Bunting**	*Emberiza pusilla*																					LJ			1874
A	**Yellow-browed Bunting**	*Emberiza chrysophrys*																							R	1871
A	**Rustic Bunting**	*Emberiza rustica*																							R	1873
AE	**Yellow-breasted Bunting**	*Emberiza aureola*																						C	R	1876
A	**Chestnut Bunting**	*Emberiza rutila*																							R	
AE	**Black-headed Bunting**	*Emberiza melanocephala*																							R	1881
AE	**Black-faced Bunting**	*Emberiza spodocephala*																							R	1853
A	**Pallas's Reed Bunting**	*Emberiza pallasi*																							R	1878
A	**Reed Bunting**	*Emberiza schoeniclus*																					RB			1877
E	**Song Sparrow**	*Melospiza melodia*																							R	1835
AE	**White-crowned Sparrow**	*Zonotrichia leucophrys*																							R	1839
AE	**White-throated Sparrow**	*Zonotrichia albicollis*																							R	1840
AE	**Dark-eyed Junco**	*Junco hyemalis*																					JU		R	1842
A	**Savannah Sparrow**	*Passerculus sandwichensis*																							R	1826
A	**Lark Sparrow**	*Chondestes grammacus*																							R	1824
A	**Eastern Towhee**	*Pipilo erythrophthalmus*																							R	1798
A	**Bobolink**	*Dolichonyx oryzivorus*																							R	1897
AE	**Baltimore Oriole**	*Icterus galbula*																							R	1918
A	**Red-winged Blackbird**	*Agelaius phoeniceus*																							R	
A	**Brown-headed Cowbird**	*Molothrus ater*																							R	1899
	Sub total																									

	NEW WORLD WARBLERS, TANAGERS		Life	2021	Jan	Feb	Mar	Apr	May	Jun	Jul	Aug	Sep	Oct	Nov	Dec	A	B	C	D	E	F	BTO	RBBP	BBRC	EU
A	**Ovenbird**	*Seiurus aurocapilla*																							R	1756
A	**Northern Waterthrush**	*Parkesia noveboracensis*																							R	1757
A	**Golden-winged Warbler**	*Vermivora chrysoptera*																							R	1722
A	**Black-and-white Warbler**	*Mniotilta varia*																							R	1720
A	**Tennessee Warbler**	*Leiothlypis peregrina*																							R	1724
A	**Common Yellowthroat**	*Geothlypis trichas*																							R	1762
A	**Hooded Warbler**	*Setophaga citrina*																							R	1771
AE	**American Redstart**	*Setophaga ruticilla*																							R	1755
A	**Cape May Warbler**	*Setophaga tigrina*																							R	1749
AE	**Northern Parula**	*Setophaga americana*																							R	1732
AE	**Magnolia Warbler**	*Setophaga magnolia*																							R	1750
A	**Bay-breasted Warbler**	*Setophaga castanea*																							R	1754
A	**Blackburnian Warbler**	*Setophaga fusca*																							R	1747
A	**Yellow Warbler**	*Setophaga aestiva*																							R	1733
A	**Chestnut-sided Warbler**	*Setophaga pensylvanica*																							R	1734
AE	**Blackpoll Warbler**	*Setophaga striata*																							R	1753
A	**Yellow-rumped Warbler**	*Setophaga coronata*																							R	1751
A	**Wilson's Warbler**	*Cardellina pusilla*																							R	1772
A	**Summer Tanager**	*Piranga rubra*																							R	1786
A	**Scarlet Tanager**	*Piranga olivacea*																							R	1788
A	**Rose-breasted Grosbeak**	*Pheucticus ludovicianus*																							R	1887
AE	**Indigo Bunting**	*Passerina cyanea*																							R	1892
	Sub total																									

	ADDITIONAL SPECIES	Life	2021	Jan	Feb	Mar	Apr	May	Jun	Jul	Aug	Sep	Oct	Nov	Dec	A	B	C	D	E	F	BTO	RBBP	BBRC	EU
	Sub total																								

BRITISH BUTTERFLY CHECKLIST

SPECIES	2021 list	Life list
Chequered Skipper		
Small Skipper		
Essex Skipper		
Lulworth Skipper		
Silver-spotted Skipper		
Large Skipper		
Dingy Skipper		
Grizzled Skipper		
Swallowtail		
Wood White		
Real's Wood White		
Clouded Yellow		
Brimstone		
Large White		
Small White		
Green-veined White		
Orange-tip		
Green Hairstreak		
Brown Hairstreak		
Purple Hairstreak		
White-letter Hairstreak		
Black Hairstreak		
Small Copper		
Small Blue		
Silver-studded Blue		
Brown Argus		
Northern Brown Argus		
Common Blue		
Chalkhill Blue		
Adonis Blue		
Holly Blue		
Duke of Burgundy		
White Admiral		
Purple Emperor		
Red Admiral		

SPECIES	2021 list	Life list
Painted Lady		
Small Tortoiseshell		
Peacock		
Comma		
Small Pearl-b'dered Fritillary		
Pearl-bordered Fritillary		
High Brown Fritillary		
Dark Green Fritillary		
Silver-washed Fritillary		
Marsh Fritillary		
Glanville Fritillary		
Heath Fritillary		
Speckled Wood		
Wall		
Mountain Ringlet		
Scotch Argus		
Marbled White		
Grayling		
Gatekeeper		
Meadow Brown		
Ringlet		
Small Heath		
Large Heath		
Additional Species		
TOTAL		

BRITISH DRAGONFLY CHECKLIST

SPECIES	2021 list	Life list
Banded Demoiselle		
Beautiful Demoiselle		
Small Red Damselfly		
Northern Damselfly		
Irish Damselfly		
Southern Damselfly		
Azure Damselfly		
Variable Damselfly		
Dainty Damselfly		
Common Blue Damselfly		
Red-eyed Damselfly		
Small Red-eyed Damselfly		
Blue-tailed Damselfly		
Scarce Blue-tailed Damselfly		
Large Red Damselfly		
Southern Emerald Damselfly		
Scarce Emerald Damselfly		
Emerald Damselfly		
Willow Emerald Damselfly		
Winter Damselfly		
White-legged Damselfly		
Southern Migrant Hawker		
Azure Hawker		
Southern Hawker		
Brown Hawker		
Norfolk Hawker		
Common Hawker		
Migrant Hawker		
Vagrant Emperor		
Emperor Dragonfly		
Lesser Emperor		
Hairy Dragonfly		
Golden-ringed Dragonfly		
Downy Emerald		
Orange-spotted Emerald		

SPECIES	2021 list	Life list
Northern Emerald		
Brilliant Emerald		
Common Club-tail		
Scarlet Darter		
White-faced Darter		
Broad-bodied Chaser		
Scarce Chaser		
Four-spotted Chaser		
Black-tailed Skimmer		
Keeled Skimmer		
Wandering Glider		
Black Darter		
Yellow-winged Darter		
Red-veined Darter		
Banded Darter		
Ruddy Darter		
Common Darter		
Additional Species		
TOTAL		

Neil Gartshore

Dungeness, on the southern tip of Kent, offers great birding prospects all year round. The area around the Bird Observatory is surrounded by shingle, scrub & gravel pits & has excellent seawatching, including 'The Patch'. The nearby gravel pits, scrub & reedbeds of the RSPB reserve have a good range of facilities. Make a day of it.

RESERVES DIRECTORY

NATURE RESERVES & BIRD OBSERVATORIES

Map of the regions

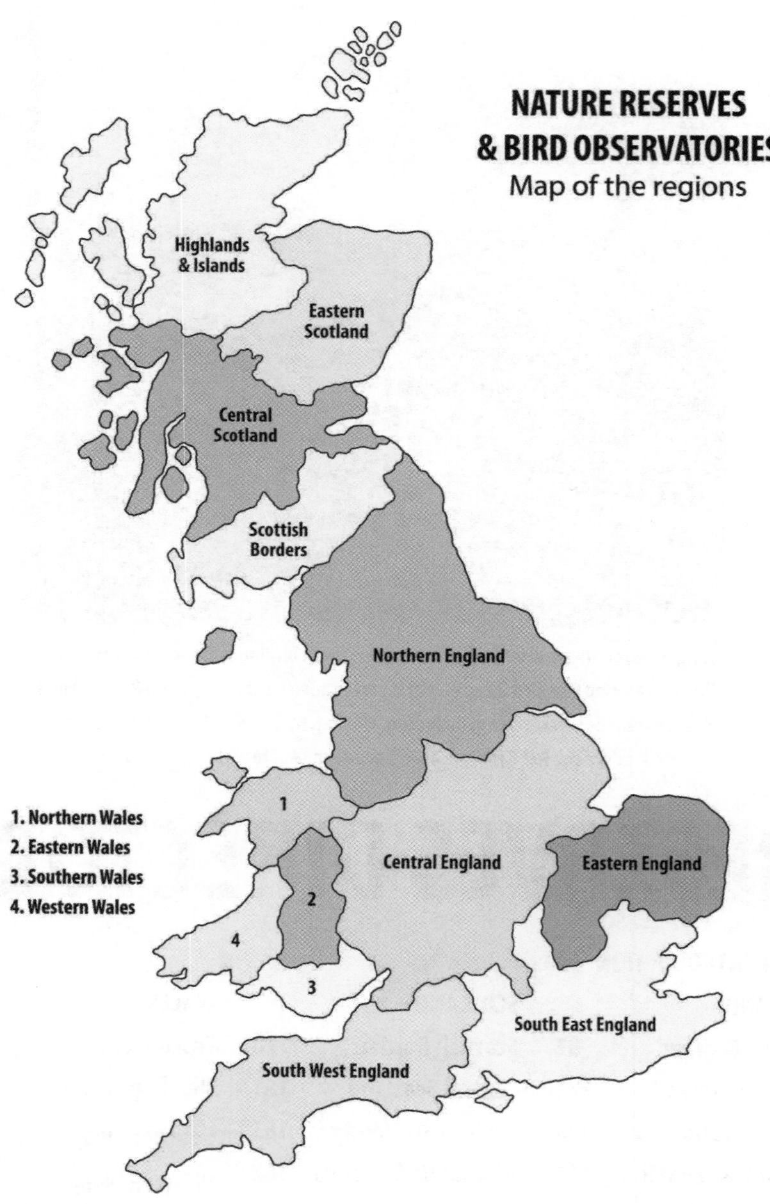

INTRODUCTION

The reserves are listed on a regional basis (see map). The aim of the directory is to give a flavour of what each county has to offer & includes many of their 'flagship' reserves.

Each entry covers:

Site name & ownership/management organisation.

Habitats: To find the greatest number of birds you will need to visit a variety of habitats - the main ones are listed for each reserve.

Birds: A small selection of the birds recorded on the reserves are highlighted along with the best time of year to see them i.e. *Summer*, *Winter*, *Passage*. Those listed tend to be the main attractions of the reserve but don't forget that there will be far more 'regular' species around.

Other: Being nature reserves they offer far more than just birds. Butterflies & dragonflies are well represented & are often fairly easy to see. Mammals can be a little more elusive but with a little patience (& for some species, with a little luck!) you may see them. Spectacular displays of flowers depend on the time of year. Rarities of individual species, of all groups, will usually depend on some knowledge of them - joining a guided walk could be a good option.

Directions: A 'sat nav' post code & grid reference are given along with a short description of how to find the reserves - use these in conjunction with a road map (unless you are happy to put your faith in your sat nav!)

Public transport: Details are noted where it's reasonably practical to get to a reserve (a short taxi ride may be necessary from the nearest bus/train stop). If it's impractical then 'none' is listed. You are strongly advised to check with the transport providers noted (or via *Traveline* - see below) before travelling as services & timetables can change - many services don't run on Sundays.

Traveline is a partnership of transport companies, local authorities & passenger groups providing a platform either by phone or online to plan your journey.

T: 0871 200 22 33 (charge of 12p/minute applies, your phone company may also add a charge).

W: www.traveline.info

Visiting: This is a catch-all section which includes information about access/opening times of the reserve & its facilities (including car parking, visitor centres, cafes, toilets, hides, viewing screens, trails, disabled access & dogs).

Wheelchair/disabled access (& pushchairs) - it is advisable to contact the reserve directly if you have any special requirements or to check the available facilities.

Dogs *(with the exception of assistance dogs)* - in many cases they are not permitted on the reserve and/or in the visitor centre or out on the reserve they may have to be kept on a (short) lead or be under 'close control'. Any dog mess should be picked up & disposed of in the bins provided... or taken offsite. Do not leave dogs unattended in cars. It is the owners responsibility to comply with these requests.

Contact: For each reserve a (T) telephone number & (E) e-mail address are listed &, in a few cases, a (W) website address.

••••••••••

Although the information has been checked, some changes (under all headings) are inevitable. It may be advisable to contact the reserve or check other sources, especially if you need to travel a distance to get there.

We welcome feedback on this section of *The Yearbook*, including any recommendations for reserves that could be included/replaced. Please send comments to the Editor (see page 6).

Central England

Derbyshire, Gloucestershire, Leicestershire & Rutland, Lincolnshire, Northamptonshire, Nottinghamshire, Oxfordshire, Shropshire, Staffordshire, Warwickshire & West Midlands, Worcestershire

Derbyshire

For its size, the county has a wide range of habitats & includes the majority of the Peak District National Park within its borders - Pied Flycatcher, Redstart & Wood Warbler can be found here. A variety of water bodies in the southern half of the county, including Carsington Water, Ogston Reservoir & Willington Gravel Pits, hold a good selection of waterfowl during the winter as well as large gull roosts that are always worth checking out.

1. CARR VALE NATURE RESERVE

Derbyshire Wildlife Trust.
Habitats: Lakes, wader flashes, reedbed, sewage farm, scrub, arable fields.
Birds: Up to 150 spp. annually, long list of rarities. *Spring/autumn:* Migrants inc. pipits & thrushes. In Sep, Swallows gather in the marsh in a large roost of 1,000-2,000 birds, which often attracts Hobby. *Early summer:* Breeding birds inc. Gadwall, Skylark, Reed & Sedge Warblers, Whitethroat & Yellowhammer. *Winter:* Large numbers of wildfowl (inc. flocks of Wigeon & Teal), Water Rail. Flocks of finches & buntings.
Other: Dragonflies, Brown Hare, Harvest Mouse, Water Shrew, Grass Snake.
Directions: Sat nav: S44 6GA. SK 459 702. 0.75 mile W of Bolsover on A632 to Chesterfield. Turn L at roundabout (follow brown tourist signs) into Riverside Way. Use the County Council's Peter Fidler car park off Riverside Way.
Public transport: Bus - nos.82, 82A & 83 serve roundabout on A632 & no.83 serves Villas Road - from Chesterfield (Stephenson Place). Stagecoach.
Visiting: Open all year. Car park, coach parking on approach road, good disabled access, paths, three viewing platforms, hides. Follow waymarked footpath around Peter Fidler reserve. Dogs only on leads.
Contact: Derbyshire WT, T: 01773 881 188;
E: enquiries@derbyshirewt.co.uk

2. CARSINGTON WATER

Severn Trent Water.
Habitats: Open water, islands, small reedbed, mixed woodland, scrub, grassland.
Birds: 220+ spp. *All year*: Willow Tit & Tree Sparrow. *Spring*: Good passage inc. Yellow & White Wagtails, Whimbrel, Black & Arctic Terns. *Summer*: Warblers & breeding waders (inc. Little Ringed Plover). Ospreys often stop-off during migration. *Winter*: Wildfowl & a large gull roost, possibility of divers & scarce grebe.
Other: Species-rich hay meadows, ancient woodlands with Bluebells, three spp. orchid, five spp. bat, 21 spp. butterflies, Water Vole.
Directions: Sat nav: DE6 1ST. SK 241 515 (visitor centre). Off B5035 Ashbourne to Wirksworth ro
Public transport: Bus - nos.110/111 (not Sun), Matlock to Ashbourne. Yourbus (T: 01773 714 013).
Visiting: Open all year (not Dec 25). Three car parks, open 7am-sunset (Apr-Oct, 7.30am in winter). Parking at visitor centre (pay-&-display) with reduced rates at Millfields & Sheepwash car parks. Visitor centre (open 10am-6pm Apr-Sep, 10am-5pm Oct-Mar): has exhibition, restaurant, four shops (inc. RSPB), play area & toilets. Good access for wheelchairs (can be borrowed at visitor centre), mobility scooters for hire. Four bird hides. Cycle & boat hire.
Contact: Carsington Water Visitor Centre,
T: 0330 6780 701;
E: carsingtonwater@severntrent.co.uk;
W: www.carsingtonbirdclub.co.uk

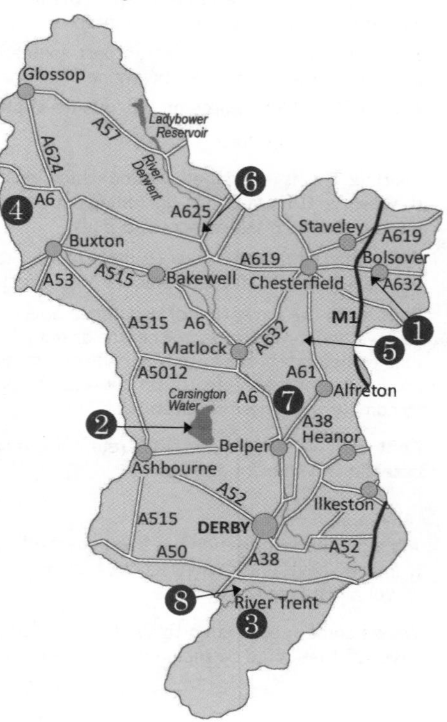

3. FOREMARK RESERVOIR & CARVER'S ROCK NR

Severn Trent Water/Derbyshire Wildlife Trust.
Habitats: FR - open water, coniferous woodland. CR - marsh, deciduous woodland, heathland.
Birds: *All Year:* Little & Great Crested Grebes, Woodcock, Barn, Little & Tawny Owls, Kingfisher. *Passage:* waders, terns, birds of prey. *Winter:* Wildfowl (inc. Goosander) & gulls with occasional scarcer spp., Siskin, Redpoll. Occasional rarities.
Other: 27 spp. butterflies & 300 spp. moths.
Directions: Sat nav: DE65 6EG. SK 336 242. Reservoir is five miles S of Derby, W of A514 at Ticknall (signed to reservoir/Milton), Carver's Rocks at S end of reservoir.
Public transport: None.
Visiting: Open all year (not 25 Dec), dawn-8pm (last admission 5pm). Pay-&-display car park (annual permit available), toilets (inc. disabled), some paths suitable for wheelchairs. Snack kiosk open Fri-Sun, Bank Hol Mondays & weekdays during school holidays.
Contact: Severn Trent Water, T: 01332 865 081;
E: staunton.foremark@severntrent.co.uk
Contact: Derbyshire Wildlife Trust (Carver's Rock) - see site 1.

4. GOYT VALLEY

Forestry England.
Habitats: River Goyt, two reservoirs, mixed conifer/broadleaved woodland, moorland.
Birds: *Spring/summer*: Breeding Wood Warbler, Pied & Spotted Flycatchers, Tree Pipit, Redstart, Cuckoo, Nightjar on restock areas & common woodland spp., Long-eared Owl & Goshawk also present. Dipper & Grey Wagtail on river, Common Sandpiper on Errwood Reservoir. Red Grouse, Curlew, Short-eared Owl, Whinchat & Ring Ouzel breed on moorland areas.
Directions: Sat nav: SK17 6SX (Errwood Hall car park, SK 011 748) for woodland birds, Derbyshire Bridge (SK 018 716) for moorland birds. From Buxton head N on A5004 (Manchester Road), then bear L on Goyt's Lane to Errwood Hall one-way system, between Errwood car park & Derbyshire Bridge.
Public transport: Train - Whaley Bridge & Buxton, both ca.3 miles from Errwood Reservoir.
Visiting: Open all year. Toilets at Derbyshire Bridge & Bonsal Cob. Several picnic sites. Footpath between Errwood Hall & Goyt's Clough Quarry. Use Old Coach Road for walk between Derbyshire Bridge & Burbage.
Contact: Forestry England, T: 0300 067 4340;
E: central.district@forestryengland.uk

5. OGSTON RESERVOIR

Severn Trent Water/Ogston Bird Club.
Habitats: Open water, pasture, mixed woodland.
Birds: *All year:* 3 spp. woodpecker, Little & Tawny Owls, Kingfisher, Grey Wagtail. *Summer:* warblers. *Passage:* raptors (inc. Osprey), terns & waders. *Winter*: Good numbers of wildfowl, tit & finch flocks. Gull roost attracts thousands of birds inc. regular Glaucous & Iceland Gulls. Top inland site for Bonaparte's Gull & also attracts birds from Caspian/Herring Gull complex.
Directions: Sat nav: DE55 6FL. SK 374 610. From Matlock, take A615 E to B6014, just after Tansley. From A61 (Alfreton to Chesterfield road), at White Bear pub, Stretton turn onto B6014 towards Tansley, cross railway, take L fork in road & continue over hill. Reservoir is on L after hill.
Public transport: Bus - no.63/63A (not Sun)Chesterfield to Matlock, both serve N end of reservoir. Hulleys (T: 01246 582 246).
Visiting: View from roads. Three car parks on N, S & W banks. Public hide (wheelchair access) reached from west bank car park (also suitable for smaller coaches). Heronry in nearby Ogston Carr Wood (private) viewable from Ogston new road, W of reservoir. Ogston BC organises monthly guided walks (see website for details) & members have access to three hides, (two wheelchair accessible) as well as club's own 1.5ha Jim Mart Nature Reserve, three miles N of Ogston.
Contact: Jenny Marshall Club Secretary, OBC),
T: 07533 973 809;
E: jen.marshall@birdinformation.co.uk;
W: www.ogstonbirdclub.co.uk

6. PADLEY GORGE (LONGSHAW ESTATE)

National Trust (East Midlands).
Habitats: Steep-sided valley containing largest area of sessile oak woodland in south Pennines.
Birds: *Spring/summer*: Pied & Spotted Flycatchers, Ring Ouzel, Redstart, Wheatear, Whinchat, Stonechat, Wood Warbler, Tree Pipit & common woodland spp.
Directions: Longshaw visitor centre - Sat nav: S11 7TZ. SK 267 800. From Sheffield, head SW on A625. After eight miles, turn L on B6521 to Nether Padley. Grindleford Station is just off B6521 (NW of Nether Padley) & one mile NE of Grindleford village.
Public transport: Bus - no.275 (not Sun) Sheffield to Bakewell. Hulleys (T: 01246 582 246). Train - Sheffield to Manchester Piccadilly stops at Grindleford Station.
Visiting: All year, dawn-dusk. Car parks, pay-&-display for non-NT members. Cafe, shop & toilets (inc. disabled) at Longshaw visitor centre. RADAR key needed for Hollin Bank, Hathersage toilets. Some paths are rocky - not suitable for disabled access or those unused to steep climbs. Dogs on leads only.
Contact: National Trust, High Peak Estate Office,
T: 01433 631 757; E: peakdistrict@nationaltrust.org.uk

7. SHINING CLIFF WOOD

Forestry England.
Habitats: Woodland - broadleaved & coniferous.
Birds: *All year:* Common woodland species inc. 3spp. Woodpecker, Woodcock. *Spring/summer*: Warblers inc. Wood & Garden, Redstart, Spotted Flycatcher. *Winter:* check feeding flocks for Firecrest. Winter thrushes, Hawfinch, Brambling, Redpoll, Siskin. [Nearby: canal path - Dipper, Kingfisher, Grey Wagtail & river: Goosander.]
Other: Woodland flora inc. Bluebell display.
Directions: Sat nav: DE56 2SR. SK 337 524. Located N of Belper on A6 to Matlock. Access wood from footpaths along minor road between Ambergate & Alderwasley.

Public transport: Bus - no.142 Belper to Alfreton stops at Ambergate (not Sun). Littles Travel (T: 0115 932 8581). Train - Whatstandwell & Ambergate (walk canal footpath between them, a Derbyshire Wildlife Trust reserve). From Ambergate, walk S on A6, turn R into Holly Lane & pick up public footpaths into wood.
Visiting: Open at all times. No formal parking facilities. Access to wood by public footpaths. Circular waymarked trail - passes by remains of 'Betty Kenny (Yew) Tree' said to be 2000 years old!
Contact: Forestry England - see site 4.

8. WILLINGTON WETLANDS

Derbyshire Wildlife Trust.
Habitats: Former gravel pits - open water, shingle island, reedbed, grassland.
Birds: *Summer:* Lapwing, Redshank, Oystercatcher, Common Tern, Cetti's, Reed & Sedge Warblers, raptors inc. Peregrine, Kestrel, Sparrowhawk & Hobby. *Passage:* up to 20 spp. waders in spring/autumn (large nos Curlew in spring). *Winter:* Large flocks of wildfowl (inc. Wigeon, Teal, Pochard & Shoveler), Bittern & waders.
Other: Short-leaved Water Starwort. Several spp. dragonflies, occasional signs of Otter.
Directions: Sat nav: DE65 6YB (Repton Road). SK 291 276. From A50 'Toyota Island' head towards Willington & Repton. Go through village towards Repton. Just before bridge over River Trent, turn R onto un-made track (Meadow Lane). Park here & walk along lane.
Public transport: Bus - no.V3 to Willington from Derby & Burton-on-Trent. Trent Barton Villager (T: 01773 712 265). Train - stops at Willington.
Visiting: Limited parking in lane. No access on site but viewing platforms situated along Meadow Lane (steps up to platforms).
Contact: Derbyshire WT - see site 1.

Gloucestershire

Lying between the River Severn & the Welsh border, the Forest of Dean/Wye Valley area is a good place to see Goshawk, Wood Warbler, Pied Flycatcher & Hawfinch. The Symonds Yat Peregrine watch point is worth a visit. On the east bank of the river, the wetlands of Slimbridge are well-known for their wintering geese & Bewick's Swans. The sand & gravel extractions of the Cotswold Water Park, partially shared with Wiltshire, is one of the largest man-made wetland complexes in the UK. They attract a wide selection of wintering waterfowl & passage waders.

1. COOMBE HILL CANAL & MEADOWS

Gloucestershire Wildlife Trust.
Habitats: Wet grassland/flood meadow, ditches, canal, scrub.
Birds: *Spring/summer:* Breeding waders inc. Oystercatcher, Lapwing, Ringed Plover, Redshank, Yellow Wagtail, warblers. *Passage:* Garganey, waders inc. Whimbrel, Ruff, Black-tailed Godwit, Common Sandpiper. *Winter:* Peregrine, wildfowl (inc. Pintail, Teal, Wigeon, Bewick's & Whooper Swans), Bittern, Water Rail,Snipe, winter thrushes.
Other: 17 spp. dragonflies inc. Hairy, Emperor & Scarce Chaser. Scarce plants inc. Fine-leaved Water-dropwort, Common Meadow-rue
Directions: Sat nav: GL19 4BB. SO 886 272. Midway between Gloucester & Tewkesbury off A38 at Coombe Hill. At crossroads in Coombe Hill take small no through road (The Wharf, by the Swan Inn) to car park. 0.5 mile walk from car park along canal towpath to entrance.
Public transport: Bus - no.71 Gloucester to Tewkesbury - stops near Swan Inn, Coombe Hill, Stagecoach (T: 01452 418 630).
Visiting: Open at all times. Small car park. Hide, paths level but can get rutted/muddy. Dogs on a lead.
Contact: Gloucestershire WT, T: 01452 383 333; E: info@gloucestershirewildlifetrust.co.uk

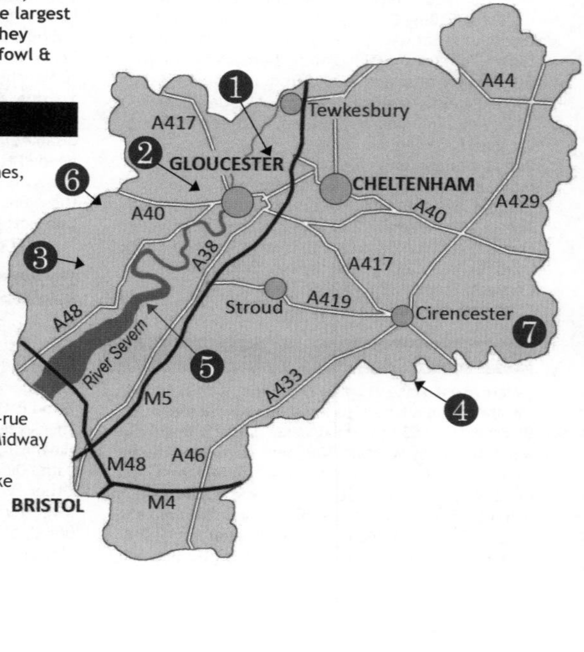

2. HIGHNAM WOODS

RSPB (South West England Office).
Habitats: Ancient woodland in Severn Vale with areas of coppice, scrub.
Birds: *All year:* Buzzard, Sparrowhawk, 3 spp. woodpecker, Marsh Tit, Raven. Hawfinch possible but elusive. *Spring/summer*: Up to 20 pairs of breeding Nightingale, Spotted Flycatcher & common migrant warblers. *Winter*: Feeding site near car park good for woodland birds.
Other: Tintern Spurge in Jun-Aug.
White Admiral & White-letter Hairstreak butterflies.
Directions: Sat nav: GL2 8AA. SO 778 190.
Signposted on A40, three miles W of Gloucester.
Public transport: Bus - nos.24 (Mon-Sun) & no.33 (Sun) Gloucester to Cinderford stops near Highnam Woods. Stagecoach.
Visiting: Open at all times. Car park, usually restricted to reserve events, can be opened for groups by arrangement (groups should book ahead). One nature trail (1.5 miles) - can be very muddy, some limited wheelchair access. One open-backed hide, 150 yards from car park. Dogs allowed on leads.
Contact: RSPB, T: 01594 562 852;
E: highnam.woods@rspb.org.uk

3. NAGSHEAD

RSPB (South West England Office).
Habitats: Much of reserve is 200-year-old oak plantations, grazed in some areas by sheep, with a mixture of open areas, conifer/mixed woodland.
Birds: *All year*: Buzzard, Goshawk, Woodcock, 3 spp. woodpecker, Raven, Hawfinch. *Spring/ Summer:* Pied Flycatcher, Wood Warbler & commoner warblers, Redstart, Tree Pipit. *Winter*: Mandarin, Siskin, Crossbill (some years), other finches.
Other: Golden-ringed Dragonfly seen annually. White Admiral, Silver-washed & Small Pearl-bordered Fritillary butterflies present. Wild Boar in the area.
Directions: Sat nav: GL15 4LA. SO 606 085. In Forest of Dean, N of Lydney. Signposted immediately W of Parkend village on B4431 road to Coleford.
Public transport: Bus - no.27 (not Sun) Lydney to Parkend. Stagecoach.
Visiting: Open at all times. Car park open dawn to dusk (coach/minibus access, advise in advance). Visitor centre (with toilets) open 10am-4pm at weekends from Easter to Sep. Two two circular waymarked nature trails (one mile & 2.25 miles) - trails hilly but there is limited wheelchair access. Two woodland hides not accessible to wheelchairs. Keep dogs on leads during bird nesting season.
Contact: RSPB, T: 01594 562 852;
E: nagshead@rspb.org.uk

4. SHORNCOTE REEDBEDS

Cotswold Water Park Trust.
Habitats: Lakes with reedbed, marsh, ditches, islands, loafing areas. [Part of CWP, covering 40 sq. miles/150 lakes, across Wilts, Gloucs & W Oxfordshire]
Birds: *Summer*: Breeding ducks, Little Grebe, warblers, Hobby, Snipe, Sand Martin, Reed Bunting. *Winter*: Common wildfowl, Bittern, Water Rail, Snipe, Peregrine, Merlin, Stonechat & Starling flocks.
Other: Otter, Water Vole, several spp. dragonflies.
Directions: Sat nav: GL7 5US (South Cerney car park). Lakes 84, 85A & 85B, Cotswold Water Park West. From A419 Cirencester to Swindon road, take B4696 towards Cotswold Water Park West. Turn R at crossroads (station Road) towards South Cerney. Follow road through village & park in playing fields car park after sharp R bend (SU 044 970). Take footpath through playing fields, cross road & continue on path through reedbeds to small lakes & hides.
Public transport: Buses - various routes from Kemble, Cheltenham, Cirencester & Swindon. Train - Kemble station four miles.
Visiting: Open at all times. Paths flood regularly in winter, wellies essential. Two hides. Toilets, refreshments, car parking/information available from nearby Cotswold Country Park (entry charge may apply). Alternative refreshments/toilets at Gateway Centre near A419 junction.
Contact: Cotswold Water Park Trust,
T: 01793 752 413; W: www.waterpark.org

5. SLIMBRIDGE

The Wildfowl & Wetlands Trust.
Habitats: Reedbed, freshwater pools, wet grassland, saltmarsh, mudflats. Captive waterfowl ponds.
Birds: 200+ spp. annually, good list of rarities. *Breeding:* Lapwing, Oystercatcher, Redshank, Little Ringed Plover, Common Tern, Kingfisher, Reed Bunting & a good range of warblers. *Passage:* Waders, terns & gulls (inc. Mediterranean & Yellow-legged). Yellow Wagtail & large passerine movements. Hobbies now reach double figures in summer. *Winter:* 30,000 to 40,000 wildfowl esp. Bewick's Swan, White-fronted Goose, Wigeon, Teal, Pintail. Waders inc. Lapwing, Golden Plover, Spotted Redshank & Little Stint. Often large roosts of Starlings & gulls.
Other: Brown Hare, Otter, Polecat & Water Vole. 22 spp. dragonflies inc. Scarce Chaser & Hairy Dragonfly.
Directions: Sat nav: GL2 7BT. SO 723 048. On banks of River Severn, S of Gloucester. Signposted from M5 (exit Junc 13 or 14). Into Slimbridge from A38.
Public transport: Local buses stop on A38. Train - stations at Cam & Dursley (4 miles).
Visiting: Open daily (not Dec 25) at 9.30am, closes 5.30pm (5pm in winter), last entry one hour before closing. Large car park with toilets. Admission charges for non-WWT members. Restaurant, shop, toilets, gallery, cinema, discovery centre. Outdoor facilities inc. a wildfowl collection of spp. from around world, an observatory & observation tower, 13 hides. Plenty of family attractions inc. a pond zone, wader aviary, commentated swan feeds in winter, Land Rover safaris & a canoe safari trail. All paths wheelchair accessible (wheelchair hire available, book in advance). Binoculars for hire. Assistance dogs only.
Contact: The Wildfowl & Wetlands Trust,
T: 01453 891 900; E: info.slimbridge@wwt.org.uk

6. SYMONDS YAT

RSPB/Forestry England.
Habitats: Cliff above the River Wye, woodland.
Birds: *Summer*: Peregrine, Buzzard, Goshawk, Sparrowhawk, Raven & woodland spp., (telescope is set up to watch nesting Peregrines).
Directions: Sat nav: HR9 6JL. SO 564 160. Hill-top site on edge of Forest of Dean, three miles N of Coleford on B4432, signposted from Coleford (brown tourist sign).
Public transport: Bus - from Coleford stops on B3342 inc. Symonds Yat car park.
Visiting: Open at all times. RSPB volunteers usually on site daily, late-Mar to early-Sep (10am-4pm). Car park (fee payable), toilets with adapted facilities for disabled visitors, picnic area, drinks & light snacks available.
Contact: RSPB, T: 01392 432 691;
E: swdatewithnature@rspb.org.uk

7. WELLFORD POOLS

Gloucestershire Wildlife Trust.
Habitats: Former gravel pit workings - two large lakes, three smaller dragonfly pools.
Birds: *Spring/summer:* Common Tern, Kingfisher, Nightingale, plus breeding Great Crested Grebe, Sedge Warbler & Reed Bunting. Artificial nesting bank for Sand Martins. *Passage:* waders. *Winter:* Wildfowl inc. Wigeon, Pochard & Tufted Ducks, occasional Bittern sightings.
Other: County's only site for Pea Mussel. Emperor, Migrant Hawker, Black-tailed Skimmer & Red-eyed Damselfly all breed.
Directions: Sat nav: GL7 4DY. SU 172 995. Lakes lie in eastern section of Cotswold Water Park between Fairford & Lechlade, from minor road S of A417.
Public transport: Cycle path from Lechlade.
Visiting: Open at all times. Car park for 12 vehicles (one disabled bay). Two bird hides. Dogs must be on leads.
Contact: Gloucestershire WT - see site 1.

Leicestershire & Rutland

These adjoining counties are well served with reservoirs, including Swithland, Eyebrook & Cropston - all attract wintering wildfowl & regular spring Black Tern passage. The jewel in the crown though is Rutland Water, home of the Bird Fair. Huge numbers of wildfowl & a good selection of passage waders can be found here while breeding Ospreys are the result of a successful re-introduction programme. The Wildlife Trust manages 35 nature reserves covering a broad range of habitats spread across the counties.

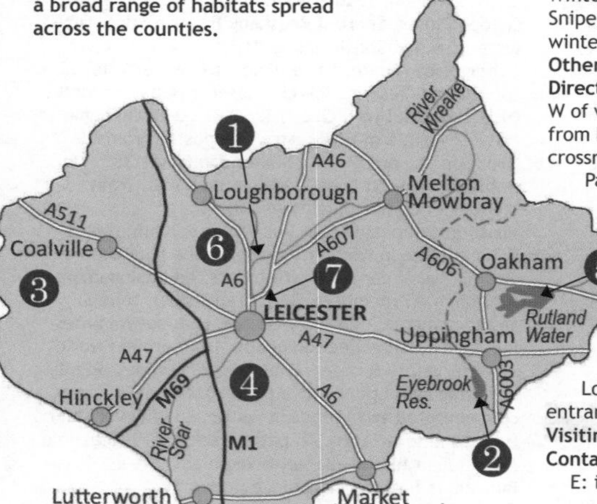

1. COSSINGTON MEADOWS

Leicestershire & Rutland Wildlife Trust.
Habitats: Deep lakes, shallow pools, lowland meadow & pasture, wet grassland, reedbed, scrub.
Birds: *All year:* Great Crested Grebe, Red-legged Partridge, Kingfisher, Reed Bunting. *Spring/autumn:* Waders inc. Common & Green Sandpipers, Ringed & Little Ringed Plovers, Redshank. Dunlin & Ruff. *Summer:* Sedge, Reed & Grasshopper Warblers. *Winter:* Wildfowl (inc. Teal, Wigeon, Goosander), Snipe, Jack Snipe, Green Sandpiper, Short-eared Owl, winter thrushes, Redpoll. Occasional rarities.
Other: Dragonflies, butterflies, Grass Snake
Directions: Sat nav: LE7 7NQ. SK 597 130. N of Leicester, W of village of Cossington, alongside River Soar. N on A6 from Leicester, take old A6 to Rothley, turn R at crossroads into Cossington Road becoming Syston Road. Park off road outside main entrance or in small public car park adjacent to Cossington Parish Church.
Public transport: Bus - no.2 (not Sun) Loughborough to Leicester stops in Cossington (alight at Garden Centre & walk along main road towards Rothley to reserve main entrance (0.3 mile). Kinchbus (T: 01509 815 637). Train - Sileby (on Leicester-Loughborough line) 1.2 mile walk to church entrance of reserve in Cossington.
Visiting: Open at all times.
Contact: Leics & Rutland WT, T: 0116 262 9968;
E: info@lrwt.org.uk

2. EYEBROOK RESERVOIR

Corby & District Water Co.
Habitats: Open water, plantations, pasture.
Birds: *Summer*: Good populations of breeding birds with sightings of Ospreys & Red Kite regular. *Passage:* waders & Black Tern. *Winter*: Wildfowl (inc. Goldeneye, Goosander, Smew), waders & gulls (often inc. less common spp.). Tree Sparrow & Yellowhammer at a LROS feeding station (SP 848 950) also Barn & Short-eared Owls may be seen hunting at dusk near Great Easton village (close to recycling centre). A good selection of rarities have turned up.
Other: Otter, Muntjac Deer, Red Darter & Blue Damselfly, Scalloped Hazel & Riband Wave moths.
Directions: Sat nav: LE15 9JG. SP 852 963. Reservoir built 1940. S of Uppingham, from unclassified road W of A6003 to Stoke Dry.
Public transport: None.
Visiting: There is no access to the private grounds but visiting by organised groups may be possible (contact first), otherwise view from road/roadside lay-bys. Fishing season Mar to Nov.
Contact: Eyebrook Trout Fishery,
T: 01536 770 264;
E: lodge@flyfisheyebrook.co.uk;
W: www.flyfisheyebrook.co.uk

3. HICKS LODGE

Forestry England.
Habitats: New native woodland, rough grassland, seasonally-grazed open fields, lakes & ponds. Largest lake has two small islands, one managed for Little Ringed Plover, other ground-nesting spp.
Birds: Raptors inc. Buzzard, Red Kite, Kestrel, Hobby, Sparrowhawk & Peregrine. Common wildfowl in winter, plus a good range of finches (inc. Crossbill), buntings, tits & summer warblers. Wader records inc. Bar-tailed Godwit, Greenshank, Ringed & Little Ringed Plovers, Common Sandpiper, Oystercatcher, Temminck's Stint, Lapwing & Golden Plover. *Passage:* migrants inc. Black Tern, Cuckoo, Wheatear, Whinchat, Stonechat, Spotted Flycatcher & hirundines.
Directions: Sat nav: LE65 2UP. SK 329 155. Within National Forest, approx 0.5 miles from Moira village. Follow brown tourist signs for National Forest Cycle Centre from Moira, Ashby-de-la-Zouch & from junc 12 of A42.
Public transport: None.
Visiting: Open all year: 8am-8pm. Height barrier at main entrance is removed when open, so no vehicle restrictions. Pay-&-display car park with designated disabled bays (5). On-site forest centre with small cafe (open 9am-5pm), toilets (inc. disabled & baby-changing facilities) & bike hire. All-ability trails & cycle trails. Most birdwatching activity occurs in front of main centre, around Hicks Lodge Loop & on the ponds/lakes & open fields. Hide, Sand Martin wall.
Contact: Forestry England, T: 0300 067 4340;
E: info_nationalforest@forestry.gsi.gov.uk

4. NARBOROUGH BOG

Leicestershire & Rutland Wildlife Trust.
Habitats: Peat bog (only substantial deposit in county), wet woodland, reedbed, dense scrub, fen meadow.
Birds: 130+ spp., inc. 3 spp. woodpecker, six spp. tit, Tawny Owl, Sparrowhawk & Kingfisher.
Other: Butterflies inc. Common Blue, Meadow Brown, Large & Small Skippers, Small Heath, Gatekeeper. Banded Demoiselle, good for moths & beetles. Harvest Mouse, Water Vole, breeding Grass Snake. Meadow Saxifrage, Common Meadow-rue, Marsh Thistle.
Directions: Sat nav: LE19 2AZ. SP 547 978. Between River Soar & M1, 5 miles S of Leicester. From city, turn L off B4114 (Leicester Road) just before going under motorway, follow track to sports club. Park near club house & walk across recreation ground to reserve entrance.
Public transport: Bus - no.X84 (not Sun) Leicester to Narborough (Abbey Rd stop), then short walk. Arriva in Midlands. Train - Narborough.
Visiting: Open at all times, keep to paths (not suitable for wheelchairs). May flood after heavy rain. Dogs on short leads only. Small bus/coach could park in sports field car park.
Contact: Leics & Rutland WT, see site 1.

5. RUTLAND WATER

Anglian Water/Leics & Rutland Wildlife Trust.
Habitats: Ramsar-designated reservoir, lagoons, scrapes, reedbeds, woods, meadows, plantations.
Birds: *Spring/autumn*: Outstanding wader passage, up to 28 spp. Wide range of raptors, owls, passerine flocks, terns (Black, Arctic, breeding Common, occasional Little & Sandwich). *Summer*: Ospreys among 70 breeding spp. *Winter*: Up to 28 spp. wildfowl (inc. internationally important numbers of Gadwall & Shoveler). Goldeneye, Smew, Goosander, rare grebes, Great Northern, Black & Red-throated Divers, Ruff.
Other: Otter, Badger, Fox, Weasel, stoat. Up to 20 spp. dragonflies & 24 spp. butterflies.
Directions: Two nature reserves on site.
1: Egleton Reserve (Sat nav: LE15 8BT). SK 878 075, from Egleton village off A6003 or A606 S of Oakham. Hosts British Birdwatching Fair in Aug.
2: Lyndon Reserve (Sat nav: LE15 8RN). SK 894 058, south shore E of Manton village off A6003 S of Oakham. Follow 'nature reserve' signs to car park.
Public transport: Train - Oakham ca.two miles.
Visiting: Day permits available. Reduced admission for disabled visitors & carers.
1: The Anglian Water Bird Watching Centre - open daily (not Dec 25/26), 9am-5pm, (4pm, Nov-Jan). Centre has toilets & disabled access, mobility scooter for hire. good network of paths. 31 hides (disabled access possible to 12 of them). Badger-watching hide, book through centre. No dogs.

2: Centre open daily 9am-5pm, mid-Mar to mid-Sep - car park open to 8pm. Interpretation centre, toilets (inc. disabled), paths, use of a mobility scooter. Seven hides, four accessible to wheelchairs. Dogs on short lead only.
Contact:
1: Egleton, T: 01572 770 651;
2: Lyndon, T: 01572 737 378; E: info@lrwt.org.uk

6. SWITHLAND RESERVOIR

Severn Trent Water.
Habitats: Large reservoir divided by Great Central Railway line, small area of woodland (Buddon Wood).
Birds: Common wildfowl are regular & has produced seaduck (inc. Common Scoter, Scaup & Long-tailed Duck) & occasional divers. Black-necked Grebe seen in late summer/autumn, Mediterranean Gull is annual, Black Tern on Spring passage. High water levels curb wader sightings but Kingfishers are regular & Ravens usually seen daily. 3 spp. woodpecker are in Buddon Wood, along with a range of woodland spp. County's best site for wintering Peregrine, also Buzzard, Sparrowhawk & Hobby (summer). Good track record of rarities in recent years.
Other: Buddon Wood along Kinchley Lane is good for Purple Hairstreak butterfly & Orange Underwing moth - look for the latter around Silver Birch.
Directions: Sat nav: LE7 7SE. SK 561 131. Lies S of Quorn, E of A6 (Leicester to Loughborough road). Use minor road between Swithland & Rothley for southern section. For northern section take Kinchley Lane along eastern shore to the dam.
Public transport: None.
Visiting: View from roads.

7. WATERMEAD COUNTRY PARK

Leicestershire County Council.
Habitats: River Soar & Grand Union Canal, 12 lakes & pools, reedbeds (one of largest in Midlands), wildflower meadow, woodland. Park stretches for nearly two miles. Wanlip Meadows can be viewed from Plover Hide.
Birds: 200 spp., inc. common wildfowl, Little Egret, Kingfisher, Water Rail, Cetti's Warbler. *Passage:* Garganey & Black Tern. Wanlip Meadows very good for waders, inc. Little Ringed Plover & is county's best site for Temminck's Stint. *Winter:* Bittern, Caspian Gull, Yellow-legged Gull, thrushes.
Other: Otters regular, but elusive. Emperor & other dragonfly spp.
Directions: LE7 1AD. SK 608 113. Located off Wanlip Road, Syston (off A46 or A607), six miles N of Leicester city centre. Watermead CP (South) is managed by Leicester City Council.
Public transport: Bus - nos.5/5A/6 from Leicester to Syston/East Goscote/Melton, regular daily. Get off at Alderton Close for south or walk from Syston for north. Arriva. Train - one mile from Syston.
Visiting: Open all year, 7am-dusk. Wanlip Road gives access to four car parks (fees payable), southern entrance in Alderton Close, Thurmaston. Wheelchair access on five miles of surfaced tracks. RADAR key needed by mobility scooter riders to negotiate kissing gates on perimeter track. Toilets, inc. disabled. Four bird hides (in nature reserve), Sand Martin nesting wall.
Contact: T: 0116 305 5000; E: via website;
W: www.leicscountryparks.org.uk

Lincolnshire

This large rural county is relatively sparsely populated & lies between the Humber to the north & the Wash to the south-east. There are many coastal sites between the two, such as Tetney Marshes, Frieston Shore & Gibraltar Point, which attract migrants & wintering wildfowl & waders. Agricultural land dominates the interior, but there are a number of reservoirs & gravel pits here which can produce interesting birds.

1. ALKBOROUGH FLATS

North Lincolnshire Council.
Habitats: 450ha managed realignment created by breaching river defences to protect homes from flooding. Inter-tidal mudflats, reedbeds, grasslands, arable land.
Birds: 200 spp. Lying on a key migration route, geese & ducks are attracted in large numbers. Long-billed Dowitcher, Lesser Yellowlegs & Marsh Sandpiper brought site's wader total to 40 spp. *Spring/autumn:* passage waders (Avocets in autumn). *Summer:* Marsh Harriers have attempted to breed, Little Egret, Bearded Tit, Reed Warbler, Water Rail. Spoonbills are regular.
Winter: Huge flocks of Lapwings (10,000 regularly) & Golden Plover (up to 14,000 but 5,000-10,000 regular), plus Marsh & Hen Harriers, Peregrine, Merlin, Teal, Wigeon, Black-tailed Godwit. Large flock of Barnacle Geese can be seen at nearby Whitton Sands.
Other: Roe deer, Badger, Brown Hare, Water Vole, Otter, Fox. Wall Brown among butterflies & Black-tailed Skimmer among dragonflies.
Directions: Sat nav: DN15 9JN. SE 887 224, main car park. Located on S bank of Humber where Rivers Trent & Ouse meet to form the Humber. Follow brown tourist signs to Alkborough Flats from A1077 near Winterton. Reach two car parks by following the duck signs through Alkborough village. Car park at bottom of Prospect Lane is mainly for disabled visitors. Main car park off Whitton Road, just N of Alkborough village. Site also accessible via a permissive footpath from Julian's Bower, Back Street, Alkborough.
Public transport: Bus - no.60 (not Sun) Scunthorpe to Alkborough. Stagecoach.
Visiting: Open at all times. Five miles of public footpaths (two miles wheelchair-friendly), three hides, with wheelchair access.
Contact: Site Manager, T: 01724 721 269.

2. COVENHAM RESERVOIR

Anglian Water.
Habitats: 81ha concrete-sided reservoir, raised above surrounding low-lying farmland, small areas of trees.
Birds: *All year:* Barn Owl. *Spring/Summer:* Yellow Wagtail, Wheatear, Ring Ouzel, Black Redstart possible on passage/Cuckoo, Tree Sparrow breeding but summer birds fairly limited. *Autumn*: Waders, inc. Common Sandpiper, Ruff, Curlew Sandpiper & Little Stint, more unusual waders may inc. Red-necked & Grey Phalaropes & Purple Sandpiper. Also Black-necked Grebe, Black Tern & Little Gull. *Winter*: Good variety of waterfowl inc. Goldeneye, Pochard, Pintail & regular Smew, Common Scoter & Long-tailed Duck plus divers, grebes (inc. red-necked), gulls & occasional geese. Short-eared Owl, finch flock with occasional Brambling & Tree Sparrow. Has attracted regular rarities inc. Red-breasted Goose, American Wigeon, Ring-necked Duck & White-winged Tern.
Directions: Sat nav: LN11 0XX. TF 340 962. Five miles N of Louth. Take minor road (Pear Tree Lane) off A16 just S of Ludborough. Continue for two miles to junction - go over junction (into Bull Bank) for a further 0.5 mile to car park on R.
Public transport: None.
Visiting: Open at all times. Top of reservoir bank reached by steps from car park. Path around the top of reservoir bank.
Contact: none.

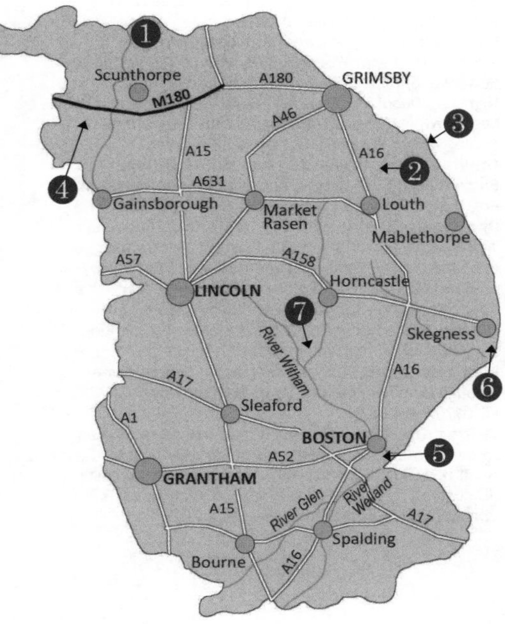

3. DONNA NOOK

Lincolnshire Wildlife Trust.
Habitats: Dunes, slacks & intertidal areas, seashore, mudflats, sandflats.
Birds: *Summer*: Little Tern, Oystercatcher. Ringed Plover, *Winter*: Brent Goose, Shelduck, Shorelark, Lapland Bunting, Linnet.
Other: One of largest & most accessible breeding colonies of Grey Seals in UK (viewing area/main car park open Oct-Dec, dawn-dusk). Badger, Stoat & Weasel, 3 spp. shrew have been identified. Common Lizard.
Directions: Sat nav: LN11 7PB. TF 422 998 (Stonebridge). Several access points off main A1031 coastal road with parking facilities at Stonebridge, Howden's Pullover (TF 449 952), Sea Lane, Saltfleet (TF 456 944) & Saltfleet Haven (TF 466 935).
Public transport: None.
Visiting: Donna Nook beach is closed on weekdays as this is an active bombing range, but dunes remain open. Some disabled access from Stonebridge car park. No dogs on viewing area.
Contact: Lincolnshire WT, T: 01507 526 667; E: info@lincstrust.co.uk

4. EPWORTH TURBARY

Lincolnshire Wildlife Trust.
Habitats: One of few relics of raised bog in county, areas of active sphagnum bog still exist. Reed swamp & mixed fen vegetation, considerable area of birch woodland of mixed ages.
Birds: *Spring/summer:* Breeding birds inc. Woodcock, Green & Great Spotted Woodpeckers, Tree Pipit, warblers & finches. Greenshank, Green Sandpiper & Little Grebe are attracted to the wet area. Around Steve's Pond, occasional Hobby & Marsh Harrier, plus Teal, Little Grebe, Tree Pipit, Sparrowhawk & Buzzard. Willow Tit, Long-tailed Tit, Reed Bunting & Willow Warbler in the woodland areas. Occasionally Corn Buntings on the adjacent farmland. *Autumn/winter:* Large corvid flocks roost in reserve. At Pantry's Pond (winter) occasional Hen Harrier & sometimes (winter) Long-eared Owls can be observed roosting close to the path. Other birds inc. Yellowhammer, Linnet & Jay.
Other: 11 spp. breeding dragonflies. Wood Tiger Moth is well established. Plants inc. Sneezewort, Yellow & Purple Loosestrife, Meadow-rue, & Devil's-bit Scabious.
Directions: Sat nav: DN9 1EA. SE 758 036. SW of Scunthorpe. Take A18 W from Scunthorpe then A161 S to Epworth. Turn R on High Street & head towards Wroot. Entrance is near bridge over Skyer's Drain. Park inside or on verge adjoining reserve, well away from corner.
Public transport: None.
Visiting: Open at all times. Car park, two hides, way-marked trail - keep to trail paths & use hides to avoid disturbing birds on ponds.
Contact: Lincolnshire WT - see site 3.

5. FRAMPTON MARSH

RSPB (Eastern England Office).
Habitats: Saltmarsh, wet grassland, freshwater scrapes, developing reedbed.
Birds: *Summer:* Breeding Redshank, Avocet, Lapwing, Skylark, Little Ringed Plover, Ringed Plover, Sand Martin & several spp. of ducks. *Passage:* waders (inc. Greenshank, Curlew Sandpiper, Wood Sandpiper, Little & Temminck's Stints, Ruff & Black-tailed Godwit), Marsh Harrier & Hobby. *Winter:* Wildfowl (inc. Whooper Swan, dark-bellied Brent Goose & Wigeon), Hen Harrier, Short-eared Owl, Merlin, Lapwing & Golden Plover, Kingfisher, Lapland Bunting, Twite.
Other: Water Vole, Brown Hare, Stoat. Dragonflies inc. Emperor, hawkers, chasers & darters. Common butterflies inc. Wall Brown, Painted Lady & Speckled Wood. Scarce Pug, Star Wort & Crescent Striped moths on saltmarsh. Important brackish water flora & fauna inc. nationally scarce Spiral Tassleweed & several rare beetles.
Directions: Sat nav: PE20 1AY. TF 356 392. Four miles SE of Boston. From A16 follow signs to Frampton then Frampton Marsh.
Public transport: None.
Visiting: Reserve open at all times. Visitor centre, inc. toilets, open daily Nov-Feb (not Dec 25) 9.30am-4pm & Mar-Oct 9.30am-4pm weekdays/5pm weekends & bank holidays. Hot drinks & snacks available, binocular hire, free information leaflets & events programmes. 60-space car park (three for disabled visitors), bicycle rack, benches, viewpoints. Footpaths & three hides open at all times, all suitable for wheelchairs.
Contact: RSPB, T: 01205 724 678;
E: lincolnshirewashreserves@rspb.org.uk

6. GIBRALTAR POINT NNR & BIRD OBSERVATORY

Lincolnshire Wildlife Trust.
Habitats: Sand dune grassland & scrub, saltmarsh & mudflats, freshwater marsh, lagoons.
Birds: Large scale visible migration during spring & autumn passage. Internationally important populations of non-breeding waders between Jul & Mar (peak Sep/Oct). Winter flocks of Brent Geese, Shelduck & Wigeon on flats & marshes with Hen Harrier, Merlin & Short-eared Owl often present. Red-throated Divers offshore (peak Feb). Colonies of Little Tern & Ringed Plover in summer. 100+ spp. can be seen in a day during May & Sep. Can be a good passage of autumn seabirds during northerly winds.
Other: Grey & Common Seal colonies, with Harbour Porpoises offshore most months. Patches of Pyramidal Orchids. Butterflies inc. Brown Argus & Green Hairstreak.
Directions: Sat nav: PE24 4SU. TF 556 580. Three miles S of Skegness, signposted from town centre.
Public transport: Train - Skegness (3.5 miles). Cycle route from Skegness.
Visiting: Open dawn-dusk all year. Charges for parking, car park closed at dusk. Free admission to reserve. Some access restrictions to sensitive sites at S end. Visitor centre & cafe open 10am-3pm (Nov-Mar) 10am-4pm (Apr-Oct), may stay open later during busy periods), toilets. shop. Public hides overlook freshwater & brackish lagoons. Wash viewpoint overlooks saltmarsh & mudflats. Four hides suitable for wheelchairs, as well as surfaced paths. Dogs on leads at all times - not permitted on beach from Apr 1st to Sep 1st. Access for coaches. Day visit groups must be booked in advance.

The Wash Study Centre Field centre is an ideal base for birdwatching/natural history groups in spring, summer & autumn. Contact Wash Study Centre for residential or day visits. T: 01754 762 763;
E: gibeducation@lincstrust.co.uk

Gibraltar Point Bird Observatory.
Kev Wilson, T: 01754 898 079;
E: kwilson@lincstrust.co.uk;
W: http://gibraltarpointbirdobservatory.blogspot.com

Contact: Reserve & wildlife:
T: 01754 898 057; E: gibnnr@lincstrust.co.uk;
Vistor Centre: T: 01754 898 057;
E: gibvc@lincstrust.co.uk

7. KIRKBY MOOR

Lincolnshire Wildlife Trust.
Habitats: Remnant heathland, mixed woodland (with adjacent coniferous plantation).
Birds: *All Year:* Sparrowhawk, Woodcock, Little & Tawny Owl, 3 spp. Woodpeckers, Willow Tit, Redpoll, Bullfinch. *Summer:* Cuckoo, Hobby, Turtle Dove, Nightjar, Woodlark, Redstart, warblers inc. Garden & Lesser Whitethroat. *Winter:* Crossbill, Brambling, Siskin, winter thrushes, occasional Firecrest.
Other: 250 spp. plants, 275 spp. moths, 20 spp. Butterflies, 11 spp dragonflies. Adder, Common Lizard, Bog Bush-cricket.
Directions: Sat nav: LN10 6YY. TF 225 629. Between Woodhall Spa & Kirkby-on-Bain (B1191), entrance gate opposite turn to Wellsyke Lane (0.9 mile W of Kirkby-on-Bain). Car park at end of track through reserve, near to reservoir (or park carefully by road if gate closed). Site adjacent to Ostler's Plantation, parking here as well (Forestry England).
Public transport: Bus - no.IC5 Lincoln-Boston passes through Woodall Spa (not Sun). Brylane Travel (T: 01205 364 087).
Visiting: Open at all times, car park, two waymarked routes (close gates behind you), hide overlooking small reservoir. Rough terrain, no wheelchair access. No dogs.
Contact: Lincolnshire WT - see site 3.

Northamptonshire

Much of the birding interest is found around the county's reservoirs & old mineral workings. These include Thrapston & Ditchford gravel pits & Stanwick Lakes Country Park in the Nene Valley, Pitsford Water & Hollowell reservoirs & are good for a range of wildfowl, especially in winter. Red Kites were re-introduced near Corby &, along with Buzzards, are spreading.

1. DAVENTRY COUNTRY PARK

Daventry District Council.
Habitats: Reservoir, woodland, meadows, orchard.
Birds: 200+ spp. *All Year*: Great Crested Grebe, Gadwall, woodland/scrub spp. *Summer*: Common Tern, warblers. *Winter*: Wildfowl (inc. Pochard, Shoveler, Wigeon, Goldeneye, Goosander) plus occasional scarcer spp., inc. Scaup, Long-tailed Duck. Gulls - check for scarcer spp. Lapwing, Golden Plover, Snipe depending on water levels. Siskin, Redpoll. Site has regularly turned up scarcer/rare spp, esp. waders.
Other: Grass Snake, amphibians.
Directions: Sat nav: NN11 2JB. SP 577 641. Located off Northern Way (A425), 1 mile NE of Daventry town centre.
Public transport: None to Park.
Visiting: Car park open daily (charge). Cafe 9am-5pm Mon-Sat (summer) & 9am-2pm (winter, Sundays & bank holidays). Toilets (inc. Disabled) open 9am-5pm (5pm winter). Facilities closed Dec 25/Jan 1). Three circular trails inc. around reservoir (2.5 miles).
Contact: Daventry District Council, T: 01327 871100.

2. NENE WETLANDS NATURE RESERVE

Beds, Cambs & Northants Wildlife Trust.
Habitats: Part of upper Nene valley floodplain, complex of old gravel pits, rough grassland, lakes, reed, scattered scrub, woodland. Joins up individual sites inc. Irthlingborough Lakes & Meadows, Ditchford Lakes & Meadows, Higham Ferrers Pits.
Birds: Great Crested & Little Grebes, Grey Heron, Redshank, Oystercatcher, Snipe. *Summer*: Common Tern, Cuckoo, Nightingale, Reed, Sedge & Cetti's Warblers, Swift, House Martin. *Autumn*: *Winter*: Wildfowl (inc. Curlew, Teal, Wigeon, Gadwall, Tufted Duck), Common Sandpiper.
Other: Hairy Dragonfly, Grass Snake, Otter. Plants inc. Marsh Woundwort, Dropwort, Great Burnet.
Directions: Sat nav: NN10 6FA. SP 938 679 (Visitor Centre). From Northampton, take A45 towards Rushden & Higham Ferrers. Take exit to Rushden Lakes Retail Park.
Public transport: Bus - nos.45, 49, 50, X46/47 from various towns inc. Northampton, Wellingborough, Kettering, Bedford to Retail Park. Stagecoach.
Visiting: Car parking at the Rushten Lakes retail park (five hrs max.). Visitor centre open daily (not Dec 25) 10am-5pm, toilets, cafe, shop. Reserve map available showing access points, inc. disabled routes. Dogs on leads.
Contact: BCN WT, T: 01933 779 587; E: nenewetlands@wildlifebcn.org

3. PITSFORD WATER

Anglian Water/Beds, Cambs & Northants Wildlife Trust.
Habitats: Open water (120 ha), marginal vegetation & reed grasses, wet woodland, grassland, mixed woodland.
Birds: Typically 165-170 spp. annually with a total list of over 250 spp. *Summer*: Breeding terns, grebes, herons, warblers. *Autumn*: Waders if water levels suitable. *Winter*: Up to 10,000 wildfowl, feeding station (Tree Sparrow & occasional Corn Bunting).
Other: 32 spp. butterflies, 392 spp. macro moths, 21 spp. dragonflies, 377 spp. flora, 404 spp. fungi, 105 spp. bryophytes. Harvest Mouse, Brown Hare.
Directions: Sat nav: NN6 9SJ. SP 787 699. Five miles N of Northampton. From A43 take turn to Holcot & Brixworth. From A508 take turn to Brixworth & Holcot.
Public transport: None.
Visiting: Reserve (N of causeway) open all year to permit holders. Wildlife Trust members can apply for free permit from HQ. Non-members can obtain day permits from fishing lodge, open mid-Mar to mid-Nov from 8am-dusk. Winter opening times variable, check in advance. No dogs. Disabled access from Lodge to first hide. Toilets available in Lodge, 15 miles of paths, eight hides & car parking.
Contact: BCN WT, T: 01604 405 285; E: northamptonshire@wildlifebcnp.org
Pitsford Water Fishing Lodge, Brixworth Road, Holcot, Northampton, NN6 9SJ. T: 01604 781 350; E: fishing@anglianwater.co.uk

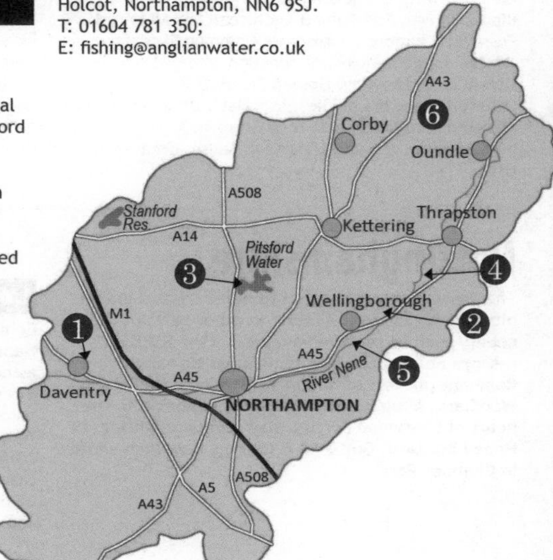

4. STANWICK LAKES

Rockingham Forest Trust.
Habitats: 300ha, countryside park includes a Ramsar-designated wetland on site of former quarry, part of Nene Valley Special Protection Area, inc. reedbeds, hedgerows, grazed areas.
Birds: *All year:* Little Egret, Kingfisher, Green & Great Spotted Woodpeckers, Grey Wagtail, Cetti's Warbler & Barn Owl. *Spring/summer:* Waders inc. Oystercatcher (breeding), Little Ringed Plover, Greenshank & Green Sandpiper. Hobby, Yellow Wagtail, hirundines & migrant warblers. *Autumn/winter:* Wildfowl inc. Pintail, Goldeneye & Goosander. Bittern, Redpoll & Siskin.
Other: Otter, Grass Snake, 150 spp. moths, dragonflies.
Directions: Sat nav: NN9 6GY. SP 967 715. Entrance off the A45, eight miles N of Wellingborough.
Public transport: None.
Visiting: Open daily (not Dec 25) 7am to 7pm (Mar & Oct), 8pm (Apr-Sep); 5pm (Nov-Feb). Visitor centre open daily (not 25/26 Dec) 10am-5pm (Mar-Oct), 10am-4pm weekdays/5pm weekends & school holidays (Nov-Feb). Charges for car & coach parking. All paths, visitor centre, gift shop, toilets & bird hide are wheelchair accessible. Disability scooter hire available.
Contact: Rockingham Forest Trust, T: 01933 625 522; E: info@rftrust.org.uk

5. SUMMER LEYS LNR

Beds, Cambs & Northants Wildlife Trust.
Habitats: Scrape, two ponds, lake, flood meadow, scrub, hedgerows.
Birds: *All year:* Tree Sparrow. *Spring/summer:* Common Tern, Black-headed Gull, Ringed & Little Ringed Plover, Redshank & Oystercatcher all breed. *Passage:* Whimbrel, Turnstone, Common Sandpiper. *Winter:* Large numbers of common wildfowl (inc. Goosander), Lapwing, Golden Plover & Ruff.
Other: 16 spp. dragonflies, inc. Hairy Dragonfly (check Marigold Pond). Common Blue & Brown Argus butterflies on grassland. Harvest Mouse, occasional Otter.
Directions: Sat nav: NN29 7TD. SP 886 634. Off Hardwater Road, Great Doddington, three miles from Wellingborough, accessible from A45 & A509.
Public transport: Bus - no.X47 Northampton to Great Doddington, about one mile away. Stagecoach. Train - Wellingborough.
Visiting: Open at all times, no permits required. Car park (open 5am-7.30pm Mar-Oct, 5am-4.30pm Nov-Feb); small tarmac circular route suitable for wheelchairs. Three hides, one feeding station. No toilets, nearest are at Irchester Country Park on A509 towards Wellingborough. Dogs on leads.
Contact: BCN WT - see site 2.

6. TOP LODGE & FINESHADE WOOD

Forestry England.
Habitats. Ancient woodland, coniferous woodland, beech woodland, open areas, small pond.
Birds: *All year*: Red Kite, Buzzard, Great Spotted Woodpecker, Goshawk, Nuthatch, Crossbill, Marsh & Willow Tit, other woodland birds. *Summer*: Turtle Dove, warblers. *Winter*: Hawfinch.
Other: Adder, Grass Snake, Slow Worm, Common Lizard. Fallow Deer, Badger. Orchids inc. Greater Butterfly, Early Purple & Common Spotted, other ancient woodland flora.
Directions: Sat nav: NN17 3BB. SP 980 983. Off A43 between Stamford & Corby. Follow brown tourist signs to Top Lodge Fineshade Wood.
Public transport: None.
Visiting: Two pay-&-display car parks. Fully accessible visitor centre open daily (not Dec 25) 9.30am-4pm weekdays/9am-5pm weekends. Toilets, Top Lodge Cafe, events/activities throughout the year. Caravan & Motorhome Club site open mid-Mar to early- Nov (see C&MC website for details). Wildlife hide in wood - Smelter's Walk is an all-ability trail leading to the hide. Electric bikes available from Fineshade Cycling shop. Orienteering course. Three way-marked walking trails (one is for all abilities, two are surfaced), one horse trail, one family cycle trail with skills loops, dedicated coach & horse box parking. Sensory garden.
Contact: Forestry England, T: 0300 067 4340; E: sherwood.fdo@forestryengland.uk

---

Nottinghamshire

The Trent Valley is dominated by a series of gravel pits which can also be found in other parts of the county such as the Idle Valley NR & the RSPB's reserve at Langford Lowfields, near Newark. Remnant pockets of heathland still hold Nightjar & Woodlark. A raptor watch point at Welbeck, in the heart of Sherwood Forest, may produce sightings of Honey Buzzard, Goshawk & Osprey. Hawfinch winter in Clumber Park.

1. ATTENBOROUGH NATURE RESERVE

Cement UK/Nottinghamshire Wildlife Trust.
Habitats: Disused flooded gravel workings with associated marginal & wetland vegetation.
Birds: *Spring/summer*: Breeding Common Tern (40+ pairs), Reed Warbler, Black Tern regular. *Winter*: Wildfowl, plus Bittern, Grey Heron colony, adjacent Cormorant roost.
Other: Smooth Newt, dragonflies inc. Four-spotted Chaser & Migrant Hawker. Brown Argus butterfly. 450+ spp. plants.

Directions: Sat nav: NG9 6DY. Car park at SK 515 339. In Nottingham alongside River Trent. Signposted from A6005 between Beeston & Long Eaton.
Public transport: Bus - no.510 (not Sun) Beeston to Stapleford, alight at Chilwell, walk 500 yards along Barton Lane. NottsBus (T: 0115 969 4390). Train - Attenborough, five mins walk.
Visiting: Open all year, 7am-dusk. Car park charge, coaches by prior appointment. Education & visitor centre with cafe & shop (accessible to wheelchair users) open (not Dec 25) 9am-5pm (4pm Nov-Mar), 6pm weekends & bank holidays. Paths suitable for disabled access. Nature trail (leaflet available), four hides inc. an elevated hide & innovative Sand Martin hide - a sunken hide within an artificial Sand Martin bank. Dogs on leads (guide dogs only in visitor centre).
Contact: Attenborough Nature Centre,
T: 01159 721 777;
E: enquiries@attenboroughnaturecentre.co.uk

2. COLWICK COUNTRY PARK

Nottingham City Council.
Habitats: Lakes, pools, woodlands, grasslands, new plantations, River Trent.
Birds: 220+ spp.*Summer*: 64 breeding spp., inc. warblers & Common Tern (15+ pairs). Good track record for rarities. *Winter*: Wildfowl (good nos. of Goldeneye) & gulls. In nature reserve look for Lesser Spotted Woodpecker, Water Rail & Kingfisher. Passage migrants inc. Stonechat & Whinchat.
Other: Pool designated a SSSI for its 14 spp. breeding dragonflies. Purple & White-letter hairstreak butterflies.
Directions: Sat nav: NG4 2DW. SK 611 398. Main access from Mile End Road/River Road, off A612 two miles E of Nottingham city centre.
Public transport: Bus - no.44 Nottingham to Netherfield/Gedling, (from stop K1 on King Street), goes through Colwick. Nottingham City Transport.
Visiting: Open at all times, 7am to dusk. Nature trails. Dogs on leads in designated areas.
Contact: Country Park, Mile End Road, Colwick, Nottingham, NG4 2DW.

3. IDLE VALLEY

Nottinghamshire Wildlife Trust/Tarmac/Private.
Habitats: Former sand & gravel quarries, restored gravel workings, conservation grazed areas, woodland, reedbed, river valley, farmland, scrub, willow plantations, open water.
Birds: 250+ spp. *Summer:* Gulls, terns, wildfowl & waders inc. breeding Little Ringed Plover & Redshank. *Passage:* waders, terns, passerines & raptors. *Winter:* Wildfowl, gulls, raptors. Wider valley has been good for rarities, which have inc. Broad-billed Sandpiper, Great White Egret, Baird's Sandpiper & Steppe Grey Shrike in recent times.
Directions: Sat nav: DN22 8SG. SK 689 830. S end of reserve is 0.5 mile N of Retford off A638 to Barnby Moor, via entrance to Tarmac. Rural Learning Centre is on R.
Public transport: Bus - no.27 Retford to Misson passes reserve entrance. Stagecoach.
Visiting: Open all year, 9am-5pm. Car park (donation welcome). Idle Valley Rural Learning Centre has toilets & cafe open 10am-4pm. Four walking routes, many wheelchair accessible. Six viewing screens, two overlooking Chainbridge NR Scrape, two at Neatholme Scrape & single screens at Neatholme Fen & Neatholme Pit. Two hides in Chainbridge Wood.
Contact: Idle Valley Rural Learning Centre, Great North Road, Retford, DN22 8RQ; T: 01777 858 245;
E: info@nottswt.co.uk

4. LANGFORD LOWFIELDS

RSPB Midlands Office/Lefarge Tarmac.
Habitats: RSPB/Tarmac working to create East Midlands largest reedbed. The site, inc. areas to be restored, currently covers 175ha on this sand & gravel quarry site. Mature woodland, flower-rich meadow, lake, shallow pools, islands.
Birds: *Summer:* Ten spp. warbler, inc. Cetti's, Grasshopper & regionally important numbers of Reed & Sedge. Cuckoo, Turtle Dove, Bearded Tit, Marsh Harrier, Hobby, hirundines & breeding Little Ringed Plover & Avocet *Winter:* Large waterfowl numbers, plus Bittern (can be heard booming into spring), Starling roosts & five owl spp.
Other: Badger, Brown Hare, 18+ spp. butterflies.

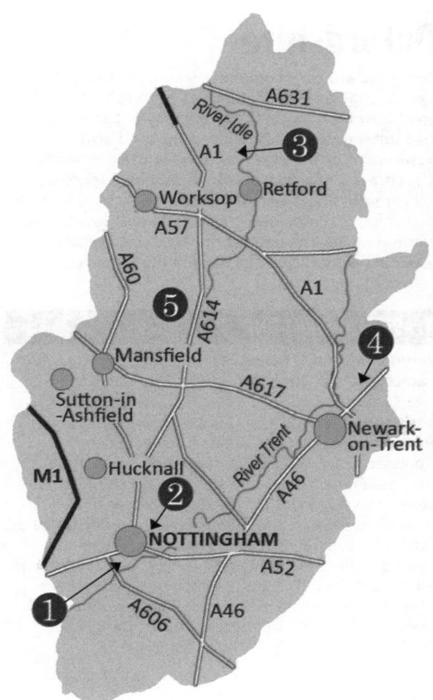

Directions: Sat nav: NG23 7QL. SK 821 601. Lies NE of Newark-on-Trent. From A1 take A46 (signposted to Lincoln) & then turn onto A1133 (to Collingham). After 2.5 miles turn L into Cottage Lane - gated car park 50m along the lane (height restriction 2.2m contact prior to visit if required).
Public transport: Bus - no. 367 Newark-Collingham will stop near to Cottage Lane junc. on request. Travel Wright T: 01636 703 813).
Visiting: Cottage Lane car park open dawn-dusk. Small hut open daily, if volunteers available, where two nature trails start (located 800m from car park). Viewing screen overlooking reedbed, floating bridge & boardwalk, pond dipping platform. No toilets.
Contact: RSPB, T: 01636 893 611;
E: langford.beckingham@rspb.org.uk

6. SHERWOOD FOREST NNR/BUDBY SOUTH FOREST

RSPB working with Nottinghamshire County Council.
Habitats: Heathland, acid grassland, rough grassland, ancient woodland & tree pasture.
Birds: *All Year:* Common woodland spp, 3 spp. woodpeckers. *Spring/summer*: Woodcock, Nightjar, Hobby, Long-eared Owl, Tree Pipit, Woodlark, Redstart, Spotted Flycatcher, warblers, Linnet, Yellowhammer. *Winter*: Redpoll, Siskin, Crossbill.
Other: Veteran Oak trees inc. 'The Major Oak' (1000 years old), fungi. .
Directions: Sat nav: NG21 9QB. SK 626 675. E of Ollerton, between A6075 & A616 (20 miles N of Nottingham). From village of Edwinstowe, follow signs to Sherwood Forest Visitor Centre, N on B6034.
Public transport: Bus - 'Sherwood Arrow' from Nottingham City Centre- Ollerton, stops at Visitor Centre (daily). From Mansfield, nos.14 & 15A to Edwinstowe (not Sun/bank hols). Stagecoach.
Visiting: Car park, across road from visitor centre (charge, RSPB members free - except during Robin Hood Festival). Sherwood Forest Visitor Centre - open daily (not Dec 25) 10.30am-5pm (Mar-Oct) 4.30pm Nov-Feb). Toilets (inc. disabled), cafe, shop. Trails., Events. Dogs on lead in breeding season/under control at other times. Parking for RSPB Budby South Forest section - 0.5 mile past Visitor Centre on L - 200 yards before junction - pull-in serves as parking area.
Contact: Sherwood Forest VC, T: 01623 677 321; RSPB, Site Manager (Budby South Forest):
T: 07718 248 953; E: chloe.ryder@rspb.org.uk

Oxfordshire

Red Kites are now common place in this largely agricultural county. The Downs in the south can be good for other raptors, particularly in the winter. Two outstanding birding locations are Farmoor Reservoir (for passage migrants, wintering wildfowl & rarities) & Otmoor (wildfowl numbers increase in winter with Short-eared Owl, Hen Harrier, Merlin & Peregrine often present. The RSPB are developing wet meadows & reedbeds on the site to benefit breeding waders such as Redshank, Snipe & Lapwing).

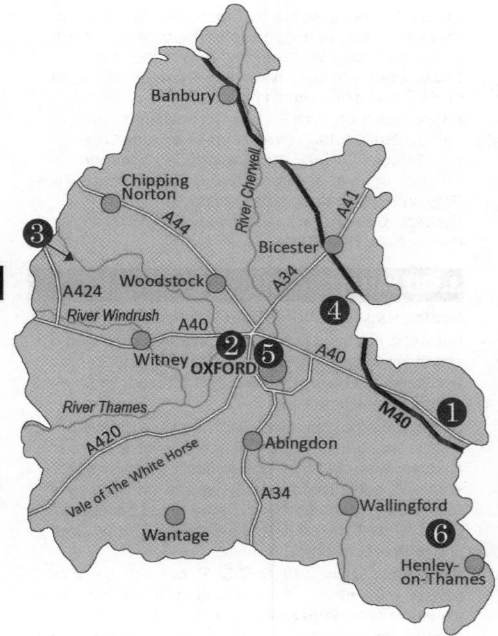

1. ASTON ROWANT NNR

Natural England (Thames Solent Team).
Habitats: Chalk grassland, chalk scrub, beech woodland.
Birds: *All year:* Red Kite, Buzzard, Sparrowhawk, Woodcock, Tawny Owl, Green & Great Spotted Woodpeckers, Skylark, Meadow Pipit, Marsh Tit. *Spring/summer:* Blackcap, other warblers, Turtle Dove. *Passage:* inc. Ring Ouzel, Wheatear & Stonechat. *Winter:* Brambling, Siskin, winter thrushes.
Other: Rich chalk grassland flora, inc. Chiltern Gentian, Clustered Bellflower & Frog, Bee, Pyramidal & Fragrant Orchids. Less common butterflies inc. Silver-spotted, Dingy & Grizzled Skippers, Chalkhill Blue, Adonis Blue, Green Hairstreak & Dark Green Fritillary.

Directions: Sat nav: HP14 3YL. SU 731 966 (for Beacon Hill car park). From the M40 Lewknor interchange at Junc 6, travel NE for a short distance & turn R onto A40. After 1.5 miles at the top of hill, turn R & R again into a narrow, metalled lane. Car park is signposted from A40. OX49 5HX. SU 726 958 (for Cowleaze Wood car park).
Public transport: Bus - no.275 High Wycombe to Oxford stops at Stokenchurch & Aston Rowant. Red Rose Travel (T: 01296 747 926) & no. Link40 High Wycombe to Thame, stops at Lewknor village. Carousel Buses (T: 01494 450 151). Short walks to reserve.
Visiting: Open all year. On-site parking at Beacon Hill & Cowleaze Wood - viewpoint, seats, interpretation panels. Some wheelchair access at Cowleaze Wood (contact for details).
Contact: Natural England, Aston Rowant NNR,
T: 01844 351 833;
E: michael.venters@naturalengland.org.uk

2. FARMOOR RESERVOIR

Thames Water.
Habitats: County's largest body of freshwater contained in two concrete basins separated by a causeway. Shallow pools in Pinkhill Reserve. Reedbed, wet grassland, pools in Shrike Meadow & Buckthorne Meadow reserves.
Birds: *Summer:* Breeding Little Ringed Plover, Common Tern & Black-headed Gull. Large numbers of hirundines, Hobby, Cuckoo. *Passage:* migrants such as White & Yellow Wagtails, Wheatear, Black Tern, Little Gull, Dunlin & Little Stint. *Winter:* Wildfowl, grebes, divers & gulls. Snipe & Water Rail at Pinkhill. A long history of rarities.
Other: Dragonflies, aquatic life-forms.
Directions: Sat nav: OX2 9NT. SP 452 061. Lies W of Oxford between A 40 & A420. Widely signposted by brown tourist signs. At mini-roundabout in Farmoor village (on B4044), turn L & look for car park at Gate 3.
Public transport: Bus - no.S1 between Oxford & Witney stop in Farmoor village (0.5 mile walk to Gate 3). Stagecoach.
Visiting: Free car parking at Gate 3. Car park off B4017. Bird hide at Pinkhill Reserve, west of reservoir.
Contact: E: hanna.jenkins@thameswater.co.uk

3. FOXHOLES RESERVE

Berks, Bucks & Oxon Wildlife Trust.
Habitats: Broad-leaved ancient woodland, grassland.
Birds: *All year:* Raven, Tawny Owl, Little Owl, Green & Greater Spotted Woodpeckers, common woodland spp. *Spring/summer:* Spotted Flycatcher, Marsh Tit & warblers. *Winter:* Redwing, Fieldfare, Woodcock.
Other: Fantastic show of Bluebells from mid-Apr & into May. Autumn fungi (200+ spp.). Silver-washed Fritillary among 23 spp. butterflies, 7 spp. bats.
Directions: Sat nav: OX7 6RW. SP 258 208. Travelling N on A424 from Burford, take R turn to Bruern. Continue past staggered crossroads towards Bruern for two miles then past R turn to Shipton-under-Wychwood. Park in lay-by after 200 yards & walk 600 yards down pot-holed track to reserve entrance - recommended not to drive along this track.
Public transport: None.
Visiting: Open all year. Car park, 1.75 mile circular wildlife walk - keep to paths (can be very muddy).
Contact: BBOWT, T: 01865 775 476;
E: info@bbowt.org.uk

4. OTMOOR NATURE RESERVE

RSPB (Central England Office).
Habitats: Wet grassland, reedbed, open water, hedgerows.
Birds: *Spring/autumn passage*: Marsh Harrier, Greenshank, Green Sandpiper & Common Sandpipers, Spotted Redshank Short-eared Owl & occasional Black Tern. *Summer*: Breeding birds inc. Cetti's & Grasshopper Warblers, Lapwing, Redshank, Curlew, Snipe, Yellow Wagtail, Shoveler, Gadwall, Pochard, Tufted Duck, Little & Great Crested Grebes. Hobby breeds locally. *Winter*: Wigeon, Teal, Shoveler, Pintail, Gadwall, Pochard, Tufted Duck, Lapwing, Golden Plover, Hen Harrier, Peregrine, Merlin.
Directions: Sat nav: OX3 9TD (Otmoor Lane). SP 570 126. Car park seven miles NE of Oxford city centre. From Junc 8 of M40, take A40 W to Wheatley, then B4027. Take turn to Horton-cum-Studley, then first L to Beckley. After 0.7 mile turn R (before the Abingdon Arms public house). After 200 yards, turn L into Otmoor Lane. Car park at the end of lane (approx one mile) - if full do not park along Otmoor Lane (emergency access).
Public transport: None.
Visiting: Open dawn-dusk, no entry fee. Small car park with cycle racks, visitor trail (three mile round trip) & two screened viewpoints. Not accessible by coach & is unsuitable for large groups. No dogs allowed on reserve visitor trail (except public rights of way). In wet conditions, visitor route can be muddy & wellingtons are essential.
Contact: RSPB, T: 01865 351 163,
E: otmoor.admin@rspb.org.uk

5. PORT MEADOW

Oxford City Council.
Habitats: Common land, on east bank of River Thames (adjacent to Thames Towpath & Burgess Field).
Birds: *All year:* Sparrowhawk, Little Owl, Reed Bunting. *Spring/summer/passage:* waders, hirundines, warblers, chats. *Winter:* When the area is wet, wildfowl & waders inc. (Wigeon, Teal, Gadwall, Snipe, Lapwing), plus occasional Goosander, Golden Plover, Water Rail.
Other: Butterflies, dragonflies, meadow plant spp.
Directions: Sat Nav: OX2 6ED. Lies on the NW outskirts of Oxford, accessed via Walton Well Road & Aristotle Lane in south or Wolvercote in north.

Public transport: Bus - no.6 from Oxford city centre (Magdalen Street, stop C3) to Wolvercote (also stops at Plantation road - short walk to south access). Oxford Bus Co.
Visiting: Open all year. Car parks off Godstow Road (north end) OX2 8PU & Walton Well Road (south end) OX2 6ED. Dogs under control.
Contact: Cutteslowe Park Offices, Harboard Road, Oxford, OX2 8ES.

6. WARBURG NATURE RESERVE

Berks, Bucks & Oxon Wildlife Trust.
Habitats: Scrub, mixed woodland, chalk grassland, ponds.
Birds: *All year:* Sparrowhawk, Red Kite, Treecreeper, Nuthatch, Tawny Owl. *Spring/summer:* Occasional Firecrest. Warblers inc. Whitethroat & Lesser Whitethroat. *Winter:* Redpoll, Siskin, sometimes Brambling, Crossbill, Woodcock.
Other: Good for orchids (15 spp.), butterflies (inc. Purple Hairstreak & Silver-washed Fritillary) & common deer spp.
Directions: Sat nav: RG9 6BJ. SU 721 878. Four miles NW of Henley-on Thames. From the A4130 turn into Bix Village. Take a L turn into Rectory Lane. Go down the steep hill & turn L at bottom, signposted Bix Bottom. Continue for about one mile until reaching car park at end of lane on R. The lane has some potholes - drive carefully.
Public transport: None.
Visiting: Open all year. Car park (not suitable for coaches) & toilets open at all times. Interpretation Centre open daily 9am-5pm, two hides (one with disabled access), children's Nature Detectives Trail, nature trail, picnic benches, leaflets. Dogs on leads. Mobility vehicle available - contact/book before visiting.
Contact: BBOWT, T: 01491 642 001; E: info@bbowt.org.uk

Shropshire

Bordering Wales to the west, & part of the area known as the 'Welsh Marches', the upland moorland of the South Shropshire Hills hold Red Grouse, Dipper & Ring Ouzel, while occasionally passage Dotterel may be encountered. The fertile lowland valleys, extensive farmland & mixed woodland hold a good mixture of species. The cluster of water bodies in the north, near Ellesmere, attracts wintering wildfowl & gulls, Venus Pools, Wood Lane & Chelmarsh attract passage waders.

1. CLUNTON COPPICE

Shropshire Wildlife Trust.
Habitats: One of county's largest sessile oak woodlands.
Birds: *All year:* Great Spotted Woodpecker, Buzzard, Red Kite, Peregrine, Raven. *Spring/summer*: Wide range of woodland birds, inc. Woodcock, Redstart, Wood Warbler, Spotted & Pied Flycatchers. *Winter:* Crossbill, Siskin, Redpoll.
Other: Hairy woodrush & broomrape, sessile oak woodland plants, bluebell, bilberry. Good for ferns, mosses & fungi. Dormouse, Roe Deer.
Directions: Sat nav: SY7 0HU. SO 337 806. From Craven Arms, take B4368 to Clunton village, at the crossroad go south, head straight over bridge & up the hill to small car park just before reserve sign.
Public transport: None.
Visiting: Open at all times. Limited parking in small quarry entrance on right, or opposite The Crown pub. Access along road & public rights of way only.
Contact: Shropshire WT, T: 01743 284 280; E: enquiries@shropshirewildlifetrust.org.uk

2. FENN'S WHIXALL & BETTISFIELD MOSSES

Natural England (West Midlands Team).
Habitats: 800ha, raised peatland meres & mosses.
Birds: *All year*: Kingfisher, Skylark, Linnet. *Spring/summer*: Breeding Teal, Mallard, Nightjar, Hobby, Curlew, Tree Sparrow. *Winter*: Short-eared Owl.
Other: Water Vole, Brown Hare, Polecat, Adder, 670 spp. moths, 27 spp. butterflies, nationally important for dragonflies (29 spp.), inc. White-faced Darter, 18 spp. bog moss.

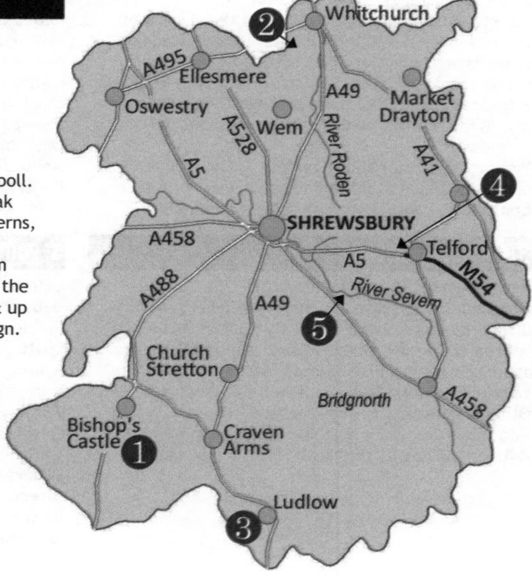

Directions: Sat nav: SY13 3NY (Fenn's Bank), SJ 505 366. Four miles SW of Whitchurch, to S of A495 between Fenn's Bank, Whixall & Bettisfield. Roadside parking at entrances, car parks at Morris's Bridge, Roundthorn Bridge, World's End & a large car park at Manor House. Disabled access by prior arrangement along railway line.
Public transport: None.
Visiting: Permit required except on Mosses Trail routes. Information panels at main entrances & leaflets are available when permits are applied for. Three interlinking Mosses Trails explore the NNR & canal from Morris's & Roundthorn bridges.
Contact: Natural England, Manor House NNR Base, T: 0300 060 0269;
E: peter.bowyer@naturalengland.org.uk

3. MORTIMER FOREST

Forestry England.
Habitats: Coniferous woodland with some broadleaved. Straddles Shropshire/Herefordshire border.
Birds: *All Year:* Sparrowhawk, Kestrel, Buzzard, Woodcock, Raven, 3 spp. woodpeckers, common woodland spp, Crossbill. *Summer:* Cuckoo, Tree Pipit, Whinchat, Redstart, Wood Warbler, Spotted & Pied Flycatcher. *Winter*: Siskin, Redpoll, occasional Hawfinch.
Other: Fallow, Roe, Muntjac Deer, Wood White.
Directions: Sat nav: SY8 2HF. SO 474 731 (Vinnalls Car Park). Forest signposted from outskirts of Ludlow. From Ludlow take B4361 towards Leominster, immediately after Ludford Bridge turn R onto unclassified road to Wigmore - Whitcliffe & Vinnalls car parks along this road or continue along B4361 to Black Pool car park.
Public transport: Bus - no.490 Ludlow-Leominster (not Sun). Stops in Overton (0.3 mile from Black Pool car park inc. 300 yards along road with no pavement). Lugg Valley Travel (T: 01568612759). Train - Ludlow.
Visiting: Open at all times. Three car parks, with picnic areas, on edge of forest, open dawn-dusk/free. Height restrictions to Vinnalls & Black Pool. Various trails from car parks inc. all ability (1 mile) trail from Vinnells.
Contact: Forestry England, T: 0300 067 6977;
E: marchesforests@forestryengland.uk

4. PRIORSLEE LAKE

Severn Trent Water/Friends of Priorslee Lake.
Habitats: A man-made balancing lake, surrounded by woodland, rough grassland & three reedbeds.
Birds: 155+ spp. (41 spp. breeding). *Summer:* Warblers, inc. Reed & Sedge. *Winter:* A nearby landfill site makes Priorslee Lake a magnet for gulls & it has a good track record for Yellow-legged, Caspian & white-winged gulls. Check the wildfowl for less common spp. such as Goosander & Pintail. Bittern & Snipe in reedbeds. Finches, tits (inc. Willow), Redpoll, Siskin in woodland.
Other: Wide range of butterflies, dragonflies & other insects. Southern Marsh, Bee & Common Spotted Orchids.
Directions: Sat nav: TF2 9NS. SJ 720 095 (Teece Drive). In Telford between M54 & A5. Leave M54 going N (B5060) at Junc 4 & park in lay-by (100 yards from Junc 4) overlooking the lake. Alternatively park - without blocking gates - by Water Sports Association entrance gate at the end of Teece Drive, Priorslee, Telford. The Flash, Priorslee is a slightly smaller lake half a mile distant. Follow the stream that comes in at western end of Priorslee Lake or head for Derwent Drive, Priorslee.
Public transport: Teece Drive entrance is about two miles from Telford bus station, 1.25 miles from Telford train station.
Visiting: Open at all times. Path around lake - can be muddy when wet.
Contact: W: http://friendsofpriorsleelake.blogspot.co.uk

5. VENUS POOL

Shropshire Ornithological Society.
Habitats: 27ha, pool, several islands, open shoreline, marshy grassland, hedgerows, woodland, scrub, species-rich meadows, field growing bird-friendly crops.
Birds: Noted for wintering wildfowl, passage waders & occasional county rarities, inc. Black-necked Grebe, Purple Heron, Spoonbill, Red Kite & Woodlark.
All year: Common ducks & waterfowl, passerines, inc. Tree Sparrow. *Spring/summer:* Passage waders inc. Curlew, Ringed Plover, Dunlin, Redshank, Green & Common Sandpipers, & both godwits. Passage Black Tern, breeding Oystercatcher, Little Ringed Plover, Lapwing, warblers, hirundines. *Autumn:* Wader passage can inc. Little Stint, Greenshank, Green, Wood, Curlew & Common Sandpipers, & possible rarities. *Winter:* Occasional Bittern. Geese inc. occasional White-fronted. Ducks inc. Wigeon, Teal, Pintail, Shoveler, Pochard, Goosander (up to 50 in evening roosts) & occasional Goldeneye. Water Rail, vagrant raptors & owls, winter thrushes & large passerine flocks inc. Lesser Redpoll, Linnet, Tree Sparrow, Reed Bunting & Yellowhammer.
Directions: Sat nav: SY5 6JT. SJ 548 062. Six miles SE of Shrewsbury in angle formed by A458 & minor road leading S to Pitchford. Entrance is 0.5 mile along minor road which leaves A458, 0.5 mile SE of Cross Houses.
Public transport: Bus - no.436 Shrewsbury to Bridgnorth, stops at Cross Houses, one mile walk from Venus Pool (partly along busy main road). Arriva Midlands North.
Visiting: Car park with height barrier, also small parking area for disabled visitors close to Main Hide. Five hides (North Hide - SOS members only). Information boards. Public access inc. four hides - keep to footpaths shown on notice boards at both entrances. Wheelchair-friendly paths to two public hides & Lena's Hide overlooking feeding station. No dogs allowed.
Contact:
W: www.shropshirebirds.com/index/guide-to-birding-sites/venus-pool-reserve/

Staffordshire

The southern part of the Peak District National Park protrudes into the northern part of the county & has Red Grouse on the moors. In the dales & valleys, including RSPB Coombes Valley, Lesser Spotted Woodpecker, Pied Flycatcher, Redstart & other songbirds can be found. The mixed habitats of Cannock Chase are good for Nightjars, Woodlark & Goshawk, & have the occasional Great Grey Shrike in winter. Belvide, Blithfield & Croxall Lakes are the best reservoirs to find wintering wildfowl & passage waders.

1. BELVIDE

Canal & Rivers Trust/West Midland Bird Club.
Habitats: Reservoir, marsh, reedbeds, woodland, scrub.
Birds: *Breeding & passage:* waders (up to 12 spp. in a day when conditions are right) & terns. Warblers breed in reedbeds & hedgerows. *Winter*: Great Northern Diver, wildfowl inc. Bewick's Swan & Goosander. Gull roost sometimes inc. Glaucous or Iceland Gulls. Recent scarcities inc. Sabine's Gull, White-winged & Whiskered Terns & Yellow-browed Warbler.
Other: Dragonflies.
Directions: Sat nav: ST19 9LX. SJ 870 098. Entrance & car park on Shutt Green Lane, Brewood (south of A5), seven miles NW of Wolverhampton.
Public transport: Bus - no.877/878 (Mon-Fri) Wolverhampton to Brewood (walk down Shutt Green Lane). Select Bus Services (T: 01785 330 764).
Visiting: Access only by permit from WMBC (members free, non-members charged) - lock combination issued to permit holders. Parking for 25-30 cars, five hides (three with wheelchair access), hard surface paths.
Contact: Michael Bevan (West Midland BC Permit Sec), E: permits@westmidlandbirdclub.org.uk; non-members, groups only - no individual permits issued.

2. BLITHFIELD RESERVOIR

South Staffs Water/West Midland Bird Club.
Habitats: Large reservoir.
Birds: 250+ spp. *Winter*: Good wildfowl numbers (inc. Bewick's Swan, Goosander, Goldeneye), large gull roost (can inc. Glaucous, Iceland, Mediterranean & Caspian). *Passage:* terns (Common, Arctic, Black) & waders, esp. in autumn (Little Stint, Curlew Sandpiper, Spotted Redshank regular).
Directions: Sat nav: WS15 3PH. SK 052 250. Close to Abbots Bromley on B5013 (Rugeley/Uttoxeter road - permit holders look for signposts to Blithfield Education Centre.
Public transport: None.
Visiting: For members of WMBC only or one-off group permit, further details from the secretary. Free car park, toilets. Walk One has partial wheelchair access.
Contact: Michael Bevan - see site 1.

3. COOMBES VALLEY

RSPB (Midlands Regional Office).
Habitats: Steep-sided valley with sessile oak woodland, unimproved pasture, meadow.
Birds: *Spring*: Displaying Woodcock, drumming Great Spotted Woodpecker, Dipper & common woodland spp. joined by migrant Pied & Spotted Flycatchers, Redstart, Tree Pipit, Grey Wagtail & Wood Warbler. *Autumn/winter:* Lesser Redpoll, Siskin, winter thrushes. *Jan-Mar:* Displaying birds of prey.
Other: Bluebells, various butterflies, Slow Worm.
Directions: Sat nav: ST13 7EU. SK 009 534. Three miles SE of Leek. From Leek take A523 towards Ashbourne. After Bradnop, turn R on minor road (cross a railway line) to Apesford & follow signs to reserve.
Public transport: Bus - no.108 (not Sun) Leek to Ashbourne. 1.2 miles from reserve (take Apesford Lane) cross disused railway & continue to reserve entrance on L). Aimee's (T: 01538 385 050).
Visiting: Open daily (not Dec 25) 9am-9pm or dusk, no charge. Coach groups by prior arrangement. Information centre open daily (until 5pm) during busy periods, but may close at times in winter; toilets & refreshments. Only guide dogs allowed off public footpaths. Most trails unsuitable for disabled visitors. Three nature trails.
Contact: RSPB, T: 01538 384 017;
E: coombes.valley@rspb.org.uk

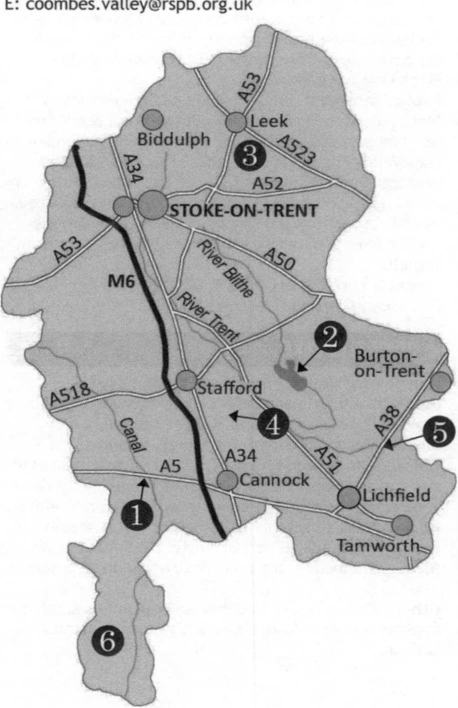

4. CANNOCK CHASE

Forestry England.
Habitats: Woodland, heathland, scrub.
Birds: *All Year:* Goshawk, Sparrowhawk, Woodcock, Tawny & Long-eared Owls, 3 spp. woodpeckers, Woodlark, Willow Tit, Raven, common woodland spp. *Spring/summer:* Hobby, Cuckoo, Nightjar, Tree Pipit, Redstart, Stonechat, warblers, Pied Flycatcher, Crossbill. *Autumn/Winter:* Snipe, winter thrushes, Brambling, Siskin, Redpoll, occasional Great Grey Shrike, Hen Harrier.
Other: Fallow & Muntjac Deer. Butterflies inc. Green Hairstreak & Small Pearl-bordered Fritillary.
Directions: Sat nav: WS15 2UQ. SK 018 171 (Birches Valley Forest Centre). The Chase is located between Stafford-Rugeley-Cannock (A513-A460-A34). Various car parks are scattered through area. Sherbrook Valley-Brocton Coppice-Seven Springs (SK 004 204) area is particularly worth a visit.
Public transport: For Forest Centre. Train - Rugeley (two miles).
Visiting: Forest Centre - open 7.30am-9pm (or dusk). Car park (pay-&-display), cafe, toilets inc. disabled access bike hire, activities, trails.
Contact: Forestry England, T: 0300 067 4340; E: info-cannock@forestryengland.uk

5. CROXALL LAKES

Staffordshire Wildlife Trust.
Habitats: Two large lakes formed from gravel pits at junction of Rivers Tame, Trent & Mease, & shallow pools, wader scrapes, reedbeds.
Birds: *Spring/summer:* Breeding spp. inc. grebes, waders such as Redshank, Oystercatcher, Ringed Plover & Lapwing. *Winter:* Substantial numbers of wildfowl, inc. Wigeon, Teal, Goldeneye, Shoveler & occasional Smew. Between Nov & Jan, Short-eared Owls hunt over rough ground.
Other: Otter, Water Vole & Harvest Mouse present but dragonflies will be easier to see.
Directions: Sat nav: WS13 8QX. SK 189139. From Lichfield head N on A38, following signs for National Memorial Arboretum. At NMA entrance, continue over river bridge & turn L on second track into car park.
Public transport: Bus - no.812 (not Sun) Lichfield to Alrewas (1.2 miles from reserve). Midland Classic (T: 01283 500 228).
Visiting: Open at all times, except to restricted areas. Small car park (8am-5pm), two bird hides. Kissing gate at entrance wide enough for wheelchairs. Surfaced access track, leading to hide overlooking main lake. Wheelchair ramps to both hides but woodland path uneven. Restricted areas for dogs.
Contact: Staffordshire WT, T: 01889 880 100; E: info@staffs-wildlife.org.uk

6. HIGHGATE COMMON

Staffordshire Wildlife Trust.
Habitats: Lowland heath with broadleaved woodland.
Birds: Cuckoo, Green Woodpecker, Tree Pipit, Skylark, Stonechat, Yellowhammer.
Other: 5,000+ spp. insects, inc. several red data book spp. bees & wasps. Glow Worm & Common Lizard.
Directions: Sat nav: DY7 5BS. SO 835 894. (Highgate Road). From A449 at Himley take B4176 towards Bridgnorth. After approx one mile, turn L at traffic lights onto Wombourne Rd, signposted towards Swindon. Continue through Swindon, along Chasepool Rd. At the T Junction turn R onto Camp Hill Road. About one mile after Camp Farm, take 1st L then R at T junction onto Highgate Rd. Take 1st entrance on R.
Public transport: None.
Visiting: Eight main car parks over the Common, network of paths. Toilets at Warden's Office, Cory Community Centre (only open when wardens on site, opening hours vary but usually 9am-4.30 pm, Mon-Sat).
Contact: Staffordshire WT - see site 4.

Warwickshire & West Midlands

Warwickshire's river valleys & gravel pits are the main focus for birds. Tame Valley sites, such as Kingsbury & Ladywalk, Draycote Water & Brandon Marsh all attract wintering wildfowl & passage waders - Cetti's Warbler are well-established at the latter. In contrast to Warwickshire's largely rural setting, the West Midlands is heavily populated but Sutton Park (one of the largest urban parks in Europe) & Sandwell Valley attract a good selection of birds.

1. BRANDON MARSH

Warwickshire Wildlife Trust.
Habitats: 105ha, pools, marsh, reedbeds, willow carr, scrub & small mixed woodland.
Birds: 230+ spp. *All year:* Cetti's Warbler, Kingfisher, Water Rail, Gadwall, Little Grebe, Buzzard. *Spring/summer:* Little Ringed Plover, Garden & Grasshopper Warblers, Whitethroat, Lesser Whitethroat, Hobby, Whinchat, Wheatear. *Autumn/winter:* Bittern, Dunlin, Ruff, Snipe, Greenshank, Green & Common Sandpipers, Wigeon, Shoveler, Pochard, Goldeneye, Siskin, Redpoll.
Other: 500 plant spp., Badger, Otter, Great Crested Newt. 20+ spp. butterflies & 18 spp. dragonflies. Lists on W: www.brandonbirding.co.uk

Directions: Sat nav: CV3 3GW. SP 386 758. Three miles SE of Coventry, 200 yards SE of A45/A46 junction (Tollbar End). Turn E off A45 (just after Texaco garage) into Brandon Lane. Reserve entrance signposted 1.25 miles on R.
Public transport: Bus - no.21 Coventry to Willenhall/ Tollbar End, then 1.25 miles walk. National Express, Coventry.
Visiting: Open 9.30am-4.30pm weekdays, 10am-4.30pm weekends (closes 4pm, Oct-Mar). Only Trust members can visit site outside these hours. Entrance charge (free to WT members). Visitor centre, tea-room (open 10am-4pm daily), shop, toilets, nature trails, eight hides. Wheelchair access to nature trails & Wright hide. No dogs. Parking for coaches, by arrangement.
Contact: Warwickshire WT, T: 024 7630 2912; E: enquiries@wkwt.org.uk

2. DRAYCOTE WATER

Severn Trent Water.
Habitats: Large storage reservoir, surrounded by grassland, wooded areas.
Birds: *All year:* Farmland & woodland spp. in surrounding countryside. *Spring & autumn passage:* inc. waders, Black & Arctic Terns & Ospreys. *Winter:* Wide range of common wildfowl, regular sightings of less common spp. such as Smew, Scaup & Black-necked Grebe. Gull roost can number in excess of 50,000 birds, scarcer spp.often seen.
Directions: Sat nav: CV23 8AB. SP 462 685. Reservoir & 8ha country park situated near Dunchurch, 3.5 miles SW of Rugby off the A426.
Public transport: Bus - no.63 Rugby to Leamington Spa stops at Kites Hardwick/Draycote Water. Stagecoach.
Visiting: Open daily (not Dec 25) 7.30am-8pm (Apr-Sep), 7.30-dusk (Oct-Mar). Cars must stop at pay-&-display car park - disabled parking allowed at Toft, close to bird hide. Visitor centre, toilets, cafe open 10am-6pm (Apr-Sep), 4pm (Oct-Mar). Access to reservoir on foot or bicycle only. Five mile road surrounding reservoir. Paths good for wheelchairs. Dogs only in Country Park.
Contact: Draycote Water, Kites Hardwick, Warwickshire CV23 8AB; T: 01788 811 107; E: draycotewater@severntrent.co.uk; W: www.draycotebirding.co.uk

3. KINGSBURY WATER PARK

Warwickshire County Council.
Habitats: Open water, numerous small pools, some with gravel islands, gravel pits, silt beds with reed mace, reed, willow & alder, grassland, rough areas.
Birds: 230 spp. inc. Kingfisher. *Summer:* Breeding warblers (nine spp.), Little Ringed Plover, Great Crested & Little Grebes. Shoveler, Shelduck & a thriving Common Tern colony. *Winter:* Wildfowl, Short-eared Owl. *Passage:* Osprey, Hobby, waders (esp. spring).
Other: Orchids.
Directions: Sat nav: B76 0DY. SP 203 960. Signposted 'Water Park' from Junc 9 M42 & A4097 NE of Birmingham.
Public transport: Bus - no.16 (not Sun) Tamworth to Kingsbury. Diamond Bus.
Visiting: Open daily (not Dec 25) generally 8am-dusk, as early as 5.30am in Jun/Jul. Pay on entry car park or annual permits in advance online. Four hides (three with wheelchair access) overlooking Cliff Pool nature reserve. Miles of flat surfaced footpaths, mobility scooters for hire. Toilets, cafe, information centre/ gift shop (opening times vary during year).
Contact: Kingsbury Water Park, T: 01827 872 660; E: parks@warwickshire.gov.uk

4. LADYWALK RESERVE

Eon Energy/West Midland Bird Club.
Habitats: 50ha, floodplain, reedbed, woodland within a loop of River Tame.
Birds: 200+ spp. *Spring/summer:* Passage waders inc. Greenshank, Curlew, godwits & plovers, plus many hirundines & other migrants. *Winter:* Hundreds of wildfowl, inc. Wigeon, Teal, Shoveler, Goldeneye & Goosander. Water Rail & Woodcock regular & lots of small bird activity at the feeding stations. Up to four Bitterns in recent years, plus Siskin, Redpoll & winter thrushes.
Other: Five spp. orchid, inc. county's only known colony of Marsh Hellebore & locally rare Yellow Bird's Nest. Butterflies plentiful & 16 spp. dragonflies.
Directions: Sat nav: B46 2BS. SP 211 916. Site of old Hams Hall power station, in Tame Valley - 10 miles from Birmingham city centre. From Junc 9 of M42, head S on A446 to Hams Hall Distribution Centre. Follow Faraday Avenue to reserve. WMBC members can use secure car park near Sainsbury's warehouse.
Public transport: None.

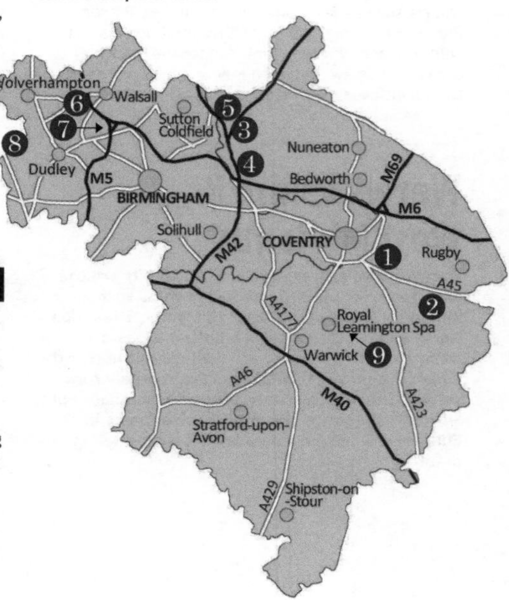

Visiting: Enter site by footbridge. Reserve open only to WMBC members, but other groups can organise visits with Sec. Non-members can observe site from public footpaths east of River Tame. No easy access on site for disabled visitors. Display permits on dashboard if using secure car park. Dogs not allowed. Six bird hides, inc. elevated River Walk Hide. Other screens for close-up viewing. Circular footpath (1.6 miles).
Contact: Michael Bevan (West Midland BC Permit Sec), E: permits@westmidlandbirdclub.org.uk; non-members, groups only - no individual permits issued.

5. MIDDLETON LAKES

RSPB (Midlands Regional Office).
Habitats: Former quarry, lakes, reedbeds, meadows, woodland.
Birds: *All year:* Barn Owls regularly seen & Cetti's Warbler frequently heard. *Spring/summer:* heronry (30+ pairs), plus common migrant warblers, Lapwing, hirundines & woodland spp. *Winter:* Lesser & Great Spotted Woodpeckers & Willow Tit on the feeders, plus peak numbers of wildfowl & waders. Raptors inc. Hen & Marsh Harriers, Merlin, Peregrine & Short-eared Owl.
Other: Bluebells & spring flowers, Grass Snake, common butterflies & moths.
Directions: Sat nav: B78 2BB. SP 192 967. Reserve lies in Tame Valley, S of Tamworth, next to Middleton Hall. Leave M42 at Junc 9 onto A446, then A4091 & finally into Bodymoor Heath Road.
Public transport: Train - Wilnecote is 2.5 miles from reserve.
Visiting: Open daily dawn/dusk. Car park for 50 - parking charge/members free, bike racks. Surfaced path from car park to Middleton Hall & heronry. Other paths are not surfaced but generally flat. Playmeadow Trail has partial wheelchair access. Four viewing screens. Lookout hide open to view northern scrapes (see RSPB website for lock combination number). Four trails, ranging from 500 yards to two miles in length. Dogs allowed on leads on parts of site. Nearest toilets at Middleton Hall.
Contact: RSPB, T: 01827 259 454; E: middletonlakes@rspb.org.uk

6. ROUGH WOOD CHASE LNR

Walsall Council.
Habitats: 28ha, oakwood - significant for W. Midlands. Reservoir, meadows, ponds/pools, marsh, scrubland.
Birds: *All year:* Great Crested & Little Grebes on pools in north end of Chase, common woodland spp. inc. Jay & Sparrowhawk. *Summer:* warblers.
Other: Great Crested & Smooth Newts, Water Vole, various dragonfly spp., Purple Hairstreak, Brimstone & Small Heath Butterflies.
Directions: Sat nav: WV12 5NX. SJ 981 008. Reserve composed of six sites on W edge of Walsall Borough. From Junc 10 of M6 head for Willenhall & A462. Turn R into Bloxwich Road North & R again into Hunts Lane. Car park on bend.
Public transport: Bus - nos.41 (not Sun)/69 Walsall & Willenhall (Short Heath Clinic stop). National Express, West Midlands.
Visiting: Open all year, circular nature trail linking all sites.
Contact: Environmental Improvement Team, T: 01922 653 344; E: eit@walsall.gov.uk

7. SANDWELL VALLEY COUNTRY PARK

Sandwell Metropolitan Borough Council.
Habitats: 268ha, pools, woodlands, grasslands, inc. three Local Nature Reserves.
Birds: *All year*: Grey Heron (small heronry), Great Crested Grebe, Lapwing, Reed Bunting, Great Spotted & Green Woodpeckers, Sparrowhawk, Kestrel. *Spring*: Little Ringed Plover, Oystercatcher, up to eight spp. breeding warbler, passage migrants. *Autumn*: Passage migrants. *Winter*: Goosander, Shoveler, Teal, Wigeon, Snipe.
Other: Common Spotted & Southern Marsh Orchid. Ringlet butterfly. Water Vole, Weasel.
Directions: Sat nav: B71 4BG (Sandwell Park Farm). Main entrances off Salter's Lane (SP 013 918) or Forge Lane (SP 022 930). Located approx one mile NE of West Bromwich town centre.
Public transport: Bus - nos.45/46 West Bromwich to Walsall/Great Barr. National Express, West Midlands. West Bromwich Central Metro stop (one mile).
Visiting: Car parks open 8am-sunset. Coach parking by appointment. Visitor centre, toilets, shop, cafe at Sandwell Park Farm open daily (not Christmas period) 10am-4.30pm. Good footpaths around LNR's & much of the country park. Wheelchair access to Priory Woods LNR, Forge Mill Lake LNR & other parts of the country park. 8ha RSPB reserve nearby (see site 9).
Contact: Sandwell Valley CP, T: 0121 569 3070.

8. SANDWELL VALLEY RSPB

RSPB (Midlands Regional Office).
Habitats: Open water, wet grassland, reedbed, dry grassland, scrub.
Birds: *Summer:* Lapwing, Little Ringed Plover, Whitethroat, Sedge & Reed Warbler, Willow Tit. *Winter:* Wildfowl inc. Goosander. Water Rail, Snipe, Jack Snipe, woodpeckers, Bullfinch. *Passage:* sandpipers, Common Tern, Yellow Wagtail, chats.
Directions: Sat nav: B43 5AG. SP 035 928. Great Barr, Birmingham. Follow signs S from M6 Junc 7 via A34. Take R at 1st junction onto A4041. Take 4th L onto Hamstead Road (B4167), then R at 1st mini roundabout onto Tanhouse Avenue.
Public transport: Bus - no.16W Birmingham to West Bromwich & no.16 to Hamstead (ask for Tanhouse Avenue). Diamond. Train - Hamstead.
Visiting: Pedestrian access open al all times. Visitor centre/car park (open Tues-Sun, 10am-5pm summer (4pm winter), toilets (inc. disabled), light refreshments. Car park charge, members free/contact for coach parking. Way-marked trails, most paths accessible to assisted & powered wheelchairs with some gradients (phone for further info). Viewing screens. Hide open when staff/volunteers available (Tues-Sun, 10.30am-3pm) - hide can be hired outside of opening hours. Dogs on leads.
Contact: RSPB, T: 0121 357 7395; E: sandwellvalley@rspb.org.uk

9. UFTON FIELDS

Warwickshire Wildlife Trust.
Habitats: Grassland, woodland, pools.
Birds: *All Year:* Little Grebe, Tufted Duck, Buzzard, Kingfisher, Bullfinch, Reed Bunting, *Summer:* Hobby, Cuckoo, warblers inc. Sedge & Reed. *Winter:* Wildfowl inc. Goosander, Wigeon - both scarce, Snipe, Woodcock, winter thrushes, Siskin, Redpoll
Other: 28 spp. butterflies, 14 spp. dragonflies, bats, Muntjac, Great Crested Newt, Grass Snake.
Directions: Sat nav: CV33 9PU. SP 378 615. W of Leamington Spa. Take A425 towards Southam, at Ufton turn R into Ufton Fields Lane to car park (0.5 mile).
Public transport: Bus - nos.63 Leamington Spa-Rugby (daily) pass Ufton, alight at 'bus shelter' stop & walk 0.5 mile along Ufton Fields Lane. Stagecoach Warwickshire (T: 01604 676 060),
Visiting: Open at all times. Small car park (height restriction). Paths are wheelchair accessible but there are wooden kissing gates at path entrance (not suitable for mobility scoters). 1.25 mile trail, two hides. Dogs under control at all times.
Contact: Warwickshire WT, T: 024 7630 2912; E: enquiries@wkwt.org.uk

Worcestershire

The Wildlife Trust manages more than 75 reserves covering a wide range of habitats in this largely rural county. Although it only has one sizeable reservoir (Bittell) there are excellent wetlands to explore at Upton Warren & Bredon's Hardwick. For the widest range of woodland species, including Pied Flycatcher, Wood Warbler & the more elusive Hawfinch, the best area is the Wyre Forest to the west of Kidderminster.

1. HILL COURT FARM & THE BLACKLANDS

Worcestershire Wildlife Trust.
Habitats: .Wet grassland, hay meadow, scrub, scrape.
Birds: *All Year:* Barn Owl, Skylark, Yellowhammer. *Spring/summer:* Lapwing, Redshank, Curlew, Reed Bunting. Autumn/*winter:* Wigeon, Teal, Pintail, Peregrine, Woodcock, Green Sandpiper, Snipe.
Other: Brown Hare, butterflies.
Directions: Sat nav: GL20 6BD. SO 825 355. From A4104 take B4211 to Longdon, Turn R into Bear Lane then R again into Marsh Lane (0.6 mile to parking area). From A438 take B4211 towards Longdon, after crossing under M50 turn L into Marsh Lane (one mile to parking area).
Public transport: None.
Visiting: Open dawn-dusk (permissive path). Parking space for 2/3 cars on Marsh Road by Longdon Brook. Access restricted to a permissive path (muddy/slippy when wet) to a viewing screen overlooking a scrape. Public bridleway between Marsh Road & Robertsend (runs along a high ridge) gives excellent views of reserve (0.6 mile E from parking area, opposite Bear Lane turn).
Contact: Worcestershire WT, T: 01905 754 919; E: enquiries@worcestershirewildlifetrust.org

2. KNAPP & PAPERMILL

Worcestershire Wildlife Trust.
Habitats: Broadleaved woodland, unimproved grassland, fast stream, old orchard in Leigh Brook Valley.
Birds: *Summer*: Breeding Grey Wagtail & Dipper, Nuthatch & common woodland spp., Kingfisher, Spotted Flycatcher, 3 spp. woodpecker. Buzzard, Sparrowhawk & Redstart.
Other: Otters have returned recently. Good numbers of dragonflies & 30+ spp. butterflies on all three meadows inc. Holly Blue, Purple Hairstreak & White Admiral. Bluebells, Green-winged & Spotted Orchids. 11 spp. bats.

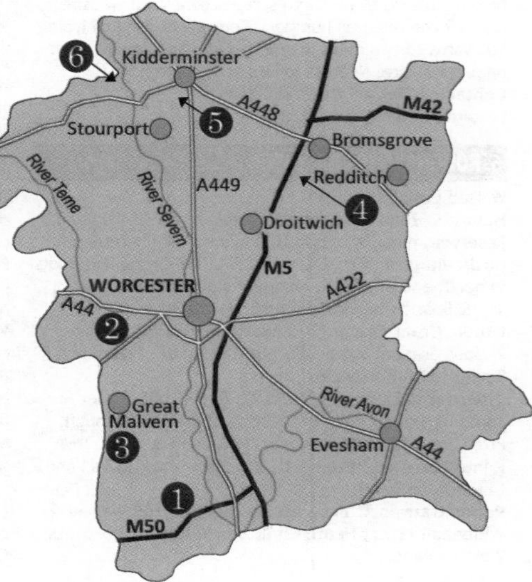

Directions: Sat nav: WR6 5HR. Take A4103 SW from Worcester, turn R at Bransford roundabout then L towards Suckley - reserve is approx three miles (do not turn off for Alfrick). Park at Bridges Stone lay-by (SO 751 522), cross road & follow path to Knapp House.
Public transport: None.
Visiting: Open dawn-dusk. Small visitor centre with toilets. Large parties should contact Warden in advance. Paths steep & uneven. Nature trail, wildlife garden, Kingfisher viewing screen. Dogs on lead at all times.
Contact: Worcestershire WT - see site 1.

3. MALVERN HILLS

Malvern Hills Trust.
Habitats: Grassland on hilltops, mixed woodland, scrub, quarries, small reservoirs & lakes.
Birds: Raptors inc. Buzzard, Sparrowhawk, Peregrine, Hobby. Ravens nest in quarries. Wooded areas hold all expected common spp., breeding flycatchers & warblers, 3 spp. woodpeckers & Tree Pipit on woodland edge. A few Nightingales hang on in areas of dense scrub, which also hold chats, pipits & Linnet. *Spring passage:* inc. Wheatear, Ring Ouzel (best in Happy Valley between Worcestershire Beacon & North Hill) & more rarely, Dotterel. *Autumn passage:* good range of migrants heading south. A winter highlight is Snow Bunting on the highest hills.
Other: Lesser Horseshoe & Barbastelle Bats, Polecat, 25 spp. butterflies, inc. High Brown Fritillary. Broad range of plants inc. Blinks, Crosswort & Common Spotted Orchid.
Directions: Sat nav: WR13 6DW (British Camp car park). SO 763 403. An eight mile long range of hills & commons lying S & W of Great Malvern, covering ca.1,200ha.
Public transport: None.
Visiting: Open all year. Many car parks (mainly open 6am-11pm) - charges/annual permit available. Public toilets with disabled access opposite British Camp car park (A449 Worcester Road). Two easy-access trails at Earnslaw (450 yards) & Blackhill (250 yards). Best birding areas inc. Castlemorton Common & Midsummer Hill.
Contact: Malvern Hills Trust, Manor House, Grange Road, Malvern WR14 3EY. T: 01684 892 002; E: info@malvernhills.org.uk, W: www.malvernhills.org.uk

4. UPTON WARREN

Worcestershire Wildlife Trust.
Habitats: Fresh & saline pools with muddy islands, some woodland, scrub.
Birds: *Spring/autumn*: Passage waders, occasional Black Tern, Osprey. *Summer:* Breeding Oystercatcher, Avocet, Redshank, Little Ringed Plover, Common Tern, Cetti's, Sedge, Reed, & Grasshopper Warblers. Hobby nearby. *Winter*: Wildfowl, Bittern, Water Rail, Snipe.
Other: Saltmarsh plants, dragonflies.
Directions: Sat nav: B61 7ET. SO 936 677. Two miles S of Bromsgrove on A38. Leave M5 at Junc 5 & head N on A38, take third exit at first roundabout.
Public transport: Bus - no.144 Birmingham to Worcester passes reserve entrance. First Bus.
Visiting: Christopher Cadbury Wetland Reserve consists of Moors Pools (freshwater) & Flashes Pools (saline). Open dawn-dusk, The Flashes car park open 9am-8pm (Apr-Sep) & 9am-4pm (Oct-Mar). Outdoor Education Centre/The Moors car parks open at all times. Non-members must obtain a day permit (Trust members - take membership card) from: Trust office, Outdoor Education Centre or volunteers on site. Six hides, maps at entrances, paths can be very muddy. Disabled access to hides at Moors Pools only by prior arrangement. Coach parking at sailing centre by arrangement. No dogs.
Contact: Worcestershire WT - see site 1.

5. WILDEN MARSH

Worcestershire Wildlife Trust.
Habitats: Dry & marshy fields with small alder & willow woods, reedbeds, many drainage ditches.
Birds: 192 spp. since 1968, about 70 spp. breed inc. Yellow Wagtail, nine spp. warbler & Redshank. *Winter:* Water Pipit, though numbers have declined recently.
Other: Plants inc. Southern Marsh Orchid, Marsh Cinquefoil, Marsh Arrow-grass, Marsh Pennywort & Lesser Water Parsnip.
Directions: Sat nav: DY13 9JT. SO 825 730. S of Kidderminster. Take A449 S from Kidderminster. At junction with A442 go straight across roundabout into Wilden Lane - very busy road with limited parking (park carefully in lay-by).
Public transport: Bus - no.15A from Kidderminster along Wilden Lane, bus stop 0.5 mile from reserve. Coniston Coaches (T: 01299 823 329).
Visiting: The reserve is complex & new visitors should consult a map. Enter over stile at gated entrance next to southern lay-by. Follow signs to leave certain areas undisturbed, no access to northern part of site. Gated entrances open at all times. Secure cattle gates at all times. Beware boggy areas, steep banks by River Stour & deep ditches.
Contact: Worcestershire WT - see site 1.

6. WYRE FOREST NNR

Natural England (West Midlands Team/Worcs Wildlife Trust.
Habitats: Ancient coppice oak woodland, conifer areas, birch heath, lowland grassland, stream.
Birds: Breeding birds inc. Redstart, Pied Flycatcher, Wood Warbler, Buzzard & Raven, with Dipper, Grey Wagtail & Kingfisher on larger streams.
Other: Mammals inc. Fallow, Roe & Muntjac Deer, Polecat, Otter, Mink, Yellow-neck Mouse, Dormouse, Water Shrew & voles. Several bat spp. inc. Pipistrelle & Daubenton's. Important for invertebrates inc. England's largest colony of Pearl-bordered Fritillary butterfly.
Directions: Sat nav: DY14 9XQ. SO 750 740 (Callow Hill/Discovery Centre). On A456 Kidderminster to Tenbury Wells road, three miles west of Bewdley.
Public transport: Bus - no.291 (not Sun) Kidderminster to Bewdley/Tenbury Wells stops at Callow Hill/DC. R&B Travel (T: 01584 890 770). Train - Kidderminster.
Visiting: Keep to paths. Toilets & refreshments (with disabled access). Several waymarked trails (some suitable for wheelchair users), regular guided walks, family cycle routes through reserve.
Contact: Wyre Forest NNR, Natural England Office, Lodge Hill Farm, Dowles Brook, Bewdley DY12 2LY; T: 01299 400 686.

Eastern England

Bedfordshire, Cambridgeshire, Essex, Hertfordshire, Norfolk, Suffolk

Bedfordshire

This is one of England's smallest counties, with a good selection of sites scattered through it. Blows Down is one of the best southern sites to see Ring Ouzel on spring passage. The RSPB's HQ at The Lodge, Sandy, is well watched & has produced a series of excellent records, Nightjars now breed on restored heathland. There are a number of country parks in the county - they can be busy but attract a good range of species.

1. BLOW'S DOWN

Beds, Cambs & Northants Wildlife Trust.
Habitats: Chalk downland, scrub & grassland - a traditional resting place for incoming spring migrants.
Birds: *Spring/autumn:* Ring Ouzel, Wheatear, Whinchat, Black Redstart, Stonechat, Willow Warbler. *Winter:* Lapwing, Meadow Pipit, Skylark. **Other:** Chalkhill Blue, Brown Argus & Marbled White butterflies. Plants inc. Small Scabious, Squinancywort, Burnet-saxifrage, Great Pignut, Common Spotted & Bee Orchids.
Directions: Sat nav: LU5 4AE. TL 030 215. On boundary between Dunstable/Luton. Take A505 from W of Luton, cross M1, straight over first roundabout, L at second continue to A5 junc., turn L - after 0.6 mile turn L into Half Moon Lane (park carefully on the verge at end of lane). Can walk 0.5 mile from Dunstable centre along A5 to same entrance.
Public transport: Bus - no.B Luton-Dunstable-Downside Estate, alight Half Moon Lane stop. Centrebus (T: 0116 410 5050).
Visiting: Open all year. Steep slopes, not suitable for wheelchairs.
Contact: BCN WT, T: 01234 364 213;
E: bedfordshire@wildlifebcnp.org

2. FLITWICK MOOR

Beds, Cambs & Northants Wildlife Trust.
Habitats: Important local wetland, mixture of fen, meadow, wet woodland & fragile peaty soil.
Birds: *Spring*: Lesser Spotted Woodpecker, Willow Warbler, Blackcap. *Summer*: Water Rail, Grasshopper & Garden Warblers, Cuckoo. *Autumn:* Brambling. *Winter*: Siskin, Water Rail, Great Spotted Woodpecker.
Other: Good variety of butterflies & dragonflies, plus Chimney Sweeper moth & Conehead Bush Cricket. Plants inc. 10 spp. sphagnum moss, Marsh Pennywort, Black Knapweed, Water Figwort plus Fly Agaric & Yellow Brain Fungus in autumn.
Directions: Sat nav: MK45 5BPZ TL 046 354.
E of Flitwick. From Flitwick town centre (Tesco roundabout) on A5120, cross railway bridge, R at roundabout, immediately L into King's Road. After 500 yards, L into Maulden Road towards A507. After quarter mile R at Folly Farm, follow track to small car park. Also footpath to reserve from Moor Lane.
Public transport: Bus - no.2 Bedford to Flitwick (not Sun). Stagecoach. Train - Flitwick & then 0.75 mile walk.
Visiting: Open all year. Car park. Stick to public paths.
Contact: BCN WT - see site 1.

3. THE LODGE, SANDY

RSPB (Central England Office).
Habitats: 220ha, mixture of woodland, heathland & acid grassland & inc. formal gardens of RSPB's UK HQ. New areas being restored to heathland.
Birds: *All year:* Woodpeckers, woodland birds. *Spring/summer:* Hobby, Nightjar, Spotted Flycatcher, breeding common woodland species & warblers. *Winter:* Winter thrushes.
Other: Natterjack Toad, rare heathland insects. Particularly good site for fungi (600 spp.) & lichens. Garden pools good for dragonflies.
Directions: Sat nav: SG19 2DL. TL 191 485. Reserve lies one mile E of Sandy, signposted from the B1042 road to Potton.
Public transport: Bus - no.73 (not Sun) Bedford to Sandy, one mile from Sandy Market Place. Stagecoach. Train - Sandy (0.5 mile). Walk in part is along trail through heathland restoration.

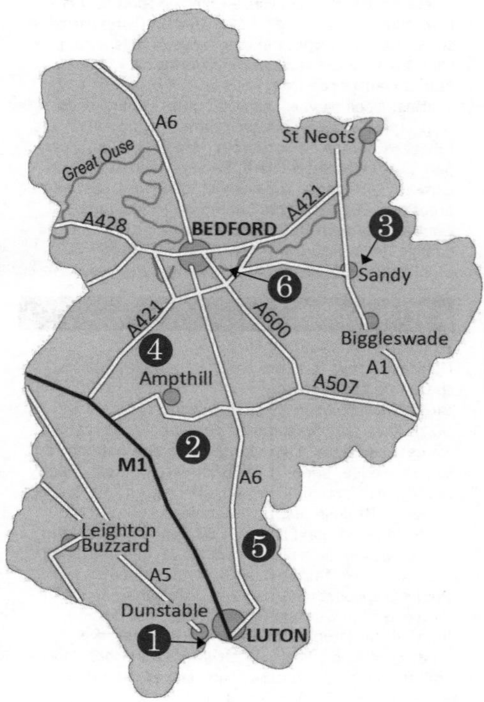

Visiting: Reserve open daily 7am-8pm (or dusk when earlier). Gatehouse: shop (with refreshments) open 9am-5pm weekdays, 10am-5pm weekends & bank holidays. Toilets (inc. disabled). Car park charge for non-members (free if only visiting shop). Five miles of nature trails. One bridleway (0.5 mile) & gardens are wheelchair/pushchair accessible. One hide (wheelchair accessible), 50 yards from car park. Bike racks. Dogs only allowed on bridleway. Coach parking at weekends by arrangement.
Contact: RSPB, T: 01767 693 333;
E: thelodgereserve@rspb.org.uk

4. MARSTON VALE MILLENIUM COUNTRY PARK

Marston Vale Trust.
Habitats: Millenium Country Park (225ha) inc. Stewartby Lake (85ha) which attracts birds when smaller waters are frozen. Reedbeds, woodland, hawthorn scrub, ponds & wet grassland.
Birds: *Spring*: Passage waders & terns (Black, Sandwich & Arctic Terns), hirundines, Wheatear, Whinchat, Osprey & Little Gull. Yellow Wagtail & Garganey occasionally breed. *Summer*: Ten species of breeding warblers, Hobby, Turtle Dove, Nightingale, Bearded Tit, Cuckoo, Barn Owl, Marsh Harrier, Water Rail, Kingfisher & common wildfowl. *Autumn*: Passage waders & terns. *Winter*: Bittern, Peregrine, Siskin, Redpoll, Stonechat, Snipe, gulls inc. Caspian, Yellow-legged & Mediterranean Gulls, thrushes, wildfowl (Gadwall, Shoveler, Pochard, Teal & Tufted Duck), Little & Great Crested Grebes. Rarer species can inc. divers, grebes, Common Scoter, Smew & Scaup. *Rarities*: Glossy Ibis, Laughing Gull, Caspian Gull, Manx Shearwater, Purple Heron & White Stork.
Other: Dingy & Grizzled Skipper butterflies, excellent for dragonflies. Also Otter & Brown Hare, plus Bee & Pyramidal Orchids & stoneworts.
Directions: Sat nav: MK43 0PS. TL 004 417. SW of Bedford off A421 at Marston Moretaine. Only five mins from Junc 13 of M1, along A421 towards Bedford. Look for brown tourist signs for the centre.
Public transport: Trains - Millbrook & Stewartby, 20 mins walk to forest centre.
Visiting: Car parking, coach parking (in advance) - charges apply - closes at 5pm. Forest Centre (cafe bar, gift shop, art gallery) open summer weekdays 9am-5pm, weekends 10am-5pm. Reduced hours in winter (closed 25/26 Dec, Jan 1). Pedestrian access to park at any time. Trails inc. a 1.25 mile Wetland Trail (entry charge, no dogs) is a level path with a compacted, loose stone surface inc. two hand gates with top latches with wheelchair & pushchair access - has four hides.
Contact: Forest Centre, T: 01234 767 037;
E: info@marstonvale.org; W: www.marstonvale.org

5. PEGSDON HILLS & HOO BIT NATURE RESERVE

Beds, Cambs & Northants Wildlife Trust.
Habitats: Chalk grassland, scrub & woodland.
Birds: *Spring*: Wheatear, Ring Ouzel, Tree Pipit, Yellowhammer. *Summer*: Turtle Dove, Grey Partridge, Lapwing, Skylark. *Winter*: Brambling, Stonechat, winter thrushes, raptors inc. Buzzard.
Other: Dark Green Fritillary, Dingy & Grizzled Skippers, Chalkhill Blue, Brown Argus & Small Heath butterflies. Glow Worm. Plants inc. Pasqueflower in spring, Fragrant & Common Spotted Orchids.
Directions: Sat Nav: SG5 3JS. TL 118 302 (lay-by). Five miles W of Hitchin. Take B655 from Hitchin towards Barton-le-Clay. Turn R to Pegsdon then immediately L & park in lay-by. Reserve entrance across B655 via footpath.
Public transport: None.
Visiting: Open at all times. Tracks/paths can be steep & uneven.
Contact: BCN WT - see site 1.

6. PRIORY COUNTRY PARK

Bedford Borough Council.
Habitats: Lakes, reedbeds, scrub & woodland, meadows adjoining River Great Ouse.
Birds: 210+ spp. Good numbers/variety of winter wildfowl, varied mix of spring passage species, with breeding warblers & woodpeckers, augmented by feeding terns, hirundines & raptors lakeside. *All year*: Cormorant, Little Egret, Grey Heron, Stock Dove, woodpeckers, Kingfisher, Grey Wagtail, Treecreeper, Goldfinch, Bullfinch. *Summer*: Hobby, Turtle Dove, Swift, hirundines, *Acrocephalus* & *Sylvia* warblers. *Passage*: Raptors, waders, terns, pipits. *Winter*: Grebes, Pochard, Shoveler, Gadwall, Merlin, Water Rail, gulls, thrushes, Chiffchaff, corvids, buntings.
Other: 23 spp. dragonflies, inc. Small Red-eyed Damselfly & Hairy Dragonfly. 20 spp. butterflies. Large plant list. Fox, Muntjac & Otter.
Directions: Sat nav: MK41 9DJ. TL 071 493. 1.5 miles SE from Bedford town centre. Signposted from A4280 & A421, car park on Barkers Lane.
Public transport: Bus - no.4 Bedford to Goldington, alight 1st stop on Riverfield Drive (200 yds). Stagecoach. Train - Bedford (approx 2.5 miles).
Visiting: Open daily. Four car parks (main one is Barkers Lane, open 5am-9pm), visitor centre, toilets, cafe (10am-4pm). Three nature trails (wheelchair accessible), hides .
Contact: Visitor Centre, Priory CP, Barkers Lane, Bedford, MK41 9DJ. T: 01234 718 012;
E: prioryrangers@bedford.gov.uk

Cambridgeshire

The Fens, including the Nene & Ouse Washes, are superb wetlands well known for wintering wildfowl, owls & raptors. The former offers the chance of Cranes, breeding Black-tailed Godwits, Spotted Crakes plus introduced Corncrakes in summer. The latter holds the largest inland concentration of wintering wildfowl in Britain. Grafham Water attracts plenty of scarce species, while Paxton Pits is probably the best place in the country to actually see Nightingales.

1. FEN DRAYTON LAKES

RSPB (Eastern England Office).
Habitats: Complex of lakes (former gravel workings) & traditional riverside meadows next to River Great Ouse.
Birds: At least 213 spp. have been recorded in area with 65 spp. being regular breeders, inc. Common Tern. Hobby, waders on passage. *Winter*: Nationally important numbers of Gadwall & Coot. Bitterns are now a regular sight, with Holywell Lake & Elney Lake being the favoured sites. *Rarities:* inc. Great Egret, Purple Heron, Glossy Ibis, Common Crane, Red-Footed Falcon, Honey Buzzard & Whiskered Tern.
Other: Good for butterflies, dragonflies & mammals.
Directions: Sat nav: CB24 4RB. TL 342 690. NW of Cambridge. Leave A14 at Junc 28, follow signs to Swavesey. Turn L in Boxworth End (signed to Fen Drayton). Turn R onto minor road (signed to Swavesey), then L into entrance to Fen Drayton Lakes. Follow signs to car park.
Public transport: Bus - route B between Huntingdon & Cambridge - has a request stop at reserve. Busway/ Stagecoach.
Visiting: Open at all times. Ten-mile network of trails, information boards give access details/trail guides & event leaflets available from car park. Dogs only allowed on public footpaths & bridleways. Five viewing screens, one hide & three open viewing shelters.
Contact: RSPB, T: 01954 233 260;
E: fendraytonlakes@rspb.org.uk

2. FERRY MEADOWS (NENE PARK)

Nene Park Trust.
Habitats: Lakes, meadows, scrub, broadleaved woodland & small wetland nature reserve.
Birds: *All year*: Good selection of woodland & water birds, Kingfisher. *Spring*: Terns, waders, Yellow Wagtail. *Winter*: Grebes, gulls, Siskin, Redpoll, Water Rail.
Other: Bluebell, Wood Anenome, Wild Garlic in woodland.
Directions: Sat nav: PE2 6YD. TL 148 973. Three miles W of Peterborough city centre & two miles E of A1. On all major routes into city, follow brown tourist signs for Nene Park or country park symbol. Also signposted on Oundle Road (A605).
Public transport: Bus - no.X4 Peterborough to Corby stops on A605 by Notcutts Nursery. 0.5 mile walk to park. Stagecoach.
Visiting: Open daily, 6.30am to 10pm (summer) & 6.30pm (winter). Car parking charges apply, height restriction. Visitor centre open 10am-5pm (Apr-Oct) & 10am-4pm (Nov-Mar), toilets (inc. disabled), cafe. Hard surface paths in park's central areas, but steep slopes in Bluebell Wood. Two wheelchair-accessible hides in nature reserve area. Electric scooters & wheelchair available - book in advance.
Contact: Nene Park Trust, T: 01733 234 193;
E: visitor.services@neneparktrust.org.uk;
W: www.neneparktrust.org.uk

3. FOWLMERE

RSPB (Eastern England Office).
Habitats: Reedbed, fen, chalk grassland, scrub.
Birds: *All year*: Water Rail, Kingfisher, Reed Bunting. *Spring/summer*: Little Grebe, Turtle Dove, ten spp.breeding warblers. *Autumn:* Yellowhammer, Corn Bunting. *Winter*: Snipe, Water Rail, raptors.
Other: Healthy population of Water Shrews & Otters. 18 spp. dragonflies.
Directions: Sat nav: SG8 6EZ. TL 406 461. Seven miles S of Cambridge. From A10, turn towards Fowlmere at Fowlmere-Shepreth crossroads (no RSPB sign); after one mile, turn R by cemetery (RSPB sign) - after another 0.6 mile, turn L into reserve.
Public transport: Bus: no.A Royston to Trumpington, alight on A10 at Shepreth, Dunsbridge Turnpike stop (one mile). Stagecoach. Walk towards Melbourn - after 300 yards, cross road & turn L on to single track road to Fowlmere (beware of traffic). After 0.75 mile, turn R into reserve (RSPB sign). Train - Shepreth, two miles.

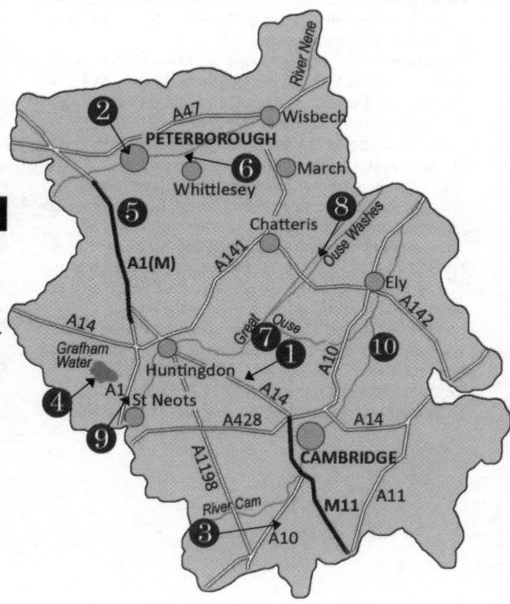

Visiting: Open at all times. Car park, charge for non-members. Visitor reception centre staffed by volunteers (usually weekends/bank holidays). Two mile signposted nature trail, three hides, toilets inc. disabled. Space for one coach, prior booking essential.
Contact: RSPB, T: 01767 693 013;
E: fowlmere@rspb.org.uk

4. GRAFHAM WATER

Beds, Cambs & Northants Wildlife Trust.
Habitats: Open water, lagoons, reedbeds, open water, wet mud & willow carr, ancient & plantation woodland, scrub, species-rich grassland.
Birds: *All year*: Common woodland birds. *Spring/summer*: Breeding Nightingale, Reed, Willow & Sedge Warblers, Common & Black Terns. *Autumn*: Passage waders. *Winter*: Waders inc. Common Sandpiper & Dunlin, Great Crested Grebe. Wildfowl inc. large flocks of common species, plus Shelduck, Goldeneye, Goosander & Smew, gulls (can be up to 30,000 roosting in mid-winter). *Rarities*: Have inc. Wilson's Phalarope, Ring-necked Duck, Great Northern Diver, Glaucous, Iceland & Mediterranean Gulls.
Other: Bee, Common Spotted & Early Purple Orchids, Common Twayblade (in woods), Cowslip. Common Blue & Marbled White butterflies, dragonflies inc. Broad-bodied Chaser, voles, Grass Snake.
Directions: Sat nav: PE28 0BX. TL 143 671. Follow signs for Grafham Water from A1 at Buckden or A14 at Ellington. Follow B661 road towards Perry & Staughtons to West Perry. As you leave village, Anglian Water's Mander car park is signposted on R.
Public transport: Bus - no.400 (Mon-Fri) Huntingdon Circular to West Perry. Go-Whippet (T: 01954 230 011).
Visiting: Open all year (not Dec 25). Car parks (8am-dusk) Use Plummer car park for lagoons, Marlow car park for dam area (good for waders/vagrants) - pay-&-display, disabled parking. Visitor centres at Mander & Plummer car parks with restaurants, shops & toilets. Six bird hides in nature reserve: three in bird sanctuary area, two in wildlife garden accessible to wheelchairs, further hide overlooks islands/scrapes in settlement lagoons. Cycle track through reserve also accessible to wheelchairs. No dogs in wildlife garden, on leads elsewhere.
Contact: Grafham Water Nature Reserve,
T: 01480 811 075; E: grafham@wildlifebcn.org

5. THE GREAT FEN

BC&N Wildlife Trust/Natural England (West Anglia Team)/Environment Agency/Hunts District Council.
Habitats: Pools formed from clay pits at Ramsey Heights; extensive birch forest (largest in lowland Britain) & reedbed at Holme Fen; mixed woodland, open waters, fen & grassland at Woodwalton.
Birds: Wide variety of common wildfowl, plus Kingfisher, Grey Heron, Bittern & wintering Goosander on meres. Marsh Harriers breed in reedbed, along with Bearded Tit & Cetti's Warbler. Hen Harriers visit in winter. Common Crane observed in recent years. Wet meadows at Darlow's Farm attractive to breeding Lapwing, Snipe & Redshank & wintering Whooper & Bewick's Swans.
Other: Great Crested Newt & rare beetles at Ramsey Heights. Otter, Brown Hare, deer spp., Water Vole. Scarce Chaser dragonfly, Small Copper & White Admiral butterflies. Wide variety of bog & heath plants.
Directions: Sat nav: PE26 2RS. TL 245 848 (Ramsey Heights), plus Holme Fen NNR & Woodwalton NNR (Chapel Road, Ramsey Heights), S of Peterborough, lying between A1 in west & Ramsey. B660 runs through centre of Great Fen.
Public transport: Bus - no.31 (Mon-Sat) Peterborough to Ramsey stops at end of Chapel Road, 0.5 mile from Countryside Centre. Stagecoach.
Visiting: Open at all times, views over farmland linking sites - Ramsey Heights Nature Reserve, Woodwalton Fen NNR, Holme Fen NNR & New Decoy Farm. Great Fen will eventiually occupy 3,700ha. All have waymarked trails - grassy paths mostly level. Countryside Centre at Ramsey Heights (open 9am-4pm), toilets. Hides at Woodwalton & Holme Fen. Dogs on leads.
Contact: Great Fen Team, T: 01487 710 420;
E: info@greatfen.org.uk; W: www.greatfen.org.uk

6. NENE WASHES

RSPB (Eastern England Office).
Habitats: Wet grassland with ditches - often flooded.
Birds: *Spring/early summer*: Corncrake release scheme, plus Spotted Crake. UK's top site for breeding Black-tailed Godwit. Other breeding waders inc. Lapwing, Redshank & Snipe. Duck (inc. Garganey), Marsh Harrier, Hobby, Yellow Wagtail & Tree Sparrow. *Autumn/winter*: Waterfowl in large numbers (inc. Bewick's Swan, Pintail, Shoveler),
Barn & Short-eared Owls, Hen Harrier, Common Crane, roost of up to 20 Marsh Harriers.
Other: Water Vole, Otter, Water Violet, Flowering Rush & Fringe Water Lily.
Directions: Sat nav: PE7 2DD. TL 318 991. Reserve is eight miles E of Peterborough & NE of Whittlesey. Car park at end of Eldernell Lane, N off A605 east of Coates.
Public transport: Bus - no.33 (not Sun) Peterborough to Chatteris runs on A605, alight at Coates, walk down Eldernell Lane (ca. one mile). Stagecoach.
Visiting: Open at all times along South Barrier Bank, accessed at Eldernell. Small car park at end of Eldernell Lane - one coach max so group visits along central path by arrangement. No access to fields or for wheelchairs along bank. Nene Valley Way path offers elevated views over reserve.
Contact: RSPB, T: 01733 205 140;
E: charlie.kitchin@rspb.org.uk

7. OUSE FEN

RSPB (Eastern England office)/Hanson.
Habitats: A working sand & gravel quarry being developed into a vast nature reserve with open water, grassland & potentially the UK's largest reedbed.
Birds: *Spring/summer*: Breeding Great Crested Grebe, Skylark, Marsh Harrier, Black-headed Gull, Reed Bunting, Bearded Tit & incoming migrants inc. Reed & Sedge Warblers, hirundines, Black-tailed Godwit, Ruff, Garganey, Common Tern & Hobby.

Autumn: Passage waders inc. Green Sandpiper, increasing numbers of common wildfowl & incoming winter thrushes. *Winter:* Good numbers of Mute Swan, Gadwall, Tufted Duck, Wigeon & Pochard & regular sightings of Smew. Large number of Little Egret, plus flocks of tits, finches & buntings. Barn Owl & Bittern regular, Short-eared Owl, Hen Harrier & Peregrine occasional.
Other: Brown Hare, Roe & Muntjac Deer. Wide range of butterflies & dragonflies.
Directions: Sat nav: PE27 4TA. TL 348 726. Located at Needingworth, near St Ives. Leave Junc 26 of A14 onto A1096 London Road. Go straight over three roundabouts. At fourth, take third exit (A1123). Cross over next roundabout & take next R onto Bluntisham Road. After 400 yards, turn L into reserve.
Public transport: Bus - no.21 (Mon-Fri, limited service) St Ives to Needingworth. Dews Coaches (T: 01487 740 241). From village bus stop follow Bluntisham Road east for 0.75 mile until signpost for reserve on R.
Visiting: Open at all times. Car park (free)), height barrier - no coaches. Two waymarked visitor trails, two viewpoints (one screened).
Contact: RSPB, T: 01954 233 260;
E: ousefen@rspb.org.uk

8. OUSE WASHES

RSPB (Eastern England Office).
Habitats: Lowland wet grassland, seasonally flooded. Open pool systems in front of some hides, particularly Stockdale's hide.
Birds: *Summer*: 70 spp. breed inc. Black-tailed Godwit, Lapwing, Redshank, Snipe, Shoveler, Gadwall, Garganey & Spotted Crake. Also Hobby & Marsh Harrier. *Autumn*: Passage waders inc. Wood & Green Sandpipers, Spotted Redshank, Greenshank, Little Stint, plus terns & Marsh & Hen Harriers. *Winter*: Large number of wildfowl (up to 100,000 birds) inc. Bewick's & Whooper Swans, Wigeon, Teal, Shoveler, Pintail, Pochard. Tree Sparrow.
Other: Good range of dragonflies, butterflies & fenland flora.
Directions: Sat nav: PE15 0NF. TL 471 860. Between Chatteris & March on A141, take B1093 to Manea. Reserve signposted from Manea. Reserve office & visitor centre located off Welches Dam.
Public transport: None to reserve entrance. Buses & trains stop at Manea, three miles from reserve.
Visiting: Open at all times. Car park (inc. two disabled bays, groups welcome - space for two small 36-seat coaches, large coaches can't pass final bend to reserve). Access reserve from visitor centre (open daily 9am-5pm, not Dec 25/26), toilets, hot drinks. Ten hides (open at all times) overlook reserve - Welches Dam hide (with disabled access) 350 yards from visitor centre, rest up to 1.8 miles away. Welches Dam to public hides approached by marked paths behind boundary bank. Boardwalk over pond is good for dragonflies in summer. Dogs on leads.
Contact: RSPB, T: 01354 680 212;
E: ouse.washes@rspb.org.uk

9. PAXTON PITS NATURE RESERVE

Huntingdonshire District Co./Friends of Paxton Pits.
Habitats: 77ha, lakes, riverside, reedbed, meadows, scrub, woodland.
Birds: 235 spp., 70 spp. breed. *Spring/summer:* Nightingale, Kingfisher, Common Tern, Sparrowhawk, Hobby, Grasshopper, Sedge & Reed Warblers, Lesser Whitethroat. Large Cormorant colony. *Winter:* Wildfowl inc. Smew, Goldeneye, Goosander, Gadwall, Pochard.
Other: Wildflowers, 27 spp. butterflies & 21 spp. dragonflies are in abundance. Common Spotted Orchids along meadow trail, Bee Orchids around car park. Otters use reserve.
Directions: Sat nav PE19 6ET. TL 196 629. Access from A1 at Little Paxton, two miles N of St Neots. Reserve signposted from edge of Little Paxton.
Public transport: Bus - no.66 (not Sun) St Neots & Huntingdon to Little Paxton. Stagecoach. Train - St Neots (two miles - can walk along Ouse Valley Way.)
Visiting: Open at all times. Car park - coaches/groups by arrangement, bike racks. Wheelchair-accessible visitor centre/toilets, small shop - books, bird seed/ feeders etc, & light refreshments. Open 10am-4.30pm (not Dec 25) - subject to volunteer availability. Three hides (always open), marked nature trails. Many paths suitable for wheelchairs, but muddy when wet. Dogs must be under control.
Contact: The Rangers, Paxton Pits Nature Reseve, High Street, Little Paxton, St Neots, Cambs PE19 6ET.
T: 01480 406 795; W: www.paxton-pits.org.uk;
E: paxtonpits@huntingdonshire.gov.uk

10. WICKEN FEN NNR

The National Trust.
Habitats: Internationally important wetland, inc. open fen meadows, sedge fields, grazing marsh, partially flooded wet grassland, reedbed, scrub, woodland.
Birds: *Spring*: Passage waders & passerines. *Summer*: Marsh Harriers, Hobbies, waders & warblers. *Winter*: Wildfowl, Hen Harriers roost on Sedge Fen, Marsh Harrier, Bittern, Black-tailed Godwit, Barn & Short-eared Owls, Cetti's Warbler.
Other: 9,000+ spp. recorded inc. 21 spp. dragonflies, 27 spp. butterflies, 1,200+ spp. moths. Water Vole, Otter.
Directions: Sat nav: CB7 5XP. TL 564 706. Lies 17 miles NE of Cambridge & ten miles S of Ely. From A10 drive E along A1123 to Wicken, turn R in village (signposted).
Public transport: None.
Visiting: Open daily dawn-dusk daily (not Dec 25). Disabled parking in main car park (close to visitor centre), coach parking limited (groups need to book). Parking/entry fee for non-NT members. Visitor centre, shop & cafe open daily (10am-5pm/dusk in winter). Toilets (inc. disabled), nine hides (three equipped for wheelchairs), boardwalk (suitable for wheelchairs), footpaths, cycle route (NCN Route 11 passes through reserve). National Dragonfly Centre open weekends during summer.
Contact: Wicken Fen Visitor Centre, T: 01353 720 274;
E: wickenfen@nationaltrust.org.uk

Essex

The county has a wide range of habitats. The Wildlife Trust manages 87 nature reserves throughout this huge county. The RSPB's coastal reserves at Rainham Marshes & Old Hall Marshes both attract a wide range of species including wintering raptors. The coast (including the Naze & Bradwell, where there is a Bird Observatory) attracts migrants, including rarities. Try seawatching along the Thames off Southend Pier. Away from the coast, Abberton Reservoir holds important numbers of wintering wildfowl & wader passage can be good. The ancient woodland of Epping Forest lies close to London.

1. ABBERTON RESERVOIR

Essex Wildlife Trust.
Habitats: 25ha on edge of expanding 485ha reservoir, with wader-friendly muddy margins.
Birds: *Spring:* Passage waders, terns, birds of prey. *Summer:* Tree-nesting Cormorant colony, raft-nesting Common Tern. Hobby, Yellow Wagtail, warblers, Nightingale, Turtle Dove, Skylark, Corn Bunting. *Autumn:* Red-crested Pochard, waders, rarities. *Winter:* Nationally important for Coot, Mallard, Teal, Wigeon, Shoveler, Gadwall, Pochard, Tufted Duck, Goldeneye. Smew, Bittern & Goosander regular. Golden Plover & Lapwing flocks on surrounding fields.
Other: Dragonflies inc. Broad-bodied Chaser, Small Red-eyed damselfly. Butterflies inc. Brown Argus & Purple Hairstreak. Roesel's Bush-cricket. Brown Hare, Smooth Newt, Wasp Spider.
Directions: Sat nav: CO2 0EU. TL 962 177. Six miles SW of Colchester on B1026 (Colchester to Maldon). Follow signs from Layer-de-la-Haye or Great Wigborough.
Public transport: None.

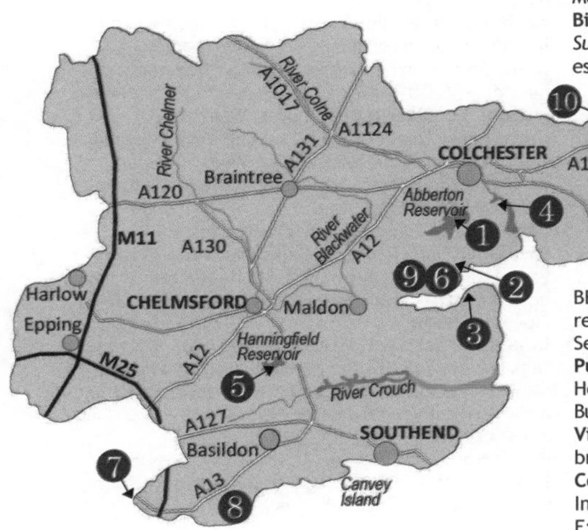

Visiting: Open daily (not Dec 25/26) 9am-5pm (4pm Nov-Jan). Ample parking, inc. disabled & coach bays. Visitor centre inc. toilets, viewing veranda, cafe & shop. Electric wheelchair for hire. Outdoor play area. Good viewing where roads cross reservoir. Nature trails with panoramic views, three hides - two overlook water, one in woodland.
Contact: Essex WT, T: 01206 738 172; E: abberton@essexwt.org.uk

2. ABBOTT'S HALL FARM

Essex Wildlife Trust.
Habitats: 280ha coastal farm - saltmarsh, saline lagoons, grazing marsh, farmland, woodland, freshwater lakes & ponds.
Birds: Skylark, Grey Partridge, Corn Bunting & other farmland species. Passage migrants & summer warblers. *Winter*: Waders & wildfowl, large roost of Little Egret.
Other: Range of butterflies, reptiles, newts, Water Vole.
Directions: Sat nav: CO5 7RZ. TL 962 146. On Blackwater estuary, seven miles SW from Colchester. Turn E off B1026 (Colchester-Maldon road) towards Peldon. Entrance, near Great Wigborough, is 0.5 mile on R.
Public transport: None.
Visiting: Wildlife Trust HQ & a working farm - take care. Weekdays (9am-5pm). Toilets, three hides (two with wheelchair ramps), information boards. Many footpaths through farmland areas. Guided walks, factsheets available. Dogs only in designated area.
Contact: Essex WT, T: 01621 862 960; E: admin@essexwt.org.uk

3. BRADWELL BIRD OBSERVATORY/SHELL BANK

Essex Birdwatching Society/Essex Wildlife Trust.
Habitats: Mudflats, saltmarsh, 12ha of shellbank. Mouth of Blackwater estuary.
Birds: *Spring/autumn:* good passage of migrants. *Summer*: Small breeding population of terns & other estuarine species, Yellow Wagtail, Reed Bunting & Linnet. *Winter*: Wildfowl (inc. Red-throated Diver, Brent Geese, Red-breasted Merganser), large numbers of waders (up to 20,000), small numbers of Twite, Snow Bunting & occasional Shore Lark on beaches. Hen Harrier, Merlin & Peregrine.
Other: Variety of dragonflies inc. Hairy Dragonfly & Scarce Emerald Damselfly.
Directions: Sat nav: CM0 7PN. TM 031 085. BBO is located on edge of Bradwell Shell Bank nature reserve, 100 yards S of St Peter's Chapel, Bradwell-on-Sea. Parking at end of East End Road.
Public transport: Bus - no.D1 (not Sun) from Maldon. Hedingham (T: 01206 769 778). No.DaRT4 (not Sun) from Burnham-on-Couch. Essex & Suffolk DaRT (T: 01621 874 411).
Visiting: Open all year. Car park. Keep to seawall in breeding season to prevent disturbance.
Contact: Graham Smith (BBO Sec), 48 The Meads, Ingatestone, Essex CM4 0AE. T: 01277 354 034; E: silaum.silaus@tesco.co.uk; Essex WT - see site 2.

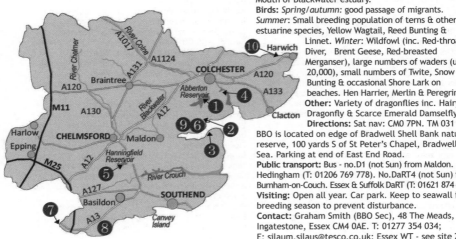

4. FINGRINGHOE WICK

Essex Wildlife Trust.
Habitats: Old gravel pit, large lake, many ponds, sallow/birch thickets, young scrub, reedbeds, saltmarsh, gorse heathland.
Birds: 200 spp. recorded. *Spring/summer*: 25+ male Nightingales. Marsh Harrier, Hobby, Turtle Dove, Cuckoo, Green & Great Spotted Woodpeckers & good variety of warblers in scrub/thickets. *Autumn/winter*: Brent Goose, waders (inc. Avocet & Golden Plover), Peregrine, Merlin, Hen Harrier, Little Egret. Little Grebe, Mute Swan, Teal, Wigeon, Shoveler, Gadwall.
Other: Swathes of Sea Lavender in summer among 350 plant spp. Numerous dragonflies & butterflies.
Directions: Sat nav: C05 7DN. TM 048 192. Reserve signposted from B1025 to Mersea Island, five miles S of Colchester.
Public transport: Nearest buses to Fingringhoe (then 45 mins walk along Gravel Pit Trail to reserve.
Visiting: Open daily (not Dec 25/26) 9am-5pm (4pm Nov-Jan). Car park. Voluntary entrance donation. Visitor centre - toilets (inc. baby changing facilities, easy access toilet), shop, light refreshments, observation room with displays overlooking saltmarsh. One wheelchair available. Seven hides, nature trails. Dogs on leads, limited to dog walk area at edge of reserve.
Contact: Fingringhoe Wick Visitor Centre, T: 01206 729 678; E: fingringhoe@essexwt.org.uk

5. HANNINGFIELD RESERVOIR

Essex Wildlife Trust/Essex & Suffolk Water.
Habitats: 45ha, mixed woodland with grassy glades & rides, adjoining 352ha Hanningfield Reservoir.
Birds: *Spring*: Good numbers & mix of woodland warblers. *Summer*: Vast numbers of Swifts, Swallows & martins feeding over the water. Hobby & Osprey. *Winter*: Good numbers & mix of waterfowl. Large gull roost.
Other: Spectacular displays of Bluebells in spring. Dragonflies around ponds. Grass Snake & Common Lizard sometimes bask on rides.
Directions: Sat nav: CM11 1WT. TQ 725 971. Three miles N of Wickford. Exit off Southend Road (Old A130) at Rettendon onto South Hanningfield Road. Follow this for two miles until reaching the T-junction with Hawkswood Road. Turn R - entrance to visitor centre & reserve is one mile on R.
Public transport: Bus - no.14 (not Sun) Chelmsford to Wickford. First Essex. Alight at Downham village & walk 0.5 mile down Crowsheath Lane.
Visiting: Open daily (not Dec 25/26) 9am-5pm (4pm Nov-Jan). Voluntary entrance donation. car park with disabled & coach parking. Visitor centre, shop, refreshments, toilets, education room. Picnic area, four bird hides (one adapted), nature trails. No dogs. No cycling.
Contact: Hanningfield Reservoir Visitor Centre, T: 01268 711 001; E: hanningfield@essexwt.org.uk

6. OLD HALL MARSHES

RSPB (Eastern England Office).
Habitats: 630ha, coastal grazing marsh, reedbed, open water, saline lagoon, saltmarsh & mudflat.
Birds: *Summer:* Breeding Avocet, Redshank, Lapwing, Pochard, Shoveler, Gadwall, Marsh Harrier, Bearded Tit & Barn Owl. *Passage:* All expected waders inc. Spotted Redshank, Green Sandpiper & Whimbrel. Yellow Wagtail, Whinchat & Wheatear. *Winter:* Large numbers of wildfowl inc. Brent Goose (ca. 4,000), Wigeon, Teal, Shoveler, Goldeneye, Red-breasted Merganser, waders, Merlin, Hen Harrier, Short-eared Owl & Twite.
Other: Brown Hare, Water Vole, Hairy Dragonfly, Scarce Emerald Damselfly, Ground Lackey moth, Cream Spot Tiger, White-letter Hairstreak among 24 spp. butterflies, Yellow Meadow Ant.
Directions: Sat nav: CM9 8TP. TL 959 122. Overlooks River Blackwater, SW of Colchester. From A12 take B1023, via Tiptree to Tolleshunt D'Arcy. Turn L at village maypole then R into Chapel Road (back road to Tollesbury). After approx 1 mile, turn L into Old Hall Lane. Continue up Old Hall Lane, through iron gates & follow signs straight ahead to car park.
Public transport: Bus - no.95 (not Sun) Maldon to Tollesbury (then two mile walk along seawall). Hedingham (T: 01206 769 778).
Visiting: Open 9am-5pm/dusk if earlier when car park gates locked. No coaches. Do not park in the lane. Two trails - three miles & 6.5 miles. Viewing screens overlooking saline lagoon area at E end of reserve. No wheelchair access or facilities. Dogs under control allowed on footpaths. Nearest toilets in Tiptree, six miles away.
Contact: RSPB, T: 01621 869 015; E: oldhallmarshes@rspb.org.uk

7. RAINHAM MARSHES

RSPB (Eastern England office).
Habitats: Former MoD shooting range, largest area of lowland wetland remaining along the Thames.
Birds: *Spring:* Marsh Harrier, Hobby, Wheatear, hirundines & other migrants. *Summer/autumn:* Many waders, inc. Black-tailed Godwit, Whimbrel, Greenshank, Snipe, Lapwing, Avocet. Yellow-legged Gull. Hunting Merlin & Peregrine. *Winter:* Waders, wildfowl, Water Pipit, Short-eared Owl, Little Egret. Penduline Tit most winters.
Other: 21 spp. dragonfly, inc. Hairy Dragonfly, Scarce Emerald & Small Red-eyed Damselfly. Marsh Frog, Water Vole, Water Shrew, Fox, Stoat, Weasel, 32 spp. butterflies, & 13 spp. orthoptera. Deadly Nightshade, Flowering Rush.
Directions: Sat nav: RM19 1SZ. TQ 547 787. Off New Tank Hill Road (A1090) in Purfleet, just off A1306 between Rainham & Lakeside. This is accessible from Aveley, Wennington & Purfleet junction of A13 & Junc 30/31 of M25.
Public transport: Bus - no.44 Grays to Lakeside. Ensignbus (T: 01708 865 656)/Arriva (on Sun). Train - Purfleet. Reserve is 20 mins walk along riverside path (signposted).

Visiting: Open 9.30am-5pm (Feb-Oct), 9.30am-4.30pm Nov-Jan (not Dec 25/26). Entry fee for non-RSPB members. Car park (four Blue Badge spaces). Award-winning visitor centre with disabled toilets, shop, cafe (10am-to 30 mins before reserve closes), picnic area, wildlife garden & children's playground. Four hides. Three signposted trails, suitable for wheelchairs & pushchairs. Guided walks - check RSPB website for details. Dogs allowed only on Thames riverside path.
Contact: RSPB, T: 01708 899 840;
E: rainham.marshes@rspb.org.uk

8. THURROCK THAMESIDE NATURE PARK

Essex Wildlife Trust/Cory Environmental Trust.
Habitats: 48ha, reclaimed landfill site covering overlooking Mucking Flats SSSI & Ramsar-designated Thames estuary. Saltmarsh, grassland, woodland, ponds & reedbed.
Birds: *All year:* Kingfisher, Barn Owl, Reed Bunting, Bearded Tit, Cetti's Warbler & Skylark. *Winter:* Wildfowl, Internationally important numbers of Ringed Plover & Avocet & nationally significant numbers of Grey Plover, Dunlin, Redshank & godwits. Short-eared Owl.
Other: Water Vole, Harvest Mouse, Shrill Carder Bee, Great Crested Newt, Adder.
Directions: Sat nav: SS17 0RN. TQ 696 806. From Basildon head SW on A13 towards Stanford-le-Hope. Take A1014 exit & follow signs for Walton Hall Farm Museum. Past museum entrance turn R into Mucking Wharf Road & take single lane entrance road to visitor centre.
Public transport: None.
Visiting: Open daily (not Dec 25/26) 9am-5pm, 4pm Nov-Jan). Visitor centre with rooftop viewing platform, toilets (inc. disabled), cafe, shop. Good access for wheelchair users to visitor centre, toilet & paths. Bird hide overlooks mudflats. Dogs on leads.
Contact: Essex WT, T: 01375 643 342;
E: ttnp@essexwt.org.uk

9. TOLLESBURY WICK MARSHES

Essex Wildlife Trust.
Habitats: Estuary with fringing saltmarsh & mudflats with some shingle. Extensive freshwater grazing marsh, brackish borrowdyke & small reedbeds.
Birds: *Summer*: Avocet, Redshank, Lapwing, Little Tern, Reed & Sedge Warblers, Reed Bunting, Barn Owl. *Passage*: Spotted Redshank, Green Sandpiper, Whimbrel. *Winter*: Large numbers of wintering wildfowl & waders, particularly Brent Geese & Wigeon, Lapwing & Golden Plover. Short-eared Owl, Hen & Marsh Harriers.
Other: Plants inc. Spiny Restharrow, Grass Vetchling, Yellow Horned-poppy, Slender Hare's-ear. Hairy Dragonfly, Roesel's & Great Green Bush-crickets. Brown Hares. Occasional Common Seals seen from sea wall.
Directions: Sat nav: CM9 8TB. TL 970 103. On Blackwater Estuary eight miles E of Maldon. Follow B1023 to Tollesbury via Tiptree, leaving A12 at Kelvedon. Then follow Woodrolfe Road S towards marina. Use small public car park at Woodrolfe Green (500 yards before reserve entrance on sea wall - suitable for mini-buses & small coaches.
Public transport: Bus - no.91 (Mon-Fri) from Witham, no. 92 (not Sun) from Colchester & no.95 (not Sun) from Maldon, all to Tollesbury. Hedingham (T: 01621 869 778).
Visiting: Open all times along exposed sea wall footpath. Motorised wheelchair access possible to Block House Bay. Hide. Public toilets at Woodrolfe Green car park.
Contact: Essex WT - see site 2.

10. WRABNESS NATURE RESERVE & MARSH

Essex Wildlife Trust.
Habitats: 24ha, grazed grassland & open scrub overlooking wader & wildfowl feeding grounds in Jacques Bay.
Birds: *Spring/summer:* Nightingale, Whitethroat, Turtle Dove, Bullfinch, Yellowhammer. *Winter:* Internationally important species inc. Brent Goose, Shelduck, Wigeon, Pintail, Black-tailed Godwit, Grey Plover, Dunlin, Turnstone & Curlew. Short-eared & Barn Owls hunt over grassland.
Other: Wildflowers, good range of butterflies & dragonflies.
Directions: Sat nav: CO11 2TD. TM 167 314. Lies on southern bank of Stour estuary. From B1352 between Bradfield & Wrabness turn down Whitesheaf Lane to the reserve. Car park is on L just beyond railway bridge.
Public transport: Bus - no.103 Colchester to Harwich, (not Sun) alight Wrabness. First Essex. Train - Wrabness - one mile walk from reserve on public footpath.
Visiting: Open all year. Car park, hide. Hard-surfaced path around site suitable for wheelchairs (RADAR NKS key required for gates).
Contact: Essex WT - see site 2.

Hertfordshire

Famous for Britain's first breeding record of Little Ringed Plover (1938) & England's first breeding record of Black-necked Grebe (1919), the Tring Reservoirs are still one of the best sites in the county. The Wildlife Trust manages over 40 nature reserves . offering residents of this urbanised Home County a welcome taste of the countryside. The wetland habitats of the Lee Valley have regular wintering Bittern & other interesting species can turn up here.

1. AMWELL NATURE RESERVE

Herts & Middlesex Wildlife Trust.
Habitats: Disused gravel pit with reedbeds & woodland.
Birds: *Spring/summer*: Ringed Plover, Little Ringed Plover, Lapwing, Common Tern. *Winter*: Bittern, Smew, Gadwall Shoveler, Snipe, Siskin.
Other: Best county site for dragonflies (21 spp. recorded), Otter, nationally scarce Marsh Dock, plus Early & Southern Marsh Orchids.

Directions: Sat nav: SG12 9SS. TL 376 127. In Lee Valley near Ware. From A10, leave at junction signposted A414 to Harlow. At first roundabout, take B181 to St Margarets & Stanstead Abbotts. On entering St Margarets, just before railway, turn L on Amwell Lane (park on lane). Reserve is on R (signposted).
Public transport: Bus - no.310 Hertford to Waltham Cross, alight St Margarets. Arriva. 5 mins walk. Train - St Margarets (0.75 mile from reserve). Walk E along B181 to towpath of River Lee Navigation, then walk N for 0.5 mile to reserve.
Visiting: Open all year. Two hides, several viewing areas. Dragonfly Trail boardwalk (May-Sep).
Contact: Herts & Middlesex WT, T: 01727 858 901; E: info@hmwt.org

2. KINGS MEAD

Herts & Middlesex Wildlife Trust.
Habitats: Largest remaining area of grazed riverside flood meadow in Hertfordshire.
Birds: 119 spp. recorded. *Summer:* Yellow Wagtail, Skylark, seven species of breeding warblers, Reed Bunting. *Winter/spring:* Gadwall, Shoveler, Wigeon, Teal, Snipe, gulls, waders, Siskin, Redpoll.
Other: 265 spp. wildflowers, 18 spp. dragonflies. Significant population of Short-winged Conehead.
Directions: Sat nav: SG12 9XD. TL 349 136. From Ware head SE on A1170 High Street, turn R into Burgage Lane shortly after Ware Museum. Park in public car park. From here pedestrian access is via the River Lee, go over the bridge, turn R & walk 250 yards. Turn L into reserve.
Public transport: Bus - no.310 Waltham Cross to Hertford, alight Hertford Regional College. Arriva in Herts & Essex. Train - Ware. Both five mins walk to reserve.
Visiting: Open all year.
Contact: Herts & Middlesex WT - see site 1.

3. MAPLE LODGE

Thames Water/
Maple Lodge Conservation Society.
Habitats: Man-made wetland habitat formed from two gravel pits & a sludge settlement area. Two lakes & a reedbed. Mixed broadleaved plantation on eastern side.
Birds: *All year:* Wildfowl (esp. winter), Sparrowhawk, Red Kite, Buzzard, Water Rail 3 spp. woodpecker, Kingfisher, Tawny Owl, variety of finches, thrushes & woodland species. *Summer:* Hobby, migrant warblers. *Passage:* Snipe, Green & Common Sandpipers. .
Other: 250 spp. moths, plus many butterflies & aquatic insects. 125 spp. wildflowers. Seven of nine bat spp. found in Herts have been recorded.
Directions: Sat nav: WD3 9SF. TQ 036 925.
S of Rickmansworth, close to village of Maple Cross. From M25 Junc 17 drive towards Denham/Uxbridge, turn L at traffic lights. Drive down Maple Lodge Close & park in social club car park on R.
Public transport: Bus - nos.432 & 724 from Rickmansworth to Maple Cross. Arriva.
Train - Maple Cross.
Visiting: Restricted to members of MLCS but visits by non-members & groups can be arranged in advance. Site can be boggy, keep to designated paths. Information centre, toilets, nine hides (two wheelchair-friendly & two more when ground dry). Winter feeding stations.
Contact: Maple Lodge Conservation Society,
T: 07580 535 986;
E: enquiries@maplelodgenaturereserve.org;
W: www.maplelodge.org

4. RYE MEADS

RSPB/Herts & Middlesex Wildlife Trust.
Habitats: Beside River Lee - marsh, willow scrub, pools, scrapes, lagoons & reedbed.
Birds: *Summer*: Breeding Water Rail, Tufted Duck, Gadwall, Common Tern, Kestrel, Kingfisher, Little Ringed Plover, nine species of warblers. Hobby. *Autumn:* Birds on passage inc. Green Sandpiper, Teal & Snipe. *Winter*: Bittern, Shoveler, Goldeneye, Teal, Water Rail, Snipe, Jack Snipe, Redpoll & Siskin. Occasional rarities.
Other: Fen vegetation, invertebrates & reptiles.
Directions: SG12 8JS. TL 389 103. Take Hoddesdon turn off A10 & follow brown duck signs. Near Rye House railway station.
Public transport: Bus - no.410 (not Sun) Harlow to Waltham Cross alight Rye Road/Rye Park, 0.5 mile. Trustybus. Train - Rye House, 0.4 mile.
Visiting: Open daily (not Dec 25/26) 9am-5pm/dusk if earlier. Gates are locked when the reserve is closed. Car park (charge for non-members), visitor centre - staffed reception, drinks machine, classrooms - toilets. Nature trails, picnic area, bird feeding area seven hides. Visitor centre, toilets & trails have disabled access. RSPB reserve has close-circuit TV on nests in summer. No dogs, except guide dogs. Access to the HMWT site.
Contact: RSPB, T: 01992 708 383;
E: rye.meads@rspb.org.uk;
Herts & Middlesex WT - see site 1.

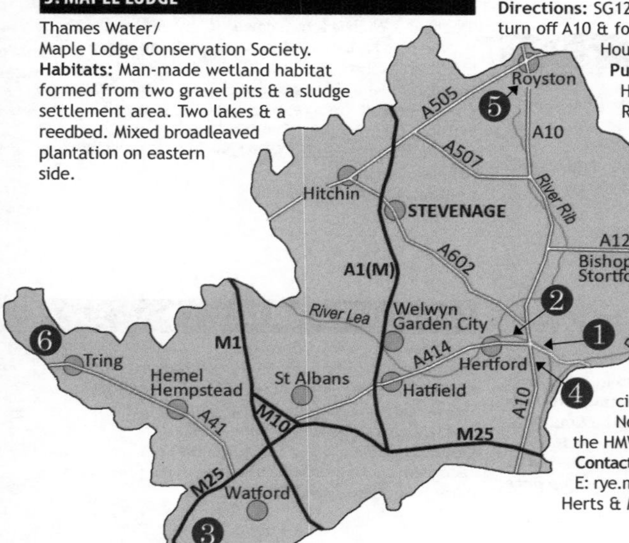

5. THERFIELD LNR

Conservators of Therfield Heath.
Habitats: Natural chalk/grass downland.
Birds: Noted stop-off site for migrants such as Ring Ouzel & Wheatear. *Spring/summer:* Breeding Skylark, Meadow Pipit, Willow Warbler, Whitethroat, Lesser Whitethroat & Grey Partridge. Good selection of raptors seen regularly, inc. Red Kite.
Other: 26 spp. butterflies inc. increasingly rare Chalkhill Blue. Several orchid spp., Pasqueflower & variety of chalk grassland flowers.
Directions: Sat nav: SG8 9NT. TL 335 400. Common land SSSI lies west & south of Royston & is accessed from A505 (Baldock Road).
Public transport: Train - Royston, two mins walk.
Visiting: Open at all times. Open downland walks, golf course & sports fields.
Contact: Conservators of Therfield Heath,
E: clerk@therfieldheath.org.uk;
W: www.therfieldheath.org.uk

5. TRING RESERVOIRS

Canals & Rivers Trust/Herts & Middlesex Wildlife Trust. [Water Treatment Works lagoon - Thames Water].
Habitats: Four reservoirs with surrounding woodland, scrub & meadows. Two of reservoirs have extensive reedbeds. WTW Lagoon with islands & dragonfly scrape, surrounding hedgerows & scrub.
Birds: *Spring/summer*: Breeding water birds, Common Terns & heronry. Regular Hobby, Black Terns & Red Kite, warblers inc. Cetti's. Occasional Marsh Harrier, Osprey. *Autumn/winter passage*: Waders, occasional White-winged Tern. *Winter*: Gull roost, large wildfowl flocks, bunting roosts, Bittern.
Other: Black Poplar trees, locally rare plants in damp areas. 18 spp. dragonflies inc. Black-tailed Skimmer, Ruddy Darter & Emerald Damselfly. Holly Blue & Speckled Wood butterflies. Chinese Water Deer, Daubenton's, Natterer's & both spp. Pipistrelle bats.
Directions: Sat nav: HP23 4NW. SP 904 134. Reservoirs two miles NW of Tring, all accessible from B489 which crosses A41 Aston Clinton by-pass. NB: exit from by-pass only southbound.
Public transport: Bus - no.164 (not Sun) Aylesbury to Tring (circular), alight Tringford Road. (0.9 miles to Wilstone, 0.4 miles to Startops). Redline Buses (T: 01296 426 786). Train - Tring (3.8 miles to Wilstone, 2.7 miles to Startops).
Visiting: Reservoirs, Marsworth / Startops End / Tringford / Wilstone, open at all times. Coaches can only drop off & pick up, contact for advice. Car parks: at Wilstone (free, height barrier), at Startop's End (pay-&-dispaly). Hides on all reservoirs. Disabled access from car park at Startops/Marsworth Reservoirs, as well as WTW Lagoon Hide.
Contact: Herts & Middlesex WT - see site 1.

Norfolk

The county is regarded as the UK's best birding area & with such iconic sites as Cley, Titchwell, The Broads & Breckland this is hard to dispute. Its east coast location ensures that no matter what time of the year your visit you will always find a wide variety of birds. During spring/autumn migration these may include many common, scarce & rare species & a 'first for Britain' wouldn't be unexpected. With breeding Bittern, Crane & Stone Curlew, passage waders & large numbers of wintering geese there is something for everyone.

1. CLEY MARSHES NNR

Norfolk Wildlife Trust.
Habitats: Reedbeds, salt & freshwater marshes, pools/scrapes & shingle ridge with international reputation as one of finest birdwatching sites in Britain.
Birds: *Breeding:* Avocet, Marsh Harrier, Spoonbill, Bearded Tit. Spring/Autumn: waders - most common species & regularly less common spp. inc. Ruff, Wood Sandpiper, Spotted Redshank & Temminck's & Little Stint. Common/scarce passage migrants and rarities can turn up at anytime. *Winter:* large numbers of wintering wildfowl inc. Wigeon, Teal, Pintail & Brent Goose. Offshore - divers, grebes, seaduck.
Directions: Sat nav: NR25 7SA. TG 054 440. Situated four miles N of Holt on A149 coast road, 0.5 mile E of Cley-next-the-Sea. Visitor centre & car park on inland side of road.
Public transport: Bus - Coastliner CH4 service Cromer-Sheringham-Wells stops at Cley. Sanders Coaches (T: 01263 712 800). Connections for train & bus services at Sheringham.
Visiting: Open dawn-dusk. Visitor Centre open daily, (not Dec 24/25) 10am-5pm/4.30 (Nov-Feb). Environmentally-friendly visitor centre (wheelchair accessible) incorporates observation area, interactive interpretation inc. remote controllable wildlife camera, toilets, cafe (closes 30 mins before centre) & sales area. Free admission to visitor centre, entrance fee charged for reserve (NWT members/children free). Five hides (three with wheelchair access), boardwalk & information boards, audio trail. Wildlife detective bumbags for children, free to hire. Reserve leaflet, regular events. No dogs on reserve but can walk Beach Road, along shingel bank & East bank.
Contact: NWT Cley Marshes Visitor Centre,
T: 01263 740 008;
Norfolk WT, T: 01603 625 540;
E: info@norfolkwildlifetrust.org.uk

2. HICKLING BROAD NNR

Norfolk Wildlife Trust.
Habitats: The largest & wildest of the Norfolk Broads with open water, reedbed, fen, grazing marsh & woodland.
Birds: *All year:* Bittern, Pochard, Water Rail, Cetti's Warbler, Bearded Tit. *Nov-Feb:* raptor roost at Stubb Mill, provides excellent views of raptors flying in to roost. Likely spp. inc. Marsh & Hen Harriers, Merlin, Crane & Pink-footed Goose. *Autumn/winter:* Wildfowl inc. Shoveler, Teal & Goldeneye.
Other: Swallowtail butterfly, Norfolk Hawker dragonfly, Marsh Orchid.
Directions: Sat nav: NR12 0BW. TG 428 222. Approx four miles SE of Stalham, just off A149 Yarmouth Road. From Hickling village, follow brown badger tourist signs into Stubb Road at Greyhound Inn. Follow Stubb Road for another mile & turn R at end for nature reserve.
Public transport: Bus - no.34 Stalham to North Walsham - stops in Hickling village. Sanders Coaches (T: 01263 712 800). 25 mins walk to reserve.
Visiting: Open daily dawn-dusk. Car & coach parking, groups welcome. Visitor centre open daily 10am-5pm from Apr-Oct & 11am-4pm Nov-Mar (weekends, Dec 26 & Jan 1). Entrance fee charged for reserve, NWT members/children free. Shop, refreshments, toilets. Picnic area, boardwalk trail through reedbeds to open water, hides - disabled access to broad, boardwalk & toilets. Dogs only allowed on Weaver's Way footpath. Water trail boat trips May to Sep (additional charge - booking advisable).
Contact: Hickling Broad Visitor Centre, T: 01692 598 276; Norfolk WT - see site 1.

3. HOLKHAM NNR

Holkham Estate/Natural England (Norfolk & Suffolk Team).
Habitats: 4,000 ha, sandflats, dunes, marshes, pinewoods, reclaimed saltmarsh.
Birds: *All year:* Marsh Harrier, Grey Heron, Lapwing, Barn Owl, Kestrel. *Summer*: Breeding Little Tern, Snipe, Oystercatcher & Ringed Plover. *Passage*: Migrants, inc. Yellow Wagtail, Wheatear, Cuckoo & many unusual species. *Winter*: Wildfowl, inc. Brent (7,000), Pink-footed (20,000) & White-fronted Geese, up to 13,000 Wigeon. Shorelark, Twite & Snow Bunting.
Other: Seablite bushes, attractive to incoming migrant birds, Sea Aster & Sea Lavender. Antlion.
Directions: Sat nav: NR23 1RH.
TF 890 447. Three miles W of Wells on A149. From Holkham village turn down Lady Ann's Drive (opposite entrance to Holkham Hall) to park. More parking at end of Wells Beach Road in Wells & at Burnham Overy.
Public transport: Bus - Coastliner 36 King's Lynn-Hunstanton-Fakenham stops at Holkham. Lynx Bus (T: 01553 611 955).
Visiting: Unrestricted, keep to paths & off grazing marshes/farmland. Pay-&-display parking, two hides. Disabled access.
Contact: Holkham Estate, Holkham Nature Reserve, T: 01328 800 730; E: j.fiennes@holkham.co.uk

4. HOLME OBSERVATORY

Norfolk Ornithologists' Association (NOA).
Habitats: Set in a 5ha reserve of pine & scrub covered dunes between shore & Broad Water (reed-fringed lagoon) making this a migration hotspot.
Birds: 300+ spp., over 150 spp. ringed. *Spring/ Autumn:* paassage migrants inc. rarities which have inc. Red-flanked Bluetail, Red-breasted Flycatcher, Yellow-browed, Pallas's, Subalpine, Arctic & Barred Warblers, Alpine Accentor, Little Bunting. *Winter:* Wildfowl & waders, Merlin, Snow Bunting, Twite.
Other: Moth trap run Mar-Oct, migrant moths & butterflies recorded annually.
Directions: Sat nav: PE36 6LQ. TF 713 449. E of Hunstanton, signposted from A149. Access from Broadwater Road, Holme. Reserve & visitors centre are beyond White House at end of track.
Public transport: Bus - Coastliner 36 service King's Lynn-Hunstanton-Fakenham stops at Holme. Lynx Bus (T: 01553 611 955).
Visiting: Open daily dawn-dusk (members) & 9am-5pm to non-members by permit from Observatory. Parties by prior arrangement. Car park, visitor centre & several hides (seawatch hide reserved for NOA members), access to beach & coastal path. Dogs on leads. Accredited Bird Observatory operating all year for bird ringing, MV moth trapping & other scientific monitoring.
Contact: Sophie Barker, Holme Bird Observatory, Broadwater Road, Holme, Hunstanton, Norfolk PE36 6LQ. T: 01485 525 406; E: info@noa.org.uk; W: www.noa.org.uk

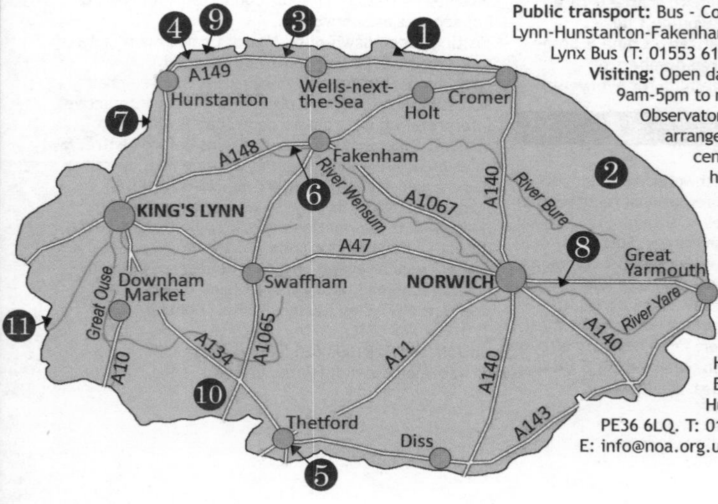

5. NUNNERY LAKES

British Trust for Ornithology.
Habitats: Flood meadows, scrape, flooded gravel pits, heathland, scrub & wet woodland.
Birds: 60 spp. breed. *All year:* Grey Heron, Egyptian Goose, Kingfisher, Green Woodpecker. *Spring*: Passage waders, hirundines, Swift, passerines. *Summer*: Warblers, Cuckoo, Oystercatcher, Lapwing, Hobby. *Winter*: Goosander, Teal, Water Rail, Snipe, Siskin.
Other: Otter, Brown Hare, Muntjac, Grass Snake, Common Lizard. Emperor Dragonfly, Red-eyed Damselfly. Speckled Wood & Orange-tip butterflies. Mossy Stonecrop.
Directions: Sat Nav: IP24 2PU. TL 873 815. On S edge of Thetford, adjacent to BTO's headquarters at The Nunnery. Main access point is via Nun's Bridges car park (off A134), cross pedestrian bridge at TL 874 821.
Public transport: Regular services to Thetford. Bus - station 0.5 mile. Train - station one mile.
Visiting: Open dawn-dusk, public access permitted on waymarked paths. Boardwalk through wet woodland, information panels, hide. Toilets on Nunnery Place at back of BTO, available office hours. Call reception in advance to arrange wheelchair access to lakes & hide. Pre-booked coaches can park in grounds. Dogs on leads at all times.
Contact: British Trust for Ornithology, The Nunnery, Thetford, Norfolk IP24 2PU. T: 01842 750 050;
E: info@bto.org

6. SCULTHORPE MOOR

Hawk & Owl Trust.
Habitats: Wetland reserve, fen containing saw sedge (European priority habitat), reedbed, wet woodland, pools, ditches & riverbank.
Birds: 90 spp. inc. breeding Marsh Harrier, Barn Owl & Tawny Owl. Buzzard, Goshawk, Hobby, Kestrel, Osprey, Sparrowhawk. Water Rail, Kingfisher, Marsh & Willow Tits, Lesser Spotted Woodpecker. Winter finches, thrushes.**Other:** Otter, Water Vole, Roe Deer, Glow Worm, 19 spp. dragonflies, butterflies inc. White Admiral. **Directions:** Sat nav: NR21 9GN. TF 900 305. In Wensum Valley, just W of Fakenham, on A148 to King's Lynn. Nature reserve signposted opposite village of Sculthorpe. Follow Turf Moor Road to visitor centre.
Public transport: Bus - no.X29 Fakenham to King's Lynn stops at end of Turf Moor Road. First Norfolk & Suffolk (T: 08456 020 121).
Visiting: Open daily (not Dec 25), 8am-5pm Apr-Oct, (4pm Nov-Mar). Late opening THurs until 8.30pm or dusk. Coach parking available. Entrance by suggested donation for adults (children & members free). Visitor centre, with adapted toilets, hot drinks, interpretive displays & live CCTV coverage from around reserve.Reserve & two hides accessible to wheelchairs & buggies via a mile of boardwalk. Bark chipping path to other hides. Guide dogs only.
Contact: The Hawk & Owl Trust, Turf Moor Road, Sculthorpe, Fakenham NR21 9GN. T: 01328 856 788;
E: sculthorpe@hawkandowl.org;
W: www.hawkandowltrust.org/reserves

7. SNETTISHAM

RSPB (Eastern England Office).
Habitats: Intertidal mudflats, saltmarsh, shingle beach, brackish lagoons, & unimproved grassland/scrub. Highest tides best for good views of waders.
Birds: *Summer*: Breeding Mediterranean Gull, Ringed Plover, Redshank, Avocet, Common Tern. Marsh Harrier regular. *Autumn/winter/spring*: Waders - particularly Knot, Bar & Black-tailed Godwits, Dunlin, Grey Plover. Wildfowl - particularly Pink-footed (40,000) & Brent Geese, Wigeon, Gadwall, Goldeneye. Peregrine, Merlin, Hen Harrier, Short-earded owl. Passage migrants in season.
Other: Yellow Horned Poppies & other shingle flora along the beach.
Directions: Sat nav: PE31 7RA. TF 650 328. Car park two miles along Beach Road, signposted off A149 S of Hunstanton, opposite Snettisham village.
Public transport: Bus - Coastliner 36 service King's Lynn-Hunstanton-Fakenham stops at Snettisham. Lynx Bus (T: 01553 611 955).
Visiting: Open at all times. Car park (charge to non-members), three trails, two hides. Coach groups by prior arrangement (contact Titchwell Reserve). Dogs on lead.
Contact: RSPB, T: 01485 210 779;
E: snettisham@rspb.org.uk

8. STRUMPSHAW FEN

RSPB (Eastern England Office).
Habitats: Reedbed/reedfen, wet grassland, woodland.
Birds: *Summer:* Bittern, Little Egret, Bearded Tit, Marsh Harrier, Hobby, Kingfisher, Cetti's Warbler & other reedbed birds. *Winter:* Bittern, wildfowl, Marsh & Hen Harriers.
Other: Rich fen flora - six spp. orchid, inc. Marsh Helleborine & Narrow-leaved Marsh Orchid. Otter, Chinese Water Deer & Water Vole. Swallowtail, White Admiral & Small Heath butterflies, Norfolk Hawker, Scarce Chaser & Variable Damselfly among 20 dragonfly spp.
Directions: Sat nav: NR13 4HS. TG 341 065. Six miles E of Norwich. Approach off A47 Great Yarmouth road - take roundabout to Brundell and continue on same road towards Strumpshaw. Just after Strumpshaw sign turn R into Stone Road & R again into Low Road. Car park 0.3 mile on R.
Public transport: Bus - nos.15 &15A from Acle/Linwood-Norwich-Wymondham. - stops 0.5 mile from reserve. First Norfolk & Suffolk (T: 08456 020 121). Train: Brundall, ca.1.5 miles from reserve.
Visiting: Open daily (not Dec 25), dawn-dusk. Entry fee for non-RSPB members. Reception hide & information centre open 9.30am-5pm Apr-Sep, 10am-4pm Oct-Mar, drinks/snacks available. Toilets, two other hides, trails. Guide dogs only. Limited wheelchair access - phone for advice.
Contact: RSPB, T: 01603 715 191;
E: strumpshaw@rspb.org.uk

9. TITCHWELL MARSH

RSPB (Eastern England Office).
Habitats: Freshwater reedbed & fresh water lagoons, extensive salt marsh, dunes, sandy beach with associated exposed peat beds.
Birds: *Spring/summer:* Breeding Avocet, Bearded Tit, Bittern, Marsh Harrier, Reed Sedge & Cetti's Warbler, Redshank, Ringed Plover & Common Tern. *Summer/ autumn:* Passage waders inc. Knot, Wood & Green Sandpiper, Little Stint, Spotted Redshank, Curlew Sandpiper & many more. *Winter:* Brent Goose, Hen/ Marsh Harrier roost, Snow Bunting. Offshore Common & Velvet Scoter, Long-tailed Duck, Great Northern & Red-throated Divers.
Other: 25 spp. butterflies, inc. all the common spp., plus Essex Skipper & annual Clouded Yellow. 21 spp. dragonflies, inc. Small Red-eyed Damselfly. Good diversity of saltmarsh plants inc. Shrubby Sea-blite & three spp. Sea Lavender.
Directions: Sat nav: PE31 8BB. TF 750 438. E of Hunstanton, signposted off A149.
Public transport: Bus - Coastliner 36 service King's Lynn-Hunstanton-Fakenham stops at Titchwell. Lynx Bus (T: 01553 611 955).
Visiting: Trails & public toilets always open. Car park charge for non-RSPB members, limited coach parking. Visitor centre open daily (not Dec 25/26) 9.30am-5pm (4pm Nov-Feb), information desk, cafe, shop - large selection of optics, birdfood & books. Four hides. Three signposted trails, suitable for wheelchairs, but beach not accessible (wheelchairs available, no charge). Groups by appointment. Dogs on leads only on west bank path (public path).
Contact: RSPB, T: 01485 210 779;
E: titchwell@rspb.org.uk

10. WEETING HEATH

Norfolk Wildlife Trust.
Habitats: Breckland grass & lichen heath.
Birds: *Spring/summer:* Stone Curlew (main attraction), Lapwing, Little Owl, Hobby, Woodlark, Tree Pipit, Spotted Flycatcher, Crossbill.
Directions: Sat nav: IP26 4NQ. TL 757 881. W of Brandon on Norfolk/Suffolk border. Head N from Brandon on A1065 to Mundford. Cross railway line on outskirts of town, then turn L to Weeting & Methwold. In Weeting, turn L to Hockwold cum Wilton - reserve is signpost off this road.
Public transport: Bus - no.40 from Brandon to Weeting (Thetford-Brandon-King's Lynn. Limited services Mon-Fri, only one on Sat). Coach Services (T: 01842 821 509). Train - Brandon.
Visiting: Open daily mid-Mar to end Jul (9.30am-4pm). Car park with coach parking (groups welcome but book first). Entrance fee for non-members, members & children free. Visitor centre open daily toilets, shop, refreshments, hides, live webcam. Disabled access to visitor centre & hides. Reserve/visitor centre opening extended into Aug if Stone Curlews still nesting.
Contact: Weeting Heath Visitor Centre,
T: 01842 827 615;
Norfolk WT - see site 1.

11. WELNEY WETLAND CENTRE

The Wildfowl & Wetlands Trust.
Habitats: 400ha, washland reserve, spring damp meadows, winter wildfowl marsh (SPA, Ramsar site, SSSI, SAC). Additional 80ha of recently created wetland habitat next to visitor centre.
Birds: *All year:* Local Cranes regularly seen, esp. post-breeding birds. *Spring/summer:* Common Tern, Avocet, Lapwing, Black-tailed Godwit, House Martin, occasional rarities. *Autumn*: waders inc Little Stint, Ruff & Curlew Sandpiper. *Winter:* Bewick's & Whooper Swans, wintering wildfowl.
Other: Purple Loosestrife, Meadow Rue, mixed grasses. Dragonflies inc. Scarce Chaser, Emperor, Banded Demoiselle, Small Red-eyed damselfly. 400 spp. moths inc. Goat Moth. Butterflies inc. Brown Argus.
Directions: Sat nav: PE14 9TN. TL 546 944. Hundred Foot Bank, 12 miles N of Ely, signposted from A10 & A1101. Check if A1101 is flooded in winter before setting off.
Public transport: None.
Visiting: Open daily (not Dec 25). Free car & coach parking. 9.30am-5pm (last entry 4.30pm) Mar-Oct, 10am-5pm (last entry 4.30pm) Mon-Wed & 10am-8pm (last entry 6.30pm) Thurs-Sun Nov-Feb). Entrance fee - WWT members free. Visitor centre (wheelchair-friendly), Blue Badge parking, wheelchairs for hire (electric scooter/manual chairs), lifts, disabled toilets, ramps. Large, heated observatory & five hides. Cafe open, 9.30am-4.30pm Mar-Oct, 10am-4.30pm Mon-Wed & 10am-6pm Thurs-Sun Nov-Feb. Access roads & paths to remote hides may be flooded so check before visiting. No dogs allowed.
Contact: WWT Welney, T: 01353 860 711;
E: info.welney@wwt.org.uk

Suffolk

The coastal hot-spots tend to get most attention from visiting birders, & rightly so. The county, in particular the RSPB reserve at Minsmere, has always been the stronghold of iconic birds like the Bittern, Marsh Harrier & Avocet, now all more widespread in the UK. Away from the coast the Suffolk Brecklands are worth a visit & there are other inland sites good for birds among the Wildlife Trust's 51 reserves.

1. BENACRE BROAD NNR

Natural England (Norfolk & Suffolk Team).
Habitats: 393ha, coastal, woodland, saline lagoons, reedbeds & heathland.
Birds: 100 spp. of breeding birds, inc. Marsh Harrier, Bearded Tit, Water Rail & wildfowl. Bittern breeds irregularly. Woodlark, Hobby & Wheatear breed on heathland areas & Little Terns fish off the coast. *Winter:* Shorelark possible on cliff-top areas, winter thrushes.
Other: Lagoon Shrimp, Starlet Sea-anemone, Yellow-horned Poppy, Grey Hair Grass.
Directions: Sat nav: NR34 7JW. TM 522 820. (Covehithe) On coast S of Kessingland. From A12 at Wrentham take minor road to Covehithe. Park near Covehithe church.
Public transport: None.
Visiting: Open at all times on permissive paths. Clifftop from Covehithe unstable, proceed with care. Elevated bird hide on southern edge of Broad - if sea has breached sandbar it is not possible to reach hide from north. Dogs on lead. Telescope needed for best views.
Contact: Natural England, T: 01502 676 171.

2. BOYTON & HOLLESLEY MARSHES

RSPB (Eastern England Office).
Habitats: 57ha, coastal grazing marsh & saltmarsh on the lower Alde-Ore estuary.
Birds: *Spring:* Breeding waders & wildfowl, inc. Lapwing, Avocet, Shoveler & Gadwall. Migrants inc. Yellow Wagtail & Whitethroat. Barn & Little Owls. *Autumn:* Wildfowl arriving, migrating waders inc. Whimbrel, Black-tailed Godwit & Greenshank. *Winter:* Wildfowl & waders, inc. Teal, Wigeon, Curlew, Dunlin & Redshank. Marsh & Hen Harriers, Short-eared Owl.
Other: Grassland butterflies inc. skippers, Wall & Meadow Brown. Dragonflies.
Directions: Sat nav: IP12 3LR.
TM 387 475. Seven miles E of Woodbridge. Follow B1084 to Butley. Turn R & follow to Capel St. Andrew before turning L towards Boyton village. Approx 0.25 mile before village, bear L down concrete track on sharp right-hand turn to car park.
Public transport: None.
Visiting: Open at all times. Car park at Boyton (eight spaces), for Hollesley, park at Shingle Street. Entrance free, donations welcome. Information boards. Public footpaths not suited to wheelchair use. Dogs only on public footpaths.
Contact: RSPB, T: 01394 450 732;
E: havergate.island@rspb.org.uk

3. CARLTON MARSHES

Suffolk Wildlife Trust.
Habitats: 141ha, meadows, wet grassland, reedbeds, marsh & woodland (together with Oulton Marsh).
Birds: 150+ spp. inc. wide range of wetland & Broadland birds, inc. Grasshopper, Reed, Sedge & Cetti's Warblers, Bearded Tit, Barn Owl, Hobby & Marsh Harrier. Breeding Lapwing & Redshank.
Other: Water Vole, 22 spp. dragonflies inc. Norfolk Hawker & rare Fen Raft Spider. Plants inc. Common Spotted & Southern Marsh Orchids, Water Soldier.
Directions: Sat Nav: NR33 8HU. TM 508 920 (Carlton). (NR32 3JP Oulton). W of Lowestoft, at W end of Oulton Broad. From Lowestoft, take A146 towards Beccles continue to Carlton Colville. Turn L off A146 down Burnt Hill Lane (signposted).
Public transport: Bus - nos. X21/X22 Norwich to Lowestoft, alight Carlton Colville. First Eastern Counties. Train - Oulton Broad South. Both within walking distance.
Visiting: Open dawn-dusk, free car park - suitable for coaches. Education centre with disabled toilet. Keep to marked paths. Firm path around part of marsh, inc. easy access gates. Disabled access route along river wall from Oulton Broad to Carlton Marshes. Dogs allowed in some areas, on lead only.
Contact: Suffolk WT, T: 01502 564 250;
E: info@suffolkwildlifetrust.org

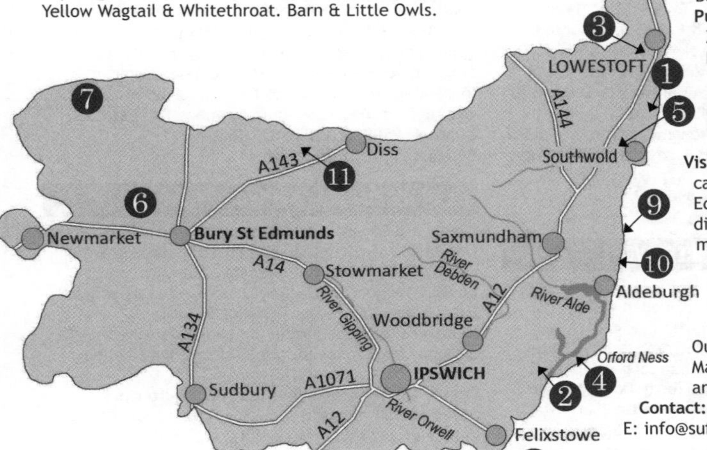

4. HAVERGATE ISLAND

RSPB (Eastern England Office)
Habitats: Small island: shallow brackish water, lagoons with islands, mudflats, saltmarsh. Part of Orfordness-Havergate Island NNR on Alde/Ore estuary.
Birds: *Summer:* Breeding gulls, Common & Sandwich Terns, Avocet, Shelduck & Oystercatcher. Flock of Spoonbills present from mid-Jul onwards. *Winter:* Wildfowl & waders inc. Wigeon, Teal, Pintail, Shoveler, Avocet, Lapwing & Black-tailed Godwit. Barn & Short-eared Owls, Marsh Harrier.
Other: Brown Hare.
Directions: Sat nav: IP12 2B. TM 425 495. Orford is 10.5 miles NE of Woodbridge, signposted off A12.
Public transport: None.
Visiting: Pre-booked 20-mins boat crossings (for max. 12 people) from Orford Quay - leaves at 10am, returns at ca. 3.20pm on first Sat of month (not May/Jun/Jul) & special event weekends (see RSPB website). Bookings made via RSPB website or search Havergate Island on Eventbrite. Reduction for RSPB members. Park in Orford's pay-&-display car park next to quay. On the island: Compost toilet with alcohol handwash - no running water, picnic area, five hides, one viewing screen, visitor trail (approx 1.25 miles).
Contact: RSPB - see site 2.

5. HEN REEDBED NNR

Suffolk Wildlife Trust.
Habitats: Reedbed, grazing marsh, scrape & estuary.
Birds: *Spring/summer:* Marsh Harrier, Bittern, Hobby, Lapwing, Snipe, Avocet, Black-tailed & Bar-tailed Godwits, Reed & Sedge warblers, Bearded Tit. *Passage:* Wood & Green Sandpipers. *Winter:* Large flocks of waders on estuary, inc. Golden & Grey Plovers, Black & Bar-tailed Godwits, Avocet & Dunlin.
Other: Otters & Water Voles regularly seen. Four-spotted Chaser & Hairy Dragonfly, occasional Norfolk Hawker. Brown Argus butterfly colony close to car park.
Directions: Sat nav: IP18 6SH. TM 471 771. Three miles from Southwold. Turn off A12 at Blythburgh & follow A1095 for two miles to signposted car park. The reserve forms part of the Suffolk Coast NNR.
Public transport: Bus - no.99A Halesworth-Southwold. First Norfolk & Suffolk (T: 08456 020 121).
Visiting: Open at all times. Viewing platforms & hides, waymarked trails. Wheelchair access to platform near car park. Dogs on lead.
Contact: Suffolk WT, T: 01473 890 089;
E: info@suffolkwildlifetrust.org

6. LACKFORD LAKES NATURE RESERVE

Suffolk Wildlife Trust.
Habitats: Restored gravel pit with open water, lagoons, islands, willow scrub, reedbeds.
Birds: *Spring/autumn*: Migrants, raptors inc. Osprey. *Summer:* Breeding Shelduck, Little Ringed Plover & reedbed warblers. Nightingale, Turtle Dove, Hobby. *Winter*: Bittern, Water Rail, Bearded Tit. Large gull roost. Wide variety of wildfowl (inc. Goosander, Pochard, Tufted Duck, Shoveler) & waders.
Other: Otter. 17 spp. dragonflies inc. Hairy & Emperor. Early Marsh & Southern Orchid.
Directions: Sat nav: IP28 6HX. TL 801 706. Five miles NW of Bury St Edmunds. Access via track off N side of A1101, between Lackford & Flempton.
Public transport: Bus - no.16 Bury St Edmunds to Mildenhall stops at Lackford - walk from church. Stephensons of Essex (T: 01440 704583).
Visiting: Open daily, dawn-dusk. Car park, coaches by arrangement. Visitor centre open 10am-5pm - viewing area upstairs, refreshments (to 4.30pm), shop, toilets. Eight hides, five trails. Wheelchair access -visitor centre, Kingfisher Trail & four hides. Limited access for dogs.
Contact: Lackford Lakes Visitor Centre,
T: 01284 728 706;
E: lackford.centre@suffolkwildlifetrust.org

7. LAKENHEATH FEN

RSPB (Eastern England Office).
Habitats: Reedbed, riverside pools, poplar woods.
Birds: *Spring/summer*: Bittern, Marsh Harrier, Cuckoo, Turtle Dove, Hobby (up to 40), Grasshopper, Reed & Sedge Warblers. *Autumn:* Harriers, Bearded Tit. *Winter*: Wildfowl inc. occasional Whooper Swan, Common Crane, Peregrine, Barn Owl, Kingfisher.
Other: 15+ spp. dragonflies & damselflies, inc. Hairy Dragonfly & Scarce Chaser. Range of fenland plants inc. Water Violet, Common Meadow-rue & Fen Ragwort. Roe Deer, Otter & Water Vole.
Directions: Sat nav: IP27 9AD. TL 724 865. W of Thetford, straddling the Norfolk/Suffolk border. From A11, head N on B1112 to Lakenheath & then two miles further. Entrance is on L, after level crossing.
Public transport: Bus - nos.200/201 Thetford-Brandon stop at Lakenheath, then two mile walk to reserve. Coach Services. Train - weekends-only some trains on Norwich-Ely service stop in Lakenheath (path links station to Visitor Centre).
Visiting: Reserve open daily dawn-dusk. Entrance fee for non-RSPB members (free if just visiting visitor centre), group bookings welcome - coaches must book oin advance. Visitor centre & toilets (inc. disabled) open 9am-5pm daily (not Dec 25-26). Events programme. Four viewpoints, one hide, picnic area, four nature trails of varied terrain - okay for wheelchairs. Dogs restricted to public footpaths.
Contact: RSPB, T: 01842 863 400;
E: lakenheath@rspb.org.uk

8. LANGUARD BIRD OBSERVATORY

Landguard Conservation Trust.
Habitats: Adjoining LNR, composed of close grazed turf, raised banks with holm oak, tamarisk, etc.
Birds: Common, scarce and occasionally rare migrants pass through area, esp. in spring & autumn. Mediterranean Gull regular on beach. In summer/autumn check for seabird & wildfowl movements offshore.
Other: 18 spp. dragonflies & 29 spp. butterflies. Several small mammal spp. plus sightings of seals & cetaceans off-shore. Nationally rare Stinking Goosefoot.

Directions: Sat nav: IP11 3TW. TM 283 317. On Landguard peninsula, off View Point Road S of Felixstowe town centre. Housed in wartime emplacements alongside Languard Fort.
Public transport: Buses & trains to Felixstowe town centre (1.5 miles away).
Visiting: Open all year providing there is a member on site to give access - contact in advance to make arrangements. Migration watch point & ringing station.
Contact: Landguard Bird Observatory, View Point Road, Felixstowe, IP11 3TW. T: 01394 673 782; E: landguardbo@yahoo.co.uk (enquiries or to arrange a visit); W: www.lbo.org.uk

9. MINSMERE

RSPB (Eastern England Office).
Habitats: Coastal lagoons, 'the scrape', freshwater reedbed, grazing marsh, vegetated dunes, heathland, arable reversion & woodland.
Birds: *All year:* Marsh Harrier, Bearded Tit, Bittern, Cetti's & Dartford Warblers, Little Egret, Green & Great Spotted Woodpeckers. *Summer:* Breeding Hobby, Avocet, Lapwing, Redshank, Common, Sandwich & Little Terns, Mediterranean Gull, Sand Martin, warblers, Nightingale, Nightjar, Woodlark, Stone Curlew (sometimes visible). *Autumn/spring:* Passage waders inc. Black-tailed Godwit, Spotted Redshank, Ruff. Regular Wryneck, Red-backed Shrike, Yellow-browed Warbler. *Winter:* Wildfowl inc. White-fronted Goose, Bewick's Swan, Smew, Hen Harrier (scarce), Water Pipit, Siskin.
Other: Red & Muntjac Deer, Otter, Water Vole, Badger. Dragonflies inc. Emperor, Norfolk Hawker & Small red-eyed Damselfly. 27 spp. butterflies inc. Purple & Green Hairstreaks & Brown Argus. Adder. Antlion. Marsh Mallow, Southern Marsh Orchid.
Directions: Sat nav: IP17 3BY. TM 473 672. Six miles NE of Saxmundham. From A12 at Yoxford or Blythburgh. Follow brown tourist signs via Westleton village. Car park is two miles from village.
Public transport: Train - Saxmundham or Darsham (five miles) then demand-responsive bus will meet local buses/trains 7am-7pm, Mon-Sat. Suffolk Links Blyth (T: 01728 635 938) - book before day of travel.
Visiting: Car park & hides open daily (not Dec 25/26) dawn-dusk. Coaches by appointment only. Visitor centre/shop open 9am-5pm (4pm Nov-Jan), cafe open 9.30am-4.30pm (3.30pm Nov-Jan). Visitor centre (free entry) - entry fee for non RSPB members to visit reserve. Car park, seven hides & viewing platform, toilets (inc. disabled). Volunteer guides, guided walks & family events (see RSPB website). Limited access for dogs.
Contact: RSPB, T: 01728 648 281; E: minsmere@rspb.org.uk

10. NORTH WARREN

RSPB (Eastern England Office).
Habitats: Grazing marsh, heath, reedbed, woodland.
Birds: *Spring/summer*: Breeding Bittern, Hobby, Marsh Harrier, Nightjar, Woodlark, Nightingale, Dartford Warbler. *Winter*: White-fronted & Tundra Bean Goose, Wigeon, Shoveler, Teal, Gadwall, Pintail, Snow Bunting.
Other: Hairy Dragonfly, Norfolk Hawker & Red-eyed Damselfly, Green & Purple Hairstreak butterflies & Southern Marsh Orchid.
Directions: Sat nav: IP15 5BH. TM 467 576. Directly N of Aldeburgh on Suffolk coast. Take A1094 to Aldebugh then follow Thorpe Road towards Thorpeness. Use signposted main car park on beach.
Public transport: Bus - no.64 Saxmundham to Aldeburgh. First Norfolk & Suffolk (T: 08456 020 121). Train - Saxmundham (six miles).
Visiting: Open at all times. Pay-&-display car parks in Aldeburgh & Thorpeness (coach spaces at the latter) Toilets in Aldeburgh & Thorpeness. Various viewing points & viewing platform adjacent to old railway line overlooking the marshes. Several circular walks on public rights of way. Beach area suitable for disabled access. Dogs only on public footpaths/bridleways.
Contact: RSPB - see site 9.

11. REDGRAVE & LOPHAM FENS

Suffolk Wildlife Trust.
Habitats: Calcareous fen with open water areas, wet acid heath, river corridor, scrub & woodland.
Birds: *All year:* Water Rail, Snipe, Teal, Shelduck, Gadwall, Woodcock, Sparrowhawk, Kestrel, Great Spotted & Green Woodpeckers, Tawny, Little & Barn Owls, Kingfisher, Bearded Tit, Willow & Marsh Tits, Reed Bunting. *Summer:* Hobby, warblers inc. Reed, Sedge & Grasshopper, Spotted Flycatcher,plus large Swallow & Starling roosts. *Winter/occasionally on passage:* Marsh Harrier, Greenshank, Green Sandpiper, Shoveler, Pintail, Garganey, Jack Snipe, Bittern, Little Ringed Plover, Oystercatcher, Wheatear, Stonechat & Whinchat.
Other: Otter, Water Vole, Roe, Muntjac & Chinese Water Deer, Stoat, Pipistrelle & Natterer's Bats. Great Crested Newt, Grass Snake, Adder, Slow Worm, Common Lizard. 300+ spp. flowering plants. 27 spp. butterflies inc. Purple & Green Hairstreaks & Brown Argus. 20+ spp. dragonfly inc. Emperor, Hairy Dragonfly, Black-tailed Skimmer & Scarce Emerald Damselfly. Fen Raft Spider.
Directions: Sat nav: IP22 2HX. TM 052 803. Five miles from Diss, signposted & easily accessed from A1066 & A143, car park on minor road off the B1113.
Public transport: Bus - no.304 (Mon-Sat) Diss to Bury St Edmunds stops at Redgrave. Simonds (T: 01379 647 300).
Visiting: Open all year. Car park with coach space, area for bikes. Education Centre, toilets (inc. disabled). Five waymarked circular trails (wheelchair-accessible gates on 'spider' trail) - trails can be muddy after heavy rain (not wheelchair accessible), boardwalk & viewing platform. Dogs on short leads.
Contact: Suffolk WT, T: 01379 687 618; E: info@suffolkwildlifetrust.org

Northern England

Cheshire & Wirral, Cumbria, Durham, Lancashire & North Merseyside, Manchester (Greater), Northumberland, Yorkshire (East Riding), Yorkshire (North), Yorkshire (South & West)

Cheshire & Wirral

Sites along the Dee & Mersey estuaries provide a spectacular wader experience at passage time & during the winter. North-westerly gales in autumn bring Leach's Petrels to the tip of the Wirral peninsula, probably the best place in Britain to see them away from their breeding sites. To the east the county border abuts the Peak District.

1. DEE ESTUARY (BURTON MERE WETLANDS)

RSPB (Northern England).
Habitats: Former farm & fishery now converted to freshwater wetland, mixed farmland & woodland.
Birds: *All year:* Little Egret. Great Spotted & Green Woodpecker. *Spring/summer:* Avocet, Grasshopper Warbler, Lesser Whitethroat & other commoner warblers, passage Black-tailed Godwit, Spotted Redshank & regular Mediterranean Gull. Hobby, Marsh Harrier, Spoonbill. *Autumn:* Passage waders (inc. Little Stint, Ruff, Spotted Redshank, Green, Curlew & Wood Sandpipers). *Winter:* Whooper & Bewick's Swans, Teal, Water Rail, Hen Harrier, Fieldfare, Redwing, Linnet, Brambling.
Other: Extensive butterfly list. Pipistrelle, Noctule, Daubenton's Bats, Water Vole, wide array of orchids. Red-eyed Damselfly.
Directions: Sat nav: CH64 5SF. SJ 319 739. Located on the Wirral. From Chester High Road (A540) follow signs for Burton Mere Wetlands. Turning down Puddington Lane, reserve's entrance is just outside Burton Village.
Public transport: Bus - no.487 Liverpool (Whitechapel) to nearest bus stop at Ness Botanic Gardens, 1.5 miles from reserve. Arriva in North West.
Visiting: Open daily 9am-9pm/dusk if earlier. Large car park, not suitable for coaches/larger minibuses (groups should ring for advice). Visitor centre open 9.30am-5pm (4.30pm Nov-Jan). Admission charge for non-RSPB members. Refreshments, toilets inc. disabled. Three hides & three viewing screens overlooking pools & wetland area, picnic tables. Signposted trails - wheelchair access to footpaths & hides. Guided walks & binocular hire. Guide dogs only.
Contact: RSPB, T: 0151 353 2720;
E: deeestuary@rspb.org.uk

2. DEE ESTUARY (HESWALL)

Wirral Council.
Habitats: Saltmarsh & mudflats.
Birds: *Autumn/winter*: Large passage & winter wader roosts (Redshank, Curlew, Black-tailed Godwit,Knot, Oystercatcher, Golden Plover), Shelduck, Teal, Red-breasted Merganser, Peregrine, Merlin, Hen Harrier, Short-eared Owl. Smaller numbers of Pintail, Wigeon, Bar-tailed Godwit, Greenshank, Spotted Redshank, Grey & Ringed Plovers, Whimbrel, Curlew Sandpiper, Little Stint, occasional Scaup & Little Egret.

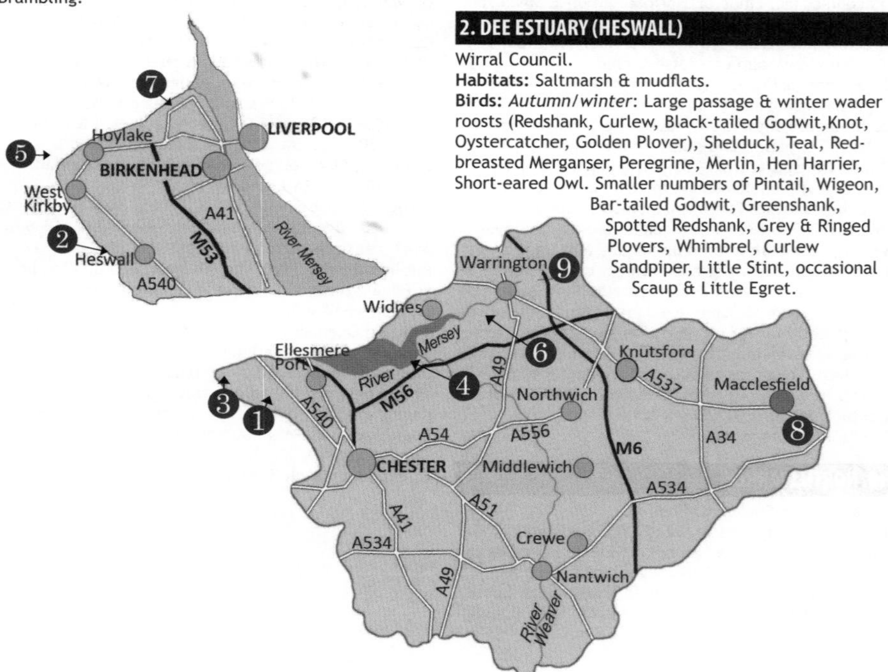

Directions: Sat nav: CH60 9JS. SJ 255 815. Leave A540 Chester to Hoylake road at Heswall & head downhill (one mile) to free car park at shore end of Banks Road. Heswall is 30 mins from South Liverpool & Chester by car.
Public transport: Buses - nos.175 & 181 from Heswall bus station to Banks Road car park. A2B Travel (T: 0151 609 0600).
Visiting: Open all times. Best viewpoint 600 yards along shore N of Banks Road arrive 2.5 hours before high tide. Coach parking available, information board. No disabled access along shore, but good birdwatching from bottom of Banks Road. Sheldrakes Restaurant, end of Banks Road, has outside terrace overlooking foreshore.
Contact: Wirral Country Park Visitor Centre, Station Road, Thustaston, Wirral CH61 0HN. T: 0151 648 4371; E: wcp@wirral.gov.uk

3. DEE ESTUARY (PARKGATE)

RSPB (Northern England).
Habitats: Estuary, saltmarsh, pools, mud, sand. Best viewed at high tide.
Birds: *Spring/summer/autumn:* Little Egret, Greenshank, Spotted Redshank, Curlew Sandpiper, Skylark, Reed Bunting. *Winter:* Pink-footed Goose, Shelduck, Teal, Wigeon, Pintail, Oystercatcher, Black-tailed Godwit, Curlew, Redshank, Merlin, Peregrine, Water Rail, Short-eared Owl, Hen Harrier.
Other: On very high tides, incoming water displaces several mammal spp. inc. Pygmy Shrew, Water Shrew, Harvest Mouse, Weasel & Stoat.
Directions: Sat nav: CH64 6RL. SJ 273 789. On W side of Wirral, S of Birkenhead. View high tide activity from Old Baths car park near Boathouse pub, Parkgate, off B5135.
Public transport: Bus - no.487 Liverpool (Whitechapel) to Parkgate. Arriva in North West. Train - station at Neston, two miles from reserve.
Visiting: Open at all times. Shared car park (closes 8pm summer/5pm winter). Toilets at Parkgate village opposite the Square. Viewing from public footpaths & car parks - don't walk on saltmarsh (dangerous tides/ nesting birds). Picnic area, group bookings, guided walks, special events, wheelchair access. Dogs only on footpaths.
Contact: RSPB - see site 1.

4. FRODSHAM MARSH

Manchester Ship Canal Company.
Habitats: Saltmarsh, mudflats, embanked tanks to hold river dredgings, reedbeds, farmland & river.
Birds: 20+ spp. wader, inc. large flocks of Redshank, Black-tailed Godwit, Dunlin. *Summer:* Breeding Oystercatcher, Ringed & Little Ringed Plovers, Grasshopper, Sedge & Reed Warblers. *Autumn:* Hobbies hunt. *Winter:* Wildfowl, inc. Whooper Swan, Pink-footed Goose, Shelduck, Pochard, Pintail, Wigeon & other common species, Raven, Short-eared Owl, Hen Harrier, Peregrine. Passage migrants inc. wagtails, pipits, terns, Garganey, Wheatear & Whinchat.
Directions: Sat nav: WA6 7BN. SJ 511 779 (Marsh Lane), SJ 520 785 (Weaver Bend/Ship Street). Large area of mixed habitat lying alongside Manchester Ship Canal, SW of Runcorn. Close to Frodsham town centre. Take Ship Street, off High Street, turn L into Weaver's Lane & cross over M56 (to access Weaver's Bend). Take Marsh Lane, off Main Street, take R fork at Marsh Green Cottages & cross over M56. (to access main marsh).
Public transport: None.
Visiting: Open at all times. Park just before concrete bridge, walk along grassy track to barrier gates & then towards vantage points overlooking Rivers Mersey & Weaver. Wheelchair access difficult.
Contact: None.
W: https://frodshammarshbirdblog.wordpress.com/

5. HILBRE ISLAND LNR

Wirral Council.
Habitats: Sandflats, rocky shore & open sea.
Birds: *Late summer/autumn:* Seabird passage inc. Gannets, terns, skuas, shearwaters & after NW gales good numbers of Leach's Petrel. *Passage:* migrants. *Winter:* Wader roosts at high tide, Purple Sandpiper, Turnstone, sea ducks, divers, grebes.
Other: Nationally scarce Rock Sea-lavender & Sea Spleenwort. Field Vole, Grey Seal. Whales & dolphins.
Directions: Sat nav: CH48 0QG. SJ 208 866 (Dee Lane, West Kirby). SJ 184 880 (main island). Three tidal islands in mouth of Dee Estuary. Park in West Kirby on A540 Chester to Hoylake road. Follow brown Marine Lake signs to Dee Lane pay-&-display car park (or free parking along promenade). Coach parking available in West Kirby.
Public transport: Bus - no.437 Liverpool (Union Court) to West Kirby, within 0.5 mile of Dee Lane slipway. Arriva in North West. Train - West Kirby.
Visiting: Two mile walk across sands from Dee Lane slipway - DO NOT cross either way within 3.5 hours of high water - tide times & suggested safe route on noticeboard at slipway. No disabled access. Permit required for groups of six or more (apply to Wirral Country Park Visitor Centre). Composting toilets on main island (Hilbre) & at Wirral Sailing Centre (end of Dee Lane, West Kirby). Leaflets & tide times available at Visitor Centre. Visits to Hilbre Bird Observatory by prior appointment only.
Contact: Wirral Country Park Visitor Centre - see site 2. Hilbre Island Bird Obs,
E: secretary@hilbrebirdobs.org.uk;
W: http://hilbrebirdobs.blogspot.co.uk

6. MOORE NATURE RESERVE

FCC Environment.
Habitats: 80ha, woodland, meadows, lakes & ponds.
Birds: 130+ spp. annually, inc. occasional rarities. *Spring/summer*: Breeding wildfowl & waders, warblers. *Autumn/winter*: Wide variety of wildfowl, Bittern. Also good for gulls, woodpeckers, owls (all five UK spp. recorded) & raptors.
Other: Flora inc. rarities. Great crested newt.
Directions: Sat nav: WA4 6XE. SJ 577 854. SW of Warrington, off A56 Warrington to Chester road. At traffic lights at Higher Walton, follow signs for Moore. Take Moore Lane over swing bridge to reserve.
Public transport: Bus - nos.62 (Mon-Fri) & 62A Warrington to Runcorn stop in Moore, less than 0.75 mile from reserve. Warrington's Own Buses (T: 01925 634 296) & Halton Transport (T: 0151 423 3333).
Visiting: Open all year. Car park, coaches by prior arrangement, paths, hides, bird feeding area. One hide suitable for wheelchairs, other parts of site unsurfaced or gravel paths.
Contact: Moore Nature Reserve, T: 01925 444 689; W: www.fccenvironment.co.uk/waste-processing/landfill/arpley-landfill/moore-nature-reserve/

7. NORTH WIRRAL COASTAL PARK

Wirral Council.
Habitats: Saltmarsh.
Birds: Important as a feeding & roosting site for passage & wintering flocks of waders, wildfowl, terns & gulls inc. wintering Knot (20,000+), Bar-tailed Godwit (2,000+) & Dunlin (10,000). Redshank (1,000+) & Turnstone (500+) feed on the rocky shore at Perch Rock & on rocky sea walls. Oystercatcher (500+), Curlew, Grey Plover & Black-tailed Godwit regularly roost here in relatively high numbers. Small numbers of wildfowl, inc. Common Scoter, Scaup & Goldeneye, Red-throated Diver & Great Crested Grebe also frequently winter.
Other: Sea Holly, Marram Grass, Storksbill, Burnet Rose & rarities like the Isle of Man Cabbage. One of two known sites in world for very rare British sub-species of Belted Beauty moth.
Directions: Sat nav: CH46 4TA. SJ 241 909. Located between outer Dee & Mersey Estuaries. From Moreton take A553 E. then A551 N. Turn L onto Tarran Way South then R onto Lingham Lane. Parking available by lighthouse. Foreshore can be viewed from footpath which runs alongside.
Public transport: Bus - routes along Leasowe Road, Pasture Road & Harrison Drive. Train - area served by Grove Road (Wallasey), Leasowe, Moreton, & Meols Merseyrail Stations.
Visiting: Open at all times. Various car parks, toilet blocks, picnic areas, extensive network of footpaths & public bridleways. Wirral Country Park Visitor Centre open daily (not Dec 25) 10am-4.45pm, located Heswall & West Kirby, off A540 - has toilets, hide, cafe, kiosk (all wheelchair accessible).
Contact: Wirral Country Park Visitor Centre - see site 2.

8. TRENTABANK RESERVOIR

Cheshire Wildlife Trust.
Habitats: Reservoir surrounded by coniferous plantation. [Other reservoirs in area (viewable from roads) & further access into Macclesfield Forest.]
Birds: Small heronry. *All year:* Raven, Crossbill, common coniferous woodland spp. *Spring/autumn:* (when water levels expose the banks) Green Sandpiper, Little Ringed Plover. *Summer:* Common Sandpiper, Woodcock (roding). *Winter:* Wildfowl inc. Goldeneye, Goosander.
Other: Red Deer, variety of butterflies & dragonflies.
Directions: Sat Nav: SK11 0NS. SJ961711. Three miles SE of Macclesfield. Head out of Macclesfield on A537 Buxton Road, take minor road signposted Tegg's Nose Country park. After 0.7 miles turn R & continue to Langley, turn L at T-junction. After another 0.8 miles turn R (by Ridgegate Reservoir) & then L for 250 yards to reservoir car park/visitor centre.
Public transport: None.
Visiting: Open all year. The woodland trail & heronry viewpoint is opposite car park entrance. Access to reservoir itself is by permit only. Visitor centre may be open on selected weekends. Toilets. Dogs on leads.
Contact: Cheshire WT, T: 01948 820 728; E: info@cheshirewt.org.uk

9. WOOLSTON EYES

Woolston Eyes Conservation Group.
Habitats: Wetland, marsh, scrubland, wildflower meadow areas.
Birds: 230 spp. *Breeding:* Black-necked Grebe, variety of duck, good number of warblers (inc. Grasshopper), raptors (Merlin, Peregrine, Marsh Harrier). *Passage:* waders. *Winter:* wildfowl, winter thrushes.
Other: 24 mammal spp. inc. four spp. bat. 241 spp. lepidoptera inc. wide variety of butterflies. 21 spp. dragonflies. Notable plants inc. Marsh & Bee Orchids, Helleborine, Snakeshead Fritillary & Cowslip.
Directions: Sat Nav: WA4 1PD. SJ 654 888. E of Warrington between River Mersey & Manchester Ship Canal. Off Junc. 21 of M6, take New Manchester Road (A57), take 2nd L into Weir Lane (footpath only) - do not park at bottom end of Weir Lane. Vehicle access via Thelwell Lane, Latchford - permit & key required. Sat Nav: WA4 1NN. SJ 638 873.
Public transport: Buses - from Warrington Bus Interchange. (Weir Lane) no.3 to Martinscroft. (Thelwall Lane) nos.1 or 2 to Westy (Whitley Ave) & walk to east end of Thelwall Lane. Warriington's Own Buses (T: 01925 634 296).
Visiting: Open all year from 8am dusk. Permits required - contact via website for details. Hides & raised platform. Dogs on lead - pick up watse & take away with you.
Contact: E: via website; W: www.woolstoneyes.com

Cumbria

Wintering wildfowl, including Barnacle & Pink-footed Geese, reach into their thousands on The Solway. The Lake District can still offer a typical range of upland birds & there is an Osprey watch point at Lake Bassenthwaite. A small seabird colony at St Bees Head holds a few Black Guillemots & Puffins. Walney, with its bird observatory, is a good place to pick up passage migrants, including occasional rarities.

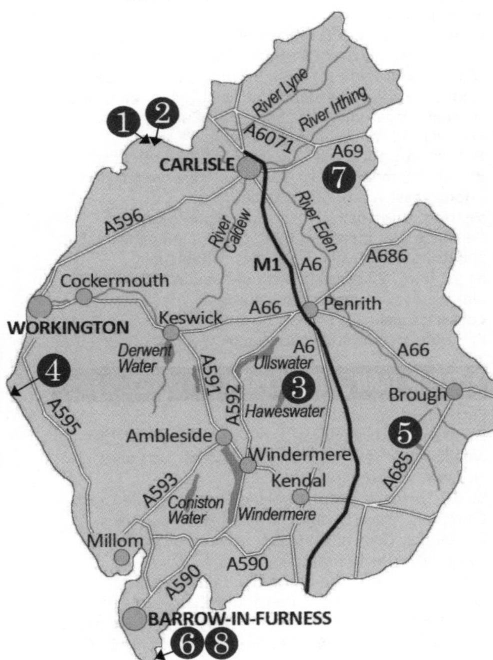

1. CAMPFIELD MARSH

RSPB (Northern England).
Habitats: Saltmarsh/intertidal areas, open water, raised peat bog, farmland, wet grassland.
Birds: *Spring/summer*: Breeding Lapwing, Curlew, Redshank, Snipe, Tree Sparrow & warblers. *Spring & autumn*: Passage waders inc. Black-tailed Godwit, Whimbrel. Look for Pomarine, Arctic, Great & Long-tailed Skuas over the Solway. *Winter*: Waders (up to 10,000 Oystercatcher among large roosting wader flocks). Wildfowl inc. Barnacle & Pink-footed Geese, Shoveler, Scaup, Grey Plover. Hen Harrier.
Other: Roe Deer, Brown Hare. Bog Rosemary, Bog Asphodel, sundews & cotton grass. Large numbers of dragonflies (inc. Azure & Emerald Damselflies & Four-spotted Chaser).
Directions: Sat nav: CA7 5AG. NY 197 615. At North Plain Farm, on S shore of Solway estuary, W of Bowness-on-Solway. Signposted on unclassified coast road from B5307 from Carlisle.
Public transport: Bus - no.93 from Carlisle terminates at reserve's eastern end, 1.5 mile walk to North Plain Farm. Stagecoach.
Visiting: Open at all times. Car park at North Plain Farm. Disabled visitors can drive to wheelchair-friendly hide to view high-tide roosts. Small visitor centre - 'Solway Wetlands Centre' - open 10am-4pm, manned most weekends. One hide, several viewing screens overlooking wetland areas, three trails (grass paths, can be muddy). Roadside lay-bys overlook wader roosts.
Contact: RSPB, T: 01697 351 330;
E: campfield.marsh@rspb.org.uk

2. DRUMBURGH MOSS NNR

Cumbria Wildlife Trust.
Habitats: One of four raised bogs south of Solway (rated best in England), woodland, wet heath, grassland.
Birds: *Summer*: Breeding Curlew, Redshank & Grasshopper Warbler. *Winter:* Geese from Solway, Short-eared Owl.
Other: Large Heath butterfly, Emperor Moth, Adder & lizards, Roe Deer, Brown Hare. Specialist plants inc. 13 spp. of sphagnum moss, sundews, cotton grass & Bog Rosemary.
Directions: Sat nav: CA7 5DR. NY 255 586. From Carlisle city centre, head W on B5307 to Kirkbride. After about one mile, turn R to Burgh by Sands. Follow road for 7.5 miles to Drumburgh village. Turn L by post box, continue down track & park on R past Moss Cottage.
Public transport: Bus - no. 93 Carlisle to Bowness-on-Solway (not Sun), stops in Drumburgh. Stagecoach.
Visiting: Open all year. Difficult terrain, so it is best to walk on paths or waymarked routes. Viewing platform. Dogs on leads.
Contact: Cumbria WT, 01228 829 570;
E: mail@cumbriawildlifetrust.org.uk

3. HAWESWATER

RSPB (Northern England)/United Utilities.
Habitats: Fells with rocky streams, steep oak & birch woodlands.
Birds: *Upland breeders*: Peregrine, Raven, Ring Ouzel, Curlew, Redshank, Snipe. *Woodlands*: Pied Flycatcher, Wood Warbler, Tree Pipit, Redstart, Buzzard, Sparrowhawk. Breeding Goosander & Dipper around lake. *Winter:* Large gull roost.
Other: Red Deer, Red Squirrel.
Directions: Sat nav: CA10 2QT. NY 469 108, (Haweswater car park). For old eagle viewpoint, go to Bampton village, 10 miles S of Penrith & five miles NW of Shap. From Bampton, head S towards Haweswater reservoir. Drive down unclassified road alongside the reservoir, road ends at a car park - walk from here.

Public transport: None.
Visiting: Majority of site is open access. Small car park at south end of Hawswater reservoir (managed by United Utilities).
Contact: RSPB, T: 01931 713 376;
E: haweswater@rspb.org.uk

4. ST BEES HEAD

RSPB (Northern England).
Habitats: Three miles of sandstone cliffs, up to 300 feet high.
Birds: *Spring/summer*: Largest seabird colony on W coast of England: Fulmar, Cormorant, Guillemot, Razorbill, Puffin, Kittiwake & England's only breeding pairs of Black Guillemot (around Fleswick Bay). Linnet, Stonechat, Whitethroat & Rock Pipit along cliff-top heath areas.
Directions: Sat nav: CA27 0ETN NX 959 118. S of Whitehaven via B3545 to St Bees village. Car park at end of Beach Road.
Public transport: Train - St Bees (0.75 mile).
Visiting: Open at all times. Pay-&-display car park, toilets next to reserve entrance. Three viewpoints overlook seabird colony - access via three mile cliff-top coast-to-coast footpath (steep in parts). Dogs only on public footpaths.
Contact: RSPB, T: 01697 351 330;
E: stbees.head@rspb.org.uk

5. SMARDALE GILL NNR

Cumbria Wildlife Trust.
Habitats: Limestone grassland, river, ancient semi-natural woodland, quarry.
Birds: *All year:* Usual woodland birds, Buzzard, Sparrowhawk, Raven, Green Woodpecker & Dipper. *Summer:* Redstart, Pied Flycatcher & commoner woodland species.
Other: Scotch Argus, Northern Brown Argus, Common Blue & Dark Green Fritillary butterflies. Fragrant Orchid, Common Rockrose, Bluebell & Bloody Cranesbill. Red Squirrel.
Directions: Sat nav: CA17 4HG. NY 742 083 (Smardale car park). Approx 2.5 miles NE of Ravenstonedale on A685 or 0.5 mile S of Kirkby Stephen station. Take turning signed to Smardale. Cross over railway & turn L to junction, ignoring turn to Waitby. Cross over railway & turn L at junction ignoring sign for Smardale. Cross disused railway, turn L immediately & L again to car park. Alternative parking - Sat Nav: CA17 4NY. NY 703 053 Newbiggin-on-Lune parking area.
Public transport: Bus - no.S5 Kirby Stephen to Kendal, alight Newbiggin-on-Lune. New Western Dales Bus (T: 01539 620 125). Train - Kirkby Stephen.
Visiting: NNR occupies a 3.75 miles stretch of disused railway between Tebay & Darlington. Railway line open to all, non-members should obtain a permit before visiting other parts of reserve. Dogs on lead.
Contact: Cumbria WT, 01539 816 300;
E: mail@cumbriawildlifetrust.org.uk

6. SOUTH WALNEY

Cumbria Wildlife Trust.
Habitats: Shingle, lagoon, sand dune, saltmarsh.
Birds: 250 spp. *Spring/autumn*: Passage migrants inc. Wheatear, Redstart, Goldcrest & Willow Warbler. *Summer*: 14,000 breeding pairs of Herring, Greater & Lesser Black-backed Gulls, Shelduck, Eider. Arctic, Little & Sandwich Terns offshore. *Winter*: Teal, Wigeon, Goldeneye, Redshank, Greenshank, Curlew, Oystercatcher, Knot, Dunlin, Merlin, Short-eared Owl, Tree Sparrow, Twite.
Other: 450 spp. of flowering plants. Grey Seal colony.
Directions: Sat nav: LA14 3YQ. SD 225 620. Six miles S of Barrow-in-Furness. From Barrow, cross Jubilee Bridge onto Walney Island, turn L at lights. Continue through Biggar village to South End Caravan Park. Follow road for one mile to reserve.
Public transport: Bus - no.1 Barrow-in-Furness to Biggar, 3.5 mile walk to South End/reserve car park (along coast road). Stagecoach.
Visiting: Open daily (10am-5pm, 4pm in winter) - entrance fee, members free. Coach parking available. Toilets, nature trails, hides (two wheelchair accessible), 200 yard boardwalk. Mobility tramper for hire. No dogs, except assistance dogs.
Contact: Cumbria WT, T: 01229 471 066;
E: mail@cumbriawildlifetrust.org.uk

7. TALKIN TARN COUNTRY PARK

Carlisle City Council.
Habitats: Natural glacial tarn, mature oak/beech woodland, orchid meadow (traditionally managed), wet mire & farmland.
Birds: *Spring/summer*: Spotted Flycatcher, Redstart, Chiffchaff, Wood Warbler. *Winter*: Grebes, swans, Goosander, Gadwall, Wigeon, occasional Smew & Long-tailed Duck. Brambling.
Other: Common Blue Damselfly, Common Darter, Small Copper butterfly, Otter, Red Squirrel.
Directions: Sat nav: CA8 1HN. NY 543 590. Nine miles E of Carlisle. From A69 E at Brampton, go S on B6413 for two miles (signposted). Talkin Tarn is on L just after level crossing.
Public transport: Train - Brampton Junction, one mile along footpath.
Visiting: Open at all times. Car park charges, coaches welcome. Tearoom, shop open 10.30am-4pm daily from Easter to Oct half term then Sat/Sun & school holidays until Easter. Toilet. Wheelchair access around tarn. Watersport activities can cause some disturbance to water birds.
Contact: Talkin Tarn Country Park, Tarn Road, Brampton, Cumbria, CA8 1HN. T: 01228 817 200;
E: talkintarn@carlisle.gov.uk;
W: www.carlisle.gov.uk/talkintarn/

8. WALNEY BIRD OBSERVATORY

Habitats: Estuarine, maritime, dunes, freshwater & brackish pools, scrub & farmland. Observatory is located in south but covers whole island.
Birds: *Spring/autumn:* Migrants - island has a proven pedigree for attracting rare & unusual species. *Summer:* Renowned Eider & gull colonies at south end. Winter: wildfowl & wader spectacular across island.
Other: Famed for Walney Geranium, but also important for coastal shingle species such as Sea Holly, Sea Rocket & Sea Kale. 500+ spp. moths inc. sand dune specialities such as Coast Dart & Sand Dart. Natterjack Toad at North Walney.
Directions: See site 6.
Public transport: See site 6.
Visiting: Access to several areas, notably golf course/ airfield, is restricted but island's narrow width means most sites are viewable from road or footpaths. Monitoring & ringing of breeding birds/migrants, with ringing opportunities for qualified visitors. For availability contact Walney Bird Obs.
Contact: Walney Bird Observatory, Coastguard Cottages, Walney Island, Barrow-in-Furness, Cumbria LA14 3YQ. E: walneyobs@gmail.com; W: http://walneybo.blogspot.co.uk

Durham

The coast around the Teesmouth area pulls in rarities & regular migrants during spring & autumn passage & large numbers of wintering wildfowl & waders. Away from the coast, Upper Teesdale still holds Black Grouse & breeding waders while the Derwent Valley has a good mixture of habitats & birds.

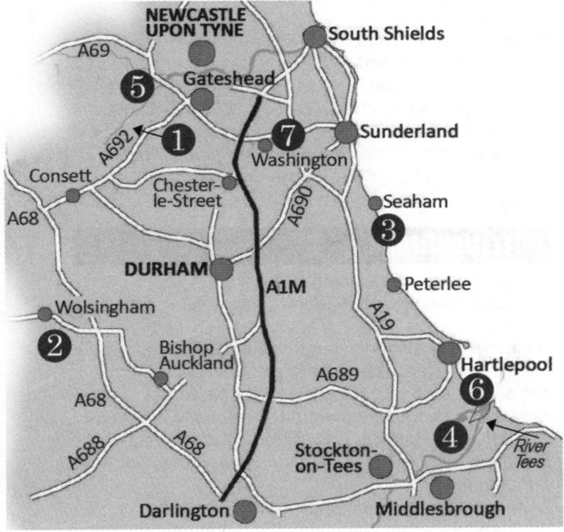

1. DERWENT WALK COUNTRY PARK & DERWENTHAUGH PARK

Gateshead Council.
Habitats: Mixed woodland, river, ponds, meadows.
Birds: *All year:* Kingfisher. *Summer*: Red Kite, Grasshopper Warbler, Lesser Whitethroat, Dipper, Great Spotted & Green Woodpeckers, Blackcap, Garden Warbler, Nuthatch. *Winter*: Teal, Tufted Duck, Goosander, Marsh Tit, Brambling, Bullfinch, Siskin.
Other: Otter, Roe Deer, Badger, woodland flowers.
Directions: Sat nav: NE39 1AU. NZ 178 604 (Thornley Woodlands Visitor Centre, near Rowlands Gill). Sat Nav: NE16 3BN. NZ 199 621 (Swalwell Visitor Centre, on B6317 beside Blaydon Rugby Club). Along River Derwent, four miles SW of Newcastle & Gateshead. Several car parks along A694. Derwent Walk follows old railtrack for 11 miles from Swalwell to Consett.
Public transport: buses - various services from Newcastle/Gateshead to Swalwell/Rowlands Gill. Bus stop Thornley Woodlands Centre. Go North East (T: 0191 420 5050).
Visiting: Open at all times. Two visitor centres. Thornley Woodlands, open daily 10am-4pm. Parking, toilets, cafe, ranger service. Swalwell, open 10am-3pm Mon-Fri only (not Christmas-New Year or bank holidays). Parking, toilets, information - open subject to staff availability. Hides at Far Pasture Ponds & Thornley feeding station - keys from Thornley. Derwent Walk & Derwenthaugh Parks both accessible to wheelchairs from Swalwell.
Contact: Thornley Woodlands Centre, T: 01207 545 212; Swalwell Visitor Centre, T: 0191 414 2106; E: countryside@gateshead.gov.uk; W: www.gateshead.gov.uk/article/4393/Derwent-Walk-Country-Park-and-Derwenthaugh-Park

2. HAMERSLEY FOREST

Forestry England.
Habitats: Commercial mixed & broadleaved woodland.
Birds: *All year*: Goshawk, Dipper, Green Woodpecker. *Spring/summer*: Chiffchaff, Willow & Wood Warblers, Redstart, Tree Pipit, Pied Flycatcher. *Winter*: Crossbill, Redwing, Fieldfare.
Other: Hay meadows have wide variety of plants inc. Globe Flower.
Directions: Sat nav: DL13 5NL (Forest Drive car park). NZ 092 312. Ten miles W of Bishop Auckland. Main entrance is five miles from A68, S of Witton-le-Wear & signposted through Hamsterley village & Bedburn.
Public transport: None.

Visiting: Open all year, dawn-dusk. Forest drive & car park open 9am-5pm - daily toll charge, higher during bank holidays. Visitor centre (main car park), information point open 9am-4pm, cafe open 10am-4pm (5pm weekends & school holidays). Toilets, shop, access for disabled. Visitors should not enter fenced farmland.
Contact: Forestry England, T: 01388 488 312; E: enquiries.hamsterley@forestryengland.uk

3. HAWTHORN DENE NATURE RESERVE

Durham Wildlife Trust.
Habitats: Extensive area of semi-natural habitat situated on magnesium limestone escarpment. Steep-sided ravine woodland & limestone grassland.
Birds: *Summer:* Green Woodpecker, Sparrowhawk, Kestrel, Skylark (important conservation site), Twite, Linnet, Yellowhammer, Whitethroat, Blackcap, Grasshopper Warbler, Tree Sparrow, Reed Bunting. *Passage:* Wheatear, Fieldfare, Redwing, Waxwing, Buzzard, Ringed Plover, Dunlin, Knot, Lapwing. *Winter (coast/offshore):* Wide variety of waders inc. Turnstone, Purple Sandpiper, Redshank, Curlew, Oystercatcher. Common Scoter, Red-throated Diver, Guillemot, Cormorant & Great Crested Grebe.
Other: Good variety of butterflies. Snowdrops, Bluebells & numerous spp. orchid, inc. Early Purple, Bird's Nest, Lesser Butterfly & Bee. Roe Deer, Badger & Brown Hare.
Directions: Sat nav: SR7 8SH. NZ 424 459. Hawthorn Dene Meadow located between Easington & Seaham on Durham coast. Leave A19 at Easington or Seaham & join B1432 to Hawthorn village. From N end of village, follow minor road E, signposted 'Quarry Traffic'. After 0.25 mile, road ends at two metal gates. Park on grass verge on opposite side to cottage. Follow track through gate for 350 yards, turn R onto trail into wood.
Public transport: Bus - nos.22/23 Sunderland to Durham/Hartlepool, pass through Hawthorn. Arriva Durham County. Short walk to reserve entrance.
Visiting: Open all year, footpaths. Dogs on leads.
Contact: Durham WT, T: 0191 584 3112; E: mail@durhamwt.co.uk

4. SALTHOLME

RSPB (Northern England).
Habitats: Wet grasslands, reedbeds, pools with tern islands, wader scrapes.
Birds: *All year:* Lapwing, Peregrine, Water Rail. *Spring/summer:* Breeding Great Crested Grebe, common wildfowl, hirundines, Snipe, Skylark, Yellow Wagtail, large colony of Common Terns. *Autumn:* Various waders inc. Black-tailed Godwits & Green Sandpipers, occasional rarer species. *Winter:* Large numbers of wildfowl & waders, inc. impressive flocks of Golden Plover & Lapwing. Starling murmuration.
Directions: Sat nav: TS2 1TP. NZ 506 231. N of River Tees between Middlesbrough & Billingham. From A19, take A689 north of Stockton & then A1185. After four miles join A178 at mini roundabout. Take third exit & reserve is 250 yards on R.
Public transport: Bus - no.1 Middlesborough-Hartlepool stops outside reserve. Stagecoach.
Visiting: Open daily (not Dec 25) 9.30am-5pm Apr-Oct (4pm Nov-Mar). Large car park, inc. Blue Badge spaces & coach parking - charge for non-members. Visitor centre, tea-room & shop open 9.30am-4pm (3.30pm winter). Toilets (inc. disabled), picnic area, bound gravel surfaces to five trails, four hides (wheelchair users may need assistance to reach them). Dogs only allowed in small exercise area.
Contact: RSPB, T: 01642 546 625; E: saltholme@rspb.org.uk

5. SHIBDON POND

Durham Wildlife Trust/Gateshead Council.
Habitats: Pond, marsh, scrub & damp grassland.
Birds: *Summer*: Reed & Sedge Warblers, Lesser Whitethroat, Grasshopper Warbler, Water Rail. Roosts of terns & Cormorants. *Autumn*: Passage waders & wildfowl, Kingfisher. *Winter*: Large numbers of wildfowl, Water Rail, occasional white-winged gulls.
Other: 17 spp. butterfly, inc. Dingy Skipper. Nine spp. dragonflies inc. Ruddy Darter, Migrant Hawker. Otter, Great Crested Newt.
Directions: Sat nav: NE21 5LU. NZ 192 628. E of Blaydon, S of Scotswood Bridge, close to A1. Car park at Blaydon swimming baths. Open access from B6317 (Shibdon Road).
Public transport: Buses - various services from Newcastle/Gateshead to Blaydon (take another short bus journey to Blaydon Baths/Shibdon Road - short walk from here). Go North East (T: 0191 420 5050).
Visiting: Open at all times. Hide (disabled access) in SW corner of pond (key required, see site 1/Thornley Woodlands Visitor Centre). Dogs on lead.
Contact: Durham WT - see site 1.

6. TEESMOUTH NNR

Natural England (Northumbria Team).
Habitats: Grazing marsh, dunes, intertidal sand & mudflats.
Birds: *Spring/summer:* Breeding Ringed Plover, Lapwing, Oystercatcher, Redshank & Snipe. *Passage:* terns & skuas in late summer, scarce passerine migrants & rarities. *Winter*: Internationally important numbers of waterbirds, inc. divers, grebes, waders & Shelduck. Merlin, Peregrine, Short-eared Owl, Snow Bunting, Twite.
Other: Northern area has large Marsh Orchid populations in damp dune grassland. Colony of Common Seals at Seal Sands (pups born in late-Jun).
Directions: Two areas - North Gare, centred on Sat Nav: TS25 2DT, NZ 535 276 & Seal Sands - centred on Sat Nav: TS25 2BY, NZ 530 260. Three & five miles S of Hartlepool, E of A178. Access to northern area from car park at NZ 533 282, 0.5 mile E of A178. Access to southern area from A178 bridge over Greatham Creek at NZ 509 254. Car park adjacent to A178 at NZ 508 251. Both car parks can accommodate coaches.
Public transport: Bus - no.1 Middlesborough-Hartlepool. Stagecoach. Train - Seaton Carew is 1.25 miles from North Gare car park.

Visiting: Open at all times. Northern area - no restrictions over most of dunes & North Gare Sands (avoid golf course, dogs must be kept under close control). Southern area - easy-access path to public hides at NZ 516 255 & NZ 516 252 (no other access). Nearest toilets at Seaton Carew, one mile to N & RSPB Saltholme (one mile to S). Interpretive panels & leaflet. Teesmouth Field Centre, T: 01429 853 847, W: www.teesmouthfieldcentre.org.uk
Contact: Natural England,
T: 01429 853 325 or 07803 228 394;
E: northumbria.hub@naturalengland.org.uk

7. WASHINGTON

The Wildfowl & Wetlands Trust.
Habitats: Wetlands, woodland & meadows.
Birds: *Spring/summer*: Nesting colony of Grey Heron, other breeders inc. Common Tern, Avocet, Oystercatcher, Lapwing. *Winter*: Goldeneye & other wildfowl. Bird-feeding station visited by Willow Tit, Siskin, Redpoll, Brambling, Bullfinch & Sparrowhawk.
Other: Wildflower meadows hold Cuckoo Flower, Bee Orchid & Yellow Rattle. Dragonfly & amphibian ponds.
Directions: Sat nav: NE38 8LE. NZ 330 564. On N bank of River Wear, four miles E of A1(M), sign-posted from A195, A19, A182 & A1231.
Public transport: None.
Visiting: Open daily (not Dec 25) 9.30am-5.30pm Apr-Oct (4.30pm Nov-Mar) - last admission one hour before closing. Admission fee for non-members, WWT members free. Good disabled access. Visitor centre, shop (open 9.30am) & cafe (open 10am), toilets, parent & baby room, four hides, woodland feeding station. Guide dogs only.
Contact: Washington Wetland Centre,
T: 0191 416 5454; E: info.washington@wwt.org.uk

Lancashire & North Merseyside

The county's numerous estuaries attract tens of thousands of wintering waders & the Mosses hold huge numbers of wintering Pink-footed Geese & Whooper Swans. Leighton Moss is one of the RSPB's flagship reserves, Bittern are regular. Seaforth Docks has a good reputation for rare gulls. Inland, Pendle Hill attracts regular Dotterel on spring passage.

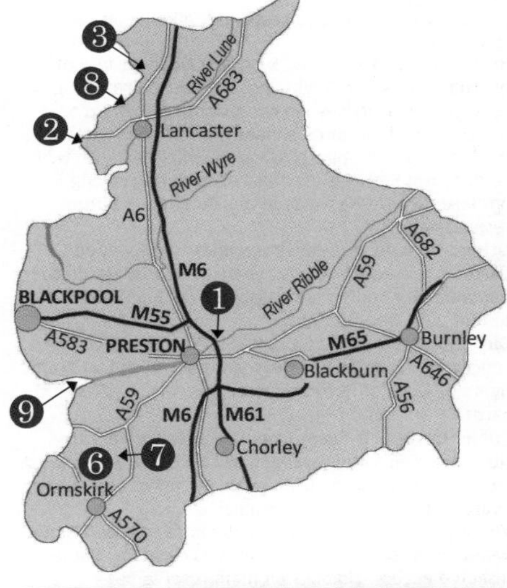

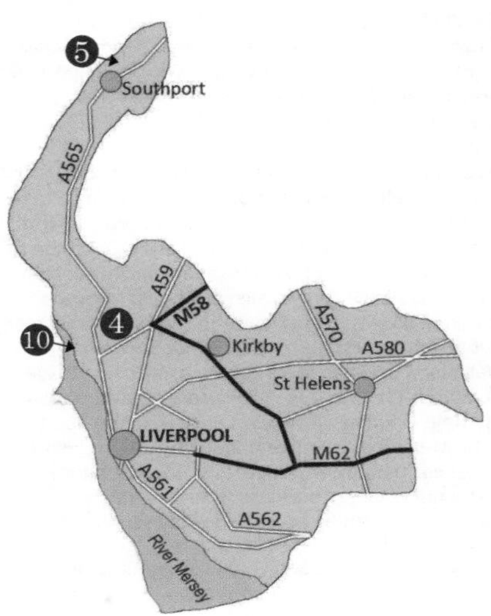

1. BROCKHOLES

Wildlife Trust for Lancashire, Manchester & N. Merseyside.
Habitats: Created from disused gravel pits, alongside River Ribble now features open water, reedbeds, wet grassland & woodland.
Birds: *Spring/summer:* Breeding Great Crested Grebe, Lapwing, Redshank, Skylark, Reed & Sedge Warblers, Reed Bunting. *Passage:* waders inc. Turnstone, Grey Plover, Greenshank, Whimbrel, Curlew, Wood, Green & Curlew Sandpipers & Black-tailed Godwit. *Winter:* Good for wildfowl, inc. Pochard, Pintail, Goldeneye & Teal.

Other: Brown Hawker & Emperor dragonflies.
Directions: Sat nav: PR5 0AG. SD 588 306. Site in Preston New Road, Samlesbury, adjacent to Junc 31 of M6. From S take A59 towards Blackburn & then first exit, signposted to reserve, & follow under southbound slip road north of River Ribble.
Public transport: Buses run close to entrance but no safe pedestrian route to reserve.
Visiting: Gates to reserve open 6am-9pm - car park charges, inc. members. Visitor Village open 10am-5pm Apr-Oct, 10am-4pm Wed to Sun, Nov-Mar (not Dec 25/26). The village - is a cluster of buildings made from sustainable materials with a village store & shop, cafe, adapted toilets. Most paths are level & surfaced - wheelchair-friendly (for larger wheelchairs a refundable deposit required for keys to access gates bypassing kissing gates), hides, Sand Martin wall, children's play area. Guided tours available, booking required. No dogs.
Contact: WT for Lancashire, Manchester & N. Merseyside; T: 01772 872 000; E: info@brockholes.org

2. HEYSHAM NR & BIRD OBSERVATORY

Wildlife Trust for Lancashire, Manchester & N. Merseyside /EDF Energy Estates.
Habitats: Wetland, acid grassland, alkaline grassland, foreshore.
Birds: 170+ spp annually. *Summer:* Good variety of breeding birds (inc. eight spp. warbler on reserve). *Passage:* Passerines when conditions right - two or three scarce land-birds annually, esp. Yellow-browed Warbler. Good seabird passage in spring, esp. Arctic Tern. Storm Petrel & Leach's Petrel during strong onshore (SW-WNW) winds in mid-summer & autumn respectively.
Other: Notable area for dragonflies - Red-veined Darter has bred for several years at nearby Middleton Community Woodland main pond SD 418 592 (mid-Jun to mid-Jul). Bee Orchid.
Directions: Sat nav: LA3 2UW. SD 407 601. W of Lancaster. Take A683 to Heysham port. Turn L at traffic lights by Duke of Rothesay pub, then first R after 300 yards.
Public transport: Buses from Lancaster to various Heysham sites within walking distance (ask for nearest stop to the harbour). Train services connect with nearby Isle of Man ferry terminal.
Visiting: Pedestrian access at all times, car park open 9am-6pm or dusk if earlier - map in car park. Limited disabled access. No dogs on main reserve but extensive off-lead area nearby. No manned visitor centre or toilet access, but someone usually in reserve office in morning (next to main car park).
Contact: WT for Lancashire, Manchester & N. Merseyside; Reserve Warden, Heysham Nature Reserve, T: 01524 855 030; E: rneville@lancswt.org.uk
Check out observatory's blogpot for virtually daily updates & detailed map at bottom of page.
http://heyshamobservatory.blogspot.co.uk/

3. LEIGHTON MOSS

RSPB (Northern England).
Habitats: Reedbed, shallow meres, woodland & scrub. Saltmarsh pools approx one mile.
Birds: *All year:* Bittern, Bearded Tit, Water Rail, Shoveler, Gadwall, Marsh Tit, Little Egret. *Summer:* Breeding Marsh Harrier, Reed & Sedge Warbler. Avocet at saltmarsh pools. *Passage:* Black-tailed Godwits in spring (good numbers), Greenshank, Ruff & godwits in autumn. *Winter:* Large flocks of Starlings roosting, hunting Peregrine & Merlin terrorise overwintering wildfowl.
Other: Otter, Red Deer.
Directions: Sat nav: LA5 0SW. SD 478 750. Four miles NW of Carnforth. Leave M6 at Junc 35. Take A6 N towards Kendal & follow brown signs for Leighton Moss off A6.
Public transport: Train - Silverdale station is 250 yards from reserve (on Manchester Airport to Barrow line).
Visiting: Open daily, dawn-dusk. Entry fee for non-members (half-price if arriving by bike or public transport). Visitor centre/cafe (free entry) open 9.30am-5pm/4.30pm Dec-Jan (not Dec 25) - shop, cafe (stair lift available), toilets (inc. disabled), binoculars for hire. Three signposted nature trails, seven hides (some wheelchair access). Dogs restricted to Causeway public footpath.
Contact: RSPB, T: 01524 701 601; E: leighton.moss@rspb.org.uk

4. LUNT MEADOWS

Wildlife Trust for Lancashire, Manchester & N. Merseyside.
Habitats: Open water/pools, reedbeds, grassland, small orchard - along the River Alt.
Birds: *All year:* Marsh Harrier, Peregrine, Barn Owl, Kingfisher, Bearded Tit, Reed Bunting. *Spring/summer:* Shelduck, Oystercatcher, Avocet, Little Ringed & Ringed Plovers. Hobby, Grasshopper, Reed & Sedge Warblers. *Passage:* Common & Green Sandpipers, Ruff, Greenshank, Black-tailed Godwit, Black Tern. *Winter:* Wildfowl & waders, Short-eared Owl.
Other: Water Vole.
Directions: Sat Nav: L29 8YA. SD 355 021. Lies just to W of Maghull. From A59/M57/M58 interchange take A5758. At roundabout, turn L (A565) then L at traffic lights towards Netherton (Green Lane). Continue to T-junction, turn L (B5422 to Maghull). In Sefton turn L into Bridge Lane (brown sign to The Punchbowl) continue on this road (1 mile) to reserve entrance on R.
Public transport: Bus - no.133 (not Sun) from Waterloo Interchange-Kirkby, stops at Lunt village. Cumfybus (T: 0151 236 7676 - Merseytravel network).
Visiting: Open at all times. Car park (free) open 9.30am-6.30pm (summer), 9.30am-4.30pm (winter) - if locked, park by entrance gate - do not park in surrounding lanes to access reserve. Paths (unsurfaced, can be rough), viewing screens, hide. Dogs on lead.
Contact: WT for Lancashire, Manchester & N. Merseyside; Reserve Warden, T: 01519 203 769; E: agraham@lancswt.org.uk

5. MARSHSIDE

RSPB (Northern England).
Habitats: Coastal grazing marsh & lagoons.
Birds: *All year:* Black-tailed Godwit. *Spring:* Breeding waders, inc. Avocet & wildfowl, Garganey, migrants. *Autumn:* Migrants. *Winter:* Wildfowl inc.Pink-footed Goose, waders inc. Golden Plover, raptors inc. Merlin, Peregrine, Kestrel & Sparrowhawk.
Other: Brown Hare, various plants inc. Marsh Orchid, Migrant Hawker dragonfly.
Directions: Sat nav: PR9 9PJ. SD 353 205. From Southport, follow minor coast road Marine Drive N (1.5 miles from Southport Pier) to small car park by sand works.
Public transport: Bus - no.44 Southport to Crossens, alight at Marshside, Elswick Road stop. Walk 0.5 mile (towards the coast) to reserve entrance. Arriva in North West.
Visiting: Open all year 8.30am-5pm (dusk if earlier), car park charge for non-members - coach parties should book in advance. Visitor centre, toilets (inc. disabled), two hides (both glazed, one doubling as visitor centre), trails accessible to wheelchairs, two viewing screens, one raised viewing platform. Dogs not permitted on path to Nel's hide or in the hides, keep on leads elsewhere.
Contact: RSPB, T: 01704 211 690;
E: Ribble.reserves@rspb.org.uk

6. MARTIN MERE

The Wildfowl & Wetlands Trust.
Habitats: Open water, wet grassland, moss, copses, reedbed, parkland.
Birds: *Spring*: Ruff, Shelduck, Little Ringed & Ringed Plovers, Lapwing, Redshank. *Summer*: Marsh Harrier, Garganey, hirundines, Tree Sparrow. Breeding Avocet, Lapwing, Redshank, Shelduck. *Autumn*: Pink-footed Goose, waders on passage. *Winter*: Whooper & Bewick's Swans, Pink-footed Goose, various ducks, Ruff, Black-tailed Godwit, Peregrine, Hen Harrier, Tree Sparrow.
Other: Whorled Caraway, Golden Dock, Tubular Dropwort, 300 spp. moth.
Directions: Sat nav: L40 0TA. SD 428 145. Off Fish Lane, Burscough, six miles N of Ormskirk via Burscough Bridge (A59). 20 miles from Liverpool & Preston. Signposted from: Junc 8 M61, Junc 3 M58, Junc 27 M6.
Public transport: Train - Burscough Bridge (2.5 miles) or Burscough Junction (three miles - walk to Burscough Bridge station first). New Lane Station (1.2 miles - no safe footpath, have to walk along a road).
Visiting: Open daily (not Dec 25) 9.30am-6pm Apr-Oct (4.30pm Nov-Mar), last admission one hour before closing. Entrance fee for non-WWT members (discount if arrive by public transport or bike), coach park available - special rates for coach parties. Visitor centre, toilets, shop, cafe, education centre, play area, nature reserve/nature trails, hides, waterfowl collection, sustainable garden. Full disabled access, hides suitable for wheelchairs. Special dawn & evening events. Guide dogs only.
Contact: WWT Martin Mere Wetland Centre,
T: 01704 895 181; E: info.martinmere@wwt.org.uk

7. MERE SANDS WOOD

Wildlife Trust for Lancashire, Manchester & N. Merseyside.
Habitats: 40ha, freshwater lakes, mixed woodland.
Birds: 170 spp., 60 spp. have bred. *All year:* Lesser Spotted Woodpecker, Willow Tit, Treecreeper, Nuthatch. *Summer*: Kingfisher. *Passage*: Most years - Osprey, Crossbill, Green Sandpiper, Greenshank. *Winter*: Regionally important for Teal & Gadwall, good range of waterfowl inc. Mandarin & Goosander. Feeding stations attract Tree Sparrow, Bullfinch, Reed Bunting, Water Rail.
Other: 18 spp. dragonflies recorded annually, Broad Bucker Fern, 200+ spp. fungi. Red Squirrel, Stoat, Water Vole.
Directions: Sat nav: L40 1TG. SD 449 161. 12 miles from Southport, 0.5 mile off A59 Preston to Liverpool road, in Rufford along B5246 (Holmeswood Road).
Public transport: Bus - no.347 Southport-Chorley (Presrton Bus) & no.2B Preston-Ormskirk (Stagecoach)stop in Rufford, 0.5 mile walk. Train: Preston-Ormskirk service stops at Rufford station, one mile walk.
Visiting: Reserve & car park open at all times (car park charge). Visitor centre open 9.30am-4.30pm Tues-Sun/bank-holiday Mons, exhibition room, shop, toilets (inc. disabled). Six viewing hides (wheelchair accessible), three trails - three miles of wheelchair-accessible footpaths, latest sightings board. Feeding stations. Guided walks for groups can be arranged. Two motorised buggies - booking essential.
Contact: WT for Lancashire, Manchester & N. Merseyside; Reserve Manager, Mere Sands Wood NR,
T: 01704 821 809; E: lbeaton@lancswt.org.uk

8. MORECAMBE BAY (HEST BANK)

RSPB (Northern England).
Habitats: Saltmarsh, estuary.
Birds: *Winter:* 250,000 waders & wildfowl winter on Britain's second-most important estuary site. Wildfowl inc. Pintail, Shelduck, Wigeon. Important high tide roost for waders inc.Oystercatcher, Curlew, Redshank, Dunlin & Bar-tailed Godwit.
Directions: Sat nav: LA2 6HN. SD 467 666. Two miles N of Morecambe at Hest Bank. Access car park from Hest Bank level crossing off A5105.
Public transport: Bus - no.5 runs between Carnforth & Morecambe. Stagecoach. Train - nearest station is Morecambe.
Visiting: Open at all times - do not go onto saltmarsh or intertidal area (dangerous channels & quicksands). Viewpoint & toilets at local council car park. Paths from car park too rough for wheelchairs. Dogs allowed. Guided walks programme.
Contact: RSPB- see site 3.

9. RIBBLE ESTUARY NNR

Natural England (Cheshire & Lancashire Team).
Habitats: One of England's largest areas of saltmarsh, & mudflats.
Birds: *Winter:* High water wader roosts of Knot, Dunlin, Black-tailed Godwit, Oystercatcher & Grey Plover are best viewed from Southport, Marshside, Lytham St Annes. Pink-footed Geese & wintering swans are present in large numbers from Oct-Feb on Banks Marsh & along River Douglas respectively. Banks Marsh can be viewed from public footpath which runs along sea defence embankment from Crossens Pumping Station to Hundred End. Large flocks of Wigeon, for which site is renowned, can be seen on high tides from Marshside but feed on saltmarsh areas at night. Good numbers of raptors.
Directions: Sat Nav: PR4 6XH. SD 380 240 (S side). Lies approx 4.5 miles W of Preston, stretching on both sides of River Ribble as far as Lytham St Anns (N side) & Crossens (S side). Take A584 & minor roads for north bank, A59/A565 & minor roads for south bank.
Public transport: Bus - no.2 Preston to Southport & no.68 Preston to Lytham St Anns. Stagecoach.
Visiting: Public footpaths open at all times, no access to saltmarsh itself. Ribble Discovery Centre at Fairhaven Lake (3.2 miles from Lytham). RSPB Marshside, adjacent to NNR - see site 5.
Contact: Natural England, T: 01704 578 774; E: dave.mercer@naturalengland.org.uk

10. SEAFORTH NATURE RESERVE

Wildlife Trust for Lancashire, Manchester & N. Merseyside.
Habitats: Saltwater & freshwater lagoons, scrub grassland & small reedbed.
Birds: Major roosting site for waders (38 spp. have been recorded) & seabirds, noted for Little Gull on passage (Apr), Roseate, Little & Black Terns. *Breeding/passage:* Common Tern (Apr-Sep). *Passage/ winter:* waders & gulls - 15 spp. of gulls recorded, with Ring-billed annual & Mediterranean seen almost daily. Passage passerines, esp. White & Yellow Wagtails, pipits, Wheatear, & a sprinkling of vagrants.
Directions: Sat nav: L21 1JD. SJ 318 971. Five miles from Liverpool city centre. From M57/M58 take A5036 to docks. Enter via Liverpool Freeport entrance in Crosby Road South.
Public transport: Buses - to dock gates from Liverpool. Train - to Waterloo or Seaforth stations from Liverpool.
Visiting: Open at all times. Permit required (visitor & vehicle passes) - members only, apply for them directly from Port Police 0151 949 6144. Organised groups must contact reserve office (below) at least seven days in advance of planned visit.
Contact: WT for Lancashire, Manchester & N. Merseyside; Reserve Warden, T: 0151 920 3769; E: seaforth@lancswt.org.uk

---

Manchester (Greater)

Despite being a largely urban area, there are good places for birdwatching. The former colliery workings of Pennington & Wigan Flashes are the area's best all-round birding sites with a wide range of species, including rarities from time to time. Etherow CP has Dipper & a good selection of woodland birds including Pied Flycatcher.

1. BROAD EES DOLE (SALE WATER PARK)

Mersey Valley Countryside Warden Service.
Habitats: Wetland site with water levels managed to provide feeding & breeding opportunities for spp. such as herons, Kingfisher, Little Ringed Plover & Lapwing.
Birds: Important site for migratory species & waders inc. Snipe & Jack Snipe. *Winter:* wildfowl inc. Mallard, Gadwall, Teal, Coot, Moorhen in LNR, wider variety on main lake of Water Park.
Other: Spotted Orchid, Smooth & Great Crested Newts. Variety of fish on main lake in Sale Water Park.
Directions: Sat nav: M33 2LX. SJ 804 926. Local Nature Reserve located close to visitor centre in Sale Water Park, Trafford. Access from Junc 6 of M60, following signs for Trafford Water Sports Centre.
Public transport: Metrolink - Sale Water Park.
Visiting: Open dawn-dusk. Sale Water Park visitor centre car park off Rifle Road. Walk to reserve by following track behind visitor centre. Small concrete hide. No paths within reserve, view from perimeter paths.
Contact: MVCWS, T: 0161 906 1100; E: info@merseyvalley.org.uk

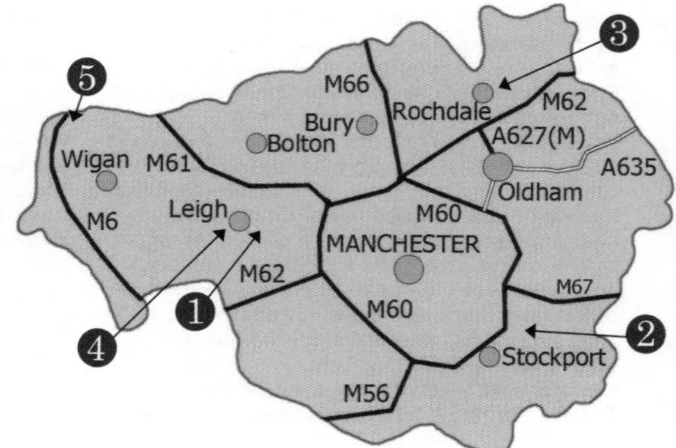

2. ETHEROW COUNTRY PARK

Stockport Metropolitan Borough Council.
Habitats: River Etherow, woodlands, marshy area, ponds & surrounding moorland.
Birds: 100+ spp. inc. Sparrowhawk, Buzzard, Woodcock, 3 spp. woodpecker, Dipper, warblers inc. Wood & Garden, Pied Flycatcher, *Winter*: Brambling, Siskin, Water Rail. Frequent sightings of Merlin & Raven over hills.
Other: 200 spp. of plants.
Directions: Sat nav: SK6 5JD. SJ 965 908. Site lies at halfway point on 12-mile Valley Way Footpath linking Stockport & Woolley Bridge. Situated at Compstall on B6104 near Romiley, Stockport.
Public transport: Bus - nos.383 & 384 Stockport, Marple/Romiley circular - alight at Compstall. Stagecoach. Train - Romiley & Marple Bridge.
Visiting: Parkland open at all times - permit required for conservation area (contact first for info). Pay-&-display car park. Visitor centre open (not Dec 25) 11am-4pm (when possible), cafe (10am-4pm summer, 10am-3pm winter) & toilets. One hide, nature trail, Keep to paths. Motorised wheelchairs available (free), book in advance.
Contact: Etherow Country Park Visitor Centre, T: 0161 427 6937.

3. HOLLINGWORTH LAKE

Hollingworth Lake/Rochdale MBC.
Habitats: Lake (47ha, inc. 17.5ha nature reserve), woodland, streams, marsh, willow scrub.
Birds: *All year*: Great Crested Grebe, Cormorant, Lapwing, Kingfisher, Little Owl, Bullfinch. Occasional Peregrine, Sedge Warbler, Water Rail, Snipe. *Spring/autumn*: Passage waders, wildfowl, Kittiwake. *Summer*: Reed Bunting, Dipper, Common Sandpiper, Curlew, Oystercatcher, Black Tern, 'Commic' Tern, Grey Partridge, Blackcap. *Winter*: Goosander, Goldeneye, Golden Plover, Siskin, Redpoll.
Directions: Sat nav: OL15 0AQ. SD 939 153 (visitor centre). On outskirts of Littleborough, four miles NE of Rochdale, signposted from A58 Halifax Road & Junc 21 of M62 (B6225 to Littleborough).
Public transport: Bus nos.455 & 458 from Rochdale stop at Hollingworth Lake. Transport for Greater Manchester (T: 0161 244 1000). Train - Littleborough or Smithy Bridge (ca 10 mins to Lake).
Visiting: Open access to lake & surroundings. Car parks, coaches by prior arrangement. Visitor centre open 10am-3pm, Fri to Tues, toilets (disabled/baby changing facilities) & cafe open at 9.30am. Hide, trails. Education service, free wheelchair hire, fishing.
Contact: Hollingworth Lake Country Park & Visitor Centre, T: 01706 373 421.

4. PENNINGTON FLASH COUNTRY PARK

Wigan Council
Habitats: Lowland lake, ponds & scrapes, fringed with reeds, rough grassland, scrub & woodland.
Birds: 240+ spp. inc. many county firsts & rarities. *All year:* Waterfowl. Feeding station attracts Willow Tit, Stock Dove & up to 40 Bullfinches. *Spring/autumn passage:* waders (14+ spp.) & terns (4+ spp.). *Summer:* Breeding inc. Common Tern, Ringed & Little Ringed Plover, nine spp. warbler. *Winter:* Peregrine, Merlin, large gull roost (with occasional white-winged gulls), Siskin, Brambling.
Other: Several spp. orchid, inc. Bee Orchid. Wide variety of butterflies & dragonflies.
Directions: Sat nav: WN7 3PA. SJ 640 990. One mile from Leigh town centre & well signposted from A580 East Lancashire Road. Main entrance on A572 (St Helens Road).
Public transport: Bus - one mile from Leigh bus station, nos. 589 & 590 stop on St Helens Road near entrance to park. Transport for Greater Manchester (T: 0161 244 1000).
Visiting: Park open at all times. Main car park pay-&-display (coach parking/group visits available if booked in advance) Toilets (inc. disabled) & information point open 9am-dusk (not Dec 25), catering. Main paths flat, suitable for disabled. Seven hides, nature trails. Site leaflet available.
Contact: Wigan Council, T: 01942 489 007

5. WIGAN FLASHES

Wildlife Trust for Lancs, Manchester & N. Merseyside/ Wigan Council.
Habitats: Open water, reedbed, fen, rough grassland, wet woodland & scrub.
Birds: 200+ spp. *Summer*: Nationally important for Willow Tit. Common Tern, Water Rail, Reed, Sedge, Cetti's & Grasshopper Warblers, Kingfisher. *Passage:* Black Tern. *Winter*: Bittern, wildfowl, especially diving duck & Gadwall.
Other: Interesting orchids, six spp. inc. Marsh & Dune Helleborine. One of UK's largest feeding assemblage of Noctule Bats. Water Vole. 18 spp. dragonflies, has inc. Red-veined Darter.
Directions: Sat nav: WN3 5NY. SD 585 030. Leave M6 at J25 head N on A49, turn R on to Poolstock Lane (B5238) - car park 0.75 mile on R. Also parking on Welham Road - after turning into Poolstock Lane turn R (0.3 mile) into Carr Lane then L into Welham Road, just before school. Can access reserve from banks of Leeds & Liverpool Canal.
Public transport: Bus - no.607 bus Wigan to Ashton Heath passes along Poolstock Lane. Diamond Bus North West (T: 01942 888 893).
Visiting: Open at all times. Poolstock Lane car park has 300 spaces - access for coaches, contact reserve manager. Network of footpaths, areas suitable for wheelchairs. Six hide screens.
Contact: WT for Lancashire, Manchester & N. Merseyside; T: 01942 233 976; E: mchampion@lancswt.org.uk

Northumberland

The county offers a lot of variety with a fantastic range of habitats. The seabird colonies on the Farne Islands & Coquet Island are teeming with birds that can be seen at close quarters. Coastal sites, such as Holy Island (Lindisfarne), Budle Bay & East Chevington, attract spring & autumn migrants, & large numbers of wintering birds. Kielder Forest is good for Crossbills & raptors, including Goshawk & Osprey, while the nearby moors hold a good selection of upland species.

1. DRURIDGE POOLS & CRESSWELL POND

Northumberland Wildlife Trust.
Habitats: 1 (Druridge): Deep lake & two wet meadows with pools behind dunes. 2 (Cresswell): Shallow brackish lagoon behind dunes fringed by saltmarsh & reedbed, some mudflats.
Birds: 1: Especially good in spring. Winter & breeding wildfowl (mostly Wigeon & Teal); passage & breeding waders. 2: Good for waders, esp. on passage. Wildfowl inc. Pink-footed Geese in winter.
Other: Sheltered sunny banks good for a range of butterflies & dragonflies in summer at Druridge Pools. Otters often seen by lakes.
Directions: Two sites lying on coast between Amble & Newbiggin, off A1068. 1: Sat nav: NE61 5EG for Druridge Pools (NZ 275 963). Roadside parking next to National Trust's Druridge Links site. 1.9 miles N of Cresswell. 2: Sat nav: NE61 5EH for Cresswell Pond (NZ 283 944). Use car park to northern end of reserve, 0.6 mile N of Cresswell & walk S along road Blakemoor Farm track.
Public transport: Bus - 1: no.X18 Alnwick to Morpeth alight Widdrington (two miles). 2: no.1 to Cresswell (Blyth to Widdrington). Arriva in North East.
Visiting: 1: Access along public footpath or short path to screen, two hides. 2: Access along short path from farm track. Wheelchair users can view northern part of Cresswell Pond from public footpath or roadside. Hide. Dogs on leads.
Contact: Northumberland WT, T: 0191 284 6884;
E: mail@northwt.org.uk

2. EAST CHEVINGTON

Northumberland Wildlife Trust.
Habitats: Ponds & reedbeds created from former open cast coal mine. Areas of scrub & grassland.
Birds: *Summer:* Breeding Skylark, Stonechat, Reed Bunting, Reed, Sedge & Grasshopper Warblers. Marsh Harrier. *Winter:* Large numbers of wildfowl, inc. Greylag & Pink-footed Geese. Short-eared Owl, Tree Sparrow, Twite.Capable of attracting rarities at any time.
Other: Coastal wildflowers & in grassland, Dyer's Greenweed.
Directions: Sat nav: NE61 5BX. NZ 270 990. Near Red Row, overlooking Druridge Bay, off A 1068 between Amble & Widdrington - park at Druridge Bay Country Park (signposted).
Public transport: Bus - X18 to Red Row (one mile). Arriva in North East.
Visiting: Main access from overflow car park at Druridge Bay Country Park (walk S). Four hides, plant ID boards.Cafe, toilets & information at Country Park (County Council).
Contact: Northumberland WT - see site 1.

3. FARNE ISLANDS

The National Trust.
Habitats: 15-28 maritime islands, depending on tide.
Birds: *Spring/summer:* ca.23 breeding spp./100,000 pairs of seabirds - Common, Arctic & Sandwich Terns, Puffin, Razorbill, Guillemot, Kittiwake, Eider, Shag. Shearwaters, skuas offshore. Rarities often turn up but usually difficult to see as a visitor.
Other: Large Grey Seal colony, breed late-Oct/early Dec.
Directions: Sat nav: NE68 7TA. NU 219 322 (Seahouses). Access by boat from Seahouses Harbour, reached from A1.
Public transport: Bus - no.X18 Berwick to Alnwick (few services on Sun). Arriva Northumbria. No.418 (not Sun) Alnwick to Belford. Travelsure (T: 01665 720 955). Trains: Alnmouth & Berwick (then use bus).
Visiting: Four boat companies run trips out of Seahouses. Islands open: Apr, Aug-Sep: Inner Farne 10.30am-5pm. May-Jul: Staple Island 10.30am-1.30pm & Inner Farne: 1.30pm-5pm. Disabled access possible on Inner Farne, contact Property Manager for details. NT charge to land on islands (free to members) - these DO NOT include boatman's fees. Toilets on Inner Farne. Dogs may be allowed on boats (check with boatman) but NOT allowed on islands.
Contact: The National Trust, The Farne Islands, Seahouses, NE68 7SR. T: 01289 389 244;
E: farneislands@nationaltrust.org.uk

4. KIELDER WATER & FOREST PARK

Forestry England.
Habitats: Commercial coniferous/broadleaved woodland.
Birds: Successful Osprey breeding programme since 2009. *All year*: Dipper, Great Spotted & Green Woodpeckers, Tawny Owl, Song Thrush, Jay, Nuthatch, Goldcrest, Siskin. *Spring/summer*: Goshawk, Raven, Chiffchaff, Willow Warbler, Redstart. *Winter*: Crossbill & winter thrushes.
Other: Impressive display of Northern Marsh Orchids at entrance to Kielder Castle. Red Squirrel, Badger, Otter, Roe Deer, seven bat spp.
Directions: Sat nav: NE48 1ER. NY 632 934 (Kielder Castle). The Castle is situated at N end of Kielder Water, NW of Bellingham, 30 miles from Hexham.
Public transport: Bus - no.880 (Mon-Sat) Hexham to Kielder Castle. Snaith's Travel (T: 01830 520 609) & Tyne Valley Coaches (T: 01434 602 217). No.714 (Sun/bank hol - limited, Newcastle to Kielder Castle. Arriva.
Visiting: Forest open all year, car parks open dawn-dusk. Car parking facilities at Kielder Castle & overflow behind Angler's Arms pub (24-hr parking ticket required) - transferable for all car parks on south shore. Toll charge for 12-mile forest drive (rough surface), closed Nov to end-Apr due to conditions.

Kielder Castle Information Centre, free exhibition, licensed Kielder Castle Cafe with live wildlife viewing screens, access for disabled & toilets inc. baby changing facilities. Many walking/mountain biking trails start from here, ask staff for more info. Kielder Cycle Centre & bike wash, post office/local shop, Angler's Arms pub, youth hostel, camp site, No.27 B&B & 24 hour (pay by card) garage. One mile multi-access Duke's Trail inc. arboretum & hide where red squirrels can usually be seen. Bakethin Nature Reserve has dipping pond.
Contact: Forestry England, T: 01434 250 209;
E: kieldercastle@forestryengland.uk
Ospreys: W: www.kielderospreys.wordpress.com
W: www.visitkielder.com

5. LINDISFARNE NNR

Natural England (Northumbria Team).
Habitats: Dunes, sand, mudflats & saltmarsh, rocky shore & open water.
Birds: *Passage & winter*: Wildfowl & waders, inc. Pale-bellied Brent Goose, Red-breasted Merganser, Long-tailed Duck & Whooper Swan. Divers, grebes, Merlin. Common, scarce & rare migrants.
Other: Butterflies inc. Dark Green Fritillary & Grayling, nine spp. orchid inc. Coralroot & Lindisfarne Helleborine. Grey Seal.
Directions: Sat nav: TD15 2SS. NU 094 430. Island access lies two miles E of A1 at Beal, signposted to Holy Island, 10 miles S of Berwick-on-Tweed.
Public transport: Bus - no.477 limited service to Holy Island from Berwick. Border Buses (T: 01289 308 719). WT2 'Lindisfarne Hoppa' service Haggerston/Beal to Holy Island. Woody's Taxis T: 01289 547009. Both mainly summer, services fit in with safe crossing times.
Visiting: NOTE - causeway to Holy Island floods at high tide, check safe crossing times BEFORE crossing. Some restricted access (bird refuges). On island - car & coach parking, toilets & visitor centre in village, hide & self-guided trail. New hide with disabled access at Fenham-le-Moor (on mainland).
Contact: Natural England, T: 01289 381 470.

6. PRESTWICK CARR

Northumberland Wildlife Trust.
Habitats: Lowland raised mire, woodland, farmland.
Birds: A noted raptor watchpoint: 2010's White-tailed Eagle became 14th bird of prey spp. recorded since 1990s. *All year:* Water Rail, Kingfisher, Stonechat, Whinchat & Willow Tit. Barn, Little, Long-eared & Tawny Owls breed. *Summer:* migrants, inc. Grasshopper Warbler. *Passage:* waders occur in large numbers if carr is flooded. *Winter:* Hen Harrier are regular between Oct-Jan. Merlin & Peregrine, Short-eared Owl.
Directions: Sat nav: NE20 9UD. NZ 192 733. Seven miles NW of Newcastle city centre between Dinnington & Pontesland. Take A696 from A1 western bypass for three miles, then minor road to Prestwick hamlet. Park on minor roads north of Prestwick & Dinnington.
Public transport: Bus - no.45 runs between Newcastle Haymarket & Dinnington (0.75 mile walk to carr's eastern end). Arriva Northumbria.
Visiting: Restricted to minor roads & bridleway across carr. No access to northern section when military firing range in use (between Prestwick Mill Farm & Berwick Hill). Viewing platform & interpretation.
Contact: Northumberland WT - see site 1.

7. WHITELEE MOOR

Northumberland Wildlife Trust.
Habitats: Blanket bog & heather moorland.
Birds: The River Rede & its tributaries add to habitat & bird diversity. Notable breeding spp. inc. Merlin, Hen Harrier, Peregrine, Red Grouse, Dunlin, Curlew, Golden Plover, Skylark, Meadow Pipit, Stonechat. Dipper & Ring Ouzel regularly visit reserve.
Other: Otters often hunt along the Rede & herd of feral Goats may be seen.
Directions: Sat nav: TD8 6PT. NT 698 068. (Carter Bar) Reserve located at head of Redesdale, S of A68 Newcastle to Jedburgh road where it crosses Scottish Border at Carter Bar.
Public transport: None.
Visiting: Remote & wild, so hill-walking experience needed if attempting long walks. Park at tourist car park at Carter Bar & on lay-bys on forest track at reservoir end. Public footpath along old track to Whitelee Limeworks - then southwards extends to site's southern boundary - eastwards to link up with bridleway from White Kielder Burn to Chattlehope Burn. Additional access on foot via Forestry road near eastern corner of reserve. Dogs on lead.
Contact: Northumberland WT - see site 1.

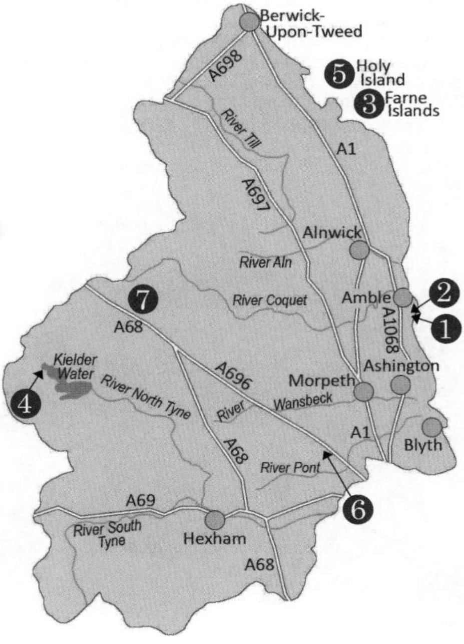

Yorkshire (East Riding)

The coast dominates the birding here - the headlands at Flamborough Head & Spurn Point are a magnet for migrants - regularly turning up rarities, especially in the autumn. Bempton Cliffs is probably the best mainland seabird colony in England, where you can get close to Puffins & Gannets. An autumn boat trip from Bridlington is worth taking to see passing shearwaters & skuas.

1. BEMPTON CLIFFS

RSPB (Northern England).
Habitats: Largest mainland seabird colony in UK & only Gannet colony in England. Sea cliffs, farmland, grassland, coastal scrub.
Birds: Breeding numbers in excess of 200,000 between Apr-Jun inc. Kittiwake, Gannet, Puffin, Guillemot, Razorbill & Fulmar, some spp. start returning to cliffs in Jan. Breeding Tree Sparrow & Corn Bunting. *Passage:* skuas, shearwaters, terns & passerine migrants.
Other: Harbour Porpoise & Grey Seal regularly offshore. Bee & Northern Marsh Orchids.
Directions: Sat nav: YO15 1JF. TA 197 738. Near Bridlington. Take Cliff Lane N from Bempton village off B1229 to car park & visitor centre.
Public transport: Train - Bempton station 1.25 miles from reserve.
Visiting: Entrance charge for non-members, coaches/ minibuses (in advance, or drop off only). Seabird Centre open daily (9.30am-5pm Mar-Oct, 9.30am-4pm Nov-Feb. Toilets (inc. disabled), light refreshments, shop, picnic area, binoculars for hire. Cliff-top public footpath with five observation points (two wheelchair accessible). Four miles of stunning chalk cliffs, highest in county. Short farmland footpath. Dogs on leads.
Contact: RSPB, T: 01262 422 212;
E: bempton.cliffs@rspb.org.uk

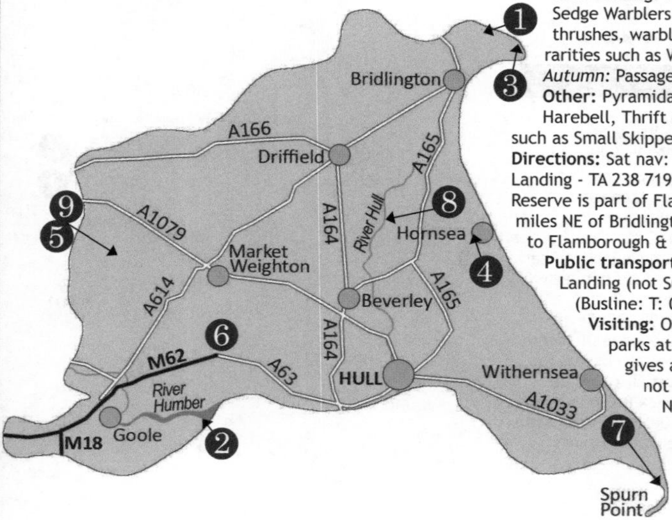

2. BLACKTOFT SANDS

RSPB (Northern England).
Habitats: Second largest tidal reedbed in UK, saline lagoons, lowland wet grassland, willow scrub.
Birds: 270 spp. *Summer*: Breeding Bittern, Avocet, Marsh Harrier, Bearded Tit, Reed & Sedge Warblers, Tree Sparrow. *Passage:* waders (exceptional list inc. rarities). *Winter*: Wildfowl, Hen Harrier, Merlin, Peregrine.
Other: Water Vole. Dragonflies & damselflies inc. Black-tailed Skimmer, Four-spotted Chaser, Large Red Damselfly. Marsh Sow Thistle easily seen from footpaths in summer. Rare Brown-veined Wainscot moth.
Directions: Sat nav: DN14 8HR. SE 843 232. Eight miles E of Goole. Follow brown tourist signs on minor road between Ousefleet & Adlingfleet.
Public transport: Bus - no.360/361 from Goole stops at reserve entrance. East Yorkshire Motor Services (Busline: T: 01482 592 929).
Visiting: Open daily (not Dec 25) 9am-9pm/dusk if earlier. Charge for non-members. Car park, toilets. Reception hide open daily 9am-5pm Apr-Sep, weekends 10am-4pm Oct-Mar. Light refreshments, binocular hire. Six hides with wheelchair spaces, one viewing screen, footpaths suitable for wheelchairs. Assistance dogs only.
Contact: RSPB, T: 01405 704 665;
E: blacktoft.sands@rspb.org.uk

3. FLAMBOROUGH HEAD

Yorkshire Wildlife Trust.
Habitats: Coastal cliffs, species-rich rough grassland & scrub, farmland.
Birds: *Summer:* Breeding Puffin, Guillemot, Razorbill, Kittiwake, Shag, Fulmar, Skylark, Meadow Pipit, Linnet, Whitethroat, Yellowhammer, Tree Sparrow, occasional Corn Bunting. Thornwick reedbeds hold Reed & Sedge Warblers & Reed Bunting. *Passage migrants:* thrushes, warblers, finches, buntings & occasional rarities such as Wryneck & Red-backed Shrike. *Autumn:* Passage divers, grebes & seaduck.
Other: Pyramidal & Northern Marsh Orchids, Harebell, Thrift on cliff tops. Migrant butterflies such as Small Skipper & Painted Lady.
Directions: Sat nav: YO15 1BJ. Car parks: North Landing - TA 238 71920 & Thornwick Bay - TA234 719. Reserve is part of Flamborough headland, approx four miles NE of Bridlington. From Bridlington take B1255 to Flamborough & follow signs for North Landing.
Public transport: Bus - no.14 Bridlington to North Landing (not Sun). East Yorkshire Motor Services, (Busline: T: 01482 592 929).
Visiting: Open all year. Pay-&-display car parks at North Landing/Thornwick Bay gives access to trails on reserve. Paths not suitable for wheelchairs. Cafe at North Landing (open Apr-Oct, 10am-5pm), toilets.
Contact: Yorkshire WT,
T: 01904 659 570;
E: info@ywt.org.uk

4. HORNSEA MERE

Wassand Hall.
Habitats: Yorkshire's largest body of freshwater, 0.6 mile inland from coast, edged by reedbeds & woodland.
Birds: *All year:* common wildfowl. *Spring/autumn passage:* Marsh Harrier, Osprey, Little Gull, terns, White & Yellow Wagtails, Wheatear, maybe rarer spp. *Winter:* common wildfowl with a chance of divers, grebes, Long-tailed Duck, Goosander & Pintail.
Directions: Sat nav: HU11 5RJ .TA 174 460 (Hall). 12 miles E of Beverley, Wassand is between Seaton & Hornsea on A1035. Mere can also be viewed from Hornsea - enter town, onto Southgate then take signposted road to car park at Kirkholme Point.
Public transport: Bus - no.246 Hull-Beverley-Hornsea - ask to stop by Wassend Hall. East Yorkshire Motor Services, (Busline: T: 01482 592 929).
Visiting: Mere is owned by nearby Wassand Hall (which is open to public on selected days through year). Cafe on site (limited winter opening), toilets. Hide & woodland trail open daily (not Dec 25) - see notices for closing times. Hide - charge for electronic code, available from 10.30am at East Lodge, first house after Wassand Estate entrance on R (parking at Hall). Dogs on leads.
Contact: T: 01964 537 474 or 07767 039 793;
E: info@wassand.co.uk; W: www.wassand.co.uk;
W: https://hornseamere.wordpress.com/

5. LOWER DERWENT VALLEY NNR

Natural England (Yorkshire & Northern Lincolnshire Team)/ Yorkshire Wildlife Trust/Carstairs Countryside Trust.
Habitats: Flood meadows, pastures, swamp, open water & alder/willow woodland.
Birds: 80+ spp. *Spring/summer*: Breeding wildfowl & waders, inc. Garganey & Snipe. Grey Partridge, Spotted Crake, Barn Owl & warblers. *Passage*: waders, inc. Whimbrel. *Winter/spring*: Bittern, 20,000+ waterfowl inc. Whooper Swan, wild geese, Teal & Wigeon. Large gull roost. Merlin, Hen Harrier, Peregrine, finches, buntings.
Other: Druridge Canal is particularly good for wide range of aquatic plants & animals. Noctule, Daubenton's & Pipistrelle bats regularly recorded. Water Vole, Pygmy Shrew & Brown Hare.
Directions: Sat nav: YO19 6FE (Bank Island). Six miles SE of York, stretching 12 miles S along River Derwent from Newton-on-Derwent to Wressle & along Pocklington Canal. Three main access points: Bank Island (SE 691 448), North Duffield Carrs (SE 697 367) & Wheldrake Ings YWT (SE 691 444 - see site 9).
Public transport: Buses (not Sun) - no.18 York to Wheldrake/North Duffield. East Yorkshire Motor Services, (Busline: T: 01482 592 929). No.36 York to Wheldrake. Pullman (T: 01904 622 992).
Visiting: Open all year. Car parks at all sites, bike stands Bank Island & North Duffield Carrs. Bank Island - RADAR key toilets, two hides, viewing tower, sightings board. North Duffield Carrs - two hides, wheelchair access. Thorganby - viewing platform. No dogs.
Contact: Natural England, T: 07917 088 021;
E: craig.ralston@naturalengland.org.uk

6. NORTH CAVE WETLANDS

Yorkshire Wildlife Trust.
Habitats: Former gravel pits converted into various lagoons for wetland birds, inc. reedbed, scrub & hedgerows, wet grassland. A developing site.
Birds: 200+ spp. Summer: Breeding spp. inc. Great Crested Grebe, Gadwall, Pochard, Common Tern, Sparrowhawk, Avocet, Little Ringed & Ringed Plover, Oystercatcher, Sedge Warbler & Reed Bunting. Large numbers of Sand Martins feed over reserve in summer. *Winter:* wildfowl & waders inc. Golden Plover, Dunlin, Ruff & Redshank. Tree Sparrow.
Other: Water Vole, dragonflies, several butterfly spp. inc. small colony of Brown Argus.
Directions: Sat nav: HU15 2LY. SE 886 328. NW of North Cave village, approx 10 miles W of Hull. From Junc 28 of M62, follow signs to North Cave on B1230. In village, turn L & follow road to next crossroads, then go L, & park in Dryham Lane.
Public transport: Bus - nos.X55 (not Sun), 155 to North Cave from Hull/Goole. East Yorkshire Motor Services, (Busline: T: 01482 592 929).
Visiting: Open all year, car park 7.30am to dusk, toilet on site. Wild Bird Cafe (mobile trailer, Wed-Sun, 7.15am-1.15pm) on Dryham Lane, adjacent to reserve. Part of circular footpath is suitable for all abilities, five hides, four wheelchair accessible. No dogs.
Contact: Yorkshire WT - see site 3.

7. SPURN NNR

Yorkshire Wildlife Trust.
Habitats: Sand dunes with marram & sea buckthorn scrub. Mudflats around Humber Estuary.
Birds: *Spring:* Many migrants on passage, inc. scarce spp. inc. Red-backed Shrike, Bluethroat. *Summer:* Little Terns feed offshore. *Autumn:* Passage migrants & rarities inc. Wryneck, Pallas's Warbler. *Winter:* Large numbers of waders, Shelduck, Brent Goose, Merlin, Peregrine, Snow Bunting.
Other: Unique habitats & geographical position makes Spurn an interesting site for butterflies (25 spp.) & moths.
Directions: Sat nav: HU12 0UH. TA 419 149. 26 miles from Hull. Take A1033 from Hull to Patrington then R on B1445 to Easington & continue along minor road to Kilnsea. Turn R at crossroads towards Spurn Discovery Centre.
Public transport: None.
Visiting: Open all year - inclement weather may result in reserve being closed. Pay-&-display car park (open dawn-dusk) on approach road to reserve, opposite Spurn Discovery Centre (members & Easington parish residents/with permit free). Coaches - book in advance. Centre open 9am-6pm (cafe 10am-5pm), toilets, shop. Cycle hire. Hides. Limited access for dogs.
Contact: Spurn Discovery Centre, Spurn Road, Kilnsea, Hull, HU12 0UH. T: 01964 650 144;
E: spurn@ywt.org.uk

8. TOPHILL LOW NATURE RESERVE

Yorkshire Water.
Habitats: Open water (two reservoirs), marshes, wet grassland, wader scrapes, woodland & thorn scrub.
Birds: 270 spp., 160 spp. annually. *Spring/early summer:* Hirundines, Black Tern & Black-necked Grebe. Breeding Little Ringed Plover, Common Tern, Kingfisher & Barn Owl with variety of warblers. *Late summer/autumn:* Up to 20 spp. of passage wader. *Winter:* wildfowl, one of UK's largest Black-headed & Common Gull roosts. Regular Bittern & Smew. Feeding station - Marsh & Willow Tit.
Other: 400+ spp. flora, 365+ spp. fungi, 16 spp. odonata inc. Hairy Hawker. Grass Snake, Otter, Water Vole, Great Crested Newt & Roe Deer.
Directions: Sat nav: YO25 9RH. TA 071 482. Located SE of Driffield & signposted (four miles) from A164 at Watton.
Public transport: None.
Visiting: Open daily (9am-6pm), other times by reserve membership only. Entrance fee, concessions available - from car park ticket machine. Coaches welcome. Toilets (inc. disabled) open daily. 12 hides (seven with wheelchair access), paths (disabled access), sightings board. No dogs.
Contact: Warden, Tophill Low NR, Watton Carrs, Hutton Cranswick, Driffield, East Yorkshire YO25 9RH. T: 01377 270 690;
E: richard.hampshire@yorkshirewater.co.uk;
W: www.tophilllow.blogspot.com

9. WELDRAKE INGS

Yorkshire Wildlife Trust.
Habitats: Flooded meadows & pools, riverside vegetation.
Birds: *All year:* Kingfisher, Little & Barn Owl. *Spring passage:* Garganey, Little Gull, terns & Wheatear. *Summer:* Breeding waders, plus Turtle Dove, Yellow Wagtail, hirundines & migrant warblers. *Autumn:* Passage waders, Hobby & wildlfowl. *Winter:* large numbers wildfowl, inc. Shelduck, Pintail & Goldeneye among commoner species. Hen Harrier, Whooper & Bewick's Swans, Little Egret.
Other: Internationally important community of meadow plants. Brown Hare.
Directions: Sat nav: YO19 6AX. SE 690 446. Eight miles SE York, four miles E of A19. From York by-pass (A64) head S on A19 towards Selby for 1.2 miles, then turn L on Wheldrake Lane. Drive through Wheldrake village & turn sharp R to reach Natural England's Bank Island car park. Alternatively continue another 250 yards, just past the water compound to Ings Lane on L - park on stoney area next to bridge over river (can be flooded).
Public transport: See site 5.
Visiting: Open all times. Paths (inc. link between car parks), hides (not suitable for wheelchairs). No dogs.
Contact: Yorkshire WT - see site 3.

Yorkshire (North)

Seawatching in autumn from Filey Brigg can produce a range of skuas & shearwaters, with divers & grebes becoming more noticeable as the season progresses. The North York Moors hold breeding waders, chats, raptors & Red Grouse. The Lower Derwent Valley has great birding throughout the year.

1. COATHAM MARSH

Tata Steel/Tees Valley Wildlife Trust.
Habitats: 54ha, freshwater pools, lakes, reedswamp.
Birds: *Spring/autumn*: Wader passage (inc. Greenshank & Wood Sandpiper). *Summer*: Passerines (inc. Sedge Warbler, Yellow Wagtail). *Winter*: Large numbers of common ducks (plus Smew). *Occasional*: Water Rail, Great White Egret, Avocet, Bearded Tit & Bittern.
Other: Lime-rich soil good for wildflowers, inc. Northern Marsh Orchid. Insects inc. Migrant Hawker dragonfly.
Directions: Sat nav: TS10 5BQ. NZ 586 247. Located on W edge of Redcar, off A1085. At crossroads with Kirkleatham Lane, turn L continue over railway bridge to next mini roundabout. Turn L onto York Road/Tod Point Road. Reserve is on L.
Public transport: Bus - nos. X3/X3A (not Sun), X4, 62/62A Redcar to Middlesbrough stop in Coatham, 0.5 mile from reserve. Arriva Durham County. Train - Redcar Central station one mile from reserve.
Visiting: Open dawn-dusk. Keep to permissive footpaths only, section along The Fleet prone to winter flooding. Nearest toilets on Redcar seafront.
Contact: Tees Valley WT, T: 01287 636 382;
E: info@teeswildlife.org

2. FILEY BIRD OBSERVATORY & GROUP

FBOG/Yorkshire Wildlife Trust (The Dams).
Habitats: Five reserves owned/managed in area inc. wetland, woodland, scrub - attractive to migrants.
Birds: The Dams: Breeding & wintering water birds, breeding Sedge Warbler, Reed Warbler & Tree Sparrow.
The Tip: Important for breeding Skylark, Meadow Pipit, common warblers & Grey Partridge. *Winter:* Buntings, inc. Lapland. **Seawatching Hide:** *(Jul-Oct)* All four skuas, shearwaters, terns. *Winter:* Divers & grebes.
Parish Wood: Common woodland residents & summer migrants inc. Grasshopper Warbler, Lesser Whitethroat. Scarce/rare migrants possible at all sites.
Directions: The Observatory recording area lies between coast & A165, centred around Filey town in N & as far as Reighton in S.
Filey Dams & East Lea: Sat nav: YO14 0DG. TA 106 807.
The Old Tip: Sat nav: YO14 9NU. TA 112 818.
Parish Wood: Sat nav: YO14 9NU. TA 112 815.
Rocket Pole Field: Sat nav: YO14 9ES. TA 121 818.

Public transport: Filey bus & train stations are within walking distance (one mile) from each site.
Visiting: Open at all times. Park at end of Wharfedale Road (Dams/East Lea), Sycamore Avenue (Parish Wood/The Old Tip) or North Cliff Country Park (Rocket Pole Field & Filey Brigg). Toilets in Country Park (Apr-Oct) & town centre. Two open-access hides at The Dams (wheelchair access to Main Hide), one hide on The Brigg (for FBOG members only). Nature trails at The Dams, Parish Wood/Old Tip. Cliff top walk for seabirds along Cleveland Way. Dogs only in Parish Wood & The Old Tip (on lead). Events held.
Contact: Bird Observatory,
E: membership.fbog@gmail.com; W: www.fbog.co.uk; Yorkshire WT, T: 01904 659 570; E: info@ywt.org.uk

3. FYLINGDALES MOOR CONSERVATION AREA

Strickland Estate/Fylingdales Moor ESS Co Ltd.
Habitats: Heather moorland (former grouse moor), with scattered trees, wooded valleys & gulleys. Now managed for wildlife & archaeological remains.
Birds: 80+ common spp. inc. Kestrel, Lapwing, Snipe, Cuckoo, Meadow Pipit, Grey Wagtail & Wood Warbler. Peregrine regular. Scarce breeding spp. inc. Hen Harrier, Merlin, Golden Plover, Red Grouse, Curlew, Wheatear, Stonechat, Whinchat, Skylark, Marsh & Willow Tit, Linnet, Bullfinch, Reed Bunting & Yellowhammer.
Other: Otter, Roe Deer, Brown Hare, stoat, Weasel & Badger, important for Water Vole. Three spp. heather, plus Cranberry, Cowberry, Moonwort and, in wetter parts, Bog Myrtle, Lesser Twayblade, Bog Asphodel, Butterwort, Marsh Helleborine & sundews. Rare orchids & sedges. Insect spp. inc. Large Heath & Small Pearl-bordered Fritillary butterflies & Emperor Moth.
Directions: Sat nav: YO22 4US. NZ 945 002 (Jugger Howe lay-by). Conservation area covers 2,750ha within National Park off A171 S of Whitby, stretching between Sneaton High Moor (Newton House Plantation) & coast at Ravenscar.
Public transport: Bus - no.X93 between Scarborough & Whitby, nearest stop at Flask Inn (approx one mile N of Jugger Howe lay-by).
Arriva North East,
(T: 0344 800 4411).
Visiting: Open access. Parking (inc. coaches) available at Jugger Howe lay-by on A171. Numerous footpaths inc. Jugger Howe Nature Trail, Lyke Wake Walk & Robin Hood's Bay Road.
Contact: None.

4. MALHAM TARN

National Trust.
Habitats: Upland pasture, woodland, lake (highest in England), limestone outcrops.
Birds: *All year:* Waterfowl inc, Great Crested Grebe, regular gull spp., Peregrine, Barn Owl. *Spring/Summer:* Oystercatcher, Lapwing, Redshank, Curlew, Redstart, warblers, Twite. *Winter:* Wildfowl (inc. Goldeneye, Pochard, Goosander), Woodcock, Water Rail, winter thrushes, Redpoll, Siskin. Occasional: harriers, Osprey on passage, Whooper Swan & Short-eared Owl (winter).
Other: Water Vole.
Directions: Sat nav: BD24 9PU. SD 894 658 (parking S side of lake). BD24 9PT. SD 882 671 (parking N side of lake/woodland. Five miles NE of Settle, two miles NW of Malham.
Public transport: Bus - irregular & seasonal Skipton to Malham.
Visiting: Open at all times, Various walks in the area, graded easy to difficult, inc. tramper route & circular walk (4.5 miles). No dogs in nature reserve. Nearest facilities in Malham, inc. National Park Centre. Malham Cove one mile N of village for limestone outcrop/Peregrine.
Contact: National Trust, T: 01729 830 416;
E: malhamtarn@nationaltrust.org.uk

5. NOSTERFIELD LNR

Lower Ure Conservation Trust.
Habitats: Wetland grassland & open water, magnesium limestone grassland, gravel banks, hedgerows & scrub.
Birds: 150 spp. annually, 225+ spp. overall. *Spring/autumn:* Up to 30 wader spp. annually, terns. *Summer:* Breeding spp. inc. Redshank, Lapwing, Avocet, Oystercatcher, Curlew, Ringed Plover, Mediterranean Gull, Shoveler, Gadwall, Barn Owl, Skylark, Lesser Whitethroat, Tree Sparrow, Linnet, Reed Bunting. *Autumn:* Passage waders inc. regular Pectoral Sandpiper.

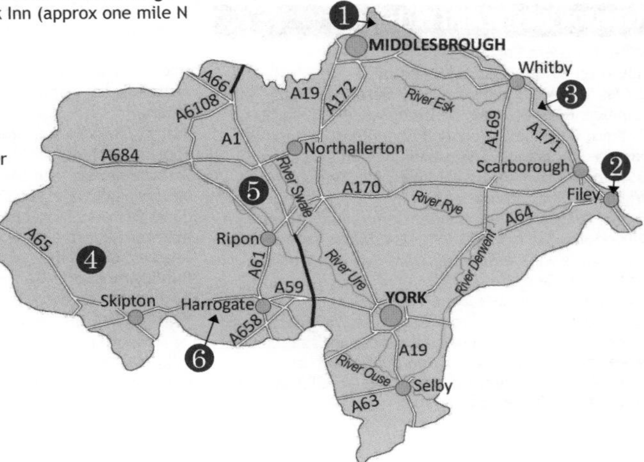

Winter: Wildfowl (Wigeon, Teal, Greylag & rarer geese), waders (Golden Plover, Lapwing, Curlew) & Peregrine.
Other: Specialist grassland & wetland flora, inc. seven spp. orchid, Mudwort, Yellow Rattle, Golden Dock. Butterflies inc. White-letter Hairstreak, Brown Argus, Wall & large colony of Common Blue. Dragonflies inc. Emperor, Black-tailed skimmer, Red-veined Darter (has bred). 480+ spp. moths. Brown Hare & Water Shrew.
Directions: Sat nav: DL8 2QZ. SE 278 795. Six miles N of Ripon, between West Tanfield & Nosterfield E of A6108 (Ripon to Masham road) & approx four miles W of A1.
Public transport: Bus - no.159 (Mon-Sat) from Ripon to Masham, alight at West Tanfield (0.5 mile walk to reserve). Proctors Coaches (T: 01677 425 203).
Visiting: Open all year. Lower viewing area beyond car park allows viewing from cars only. Coaches, book in advance. Footpath (approx one mile) is wheelchair-friendly. Two disabled-friendly hides, interpretation panels (main hide).
Contact: Warden, E: simon.warwick@luct.org.uk; T: 01765 602 832; W: www.luct.org.uk

6. TIMBLE INGS

Yorkshire Water.
Habitats: Upland woodlands of pine, larch & spruce & nearby reservoirs (Fewston/Swinsty). SW corner of wood a good place to observe visible migration in autumn.
Birds: Bradford Ornithological Group spp. list stands at 134. Yorkshire Water habitat management makes site attractive to Long-eared & Tawny Owls, Nightjar & Tree Pipit. Buzzard breed & Red Kite regular but Goshawk numbers in decline. *Summer:* Breeding species inc. Redpoll, Siskin, Crossbill, Woodcock, Redstart & Grasshopper Warbler. Short-eared Owl hunt adjacent moorland. *Winter:* Fieldfare, Redwing, Brambling, occasional Waxwing & Hawfinch.
Other: Roe Deer, Badger, Brown Hare, shrew, vole & mouse spp. (all detected from owl pellets). Ponds attractive to amphibians & dragonflies, inc. Broad-bodied Chaser, Emperor & Black Darter.
Directions: Sat nav: LS21 2PP. SE 170 542 (parking opposite Anchor Farm). W of Harrogate, N of Otley, off A59 S of Blubberhouses, near Timble village.
Public transport: None.
Visiting: Open at all times, hard forest tracks. Toilets, cafes, pubs, coach parking nearby.
Contact: Recreation Officer, Yorkshire Water, E: Geoff.D.Lomas@yorkshirewater.co.uk

Yorkshire (South & West)

Found in the heart of the industrial north, dominated by a large number of towns, the area still manages to offer birdwatchers a surprising number of interesting sites. There are a large number of water meadows & marshes (ings), many the result of the areas industrial past. Sites such as RSPB Fairburn Ings (next to the A1), Potteric Carr, RSPB Old Moor reserve & Bolton Ings all have a year-round birding interest.

1. BOLTON INGS (DEARNE VALLEY)

RSPB (Northern England).
Habitats: 43 ha, reedbed & scrub.
Birds: *All year:* Kingfisher, Grey Heron. *Spring/summer:* Reed Bunting. breeding waders & warblers, Cuckoo, Garganey. Avocets & Spoonbills. *Autumn:* Passage waders inc.Greenshank, Green Sandpiper, Golden Plover. *Winter:* Wildfowl, inc. Goosander, Wigeon & Teal, Stonechat.
Other: Dragonflies inc. Banded Demoiselle, Brown Hare.
Directions: Sat nav: S73 0YF. SE 425 020. Park at RSPB Old Moor & walk east along Trans-Pennine Trail to Bolton Ings. See site 6.
Public transport: See site 6 (Old Moor).
Visiting: Open all year round. Dearne Way footpath & Trans-Pennine Trail open at all times, not suitable for wheelchair users. Dogs only on public footpaths. Cormorant View hide. More facilities at RSPB Old Moor.
Contact: RSPB - see site 6.

2. DENABY INGS

Yorkshire Wildlife Trust.
Habitats: Riverside meadows, hay meadows, open water, deciduous woodland, marsh, willows.
Birds: *All year:* common woodland birds, 3 spp. woodpecker, possible Willow Tit, Corn Bunting, Yellowhammer. *Spring/summer:* Waterfowl, Kingfisher, Barn & Tawny Owls, Sand Martin, Swallow, Whinchat, Grasshopper Warbler, Lesser Whitethroat, Whitethroat, other warblers *Passage:* waders, Common, Arctic & Black Terns, Redstart, Wheatear. *Winter:* Wildfowl (inc. Whooper Swan & Goosander), Jack Snipe & other waders, Grey Wagtail, Fieldfare, Redwing, Brambling, Siskin.
Other: Grass Snake, Bee, Pyramidal & Common Spotted Orchids.
Directions: Sat nav: S64 0JJ. SE 496 008. NE of Mexborough. Take A6023 from Mexborough, turn L down Pastures Road on outskirts of town. After one mile turn R into car park (shortly after crossing River Dearne). Climb flight of concrete steps to enter reserve.
Public transport: Train - Conisbrough or Mexborough, 30 mins to reserve.
Visiting: Open all year. Car park, interpretation panels, two hides/one viewing screen, circular trail. Dogs on leads.
Contact: Yorkshire WT, T: 01904 659 570; E: info@ywt.org.uk

3. FAIRBURN INGS

RSPB (Northern England).
Habitats: Open water, wet grassland, marshand fen scrub, reedbed, reclaimed colliery spoil heaps.
Birds: *All year:* Kingfisher, Green Woodpecker, Tree Sparrow, Willow Tit, Bullfinch. *Spring:* Osprey, Little Gull, Wheatear, five spp. tern inc. annual Black Tern, Garganey, Little Ringed Plover. *Summer:* Nine spp. breeding warbler, Grey Heron, Gadwall, Little Ringed Plover. *Autumn:* Thousands of waders on passage inc Green Sandpiper, Little Ringed Plover & Black-tailed Godwit. *Winter*: Smew, Goldeneye, Goosander, Wigeon, Peregrine.
Other: Brown Hare, Harvest Mouse, Roe Deer, Leisler's & Daubenton's Bats, 28 spp. butterflies & 20 spp. dragonflies.
Directions: Sat nav: WF10 2BH. SE 451 277. 12 miles from Leeds, six miles from Pontefract, three miles from Castleford. Next to A1246 from Junc 42 of A1.
Public transport: Bus - no.493 from Pontefract to Fairburn (Mon-Sat). Arriva in Yorkshire. Train - Castleford, three miles.
Visiting: Open daily (not Dec 25/26). Car parking (inc. coaches) 9.30am-8pm Feb-Oct, 9.30am-4pm Nov-Jan - charge for non-members (after 30 mins), free for disabled badge holders. Visitor centre/shop open 9am-5pm Mar-Oct, 9am-4pm Nov-Feb. Hot/cold drinks & snacks available. Toilets inc. disabled & baby-changing facilities. Wildlife garden, pond-dipping & mini beast areas, duck feeding platform. Boardwalks leading to Pickup Pool, feeding station & Kingfisher viewpoint are wheelchair-friendly. Four hides/four shelters, two public trails (one accessible to wheelchairs). Mobility Scoter available - call to book. Dogs on leads.
Contact: RSPB, T: 01977 628 191; E: fairburnings@rspb.org.uk

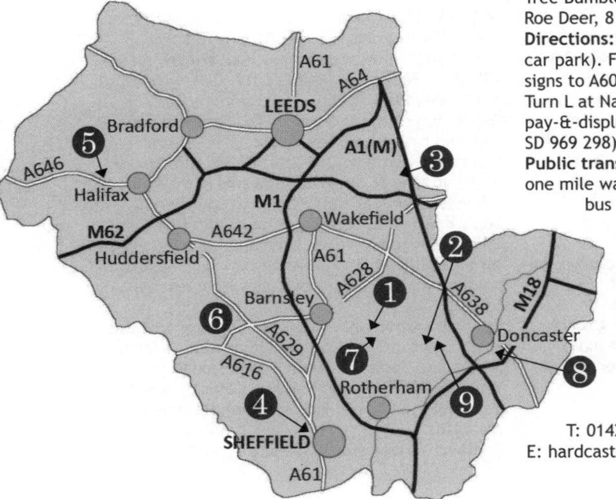

4. GRENO WOODS

Sheffield & Rotherham Wildlife Trust.
Habitats: 170ha, ancient woodland, some heathland.
Birds: Inc. wider area - *All year:* Common woodland spp., Tawny Owl, Willow Tit, Crossbill. *Summer:* Woodcock, Nightjar, Cuckoo, warblers inc. Whitethroat & Willow Warbler, Tree Pipit. *Winter:* Winter thrushes, Stonechat, Redpoll.
Other: woodland plants inc. Bluebells & Cow Wheat.
Directions: Sat nav: S35 7DS. SK 325 949. Lies on N outskirts of Sheffield (adjacent to Wharncliffe & Wheata Woods - covering total area of 700ha). Head N from Shefield on A61 (Penistone Road) until it becomes Halifax Road, then turn L into Foxhill Road - continue on to Main Street & then on to Woodhead Road. After one mile, Forestry England car park is on L. Most of wood lies between Woodhead Road & A61.
Public transport: Bus - no.85 runs from Sheffield city centre to Grenoside village. No.86 run along the A61 with stops adjacent to reserve. Stagecoach.
Visiting: Open all times. Network of footpaths & bridleways - also three downhill mountain bike trails.
Contact: Sheffield & Rotherham Wildlife Trust, T: 0114 263 4335; E: mail@wildsheffield.com

5. HARDCASTLE CRAGS

National Trust.
Habitats: 160ha, unspoilt wooded valleys, ravines, streams, hay meadows & moorland edge.
Birds: *All year*: Sparrowhawk, Kestrel, Tawny, Barn & Little Owls, Green & Great Spotted Woodpeckers, Dipper, Grey Wagtail, Jay other woodland species. Goshawk in Crimsworth Dean. *Spring/summer*: Cuckoo, Redstart, Lesser Whitethroat, Garden Warbler, Blackcap, Wood Warbler, Chiffchaff, Spotted & Pied Flycatchers.
Other: Northern Hairy Wood Ant, Moss Carder Bee, Tree Bumblebee, Killarney Fern, Brittle Bladder Fern, Roe Deer, 8 spp. bat.
Directions: Sat nav: HX7 7AL. SD 988 291 (Midgehole car park). From Hebden Bridge follow National Trust signs to A6033 Keighley Road. Follow for 0.75 mile. Turn L at National Trust sign to car parks. Alternate pay-&-display car park at Clough Hole (HX7 7AZ. SD 969 298)) on Widdop Road, Heptonstall.
Public transport: Bus/train - to Hebden Bridge, then one mile walk to Midgehole. Sat/Sun & bank holidays bus (approx. May-Oct)- no.906 Widdop Reservoir-Hardcastle Crags-Hebden Bridge. TLC Travel (T: 0113 245 7676).
Visiting: Open all year. Two small car parks, NT car park charges - free for members & disabled badge holders. Cycle racks, several way-marked trails. Gibson Mill visitor centre has toilets, cafe, exhibitions & limited disabled parking (pre-book). Dogs under control.
Contact: National Trust, Hardcastle Crags, T: 01422 846 236; E: hardcastlecrags@nationaltrust.org.uk

6. INGBIRCHWORTH RESERVOIR

Yorkshire Water.
Habitats: Reservoir, small strip deciduous woodland.
Birds: *Spring/summer*: Whinchat, warblers, woodland birds, House Martin. *Spring/autumn passage*: Little Ringed Plover, Ringed Plover, Dotterel, other waders, Common Tern, Arctic Tern, Black Tern, Yellow Wagtail, Wheatear. *Winter*: Wildfowl, Golden Plover, waders, occasional rare gull such as Iceland or Glaucous, Grey Wagtail, Fieldfare, Redwing, Brambling, Redpoll.
Other: Woodland wildflowers, inc. Bluebells.
Directions: Sat nav: S36 7GS. SE 217 062. Leave M1 at Junc 37 & take A628 towards Manchester. After five miles turn R at roundabout onto A629 Huddersfield road. Drive 2.5 miles to Ingbirchworth. Turn L into Wellthorne Lane (signed to 'Inn'). Park on roadside just past The Fountain Inn, continue on foot to where road bears L (to cross the dam), go straight forward here onto track which follow N edge of reservoir. Can also walk across dam & onto a footpath through narrow strip of woodland at end of dam.
Public transport: Bus - no.24 Barnsley to Ingbirchworth (Mon-Sat). Stagecoach.
Visiting: Open all year. Car park, picnic tables. One of few reservoirs in area with footpath access.
Contact: Recreation Officer, Yorkshire Water, E: Geoff.D.Lomas@yorkshirewater.co.uk

7. OLD MOOR (DEARNE VALLEY)

RSPB (Northern England).
Habitats: Lakes & flood meadows, wader scrape & reedbeds.
Birds: *All year:* Kingfisher, Barn & Little Owl.s *Summer:* Breeding Bittern, Sand Martin waders, inc. Little Ringed Plover & drumming Snipe, migrant warblers & wildfowl. *Autumn:* passage waders. *Winter:* Large numbers of wildfowl, spectacular flocks of Lapwing & Golden Plover (up to 8,000 birds), Peregrine, Tree Sparrow (in garden feeding area).
Other: Water Vole, Brown Hare, Weasel, Pygmy Shrew, wildflowers inc. orchids & Adders Tongue Fern.
Directions: Sat nav: S73 0YF. SE 422 022. Old Moor is just off Manvers Way (A633). From M1, take Junc 36 & take A61. At next roundabout follow Old Moor signs for ca four miles. From A1M, take Junc 37 & follow A635 towards Barnsley, then follow RSPB Old Moor signs.
Public transport: Bus - no.X20 to Old Moor reserve from Barnsley-Doncaster (not Sun). Stagecoach (T: 01709 515 151). Train - Wombwell & Swinton stations approx three miles from reserve.
Visiting: Open until 8pm Apr-Oct. Entrance charge, for non-members. Visitor centre open daily (not Dec 25/26) 9.30am-5pm . Cafe open 9.30am-3.00pm. Shop, accessible toilets, education & meeting rooms, mobility scooter for hire. Two trails with ten hides/ viewing screens - suitable for wheelchair users. Guide dogs only.
Contact: RSPB, T: 01226 751 593; E: old.moor@rspb.org.uk

8. POTTERIC CARR

Yorkshire Wildlife Trust.
Habitats: Flood plain of River Tome, with reed fen, subsidence ponds, artificial pools, grassland, woodland.
Birds: 230 spp. 102 spp. have bred - waterfowl (inc. Shoveler, Gadwall, Pochard, Water Rail, Kingfisher, 3 spp.woodpecker, Lesser Whitethroat, Reed & Sedge Warblers, Willow Tit. *Passage/winter*: Bittern, Marsh Harrier, Black Tern, wildfowl & waders.
Other: 21 spp. dragonflies, 28 spp. butterflies inc. Purple Hairstreak & Dingy Skipper. Palmate & Great Crested Newt. Common Spotted & Bee Orchids.
Directions: Sat nav: DN4 8DB. SE 588 005. From M18, Junc 3 take A6182 (Doncaster) & at first roundabout turn R. Entrance & car park are on R after 50 yards.
Public transport: Bus - nos.72 & 73 from Doncaster Interchange, alight at B&Q on Woodfield Way. Cross White Rose Way, walk down Mallard Way. Cross car park to reserve entrance in Sedum House. First South Yorkshire. Train - Doncaster.
Visiting: Open daily (not Dec 24-27) 9am-5pm. Car park locked at 5pm but ask (before 5pm) if you would like to stay later. Visitor centre/cafe/shop free, non-members entrance fee to reserve. Groups of ten or more should book in advance. Cafe open daily (9am-4pm). Toilets at entrance reception, in cafe & outside. Around five miles of paths (3.2 miles accessible to wheelchairs, unassisted), 14 viewing hides (10 suitable for disabled). Guide dogs only.
Contact: Potteric Carr Nature Reserve, T: 01302 325 736; E: potteric.carr@ywt.org.uk

9. SPOTBOROUGH FLASH & DON GORGE

Yorkshire Wildlife Trust.
Habitats: Limestone gorge, limestone grassland on plateau, woodland, wetland & open water.
Birds: *Spring/autumn passage:* waders inc. Little Ringed Plover, Dunlin, Greenshank, Green Sandpiper, Yellow Wagtail. *Summer:* Hirundines, Whitethroat, Lesser Whitethroat, Garden Warbler, Blackcap, Chiffchaff, Willow Warbler, Cuckoo. *Winter/all year:* Wildfowl, Water Rail, Snipe, Little Owl, Tawny Owl, 3 spp. woodpecker, thrushes, Siskin.
Other: Brown Hare, Grass Snake, flora inc. Cowslip, common twayblade, bee orchid.
Directions: Sat nav: DN5 7NB. SE 537 015. Leave A1(M) at Junc 36 onto A630 towards Rotherham. After 0.5 mile, turn R at traffic lights to Sprotborough. After approx two miles road drops down into Don Gorge. Cross a bridge over river, then another over a canal, turn immediately L. Public car park on L next to toll house in Nursery Lane - two mins from reserve along towpath.
Public transport: Bus - no.219 Doncaster to Barnsley, alight Sprotbrough village (10 mins walk to reserve). Stagecoach Yorkshire. Train - Conisbrough (two miles).
Visiting: Open all year. Two hides along towpath, accessible to wheelchairs, interpretation panels, footpaths.
Contact: Yorkshire WT - see site 2.

South East England

Berkshire, Buckinghamshire, Hampshire, Kent, London (Greater), Surrey, Sussex (East), Sussex (West)

Berkshire

Despite being close to London, & with the M4 running through its centre, the county has a decent range of habitats. These include heathland & downland but it is the gravel pits that attract the widest range of bird species & where wintering Smew & Goosander can be regular visitors.

1. DINTON PASTURES

Wokingham Borough Council.
Habitats: 135ha, woodland, meadow & lakes on banks of River Loddon. Sandford Lake managed for wildfowl, Lavell's Lake (see site 3) best for waders & scrub species.
Birds: *All year:* Kingfisher, Water Rail, Barn Owl. *Spring/summer*: Hobby, Little Ringed Plover, Common Tern, Nightingale, common warblers. *Winter*: Bittern, wildfowl (inc. Goldeneye, Wigeon, Teal, Gadwall), thrushes. Waders inc. Green & Common Sandpipers, Snipe, Redshank.
Other: Water Vole, Harvest Mouse, Great Crested Newt, Loddon Pondweed & Loddon Lily. 18 spp. dragonflies inc. Emperor, Black-tailed Skimmer, Migrant Hawker, White-legged Damselfly & Banded Demoiselle.
Directions: Sat nav: RG10 0TH. SU 784 718. From Junc 10 of M4 head towards Reading, then follow sign to Winnersh on A329. Park is signposted off B3030 between Hurst & Winnersh.
Public transport: Bus - nos.127/128/129 between Reading & Wokingham stop near main entrance, Courtney Bus (T: 0118 973 3486). Train - Winnersh station is 15 mins walk.
Visiting: Open all year, dawn-dusk. Car park charges apply 6am-10pm daily. Information centre, cafe open daily 8.30am-5pm (4pm in winter), toilets (suitable for wheelchairs). Various trails between one & three miles, one hide (overlooking Sandford Lake). Electric buggies for hire, walks leaflet. Dogs allowed.
Contact: Dinton Pastures Country Park, T: 0118 974 2016; E: countryside@wokingham.gov.uk; W: www.dinton-pastures.co.uk

2. LAVELL'S LAKE

Wokingham Borough Council/Lavell's Wetland Trust.
Habitats: 10 ha, composed of gravel pits, two wader scrapes, reed beds, rough grassland, marshy area, sand martin banks, between River Loddon & Emm Brook. To N of Lavell's Lake, gravel pits are being restored to attract birds. The lake at Lea Farm is viewable walking N along the River Loddon from Lavell's Lake over small green bridge - on R & can be seen through a viewing screen & members only hide for members of Lavell's Wetland Trust - no access.
Birds: *All year*: Great Crested Grebe, Gadwall, Sparrowhawk, Kingfisher, Red Kite, Buzzard, Cetti's Warbler. *Summer:* Common Tern, Redshank, Lapwing, Hobby, warblers inc. Reed, Sedge, Whitethroat. *Passage*: Garganey, Little Ringed Plover, Common & Green Sandpiper & Greenshank. *Winter:* Water Rail, Bittern, Little Egret, Teal, Shoveler, Pochard, Goldeneye, occasional Smew & Goosander. Along River Loddon - Siskin, Lesser Redpoll, Fieldfare & Redwing.
Directions: Sat nav: RG10 0SU. SU 785 727. Parking on Sandford Lane off B3030 between Hurst & Winnersh, E of Reading or walk from Dinton Pastures, see site 1.
Public transport: See site 1.
Visiting: Open dawn-dusk. Car park open 9am-5pm, three hides, one with disabled access, Lea Farm hide open to LWT members only. Dogs on leads at all times.
Contact: Dinton Pastures Country Park - see site 1.
W: www.lavells.org.uk/

3. MOOR GREEN LAKES

Lakes Group Moor Green/Blackwater Valley Countryside Partnership.
Habitats: 36ha, three lakes with gravel islands, beaches & scrapes. River Blackwater, grassland, surrounded by willow, ash, hazel & thorn hedgerows.

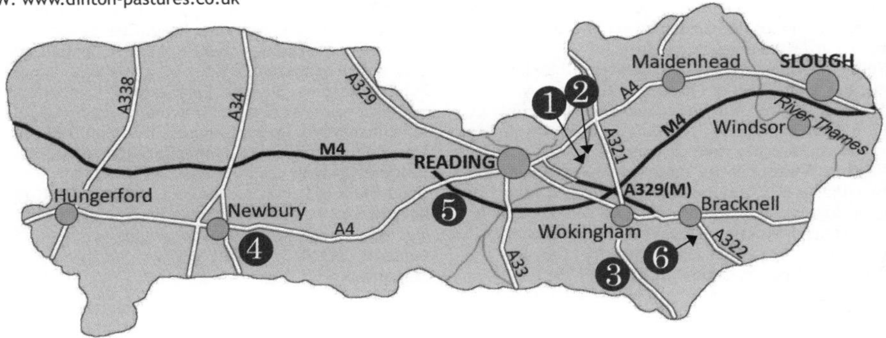

Birds: 200+ spp., 60 spp. regularly breeding. *Spring/summer:* Little Ringed Plover, Reed Warbler & Hobby. Whitethroat, Sedge Warbler, Common Sandpiper. Mandarin Duck, Common Tern & Barn Owl breed on site. Dunlin & Green Sandpiper on passage. *Winter:* Wigeon, Teal, Gadwall & of particular interest, a roost of Goosander on Grove Lake. Little Egret regular, Snipe, Lapwing & Green Sandpiper. Gull roost on adjacent Manor Farm workings inc. up to 1,000 Lesser Black-backed.
Other: 31 spp. butterflies & 15 spp. dragonflies.
Directions: Sat nav: RG40 3TF. SU 805 628 (free car park in Lower Sandhurst Road, Finchampstead (open 8am-dusk). Alternatively use Horseshoe Lakes free car park in Mill Lane, Sandhurst (Sat nav: GU47 8JW, SU 820 620). Lies ca one mile NW of Sandhurst - take A321 N from Sandhurst, from High Street turn L along Lower Church Road. At T-junction turn L for Mill Road car park or R for Lower Sandhurst Road car park.
Public transport: Train - nearest stations, Crowthorne & Sandhurst - both a one mile walk .
Visiting: No access to lakes, view from footpaths bordering E, S & W sides - paths can be used by wheelchairs though surface not particularly suitable. Southern path forms part of Blackwater Valley long distance footpath. Two bird hides open to MGLG members, two public viewing screens. Feeding station viewable from bench on western path.
Contact: Moor Green Lakes Group,
E: via website; W: www.mglg.org.uk
Blackwater Valley Countryside Partnership,
T: 01252 331 353; E: blackwater.valley@hants.gov.uk;
W: www.blackwatervalleycountryside.wordpress.com/

4. NATURE DISCOVERY CENTRE & THATCHAM REEDBEDS

Berks, Bucks & Oxon Wildlife Trust.
Habitats: Lakes, reedbeds, scrub.
Birds: *All year:* Red Kite, Egyptian Goose, common wildfowl, Grey Heron, Great Crested & Little Grebe, Water Rail, Kingfisher, Cetti's Warbler, Reed Bunting. *Spring/summer:* Common Tern, hirundines, Reed & Sedge Warblers. *Winter:* Wildfowl inc Pochard, occasional Bittern.
Other: Moths inc. Garden Tiger, butterflies, & dragonflies inc. demoiselles, Desmoulin's Snail.
Directions: Sat nav: RG19 3FU. SU 506 672. E of Newbury: from A339, take A4 towards Thatcham. Turn R after 1.2 miles (signposted Lower Way & Centre) then R after 0.8 miles into Centre.
Public transport: Bus - no.1c Newbury-Thatcham circular, alight Derwent Road stop (Lower Way, Thatcham - short walk to centre. Newbury & District (T: 01635 33855) Train - Newbury & Thatcham stations - short walks to bus stops on route 1c.
Visiting: Visitor centre, shop, cafe open 10.30am-5pm (Apr-Oct) & 10.30am-4pm (Nov-Mar, closed Mon). Car park, toilets, waymarked trails (flat/level), picnic & play areas. Dogs under close control - keep out of lake. Small car park beyond centre for reedbeds.
Contact: Discovery Centre, T: 01635 874 381;
E: ndc@bbowt.org.uk

5. THEALE GRAVEL PITS

Theale Area Bird Conservation Group.
Habitats: Three complexes of various sized gravel pits spread out across Theale flood plain.
Birds: *Spring/summer:* Migrant warblers, breeding Nightingale & Common Tern, passage Arctic & Black Terns, large number of hirundines, resident Peregrine favours pylon area. *Autumn:* Dunlin, Common Sandpiper & other passage waders. Little Gull, Osprey, along with terns on passage. *Winter:* Large numbers of wildfowl, inc. Goldeneye & Goosander. Thousands of gulls on nearby Moatlands pit. Bittern sometimes recorded in Hosehill Lake LNR reedbed.
Other: Good variety of dragonflies & butterflies. Grass Vetchling worthy of note.
Directions: Sat nav: RG7 4GB. SU 646 699 (lay-by parking). Group of pits, S of Reading, situated between Juncs 11 & 12 of M4, immediately S of Theale town centre. From Theale town centre head S on Station Road/Hanger Road & park in lay-bys in Dean Copse Road, by Fox & Hounds Pub - main pit & Hosehill Lake LNR.
Public transport: Train - Theale station, short walk to nearest pits.
Visiting: Open all times. Parking for a few vehicles in lay-bys near Fox & Hounds pub. Tern rafts, Sand Martin bank & wildflower meadow in Hosehill Lake LNR, with information boards/benches on mile-long circular walk.
Contact: TABCC Sec, Cathy McEwan T: 01189 415 792;
E: tabcgsec@yahoo.com;
W: https://tabcg.webs.com/thealesites.htm

6. WILDMOOR HEATH

Berks, Bucks & Oxon Wildlife Trust.
Habitats: 91 ha, wet & dry lowland heath, bog, mixed woodland & mature Scots pine plantation.
Birds: *Spring/summer:* 55 spp. inc. Hobby, Nightjar, Woodlark, Tree Pipit, Stonechat, Dartford Warbler, Reed Bunting.
Other: 20 spp. dragonflies, Silver-studded Blue butterfly, Slow Worm, Adder, Grass Snake, Common Lizard, Roe Deer. Bog plants inc. sundews.
Directions: Sat nav: RG45 7PW. SU 838 630. Between Bracknell & Sandhurst. From Sandhurst shopping area, take A321 NW towards Wokingham. Turn R at mini-roundabout on to Crowthorne Road. Continue for about one mile through one set of traffic lights. Car park is on R at bottom of hill.
Public transport: Bus - no.194 Bracknell-Camberley runs past reserve car park (Crowthorne Road/ Sandhurst Road). Courtney Buses (T: 0118 973 3486). Train - Sandhurst station, one mile S of reserve.
Visiting: Open all year. Car park. No access to woodland N of Rackstraw Road at Broadmoor Bottom. Not suitable for wheelchairs due to slope of site & muddy, uneven terrain. Dogs on a lead.
Contact: BBOWT, T: 01628 829 574;
E: info@bbowt.org.uk

Buckinghamshire

Between the River Thames to the south & the River Ouse to the north, the county offers a good selection of woodlands, lakes & gravel pits. The higher ground of the Chiltern escarpment is an excellent place to watch Red Kites. Some interesting species breed in the county including Little Ringed Plover, Firecrest & Hawfinch.

1. BURNHAM BEECHES NNR

City of London Corporation.
Habitats: Ancient woodland, streams, pools, heathland (Stoke Common), grassland, scrub.
Birds: *All year*: Mandarin (good nos.), Sparrowhawk, 3 spp. woodpecker. *Spring/summer*: Cuckoo, possible Turtle Dove. *Winter*: Siskin, Crossbill, Brambling. Red Kite & Buzzard, possible Woodcock. Marsh & Willow Tits.
Other: Ancient Beech & Oak pollards with associated wildlife. Rich array of fungi.
Directions: Sat nav: SL2 3PS. SU 958 850. 2.5 miles N of Slough & on W side of A355, running between Junc 2 of M40 & Junc 6 of M4. Entry from A355 via Beeches Road. Also smaller parking areas in Hawthorn Lane & Pumpkin Hill to the S & Park Lane to the W.
Public transport: Bus - no.X74 Slough to Farnham Common. First Berkshire & Thames Valley. Train - Slough.
Visiting: Open all year (not Dec 25). Main Lord Mayor's Drive open 8am-dusk. Coach parking. Visitor centre, Beeches Cafe, public toilets & information point open 10am-5pm. Network of wheelchair accessible roads & paths, most start at Victory Cross. Motorised buggy available for hire.
Contact: Burnham Beeches Office, Hawthorn Lane, Farnham Common, SL2 3TE. T: 01753 647 358;
E: burnham.beeches@cityoflondon.gov.uk;
W: www.cityoflondon.gov.uk

2. CHURCH WOOD

RSPB (Midlands Regional Office).
Habitats: 14ha, mixed woodland.
Birds: *All year*: Common woodland spp., inc. Green & Great Spotted Woodpeckers, Nuthatch, Treecreeper. *Spring/summer*: Red Kite, Buzzard, Swallow, Blackcap, Garden Warbler. *Winter*: Winter thrushes, Redpoll, Siskin.
Other: Wood Anenome, Wood Sorrel, Bluebell & other woodland plants. Brimstone, Comma & White Admiral butterflies. Good range of fungi spp.
Directions: Sat nav: SL2 3UY. SU 971 872. Reserve lies three miles from Junc 2 of M40 in Hedgerley. Park in village, walk down small track to R of village pond for approx 200 yards. Reserve entrance is on L.
Public transport: Bus - no.583 (Mon-Sat) Slough to Hedgerley. Redline (T: 01296 426 786). Alternatively: bus - no.X74 Slough to Farnham Common (1.25 miles from reserve). First Berkshire & Thames Valley.
Visiting: Open at all times. One marked trail (1.25 miles) with some inclines, not suitable for wheelchairs. Keep dogs on leads (Apr-Jun).
Contact: RSPB, T: 01865 351 163;
E: admin.otmoor@rspb.org.uk

3. COLLEGE LAKE

Berks, Bucks & Oxon Wildlife Trust.
Habitats: Deep lake in former chalk pit, shallow pools, chalk & rough grasslands, woodlands, scrub.
Birds: *Spring/summer:* Breeding Lapwing, Redshank & Little Ringed Plover. Sand Martin, Hobby, Common Tern, Skylark & Shelduck. *Winter:* Wildfowl (Wigeon, Shoveler, Teal, Gadwall), waders inc. Snipe, Peregrine. Scarcer birds turn up regularly.
Other: Chalk grassland flowers. Arable Weed Project inc. displays of cornfield flowers in Jun/Jul. Butterflies inc. Small Blue & Green Hairstreak. 16 spp. dragonflies. Brown Hare.
Directions: Sat nav: HP23 5QG. SP 935 139. Two miles N of Tring on B488, 0.25 mile N of canal bridge at Bulbourne turn L into gated entrance. Marked with brown tourist signs.
Public transport: Train - Tring, two mile walk mostly on canal towpath.
Visiting: Open daily, 9.30am-5pm (4pm in winter). Large car park, coach park. Visitor centre/shop, toilets inc. disabled. Cafe open daily (not 24-31 Dec) 9.30am-4pm Feb-Oct & 10am-3pm Nov-Jan. Interactive interpretation, 10 hides (some with wheelchair access). Network of wheelchair-friendly trails. Electric tramper available, phone to book.
Contact: BBOWT, T: 01442 826 774;
E: collegelake@bbowt.org.uk

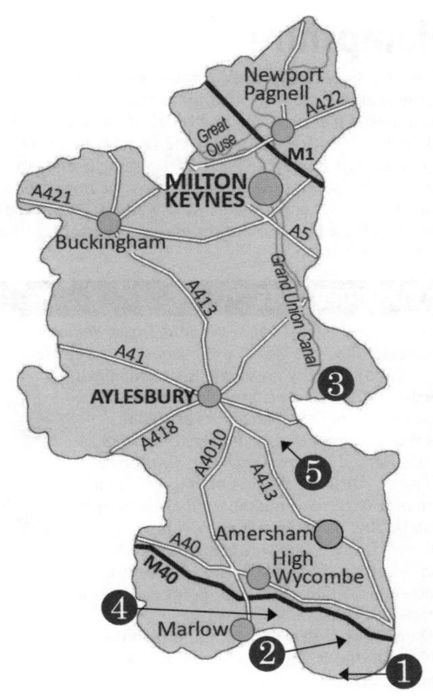

4. LITTLE MARLOW LAKES COUNTRY PARK

Lefarge Aggregates/private ownership.
Habitats: Gravel pit with sand spit (best viewed from west bank), lake, scrub.
Birds: *Spring*: Passage migrants inc. Whimbrel, Wheatear, Whinchat, Sand Martin, Garganey, Hobby. *Summer*: Reedbed warblers, Kingfisher, wildfowl. *Autumn:* Passage migrants. *Winter*: Wildfowl, possible Smew, Goldeneye, Water Rail, Yellow-legged Gull among large gull flocks, Lapwing, Snipe.
Directions: Sat nav: SL8 5PS. SU 884 877. NE of Marlow from Junc 4 of M40 tale A404 S to Marlow then turn L onto A4155 to Little Marlow. After ca 1.5 miles turn R into Coldmoorholme Lane - Spade Oak car park on R after pub. Use permissive path from Coldmoorholme Lane to Little Marlow village. Follow path over wooden bridge to N end of lake. Permissive path ends just past cottages where it joins a concrete road to sewage treatment works. Be careful at all times when walking round lake.
Public transport: Buses & trains to Bourne End (one mile walk to Coldmoorholme Lane, along riverside path).
Visiting: Open all year, permissive footpath. Do not enter gravel works & look out for heavy traffic when crossing site's entrance road.
Contact: Little Marlow Lakes Country Park,
E: littlemarlowlakescountrypark@hotmail.co.uk

5. WENDOVER WOODS

Forestry England.
Habitats: Large mixed woodland, largely coniferous with some broad-leaved & scrub.
Birds: Firecrest, Sparrowhawk, Buzzard, Goshawk, Red Kite, Woodcock, 3 spp. Woodpeckers, Hawfinch (rare), Crossbill, common woodland spp. *Summer:* Cuckoo, Tree Pipit, warblers. *Spring/autumn:* passage migrants. *Winter:* Siskin, Redpoll, Brambling, winter thrushes.
Other: Bluebell display. .
Directions: Sat nav: HP22 5NQ. SP 890 090. From Wendover (A413) take B4009 towards Tring, turn R ca. one mile N of RAF Halton, signposted Wendover Woods & St Leonards.
Public transport: Bus- nos.8/8A Aylesbury bus station to RAF Halton (ca 1.3 miles from visitor centre) - Arriva (Mon-Sat, T: 0344 800 4411)), Redline (Sun, T: 01296 426 786).
Train - Wendover.
Visiting: Open daily (not 25 Dec) 8.00am to dusk. Large car park - charges apply. Toilets, play area, cafe, walking & cycling trails, picnic area, wildlife hides, Firecrest Trail.
Contact: Forestry England, T: 01296 696 184:
E: wendoverwoods@forestryengland.uk

Hampshire

The New Forest dominates this huge county & holds many scarce breeding birds including Honey Buzzard, Goshawk, Firecrest, Hawfinch, Dartford Warbler & Nightjar, with Great Grey Shrike regular in winter. The marshes at Keyhaven & Farlington, & elsewhere around the Solent are the best sites for migrants as well as for wintering wildfowl & waders. Blashford Lakes holds a good selection of waterbirds including wintering Bittern.

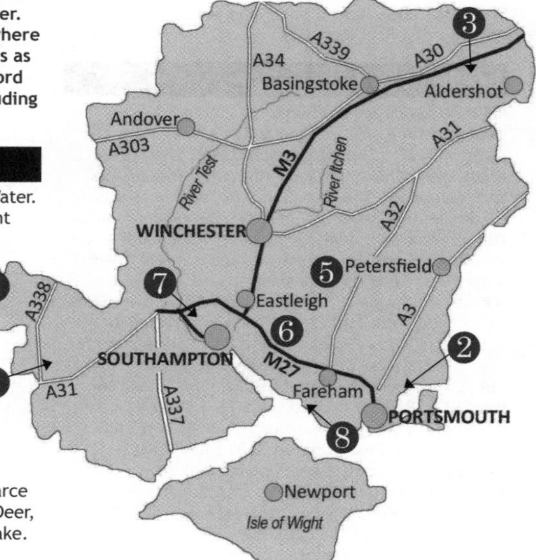

1. BLASHFORD LAKES

Hampshire & Isle of Wight Wildlife Trust/Wessex Water.
Habitats: Flooded gravel pits, areas of wet ancient woodland, also dry grassland & lichen heath.
Birds: *Spring/summer*: Breeding birds inc. Common Tern, Sand Martin (in artificial bank), Lapwing, Redshank, Oystercatcher, Little Ringed Plover. Kingfisher, Garden Warbler. *Autumn*: Waders on migration inc. Green & Common Sandpipers & Greenshank, also Hobby, Black Tern & passerines. *Winter*: Up to 5,000 wintering wildfowl, inc. internationally important numbers of Gadwall. Grey Heron, Little Egret & Bittern. Large gull roost on Ibsley Water.
Other: 25 spp. dragonflies inc. Brown Hawker, Scarce Chaser, Large & Small Red-eyed damselflies. Roe Deer, Badger, Otter, Fox, reptiles inc. Adder & Grass Snake.

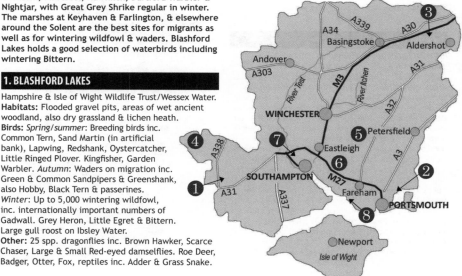

Directions: Sat nav: BH24 3PJ. SU 151 083. From Ringwood take A338 for two miles towards Fordingbridge/Salisbury, pass Ivy Lane on R & take next R at Ellingham Cross, into Ellingham Drove. The main car park for hides is first L after 400 yards.
Public transport: Bus - no.X3 Bournemouth-Salisbury at Ellingham Cross, 500 yards W of main entrance. More Bus (T: 01202 338 420).
Visiting: Car parks (coaches/groups by arrangement). Education centre/toilets, six hides open daily (not Dec 25) 9am-4.30pm. Paths open outside these hours but no vehicle access. RADAR keys needed to open kissing gates for wheelchairs. Viewing screens, recent sightings board, webcams. No dogs.
Contact: Hampshire & Isle of Wight WT, T: 01425 472 760; E: Robert.Chapman@hiwwt.org.uk

2. FARLINGTON MARSHES

Hampshire & Isle of Wight Wildlife Trust.
Habitats: Coastal grazing marsh with pools & reedbeds. Views over saltmarsh/intertidal mudflats of Langstone Harbour.
Birds: *Summer*: Breeding waders & wildfowl (inc. Lapwing, Redshank & Shelduck) & Cetti's, Sedge & Reed Warblers, Bearded Tit. *Late summer:* Passage migrants (Yellow Wagtail, Whinchat, Wheatear etc) & returning waders, always a chance of rarities/less common spp. inc. Spotted Crake, Curlew Sandpiper, stints. *Autumn/ winter:* Waders & wildfowl, good numbers of Teal, Wigeon, Pintail, Marsh Harrier, Short-eared Owl regular visitors. Internationally-important numbers of Dark-bellied Brent Goose & Bar-tailed Godwit. Important high tide roost site, best viewed over high spring tides.
Other: Corky Fruited Waterdropwort, Slender Hares-ear, Southern Marsh & Early Marsh Orchids. Water Vole.
Directions: Sat nav: PO6 1RN. SU 685 045. N of Langstone Harbour. Main entrance off roundabout junction A2030/A27 - tale is small lane between the A27 westbound & A2030 Portsmouth road - height restriction barrier, three parking areas available.
Public transport: Bus - no.21 Portsmouth to Havant stops by Farlington Sainsbury's (north of A27), 20 mins walk to reserve. Stagecoach South (T: 0345 121 0190). Train - Hilsea is 1.5 miles from reserve.
Visiting: Open all times. 2.5 mile circular walk around sea wall, plenty of benches - exposed to wing & sea spray. Information at entrance & shelter. Paths mostly level but main track along sea wall uneven in places, muddy when wet. Short slopes up to sea wall. Wheelchair access via RADAR gates. Dogs on leads at all times.
Contact: Hampshire & Isle of Wight Wildlife Trust, T: 07917 616 696; E: Christopher.Lycett@hiwwt.org.uk

3. FLEET POND LNR

Hart District Council Service/Fleet Pond Society.
Habitats: Largest freshwater lake in Hampshire - marsh, reedbed, heathland, wet & dry woodland.
Birds: 180 spp. Woodcock, Kingfisher. 3 spp woodpecker. *Spring/autumn:* Migrant waders inc. Little Ringed Plover, Dunlin, Greenshank. Little Gull, occasional Kittiwake, terns, occasional Ring Ouzel, Pied Flycatcher, Firecrest, *Summer:* Hobby, Common Tern, Tree Pipit, occasional Red Kite & Osprey. *Winter:* Bittern, wildfowl inc. occasional Smew, Snipe, occasional Jack Snipe, Siskin, Redpoll.
Other: Dragonflies in wet areas of marshes/heathland (21 spp.), 26 spp. butterflies, 400+ plant spp.
Directions: Sat nav: GU51 2RR. SU 823 553. Located in Fleet, W of Farnborough. Main site car park (free) is off Cove Road B3013/A327 (follow brown signs).
Public transport: Train - Fleet lies just to NW of site.
Visiting: Open all year. Additional parking in Wellington Avenue, Chestnut Grove, Kenilworth Road & Westover Road (take A3013 S from train station (0.25 mile), turn L into Avondale Road - roads are on L off this road. Some times restrictions/charges may apply). Some surfaced paths, boardwalks in wet areas.
Contact: Hart District Council,
T: 01252 623 443;
E: countryside@hart.gov.uk;
W: www.hart.gov.uk/fleet-pond;
W: www.fleetpond.org.uk/

4. MARTIN DOWN NNR

Natural England (Thames Solent Team)/Hampshire County Council.
Habitats: 350ha, unimproved chalk downland & scrub.
Birds: *All year:* Yellowhammer, Skylark. *Spring/ summer:* Grey Partridge, Turtle Dove, Nightingale (all now scarce), Cuckoo, plus warblers inc. Lesser Whitethroat. *Winter:* Occasional Merlin, Hen Harrier.
Other: Species-rich chalk downland with variety of orchids, plus Pasqueflower & Milkwort. 20+ spp. butterflies.
Directions: Sat nav: SP5 5RH. SU 036 200 (main car park). Fourteen miles SW of Salisbury, 0.6 mile W of Martin village. N part of site is crossed by the A354. Main car park is on A354 & another at end of Sillens Lane, a minor road from Martin village.
Public transport: Bus - no.20 (Mon-Fri) Salisbury to Blandford. Damory (T: 01202 338 420).
Visiting: Open access, but organised groups of 10+ should book in advance. Two car parks, interpretative boards. Main car park height barrier (7ft 6 ins), coaches by prior arrangement. Hard flat track from A354 car park suitable for wheelchairs.
Contact: Hampshire County Council, T: 01590 674 656; E: centralcountrysidesites@hants.gov.uk

5. OLD WINCHESTER HILL NNR

Natural England (Thames Solent Team).
Habitats: Chalk grassland, scrub, woodland. Iron Age hill-fort. In South Downs National Park.
Birds: *All year:* Red Kite, Buzzard, Raven, Grey Partridge, Yellowhammer. *Summer/breeding:* Hobby, Turtle Dove, Whitethroat & other regular 'scrub' spp. *Passage:* Migrants inc. Wheatear, Redstart, Whinchat, Ring Ouzel. Rarities have turned up from time to time. *Winter:* Raptors inc. Hen Harrier (occasional), Peregrine, Merlin, winter thrushes.

Other: Species-rich chalk downland with variety of orchids, scarcities inc. Round-headed Rampion & Field Fleawort, butterflies (37 spp recorded) inc. Chalkhill Blue & Silver-spotted Skipper.
Directions: Sat nav: GU32 1HW. SU 646 214. Mid-way between Winchester & Petersfield. Approach off A32 Fareham to Alton road at Warnford. Just E of George & Falcon pub take Hayden Lane towards Clanfield. Small car park after 1.8 miles on R.
Public transport: Bus - no.67 Winchester-Petersfield (not Sun) - stops at West Meon (two miles from reserve). Stagecoach in Hampshire (T: 0345 121 0190).
Visiting: Open at all times. Car park (height barrier), picnic area & interpretation, well-marked footpaths. Fully accessible trail (towards hill-fort) at southern side of reserve with allocated disabled parking (RADAR key holders) - further along the lane from main car park. Dogs under close control (grazing stock).
Contact: Natural England. T: 0300 060 6000; E: enquiries@naturalengland.org.uk

6. SWANWICK LAKES NATURE RESERVE

Hampshire & Isle of Wight Wildlife Trust.
Habitats: Mixed woodland, flower-rich meadows & deep lakes.
Birds: Good variety of birds inc. Little Grebe, Gadwall, Buzzard, Kingfisher, Great Spotted & Green Woodpeckers, Nuthatch, Treecreeper, finches & tits.
Other: Common butterflies, with occasional Purple Emperor & Silver-washed Fritillary, common dragonflies & other insects inc. mining bees. Great Crested Newts. Common Spotted Orchid. Rich variety of fungi. Roe Deer.
Directions: Sat nav: SO31 7AY. SU 507 099. SE from Southampton. About two miles from Bursledon & seven miles from Fareham. From Junc 8 of M27, follow signs to A3024 Southampton & Hamble & then A27 to Park Gate. At lights by The Navigator pub turn L onto Swanwick Lane. Cross motorway then L onto Sopwith Way. Turn R at mini roundabout by security gates. From Junc 9 follow signs for Southampton A27 up to Park Gate. Take road to Botley. At Elm Tree pub turn L onto Swanwick Lane. After about a mile, turn R onto Sopwith Way. Turn R at mini roundabout by security gates.
Public transport: Bus - nos X4, X5 from Southampton stop on A27, at bottom of Swanwick Lane. First (T: 0345 646 0707). Train - about 30 mins walk from Swanwick. From station turn R at end of access road then continue to Elm Tree Pub. Turn L onto Swanwick Lane then continue as above.
Visiting: Car park closed at dusk. Toilets available when education centre open. Network of surfaced (suitable for wheelchairs) & unsurfaced paths, three waymarked trails,benches, viewpoints. Groups by arrangement. Dogs may need to be on lead if schools visiting.
Contact: Hampshire & Isle of Wight Wildlife Trust, T: 01489 570 240; E: swanwickLakes@hiwwt.org.uk

7. TESTWOOD LAKES NATURE RESERVE

Southern Water/
Hampshire & Isle of Wight Wildlife Trust.
Habitats: Flooded gravel pits, scrapes, wet & dry grasslands, woodland & hedgerows.
Birds: *Spring:* Shelduck, Little Ringed Plover, Lapwing, Sand Martin, Willow Warbler. *Summer:* Swift, Swallow, Blackcap, Whitethroat. *Autumn:* Wheatear, Yellow Wagtail, Goldfinch. *Winter:* Wildfowl (inc. Tufted Duck, Wigeon, Pochard, Teal, Gadwall, Goosander), Common & Green Sandpipers, Meadow Pipit, Redwing, Fieldfare, Siskin, Hawfinch.
Other: Variety of butterflies & dragonflies inc. Emperor, Scarce Chaser, Migrant Hawker & Golden-ringed.
Directions: Sat nav: SO40 3YD. SU 347 155. Take M271 West Junc 2 towards Totton. L at first roundabout, then L onto A36. L at next roundabout onto Brunel Rd. Entrance on L after 0.25 mile.
Public transport: Bus - nos.12 / X7 (not Sun) from Southampton stop at Testwood Crescent (0.5 mile from reserve) - Bluestar (T: 01202 338421) / Salisbury Reds. Train - Totton is 1.5 miles from reserve.
Visiting: Car parks open 8am-5pm (4pm winter) - height restriction. Two hides (open 10am-4pm daily), two screens. Surfaced paths around lakes & to hides relatively flat - RADAR key (available at centre) needed for wheelchair users to get through gates. Testwood Lakes Centre open 9am-4pm Mon-Fri & 1pm-4pm Sun (summer), 12pm-3pm (winter) - weekday access may not be possible if school groups in attendance. Disabled toilet in Education Centre, mobility vehicle available (book in advance). No dogs in conservation & education areas.
Contact: Hampshire & Isle of Wight Wildlife Trust, T: 02380 667 929; E: TestwoodLakes@hiwwt.org.uk

8. TITCHFIELD HAVEN NNR

Hampshire County Council.
Habitats: 150ha, in Lower Meon valley. Shoreline, reedbeds, freshwater scrapes, wet grazing meadows.
Birds: 200+ spp. *Spring/summer:* Waders (inc. Avocet & Black-tailed Godwit), wildfowl, Common Tern, breeding Cetti's Warbler, Water Rail. *Autumn/winter:* Bittern, Kingfisher, Bearded Tit, Brent Geese, Wigeon, Teal, Shoveler & Snipe. Occasional rarities at any time.
Other: Six spp. nationally rare plant, Roe Deer, Badger & Pipistrelle Bat. Water Voles released in 2013. 19 spp. dragonflies & 30+ spp. butterflies.
Directions: Sat nav: PO14 3JT. SU 532 022. Located on Cliff Road, Hill Head in Fareham. Reach from A27 & B3334 W of Fareham. Car park adjacent to Hill Head Sailing Club (free for blue badge holders).
Public transport: Bus - no.21 (not Sun) Stubbington to Fareham stops in Solent Road, 200 yards from reserve. First Bus.
Visiting: Free entry to visitor centre, charge for reserve. Open daily 9.30am-5pm Apr-Oct, 9.30am-4pm (Nov-Mar, not Dec 25/26). Centre has information desk, toilets, cafe, shop. Seven hides (wheelchair access). Guided walks. Public footpath follows derelict canal along W of reserve & road skirts S edge. Guide dogs only.
Contact: Titchfield Haven, T: 01329 662 145; E: titchfield.enquiries@hants.gov.uk

Kent

A great county for birders. The Dungeness area offers excellent birding with an RSPB reserve & a bird observatory ensuring that it is well watched. Seawatching from the shingle spit here will pick up divers, seaduck, shearwaters, skuas & terns as they move through the Channel. There is another observatory at Sandwich Bay, marshes all along the north coast (where a wide selection of birds of prey winter on the Isle of Sheppey), & reedbeds at Stodmarsh.

1. BOUGH BEECH RESERVOIR

Kent Wildlife Trust.
Habitats: Reserve occupies northern end of reservoir & adjacent woodland & farmland.
Birds: 60 spp. breed annually in/around reserve, with Tufted Duck, Mandarin & Great Crested Grebe notable amongst waterfowl. Little Ringed Plover breed most years. *Autumn*: Good for waders inc. Green & Common Sandpipers & Greenshank. Osprey most years. Many rarities have been recorded. *Winter:* wildfowl numbers much higher than summer & inc. Goldeneye & Goosander.
Other: Great Crested Newt, Common Toad, dragonflies (Black-tailed Skimmer, Ruddy Darter, Emperor, Southern & Migrant Hawkers, Red-eyed damselfly), Common Lizard, Roesel's Bush Cricket, Long-winged Conehead, Dormouse, Water Shrew, White Admiral butterfly, Glow-worm, bats (Pipistrelle, Daubenton, Noctule, Brown Long-eared).
Directions: Sat nav: TN14 6LD. TQ 496 489. Lying SW of Sevenoaks, Bough Beech is situated 3.5 miles S of Ide Hill, signposted off B2042.
Public transport: Train - Penshurst (The Causeway is 2.5 miles to NW).
Visiting: Roadside parking along The Causeway. Circular nature trail - paths uneven & can be muddy. Hide overlooks wader scrape, wheelchair accessible. Dogs on lead at all times.
Contact: Kent WT, T: 01622 662 012;
E: info@kentwildlife.org.uk

2. CLIFFE POOLS

RSPB (South East Region Office).
Habitats: A mix of saline lagoons, freshwater pools, grassland, saltmarsh & scrub.
Birds: *Spring/autumn passage:* Good variety of spp. *Summer:* Breeding spp. inc. Lapwing, Redshank, Avocet, Ringed Plover, Shelduck. Hobby, Mediterranean Gull, Cuckoo, Turtle Dove, Nightingale. *Winter:* Massed flocks of waders inc. Black-tailed Godwit & Dunlin in thousands, wide variety of wildfowl. Hen & Marsh Harriers, Merlin.
Other: Good range of insects (rare bees inc. Shrill & Brown-banded Carder Bees). Butterflies, inc. Marbled White, Common Blue, Essex Skipper & Clouded Yellow, grasshoppers & bush crickets, inc. Roesel's.
Directions: Sat nav: ME3 7SX. TQ 722 757. From coastbound A2, take A289 near Strood. From A289 follow signs for Wainscott & Cliffe onto B2000. At T-junction turn L to Cliffe. At crossroads, turn L to Higham. Before entering Cliffe, take 2nd L after Cliffe sign. Turn L at next T-junction & L again into Salt Road. Car park is on L just past a sharp right-hand bend.
Public transport: Bus - no.133 (Mon-Sat) from Chatham, Rochester & Strood stops in Cliffe (1.5 miles from reserve). Arriva in Kent & Surrey.
Visiting: Car park (free) open daily 9am-5pm (not Christmas period). Group bookings welcome, monthly guided walks available. Six viewing points. Public rights of way encircle & bisect reserve, pushchair friendly. Dogs only on public footpaths.
Contact: RSPB, T: 01634 222 480;
E: northkentmarshes@rspb.org.uk

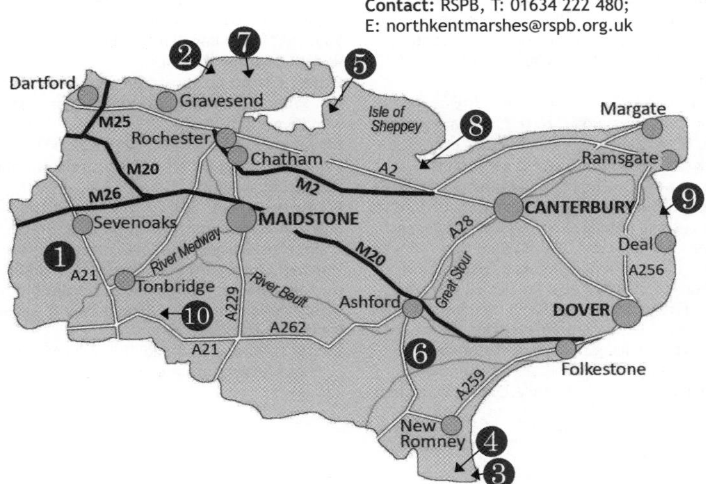

3. DUNGENESS BIRD OBSERVATORY

Dungeness Bird Observatory Trust.
Habitats: Shingle promontory with scrub & gravel pits.
Birds: *Summer:* Breeding spp. inc. Raven, Wheatear & Black Redstart. *Passage:* Important migration site, regular overshoots inc. Bee-eater, Hoopoe, Purple Heron & Red-rumped Swallow. Excellent seawatching when weather conditions suitable. Power station outfall, 'The Patch' good for terns & gulls, inc. Mediterranean, Caspian & Yellow-legged.
Other: Long Pits are excellent for dragonflies, inc. Small Red-eyed damselfly. Moth trapping throughout year.
Directions: Sat nav: TN29 9NA. TR 085 173. Three miles SE of Lydd. Turn S off main Dungeness Road just before Pilot Inn - continue to end of road, past two lighthouses.
Public transport: Bus - see site 3 - alight at Pilot Inn, 1.75 miles from Observatory.
Visiting: Observatory open throughout year. Wardens on site between Mar & Nov. Accommodation for up to nine people (reduced charges for Friends). Apply in writing to the warden or by phone. No wheelchair access. Bring own sleeping bag/sheets & toiletries. Shared facilities inc. a fully-equipped kitchen. Coach parking available at mini-railway station.
Contact: Dungeness Bird Observatory, 11 RNSSS Cottages, Dungeness, Romney Marsh, Kent TN29 9NA. T: 01797 321 309; E: dungenessobs@vfast.co.uk; W: www.dungenessbirdobs.org.uk

4. DUNGENESS NNR

RSPB (South East Region Office).
Habitats: Shingle, 90 flooded gravel pits, sallow scrub, newly-extended reedbed on Denge Marsh, wet grassland.
Birds: *All year:* Bittern, Marsh Harrier, Bearded Tit, Cetti's Warbler. *Spring:* Garganey, Little Ringed Plover among a wide variety of waders, Wheatear, Yellow Wagtail, Lesser Whitethroat, Black Redstart. *Autumn:* Migrant waders & passerines, inc. large flocks of swallows & martins. *Winter:* Smew, Goldeneye, Black-necked & Slavonian Grebes, Wigeon, Goosander, Bewick's Swan, Marsh & Hen Harriers, other raptors.
Other: Jersey Cudweed, Nottingham Catchfly, endemic leafhopper.
Directions: Sat nav: TN29 9PN. TR 062 197. One mile out of Lydd on Dungeness Road, turn R for main site. Visitor centre & car park are one mile along entrance track. Entrance to Hanson ARC site & car park is opposite main reserve entrance on L of Dungeness Road.
Public transport: Bus - no.11 (not Sun) from Ashford via Lydd stops at reserve entrance on request. Stagecoach.
Visiting: Open daily (not Dec 25/26) 9am-9pm/sunset when earlier. Coach parking available. Visitor centre open 10am-5pm (4pm Nov-Feb). Parties 12+ by prior arrangement. Entry fee for non-RSPB members. Visitor centre, fully equipped classroom/meeting room, toilets (inc. disabled access), light refreshments, shop. Six hides (wheelchair accessible), viewing screen, two nature trails. Assistance dogs only. Hide & viewing screen at Hanson ARC site.
Contact: RSPB, T: 01797 320 588; E: dungeness@rspb.org.uk

5. ELMLEY MARSHES NNR

Private.
Habitats: 1335ha estate - coastal grazing marsh, ditches & pools alongside Swale Estuary with extensive intertidal mudflats & saltmarsh.
Birds: *Spring/summer:* Breeding waders - Redshank, Lapwing, Avocet plus passage waders. Hobby, , Yellow Wagtail. *Autumn:* Passage waders. *Winter:* Spectacular numbers of wildfowl, especially Wigeon & White-fronted Goose. Waders. Hunting raptors - Peregrine, Merlin, Hen Harrier & Short-eared Owl.
Other: Water Vole.
Directions: Sat nav: ME12 3RW. TQ 937 680. From Junc 5 of M2, follow A249 towards Sheerness. Reserve signposted from exit for Iwade & Ridham Dock, immediately before Sheppey bridge. At roundabout, take second exit onto old road bridge. On Isle of Sheppey, after 1.25 miles, turn R following reserve sign. Follow rough track for approx two miles to car park at Kingshill Farm. do not leave car on entrance track.
Public transport: Train - Swale nearest station, Sittingbourne-Sheerness line - three miles to reserve.
Visiting: Open daily (not Tues or Dec 25/26) 9am-5pm. Honesty box in car park for parking fee. Groups by appointment. Toilets in car park. Four hides, nearest one mile from car park. Disabled access to Wellmarsh hide, Blue Badge holders may drive to hide. Swale viewing screen 200 yrds from car park. Paths pushchair friendly. Guide dogs only.
Contact: T: 01795 664 896; E: info@elmleynaturereserve.co.uk; W: www.elmleynaturereserve.co.uk

6. HAM STREET WOODS NNR

Natural England (Sussex & Kent Team).
Habitats: Ancient woodland.
Birds: *All year:* Common woodland spp. inc. 3 spp. Woodpeckers, Marsh Tit. Sparrowhawk, Tawny Owl. *Spring/summer*: Hobhby, Turtle Dove, Tree Pipit, Nightingale, warblers inc. Garden & Whitethroat, Spotted Flycatcher. *Winter*: Brambling, Siskin, Redpoll, winter thrushes.
Other: Dormouse, Great Crested Newt, butterflies inc. White Admiral & Purple Emperor, ancient woodland flora, fungi.
Directions: Sat nav: TN26 2HH. TR 003 337. Six miles S Ashford. Car park off B2067 at end of Bourne Lane in Hamstreet village.
Public transport: Bus - no.11 Asfford-Lydd (not Sun), alight at Hamstreet railway station. Stagecoach. Train: Ham Street - 0.3 miles from reserve.
Visiting: Open all times. Three waymarked trails through reserve - rough paths, unsuitable for wheelchairs. Both Saxon Shore Way & Greensand Way trails pass through.
Contact: Natural England, T: 0300 060 3900; E: enquiries@naturalengland.org.uk

7. NORTHWARD HILL

RSPB (South East Region Office).
Habitats: Ancient & scrub woodland overlooking grazing marsh.
Birds: *Spring/summer:* Wood holds UK's largest heronry, with c150 pairs of Grey Heron & c50 pairs of Little Egret. Breeding Nightingale (ca 20 pairs), Turtle Dove, scrub warblers & woodpeckers. Marshes - breeding Lapwing, Redshank, Avocet, Marsh Harrier, Shoveler, Pochard. *Winter:* Wigeon, Teal, Shoveler. Passage waders, inc. Black-tailed Godwit, raptors, Corn Bunting. Long-eared Owl.
Other: Good variety of dragonflies over marsh, White-letter Hairstreak butterfly in woods.
Directions: Sat nav: ME3 8DS. TQ 768 765. Four miles NE of Rochester. Leave M2 at Junc 1 & join A228, signposted Grain. Turn off A228 for High Halstow then L in village into Cooling Road - reserve signposted ca one mile on R.
Public transport: Difficult, contact reserve for more info.
Visiting: Open all times. Car park (dawn-dusk), toilets. Trails in public area of wood joining Saxon Shoreway link to grazing marsh. Three trails, from 0.7 to 2.3 miles - often steep, not suitable for wheelchairs. Four viewpoints with benches. Dogs only allowed on Saxon Shoreway.
Contact: RSPB, T: 01634 222 480;
E: northkentmarshes@rspb.org.uk

8. OARE MARSHES LNR

Kent Wildlife Trust.
Habitats: Grazing marsh, freshwater dykes, open water scrapes, reedbed, mudflats/Swale Sea Channel.
Birds: *All year*: Waders & wildfowl, Little Egret, Marsh Harrier, Water Rail, Barn & Little Owls. *Spring/summer*: Avocet, Garganey, Green, Wood & Curlew Sandpipers, Little Stint, Black-tailed Godwit, Little Tern. *Winter*: Brent Goose, Red-breasted Merganser, Hen Harrier, Merlin, Peregrine, Short-eared Owl, Bittern, Stonechat. Divers, grebes & sea ducks on Swale. Good record for attracting rarities.
Other: Dragonflies, Common Seal on sandbank.
Directions: Sat nav: ME13 0QA. TR 013 647 (car park). Off Church Road, Oare, two miles N of Faversham. From A2 follow signs to Oare & Harty Ferry.
Public transport: Bus - no.3 (not Sun) Sittingbourne-Canterbury stops in Oare, one mile from reserve). Stagecoach in East Kent. Train - Faversham (three miles).
Visiting: Open all times. Car park opposite Watch House near seawall, restricted turning space (not suitable for coaches). Disabled-only car park 300 yards from East Flood hide. Three hides. Roadside viewpoint of East Hide accessible to wheelchair users. Those with pneumatic tyres can reach seawall path & hide. Access along marked paths only. Dogs on leads.
Contact: Kent WT, T: 01622 662 012;
E: info@kentwildlife.org.uk

9. SANDWICH BAY BIRD OBSERVATORY

Sandwich Bay Bird Observatory Trust.
Habitats: Coastal, dune land, farmland, marsh, two small scrapes.
Birds: *All year:* Breeding residents inc. Oystercatcher, Grey Partridge, Stonechat, Stock Dove, Little Owl, Corn Bunting. *Spring/autumn passage*: Good variety of migrants & waders. Annual Golden Oriole. Firecrest & Yellow-browed Warbler occur in The Elms. *Summer:* Little Ringed Plover. *Winter*: Waders, Short-eared & Long-eared Owl.
Other: Sand dune plants inc. Lady's Bedstraw & Sand Sedge. Small Heath butterfly, Red-veined Darter.
Directions: Sat nav: CT13 9PF. TR 355 575. 2.5 miles from Sandwich, five miles from Deal. A256 to Sandwich from Dover or Ramsgate. From Sandwich follow signs to Golf Courses, continue on into Sandwich Bay Estate, turn R after 0.25 mile. There is small fee at Tollgate for non-members visiting Obs.
Public transport: Train - Sandwich two miles from Observatory.
Visiting: Aim to open daily 10am-6pm (summer) 10am-1pm/4pm on Sat, (winter), disabled access. Field Study Centre - toilets, refreshments, hostel-type accommodation & self-contained flat.
Contact: Sandwich Bay Bird Obs, Guildford Road, Sandwich, CT13 9PF; T: 01304 617 341;
E: info@sbbot.org.uk; W: www.sbbot.org.uk

10. TUDELEY WOODS & PEMBURY HEATH

RSPB (South East Region Office).
Habitats: Ancient, semi-natural mixed woodland, heathland.
Birds: *All year*: Common woodland species, 3 spp. woodpeckers, Marsh Tit. *Spring/summer*: Turtle Dove, Spotted Flycatcher, common warblers, inc. Garden. Nightjar & Tree Pipit on heath. *Winter:* Woodcock, winter thrushes & finches, Crossbill.
Other: Butterflies, inc. White Admiral & Silver-washed Fritillary. Golden-ringed Dragonfly, 1000+ spp. fungi. Bluebells, orchids & other woodland plants. Dormouse.
Directions: Sat nav: TN11 0PT. TQ 617 433. 0.5 mile SW Tonbridge. Take A21 from Tonbridge towards Tunbridge Wells. Take L turn (signposted to Chapel) into Half Moon Lane - also known as Dislinbgbury Road - (immediately before petrol station). Parking area 0.3 mile on L. Pembury Heath can be accessed from here, footpath to S of the road links to trail.
Public transport: None.
Visiting: Open all times. Car park can be opened for groups by arrangement, limited parking outside gate. Three trails of one, 1.5 & three miles. Dogs allowed on public footpaths/bridleways & some parts of reserve - contact for info.
Contact: RSPB, T: 01892 752 430.

London (Greater)

The London Natural History Society, publishers of the London Bird report, base their recording area on a 20-mile radius from St Paul's Cathedral (which overlaps with some of the surrounding counties). Despite being a sprawling city, it offers a number of green spaces & purpose-built reservoirs, all attractive to the capital's birds & the occasional oddity that turns up from time to time.

1. BEDFONT LAKES COUNTRY PARK

London Borough of Hounslow.
Habitats: Country Park inc. a private nature reserve - 73ha of lakes, reedbed, wildflower meadows, scrub, wet woodland.
Birds: 155 spp. *Summer*: Common Tern, Willow, Garden, Reed & Sedge Warblers, Whitethroat, Lesser Whitethroat, hirundines, Hobby, Blackcap, Chiffchaff, Skylark. *Passage*: Wheatear, Wood Warbler, Spotted Flycatcher, Ring Ouzel, Redstart, Yellow Wagtail. *Winter*: Water Rail, Bittern, Smew & other wildfowl, Meadow Pipit.
Other: 350 plant spp. inc. Bee & Pyramidal Orchids. Nathusius Pipistrelle Bat, butterflies & dragonflies (inc. Emperor).
Directions: Sat nav: TW14 8QA. TQ 076 724 (Clockhouse Lane). From M25 take Junc 13 (A30) towards central London. Continue through Crooked Billet traffic light complex, past Ashford Hospital & take B3003 (Clockhouse Lane) from Clockhouse roundabout.
Public transport: Bus - no.H26 Feltham to Hatton Cross & no.116 from Hounslow to Ashford Hospital. Transport for London. Train - Ashford (Surrey) station one mile.
Visiting: Nature reserve - access by BLCP membership or annual fee only. Country park - open daily (not Dec 25) 8am-4.30pm. Toilets, information centre, several hides, nature trail, free parking, up-to-date information. Disabled friendly. Dogs on leads.
Contact: Bedfont Lakes Country Park LNR, managed by Lampton Greenspace 360, T: 020 8583 2000; Friends of BLCP: E: info@bedfontlakes.co.uk; W: www.bedfontlakes.co.uk

2. BRENT RESERVOIR (WELSH HARP)

Canal & River Trust.
Habitats: Reservoir surrounded by marshland, woodland, unimproved grassland & playing fields.
Birds: 250+ spp. *Spring/summer:* Breeding Great Crested Grebe, Gadwall, Shoveler, Pochard, Common Tern, woodland species & up to eight spp. warbler. Long history of rare birds inc. London's first Great Egret in 1997 & UK's first Iberian Chiffchaff in 1972. *Winter:* Good variety of wildfowl & gull spp.
Other: 28 spp. butterflies, inc. Marbled White & Ringlet, 15 spp. dragonflies. A notable site for bats.
Directions: Sat nav: NW9 8SE. TQ 208 870 (Birchen Grove). NW London close to M1/junc 1 - take A406 (N Circular Rd) towards Neasden, then 2nd slip road on L onto A4088 (brown sign to reservoir), continue to next brown sign, turn R into Birchen Grove continue to car park.
Public transport: Train - Hendon station (Thameslink) & Neasdon (Underground) at opposite ends of the reservoir.
Visiting: Open access at all times. Park in Birchen Grove to access Welsh Harp Open Space nature reserve. Raised viewing platform & permanently open public hide overlooks northern marsh. Circular walk.
Contact: Welsh Harp Conservation Group, E: via website; W: https://brentres.wordpress.com/ (see website for other access arrangements)

3. DAGENHAM CHASE LNR

London Borough of Barking & Dagenham.
Habitats: Shallow wetlands, reedbeds, horse-grazed pasture, scrub & wetland.
Birds: 190 spp. *Summer*: Breeding Reed Warbler, Lapwing, Water Rail, Lesser Whitethroat, Little Ringed Plover, Kingfisher, Reed Bunting. *Spring/autumn passage*: Yellow Wagtail, Wheatear, Ruff, Wood Sandpiper, Sand Martin, Ring Ouzel, Black Redstart & Hobby regular. *Winter*: Good numbers of Teal, Shoveler, Snipe, Redwing & Fieldfare.
Other: 140 plant spp., the nationally rare black poplar tree. Wasp Spider, butterflies & dragonflies.
Directions: Sat nav: RM7 0SS. TQ 509 860 (Millennium Centre). Lies in Dagenham Corridor S of A124 between A1112 & A125, an area of green belt between London Boroughs of Barking, Dagenham & Havering.
Public transport: Bus - no.174 from Romford or Dagenham, five mins walk. Transport for London.Train - Dagenham East (District Line), 15 mins walk.
Visiting: Open all times, not suitable for wheelchairs. Eastbrookend & Beam Valley Country Parks border site - surfaced footpaths suitable for wheelchairs. Millennium Centre (T: 0208 595 4155) in Eastbrookend CP, toilets, car parking, Timberland Trail walk.
Contact: LBB&D, T: 0208 227 2332; E: parksandcountryside@lbbd.gov.uk

4. LONDON WETLAND CENTRE

The Wildfowl & Wetlands Trust.
Habitats: Main lake, reedbeds, wader scrape, open water lakes, wet woodland, grazing marsh.
Birds: *All year:* Cetti's Warbler. *Summer:* Important numbers of wetland breeding spp. inc. grebes, swans, variety of duck (inc. Pochard), Lapwing, Little Ringed Plover, Redshank, warblers, Reed Bunting. Artificial nesting bank for Sand Martins & rafts for nesting terns. Peregrines which nest on Charing Cross Hospital sighted regularly. *Winter:* Nationally important numbers of waterfowl, inc. Gadwall & Shoveler. Bittern, Jack Snipe, Water Pipit.
Other: Water Voles, Slow Worm, Grass Snake, Common Lizard. Seven spp. bat, 22 spp. dragonflies & 25 spp. butterflies. Notable plants inc. Snake's Head Fritillaries, Cowslip, Pyramidal & Bee Orchids.
Directions: Sat nav: SW13 9WT. TQ 226 768. Less than one mile N of South Circular Road (A205), take A306 N, signposted into Queen Elizabeth's Walk, Barnes. In London Zone 2/3, one mile from Hammersmith.

Public transport: Bus - no.485 (not Sun/bank hol) comes into centre. Others from Hammersmith nos.33 & 209; from Richmond no.33. Train: Barnes. Tube: Hammersmith. Transport for London.
Visiting: Coaches by arrangement. Open 9.30am-5.30pm Mar-Oct, 9.30am-4.30pm Nov-Feb (not Dec 25), last admission one hour before closing. Admission charge for non-WWT members. Visitor centre, discovery centre & children's adventure area, restaurant (hot/cold food), cinema, shop, observatory building, six hides (all wheelchair accessible), sustainable gardens, interactive pond zone, three interpretative buildings, nature trails. Events. Assistance dogs only.
Contact: London Wetland Centre, T: 020 8409 4400; E: info.london@wwt.org.uk

5. WOODBERRY WETLANDS

London Wildlife Trust.
Habitats: A working Reservoir, reedbeds.
Birds: *All year*: Great Crested Grebe, Sparrowhawk, Peregrine, Kestrel, Kingfisher, Reed Bunting. *Summer*: Hobby, Reed, Sedge & Cetti's Warblers. *Passage:* Common Sandpiper, occasionally other waders, terns. Hirundines,.*Winter*: Wildfowl, gulls, Bittern.
Other: Bats, Fox, amphibians.
Directions: Sat nav: N16 5HQ. TQ 326 873. Off A503 (Seven Sisters Road), Woodberry Down - turn S into Woodburry Grove/Lordship Road. Two entrances on to New River Path - one from Lordship Road & one from Newnton Close.
Public transport: Bus - nos.253, 254, 259 & 279 stop in nearby Seven Sisters Road. Train - Manor House Underground (Piccadilly line) five min walk from west entrance & Stamford Hill station five min walk from north entrance.
Transport for London.
Visiting: Open daily 9.00am to 4.30pm. Visitor centre, toilets (inc. Disabled, baby changing facilities), shop, cafe/refreshments, picnic area. Guide dogs only. Wheelchair accessible path, seating.
Contact: London WT, T: 020 7261 0477; E: enquiries@wildlondon.org.uk

---

Surrey

London's urban sprawl has continued to spread into much of the north of the county, but reservoirs & the sewage farm at Beddington still offer opportunities for birders. To the west, the heathlands at Thursley Common & around Frensham are good for finding the specialities - Hobby, Nightjar, Woodlark & Dartford Warbler.

1. CHOBHAM COMMON NNR

Surrey Wildlife Trust.
Habitats: Largest NNR in south-east England (575ha). Lowland wet & dry heath, with pools, mixed broadleaved & pine woodlands.
Birds: 115+ spp. inc. Hobby, Nightjar, Woodlark & Dartford Warbler. Also Cuckoo, Lesser Spotted Woodpecker, Skylark, Stonechat, Linnet & Yellowhammer.
Other: 350+ spp. flowering plants, 25 spp. mammal, 29 spp. butterflies inc. Silver-studded Blue & 22 spp. dragonflies, Raft Spider.
Directions: Sat nav: KT16 0ED. SU 973 648 (Staple Hill car park). From Junc 3 of M3 head N on A322 & A30 in direction of Sunningdale. From Broomhall turn R into Chobham Road (B383) then L at roundabout (B386) & R at next roundabout over M3 - R into Staple Hill Road. Other car parks in area.
Public transport: Buses - Woking to Chobham. No.73, Falcon Buses (T: 01932 787 752). No.37A (Mon-Fri, limited). Stagecoach. Both stop in Bowling Green Road, S of Common. Services to Sunningdale from Ascot, Windsor, Camberley & Staines. Train - Sunningdale, 0.5 mile from NW corner of Common.
Visiting: Open at all times. Six car parks with information boards (parking charges apply), three self-guided trails. Site leaflet available from rangers.
Contact: Surrey WT, T: 01483 795 440; E: info@surreywt.org.uk

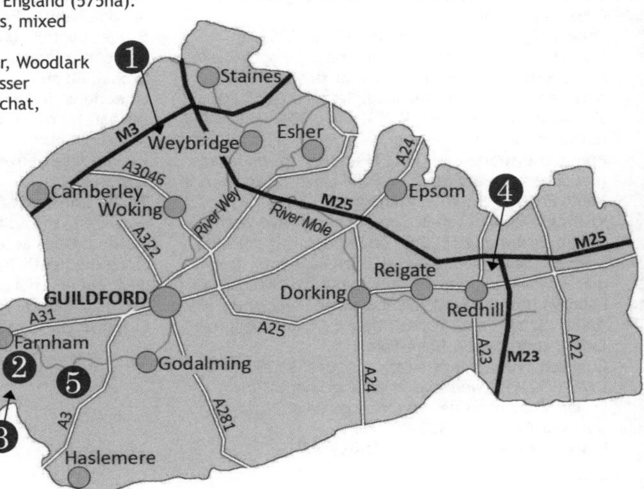

2. FARNHAM HEATH

RSPB (South East Region Office).
Habitats: Heathland & pine woodland.
Birds: *Spring/Summer*: Woodcock, Nightjar, Woodlark, Tree Pipit, Dartford Warbler, woodland birds, inc. Stock Dove, Green & Great Spotted Woodpeckers, Blackcap. *Winter*: Crossbills in pine woods, winter finches & thrushes, inc. Brambling around feeders.
Other: 150+ spp. fungi. Bats in summer. Sand Lizard, plus variety of butterflies inc. Grayling.
Directions: Sat nav: GU10 2DL. SU 859 433. Take B3001 SE from Farnham. Take R hand fork, signposted Tilford, immediately past level crossing. Keep to that road. Just outside Tilford village look for sign to Rural Life Centre. Entrance is on R after 0.5 mile.
Public transport: Bus - no.19 Farnham to Hindhead (not Sun) stops in Millbridge village, outside entrance to Pierrepont House. Reserve is a mile away, along Reeds Road (follow signs to Rural Life Centre). Stagecoach in Hants & Surrey. Train - Farnham.
Visiting: Open all times. Large grass car park, shared with adjacent Rural Life Centre (open 9.30am weekdays, 10.30am weekends - some parking lay-bys on adjacent roads outside of these hours). Three way-marked trails - good for walking, pushchair friendly. Rural Life Centre open Wed-Sun 11am-4pm (Apr-Sep) & Wed, Thurs & Sun (Oct-Mar). Cafe, toilets (inc. disabled), picnic area. Group bookings accepted, guided walks available.
Contact: RSPB, T: 01252 795 632;
E: farnham.heath@rspb.org.uk

3. FRENSHAM COMMON & PONDS

Waverley Borough Council/National Trust.
Habitats: 400ha, dry & humid heath, woodland, two large ponds, reedbeds.
Birds: *Summer*: Common Tern, Hobby, Nightjar, Dartford Warbler, Woodlark, Stonechat, Spotted Flycatcher, Sedge & Reed Warblers, Reed Bunting. *Winter*: Wildfowl (inc. occasional Smew), Bittern, Great Grey Shrike.
Other: Tiger Beetle, Purple Hairstreak & Silver-studded Blue butterflies, Sand Lizard, Smooth Snake.
Directions: Common lies on either side of A287 between Farnham & Hindhead. Sat nav: GU10 2QD. SU 844 405 (Great Pond, WBC). GU10 3BT. SU 856 418 (Little Pond, NT).
Public transport: Bus - no.19 Farnham to Hindhead (not Sun) stops at Frensham Pond Lane. Stagecoach in Hants & Surrey. Train - Farnham.
Visiting: Open all times. Keep to paths, many are smooth & fairly level. Dogs on leads during breeding season. *Great Pond:* car park open 8am-9pm, free during week, charges 9.30am-4pm at weekends/bank holidays (Apr-Sep). NT members free. Snack bar, toilets. *Little Pond:* Pay-&-display, NT members free. Cafe & toilets open 10am-5pm.
Contact: WBC - Rangers Office, T: 01483 523 394 or 01252 792 416 (weekend in summer months);
E: parks&countryside@waverley.gov.uk;
National Trust, T: 01428 681 050;
E: frensham@nationaltrust.org.uk

4. NUTFIELD MARSHES

Surrey Wildlife Trust.
Habitats: Flooded sand pits, scrub, grassland.
Birds: *All year*: Little & Great Crested Grebes, Kingfisher, Ring-necked Parakeet, Grey Wagtail, Reed Bunting. *Summer*: Common Tern, hirundines, warblers inc Garden & Lesser Whitethroat. *Passage:* Waders inc. Common Sandpiper, possible godwits, Whimbrel & Spotted Redshank. *Winter*: Wildfowl inc. Goldeneye, Pochard, occasional Scaup, Smew & divers, Red-necked & Black-necked Grebes. Gulls, Green Sandpiper, Lapwing, Snipe, occasional Jack Snipe, Golden Plover, Fieldfare, Redwing, Brambling .
Other: Dragonflies & butterflies, Grass Snake.
Directions: Sat nav: RH1 4EU. TQ 299 517 (Mercer's Country Park car park). Located between M25 & M23. From A25 take Nutfield Marsh Road, after one mile turn R into Mercer's CP (walk the site from here).
Public transport: Bus - nos.430/435 Redhill to Merstham, alight at Watercolour. Metrobus (T: 01293 449 191). Train - Redhill & Merstham.
Visiting: Open at all times, three sites - The Moors, Spynes Mere & Holmethorpe Lagoons - part of a complex with Mercer's Country Park. Car park, toilets, cafe at Mercer's CP.
Contact: Surrey WT, T: 01483 795 440;
E: info@surreywt.org.uk

5. THURSLEY NNR

Natural England (Thames Solent Team).
Habitats: Wet & dry heathland, woodland, peat bog.
Birds: *Summer*: Hobby, Lapwing, Curlew, Snipe, Nightjar, Woodlark, Spotted Flycatcher, Stonechat, Redstart, Crossbill. *Passage:* waders inc. Redshank, Greenshank, Wood & Common Sandpipers.
Winter: Hen & Marsh Harriers, Great Grey Shrike.
Other: Large populations of Silver-studded Blue, Grayling & Purple Emperor butterflies can be seen, alongside 26 spp. dragonflies. Sandier sites on reserve provide habitat for many spp. of solitary bees & wasps & tiger beetles. Damp areas support carnivorous sundews & large population (1,000's) of Early Marsh Orchid. All six native reptiles.
Directions: Sat nav: GU8 6LW. SU 898 417 (The Moat car park). From Guildford, take A3 SW to B3001 (Elstead/Churt road). Moat car park, S of Elstead village. Alternative parking on recreation ground in Thursley.
Public transport: Bus - no.46 (not Sun) Guildford/ Godalming to Farnham stops in Elstead. Stagecoach.
Visiting: Open access. Boardwalk in wetter areas along the Heath Trail (2.25 miles in length). Parties must obtain prior permission.
Contact: Natural England, T: 01428 685 675;
E: james.giles@naturalengland.org.uk

Sussex

The county, usually referred to as 'East Sussex' & 'West Sussex, is dominated by the chalk hills of the South Downs. Coastal sites from Chichester Harbour in the west to Rye Harbour in the east guarantee a good day's birdwatching, with an interesting mix of wildfowl, waders, raptors, terns & Bittern, depending on the season. Selsey Bill (west) is good for migrants & a good spot for seawatching from where there is a noticeable skua passage in the spring & Beachy Head (east) also attracts spring & autumn migrants. Ashdown Forest offers a fine mix of woodland & heathland birds while RSPB Pulborough Brooks holds important numbers of wintering wildfowl, with a chance of Bewick's Swans.

West

1. ARUNDEL WETLAND CENTRE

Wildfowl & Wetland Trust.
Habitats: 26ha, lakes, wader scrapes, reedbed.
Birds: *All year:* 3 spp. woodpecker, Kingfisher. *Summer*: Breeding Redshank, Lapwing, Oystercatcher, Common Tern, Sedge, Reed & Cetti's Warblers, Peregrine, Hobby. *Winter*: Teal, Wigeon, Reed Bunting, Water Rail, Cetti's Warbler & occasionally Bewick's Swan.
Other: Bee Orchid, Water Shrew, Palmate & Smooth Newts, Grass Snake, 6 spp. bats.
Directions: Sat nav: BN18 9PB. TQ 020 081. Centre on Mill Road clearly signed from Arundel, just N of A27.
Public transport: Bus - no.85 Chichester to Arundel (Mon-Fri). Compass Travel (T: 01903 690 025). No.9 Littlehampton to Arundel. Stagecoach. Train - Arundel, 20 mins walk.
Visiting: Open daily (not Dec 25) 9.30am-5.30pm (4.30pm winter), last admissions 30 mins before closing. Admission charges for non-WWT members. Visitor centre, cafe, shop, hides, picnic area, seasonal nature trails. Corporate hire facilities. Electric boat safaris. Manual wheelchairs available. Approx 1.5 miles of level footpaths, suitable for wheelchairs. Guide dogs only.
Contact: Arundel Wetland Centre, T: 01903 883 355; E: info.arundel@wwt.org.uk

2. CHICHESTER HARBOUR

Chichester Harbour Conservancy.
Habitats: Deep saltwater channels, mud banks, sand dunes & shingle.
Birds: Internationally-important for birds, with an estimated 55,000 birds residing or passing through each year. *Spring/summer:* Little, Sandwich & Common Terns breed. Dartford Warbler breeds at Sandy Point NR. *Autumn/winter:* Waders inc. Lapwing, Golden Plover, Curlew, Whimbrel, Black & Bar-tailed Godwits, Oystercatcher, Turnstone, Snipe, Dunlin & Sanderling. Up to 10,000 Brent Geese, Red-breasted Merganser & common wildfowl species. Kingfisher, Short-eared owl, Hen Harrier, Skylark.
Other: Common Seal, Water Vole, Stoat, Marsh Samphire, Sea Purslane, Sea Lavender & Sea Aster.
Directions: West of Chichester, with various viewing points along 47 miles of coastline to Hayling Island. East Head/West Wittering good for birding - from A27 S of Chichester, follow brown signs for West Wittering Beach. Sandy Point NR in SE corner of Hayling Island can only be visited on guided walks.
Public transport: Various Stagecoach services in area.
Visiting: Five paths suitable for wheelchairs: Cobnor Point/ Itchenor/ Prinsted/ North Common, Northney/ Sandy Point, Hayling Island. Wheelchair-accessible viewing platform & toilet at Itchenor. RADAR-key toilet at Dell Quay.
Contact: Harbour Office (inc Friends of Chichester Hbr), Itchenor, PO20 7AW. T: 01243 512 301;
E: info@conservancy.co.uk;
W: www.conservancy.co.uk;
E: info@friendsch.org; W: www.friendsch.org

3. KINGLEY VALE NNR

Natural England (Sussex & Kent Team).
Habitats: Greatest yew forest in W.Europe (30,000+ yew trees). Chalk grassland, mixed oak/ash woodland & scrub. Chalk heath. Part of South Downs National Park.
Birds: *All year:* Common woodland spp. inc. Green Woodpecker, Treecreeper, Nuthatch, Goldcrest, Firecrest, Bullfinch. Woodcock, Buzzard, Red Kite, Barn & Tawny Owls, Hawfinch, Raven.

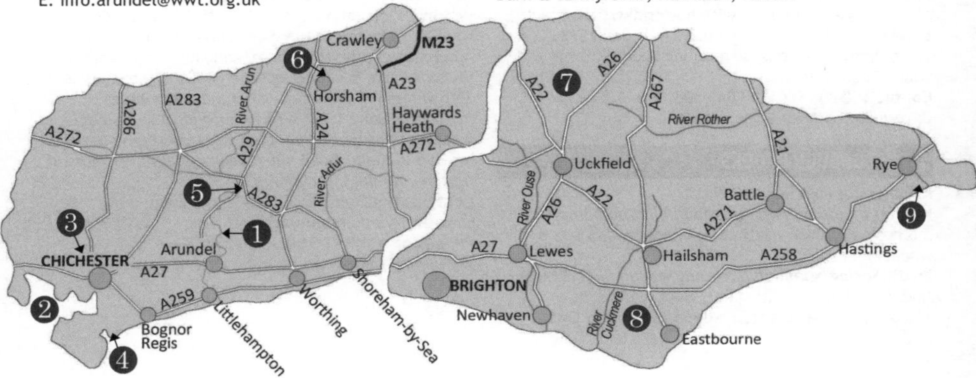

Spring/summer: Nightingale, Grasshopper Warbler, Whitethroat, Lesser Whitethroat, Blackcap. *Autumn passage*: Osprey, Hen Harrier & Hobby. *Winter*: Redwing, Fieldfare, other thrushes (attracted to Yew berries).
Other: Ancient Yew trees, Yellow Meadow Ant, 39 spp. butterflies inc. Brown Argus & Chalkhill Blue, 11 spp. orchid, Brown Hare, Dormouse, Fallow & Roe Deer, bats.
Directions: Sat nav: PO18 9BE. SU 825 087 (West Stoke car park). Approx five miles NW of Chichester town centre. N from Chichester on A286 to Mid Lavant, then turn L by church on to Downs Road, follow to West Stoke. Turn R at junction after church to West Stoke car park - 0.6 mile from reserve entrance).
Public transport: Train - Chichester (three miles)
Visiting: Via footpath from car park, bridleway access via Woodend. No disabled access. Nature trail & an unmanned information centre, leaflets & nature trail guides. Dogs on lead.
Contact: Natural England, T: 0300 060 6000;
E: enquiries@naturalengland.org.uk;
South Downs National Park Authority, T: 01730 814 810;
E: info@southdowns.gov.uk

4. PAGHAM HARBOUR

West Sussex County Council/RSPB.
Habitats: Mudflats, intertidal saltmarsh, shingle beaches, lagoons, grassland & farmland.
Birds: *All year:* Little Egret. *Spring*: Passage migrants (warblers, hirundines, Wheatear). *Summer*: Breeding Little & Common Terns. *Autumn*: Passage waders inc. Curlew Sandpiper, Ruff & Little Stint, wildfowl, migrants, inc. Pied & Spotted Flycatchers. *Winter*: 20,000 wildfowl & waders inc. Brent Goose. Slavonian Grebe.
Other: Common & Grey Seals (winter). Wide variety of grasses, butterflies & dragonflies (inc. Emperor, Broad-bodied Chaser & Hairy Dragonfly).
Directions: Sat nav: PO20 7NE. SZ 856 966. Five miles S of Chichester on B2145 towards Selsey. After 0.5 mile turn R at first roundabout still following Selsey. Look for entrance just after leaving Sidlesham after speed limit increases to 50mph.
Public transport: Bus - no.51 (Chichester-Selsey) stops by visitor centre. Stagecoach. Train - Chichester.
Visiting: Sidlesham Ferry & Church Norton car parks open all times. Groups & coach parties must book in advance. Visitor centre, with hot drinks/light snacks, toilets (inc. disabled) open daily (not Dec 25/26), 10am-4pm. Two hides, several viewpoints, three trails. Dogs on leads.
Contact: RSPB, T: 01243 641 508;
E: pagham.harbour@rspb.org.uk

5. PULBOROUGH BROOKS

RSPB (South East Region Office).
Habitats: Lowland wet grassland (wet meadows/ ditches). Restored heathland, hedgerows, scrub & woodland.
Birds: *Spring/summer*: Breeding waders & songbirds (inc. Lapwing & Nightingale), Hobby, Nightjar, Woodlark, Lesser-spotted Woodpecker, Barn Owl. *Autumn*: Passage waders, Redstart, Whinchat, Yellow Wagtail, incoming wildfowl spp. *Winter*: Thousands of wildfowl & waders, Bewick's Swan. Peregrine, Hen Harrier, Merlin & Short-eared Owl hunt regularly.
Other: Good variety of butterflies & dragonflies (inc. Emperor, Four-spotted Chaser & Downy Emerald).
Directions: Sat nav: RH20 2EL. TQ 058 164. Part of South Downs National Park, signposted on A283 between Pulborough (via A29) & Storrington (via A24). Two miles SE of Pulborough.
Public transport: Train - Pulborough (two miles) with connecting bus no.100 (Burgess Hill to Horsham, not Sun) - request stop, ask driver to stop outside reserve entrance. Compass Travel (T: 01903 690 025).
Visiting: Two trails, four hides, two viewpoints open dawn-dusk (not Dec 25). Large car park inc. coach area, cycle stands. Admission fee for nature trails (RSPB members free). Visitor centre open daily (not Dec 25/26) 9.30am-5pm (inc. shop, cafe until 4.30pm), displays, toilets. Play & picnic areas. Electric buggy available for hire - book in advance, only suitable on wetland trail. Assistance dogs only on wetland trail, access on lead to parts of wooded heathland trail/public footpaths.
Contact: RSPB - see site 1.

6. WARNHAM LNR

Horsham District Council.
Habitats: 37ha inc. 7ha millpond, reedbeds, marsh, meadow & woodland (deciduous & coniferous).
Birds: 170 spp. *Summer*: Mandarin Duck, Common Tern, Hobby, Kingfisher, woodpeckers, Marsh Tit, Goldcrest, hirundines, warblers. *Passage*: Waders, terns, pipits & hirundines. *Winter*: Wildfowl, Cormorant, Little Grebe, gulls, Water Rail, Brambling, Siskin, Redpoll, thrushes.
Other: Extensive invertebrate interest, inc. 35 spp. butterfly & 25 spp. dragonfly. 32 spp. mammals inc. Harvest Mouse & Water Shrew. 450+ spp. plants, inc. Broad-leaved Helleborine & Common Spotted Orchid.
Directions: Sat nav: RH12 2RA. TQ 167 323. 1.5 mile NW of Horsham town centre on B2237, just off A24 'Robin Hood' roundabout.
Public transport: Bus - nos.51 & 62 (not Sun) from Horsham town centre stop close to reserve. Metrobus (T: 01293 449 191). Train - Horsham (one mile - along Hurst Road, with R turn onto Warnham Road).
Visiting: Open all year (not Dec 25/26) 10am-6pm Mar-Oct, 10am-5pm Nov-Feb. Large car park. Admission charge to reserve/annual permit available. Visitor centre & cafe (free entry -10am-4pm summer/ 3pm winter). Toilets (inc. disabled), four hides, millpond nature trail, bird feeding station, wader scrapes, boardwalks, benches & hardstanding paths, reserve leaflets. Good wheelchair access over most of reserve. No dogs or cycling.
Contact: Horsham DC, T: 01403 215 256;
E: parks@horsham.gov.uk;
Friends of WLNR, T 01403 756 238;
W: www.warnhamnaturereservefriends.org.uk

East

7. ASHDOWN FOREST

Conservators of Ashdown Forest - responsible for its management.
Habitats: 2500ha, heathland (60%), woodland (40%).
Birds: *All year:* Buzzard, Sparrowhawk, Red Kite, Raven, Stonechat, Crossbill, Yellowhammer, woodland species inc. Marsh Tit. *Spring/summer:* Hobby, Woodcock, Cuckoo, Turtle Dove, Nightjar, Woodlark, Redstart, Tree Pipit, Spotted Flycatcher, warblers. *Winter:* Hen Harrier, Great Grey Shrike, winter thrushes, Brambling, Redpoll, Siskin.
Other: Deer (Fallow, Roe, Sika, Muntjac), Dormouse, bats. Dragonflies, Raft Spider. 34 spp. Butterflies inc. Purple Emperor, Silver-studded Blue, White Admiral.
Directions: Forest lies between Crowborough, Forest Row & Maresfield - crossed by A22 & A275. The Forest Centre (Sat nav: RH18 5JP. TQ 432 323) is one mile E of Wych Cross traffic lights on A22, opposite Ashdown Park Hotel.
Public transport: Bus - various services run through Forest. Stagecoach no.54; Metrobus nos.270 & 291; Sussex Bus no.31; Brighton & Hove Buses (Regency) no.29; Compass Travel no.261.
Visiting: Open all year, over 40 signposted car parks, many walks throughout Forest (various maps available - downloadable for small donation). Dogs should be under control at all times - grazing stock present. Forest Centre - information barn, toilets.
Contact: The Ashdown Forest Centre, Coleman's Hatch Road, Wych Cross, Forest Row, East Sussex, RH18 5JP: T: 01342 823 583; E: conservators@ashdownforest.org; W: www.ashdownforest.org;
Ashdown Forest Bird Group,
W: www.ashdown-forest.co.uk;
Friends of Ashdown Forest,
W: www.friendsofashdownforest.co.uk/

8. LULLINGTON HEATH NNR

Natural England (Sussex & Kent Team).
Habitats: Grazed chalk downland/heath, scrub/gorse.
Birds: *Summer*: Breeding Nightingale, Turtle Dove, Cuckoo, Garden Warbler, Yellowhammer. *Passage:* migrants inc. Wheatear, Redstart, Ring Ouzel. *Winter*: Woodcock, Brambling (adjacent forest).
Other: Bell Heather, Ling, gorse on chalk heath, orchids.**Directions:** Sat nav: BN26 5QJ. TQ 562 013 (Jevington). Five miles NW of Eastbourne, between Jevington & Litlington, on N edge of Friston Forest. Turn off A259 at Friston and head to Jevington - park here. Walk past church (on South Downs Way), after ca 0.5 mile, once out of trees, continue straight (SDW goes off to R) on for 0.25 mile to reserve. Alternative parking around Friston Forest, inc. Seven Sisters CP visitor centre on A259.
Public transport: Bus - nos.12/12X Brighton to Eastbourne stop at Friston/Seven Sisters CP. Brighton & Hove Buses (T: 01273 886 200).
Visiting: Access on foot via footpaths & bridleways (some steep). Nearest toilets/refreshments at pubs in Jevington, Litlington or Seven Sisters CP, 1.25 miles to S.
Contact: Natural England, T: 01323 423 962.

9. RYE HARBOUR

Sussex Wildlife Trust/Environment Agency/ East Sussex County Council/Rother District Council - main partners of management agreement. [Inc. Castle Water (88ha) owned by Sussex Wildlife Trust.]
Habitats: 465ha, sea, sand, shingle, saline lagoons, saltmarsh, coastal grazing marsh, ditches, freshwater gravel pits & reedbeds.
Birds: 280 spp., 70 spp. have bred. *Spring*: Passage waders, especially roosting Whimbrel. *Summer*: Turtle Dove, breeding terns (three spp), waders (seven spp. inc. Avocet), gulls (six spp. inc Mediterranean), Garganey, Shoveler, Cetti's Warbler, Bearded Tit, Wheatear. *Winter*: Wildfowl & waders, inc. nationally important numbers of Shoveler & Sanderling. Smew, Water Rail, Bittern, Barn & Short-eared Owls.
Other: Good shingle flora inc. endangered Least Lettuce & Stinging Hawksbeard. Saltmarsh supports unusual plants inc. Marsh Mallow & Sea-heath & specialist insects inc. Saltmarsh Bee & Star-wort Moth. Dragonflies inc. Red-veined Darter & Scarce Emerald Damselfly.
Directions: Sat nav: TN31 7TX. TQ 942 189. Main access (large car park) is 1.5 miles SE Rye, off A259 along Harbour Road (to the end) - signposted Rye Harbour. Access also from Winchelsea (SW of site).
Public transport: Bus - no.313 Rye (train station) to Rye Harbour. Stagecoach in Hastings. Train - Rye & Winchelsea.
Visiting: Open all times - public footpaths & two trails: short trail (2.5 miles) & long trail (5.5 miles). Car park with information kiosk in Rye Harbour village, local facilities inc. shop, pubs, toilets & disabled facilities near car park. New Discovery Centre (due for completion in early 2020). Site is flat with some wheelchair access to four hides on eastern side, although there are stiles where stock is grazing. One hide & viewpoint on Castle Water side. Organised groups should book in advance.
Contact: Sussex WT, T: 07884 494 982; E; via website; Friends of Rye Harbour, W: www.rhnrfriends.co.uk

South West England

Cornwall, Devon, Dorset, Somerset, Wiltshire

Cornwall

For the seawatching enthusiast an autumn visit to a Cornish headland, such as St Ives or Porthgwarra, is a must with a good chance of Cory's, Great & Sooty Shearwaters, skuas, terns & gulls or even something much rarer. Spring &, particularly, autumn brings many migrants passing through the county & birds (including rarities) can turn up anywhere - migrant hot-spots near Land's End include Cot & Nanquidno Valleys. Choughs have recolonised the Lizard & Cirl Buntings are beginning to spread as the result of a re-introduction programme.

1. CROWDY RESERVOIR

South West Lakes Trust.
Habitats: Reservoir, bog, moorland, forestry.
Birds: *Spring*: Passage migrants, inc. Wheatear, Whimbrel, Ruff. *Summer*: Black-headed Gull, Grasshopper, Reed & Sedge Warblers, returning waders. *Autumn*: Waders, raptors possible inc. Peregrine, Goshawk, Merlin. *Winter*: Wildfowl, inc. Goosander & possible Smew. Golden Plover, Woodcock, Fieldfare, Redwing. Starling murmuration (nearby Rough Tor).
Other: Mire floral communities. Marsh Fritillary.
Directions: Sat nav. PL32 9XJ. SX 138 833. Follow signs from A39 at Camelford to Davidstow Airfield & pick up signs to reservoir. Park in main car park or continue to edge of forestry plantation & park in pull-in spot near cattle grid - track leads to hide via stiles from here.
Public transport: Buses - to Camelford (2.25 miles).
Visiting: Open all year. Hide (N side). Access along reservoir banks (unsuitable for wheelchairs).
Contact: South West Lakes Trust, T: 01566 771 930;
E: info@swlakestrust.org.uk;
W: www.swlakestrust.org.uk

2. HAYLE ESTUARY

RSPB (South West England Office).
Habitats: Intertidal mudflats, saltmarsh, lagoon & islands (access to Ryan's Field, Lelant Water, Carnsew Pool, Copperhouse Pool).
Birds: *Spring/summer*: Migrant waders, breeding Shelduck. *Autumn*: Rare waders, often from North America, terns, gulls (inc. Mediterranean). *Winter*: Large numbers of wildfowl & waders. Top UK site for Ring-billed Gull, but not annual. Other gull spp., Kingfisher, Great Northern Diver.
Directions: Sat nav: TR27 6JF. SW 551 364. Follow signs to Hayle from A30. Take B3301 through Hayle past Tempest factory, turn L into Chenalls Road signposted St Erth & Hayle Estuary NR, turn R after 200 yeards into Ryans Field car park. Other parking in Hayle & Lelant.
Public transport: Bus - services to Hayle. Train - Hayle (limited stops) & St Erth (one mile).
Visiting: Open all times. Ryan's Field: no coaches. Eric Grace Memorial Hide (information board) overlooks Ryan's Field but birds here only at high tide. Not suitable for wheelchair users. Circular walk around Ryan's Field. Public footpath around Carnsew Pool. Dogs on leads restricted to public footpaths.
Contact: RSPB, T: 01736 360 624;
E: hayle.estuary@rspb.org.uk

3. HELMAN TOR NATURE RESERVE

Cornwall Wildlife Trust.
Habitats: 217ha, inc. wetland, grassland, heath & scrub.
Birds: Curlew, Sparrowhawk, Nightjar, Tree Pipit, Lesser Whitethroat, Willow Tit.
Other: Butterflies (inc. Marsh & Small Pearl-bordered Fritillaries, Silver-studded Blue). Royal Fern, sundews & other bog plants.
Directions: Sat nav: PL30 5DF. SX 062 615 (Tor car park). Large wetland complex spreading from slopes of Helman Tor inc. Breney Common & Red Moor Memorial Reserve. 2.5 miles S of Bodmin. From A30/A391 (Innis Downs) roundabout south of Bodmin, turn N to Lanivet & take first R under A30 bridge. For Breney Common entrance, turn R at Reperry Cross, then L fork to Trebell Green & on towards Gurtla. Entrance track is on L in Gurtla, after Methodist church, opposite The Barn (SX 053 610).
Public transport: None.
Visiting: Open all times, keep to paths. Small car park at Helman Tor, Wilderness trail from here can be very muddy after heavy rain - boardwalk sections only suitable surface for wheelchairs (can be slippery when wet).
Contact: Cornwall WT,
T: 01872 273 939;
E: info@cornwallwildlifetrust.org.uk

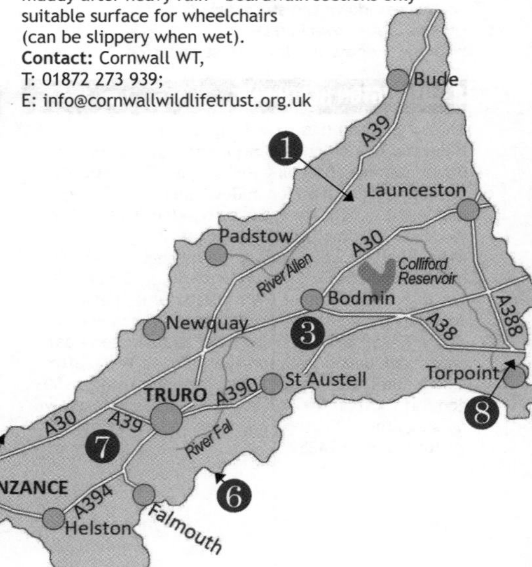

4. THE LIZARD NNR

Natural England/National Trust/Cornwall Wildlife Trust.
Habitats: Heathland, coastal grassland, cliffs & coves, puddles & ponds.
Birds: *All year*: Chough, Raven, Gannet, Barn Owl, Dartford Warbler. *Spring/autumn passage:* migrants, seabirds often inc. scarce/rare spp. *Summer*: Wheatear, warblers, Puffin (offshore). *Winter*: Divers, Razorbill, Guillemot, Hen Harrier, Merlin, Peregrine, Short-eared Owl, Purple Sandpiper, winter thrushes.
Other: 250 spp. of national/international importance esp. coastal flora, Cornish Heath. Adder, Common Lizard.
Directions: Main route to The Lizard is by heading S on A3083/B3293 from A394 at Helston. NNR (2500ha) is scattered across area. Sat nav: places of interest inc. Goonhilly Downs TR12 6RW (SW 736 201); Kynance Cove TR12 7PJ (SW 687 132); Lizard Village TR12 7NU (SW 701 116); Windmill Farm TR12 7LH (SW 694 152); but birds can turn up anywhere!
Public transport: Bus - no.34 Helston-Lizard village (not Sun). Plymouth Citibus (T: 01752 662 271).
Visiting: Open all year. Car parks, most with toilets, spread around area. Cafe/refreshments in Lizard Village - Chough watch point to S of village.
Contact: Natural England, T: 01326 240 808;
E: steve.townsend@naturalengland.org.uk;
National Trust, T: 01326 222 170;
E: lizard@nationaltrust.org.uk;
Cornwall Wildlife Trust - see site 3.

5. MARAZION MARSH

RSPB (South West England Office).
Habitats: Wet reedbed, willow carr.
Birds: 250+ spp. *Spring/summer*: Breeding Reed, Sedge & Cetti's Warblers, herons, swans. *Autumn*: Large roost of Swallows & martins in reedbeds, migrant warblers (inc. regular Aquatic, difficult to see) & Water Rail. *Winter*: Wildfowl, Snipe, occasional Bittern, impressive pre-roost flocks of Starlings up to New Year Buzzard & Sparrowhawk.
Other: 22 spp. dragonflies, 500 spp. vascular plants, inc. Lawn Camomile & Yellow Flag.
Directions: Sat nav: TR17 0AA. SW 510 312. Reserve is one mile E of Penzance, 500 yards W of Marazion. Entrance off seafront road near Marazion.
Public transport: Bus - nos. A2 & U4 from Penzance bus station to Marazion. Alight Godolphin Place (opp. St MIchael's Mount car park). First Group.
Visiting: Open all times, not suitable for wheelchair users. Park in car parks within walking distance. No coaches. Viewing bay on seafront pavement overlooks pools & reedbeds of sanctuary area. Dogs on leads. Nearest toilets in Marazion & seafront car park.
Contact: RSPB, 01736 360 624;
E: marazion.marsh@rspb.org.uk

6. NARE HEAD

National Trust.
Habitats: Headland, open sea.
Birds: *Spring/summer*: Razorbill, Guillemot, Shag, Sandwich, Common & Arctic Terns, possible Whimbrel, Fulmar, occasional Chough. *Passage:* Migrants. *Winter*: Great Northern, Black & Red-throated Divers, Slavonian, Black-necked & Red-necked Grebes, Common & Velvet Scoter.
Directions: Sat nav: TR2 5PQ. SW 919 378 (Nare Head car park). Parking also in Carne. Part of NT's Roseland estate. Approx ten miles SE of Truro. From A390 head S on A307 to two miles S of Tregony just past garage. Follow signs to Veryan then L signposted to Carne. Go straight over at crossroad, following Carne & Pendower. Turn L on a bend following NT signs for Nare Head. Bearing R, cross over a cattle grid to car park (Nare Head is about four miles from garage).
Public transport: None.
Visiting: Open daily. Car Park. Unstable cliff edges approach with care.
Contact: National Trust, T: 01872 580 553;
E: roseland@nationaltrust.org.uk

7. STITHIANS RESERVOIR

South West Lakes Trust.
Habitats: Open water, marshland, meadows, wet woodland, heathland.
Birds: *Passage:* Good for waders inc. Common, Green & Wood Sandpipers. Osprey, Black Tern, Garganey. *Winter*: County's best open water site for wildfowl. Winter gull flocks inc. Mediterranean. Reservoir has good track record for *rarities*: inc. Pied-billed Grebe, Pectoral, White-rumped & Semipalmated Sandpipers, Lesser Yellowlegs, Wilson's Phalarope, Caspian Tern & Black Kite.
Directions: Sat nav: TR16 6NW. SS 709 369. Signposted from B3297 S of Redruth.
Public transport: None.
Visiting: Good viewing from causeway. Hide near main centre (opposite Golden Lion Inn), open to all. Two other hides for members of CBWPS. Toilets, cafe (9am-4pm). Footpath around reservoir.
Contact: Stithians Activity Centre, T: 01209 860 301;
South West Lakes Trust - see site 1.

8. TAMAR ESTUARY

Cornwall Wildlife Trust.
Habitats: 110ha, tidal mudflats, some saltmarsh.
Birds: *Spring/summer:* Breeding Shelduck. *Winter*: Waders - inc. large nos. of Avocet. Black-tailed Godwit, Redshank, Dunlin, Curlew, Whimbrel, Spotted Redshank, Green Sandpiper, Golden Plover, Snipe, Kingfisher.
Directions: Sat nav: PL12 6LJ. SX 431 614 (Landulph). PL12 6NX. SX 436 626 (Cargreen). N of Saltash. From Plymouth head W on A38, after Saltash turn R on to A388. Access parking at Cargreen & Landulph from minor roads off A388.
Public transport: None.
Visiting: Open all times. Footpath from Cargreen to Landulph. Also access to two hides (from China Fleet Club car park, Saltash PL12 6LJ. SX428 604). Follow path alongside golf course (keep off course). Combination number for hide locks available at club reception. Two hides on foreshore, first (0.25 mile from car park - NOW UNSAFE) overlooks estuary, second (0.5 mile) has views across Kingsmill Lake.
Contact: Cornwall WT - see site 3.

Devon

The county has a wide variety of habitats including the marshes of the Exe estuary, near Exeter (wildfowl & waders), the pebblebed heathlands (Dartford Warbler) in the east, the moorlands of Exmoor, that spread into west Somerset, & Dartmoor (where Red-backed Shrikes are attempting to re-establish themselves). The south coast holds localised but increasing pockets of Cirl Buntings. The island of Lundy in the Bristol Channel regularly turns up rarities.

1. AYLESBEARE COMMON

RSPB (South West England Office).
Habitats: Heathland, wood fringes, streams & ponds.
Birds: *All year*: Buzzard, Dartford Warbler, Yellowhammer. *Spring/summer*: Hobby, Nightjar, Tree Pipit, Stonechat. *Winter*: Possible Hen Harrier.
Other: Good variety of dragonflies (inc Southern Damselfly) & butterflies.
Directions: Sat nav: EX5 2JS. SY 057 897. Five miles E of Junc 30 of M5 at Exeter, 0.5 mile past Halfway Inn on B3052. Turn R to Hawkerland, car park is on L. Reserve is on opposite side of main road.
Public transport: Bus - nos.9 & 9A Exeter to Seaton/ Honiton request stop at Joneys Cross (reserve entrance). Stagecoach South West.
Visiting: Open all year. Car park, two trails, picnic area, group bookings, guided walks & special events. One track suitable for wheelchairs & pushchairs, disabled access via metalled track to private farm. Dogs on lead.
Contact: RSPB, T: 01395 233 655;
E: aylesbeare.common@rspb.org.uk

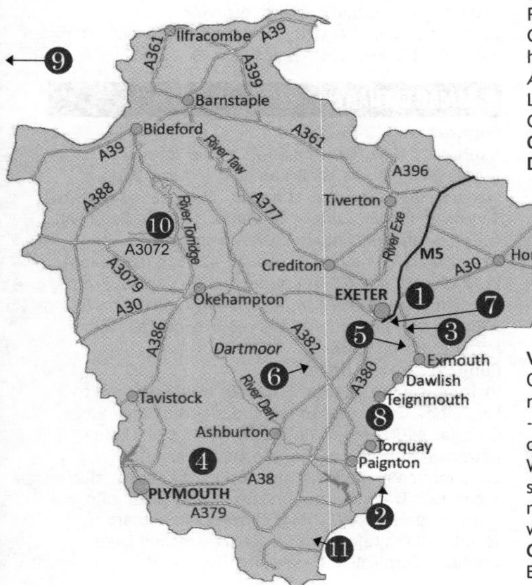

2. BERRY HEAD NNR

Torbay Coast & Countryside Trust.
Habitats: Limestone cliffs (200ft), grassland, quarry.
Birds: *All year:* Cirl Bunting (in flocks in winter), Peregrine (hunting in quarry area), Fulmar. *Spring/ summer:* Up to 1,200 nesting Guillemots on cliffs below Southern Fort. *Passage:* Well known for migrants.
Other: Limestone flora inc. eight spp. orchid, Small Hare's-ear. Harbour Porpoise, Common Dolphin, Greater & Lesser Horseshoe Bats (walks arranged), Bloody Nose Beetle & variety of butterflies.
Directions: Sat nav: TQ5 9AP. SX 940 561 (Berry Head car park). Signposted from Brixham on minor roads from A3022 & A379. Located at end of Gillard Road, past Landscove Holiday Village.
Public transport: Bus - no.17 from Brixham to Victoria Road (0.5 mile walk to Berry Head: some steep sections). Stagecoach South West.
Visiting: Open all year. Pay-&-display car park. Guardhouse visitor centre open Easter-Oct 10am-4pm Tues-Sun/1pm-4pm Mon & Oct-Easter 10am-4pm Sat/ Sun only. CCTV images of nesting seabirds, cafe & toilets. Wheelchair-friendly 300 yards path from car park to visitor centre & cafe. Two mobility vehicles for hire (pre-book). Bird hide overlooking cliffs.
Contact: Berry Head NNR, T: 01803 882 619;
E: berryhead@countryside-trust.org.uk;
W:www.countryside-trust.org.uk/explore/berry-head/

3. BOWLING GREEN & GOOSEMOOR

RSPB (South West England Office).
Habitats: Coastal grassland, open water/marsh.
Birds: *Spring*: Shelduck, passage waders inc. Little Stint, Ringed Plover, Ruff & sandpipers, Whimbrel, passage Garganey & Yellow Wagtail. *Summer*: Gull/tern roosts, high tide wader roosts contain many passage birds. *Autumn*: Wildfowl, Peregrine, wader roosts. *Winter*: Large numbers of Wigeon, Shoveler, Teal, Black-tailed Godwit, Curlew, Golden Plover. Avocet & Brent Geese.
Other: Hairy Dragonfly, Wasp Spider.
Directions: Sat nav: EX3 0EN. SX 683 825 (Holman Way car park). On E side of River Exe, four miles SE of Exeter in Bowling Green Road, Topsham.
Public transport: Bus - no.57 Exeter to Topsham, alight at Elm Grove Road (0.6 mile from reserve). Also stops at Darts Farm Shopping Village (inc. RSPB shop). Stagecoach. Train - Exeter to Exmouth stops at Topsham (reserve - one mile).
Visiting: Open all times. Park at Holman Way or The Quay public car parks in Topsham, not in lane by reserve. Lookout Hide located on Bowling Green Road - short walk from parking areas (Blue Badge bay outside). Nearest RADAR toilets at The Quay car park. Wheelchair accessible hide/viewing platform. RSPB shop at Darts Farm (EX3 0QH, T: 01392 879 438), one mile from reserve, E of Topsham across River Clyst - weekly guided walks from here.
Contact: RSPB, T: 01392 833 311;
E: exe.estuary@rspb.org.uk

4. BURRATOR RESERVOIR

South West Lakes Trust.
Habitats: Pine forests, wooded streams, open moorland scrub.
Birds: *All year*: 3 spp. woodpecker, Buzzard, Kestrel, Sparrowhawk, Barn Owl, Tree Sparrow. *Winter*: Goosander, Dipper, Grey Wagtail, Green Sandpiper, Brambling, Crossbill, Siskin, Redpoll.
Other: Marsh Fritillary butterfly, dragonflies, esp. in arboretum, bats, Otter.
Directions: Sat nav: PL20 6PE. SX 552 685 (Discovery Centre). On S side of Dartmoor, 10 miles NE of Plymouth, off A386 (Tavistock road). At Yelverton take B3212 towards Princeton. Turn R at Burrator Inn (Dousland) & follow signs to reservoir.
Public transport: Bus - no.1 Plymouth/Tavistock to Yelverton - Stagecoach South West - then no.56 (limited) Yelverton to Dousland (1.5 miles from reservoir/not Sun). Target Travel (T: 01752 242 000).
Visiting: Open all year. Car park around reservoir (inc. Norsworthy Bridge, Arboretum & Quarry car parks, (free/donations welcome). Visitor centre (opening times/days vary depending on time of year), toilets (inc disabled). Snack & ice-cream vans during summer. Main circular route, though suitable for disabled access, is used by cars & cyclists. One mile wildlife trail in Arboretum suitable for wheelchairs.
Contact: Burrator Discovery Centre,
T: 01822 855 700; E: heritage@swlakestrust.org.uk;
W: www.swlakestrust.org.uk

5. DAWLISH WARREN NNR

Teignbridge District Council.
Habitats: High tide roost site for wildfowl & waders of Exe estuary on mudflats & shore. Dunes, dune grassland, woodland, scrub, ponds.
Birds: Excellent variety of birds all year, esp. on migration. *Summer*: Particularly good for terns. *Winter*: Waders & wildfowl in large numbers. Also good for divers & Slavonian Grebe offshore.
Directions: Sat nav: EX7 0NF. SX 983 788. On S side of Exe estuary mouth. Turn off A379 just N of Dawlish (signposted to Dawlish Warren). At mini-roundabout, just after Welcome Inn, turn R. Pass under tunnel (by train station) then turn L (away from amusements) & park at far end of car park & walk through gates.
Public transport: Bus - no.22 Torquay/Paignton to DW. Stagecoach South West. Train - Dawlish Warren.
Visiting: Open public access, but avoid mudflats & beach beyond groyne nine around high tide (roosting birds). Pay-&-display car park. Visitor centre open Apr-Aug 2pm-5pm/Sat-Sun, 2pm-4pm/Wed-Fri (closed Mon-Tues) Sep-Mar 1pm-4pm/Sat-Sun (may be closed if in use by groups or wardens out on site). Toilets at entrance tunnel & in resort area. Hide one mile NE of visitor centre, open at all times - best around high tide. No dogs on beach or dunes between ninth groyne at any time (inc. hide).
Contact: Teignbridge District Council, T: 01626 215 751;
E: greenspaces@teignbridge.gov.uk;
W: www.dawlishwarren.co.uk (DW Recording Group).

6. EAST DARTMOOR WOODS & HEATHS NNR

Natural England (Devon, Cornwall & Isles of Scilly Team).
Habitats: Three connected sites (Yarner Wood, Trendlebere Down & Bovey Valley Woodlands), 365 ha of upland oakwood, heathland, bogs & streams.
Birds: *All year*: Raven, Buzzard, Sparrowhawk, Goshawk, 3 spp. woodpecker, Dipper, Grey Wagtail & Dartford Warbler (Trendlebere Down). *Spring/summer*: Cuckoo, Tree Pipit, Skylark, Pied Flycatcher, Redstart, Stonechat, Whitethroat, Wood Warbler, Linnet. Nightjar on heaths. *Autumn/winter*: Good variety of birds feeding at Yarner Wood hide, inc. Siskin, Redpoll. Hen Harrier (Trendlebere Down).
Other: Good for butterflies inc. fritillaries & Grayling.
Directions: Sat nav: TQ13 9LJ. SX 785 788 (Yarner Wood). NNR is two miles from Bovey Tracey on road to Becky Falls & Manaton. Road continues across Trendlebere Down - three roadside car parks & adjacent paths.
Public transport: None.
Visiting: Yarner Wood car park open 7.30am-7.30pm/ dusk if earlier - outside these hours, access on foot from Trendlebere Down. Information/interpretation display & self-guided trails available in Yarner Wood car park & hide with feeding station (Nov-Mar). Dogs under close control.
Contact: Natural England, Yarner Wood,
T: 01626 832 330.

7. EXMINSTER & POWDERHAM MARSHES

RSPB (South West England Office).
Habitats: Coastal grazing marsh with freshwater ditches & pools, reeds, scrub-covered canal banks, winter stubble/crops managed for farmland birds.
Birds: *Spring*: Lapwing, Redshank & wildfowl breed, Cetti's Warbler on canal banks. *Summer*: Gull roosts, passage waders, hirundines, Hobby. *Autumn/Winter*: Peregrine, Short-eared Owl, finch flocks (inc. Cirl Bunting. *Winter*: Hundreds of Brent Geese & Wigeon, smaller numbers of common ducks, Water Rail, Short-eared Owl, winter thrushes.
Other: 23 spp. dragonflies inc. Hairy & Scarce Chaser.
Directions: Sat nav: EX6 8DZ. SX 954 872. Five miles S of Exeter on W bank of River Exe, on outskirts of Exminster. At S end of village take Station Road exit off A379 from Swans Nest roundabout. Go past Swans Nest Inn, over railway bridge - lane to car park immediately on R (signposted). Powderham Marsh is accessed from car park behind Swan's Nest Inn.
Public transport: Bus - no.2 Exeter to Newton Abbot, Swan's Nest roundabout stop is 400 yards from reserve car park - walk down Station Road (past Swans Nest Inn). Stagecoach South West.
Visiting: Open all times (except permissive path at Powderham). Information in RSPB car park (Exminster), marked footpaths across reserve , viewing screen - 2.5 mile circular walk takes 90 mins. No dogs at Powderham Marshes, one mile trail, viewing platform. Refreshments & toilets at Swans Nest Inn & Turf pub.
Contact: RSPB - see site 3.

8. LABRADOR BAY

RSPB (South West England Office).
Habitats: Reserve covers 1.25 miles of coastline. Part of a working farm grazed by cattle in summer, sheep in winter with coastal cliff top, woodland, scrub, arable & semi-improved grassland.
Birds: Purchased to help secure future of Cirl Buntings that can be seen all year round - breeding pairs in spring/summer & in flocks during autumn/winter when they feed on stubble with other farmland birds inc. Skylark, Chaffinch & Yellowhammer. Peregrine & Buzzard also regular.
Other: Offshore - Dolphins, Basking Shark.
Directions: Sat nav: TQ1 4TP. SX 931 705. The bay lies 2.7 miles S of Teignmouth on the A379 coast road between Shaldon & Maidencombe.
Public transport: Train - Teignmouth is two miles away, then use SW Coast Path (no bus services).
Visiting: Open at all times. Pay-&-display car park, nearest toilets one mile (Maidencombe, summer only). Several walks around the site, longest inc. three miles of South West Coast Path.
Contact: RSPB - see site 3.

9. LUNDY

Owned by National Trust/managed by Landmark Trust.
Habitats: Island (3.5 miles long, 0.5 miles wide), 12 miles N of Hartland Point in Bristol Channel. Farmed area in S, moorland to N & Marine Protected Area.
Birds: 140 spp. annually. *Breeding:* Seabirds, inc. Manx Shearwater (5,500 pr) & Puffin (400 pr)- both recovering after rat eradication. Fulmar, Shag,Gannet (offshore), Razorbill,Guillemot, Kittiwake, Storm Petrel (possibly breeds, occasionally offshore). *Spring/autumn passage:* Regular common migrants pass through, always with a chance of scarce or rare spp. Sometimes large 'falls' of birds occur.
Other: Endemic Lundy Cabbage & Bronze Lundy Cabbage Flea Beetle.
Directions: Sat nav: EX39 2EY (Bideford Office). TQ7 2QP (Ilfracombe Office). Parking in both towns.
Public transport: None.
Visiting: Lundy's own ferry/supply ship MV Oldenburg sails at least three times pw from either Bideford or Ilfracombe (crossing takes ca. two hours each way). *Day trips.* Boat runs from Apr-Sep, onshore time limited to four/six hours depending on sailing. *Residential trips* (accommodation available). Boat runs from Apr-Oct & helicopter from late-Jan to Mar & Nov to early Jan (Fri/Mon only). Contact/see website for sailing/flight dates, times, costs & for accommodation options. Crossings may be cancelled during bad weather.
Contact: Booking Office - T: 01271 863 636;
E: info@lundyisland.co.uk;
W: www.landmarktrust.org.uk/Lundyisland;
Lundy Field Society,
E: secretary@lundy.org.uk;
W: www.lundy.org.uk

10. MEETH QUARRY

Devon Wildlife Trust.
Habitats: Lakes (flooded quarry), ponds, woodland, grassland. Adjoins DWT Ash Moor reserve.
Birds: *All Year:* Great Crested & Little Grebe, Barn Owl, Kingfisher, Yellowhammer. *Summer:* Hobby, hirundines, warblers. *Winter:* Wildfowl (inc. Goosander, Pochard, Tufted Duck), Woodcock, Snipe.
Other: Roe Deer, Brown Hare, 14 spp. Dragonflies, butterflies, Otter.
Directions: Sat nav: EX20 3ER. SS 546 078. Eight miles NW Okehampton. From A386 Hatherleigh-Great Torrington road at Meeth look for sign to Tarka Trail & Meeth Quarry NR. Enter service road here & drive for ca. one mile to reach reserve/car park.
Public transport: Bus - no.75A Okehamption-Great Torrington passes through Meeth - alight at Meeth Village stop & walk down service road lane to reserve entrance (ca one mile).
Visiting: Open all year. Car park at reserve entrance open 8am-8pm weekends, 9am-5pm weekdays. Toilet (inc. disabled), picnic area, hide. Colour-coded trails (pushchair friendly) - red trail suitable for wheelchairs/mobility scooters. A 3 mile 'Meeth Quarry Wild Walk' is good introduction to area. 'Tarka Trail' cycle route starts/ends in Meeth & cuts through reserve. Dogs on lead.
Contact: Devon WT, T: 01392 279 244;
E: contactus@devonwildlife trust.org

11. SLAPTON LEY NNR

Field Studies Council/Natural England (Devon, Cornwall & Isles of Scilly Team).
Habitats: Freshwater lake, reedbeds, marsh & woodland.
Birds: *All year:* Cirl Bunting, Cetti's Warbler. Most south-westerly population of Great Crested Grebe. *Spring/summer:* Migrant warblers. Good seawatching in favourable conditions in spring & autumn, migrants on passage. Large gathering of Swallows in autumn roosts. *Winter:* Divers & grebes on sea, Bittern at Higher Ley. Diving ducks & grebes on Lower Ley.
Other: UK's only site for Strapwort. Otter, Dormouse.
Directions: Sat nav: TQ7 2QP. SX 825 448 (Field Centre). Largest freshwater lake in SW England, lying S of Dartmouth on south coast, is separated from Start Bay by a shingle bank which carries A379.
Public transport: Bus - no.3 from Plymouth/ Kingsbridge to Dartmouth stops at Slapton (outside field centre - limited on Sun)). Stagecoach South West.
Visiting: Pay-&-display car parks off A379 at Torcross & Slapton Sands. Higher Ley is closed to public, but can be viewed from public footpath. Hides overlooking Torcross & Stokely Bay areas of lagoon & surrounding backdrops. Field Centre offers variety of residential courses.
Contact: Slapton Ley Field Centre, T: 01548 580 466;
E: enquiries.sl@field-studies-council.org;
W: www.slnnr.org.uk

Dorset

The county holds internationally important habitats & the Isle of Portland is a migration hot-spot - making this one of England's top birding destinations. The heathlands hold Dartford Warbler, Woodlark & Nightjar, Poole Harbour attracts internationally important numbers of wintering waders & wildfowl. Two RSPB reserves in Weymouth (Lodmoor & Radipole) are probably the best urban birding sites in the country & the Portland Bird Observatory is the place to be at migration time. Ospreys are being re-introduced in to Poole Harbour.

1. ARNE

RSPB (South West England Office).
Habitats: Lowland heath, woodland, reedbed & saltmarsh, extensive mudflats of Poole Harbour.
Birds: *All year*: Little Egret, Spoonbill, Marsh Harrier (breed in harbour), Barn Owl, Dartford Warbler, Stonechat. *Summer*: Sandwich & Common Terns, Hobby, Nightjar, hirundines, warblers. *Passage*: Osprey, Spotted Redshank, Whimbrel, Greenshank. *Winter*: 30,000 waders/wildfowl use Poole Harbour, many seen from Arne inc. grebes, divers, Brent Goose, Black-tailed Godwit, Avocet, plus occasional Eider, Scaup & Long-tailed Duck. Hen Harrier, winter thrushes & finches. A five-year Osprey re-introduction programmed started in Poole Harbour in 2017.
Other: Sika Deer, all six spp. UK reptile, 32 spp. butterflies inc. Silver-studded Blue, 23 spp. dragonflies, 850 spp. moths & 500 spp. flowering plants.
Directions: Sat nav: BH20 5BJ. SY 971 876. Head S from Wareham over causeway, turn off L at Stoborough to Ridge continue to Arne.
Public transport: None to reserve. Train - nearest station is Wareham (four miles).
Visiting: Trails open all times. Pay-&-display car park open 8.30am-6pm Nov-Mar/ 10pm Apr-Oct (free for RSPB members). Coaches & escorted parties by prior arrangement. Shop open daily (not Dec 25/26) 9.30am-5pm/cafe 9.30am-4.30pm (opposite car park), small Welcome Hut (9am-4.30pm) & toilets in car park/cafe. Seven signposted trails, limited wheelchair access on trails. Two hides, one viewpoint & two viewing screens. Dogs on leads/no dogs on new Hyde Heath extension, take dog waste away.
Contact: RSPB, T: 01929 553 360; E: arne@rspb.org.uk

2. BROWNSEA ISLAND NATURE RESERVE

Dorset Wildlife Trust/National Trust.
Habitats: 101ha, saline lagoon, reedbed, lakes, coniferous & mixed woodland.
Birds: *All year*: Spoonbill, Little Egret, Golden Pheasant. *Summer*: Common & Sandwich Terns, Little Grebe, Mediterranean Gull. *Autumn*: Curlew Sandpiper, Little Stint & rarities often turn up on DWT Lagoon. *Winter*: Avocet, Black-tailed Godwit, Spotted Redshank & other waders, Water Rail, gulls & wildfowl.
Other: Red Squirrel (up to 250 on island), Water Vole, Bechstein's Bat. Good variety of butterflies & dragonflies.
Directions: Sat nav: BH15 1HJ. SZ 010 902 (Poole Quay). Brownsea Island Ferries (T: 01929 462 383): half hourly crossings from Poole Quay/Sandbanks Quay (BH13 7QN. SZ 037 870 by Studland chain-ferry). Greenslade Pleasure Boats (T: 01202 669 955): half hourly crossings from Poole Quay. Boat charges apply in addition to landing fee.
Public transport: Poole - bus & train stations are short walk from Poole Quay/boats (mainly down pedestrian shopping area to the Old Town).

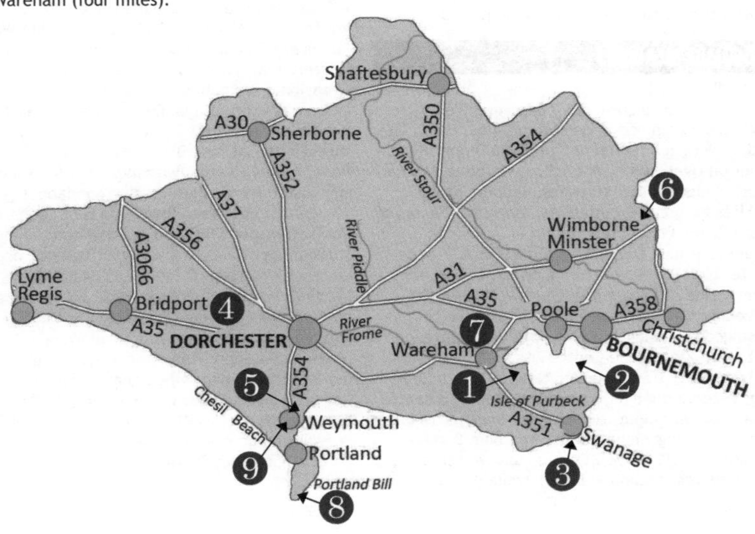

Visiting: Island open late-Mar to end-Oct, 10am-5pm. Landing fee (free for NT members). Free admission to nature reserve for DWT members (show card to NT staff) but landing fee must be paid if visiting rest of island. Toilets, information centre, cafe, gift shop, five hides, nature trail. Assistance dogs only.
Contact: Dorset WT, T: 01202 709 445;
E: info@dorsetwildlifetrust.org.uk;
National Trust, T: 01202 707 744;
E: brownseaisland@nationaltrust.org.uk

3. DURLSTON NNR & COUNTRY PARK

Dorset County Council.
Habitats: 113ha, sea cliffs, woodland, grassland, hedges, cliff, meadows & downland.
Birds: *All year:* Peregrine, Kestrel, Raven, woodland species. *Spring/autumn passage:* migrants (esp. important site for visible migration in autumn). *Summer:* Cliff-nesting seabird colonies inc. Fulmar, Guillemot, Razorbill & Shag, good variety of scrub & woodland breeding spp. Can be good for seabird passage - esp. Apr/May & Aug/Nov.
Other: 34 spp. butterflies inc. Lulworth Skipper, 800 spp. moths & 500+ spp. flowering plants, inc. nine spp. orchid. Bottlenose Dolphin.
Directions: Sat nav: BH19 2JL. SZ 032 773. Lighthouse Road, Swanage, one mile S of town centre (signposted).
Public transport: Bus - Durlston Explorer 5 runs between end-May to end-Sep (half-hourly from pick-up points in Swanage running approx. 10am-5pm).
Visiting: Open dawn-dusk. Pay-&-display parking. Durlston Castle: visitor centre open daily (not Dec 25/26) 10am-5pm Apr-Oct, 10am-4pm Nov-Mar. Cafe (in Castle) open daily (not Dec 25/26) 9.30am-5pm & Fri/Sat evenings Apr-mid Oct. Toilets, exhibitions, art displays & shop. Dolphin watch point hide, waymarked trails. Walks & events.
Contact: Durlston CP, T: 01929 424 443;
E: info@durlston.co.uk; W: www.durlston.co.uk

4. KINGCOMBE MEADOWS

Dorset Wildlife Trust.
Habitats: Unimproved grassland, hedgerows, fields, river.
Birds: *All year:* Common woodland spp. (inc. Marsh Tit), Buzzard, Raven, Yellowhammer, possible Dipper & Kingfisher on river. *Summer:* Cuckoo, warblers. *Winter:* Woodcock, Snipe, winter thrushes, Redpoll, Siskin.
Other: Flora inc orchids, butterflies, fungi (inc. 27 spp. of wax-caps), Otter, Dormouse.
Directions: Sat nav: DT2 0EQ. SY 554 990. A37 from Dorchester towards Yeovil, turn L on to A356 after Grimstone. One mile past Maiden Newton turn L to Toller Procorum (Toller Lane) then R in village to Lower Kingcombe (Kingcombe Road). Info Centre/car park 1st on R, Kingcombe Centre 2nd on R.
Public transport: Train - Maiden Newton (3.5 miles)
Visiting: Reserve open all times. Car park. Info centre & toilets open 9am-5pm, two circular marked trails. Dogs on leads. Kingcombe Centre: tearoom & shop open 10am-4pm (Mar-Dec). Centre runs workshops, courses & events, accommodation available.
Contact: Dorset WT, T: 01305 264 620;
E: info@dorsetwildlifetrust.org.uk
Kingcombe Centre, T: 01300 320 684;
E: kingcombe@dorsetwildlifetrust.org.uk;
W: www.kingcombe.org

5. LODMOOR NATURE RESERVE

RSPB (South West England Office).
Habitats: Marsh, shallow pools, large reedbed & scrub, remnant saltmarsh.
Birds: *All year:* Little Egret, Marsh Harrier (breeding), Kingfisher, Cetti's Warbler, Bearded Tit. *Spring/summer*: Common Tern colony, warblers (inc. Reed, Sedge, Lesser Whitethroat, occasionally Grasshopper), Hobby. *Passage*: Waders (inc. Black-tailed Godwit, Green & Wood Sandpipers) - other migrants & rarities regularly turn up. *Winter*: Wildfowl, waders, Bittern.
Directions: Sat nav: DT3 6HS. SY 688 809. NE of Weymouth, one mile from town centre adjacent to A3155 (Preston Road).
Public transport: Bus - frequent local service to Overcombe Corner, Lodmoor Country Park from Weymouth seafront. Train - Weymouth, bus or easy walk along seafront to reserve (one mile).
Visiting: Open all times. Pay-&-display car parks nearby, street parking on N side (Southdown Ave). One viewing shelter, trails mostly accessible to wheelchairs.
Contact: RSPB, T: 01305 778 313;
E: weymouth.reserves@rspb.org.uk

6. MOORS VALLEY COUNTRY PARK & FOREST

East Dorset Council/England.
Habitats: Lakes, ponds, river, scrub, deciduous woodland, coniferous forest, meadow, heathland.
Birds: *All year*: Buzzard, Lapwing, Woodcock, Little Owl, Grey Wagtail, Kingfisher, Dartford Warbler, Crossbill, usual woodland species. *Spring/summer*: Cuckoo, Nightjar, Sand Martin, Tree Pipit, Whitethroat. Occasional Woodlark, Sedge Warbler. *Passage*: Whimbrel, Common Sandpiper, waders. *Winter*: Teal, Pochard, Gadwall, Snipe, Redpoll. Occasional Brambling, Goosander.
Other: 20+ spp. dragonflies. Good number butterflies & other invertebrates. Roe Deer, Badger, reptiles.
Directions: Sat nav: BH24 2ET. SU108 047 - on Horton Road, Ashley Heath. Two miles W of Ringwood, signposted from Ashley Heath roundabout (junction of A31 & A338) between Ringwood & St Leonards.
Public transport: Bus - no.38 Ringwood to Ferndown stops at Lions Lane, at Castleman Trailway, near main entrance. Morebus (T: 01202 338 240).
Visiting: Pay-&-display car park, accessible parking spaces, coach parking. Open daily (not Dec 25) 8am-5pm Sep-Mar, (6pm Apr-May & 7pm Jun-Aug). Visitor centre open 9am-4.30pm, toilets, restaurant, gift shop. Way-marked trails, many wheelchair friendly.
Contact: Moors Valley Country Park, T: 01425 470 721,
E: rangers@moors-valley.co.uk;
W: www.moors-valley.co.uk;
Forestry England, T: 0300 067 4600.

7. MORDEN BOG NNR (WAREHAM FOREST)

Natural England (Wessex Team).
Habitats: NNR - mainly lowland heath (dry & wet heath, bog & valley mire), large decoy pond with surrounding area consisting of coniferous forest & lowland heath.
Birds: *All year*: Buzzard, Dartford Warbler, Meadow Pipit, Stonechat, Siskin, Lesser Spotted Woodpecker (by Sherford Bridge - best in spring). *Spring/summer*: Hobby, Nightjar, Woodlark, Tree Pipit, Redstart. *Winter*: Great Grey Shrike (almost annual).
Other: Butterflies, inc. Silver-studded Blue, Grayling, dragonflies, & all six British reptile spp.
Directions: Sat nav: BH20 7ES. SY 919 926 (parking area). N of Wareham, part of a wider Wareham Forest site. From Wareham take A351 to Sandford then turn L onto B3075 towards Morden. Drive through forest until reaching lay-by (on R) at Sherford Bridge. Park & cross road through metal gate.
Public transport: Can access forest from Wareham train station follow blue signs (bus stop here as well).
Visiting: Open at all times, many footpaths.
Contact: Natural England (main enquiries), T: 0300 060 3900; E: enquiries@naturalengland.org.uk

8. PORTLAND BIRD OBSERVATORY

Portland Bird Observatory.
Habitats: Portland - cliffs, scrub, quarries, open fields. Migration watch point, seawatching.
Birds: 355+ spp. on Portland. *All year:* Little Owl. *Spring/autumn*: Most of regular common & scarce migrants recorded annually, national rarities frequently turn up. Good selection of offshore passage inc. divers, Common Scoter, shearwaters (inc. Balearic), skuas (inc. Pomarine & occasional Long-tailed), terns (inc. Arctic & Black). *Summer*: Breeding Razorbill, Guillemot, Fulmar, Shag, Little Tern (Ferrybridge). Puffin (occasionally at the Bill). *Winter*: Purple Sandpiper, Short-eared Owl, Black Redstart, Mediterranean Gull (large numbers at Ferrybridge), divers, grebes, Red-breasted Merganser (Portland Harbour).
Directions: Sat nav: DT5 2JT. SY 681 690. Six miles S of Weymouth, Observatory on road to Portland Bill.
Public transport: Bus - no.1 Weymouth to The Bill. First Wessex, Dorset & Somerset.
Visiting: Open at all times. Parking only for Portland Bird Obs members. Self-catering accommodation available - take own towels, sheets, sleeping bags. Information, toilets, natural history bookshop. Large pay-&-display car park & toilets at The Bill.
Contact: Martin Cade (Warden PBO), T: 01305 820 553; E: obs@btinternet.com; W: http://portlandbirdobs.blogspot.co.uk/

9. RADIPOLE LAKE

RSPB (South West England Office).
Habitats: Lake, reedbeds.
Birds: Excellent for rare/scarce gulls, regular rarities. *All year:* Marsh Harrier, Bearded Tit, Cetti's Warbler. *Spring/summer/autumn*: Hirundines, Reed & Sedge warblers, passage waders & other migrants. Garganey regular in spring. *Winter*: Bittern, wildfowl, Water Rail, pre-roost gatherings of gulls & Pied Wagtail.
Directions: Sat nav: DT4 7TZ. SY 675 795. In Radipole Park Drive, Weymouth (signposted with brown signs). Enter footpaths from Swannery car park.
Public transport: Train - station 400 yards from reserve, serving London & Bristol.
Visiting: Public footpaths open all times. Public pay-&-display car park. Discovery Centre open daily (not 24-26 Dec) 9.30am-5pm (4pm Nov-Jan). Centre has small cafe & disabled toilets. Network of wheelchair friendly paths, two signposted trails, one viewing shelter, viewpoints. Dogs on leads.
Contact: RSPB - see site 5.

Somerset

Habitat restoration on the old peat workings of the Somerset Levels has changed the area dramatically. Breeding Bitterns & Common Cranes (from a successful re-introduction programme) have been boosted by this work & a variety of herons & egrets are colonising the area. In winter the Levels hold large numbers of wildfowl & are worth a visit to witness a spectacular Starling murmuration. Coastal sites attract wintering waders & wildfowl.

1. BREAN DOWN

National Trust.
Habitats: Extension of Mendips hard limestone, featuring calcareous grassland, scrub & steep cliffs.
Birds: *All year:* Peregrine, Raven. *Summer:* Blackcap, Garden Warbler, Whitethroat, Stonechat. *Passage:* Gannet, divers, shearwaters, waders, skuas, gulls & passerines. *Winter:* Shelduck, Curlew, Dunlin on mudflats.
Other: Chalkhill Blue, Marbled White & other butterflies. Three rare plants - White Rock Rose, Somerset Hair Grass, Dwarf Sedge.
Directions: Sat nav: TA8 2RS. ST 296 586. 300ft high promontory jutting into Bristol Channel, five miles N of Burnham-on-Sea. From junc 22 of M5, head for Weston-super-Mare on A38/A370. Turn off at Lympsham & head for Brean. In Brean head N to car park at bottom of Brean Down.
Public transport: Bus - no.20 Burnham-on-Sea to Weston-super-Mare, alight at Brean - 1.75 miles to reserve). First Bristol, Bath & the West.
Visiting: Open all year. Pay-&-display car park opens with shop & cafe (9am-5pm), NT members free. Toilet (inc. disabled) at bottom of Brean Down. Steep slope not recommended for wheelchair users. Dogs on lead.
Contact: National Trust, T: 01278 751 874; E: breandown@nationaltrust.org.uk

2. BRIDGEWATER BAY NNR

Natural England (Wessex Team).
Habitats: 2,560ha, Parrett River estuary, intertidal mudflats, saltmarsh.
Birds: 200 spp. *All year*: Curlew, Oystercatcher, Avocet. Shelduck (Europe's second largest moulting ground with up to 2,000 birds in Jul). *Spring/autumn*: Passage migrants, inc. occasional vagrants. Waders inc. internationally important numbers of Whimbrel & Black-tailed Godwit. *Winter:* Raptors inc. Peregrine, harriers & Short-eared Owl. Waders & wildfowl inc. nationally important numbers of Wigeon.
Other: Saltmarsh flora. Rare invertebrates inc. Great Silver Water Beetle, Aquatic Snail & Hairy Dragonfly.
Directions: Sat nav: TA5 2PL. ST 257 408. 3.25 miles N of Bridgwater & extends to Burnham-on-Sea. Take Junc 23 or 24 off M5. Turn N off A39 at Cannington & take minor roads to car park at Steart.
Public transport: None.
Visiting: Car park, interpretive panels, leaflet dispenser at Steart - follow footpath approx 0.5 mile to tower hide & three other hides at mouth of River Parrett. Hides open daily (not Dec 25). Permits needed for Steart Island (by boat only). Dogs on leads. Disabled access to hides by arrangement, other areas accessible.
Contact: Natural England, T: 01458 860 120;
E: somersetavonandwiltshire@naturalengland.org.uk

3. CHEW VALLEY LAKE

Avon Wildlife Trust/Bristol Water Plc.
Habitats: Largest artificial lake in SW England with important reedbed.
Birds: 270+ spp. - often attracts rarities. *Summer*: Breeding Great Crested & Little Grebes, Gadwall, Tufted Duck, Shoveler, Pochard, Reed Warbler. Hobby hunt in late summer. When mud exposed can attract waders inc. Dunlin, Ringed Plover & Green Sandpiper. *Winter & passage*: Wildfowl inc. important numbers of Shoveler, Gadwall, Teal & Tufted Duck. Large numbers of Goosander, Great Crested Grebe & Cormorant. Bewick's Swan, Goldeneye, Smew. Large winter gull roost (up to 50,000+), mostly Black-headed, Common & Mediterranean.
Other: Ruddy Darter & Migrant Hawker dragonflies.
Directions: Sat nav: BS40 6HN. ST 570 581. (Avon WT reserve at Herriotts Bridge). Nine miles S of Bristol. Take B3114 south from Chew Stoke, bear L for West Harptree & head NE on A368.
View reserve from causeway at Herriotts Bridge where there is car parking.
Public transport: None.
Visiting: Permit (fee) required to enter reservoir enclosure & to use access road, paths & five hides - available to members of recognised ornithological/naturalist societies - contact Bristol Water. Roadside viewing at Herons Green Bay (parking for coaches) & Harriotts Bridge.
Public trails/hide (Hollow Brook), E shore: Grebe Trail (0.75 mile long), hard surface for wheelchairs, dogs on leads. Unsurfaced Bittern Trail (one mile) leads to hide - can be muddy. No dogs.
Contact: Avon WT, T: 0117 917 7270;
E: hello@avonwildlifetrust.org.uk;
Bristol Water, Woodford Lodge, Chew Stoke, BS18 8SH. T: 01275 332 339.

4. DUNKERY & HORNER WOOD NNR

National Trust.
Habitats: 1,600ha, ancient oak woodland, moorland, part of 4,850ha NT Holnicote Estate in Exmoor National Park.
Birds: *All year*: Dipper, Grey Wagtail, woodpeckers, Buzzard, Sparrowhawk. *Spring/summer*: Redstart, Stonechat, Whinchat, Tree Pipit, Pied Flycatcher, Wood Warbler. Dartford Warbler possible.
Other: Holnicote estate holds 15 of UK's bat spp. Silver-washed & Heath Fritillary butterflies. Red Deer.
Directions: Sat nav: TA24 8HY. SS 898 309 (Horner). 4.5 miles W of Minehead. Take A39 W to minor road 0.5 mile E of Porlock signposted to Horner. Park in village.
Public transport: Bus - no.10 (not Sun) between Minehead to Porlock. Operated by various companies - First Buses of Somerset, Atwest & W Ridler & Sons.
Visiting: Open all year. Pay-&-display car parks at Bossington (SS 920 469) & Horner (SS 920 469), inc. toilets. Free small car parks at Allerford, Selworthy (overflow only), Selworthy Beacon, Webbers Post, 150 miles of footpaths. Webber's Post circular walk suitable for wheelchairs. Rugged terrain to Dunkery Beacon.
Contact: National Trust, T: 01643 862 452;
E: holnicote@nationaltrust.org.uk

5. GREYLAKE

RSPB (South West England Office).
Habitats: Wet grassland, formerly arable farmland.
Birds: *Spring/summer:* Kingfisher, Grey Heron, Little Egret & breeding Garganey, Snipe, Lapwing, Redshank, Skylark, Meadow Pipit, Yellow Wagtail.

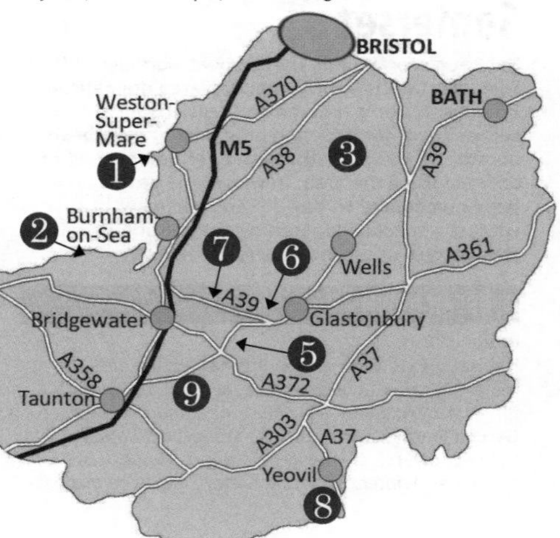

Autumn: Green Sandpiper, waders on passage. *Winter:* Waders & wildfowl (inc. Lapwing, Golden Plover, Teal, Pintail, Shoveler,& Wigeon). Peregrine, Merlin, Hen Harrier. Cranes re-introduced in area sometimes seen.
Other: Roe Deer, Water Vole, Stoat, Otter, dragonflies inc. Four-spotted Chaser.
Directions: Sat nav: TA7 9PB. ST 399 346. Off A361 Taunton to Glastonbury road, midway Othery & Greinton.
Public transport: Bus - no.29 (not Sun) Taunton to Glastonbury stops in Greinton (by phone box) or Othery (by London Inn) - driver may stop at reserve on request otherwise two mile walk along A361 (NOT ADVISABLE - fast road, no path). First Buses of Somerset.
Visiting: Open all year, dawn-dusk. Two circular trails interpretive signs, two hides, one viewing platform, easy-access trail suitable for wheelchairs. Assistance dogs only, on leads.
Contact: RSPB, T: 01458 252 805;
E: greylake@rspb.org.uk

6. HAM WALL

RSPB (South West England Office).
Habitats: 265ha, wetland, inc. SW's largest reedbed.
Birds: *All year:* Bittern, Great & Little Egret, Cetti's Warbler, Water Rail, Barn Owl. *Spring/summer:* Migrant warblers, hirundines, Hobby, Whimbrel, sandpipers. Possible rare herons. *Autumn:* Migrant thrushes, Redpoll, Siskin, Kingfisher, Bearded Tit. *Winter:* Wildfowl, million-plus Starling roost, Peregrine, Merlin, Short-eared Owl. Cranes re-introduced in area sometimes seen.
Other: Otter, Roe Deer, Water Vole, dragonflies, butterflies.
Directions: Sat nav: BA6 9SX. ST 449 397. W of Glastonbury. From A39 turn N in Ashcott & follow road onto moor (towards Meare). After three miles pass Church Farm Horticultural building. Shortly after, at metal bridge, reserve is opposite side of road to Shapwick Heath NNR (also has car park) .
Public transport: Bus - no.75 (not Sun) Wells to Bridgwater stops in Ashcott - two miles to reserve. First Buses Somerset. No.688 (Mon-Fri) Glastonbury to Meare - 1.5 miles to reserve. Libra Travel (T: 01373 812 255).
Visiting: Open all year. Car park open 5am-6.30pm (Oct-Jan), 5am-8pm (Feb-Mar), 5am-10pm (Apr-Sep), parking charge for non-RSPB members). Alternative car park operated by Natural England available outside of Ham Wall opening times. Coach parking - check with reserve. Welcome Building with drink machine/light snacks open weekends 10am-4pm, weekdays when volunteers available. Toilets. Five viewing screens, two raised hides, four trails.Wheelchair users can access viewing areas from main track (use RADAR key/can be borrowed from Welcome Building when open). Assistance dogs welcome on all parts of reserve. Other dogs (short lead) on main path & public footpath (Ham Wall loop) only - take waste away.
Contact: RSPB, T: 01458 860 494;
E: ham.wall@rspb.org.uk

7. SHAPWICK MOOR

Hawk & Owl Trust.
Habitats: 54ha, wet grassland - grazing pasture, hay meadows with rough grass edges, fen, open ditches, pollard willows & hedges.
Birds: *All year:* Buzzard, Kestrel, Sparrowhawk, Kingfisher, Lapwing, Grey Heron, Mute Swan. *Spring/summer:* Hobby, Barn Owl, Whimbrel & other waders on passage. Skylark, Cetti's Warbler, Bullfinch, Reed Bunting & Yellowhammer. *Autumn/winter:* Finch flocks, Snipe, Shoveler, Gadwall, Stonechat, Brambling. Peregrine & harriers may fly over.
Other: Roe Deer, Brown Hare, Stoat, Badger, Otter & Water Vole.
Directions: Sat nav: TA7 9NW. ST 417 398. From Junc 23 of M5 take A39 towards Glastonbury, after six miles turn N signposted Shapwick, on to minor road, straight over cross-roads & through Shapwick village, turn L at T-junction following signs for 'Avalon Marshes Centre'. Reserve is about half way between Shapwick village & AM Centre.
Public transport: Bus - no.75 (not Sun) Wells to Bridgwater stops in Shapwick - one mile to reserve, two mile to AM Centre. First Buses Somerset.
Visiting: Open all year (not Dec 25). Car park. Access only along public footpaths & permissive path. Dogs on leads only. Information panels, two hides. Toilets at AM Centre (BA6 9TT, ST 425 414).
Contact: Hawk & Owl Trust, T: 01328 856 788;
E: enquiries@hawkandowl.org;
W: www.hawkandowl.org

8. SUTTON BINGHAM RESERVOIR

Wessex Water.
Habitats: Reservoir, hay meadow, surrounding farmland, mature hedgerows. Southern tip of reservoir is in Dorset.
Birds: *All year:* Great Crested Grebe, Buzzard, Peregrine, Sparrowhawk, Grey Heron, Little Egret, Kingfisher. *Spring/autumn passage*: Hirundines, waders (esp. when water levels low, inc. Green & Common Sandpipers, Redshank), Osprey. *Summer:* Hobby, warblers. *Winter*: Wildfowl, gulls (worth checking through), Snipe, winter thrushes, Siskin & Redpoll. Has turn up intersting birds in past.
Other: Bats, butterflies, meadow flora.
Directions: Sat nav: BA22 9QL. ST 548 111. Two miles S of Yeovil. Head S from Yeovil (for ca. one mile) or N from Dorchester on A37. Take turn signed to Sutton Bingham/East Coker. Follow minor road SW for 2 miles to car park (just beyond causeway).
Public transport: None.
Visiting: Car park (height restriction), toilets, nature trail, picnic area. Parts of reservoir viewable from road (care when stopping). No dogs.
Contact: Wessex Water, T: 01935 872 389.

9. SWELL WOOD

RSPB (South West England Office).
Habitats: Semi-natural ancient oak woodland & views across wet grassland from woodland trails. Part of Somerset Levels & Moors.
Birds: Largest heronry in SW England - up to 100 pairs of Grey Heron & small number of Little Egret. *All year:* common woodland spp. inc. Treecreeper, Green & Great Spotted Woodpeckers, Nuthatch. *Spring/ summer:* Breeding Buzzard, Bullfinch, Spotted Flycatcher, Song Thrush, warblers inc. Chiffchaff, Blackcap & Garden Warbler. *[On escorted walks]:* Curlew, Snipe, Sedge Warbler, Yellow Wagtail, Skylark, Nightingale.
Other: Roe Deer, Dormouse, woodland flora inc. Bluebells, Wood Anemone, Lesser Celandine. Dragonflies & butterflies.
Directions: Sat nav: TA3 6PX. ST 360 238. Reserve lies 11 mile E of Taunton. From A378 (Taunton) to Langport road, take minor road one mile E of Fivehead (signposted to car park).
Public transport: Bus - no.54 (not Sun) from Taunton stops on A378 at Swell where reserve can be accessed via stile onto Scarp Trail. First Buses of Somerset.
Visiting: Swell Wood car park & heronry hide open all year (dawn-dusk), disabled parking area. Coach parking in lay-by across main road. Heronry hide & part of woodland trail are wheelchair accessible. Scarp Trail (only path accessible to dogs) links to public footpaths.
Contact: RSPB, T: 01458 252 805;
E: swell.wood@rspb.org.uk

Wiltshire

The chalk downlands of Marlborough Downs & the extensive Salisbury Plain are internationally threatened habitats & make up most of the county. The latter is used extensively by the Army & has limited public access so the birds, including breeding Quail & Stone Curlew, are subject to less disturbance than the former. The re-introduction of Great Bustards is being undertaken on the Plain. The Wildlife Trust manage nearly 40 reserves across the county.

1. CLEVELAND LAKES

Cotswold Water Park Trust.
Habitats: Lakes with islands, scrapes, lagoons, reedbed, marsh, ditches, loafing areas. [Part of CWP, covering 40 sq. miles/150 lakes, across Wilts, Gloucs & W Oxfordshire]
Birds: *Summer:* Breeding ducks, Great Crested Grebe, Hobby, Sand Martin, warblers, Reed Bunting, Little Egret, Grey Heron. *Winter:* Large numbers wildfowl spp., plus Bittern, Water Rail, Stonechat. These & passage waders also viewable from "Twitchers' Gate" on lane to N of Lake 74 (SU 065 946).
Other: Otter, Water Vole, several spp. of dragonflies & butterflies.
Directions: Sat nav: SN6 6QW. SU 059 933 (Waterhay Car Park). Lakes 68A/B & 74 of Cotswold Water Park. From A419 Cirencester to Swindon road, take B4696 towards Cotswold Water Park West (passing Gateway Centre). After 1.5 miles turn L on to Fridays Ham Lane. Follow road to Ashton Keynes village & turn L to Cricklade/Leigh road. Waterhay Car Park is on L next to River Thames. Take bridleway north to kissing gate on R. Permissive path follows southern edge of Lake 68A/B before turning N towards hide.
Public transport: Bus - no.51 between Swindon, Cheltenham, Cirencester stops at Gateway Centre. Stagecoach West.
Visiting: Open at all times. Car park, most paths firm & flat but subject to severe flooding in winter. Dogs on short leads at all times. Toilets, refreshments & information available at Gateway Centre next to A419.
Contact: Cotswold Water Park Trust,
T: 01793 752 413; E: info@waterpark.org;
W: www.waterpark.org

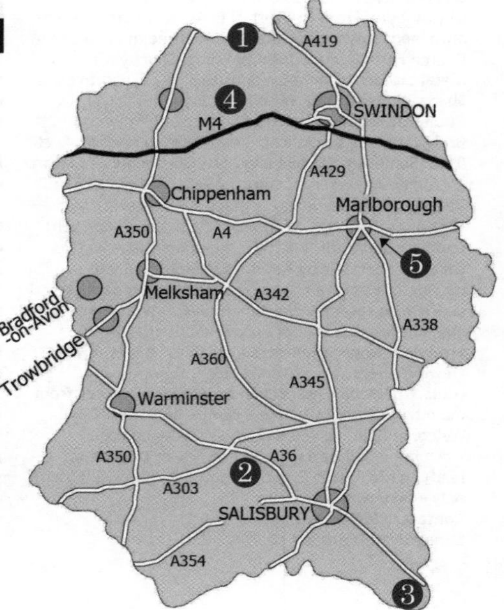

2. LANGFORD LAKES

Wiltshire Wildlife Trust.
Habitats: Four former gravel pits, with islands & reed fringes. 12ha, open water, wet woodland, scrub, chalk river.
Birds: 150+ spp. *Summer*: Breeding Coot, Moorhen, Tufted Duck, Pochard, Gadwall, Little & Great Crested Grebe. Kingfisher, Common Sandpiper, Grey Wagtail, warblers (eight spp.). *Passage*: Sand Martin, Green Sandpiper & other waders, Black Tern. *Winter*: Common wildfowl - Wigeon, Shoveler, Teal, Water Rail, Little Egret, occasionally Bittern.
Other: Otter, Water Vole, Water Shrew. Spawning Salmon & Trout in river.
Directions: Sat nav: SP3 4NH. SU 037 370. Nr Steeple Langford, S of A36, approx eight miles W of Salisbury. In centre of village, turn S into Duck Street, signposted Hanging Langford. Langford Lakes is first L just after small bridge.
Public transport: Bus - no.265 (not Sun) Salisbury to Bath stops in Steeple Langford (0.3 mile from reserve). First West of England.
Visiting: Main gates open during day. Advance notice required for coaches. Visitor centre, cafe, toilets, education centre. Trails & five hides, accessible to wheelchairs. Cycle racks (reserve 250 yards from Wiltshire Cycleway between Great Wishford & Hanging Langford). No dogs.
Contact: Wiltshire WT, T: 01380 725 670;
E: info@wiltshirewildlife.org

3. LANGLEY WOOD NNR

Natural England.
Habitats: Ancient Oak woodland (marks northern tip of New Forest).
Birds: *All Year:* Buzzard, Sparrowhawk, common woodland spp., 3 spp. woodpeckers, Hawfinch, Crossbill, Siskin. *Summer*: Hobby (open areas), Woodcock, Cuckoo, Nightjar, Tree Pipit, Redstart, warblers (inc. Wood), Spotted Flycatcher, Firecrest. *Winter*: Redpoll.
Other: 600 spp. fungi, flora (inc. Bluebell spectacle, Yellow Bird's Nest), butterflies (inc. Silver-washed & Pearl-bordered Fritillaries), 5 spp. deer, Dormouse, bats.
Directions: Sat nav: SP5 2PB. SU 219 203. Ten miles SE Salisbury. From A36 between Salisbury & Southampton take B3079 at Landford. Take 1st on R (Hamptworth Road) & follow to reserve entrance - 2.5 miles along this road.
Public transport: Bus - no.44 Salisbury-Woodfalls (not Sun/bank hols) stops at Lover (Redlynch Church stop, 0.6 mile from reserve gate - CARE no pavement). Salisbury Reds (T: 01202 338 420).
Visiting: Open all times. Small area for car parking by gate (noticeboard showing paths). Paths can be muddy when wet.
Contact: Natural England, T: 07771 944 557.

4. RAVENSROOST WOOD & MEADOWS

Wiltshire Wildlife Trust.
Habitats: Woodland, both coppice & high oak forest, & ponds. Surrounding meadows rich in wildflowers.
Birds: *Summer:* Woodland birds inc. Blackcap, Chiffchaff, Willow & Garden Warbler. *Winter:* mixed flocks of tits, Nuthatch, & Treecreeper move noisily through wood & Woodcock (wet, muddy areas).
Other: Butterflies inc. Silver-washed Fritillary & White Admiral. Good display of spring flowers inc. Bluebells, Wood Anemone, Wood Sorrel, Sanicle, violets & Primrose. Common spotted, Early Purple & Greater Butterfly Orchids, Hemp Agrimony & Betony.
Directions: Sat nav: SN16 9RN. SU 024 876 & SU 020 876 (parking - Ravensroost Wood, Meadows & Avis Meadows). NW of Swindon. Take B4696 Ashton Keynes road N from Wootton Bassett. After two miles take second turn L to Minety. Go straight on when main road turns R. Go straight over next crossroads - car park is 0.25 mile on R. Sat nav: SN16 9RH. SU 031 892 & SU 032 895 (parking - Distillery & Warbler Meadows). One mile S of Minety. In Minety turn S off B4040, after ca.0.3 mile turn R (to Brinkworth). Hill Ground part of reserve is first field on R (parking in gateways). Rest of reserve is about 0.25 mile down lane to double gateway entrance to reserve R.
Public transport: None.
Visiting: Sites connected - open at all times.
Contact: Wiltshire WT - see site 2.

5. SAVERNAKE FOREST

Savernake Estate.
Habitats: Ancient woodland, with one of largest collections of veteran trees in Britain. Four mile Beech avenue - longest in UK.
Birds: *All year:* Sparrowhawk, Buzzard, Red Kite, Woodcock, owls, 3 spp. woodpecker, Marsh & Willow Tits, Jay, other woodland birds. *Spring/summer:* Garden Warbler, Blackcap, Willow Warbler, Chiffchaff, Wood Warbler, Redstart, occasional Nightingale, Tree Pipit, Spotted Flycatcher. *Winter:* Finch flocks possibly inc. Siskin, Redpoll, Brambling & Hawfinch.
Other: Rare lichens & fungi, all main deer spp., Badger, Fox. Ancient trees.
Directions: Sat nav: SN8 3HN. SU 210 683 (entrance to Grand Avenue). From Marlborough, A4 Hungerford road runs along N side of forest. Two pillars mark Forest Hill entrance on A4, 1.5 mile E of A346/A4 junction. The 'Grand Avenue' leads straight through middle of woodland to join minor road from Stibb.
Public transport: None.
Visiting: Privately owned - no vehicular rights of way or public footpaths but open all year to public. Car park, picnic site at NW end by A346. Visitors can drive along main avenues, but all roads closed on one day a year - usually first working day of year. Only enter fenced-off areas if there is a footpath.
Contact: Savernake Estate Office, T: 01672 512 161;
E: savernakeestate1@gmail.com;
W: www.savernakeestate.co.uk

Scottish Borders

Borders, Dumfries & Galloway

Borders

This area is often overlooked as birders head north on the A1 but there are many good sites to make a stopover (or a visit) worthwhile. St Abb's Head holds a large summer seabird colony, while migrants move past in spring & autumn. Goosander is present all year, joined in the winter by Whooper Swan, geese & other wildfowl.

1. BEMERSYDE MOSS

Scottish Wildlife Trust.
Habitats: Long narrow strip of marsh, willow scrub, open water.
Birds: *Summer:* Breeding spp. inc. Black-necked Grebe, Lapwing, Curlew, Spotted Flycatcher, Tree Sparrow, Yellowhammer, Reed Bunting, Grasshopper Warbler & up to 15,000 pairs of Black-headed Gulls. *Winter:* wildfowl inc. large numbers of Wigeon & Greylag Goose.
Other: Otter, Water Vole.
Directions: Sat nav: TD6 9DS. NT 614 340. Located eight miles E of Melrose. Head S on A68 to St Boswells, then take B6404 across the Tweed into minor road to Maidenhall. At T-junction turn R & reserve is 0.5 mile ahead (lay-by on sharp bend).
Public transport: None.
Visiting: Open at all times. Limited parking in lay-by on southern edge of loch. Boardwalk leads to wheelchair-friendly bird hide.
Contact: Scottish WT, T: 0131 312 7765;
E: enquiries@scottishwildlifetrust.org.uk

2. DUNS CASTLE NATURE RESERVE

Private.
Habitats: Two man-made lochs (Heron Pool (Hen Poo) & Mill Dam), woodland.
Birds: *All year:* woodland spp. inc. Green & Great Spotted Woodpeckers, Goldcrest. *Summer:* Redstart, Pied Flycatcher & warblers. *Winter:* wildfowl.
Other: Red Squirrel, Roe Deer, occasional Otter. Woodland rich in wild flowers.
Directions: Sat nav: TD11 3NW. NT 778 550. Duns lies W of Berwick-upon-Tweed. From town centre head N on Castle Street & North Castle Street. Alternatively drive N on A6112 for one mile & turn L on B6365 to car park on northern edge of reserve.
Public transport: Bus - no.60 Galashiels to Tweedmouth stops at Duns. Borders Buses (T: 01896 754 350).
Visiting: Grounds open all year. Network of well-marked paths, some suitable for wheelchairs.
Contact: Duns Castle,
T: 01361 883 211;
info@dunscastle.co.uk;
W: www.dunscastle.co.uk

3. ETTRICK MARSHES

Habitats: 125ha, floodplain mosaic of woodland, wetland, grassland, open water.
Birds: 80 spp. *All year:* Goosander, Kingfisher, Buzzard, Crossbill, Dipper, occasional Goshawk.*Summer:* Redstart, Sedge Warbler, Sand Martin & occasional Osprey.
Other: Red Squirrel, Otter. Moths & plants at northern edge of range.
Directions: Sat nav: TD7 5HU. NT 294 167 (by Honey Cottage caravan park). Sited in Ettrick Valley, off B7009, approx 16 miles SW of Selkirk.
Public transport: None.
Visiting: Open all times. Two car parks, network of footpaths & board walk (best access from main car park by Honey Cottage - other car park at Tima Water end of site). Can flood quickly after heavy rain.

4. GUNKNOWE LOCH & PARK

Scottish Borders Council.
Habitats: River, loch, parkland, scrub, woodland.
Birds: *All year:* Goosander, Great Spotted & Green Woodpeckers, Redpoll, possible Marsh Tit. *Spring/ summer:* Grey Wagtail, Kingfisher, Sand Martin, Blackcap, Sedge & Grasshopper Warblers. *Passage:* Yellow Wagtail, Whinchat, Wheatear. *Winter:* Wigeon, Tufted Duck, Pochard, Goldeneye, thrushes, Brambling.
Directions: Sat nav: TD1 3SZ. NT 517 345. In Tweedbank, two miles from Galashiels on A6091. Park at Gunknowe Loch (Tweedbank Road, off roundabout on A6091).
Public transport: Bus - no.X62 Melrose to Galashiels stops in Tweedbank. Borders Buses (T: 01896 754 350).
Visiting: Open all year. Car park, Various surfaced paths suitable for wheelchairs.
Contact: Ranger Service,
T: 01835 825 070.

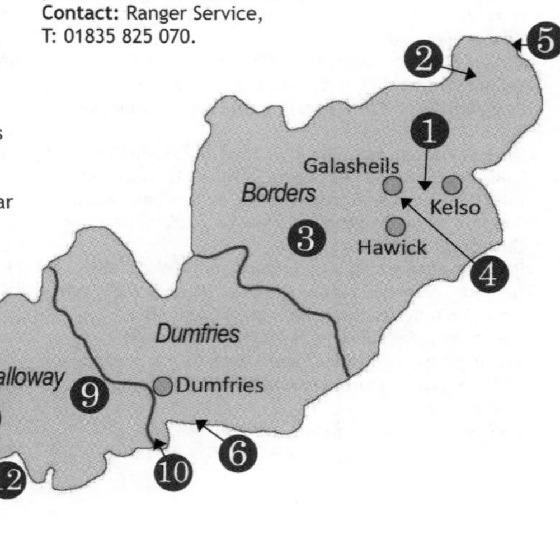

5. ST ABB'S HEAD

National Trust for Scotland.
Habitats: Cliffs, coastal grasslands, freshwater loch.
Birds: *Apr-Aug:* Seabird colonies with large number of Guillemot & Kittiwake, also Shag, Razorbill, Fulmar. *Apr-May & Sep-Oct:* Good seawatching.
Other: Common Rock-rose, Purple Milk-vetch, Spring Sandwort. Northern Brown Argus butterfly.
Directions: Sat nav: TD14 5QF. NT 913 674 for car park/bus stop. Lies five miles N of Eyemouth. Follow A1107 from A1 then take B6438 to St Abbs.
Public transport: Bus - no.235 from Berwick-upon-Tweed. Borders Buses (T: 01896 754 350). Train - Berwick-upon-Tweed.
Visiting: Open all year. Car park (free for members, coach parking arrangements - contact Old Smiddy Coffee Shop (T: 07773 347 209). Nature Centre open daily (usually unmanned) 10am-5pm Easter-Oct, public toilets (inc. disabled). All-ability path to viewpoint at Starney Bay. Dogs welcome, keep under control - ensure waste is taken to bins in car park.
Contact: NTS, T: 01890 771 443;
E: st.abbs@nts.org.uk

Dumfries & Galloway

Barnacle Geese winter on The Solway in nationally important numbers, WWT Caerlaverock & RSPB Mersehead are the best sites to see them. Ospreys & Red Kites are colonising & there is a chance of a Golden Eagle over upland areas or a Hen Harrier on moorland. The Mull of Galloway has fine seabird cliffs, while the Ken/Dee Marshes have wintering Greenland White-fronted & Pink-footed Geese, & Whooper Swan plus resident Willow Tit.

6. CAERLAVEROCK WETLAND CENTRE

The Wildfowl & Wetlands Trust.
Habitats: Saltmarsh, grassland, wetland.
Birds: *Summer:* Osprey, Barn Owl, Skylark, Tree Sparrow, migrant warblers. *Winter:* Wildfowl esp. Barnacle (up to 40,000) & Pink-footed Geese, Whooper Swan.
Other: Natterjack Toad, Badger, Tadpole Shrimp, bats. Northern Marsh, Common Spotted & Twayblade Orchids.
Directions: Sat nav: DG1 4UF. NY 051 656. Overlooks the Solway. From St Michael's church in Dumfries take B725 towards Bankend, following tourist signs. Also signposted from A75 W of Annan.
Public transport: Bus - no.6A (not Sun) from Dumfries stops one mile from reserve. Stagecoach West Scotland.
Visiting: Open daily (not Dec 25), 10am-5pm. Parking for coaches. Charge for non-WWT members. Visitor centre & Cathan coffee shop (10.30am-4.30pm), gift shop. Binocular hire. Live CCTV pictures inc Ospreys. 20 Hides, four towers, heated observatory & sheltered picnic area. Self-catering farmhouse accommodation. Summer meadow walk May-Aug, wild swan feeds Oct-Apr. Assistance dogs only.
Contact: WWT Caerlaverock, T: 01387 770 200;
E: info.caerlaverock@wwt.org.uk

7. CROOK OF BALDOON

RSPB (South & West Scotland).
Habitats: Saltmarsh, wet grassland.
Birds: *Summer:* Osprey (possible), Lapwing, Redshank, Skylark, Wheatear, Linnet. *Winter:* Pink-footed & Barnacle Geese, Shelduck, Whooper Swan, Golden Plover, Curlew, Lapwing, Hen Harrier, Peregrine, Merlin, Twite.
Other: Thrift, Sea-lavender.
Directions: Sat Nav: xxx xx NX 442 530. Four miles S of Wigtown. From Wigtown, head S along A714. Go through Bladnoch, then take minor road to L (at Penkiln Sawmill sign) - follow this road down to Crook of Baldoon car park (ignoring left hand turns).
Public transport: None.
Visiting: Open at all times. Car park, viewing point & picnic tables. Not suitable for disabled access. Dogs under close control.
Contact: RSPB, T: 01988 402 130;
E: crookofbaldoon@rspb.org.uk

8. GLENTROOL

Forestry & Land Scotland.
Habitats: Part of Galloway Forest Park. Loch, waterfalls, conifer & oak woodlands, moorland.
Birds: *All year:* Common woodland spp., Peregrine, Hen Harrier, Siskin, Crossbill. *Summer:* Redstart, Pied Flycatcher, Wood Warbler.
Other: Red Squirrel, Roe Deer.
Directions: Sat nav: DG8 6SX. NX 371 786. Eight miles NW of Newton Stewart. Leave A714 at Bargrennan to Glentrool - visitor centre signposted from unclassifield road that passes N from village.
Public transport: None.
Visiting: Open all times. Car parking (charge), visitor centre with toilets & cafe - open 10.30am-5pm Easter to end-Aug. Various trails of between 1.75 miles & 5.75 miles. Single track road (with passing places) continues past visitor centre along N side of Loch Trool to two other parking areas.
Contact: Forestry & Land Scotland, T: 0131 370 5900;
E: enquiries.south@forestryandland.gov.scot

9. KEN-DEE MARSHES

RSPB (South & West Scotland).
Habitats: Open water, marsh, grassland, woodland.
Birds: *All year:* Mallard, Grey Heron, Buzzard, Nuthatch, Willow Tit. *Spring/summer:* Lapwing & Oystercatcher nest in fields. Pied Flycatcher, Redstart, Tree Pipit, Sedge Warbler. *Winter:* Greenland White-fronted & Greylag Geese, raptors (Hen Harrier, Peregrine, Merlin, Red Kite).
Other: Red Squirrel, Roe Deer, Otter.
Directions: Sat nav: DG7 2LY. NX 699 684. Six miles NW of Castle Douglas. On minor road off A762 (N of Laurieston) or off B795 (at Glenlochar), parking at Mains of Duchrae.
Public transport: None.

Visiting: Open dawn/dusk. Car park at entrance to Mains of Duchrae farm. Two hides (one wheelchair-accessible, limited parking for elderly/disabled next to first hide), viewing platform, three miles of trails. Dogs under close control. Part of Galloway Kite Trail.
Contact: RSPB, T: 01988 402 130;
E: wood.cree@rspb.org.uk

10. MERSEHEAD

RSPB (South & West Scotland).
Habitats: Wet grassland, arable farmland, saltmarsh, intertidal mudflats.
Birds: *Summer*: Breeding birds inc. Lapwing, Redshank, Skylark. *Winter*: Whooper Swan, 9,500 Barnacle Geese, 4,000 Teal, 2,000 Wigeon, 1,000 Pintail, waders (inc. Dunlin, Knot, Oystercatcher), Hen Harrier.
Other: Natterjack Toad, Otter.
Directions: Sat nav: DG2 8AH. NX 928 566. From Dumfries take A710 S for about 16 miles. Reserve is signposted from New Abbey & then on L just before Caulkerbush village. Single track road with passing places runs for one mile to car park, adjacent to visitor centre. From Castle Douglas, take A745, then A711 to Dalbeattie. Follow signs from Dalbeattie before joining A710.
Public transport: Bus - no.372 Dalbeattie to Dumfries. Bus stop at Caulkerbush (Southwick), ca one mile from visitor centre. Houstons Coaches (T: 01576 203 874).
Visiting: Dawn-dusk daily (not Dec 25). Car park (members free). Visitor centre open 10am-4pm, occasionally unmanned - viewing room, toilets, refreshments (when manned). Wheelchair-friendly hides/trails, open all times, Blue Badge parking spaces within 400 yards of hides & next to visitor centre.
Contact: RSPB, T: 01387 780 579;
E: mersehead@rspb.org.uk

11. MULL OF GALLOWAY

RSPB (Scotland).
Habitats: Sea cliffs, coastal heath.
Birds: *All year*: Peregrine. *Spring/summer*: Fulmar, Shag, Guillemot, Razorbill, Black Guillemot, Puffin, Kittiwake, Raven, Wheatear, Rock Pipit, Twite. Gannet (feeding offshore). *Early Autumn:* Departing Manx Shearwater gather offshore.
Other: Harbour Porpoise, dolphins, Grey Seal.
Directions: Sat nav: DG9 9HP. NX 156 305. Most southerly tip of Scotland - follow brown signs for five miles from village of Drummore, S of Stranraer.
Public transport: None.
Visiting: Open all times. Blue Badge parking by centre. Visitor centre open Easter-Oct, toilets, nature trail, CCTV on cliffs. Small shop in Gallie Craig cafe (not RSPB). Steep stairway to foghorn viewing platform overlooking seabird colonies. Trail uneven.
Contact: RSPB, T: 01988 402 130 or 01776 840 539 Easter to end-Oct); E: mullofgalloway@rspb.org.uk

12. WIGTOWN BAY LNR

Dumfries & Galloway Council.
Habitats: 2,845ha, largest LNR in Britain - estuary with extensive saltmarsh/merse, mudflats & a freshwater wetland at Wigtown Harbour.
Birds: *Summer*: Breeding Osprey, Peregrine, waders & duck. *Winter*: Internationally important for Pink-footed Goose, nationally important for Curlew, Whooper Swan & Pintail, with major gull roost & other migratory coastal birds. Small Twite flock.
Other: Fish inc. Smelt & Shad. Lax-flowered Sea-lavender, Sea Aster.
Directions: Sat nav: DG8 9ED. NX 438 548. Between Wigtown & Creetown, S of Newton Stewart. The A75 runs along E side, with A714 S to Wigtown & B7004 providing views of LNR.
Public transport: Bus - no.415 from Newton Stewart to Wigtown. Stagecoach West Scotland.
Visiting: Open all times. Main access points: roadside lay-bys on A75 near Creetown, parking at Martyr's Stake (on B7004 just out of Wigtown) & Wigtown Harbour - suitable for coaches. Visitor Centre - open Mon-Sat 10am-5pm (later some days), Sun 2pm-5pm - located in Wigtown County Building has coach parking plus full disabled access, inc. lift & toilets. CCTV of Ospreys breeding in Galloway during summer & wetland birds in winter. Hide at Wigtown Harbour overlooking River Bladnoch, saltmarsh & fresh water wetland has disabled access from harbour car park. Another hide at Martyr's Stake car park.
Contact: D&G Council, T: 0303 333 3000;
E: contact@dumgal.gov.uk

13. WOOD OF CREE

RSPB (Scotland).
Habitats: Deciduous oak woodland, riverside meadow, streams, moorland.
Birds: *All year*: Sparrowhawk, Buzzard, Woodcock, Barn & Tawny Owls, Great Spotted Woodpecker, Willow Tit. Black Grouse on moorland. *Summer*: Redstart, Tree Pipit, Pied Flycatcher, Wood & Grasshopper Warblers, Dipper, Grey Wagtail, Common Sandpiper. *Autumn/winter*: Whooper Swan, Goldeneye.
Other: Otter, Roe Deer, Red Squirrel, eight spp. bats inc. Leisler's. Bluebells & woodland flowers in spring.
Directions: Sat nav: DG8 6SW. NX 381 708. Travel N along minor road from Newton Stewart through Old Minnigaff. Turn L past Monigaff church, continue three miles along minor road until reaching Wood of Cree car park (go past Barclye car park on way - at NX 386 694).
Public transport: None.
Visiting: Open all times. Main car park at Wood of Cree. Keep to trails - 1.25 waymarked woodland trail can be extended to 3.5 mile walk inc. scrubland trail - steep, rough & uneven in parts. Another car park at Barclye Wood - one mile before Wood of Cree. Dogs under control, esp. during breeding season.
Contact: RSPB - see site 9.

Central Scotland

Argyll, Ayrshire, Clyde, Fife, Forth, Lothian

Argyll

Islands take the birding honours for this area - Coll, Tiree, Islay & Mull all have excellent birding. Islay is renowned for its wintering wildfowl, which includes huge numbers of Barnacle & White-fronted Geese. Choughs, raptors & Corncrakes are other island specialities although the latter has a better chance of being seen at RSPB reserve on Coll. Mull is home to the highest breeding densities of Golden & White-tailed Eagles in Britain.

1. COLL RESERVE

RSPB (South & West Scotland).
Habitats: Sand dunes, beaches, machair grassland, moorland, farmland.
Birds: *Spring:* Great Northern Diver offshore. Corncrake arrive in late Apr. Displaying waders, inc. Redshank, Lapwing, Snipe. *Summer:* Auks offshore, plus Gannet, shearwaters & terns. *Autumn:* Barnacle & Greenland White-fronted Geese arrive, thrushes on passage. Waders inc. Purple Sandpiper. *Winter:* Long-tailed Duck, divers offshore. Hunting Hen Harrier & Merlin. Twite.
Other: Good for cetaceans & Basking Shark. Otter, 300+ spp. machair wildflowers inc. rare orchids, Great Yellow Bumblebee.
Directions: Sat nav: PA78 6TB, NM 167 563. By ferry from Oban to Coll. Take B8070 W from Arinagour for five miles. Turn R at Arileod. Continue for about one mile. Park at end of road. Reception point at Totronald.
Public transport: Ferry from Oban - Caledonian MacBrayne (T: 08705 650 000; W: www.calmac.co.uk)
Visiting: Open all year. Two car parks, info bothy at Totronald, guided walks in summer. Corncrake viewing bench. Natural site with unimproved paths not suitable for wheelchairs. Avoid walking through fields & crops.
Contact: RSPB, T: 01879 230 301.

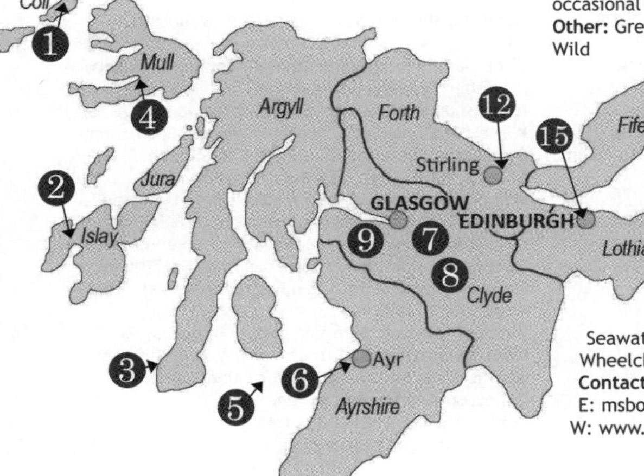

2. LOCH GRUINART, ISLAY

RSPB (South & West Scotland).
Habitats: Lowland wet grassland, sea loch, farmland, moorland.
Birds: *All year:* Birds of prey, esp, Hen Harrier & Peregrine, Chough feed in nearby fields. *Spring/ summer:* displaying Snipe, Lapwing, Curlew & Redshank. Corncrake. *Sep-Nov:* Passage migrants & arriving wildfowl. *Oct-Apr:* Large numbers of Barnacle & White-fronted Geese, other wildfowl & waders.
Other: Otter, Red & Roe Deer. Marsh Fritillary butterfly.
Directions: Sat nav: PA44 7PP. NR 275 672. On N coast of Islay, seven miles NW of Bridgend. Signposted from A847 Bridgend to Bruichladdich road, three miles from turn-off.
Public transport: Ferry from Kennacraig - Caledonian MacBrayne (T: 08705 650 000; W: www.calmac.co.uk)
Visiting: Open all times. Car parking at centre & start of trails, coaches at visitor centre only. Visitor centre open daily 10am-5pm (not Christmas/New Year), manned Apr-Oct. Toilets (inc. disabled), two hides, two trails, viewpoints. Weekly guided walks Apr-Oct, group bookings accepted. Disabled access to south hide, viewing area. No dogs in hides & under close control on trails.
Contact: RSPB, T: 01496 850 505:
E: loch.gruinart@rspb.org.uk

3. MACHRIHANISH SEABIRD/WILDLIFE OBSERVATORY

Eddie Maguire (sponsored by SNH).
Habitats: Marine, rocky shore, upland habitats.
Birds: *Summer*: Golden Eagle, Peregrine, Storm Petrel, Twite. *Autumn*: Passage seabirds & waders. On-shore gales/squalls often produce inshore movements of Leach's Petrel & other scarce seabirds, inc. Balearic Shearwater, Sabine's Gull, Grey Phalarope. *Winter*: Great Northern Diver, Purple Sandpiper, Turnstone, occasional Glaucous & Iceland Gulls.
Other: Grey & Common Seals, Bottlenose Dolphin, Otter, Wild Goat.
Directions: Sat nav: PA28 6PZ. NR 608 209. SW Kintyre, Argyll. Six miles W of Campbeltown on A83, then B843 to Machrihanish. Signposted from village.
Public transport: Bus - from Campbeltown. West Coast Motors (T: 01586 552 319).
Visiting: Open daily Apr-Oct. Parking for three cars. Coach parking. Seawatching hide, toilets in nearby village. Wheelchair access. Dogs welcome.
Contact: Eddie Maguire, Warden, T: 07895 952 640; E: msbowarden@gmail.com; W: www.machrihanishbirdobservatory.org.uk/

4. MULL EAGLE WATCH

RSPB (South & West Scotland)/Forestry & Land Scotland/SNH/MICT/Police Scotland/Craignure Golf Club.
Habitats: Large sea loch with tidal mudflats at its head (Loch Beg).
Birds: *All year:* Apart from White-tailed Eagles, other raptors in area inc. Golden Eagle, Hen Harrier & Buzzard. Waders on muddy areas. *Winter/early spring:* (on loch) three spp. diver, Slavonian Grebe, Eider, Red-breasted Merganser.
Other: Otter sightings are common here.
Directions: Sat nav: PA65 6BA. Tours are hosted from Craignure Golf Club on outskirts of Craignure (one mile from ferry terminal). Further details of when/where to meet are given when booking made.
Public transport: Ferry from Oban - Caledonian MacBrayne (T: 08705 650 000; W: www.calmac.co.uk).
Visiting: Tours for observing nesting White-tailed Eagles - ranger led trips run daily (not Sat) 11am & 2pm (Apr-Sep) - booking required, charges apply.
Contact: Booking (essential) through Visit Scotland Information Centre at Craignure, T: 01680 812 556; W: www.mulleaglewatch.com

Ayrshire

The best known site is the island of Ailsa Craig, which boasts a huge gannetry & plenty of other breeding seabirds. The shore at Barassie & Troon sees a large build-up of passage waders in spring & autumn & seawatching here in the autumn can be rewarding whilst white-winged gulls often turn up in winter. Martnaham Loch is good for wildfowl & a range of common species & Turnberry Point for seawatching, plus Twite. The river valleys and inland woodlands offer other birding opportunities.

5. AILSA CRAIG

Private.
Habitats: Volcanic plug (350ft high) provides nest sites for seabirds.
Birds: *Summer:* Hosts third largest gannetry in UK (up to 36,000 pairs of Gannets). Other breeding seabirds inc. Guillemot, Razorbill, Puffin, Black Guillemot, Kittiwake. Twite.
Other: Slow Worm.
Directions: Sat nav: KA26 9AJ. NX 181 981 (Girvan Hbr). Island is nine miles offshore. Girvan, nearest town on mainland.
Public transport: None.
Visiting: No formal arrangements - accessible only by boat during summer:

Ailsa Craig Trips/MFV Glorious (T: 01465 713 219 or 07773 794 358; E: mccrindlem@aol.com)

JAG Charters Ltd (T: 01465 713 174; E: info@seafishingchartersscotland.com)

6. CULZEAN CASTLE COUNTRY PARK

National Trust for Scotland.
Habitats: 260ha estate - shoreline, parkland, woodland, gardens, streams, ponds.
Birds: *All year:* Good numbers of common woodland species inc. Jay, Great Spotted Woodpecker & thrushes. *Spring/summer:* Arriving migrants, esp. Blackcap, Chiffchaff & Willow Warbler. Nesting Raven & Gannet on cliffs, Gannet & terns offshore. *Autumn/winter:* Wildfowl on pond inc. Little Grebe, Tufted Duck, Goldeneye. Crossbill, regular flocks of winter thrushes. Offshore divers & Eider.
Other: Roe Deer, Otter, Water Vole, several spp. of bat. Shoreline SSSI rich in rock pool life.
Directions: Sat nav: KA19 8LE. NS 234 103. 12 miles SW of Ayr off A719.
Public transport: Bus - no.60 (Ayr to Girvan) stops at site entrance. One mile walk downhill to castle. Stagecoach West Scotland.
Visiting: Open 9am-5pm. Entrance fee to country park (members free). Three car parks, cafe/shops open daily (not Dec 25/26, Jan 1), children's playground, picnic areas, many footpaths & estate tracks, ranging from unsurfaced woodland paths to metalled roads. Access leaflet available.
Contact: NTS Culzean, T: 01655 884 455; E: culzean@nts.org.uk

Clyde

The two RSPB reserves of Lochwinnoch & Baron's Haugh offer a good selection of commoner species throughout the year, with breeding Whinchat at the latter. The Scottish Wildlife Trust's Falls of Clyde reserve has a good selection of woodland birds, with Dippers & Kingfishers along the river. Cloch Point can be good for passing seabirds in late summer/early autumn.

7. BARON'S HAUGH

RSPB (South & West Scotland).
Habitats: Marshland, flooded areas, woodland, parkland, meadows, scrub, river.
Birds: *Summer:* Breeding Gadwall, Common Sandpiper, Kingfisher, Sand Martin, Whinchat, warblers (inc. Garden & Grasshopper). *Autumn:* Excellent for waders (22 spp.). *Winter:* Whooper Swan, Pochard, Wigeon, Sparrowhawk.
Directions: Sat nav: ML1 2PZ. NS 756 553. On SW edge of Motherwell. From M74/Junc 6 take road to Motherwell. Bear R at next traffic lights signposted to Wishaw. Turn R at third mini-roundabout & follow road to junction, turn L then immediately R to enter reserve.
Public transport: Buses - various from Motherwell stop in Airbles estate (0.5 mile from reserve). Train - Airbles ca.15 mins walk.
Visiting: Open all year. Car park, info boards, four hides (two with steps), four trails. Most paths are wide & surfaced, except longer circuit (steeper slopes, soft surfaces & gates).
Contact: RSPB, T: 0141 331 0993; E: baronshaugh@rspb.org.uk

8. FALLS OF CLYDE

Wildlife Trust.
Habitats: Reserve stretches along both sides of an ancient gorge, with waterfalls, meadow, wet woodland.
Birds: 100+ spp. *Summer:* Goosander, Kingfisher, Dipper, Jay, Spotted Flycatcher, Grey Wagtail
Other: Badger, Otter, bats & wildflowers.
Directions: Sat nav: ML11 9DB. NS 881 423 (visitor centre). Reserve covers both sides of Clyde Gorge from New Lanark to Bonnington Weir, approx one mile S of Lanark. From Glasgow travel S on M74 until Junc 7, then along A72, following signs for New Lanark.
Public transport: Bus - no.135 Lanark to New Lanark. Stuarts Coaches (T: 01555 773 533). Train - Lanark.
Visiting: Open daily. From New Lanark car park, walk into village, through iron gates & down steps to R of New Lanark Visitor Centre, follow road to Falls of Clyde Visitor Centre (open daily 10am-4pm, admission charge for non-SWT members, wheelchair friendly inc. toilet facilities). Woodland trails & range of guided walks (inc. self-guided) & badger watches. Reserve terrain unsuitable for wheelchairs.
Contact: Falls of Clyde Visitor Centre, T: 01555 665 262; E: fallsofclyde@scottishwildlifetrust.co.uk

9. LOCHWINNOCH

RSPB (Scotland).
Habitats: Shallow lochs, marsh, mixed woodland.
Birds: *Summer:* Breeding Great Crested Grebe, Water Rail, Sedge & Grasshopper Warblers, Reed Bunting. *Passage*: Occasional migrants inc. Greenshank, Whimbrel. *Winter*: Wildfowl (inc. Whooper Swan, Wigeon, Goosander, Goldeneye). Hen Harrier, Kingfisher.
Other: Roe Deer, small mammals, possible Otter, butterflies, moths & dragonflies.
Directions: Sat nav: PA12 4JF. NS 358 580. 18 miles SW of Glasgow, adjacent to A760 Largs Road, off A737 (Irvine Road). Leave M8 at Junc 28A.
Public transport: Bus - nos X34/X36 Glasgow to Irvine/ Ardrossan, alight Roadhead roundabout, 0.5 mile from reserve. Stagecoach West Scotland. Bus - no.4 (not Sun) Johnstone to Lochwinnoch (Key Coaches T: 01505 358 589) & no.307 (Sun) McGills. Train - Lochwinnoch.
Visiting: Open all times (charge for non-RSPB members). Visitor centre open daily (not Dec 25/26, Jan 1/2) 9.30am-5pm, refreshments, shop, toilets. Three trails, two hides & toilets - all have disabled access.
Contact: RSPB, T: 01505 842 663;
E: lochwinnoch@rspb.org.uk

Fife

The county's coastline has a number of interesting sites: Fife Ness is good for seawatching & autumn migrants; the Eden Estuary holds good numbers of wildfowl & waders throughout the year but especially in winter, & wintering flocks of seaduck off Ruddons Point (Largo Bay) often hold a few Surf Scoters among the more numerous Common & Velvet Scoters. Tentsmuir offers an unusual mix of woodland (scarce in the county) & coastal habitats.

10. EDEN ESTUARY LNR

Fife Coast & Countryside Trust.
Habitats: 891ha, mainly intertidal mud & sandflats with saltmarsh, river, reed, sand dunes, wetland.
Birds: *Winter/passage:* Significant numbers of waders & wildfowl. Outer estuary - seaduck inc. scoters, Eider, Long-tailed Duck, Red-breasted Merganser & Gannet, terns, skuas. Mudflats - godwits, plovers, sandpipers, Redshank, Shelduck. River - Common Sandpiper, Kingfisher, Goosander. Surrounding area attracts Short & Long-eared Owls, Peregrine, Merlin, Marsh Harrier & White-tailed Eagle. Osprey regular visitor.
Other: Northern Marsh Orchid, dune grasses & herbs. Common & Grey Seals, Bottlenose Dolphin, Harbour Porpoise, Brown Hare, Stoat & Otter. Butterflies inc. Grayling, Small pearl-bordered & Dark Green Fritillaries.
Directions: Sat nav: KY16 0UG. NO 450 192 (Eden Estuary Centre). Centre is off main street in Guardbridge, two miles from St Andrews on A91, & from Leuchars via Tentsmuir Forest off A919 (four miles). Use Outhead at St Andrews, off West Sands beach, to access Balgove Bay.
Public transport: Bus - regular services from Cupar, Dundee & St Andrews. Train - Leuchars (1.5 miles),
Visiting: Eden Estuary Centre, Guardbridge open daily, not Dec 25/26/31, Jan 1) 9am-5pm (4pm Nov-Mar) - (access code for centre from local ranger). Evans Hide at Balgove Bay: NO 482 181, parking at Pilmuir Links golf course car park. Viewing platform & picnic area at Outhead.
Contact: Ranald Strachan, Ranger, T: 07985 707 593; E: Ranald.Strachan@fifecountryside.co.uk

11. ISLE OF MAY NNR

Scottish Natural Heritage.
Habitats: Island, sea cliffs, rocky shoreline.
Birds: *Spring*/autumn: Weather-related migrations inc. rarities each year. *Summer*: Breeding Shag, Eider, Fulmar, Kittiwake, other gulls, terns, auks (inc. 45,000+ pairs of Puffin),
Directions: KY10 3RR. NT 655 995 (island). Small island lying five miles E of Anstruther in Firth of Forth.
Public transport: Bus - regular services to Anstruther & North Berwick harbours.
Visiting: Ferries (Apr-Sep). Trips take 4-5 hours, inc. time to explore island. From Anstruther (5 miles): Anstruther Pleasure Cruises (T: 07957 585200, E: info@isleofmayferry.com) & Osprey of Anstruther (T: 07473 631 671, E info@isleofmayboattrips.co.uk). From North Berwick (13 miles) - check with Scottish Seabird Centre (T: 01620 890 202).
If staying at Observatory delays getting on/off island are possible due to weather. Keep to paths, no dogs, no camping/fires. Permission required to carry out scientific work or filming.
Contact: Obs accomodation Bookings Sec: Mark Newell. T: 07909 707 971; E: bookings@isleofmaybirdobs.org; W: www.isleofmaybirdobs.org
Other enquiries: Reserve Manager, T: 01738 458 800; E: nnr@nature.scot;
W: www.nature.scot/enjoying-outdoors/scotlands-national-nature-reserves/isle-may-national-nature-reserve

Forth

The RSPB reserve at Inversnaid is good for Black Grouse, Redstart, Wood Warbler, Pied Flycatcher & Twite, A Red Kite feeding station at Argaty provides visitors with close-up views. Cambus Pools attract passage waders & winter wildfowl, while high tide at Kinneil produces good numbers of waders in spring & autumn.

12. CAMBUS POOLS

Scottish Wildlife Trust.
Habitats: Wet grassland, reedbeds & two salty pools.
Birds: *Spring/autumn:* Used extensively by migrants. Wildfowl inc. Mute & Whooper Swans, Goldeneye, Teal, Shelduck, waders inc. Black-tailed Godwit, Oystercatcher, Greenshank. Kingfisher regularly seen. Gadwall have bred, Small birds inc. Yellowhammer & Reed Bunting.
Other: Brown Hare, Stoat, Short-tailed vole, 115 spp. of vascular plants. Harbour Porpoise seen in Forth.
Directions: Sat nav: FK10 2PG. NS 846 937. From Stirling, take A907 east towards Alloa. From roundabout drive 0.6 mile to where B9096 leads off to Tullibody. Take minor road (Station Road) R to small village of Cambus.
Public transport: None.
Visiting: Open all year. Cross River Devon by bridge at NS 853 940 & walk down stream on R bank past bonded warehouses. Best viewing around high tide. Bench on S side of western pool. Dogs under control.
Contact: Scottish WT, T: 0131 312 7765;
E: enquiries@scottishwildlifetrust.org.uk

Lothian

More than 250 species have been recorded at Aberlady Bay, where thousands of geese gather in winter. The Seabird Centre at North Berwick is worth a visit & a boat can be taken out from here to the gannetry at Bass Rock. The Lammermuir Hills hold a range of upland species including Red Grouse, Whinchat & Ring Ouzel.

13. ABERLADY BAY LNR

East Lothian Council.
Habitats: Tidal mudflats, saltmarsh, freshwater marsh, dune grassland, scrub, open sea.
Birds: *Summer*: Breeding spp. inc. Shelduck, Eider, Reed Bunting & up to eight spp. of warbler. *Passage:* waders inc. Green, Wood & Curlew Sandpipers, Little Stint, Greenshank, Whimbrel, Black-tailed Godwit. *Winter*: Divers (esp. Red-throated), Red-necked & Slavonian Grebes & geese (in autumn 30,000+ Pink-feet roost & feed before moving on), sea-duck, waders.
Directions: Sat nav: EH32 0QB. NT 471 804. From Edinburgh take A198 E to Aberlady. Reserve car park is on A198 just to E of Aberlady village.
Public transport: Bus - nos.124/X24 Edinburgh to N Berwick pass reserve (ask to be dropped nearby). East Coast Buses.
Visiting: Open all times. Small (free) car park & toilets. Notice board with recent sightings at end of footbridge. Stay on footpaths to avoid disturbance. Disabled access from reserve car park. No dogs. The Scottish Ornithologists' Club (SOC) HQ, Waterston House, is located W of Aberlady village, open daily (not Dec 25/26, Jan 1) 10am-4pm inc. shop, library, gallery, hot/cold drinks. T: 01875 871 330.
Contact: Countryside Rangers, T: 01620 827 279;
E: ranger@eastlothian.gov.uk

14. BASS ROCK/SCOTTISH SEABIRD CENTRE

Private.
Habitats: Sea cliffs.
Birds: The spectacular cliffs hold a massive Gannet colony (up to 150,000 birds, largest in world). Fulmar, Shag, Puffin, Guillemot, Razorbill, Kittiwake, Common Tern.
Directions: NT 602 873. Island NE of North Berwick. Scottish Seabird Centre is located in North Berwick Harbour (Sat nav: EH39 4SS. NT554 856).
Public transport: None.
Visiting: Bass Rock is private - contact Seabird Centre/check website for details of exclusive Bass Rock landing trips (inc. three hours on island). Terms & conditions apply to bookings. Sailings/landings are subject to weather conditions. No facilities on island. Seabird Centre - entrance fee: open Jan 11am-4pm; Feb/Mar & Sep/Oct 10am-5pm; Apr-Aug 10am-6pm; Nov-Dec (not Dec 25) 10am-4pm. Aquaria, telescope deck & toilets. Free to visit cafe & shop.
Contact: The Scottish Seabird Centre,
T: 01620 890 202; E: info@seabird.org;
boat trips: E: boats@seabird.org; W: www.seabird.org

15. BAWSINCH RESERVE & DUDDINGSTON LOCH

Scottish Wildlife Trust.
Habitats: Edinburgh's only natural freshwater loch. Reedbed, marsh, ponds, mixed woodland, flower meadow & scrub. Bawsinch reserve developed from former industrial wasteland.
Birds: *Summer:* Heronry, breeding swans, geese, ducks, grebes & Water Rail. Kingfisher. Migrants inc. Spotted Flycatcher, hirundines, warblers, inc. occasional Grasshopper Warbler. *Winter*: Bittern, wildfowl, gulls.
Other: Fox, Water Vole & Otter. Dragonflies, four spp. of amphibian.
Directions: Sat nav: EH15 3PY. NT 282 726. Two miles from centre of Edinburgh, below Arthur's Seat. Use car park just W of Duddingston Village on Duddingston Low Road.
Public transport: Bus - no.42 Edinburgh to Portabello, alight Duddingston Village (by Holyrood School). Lothian Buses (T: 0131 555 6363).
Visiting: Open access to north shore of loch. Southern shore (& hide) by prior arrangement with SWT.
Contact: Scottish WT - see site 12.

Eastern Scotland

Angus & Dundee, Moray & Nairn, NE Scotland, Perth & Kinross

Angus & Dundee

The Angus glens hold a typical range of upland species, including Ring Ouzel, grouse, chats & Golden Eagle. Black-necked Grebe breeds at RSPB Loch of Kinnordy & Ospreys regularly fish there. Montrose Basin is a flagship Scottish Wildlife Trust reserve, with a good selection of wildfowl ever present & waders on passage.

1. LOCH OF LINTRATEN

Scottish Water/Scottish Wildlife Trust.
Habitats: Oligotrophic-mesotrophic loch. Surrounded by mainly coniferous woodland in foothills of Braes of Angus.
Birds: *Summer*: Grey Heron, Great Crested Grebe & other water birds. Osprey occasionally. *Winter*: Internationally-important numbers of Icelandic Greylag Geese (up to 3,000), Pink-footed Goose, Goosander, Whooper Swan, Wigeon, Teal, other wildfowl. Birds feed on surrounding farmland during day.
Other: Red Squirrel, Otter, Pipistrelle Bat.
Directions: Sat nav: DD8 5JH. NO 278 550. Located next to Bridgend of Lintrathen, seven miles W of Kirriemuir. Take B951 & choose circular route on unclassified roads round loch.
Public transport: None.
Visiting: Roadside parking at NO 276 557 off a minor road W of loch, forest track leads to hide. Second hide (wheelchair accessible) on E side of loch. Hides open all times. Rest of reserve is private, but good views possible from unclassified roads. Viewpoint can accommodate five cars.
Contact: Scottish WT, T: 0131 312 7765;
E: enquiries@scottishwildlifetrust.org.uk

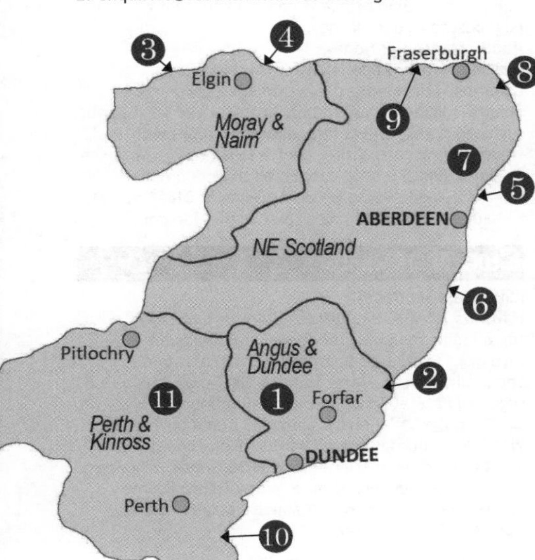

2. MONTROSE BASIN

Scottish Wildlife Trust/Angus Council.
Habitats: Estuary, saltmarsh, reedbeds, farmland.
Birds: *Summer:* Breeding Common & Arctic terns, gulls, Shelduck, Goldeneye, Eider (up to 2,000), Grey Partridge in surrounding fields. Nationally important moulting site for Mute Swan (approx 300 birds). *Winter:* Wildfowl & waders (Curlew peak numbers in Aug, Dunlin in Feb). Internationally important for Pink-footed Goose, Knot & Redshank.
Directions: Sat nav: DD10 9TA. NO 700 564. SWT Wildlife Centre on A92, one mile S of Montrose. Main car park for western end at Old Mill, Mains of Dun (DD10 9LQ. NO 668 591).
Public transport: Bus - no.30 Arbroath to Montrose, request stop outside Visitor Centre. Stagecoach East Scotland. Train - Montrose (1.5 miles).
Visiting: Admission fee (non-members) to visitor centre open, daily 10.30am-5pm mid-Feb to Oct & 10.30am-4pm, Fri-Mon, Nov to mid-Feb (not Dec 25/26 & Jan 1/2). Shop, fair-trade drinks/snacks, toilets, disabled access to centre. Rest so reserve open at all time inc. two hides on western half of reserve.
Contact: Montrose Basin Wildlife Centre,
T: 01674 676 336;
E: montrosebasin@scottishwildlifetrust.org.uk

Moray & Nairn

Two rivers, the Spey & the Findhorn, flow into the Moray Firth - the bays they flow into attract passage waders, terns, Ospreys, seabirds & wildfowl. More than half of the area is over 250m. Lochindorb is the best area of moorland to explore, with breeding grouse, raptors, divers & waders. Extensive woodlands hold Crested Tit (conifer) & Tree Pipit & Redstart (birch).

3. CULBIN SANDS

RSPB (East Scotland).
Habitats: Saltmarsh, sandflats, dunes.
Birds: *Spring:* Terns, esp. Sandwich, passage waders. *Summer*: Breeding Eider, Ringed Plover, Oystercatcher. Osprey on passage. *Winter*: Common Scoter, Long-tailed Duck, Red-breasted Merganser, Knot, Bar-tailed Godwit. Raptors inc. Peregrine, Merlin & Hen Harrier attracted by wader flocks. Roosting geese, Snow Bunting.
Other: Dolphins, Grey & Common Seals in Firth. Otters sometimes seen.
Directions: Sat nav: IV12 5BX. NH 900 576. Approx 1.5 miles NE of Nairn, overlooking Moray Firth. Use East Beach car park, signed off A96. Follow road through Maggot Road caravan park (car park at end of road). Track along dunes & saltmarsh - from far end of car park take 0.5 mile 'all abilities footpath' to reach reserve.

Public transport: Bus - from Inverness to Nairn - stops in Nairn, one mile W of site. No.10. Stagecoach North Scotland. No.11. Stagecoach Highlands. Train - Nairn, 1.5 miles W of reserve.
Visiting: Open all times. Car park with bike racks, seasonal toilets (inc. disabled, RADAR key).
Contact: RSPB, T: 01463 715 000; E: nsro@rspb.org.uk

4. SPEY BAY

Scottish Wildlife Trust.
Habitats: Shingle, rivermouth, coastal habitats.
Birds: *Summer*: Osprey, waders, wildfowl, terns. *Winter*: Seaduck & divers offshore, esp. Long-tailed Duck, Common & Velvet Scoters, Red-throated Diver.
Other: Dolphins offshore. Otter, dragonflies.
Directions: Eight miles NE of Elgin. Sat nav: IV32 7NW. NJ 334 656 (Kingston - west side) - from Elgin take A96 & B9015 to Kingston. Sat nav: IV32 7PJ. NJ 347 654 (Tugnet - east side) - from Elgin take A96 & B9014 to Spey Bay, Scottish Dolphin Centre located by car park, T: 01343 820 339; W: https://dolphincentre.whales.org/
Public transport: Bus - no.224 Elgin to Garmouth/ Kingston (west side). Moray Council (T: 01343 562 534).
Visiting: Reserve open at all times.
Contact: Scottish WT - see site 1.

NE Scotland

Troup Head holds Scotland's only mainland gannetry &, together with Fowlsheugh, has a good variety of other seabirds. The RSPB's Loch of Strathbeg sees the arrival in autumn of huge numbers of Pink-footed Geese. The Ythan Estuary is good for breeding terns, Eider, & passage & wintering waders. Inland, Deeside holds most of the typical highland species.

5. FORVIE NNR

Scottish Natural Heritage.
Habitats: 1,000ha, estuary, dunes, coastal heath.
Birds: *Spring/summer*: Breeding Eider & terns, migrant waders & seabirds offshore. *Autumn:* Pink-footed Goose, migrant seabirds, waders & passerines inc. occasional scarce/rare spp. *Winter*: Waders & wildfowl, inc. Whooper Swan, Long-tailed Duck, Golden Plover.
Other: Occasional cetaceans offshore, esp. summer.
Directions: 12 miles N of Aberdeen, inc. Ythan Estuary. Access inc. Sat nav: AB41 8RU. NK 034 289 (Forvie Visitor Centre) - three miles NE of Newburgh at Collieston. Waterside car park (AB41 6AB, NK 003 270) one mile N of Newburgh. Waulkmill hide (AB41 8RL. NK 004 287) - turn L off A975 opp. Collieston junction.
Public transport: Bus - no.63 Aberdeen to Peterhead (via Cruden Bay) stops in Newburgh & at Collieston crossroads. Stagecoach North Scotland.
Visiting: Open all times, ternery closed Apr to end-Aug. Coach parking at Forvie Visitor Centre: open daily Apr-Oct, toilets, interpretive display. Hide, waymarked trails - short trail & hide wheelchair-accessible.
Contact: SNH Reserve Manager, T: 01358 751 330; E: nnr@nature.scot; W: www.nature.scot/

6. FOWLSHEUGH

RSPB (East Scotland).
Habitats: Sea cliffs.
Birds: Peregrine regular throughout year. *Summer:* Spectacular 130,000 strong seabird colony, mainly Kittiwake & Guillemot with Razorbill, Fulmar, Puffin. Gannet, Eider & skuas offshore, *Autumn:* Red-throated Diver on sea, terns on passage.
Other: Grey & Common Seals, Bottlenose Dolphin. White-beaked Dolphin & Minke Whale occasional (summer).
Directions: Sat nav: AB39 2TP. NO 879 808. Reserve is three miles S of Stonehaven. From A92 take minor road signposted Crawton. Car park just before end of road.
Public transport: Bus - no. 747 request stop on A92 Crawton turn-off (Stonehaven to Johnshaven). Stagecoach North East. One mile to reserve entrance.
Visiting: Open at all times, not suitable for wheelchairs. Car park 200 yards from reserve. Viewing shelter at end of footpath (one mile). Toilets in Stonehaven. Dogs under close control.
Contact: RSPB, T: 01346 532 017; E: strathbeg@rspb.org.uk

7. HADDO COUNTRY PARK

Aberdeenshire Council.
Habitats: Parkland, woodland, wetland, loch, ponds.
Birds: *All year:* Goosander, Grey Heron, Cormorant, Buzzard, Sparrowhawk, Grey Partridge, Great Spotted Woodpecker, Tawny Owl, Grey Wagtail. *Spring/summer:* Osprey, Lapwing, Sedge Warbler, Blackcap, Chiffchaff. *Winter:* Canada & Greylag Geese, Teal, Wigeon, Goldeneye, Brambling.
Other: Red Squirrel, Otter, Pipistrelle & Daubenton's Bats. Meadow Brown, Ringlet & Common Blue butterflies.
Directions: Sat nav: AB41 7EQ. NJ 875 345. From Ellon (off A90) follow signs for Metlick & B9005. Once out of Ellon, cross Ythan bridge & continue straight on (signposted Haddo House).
Public transport: None.
Visiting: Grounds open daily dawn-dusk. Car park (free/ donation welcomed) - if busy, do not park on road verges, coach parking, display boards, over 3.2 miles of surfaced paths, toilets (inc. disabled), hides with wheelchair access. Visitor centre (10am-4pm), tearoom (10am-4.30pm) & shop connected to Haddo House.
Contact: Haddo House & Country Park, T: 01651 851 041; E: haddo@visithaddo.com; www.visithaddo.com

8. LOCH OF STRATHBEG

RSPB (East Scotland).
Habitats: 894ha, inc. Britain's largest dune loch, with surrounding marshes, reedbeds, grasslands.
Birds: *All year:* Tree Sparrow. *Spring/autumn*: Spoonbill, Avocet, Marsh Harrier, Garganey, Little Gull, regular Pectoral Sandpiper. Osprey (almost daily), Common Crane (annual). *Summer*: Common Tern, Water Rail, Corn Bunting. *Winter*: Pink-footed (up to 20% of world population) & Barnacle Geese, Whooper Swan, large numbers of duck. Snow Goose & Smew annual. Raptors inc. Hen & Marsh Harriers. Great Northern Diver offshore.

Other: Otter, Badger, Stoat, Roe Deer. Early Purple, Butterfly & Northern Marsh Orchids, Dark Green Fritillary butterfly.
Directions: Sat nav: AB43 8QN. NK 055 577. Near Crimond on A90, nine miles S of Fraserburgh. Reserve signposted from village - at T-junction at end of road turn L, after ca.0.3 mile turn R at reserve entrance.
Public transport: Bus - no.69 Fraserburgh to Peterhead stops in Crimond, one mile from centre. Stagecoach North Scotland.
Visiting: Open all times (not Dec 25/26). Visitor Centre open daily (not Dec 25/26) 9am-5pm, inc. observation room, toilets, coffee machine. Wildlife garden, indoor children's area. Tower Pool hide offers panoramic views, open dawn-dusk (0.5 mile from centre). Willow hide (200 yards from centre), Fen & Bay hides (500 yards from airfield car park - footpath from centre to airfield hides open Easter-end Jul). Beach & dune walks accessible from Rattray or St Combs.
Contact: RSPB - see site 6.

9. TROUP HEAD

RSPB (East Scotland).
Habitats: Sea cliffs, farmland.
Birds: Spectacular seabird colony, inc. Scotland's largest mainland Gannet colony (2000+ pairs). Fulmar, Kittiwake, Guillemot, Razorbill, Puffin. Bonxies may linger in summer. Migrants occur during spring/autumn.
Other: Impressive common flower assemblage in spring. cetaceans possible offshore in summer inc. Minke Whale. Brown Hare.
Directions: Sat nav: AB45 3JJ. NJ 822 665. Troup Head is between Pennan & Gardenstown on B9031, E along coast from Macduff. It is signposted off B9031 - look for small RSPB signs (& sign for Northfield Farm). At farm go through farmyard & onto a rough track to car park.
Public transport: None.
Visiting: Open at all times, not suitable for wheelchairs. Parking for small number of cars, but not coaches.
Contact: RSPB - see site 6.

Perth & Kinross

Loch Leven NNR (including the RSPB's Vane Farm) is the region's best known reserve & holds 1000+ breeding duck & large numbers of wintering geese, ducks & swans. Ospreys fish there too but the well-known watch point of Loch of the Lowes offers views of birds on the nest. Woodland & moorland species are well represented including Woodcock, Redstart, Wood Warbler, Red & Black Grouse (the latter can be elusive).

10. LOCH LEVEN (VANE FARM)

RSPB (East Scotland).
Habitats: Wet grassland & flooded areas by Loch Leven. Arable farmland, native woodland, moorland. Part of Loch Leven NNR.
Birds: *Spring/summer:* Breeding & passage waders (inc. Lapwing, Redshank, Snipe, Curlew), hirundines, Great Crested Grebe, Osprey. Farmland birds (inc. Skylark & Yellowhammer), Tree Pipit. *Autumn:* Migrating waders on exposed mud. *Winter:* Major fuelling stop for Pink-footed Geese (around 20,000 in late autumn). Whooper Swan (6% of Scotland's wintering population), Bewick's Swan, White-tailed Eagle, finch & tit flocks.
Other: 237 spp. butterflies & moths, 25 spp. mammal inc. Pipistrelle Bat & Roe Deer.
Directions: Sat nav: KY13 9LX. NT 160 990. Halfway between Perth & Edinburgh, seven miles from Cowdenbeath, signposted two miles E Junc 5 of M90 follow signs for B9097 towards Glenrothes. Drive for approx two miles, car park on R (signposted).
Public transport: Bus - from Edinburgh, Perth & nearby towns to Kinross. Can walk Loch Leven Heritage Trail from here to reserve (ca. four miles).
Visiting: Trails & hides open all times. Free car parking, coach parking available. Visitor centre open daily (not Dec 25/26, Jan 1/2) 10am-5pm. Entry fee to reserve, RSPB members free. Disabled access to shop, toilets, cafe (open 10am-4pm) & observation room with telescopes overlooking Loch Leven & reserve. Binocular hire. 1.25 mile Hill Trail through woodland/moorland. Wetland Trail has three hides. Eight-mile cycle path around loch. Other than assistance dogs, dogs not permitted in visitor centre (but can use courtyard) or on Wetland Trail. Permitted on Loch Leven Heritage Trail & Sleeping Giant Path (both accessed from centre).
Contact: RSPB, T: 01577 862 355;
E: lochleven@rspb.org.uk

11. LOCH OF THE LOWES

Scottish Wildlife Trust.
Habitats: Freshwater loch fringed by areas of fen, reedbeds, semi-natural woodland.
Birds: Breeding Ospreys (Apr-end Aug) nest 200 yards from hide. Wildfowl & woodland birds.
Other: Red Squirrel, Beaver.
Directions: Sat nav: PH8 0HH. NO 041 435. Sixteen miles N of Perth, two miles NE of Dunkeld, just off A923 Dunkeld to Blairgowrie road (signposted from A9).
Public transport: Bus - no.23 Perth to Dunkeld, two miles via Fungarth Path. Stagecoach. Train - Dunkeld, three miles via Fungarth Path.
Visiting: Entrance fee for non-members. Visitor Centre open daily (not Dec 25/26, Jan 1/2) 10.30am-5pm Mar-Oct & Fri to Sun 10.30am-4pm Nov-Feb. Light refreshments, exhibition, shop & toilets. Observation hide open daily during daylight hours, Crannog hide accessible during visitor centre opening hours. Full access for wheelchairs. No dogs in centre/hides, keep under control on reserve.
Contact: Loch of the Lowes Visitor Centre, T: 01350 727 337;
E: lochofthelowes@scottishwildlifetrust.org.uk

Highlands & Islands

Highlands, Orkney, Outer Hebrides, Shetland

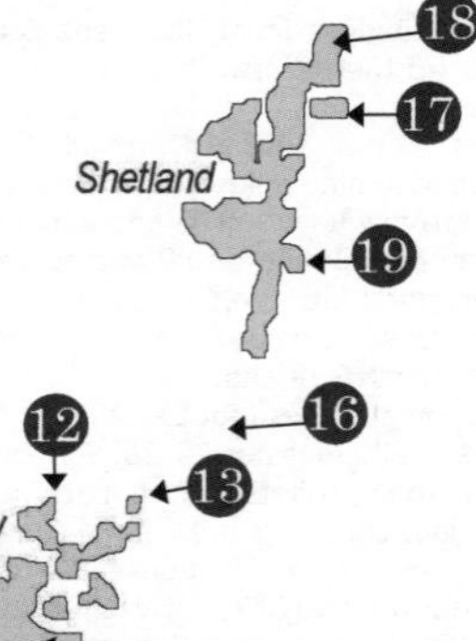

Highlands

Habitats, unique in Britain, hold a range of scarce species: Dotterel, Ptarmigan & Snow Buntings on the high tops, Crested Tit, the endemic Scottish Crossbill & Capercaillie in the Caledonian pine forests. The boggy Flow Country of Caithness & Sutherland attracts breeding Red & Black-throated Divers, Common Scoter, Greenshank. Handa Island holds important numbers of seabirds.

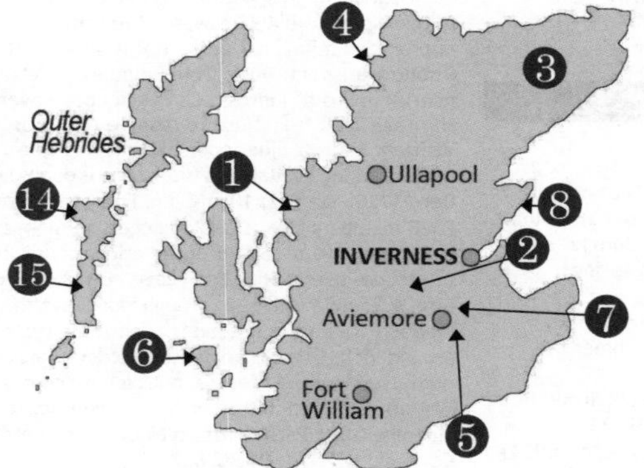

1. BEINN EIGHE & LOCH MAREE ISLANDS NNR

Scottish Natural Heritage.
Habitats: Caledonian forest, moorland, mountain tops, freshwater loch shore.
Birds: *All year*: Golden & White-tailed Eagles, Scottish Crossbill, Ptarmigan, Red Grouse, Siskin. *Summer*: Black-throated Diver, Golden Plover, Redwing, Snow Bunting.
Other: Wide range of dragonflies inc. Northern Emerald, Golden-ringed & Common Hawker. Red Deer, Pine Marten, Mountain Hare.
Directions: Sat nav: NH 019 630. IV22 2PD. Complex mountain massif. Visitor centre two miles NW of village of Kinlochewe, Wester Ross, 50 miles from Inverness & 20 miles from Gairloch on A832.
Public transport: Bus - very limited, Inverness to Kinlochewe.
Visiting: Open all times. Visitor centre open 10am-5pm Mar-Oct (T: 01445 760 258). Toilets. Two woodland trails from visitor centre. From shore of Loch Maree (continue N on A832 to Coille na Glas-Leitir) - self-guides woodland walk & mountain trail - leaflets from visitor centre.
Contact: SNH, T: 01463 701 660;
E: nnr@nature.scot; W: www.nature.scot/

2. CORRIMONY

RSPB (North Scotland).
Habitats: 1,531ha, Caledonian forest, moorland, blanket bog.
Birds: *Spring/summer:* Red-throated Diver, Goosander. Greenshank, Black (30+ displaying males) & Red Grouse, Tree Pipit, Whinchat, Crested Tit, Scottish Crossbill, occasional Golden Eagle & Osprey. *Autumn/ Winter:* Whooper Swan, Pink-footed Goose, Woodcock.
Other: Red Deer, Pine Marten, many orchids in Jul.
Directions: Sat nav: IV63 6TW (Corrimony village). NH 384 303 (car park). Lies 22 miles SW of Inverness between Cannich & Glen Urquhart, off A 831. Park in Corrimony Cairns car park.
Public transport: Bus - no.17 (not Sun) from Inverness to Cannich stops 1.5 miles from reserve (request stop). Stagecoach Highlands.
Visiting: Open all times. Waymarked trail (8.5 miles) passes through farm, suitable for wheelchairs but unimproved paths may not be suitable. Leave gates as you find them.
Contact: RSPB, T: 01463 715 000;
E: nsro@rspb.org.uk

3. FORSINARD FLOWS

RSPB (North Scotland).
Habitats: Blanket bog, upland hill farm.
Birds: *All year:* Red Grouse, Golden Eagle, Raven & Buzzard. *May-Jul:* Join a guided walk for best chance of Red-throated Diver, Golden Plover, Greenshank, Dunlin, Hen Harrier, Merlin, Short-eared Owl, Dipper.
Other: Red Deer, Otter, Water Vole, Azure Hawker dragonfly, Emperor Moth, bog plants inc. sundews.
Directions: Sat nav: KW11 6UE. NC 891 425.
30 miles SW of Thurso on A897. From S turn off A9 at Helmsdale (24 miles) or from N coast road turn off A836, two miles E of Melvich (14 miles).
Public transport: Train - between Inverness & Thurso stop at Forsinard.
Visiting: Open all times. Contact reserve office during breeding season (mid-Apr/end-Jul) & during the deer stalking season (Jul-Feb 15) for advice. Visitor centre situated in Forsinard station open daily 9am-5pm, Apr-Oct. Wheelchair access to centre & toilet. Two self-guided trails open all year. Boardwalk access to viewpoint on Dubh Lochan Trail (one mile walk). Forsinain Trail starts at roadside car park four mile N of Forsinard (four mile walk). Stay on trails. Guided walks. Dogs under control at all times.
Contact: RSPB, T: 01641 571 225;
E: forsinard@rspb.org.uk

4. HANDA

Scourie Estate/Scottish Wildlife Trust.
Habitats: Island - sea cliffs, blanket bog & heath, small sandy beaches, coastal grassland.
Birds: *Spring/summer*: 100,000 seabirds: largest Guillemot & Razorbill colony in Britain. Nationally important for Kittiwake, Arctic & Great Skuas. Puffin, Shag, Fulmar, Common & Arctic Terns.
Directions: Sat nav: IV27 4SS. NC 164 488 (Tarbet). Island accessible by boat from Tarbet, near Scourie - follow A835/A894 N from Ullapool for 40 miles. Turn L down single track road, continue another three miles to Tarbet.
Public transport: Post bus (hail & ride) - no.806 (Mon-Fri) Lairg to Durness via Scourie. No transport between Scourie & Tarbet (three miles). The Far North Bus (T: 07782 110 007). Train - Inverness to Lairg connects with service.
Visiting: Open Apr-Aug, no Sun sailings (& subject to weather). Ferry runs 9.30am-16.45pm (last boat to island at 2pm) - part of ferry ticket price goes to SWT. Visitors given introductory talk & leaflet with map on arrival. Three mile circular path, visitor shelter, compost toilet. Not suitable for disabled due to uneven terrain. No dogs.
Contact: Handa Ranger (Apr-Aug), T: 07920 468 572;
E: handaranger@scottishwildlifetrust.org.uk;
Ferry operator: Roger Tebay, T: 07780 967 800;
E: info@handa-ferry.com

5. INSH MARSHES

RSPB (North Scotland).
Habitats: 1,000+ha, marsh, woodland, river, open water.
Birds: *Spring/summer:* Waders (Lapwing, Curlew, Redshank, Snipe), wildfowl (inc. Goldeneye & Wigeon), Osprey, Wood Warbler, Redstart, Tree Pipit. *Winter:* Hen Harrier, Whooper Swan, Greylag Goose, Teal, Wigeon, other wildfowl.
Other: Roe Deer. Black Darter dragonfly & Northern Brown Argus butterfly along Invertromie trail. Five spp. orchid in Tromie Meadow.
Directions: Sat nav: PH21 1NTS. NN 775 998. In Spey Valley. From A9 take exit to Kingussie. Follow B970 S from village & then beyond Ruthven Barracks. Entrance to reserve is 0.6 mile further on.
Public transport: Bus - no.32 Newtownmore to Carrbridge stops at Kingussie. Stagecoach Highlands. Train - Kingussie. Both one mile.
Visiting: Open all times. Car park, coach parking. Disabled access to unmanned information viewpoint. Two hides, three trails.
Contact: RSPB, T: 01540 661 518; E: insh@rspb.org.uk

6. ISLE OF RUM NNR

Scottish Natural Heritage.
Habitats: Island - wild/rugged dominated by mountains. Blanket bog, grassland, woodland, wet & dry heath, scree & rocky slopes.
Birds: *Breeding:* Golden & White-tailed Eagles, Merlin, Hen Harrier, Peregrine, Golden Plover, Twite. Red-throated Diver, 70,000 pairs Manx Shearwater. & small number of other seabirds inc. Guillemot, Razorbill, Fulmar, Kittiwake.
Other: Red Deer, Wild Goat. 2,000+ spp invertebrates inc. 11spp. dragonfly, 19 spp. butterfly.
Directions: Sat nav: PH41 4RA. NM674 969 (Mallaig).
Public transport: Ferry from Mallaig to Rum - Caledonian MacBrayne (T: 08705 650 000;
W: www.calmac.co.uk). No cars permitted on island - parking for ferry passengers in Mallaig.
Visiting: SNH owns & manages most of island. Isle of Rum Community Trust owns some property & land in & around village at Kinloch. Access all times. Visitor centre on lower shore road near old pier, open daily in summer. Toilets at village campsite (10 mins from ferry terminal). Otter hide one mile through woods to S of main pier.
Contact: SNH, T: 0131 314 4181; E: nnr@nature.scot;
W: www.nature.scot/

7. LOCH GARTEN & ABERNETHY FOREST

RSPB (North Scotland).
Habitats: Caledonian pine forest.
Birds: *Spring/summer:* Ospreys nesting from Apr-Aug, Crested Tit, Redstart, Spotted Flycatcher, Tree Pipit, Scottish Crossbill. Possible views of Capercaillie from Osprey Centre (Apr/mid-May). On loch - Wigeon, Goldeneye & Common Sandpiper. *Autumn/winter:* Greylag & Pink-footed Geese roost on loch, Whooper Swan, various duck spp.Wider Cairngorm area: Golden Eagle, Black & Red Grouse, Ptarmigan, Dotterel.

Other: Red Squirrel, Roe Deer, Otter. Fungi.
Directions: Sat nav: PH25 3HA. NH 978 183. 2.5 miles from Boat of Garten, eight miles from Aviemore. Off B970, follow 'RSPB Ospreys' road signs (Apr-Aug only).
Public transport: Bus - nearest stop is on B970, no.34 Aviemore to Grantown on Spey (ask for Raebreck junction) - from here dedicated footpath leads to Osprey Centre (1.6 miles). Stagecoach Highland.
Visiting: Osprey Centre (overlooking Osprey nest) open daily 10am-6pm (Apr to first Sunday in Sep). Entrance fee, RSPB members free. Optics & CCTV live pictures, shop & light refreshments (closes 5pm), toilets. Disabled access. Guide dogs only. On reserve: three way-marked trails open all year. Dogs on leads.
Contact: RSPB, T: 01479 821 409 (Reserve); T: 01479 831 476 (Osprey Centre); E: abernethy@rspb.co.uk

8. UDALE BAY

RSPB (Scotland).
Habitats: Mudflat, saltmarsh, wet grassland.
Birds: *Spring/summer*: 10,000 Pink-footed Goose on passage, other wildfowl, Oystercatcher, Redshank, waders. Possible Osprey. *Autumn/winter*: Large flocks of wildfowl (inc. 10,000 Wigeon & Scaup), geese, waders inc. Oystercatcher, Knot, Bar-tailed Godwit & Dunlin. Peregrine.
Directions: Sat nav: IV7 8LU. NH 712 651. On Black Isle, one mile W of Jemimaville on the B9163.
Public transport: None.
Visiting: Open all year. Limited parking: Main hide Highland Council lay-by (wheelchair accessible hide). Kirkmichael Viewing Screen. Ivy Cottage - Highland Council car park Newhall Point - Highland Council car park.
Contact: RSPB - see site 2.

Orkney

Breeding seabirds, moorland specialities & passage migrants make the islands an attractive destination. Hen Harriers breed here in good numbers, other scarce breeders include Whimbrel, Great & Arctic Skuas & Red-throated Diver. For seabirds, Marwick Head (mainland) & North Hill (Papa Westray) are worth a visit. North Ronaldsay Bird Observatory is a good base to stay to look for rare migrants.

9. HOBBISTER

RSPB (East Scotland).
Habitats: Moorland, bog, fen, saltmarsh, sandflats, sea cliffs, scrub.
Birds: *Summer*: Breeding Red-throated Diver, Eider, Red-breasted Merganser, Black Guillemot, Merlin, Hen Harrier, Short-eared Owl, Red Grouse, Twite. *Autumn/winter*: Waulkmill Bay for wildfowl & waders, sea ducks, divers, auks & grebes (inc. Great Northern, Red & Black-throated Divers, Slavonian Grebe, Long-tailed Duck).
Other: Otter, Grey & Common Seals.
Directions: Sat nav: KW17 2RA. HY 395 069 (car park) or HY 382 068 (Waukmill Bay) - are main access points. Overlooking Scarpa Flow 3.2 miles W of Kirkwall on A964.
Public transport: Bus - no.2 Kirkwall to Houton Ferry along A964 passes reserve. Stagecoach (T: 01856 870 555).
Visiting: Open access between A964 & sea. Two car parks - circular walk from RSPB car park along cliff top & Scapa Flow. A council-maintained footpath to Waulkmill Bay. Dogs on leads.
Contact: RSPB, T: 01856 850 176; E: orkney@rspb.org.uk

10. HOY

RSPB (East Scotland).
Habitats: 3,920ha covering entire NW of Hoy: sea cliffs, moorland.
Birds: *All year:* Hen Harrier. *Summer*: Red-throated Diver, White-tailed Eagle, Fulmar, Puffin, Guillemot, Razorbill, Kittiwake, Black Guillemot, Arctic & Great Skuas, Stonechat. *Autumn/winter:* Finches & thrushes, Great Northern Diver, Long-tailed Duck, Merlin.
Other: Primroses & Arctic alpine flowers. Old Man of Hoy landmark.
Directions: Sat nav: KW16 3NJ. HY 222 034. Hoy reached from mainland by Houton car ferry or Stromness passenger ferry to Moaness, 1.5 miles to N part of reserve). From Lyness ferry turn R (signposted 'Hoy') onto B9047 & take first L after 8.5 miles (signposted Dwarfie Stone) toward Rackwick. Car parks at Dwarfie Stone & Rackwick beach.
Public transport: Bus (limited) - Hoy Community Bus service, T: 01856 701 356 (office), 07833 777 760 (driver).
Visiting: Access all times. Local car parks (not RSPB). Three trails - five miles return (to Old Man of Hoy) - from Rackwick); 2.5 miles Old Post Road (crosses moorland); & 0.6 mile return path to Dwarfie Stone). Rough terrain not suitable for wheelchairs. Dogs under control at all times.
Contact: RSPB - see site 9.

11. MARWICK HEAD

RSPB (East Scotland).
Habitats: Orkney's largest cliff-side seabird colony: rocky bay, sandstone cliffs. The Choin low-tide lagoon good for waders & ducks.
Birds: *May-Jul:* up to 25,000 seabirds. Large numbers of Kittiwake & auks, inc. Puffin, also Fulmar, skuas, Rock Dove, Raven, Rock Pipit, Short-eared Owl.
Other: Cetaceans possibility from Marwick with Harbour Porpoise & Minke Whale occasionally seen. Beach path for Great Yellow Bumblebee in Aug.
Directions: Sat nav: KW17 2NB. HY 229 240 (Marwick car park). Lies four miles N of Skara Brae (neolithic village) on W coast of mainland Orkney, NW of Dounby. Path N from Marwick Bay, or from council car park at Cumlaquoy at HY 232 251 (best for Kitchener Memorial).
Public transport: Bus - no.8S (Mon, Thurs, Sat - limited) stops at Marwick. Stagecoach (T: 01856 870 555).
Visiting: Open all year. Info board in Marwick car park. Cliff top path. Rough terrain not suitable for wheelchairs.
Contact: RSPB - see site 9.

12. NORTH HILL, PAPA WESTRAY

RSPB (East Scotland).
Habitats: Sea cliffs, maritime heath.
Birds: *Summer*: Close views of Puffin, Guillemot, Razorbill & Kittiwake. Black Guillemot nest under flagstones around reserve's coastline. One of UK's largest colonies of Arctic Tern. Arctic & Great Skuas. Breeding Lapwing, Redshank & Snipe in grazed areas. *Winter:* Gannet, Fulmar, Eider & winter thrushes.
Other: One of best areas (Fowl Craig) to see Scottish Primrose (*primula scotica*) - two flowering periods that just overlap (May to Aug). Whales on migration in autumn, inc. Killer Whale. Grey & Common seals.
Directions: Sat nav: KW17 2BU. HY 495 538. From pier or airfield travel N along main road. From shop/ hostel, take road N to junction at Holland Farm & turn R onto main road. Continue past Rose Cottage to reserve entrance.
Public transport: Ferry - Kirkwall to Papa Westray (car ferry, Tues & Fri). Pierowall (Westray) to Papa Westray passenger ferry (daily). Orkney Ferries (T: 01856 872 044). Flights - daily (end-Feb-Oct) from Kirkwall to North Ronaldsay. Loganair (T: 01856 872 494 or 01856 873 457).
Visiting: Access all times. Limited parking. Two trails (Coastal - 3.5 miles, around N peninsula of Papa Westray) & Fowl Craig (1.5 miles loop for nesting seabirds). Also additional short walk (200 yards each way) to North Hill hide. Not suitable for wheelchairs.Trail guide & info available in hide.
Contact: RSPB - see site 9.

13. NORTH RONALDSAY BIRD OBSERVATORY

North Ronaldsay Bird Observatory.
Habitats: Crofting island with a number of eutrophic & oligotrophic wetlands. Sandy bays & rocky shores.
Birds: *Spring/autumn:* Prime migration site inc. many rarities & sub-rarities. Walled gardens concentrate passerines. *Summer:* breeding seabirds, wildfowl & waders. *Winter*: Waders & wildfowl inc. Whooper Swan.
Directions: Sat nav: KW17 2BE. HY 748 524. Observatory in SW of island, at Twingness.
Public transport: Ferry - Kirkwall to North Ronaldsay (car ferry, Tues & Fri May-Sep, Fri only Oct-Apr). Flights - daily (end-Feb-Oct) from Kirkwall to North Ronaldsay. Loganair (T: 01856 872 494 or 01856 873 457).
Visiting: Open all year (not Christmas). Guest house & hostel accommodation, fully licenced restaurant, cafe.
Contact: North Ronaldsay Bird Observatory, T: 01857 633 200; E: enquiries@nrbo.org.uk; W: www.nrbo.co.uk

Outer Hebrides

These attractive islands are the stronghold of the Corncrake in Britain... they should be heard easily enough but can be much harder to see! May sees a strong passage of Long-tailed & Pomarine Skuas past RSPB Balranald. Black Guillemot, Hen Harrier, Short-eared Owl, Twite & passage waders all provide added interest.

14. BALRANALD

RSPB (North Scotland).
Habitats: Freshwater loch, machair, coast, crofts.
Birds: *Spring:* Skuas & divers at sea, waders inc. Purple Sandpiper, Turnstone, Dunlin. *Summer*: Corncrake, Lapwing, Oystercatcher, Dunlin, Ringed Plover, Redshank, Snipe, terns, Corn Bunting. *Autumn*: Hen Harrier, Peregrine, Greylag Goose. *Passage*: Barnacle Goose, Pomarine & Long-tailed Skuas. *Winter*: Whooper Swan, Greylag Goose, Wigeon, Teal, Shoveler, Merlin, Twite, Snow Bunting. Golden & White-tailed Eagles more regular.
Other: Blanket bog & machair plants reach their peak in Jul. Look for rare Great Yellow Bumblebee on wildflowers. Otters on freshwater lochs.
Directions: Sat nav: HS6 5DL. NF 706 707. On W coast of North Uist, three miles N of Bayhead. Follow A865 N from Clachan towards Sollas. Take L turn for Hogha Gearraigh township & another L for signposted visitor centre prior to reaching Hogha Gearraigh.
Public transport: Bus - runs across Outer Hebrides - Grenitote Travel (T: 01876 560 244) - contact on morning of travel to ensure bus will stop at Balranald. Ferry from Mallaig to Lochboisdale - Caledonian MacBrayne (T: 08705 650 000; W: www.calmac.co.uk).
Visiting: Open all times. Visitor centre open all year. Toilets (inc. disabled), group bookings welcome. Marked circular nature trail (three miles), not suitable for wheelchairs. Dogs on leads.
Contact: RSPB, T: 01876 560 422; E: jamie.boyle@rspb.org.uk

15. LOCH DRUIDIBEG NNR

Stòras Uibhist (community ownership)/RSPB (Scotland).
Habitats: 1,677ha, coast, freshwater lochs, marshes, machair, moorland.
Birds: *Spring/autumn*: Migrant waders & wildfowl. *Summer*: Breeding waders, Corncrake, Black-throated Diver, Greylag Goose, wildfowl, terns & raptors. *Winter*: Waders, wildfowl, raptors inc. Golden Eagle & Hen Harrier.
Directions: Sat nav: HS8 5RS. NF 789 382. Lies just N of Kildonan on South Uist. Turn off A865 in Stillgarry at B890 road for Loch Sgioport. Track is 1.5 miles further on - park at side of road.
Public transport: Bus - no.W17 (not Sun) Benbecula to Lochboisdale stops at Stillgarry (for NNR). DA Travel (T: 01878 700 357 or 01878 700 599). Ferry from Mallaig to Lochboisdale - Caledonian MacBrayne (T: 08705 650 000; W: www.calmac.co.uk).
Visiting: Open all year. View E part of reserve from public roads but parking & turning areas for coaches is limited. Several tracks & one walk covering a range of habitats - most not suitable for wheelchairs. Stout footwear essential. Guided walks.
Contact: RSPB, T: 01870 610 318; E: lochdruidibeg@rspb.org.uk

Shetland

With its large seabird colonies, a summer visit to Britain's most northerly islands will always be a fantastic experience. Apart from the huge numbers of the common species, Arctic and Great Skuas breed here - particularly around Hermaness (Unst) - & an evening visit to the small island of Mousa is a great way to catch up with the largely nocturnal Storm Petrel. The islands, in particular Fair Isle, always attract a large number of common, scarce & rare migrants annually in the spring & autumn. Many UK 'firsts' have been recorded here.

16. FAIR ISLE BIRD OBSERVATORY

Fair Isle Bird Observatory.
Habitats: Heather moor & lowland pasture/crofting land, sea cliffs.
Birds: *Summer:* Large seabird colonies (Gannet, Shag, Arctic & Great Skuas, Kittiwake, Arctic Tern, auks). *Spring (Apr to early-Jun) & Autumn (late-Aug to Nov):* Many common, scarce & rare migrants annually.
Other: Northern Marsh, Heath Spotted & Frog Orchid, Lesser Twayblade, Small Adders Tongue, Oyster Plant. Killer & Minke Whales, White-backed, White-sided & Risso's Dolphins. Endemic Field Mouse.
Directions: SE of Shetland/NW of Orkney - midway between them, access from Shetland.
Public transport: Regular UK flights to Sumburgh, Shetland or ferry from Aberdeen to Lerwick.
To Fair Isle: by air - Airtask services from Tingwell (nr Lerwick) - contact for details, T: 01595 840 246. By sea - Good Shepherd ferry (12 passengers) from Grutness, Shetland on Tues, Thurs, Sat (May-Sep) - contact for details (T: 01595 760 363).
Visiting: *NOTE:* Due to the fire that destroyed the Observatory in March 2019 accommodation will not be available for the forseeable future, check out the Obs website for alternative options. Public toilets at the airstrip & Stackhoull Stores (shop).
Contact: Fair Isle Bird Obs, T: none at present;
E: warden@fairislebirdobs.co.uk;
W: www.fairislebirdobs.co.uk

17. FETLAR

RSPB (East Scotland).
Habitats: Serpentine heath, rough hill land, upland mire.
Birds: *Summer*: Breeding Red-throated Diver, Eider, Shag, Manx Shearwater, Storm Petrel, Whimbrel, Dunlin, Golden Plover, Arctic & Great Skuas. Red-necked Phalarope on Loch of Funzie, viewed from road or hide overlooking Mires of Funzie. *Autumn to Spring:* Whooper Swan, Goldeneye, Long-tailed Duck, Great Northern Diver, passage migrants.
Other: Heath spotted orchid & autumn gentian. Otters common, Grey & Common seals breed.
Directions: ZE2 9DJ HU 655 900. Small island lying E of Yell. Take car ferry from Gutcher on Yell to Hamarsness, then drive six miles E to small car park W of Loch of Funzie. Ferry times & booking, T: 01595 745 804.
Public transport: None.
Visiting: Open at all Times. Car park, 500 yards from reserve. Hide open Apr-Oct (0.3 mile from car park). Loch of Funzie can be observed from road. Toilets & payphone at ferry terminal. Shop & cafe on island.
Contact: RSPB, T: 01950 460 800;
E: shetland@rspb.org.uk

18. HERMANESS

Scottish Natural Heritage.
Habitats: Sea cliffs, moorland/grassland, blanket bog.
Birds: *Summer*: 100,000 seabirds. Fulmar, Gannet, Shag, Guillemot, Razorbill, Puffin, Kittiwake. Arctic & Great Skuas, Dunlin, Golden Plover, Snipe.
Other: Spring Squill. Grey Seal.
Directions: Sat nav: ZE2 9EQ. HP 612 149. On northern island of Unst (from Lerwick via Yell & Unst ferries). On Unst, head N on A968 through Baltasound, turn on to B9086 just before Haroldswick signposted Burrafirth & Hermaness. Continue to fork in road, go straight to reserve car park.
Public transport: None to reserve (bus - Lerwick to Baltasound but overnight stay needed).
Visiting: Access all times. Walk to cliffs starts in car park (notice board/leaflets). Gravel path N to Winnaswarta Dale then boardwalk takes you across reserve to western cliffs - keep to boardwalk to avoid damaging vegetation (moderate walk). Can explore coast from cliffs (strenuous walk), N tip overlooks Muckle Flugga (UK's most northerly lighthouse).
Contact: SNH Reserve Manager, T: 01595 693 345;
E: nnr@nature.scot; W: www.nature.scot/

19. NOSS NNR

Scottish Natural Heritage.
Habitats: Dune & coastal grassland, moorland, heath, blanket bog, sea cliffs.
Birds: *Spring/summer*: Breeding Fulmar, Shag, Gannet, Arctic Tern, Kittiwake, Herring & Great Black-backed Gulls, Great & Arctic Skuas, Guillemot, Razorbill, Puffin, Black Guillemot, Eider, Lapwing, Dunlin, Snipe, Wheatear, Twite plus migrants.
Other: Grey & Common seals, Otter, Harbour Porpoise, Killer Whales (annual).
Directions: Sat nav: ZE2 9ES. HU 525 408 (Bressay parking for Noss). Take car ferry to Bressay from Lerwick & follow signs for Noss (3.2 miles). At end of road walk to shore (600 yards) where inflatable ferry (passenger only) to island will collect you. If red flag is flying, island is closed due to sea conditions.
Public transport: None.
Visiting: Car park on Bressay side. Access to island, subject to weather, by small inflatable 10am to 5pm, May to end-Aug (not Mon or Thurs). Daily update on crossings by 9am - Noss Ferry Line: 0800 107 7818. Visitor centre, toilets (open during sailing times). Steep rough track down to ferry. Walk around island ca. three hours. No dogs on ferry.
Contact: SNH Reserve Manager - see site 18.

Wales

Breconshire, Montgomeryshire, Radnorshire

Eastern

The County of Powys, formed from these three counties, is largely a rural upland area of mountains, bogs, coniferous forest plantations & typical Welsh woodlands (home to Pied flycatcher, Wood Warbler & Redstart). Birds of prey are well represented - Hen Harrier, Merlin, Red Kite & Peregrine are all well established, while Cors Dyfi is a successful breeding site for Osprey.

1. CORS DYFI NATURE RESERVE

Montgomeryshire Wildlife Trust.
Habitats: Bog, wet woodland & scrub.
Birds: *Spring/summer:* Osprey (first bred 2011), Snipe, Nightjar, Grasshopper, Sedge & Reed Warblers, Stonechat, Reed Bunting.
Other: Common Lizard, Four-spotted Chaser dragonfly.
Directions: Sat nav: SY20 8PZ. SN 704 984. Lies 3.5 miles SW of Machynlleth on A487 Abersytwyth road. Approx 2.5 miles S of Derwenlas, turn R after caravan park.
Public transport: Bus - X28 Cambrian Coastliner, Machynlleth to Aberystwyth will stop at Osprey Project (not Sun). Lloyds Coaches (T: 01654 702 100).

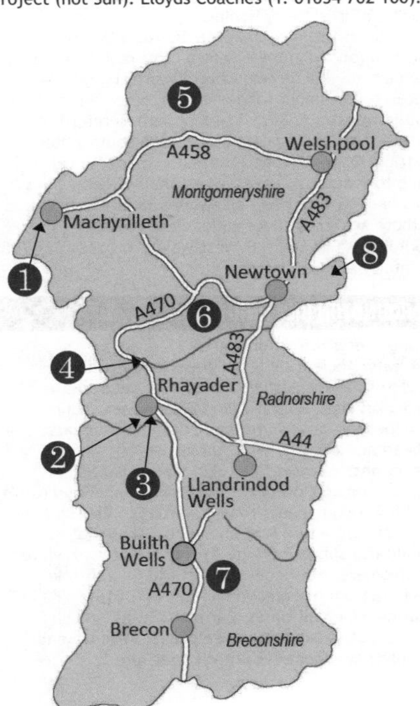

Visiting: Open 10am-5.30pm Apr-Aug & weekends Oct-Mar. Programme of special events in winter. Car park (no large coaches), visitor centre, toilets (inc. disabled), small cafe, hides, 360 degree observatory. Extensive boardwalks, site wheelchair-accessible apart from elevated hide. Assistance dogs only. The new centre due to open March 2021.
Contact: Montgomeryshire WT, T: 01938 555 654; E: info@montwt.co.uk;
Osprey Project (Mar-Aug),
E: enquiries@dyfiospreyproject.com;
W: www.dyfiospreyproject.com/

2. ELAN VALLEY

Elan Valley Trust/Welsh Water.
Habitats: 18,000ha, moorland, bog, woodland, river & reservoir.
Birds: 180 spp. *All year:* Red Kite, Buzzard, Sparrowhawk, Peregrine, Tawney & Barn Owls, Raven, Green Woodpecker, Dipper, Grey Wagtail & Marsh Tit. Common woodland spp. *Spring/summer:* Cuckoo, Pied & Spotted Flycatchers, Wood Warbler, Redstart, Tree Pipit. Upland birds inc. Curlew, Golden Plover & Dunlin. *Autumn/winter:* Short-eared Owl, Ring Ouzel (autumn), Fieldfare, Redwing.
Other: Internationally important oak woodlands. 3,000+ spp. of flora & fauna recorded.
Directions: Sat nav: LD6 5HP. SN 928 646. Three miles SW of Rhayader (A470), take B4518 - don't cross iron bridge, drive over cattle grid to visitor centre.
Public transport: None.
Visiting: Mostly open access. Pay-&-display car park with Blue Badge spaces. Coaches, contact in advance for access advice. Visitor centre, cafe, shop & toilets open daily (not Dec 25) 9am-5pm. Nature trails. Dogs, keep under close control.
Contact: Visitor Centre, T: 01597 810 880;
E: elanrangers@dwrcymru.com;
W: www.elanvalley.org.uk

3. GIGRIN FARM

Private.
Habitats: 80ha, upland sheep farm rising to 1,200ft asl.
Birds: Daily feeds attract Red Kite, numbers can vary from a few dozen to 100's when weather is bad. Other species inc. Buzzard, Raven, Jackdaw, Carrion Crow. Other feeding stations attract small birds inc. Brambling, Yellowhammer & Siskin. A wetland area attracts wild ducks, Grey Heron & wagtails.
Directions: Sat nav: LD6 5BL. SN 978 676. Farm lies 0.5 mile south of Rhayader, Powys off A470.
Public transport: Bus - X47 (not Sun) Llandrindod Wells to Aberystwyth stops at Rhayader. Celtic Travel (T: 01686 412 231).
Visiting: Gigrin has been an official Red Kite feeding station for Wales since early 1990's, helping young birds survive in winter. By attracting large numbers of birdwatchers it relieves pressure on nest sites in summer. Open for kite feeding sessions 1pm-5pm Sat-Thurs (closed Tues/Wed) & daily during school holidays - 27th Dec to end-Nov (closed 1-26 Dec).

Feeding times: 2pm (winter) & 3pm (summer). No booking required. Admission charge. Red Kite Shop, five hides (three with disabled access), plus specialist photography hides (fee applies). Dogs on leads. 1.5 mile trail offers views of Elan Valley & Cambrian Hills - rough terrain.
Contact: Chris Powell, Gigrin Farm, South Street, Rhayader, Powys LD6 5BL. T: 01597 810 243; E: chris@gigrin.co.uk; W: www.gigrin.co.uk

4. GILFACH FARM RESERVE

Radnorshire Wildlife Trust.
Habitats: 165ha, working organic hill farm, grassland, moorland, river, oak woods, meadows.
Birds: 73 spp., 55 breed regularly, inc. Barn Owl, Common Sandpiper, Stock Dove, Grey Wagtail, Dipper, Pied & Spotted Flycatchers, Redstart, Tree Pipit, Wheatear, Whinchat, Stonechat, Wood Warbler, Marsh & Willow Tits, Raven, Linnet, Yellowhammer, Siskin, Redpoll. Other spp. inc. Goosander, Curlew, Merlin, Red Kite, Goshawk, Sparrowhawk, Peregrine, Kingfisher, Reed Bunting.
Other: Green Hairstreak, Wall Brown & Ringlet butterflies, Mountain Pansy, Bloody-nosed Beetle. Welsh Clearwing Moth - first record for Radnorshire.
Directions: Sat nav: LD6 5LF. SN 965 716 (Old Farmyard). Gilfach is just off A470, three miles N of Rhayader (signposted for St Harmon). Follow brown reserve signs. Parking just off A470 (Pont Marteg) just after cattle grid.
Public transport: Bus - X47 (not Sun) Llandrindod Wells to Aberystwyth passes entrance. Celtic Travel (T: 01686 412 231).
Visiting: Open daily. Small car park at Old Farmyard with some visitor facilities. Disabled access to centre, toilets & purpose-built trail. Several waymarked trails. Wye Valley Walk & Gwastedyn Church Trail pass through reserve. Dogs on leads.
Contact: Radnorshire WT, T: 01597 823 298; E: info@rwtwales.org

5. LAKE VYRNWY

Severn Trent/RSPB (Wales HQ).
Habitats: Heather moorland, woodland, meadows, rocky streams & large reservoir.
Birds: *All year:* Buzzard, Red & Black Grouse, Raven. *Spring/summer:* Hen Harrier, Peregrine, Hobby, Curlew, Common Sandpiper, Cuckoo, Whinchat, Dipper, Kingfisher, Ring Ouzel, Pied Flycatcher, Wood Warbler, Redstart.
Other: Otter, polecat, brown hare. Golden-ringed dragonfly.
Directions: Sat nav: SY10 0LZ. SJ 016 192. WSW of Oswestry. Nearest village is Llanfyllin on A490. Take B4393 to Llanwddyn & at dam, turn L & L again.
Public transport: None.
Visiting: Open at all times. Visitor centre open (not Dec 24/27, Jan 1) 10.30am-5pm Apr-Oct, 4pm Nov-Mar), toilets, shop, cafe (nearby), six waymarked trails, three hides (one with wheelchair access).
Contact: RSPB, T: 01691 870 278; E: vyrnwy@rspb.org.uk

6. LLANDINAM GRAVELS

Montgomeryshire Wildlife Trust.
Habitats: River meadows, river shingle.
Birds: *All year:* Dipper, Grey Wagtail, Reed Bunting. *Summer:* Little Ringed Plover, Common Sandpiper, Sand Martin, Yellow Wagtail. *Passage:* Green Sandpiper, Wheatear, Whinchat. *Winter:* Goosander, winter thrushes.
Other: Rich in flora. Dragonflies. Otter.
Directions: Sat nav: SY17 5AU. SO 022 876. Beside River Severn at Llandinam. Turn off A470 at Llandinam (over narrow bridge by statue) & follow signs to reserve.
Public transport: Bus - no.X75 Welshpool-Llanidloes stops at Llandinam (not Sun) - ca. 0.5 mile walk to reserve. Celtic Travel (T: 01686 412 231).
Visiting: Open at all times. Small parking area, waymarked paths across meadows (mainly flat).
Contact: Montgomeryshire WT - see site 1.

7. PWLL-Y-WRACH

Wildlife Trust of South & West Wales
Habitats: 17.5ha, ancient woodland, river & spectacular Witches Pool waterfall.
Birds: *All year:* Dipper, Kingfisher, common woodland spp. inc. Great Spotted Woodpecker, Mistle & Song Thrushes, Nuthatch. *Spring/summer:* Chiffchaff, Wood Warbler, Pied Flycatcher.
Other: Otter, Dormouse, bats, Common Lizard. Early Purple & Birds' Nest Orchids.
Directions: Sat nav: LD3 0DU. SO 165 326. From Talgarth (on A479) town centre cross over River Enig, then L turn Bell Street. After 50 yards L (opp. Bell Hotel) follow minor road one mile, reserve is on R.
Public transport: Bus - T14 (not Sun) Hereford to Cardiff stops at Talgarth. Stagecoach South Wales.
Visiting: Open all year. Information panel in car park. Keep to footpaths. Level, wheelchair-friendly path runs halfway into site - elsewhere paths can be muddy & there are steps. Dogs under close control.
Contact: WT of South & West Wales, T: 01874 625 708; E: info@welshwildlife.org

8. ROUNDTON HILL NNR

Montgomeryshire Wildlife Trust.
Habitats: Ancient hillfort - grassland, woodland, stream-side wet flushes, scree, rock outcrops.
Birds: *All year:* Buzzard, Red Kite, Raven, 3 spp. woodpecker, Tawny Owl, Linnet. *Spring/summer:* Wheatear, Redstart, Whitethroat.
Directions: Sat nav: SY15 6EL. SO 293 946. SE of Montgomery. Follow brown duck signs from Churchstoke on A489, taking minor road towards Old Churchstoke. After one mile turn R at phone box, then first R.
Public transport: Bus - no.81 (not Sun) Newtown to Montgomery/Welshpool stops at Old Churchstoke, 0.3 mile from reserve. Tanat Valley (T: 01691 780 212).
Visiting: Open all times. Car park. Trails - rough in places, not suitable for wheelchairs. Dogs on leads.
Contact: Montgomeryshire WT - see site 1.

Anglesey, Caernarfonshireshire, Denbighshire, Flintshire, Merioneth

Northern

Anglesey holds many of the areas highlights including a seabird colony (with Choughs) at South Stack, terns at Cemlyn Bay & waders at Malltraeth. On the mainland, the RSPB's man-made Conwy reserve has good selection of wildfowl & waders, with rarities often turning up. Bardsey Island is a migrant hot-spot & the Mawddach Valley area has the typical Welsh woodland species.

1. BARDSEY BIRD OBSERVATORY

Bardsey Bird Observatory.
Habitats: 180ha island, sea-bird cliffs viewable from boat only. Farm & scrubland, spruce plantation, willow copses & gorse-covered hillside.
Birds: *All year:* Chough, Peregrine. *Spring/summer:* Night walks to see Manx Shearwaters (20,000 pairs). Other seabirds, migrant warblers, chats, thrushes. *Autumn:* Common migrants, many rarities (have inc. Eye-browed Thrush, Lanceolated Warbler, American Robin, Yellowthroat, Summer Tanager).
Other: Autumn Ladies' Tresses. Grey Seal. Moths.
Directions: 15 miles SW of Pwllheli. 30 mins boat crossing from Porth Meudwy, near Aberdaron - sat nav: LL53 8DA. SH163 255. From Aberdaron (Spar on your L) go over first bridge & turn sharp R, signposted Whistling Sands. Follow road uphill & for another 0.5 mile, take first L, signposted Uwchmynydd. After 400 yards take first L signposted Tir Glyn campsite. After 0.5 mile look out for Cwrt Farm on R. Porth Meudwy car park 75 yards further on L.
Bardsey Ferries, Colin Evans
T: 07971 769 895 (sailings subject to weather).
Public transport: Bus - no.17 (not Sun) Pwllheli to Aberdaron 1.6 miles to boat (one mile along coast path). Berwyn (T: 01286 660 315).
Visiting: Private island, open Mar-Nov. Day trips allow 3 to 4 hours on island. Public toilets available for day visitors. Three hides, one on small bay, two seawatching. Gift shop, payphone. No dogs.
Staying at Obs: Hostel-style accommodation available (Sat-Sat, end-Mar to end-Oct): two singles, two doubles, two four bed dorms).
Bookings - Alicia Normand, T: 01626 773 908;
E: stay@bbfo.org.uk
Contact: Steven Stansfield (Warden), T: 07855 264 151; E: warden@bbfo.org.uk; W: www.bbfo.org.uk

2. CEMLYN

North Wales Wildlife Trust.
Habitats: Brackish lagoon, shingle ridge, salt marsh, mixed scrub.
Birds: *Spring:* Wheatear, Whitethroat, Sedge Warbler, Manx Shearwater, Black-tailed Godwit, Whimbrel, Dunlin, Knot, passage migrants. *Summer:* Breeding Arctic, Common & Sandwich Terns, Black-headed Gull, Oystercatcher, Ringed Plover. *Autumn:* Golden Plover, Lapwing, Curlew, Manx Shearwater, Gannet, Kittiwake, Guillemot, passage migrants. *Winter:* Wildfowl inc. Shoveler, Shelduck, Red-breasted Merganser. Little & Great Crested Grebes, Purple Sandpiper, Turnstone.
Other: 20 spp. butterflies. Sea Kale, Yellow Horned Poppy, Sea Purslane, Sea Beet, Glasswort. Grey Seal, Harbour Porpoise, Bottlenose Dolphin.
Directions: Sat Nav: LL67 0DX. SH 336 931. Cemlyn on N coast of Anglesey, signposted from Tregele on A5025 between Valley & Amlwch. 'Beach' (east) car park, follow road taking sharp R at first fork. 'Bryn Aber' car park (west/closest to warden's viewpoint, SH 329 935), continue L, taking R turns at next two forks.
Public transport: Bus - no.61 (not Sun) Amlwch to Holyhead stops at Tregele (1.5 miles to reserve). Goodsir (T: 01407 764 340) & Lewis Y Llan (T: 01407 832 181).
Visiting: Open all year. In summer walk on seaward side of shingle ridge to minimise disturbance. Dogs on leads.
Contact: North Wales WT, T: 01248 351 541;
E: info@northwaleswildlifetrust.org.uk

3. CONNAH'S QUAY POWER STATION RESERVE

EON/Deeside Naturalists Society.
Habitats: Saltmarsh, mudflats, grassland scrub, open water, wetland meadow.
Birds: *Summer*: Small roosts of non-breeding estuarine birds. *Winter*: High water roosts of waders & wildfowl inc. Black-tailed Godwit, Oystercatcher, Redshank, Spotted Redshank, Curlew, Lapwing, Teal, Pintail & Wigeon.
Other: 17 spp. butterflies.

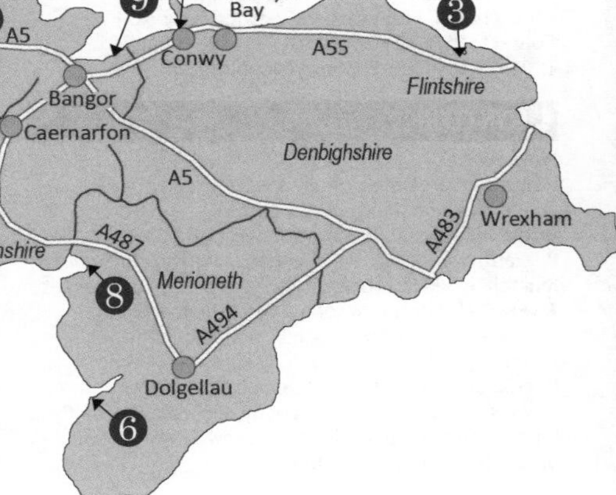

Directions: Sat nav: CH6 5TE. SJ 271 713. Travel W to end of M56 which then becomes A494. Follow signposts for Flint. Take first slip road to L joining large roundabout & turn R onto A548. Continue straight on this road (there are several roundabouts) After crossing the River Dee take first slip road & turn R at first roundabout & then straight on at second roundabout. Follow signs for power station: reserve entrance is on L at next roundabout. If approaching from W follow A548, exiting on slip road for Connah's Quay. Turn L at roundabout & follow power station signs.
Public transport: Bus - no.10A (10 on Sun, longer walk) Chester to Connah's Quay (Swan Inn). Arriva in Wales.
Visiting: Entry for DNS members only but group bookings possible in advance from DNS. Public welcome on open days - see website for details. Field studies centre, five hides. Wheelchair access.
Contact: Secretary, Deeside Naturalists' Society, E: secretary@deenats.org.uk

4. CONWY

RSPB (North Wales).
Habitats: Lagoons, islands, reedbed, scrub, estuary.
Birds: *Spring*: Passage waders, hirundines & wagtails. *Summer*: Lapwing, waterbirds & warblers. *Autumn:* Black-tailed Godwit & other passage waders. *Winter*: Kingfisher, Goldeneye, Water Rail, Red-breasted Merganser, wildfowl, huge Starling roost.
Other: Common butterflies through summer, esp. Common Blue. Great display of Cowslips in Mar, Bee Orchids in summer. Otters seen early mornings.
Directions: Sat nav: LL31 9XZ. SH 797 773. On E bank of Conwy Estuary. Exit 18 (Conwy & Deganwy) of A55, reserve on S side of roundabout (signposted).
Public transport: Bus - no.27 Conwy to Colwyn Bay & no.24 Colwyn Bay to Llandudno Junction both stop at Tesco, Llandudno Junction (five mins walk from reserve). Arriva in Wales. Train - Llandudno Junction, 0.5 mile from reserve.
Visiting: Car park open daily (not Dec 25) 9am-5pm. Coach parking. Visitor centre (9.30am-5pm), shop, toilets inc. disabled, cafe (10am-4.30/ 4pm Nov-Mar). Three trails firm/level, though a little rough in places & wet in winter. Four hides (accessible to wheelchairs) with adjacent viewing screens.
Contact: RSPB, T: 01492 584 091; for events T: 01492 581 025; E: conwy@rspb.org.uk

5. LLYN CEFNI

Welsh Water.
Habitats: Large area of open water, reedy bays, coniferous woodland, scrub, carr.
Birds: *All year*: Common wildfowl, Little Grebe, Buzzard, Stonechat, Treecreeper, Song Thrush. *Summer*: Kingfisher, Sedge & Grasshopper Warblers, Whitethroat, Tawny Owl. *Winter*: Wildfowl inc. Whooper Swan, Goldeneye, Redwing, Crossbill, Redpoll, Siskin.
Other: Northern Marsh Orchid, Rustyback Fern, Needle Spikerush. Banded Demoiselle, Migrant Hawker, Golden-ringed Dragonfly, Emerald Damselfly. Ringlet, Gatekeeper, Clouded Yellow & Wall Brown butterflies. Bloody-nose Beetle.
Directions: Sat nav: LL77 7RQ. SH 451 782 (Rhosmeirch car park). Reservoir located two miles NW of Llangefni, in central Anglesey. NE section of reservoir managed as nature reserve - entrance just N of Rhosmeirch. Follow B5111 from village.
Public transport: Bus - nos.4/4A/X4 Bangor to Holyhead alight Llangefni (1.5 miles to reservoir see visiting). Arriva in Wales.
Visiting: Open all times. Two picnic sites, coach parking at Rhosmeirch car park. Good footpath (wheelchair accessible) for most of site, bridges over streams. Walkers can reach reservoir from Dingle nature reserve, Llangefni, on boardwalks & cycle route (one mile). Dogs allowed except in sanctuary area.
Contact: none.

6. MAWDDACH VALLEY

RSPB (North Wales).
Habitats: Oak woodland, bracken & heathland at Coed Garth Gell. Willow & alder scrub & raised bog at Arthog Bog.
Birds: 1: Coed Garth Gell. *All year:* Buzzard, Peregrine, Sparrowhawk, Lesser Spotted Woodpecker, Grey Wagtail, Dipper, Raven, Hawfinch. *Summer:* Cuckoo, Pied & Spotted Flycatchers, Wood Warbler, Redstart, Tree Pipit. 2: Arthog Bog. *All year:* Raven, Buzzard, Sparrowhawk, Peregrine. *Summer:* migrants inc. Cuckoo, Tree Pipit, Grasshopper Warbler. *Winter:* Redpoll, Siskin. Little Egret & Red-breasted Merganser on nearby estuary.
Other: Coed Garth Gell has Tunbridge Filmy & Beech Ferns. Butterflies. Golden-ringed dragonfly regular.
Directions: 1: Coed Garth Gell sat nav: LL40 2TT. SH 683 192 (on A496 between Taicynhaeaf & Bontddu), N side of Mawddach Estuary, (park in lay-bys/parking spaces). 2: Arthog Bog (LL39 1BQ. SH 630 138) off Dolgellau-to-Tywyn road (A493) west of Arthog. Park at Morfa Mawddach station.
Public transport: 1: Bus - no.T3 Dolgellau to Barmouth alight Taicynhaeaf (0.5 mile to reserve). 2: Bus - no.28 Dolgellau to Twywn, alight Arthog (0.25 mile from reserve). Lloyds Coaches (T: 01654 702 100).
Visiting: Trails on both sites, open all times. Dogs on leads. Information boards.
Contact: RSPB, T: 01654 700 222; E: mawddach@rspb.org.uk

7. SOUTH STACK CLIFFS

RSPB (North Wales).
Habitats: Sea cliffs, maritime grassland, maritime & lowland heath.
Birds: *Spring/summer/autumn:* Peregrine, Chough, Shag, Fulmar, Puffin, Guillemot, Razorbill, Skylark, Rock Pipit, Stonechat, Linnet, migrant warblers & passage seabirds.
Other: Spathulate Fleawort, endemic to South Stack, Adder, lizards, Harbour Porpoise.
Directions: Sat nav: LL65 1YH. SH 211 818 (visitor centre), SH 206 820 (Ellin's Tower info centre). Follow A55 to W end in Holyhead, proceed straight on at roundabout, continue straight on through traffic lights. After another 0.5 mile turn L & follow brown tourist signs for RSPB South Stack.
Public transport: None.

Visiting: RSPB car park (free), Blue Badge parking. Visitor centre, cafe, shop open daily 10am-5pm (not Dec 25). Ellin's Tower Seabird Centre has windows overlooking main auk colony, open daily 10am-5pm, Easter to Sep - access via staircase. Reserve covered by extensive network of paths, some accessible to wheelchairs. 'Access for all' track to viewing area overlooking the lighthouse.
Contact: RSPB, T: 01407 762 100;
E: south.stack@rspb.org.uk

8. TRAETH GLASLYN

North Wales Wildlife Trust.
Habitats: Flood meadow - saltmarsh, mudflats, wet grassland, wet willow woodland.
Birds: *Spring/summer:* Sandwich & Common Terns, Osprey - breed up river at Pont Croesor (visitor centre here on B4410 N of Porthmadog). *Autumn/winter:* Good nos. of wintering wildfowl & waders inc. Teal, Wigeon, Pintail, Goldeneye, Red-breasted Merganser, Redshank, Ruff, Curlew, Dunlin, Black-tailed Godwit.
Other: Flora inc. Ragged Robin, Selfheal.
Directions: Sat nav: LL48 6HT. SH 584 379. SE of Porthmadog. At end of Cobb park in layby on A497 just past toll cottage. For N part of reserve walk N along road (along estuary, ca. one mile), then turn L at crossroads to reserve boundary (SH 592 389).
Public transport: Bus - no.3b from Portmadog stops at Tollgate & Minffordd (not Sun). Arriva. Train: Porthmadog or Minffordd.
Visiting: Open all year. Hide accessible via small gate neat toll cottage. Site is TIDAL and can get completely submerged at high tide - check tides before visiting. Paths are muddy - STAY on them. No dogs.
Contact: North Wales WT - see site 2.

9. TRAETH LAFAN LNR

Gwynedd Council.
Habitats: 2,500ha, intertidal sands & mudflats, (adjacent to Spinnies, Morfa Aber NNR & Morfa Madryn NNR).
Birds: *Summer:* Breeding Lapwing (Morfa Madryn). *Autumn:* nationally important for moulting Great Crested Grebe & Red-breasted Merganser. *Winter:* Goldeneye, waders inc. Greenshank, internationally important for Oystercatcher & Curlew, regionally significance for Black & Red-throated & Great Northern Divers, Black-necked & Slavonian Grebes.
Directions: NE of Bangor, stretching six miles to Llanfairfechan. 1: Spinnies - (LL57 3YH. SH 6213 720). 2: Morfa Aber (LL33 0LB. SH 647 731) follow brown signs from junc 13 of A55. 3: Access to Morfa Madryn is on foot one mile W from Llanfairfechan promenade (LL33 0DA. SH 678 754).
Public transport: Bus - no.5/5X Bangor to Llandudno. 1: stops by minor road to reserve. 2: stops at Abergwyngregyn. 3: stops at Llanfairfachan. Arriva Buses. Train: Llanfairfachan.
Visiting: Open access, Wales Coastal Path. 1: Car park, hides 200 yards away at Spinnies. 2: Car park, hide. 3: Car & coach park, toilets, cafe, hides. All sites are wheelchair accessible.
Contact: Gwynedd Council, T: 01766 771 000.

Glamorgan, Gower, Gwent

Southern

The Gower coastline has breeding seabirds, Peregrines &, offshore, thousands of Manx Shearwaters. Cardiff Bay is good for passage & wintering waders & the Newport Wetlands Reserve/ Gwent Levels has good numbers of wintering wildfowl & waders. Kenfig Pools have a history of turning up rarities.

1. CWM CLYDACH

RSPB (Wales HQ).
Habitats: Oak & beech woodland on steep slopes along banks of fast-flowing Lower Clydach River.
Birds: *All year:* Red Kite, Sparrowhawk, Buzzard, Raven, Green Woodpecker, Dipper & Grey Wagtail. *Summer:* Spotted Flycatcher, Garden Warbler, Wood Warbler, Cuckoo. *Winter:* Woodcock, Siskin, Redpoll.
Other: Fungi, Wood Sorrel, Silver-washed Fritillary & Speckled Wood butterflies.
Directions: Sat nav: SA6 5SU. SN 684 026. N of Swansea. Three miles N of Junc 45 of M4, through village of Clydach on B4291, follow signs for Craig-cefn-Parc. Car park is close to New Inn pub.
Public transport: Bus - no.214 & X6C (not Sun) Graig Felen to Craig Cefn Parc stops at reserve entrance. South Wales Transport (T: 01792 799 575).
Visiting: Open all times. Car park (no coaches). Two trails link to network of public footpaths - not suitable for wheelchairs. Dogs on leads.
Contact: RSPB, T: 029 2035 3000;
E: cwm.clydach@rspb.org.uk

2. CWM COLHUW

The Wildlife Trust of South & West Wales.
Habitats: Unimproved calcareous grassland, woodland, scrub & Jurassic blue lias cliff. Iron Age promontory fort on site overlooking Bristol Channel.
Birds: *All year:* Peregrine. *Summer:* Cliff-nesting Fulmar, Whitethroat, Grasshopper Warbler, Linnet, Yellowhammer, House Martin colony. *Autumn:* Large passerine passage. Seawatching vantage point, occasional passing Chough.
Other: Wild Cabbage. Butterflies inc. Small Blue.
Directions: Sat nav: CF61 1YX. SS 956 674. SE of Bridgend. From Bridgend take B4265 S to Llanwit Major (0.6 mile SW of village). Follow beach road from village to car park.
Public transport: Bus - no.303 from Bridgend to Barry, alight Llantwit Major & no.321 (not Sun) from Talbot Green to Llantwit Major. Then walk towards beach. New Adventure Travel (T: 02920 442 040). Train - Llantwit Major.
Visiting: Open all year. Includes part of Wales Coast Path. Access from stile at head of valley (SS 968 678) or by steps from car park - unsuitable for wheelchairs. Information boards. Toilets.
Contact: WT of S&W Wales, T: 01656 724 100;
E: info@welshwildlife.org

3. KENFIG NNR

Bridgend County Borough Council.
Habitats: 526ha, sand dune system, freshwater lake with reeds, numerous wet dune slacks, sandy coastline with some rocky outcrops.
Birds: *Summer*: Warblers inc. Cetti's, Sedge, Reed, Grasshopper & Willow Warbler, Blackcap & Whitethroat. *Winter*: Wildfowl, Water Rail, Bittern, grebes.
Other: 16 spp. orchid (inc. Fen), Hairy Dragonfly, Red-veined & Ruddy Darters, Small Blue, Dark Green Fritillary, Grayling & Brown Argus butterflies.
Directions: Sat nav: CF33 4PT. SS 802 811. Seven miles W of Bridgend. From Junc 37 of M4, take A4229 towards Porthcawl, then R at roundabout on B4283 to North Cornelly, signposted from here.
Public transport: Bus - no.63 Bridgend to Porthcawl stops at North Cornelly (1.5 miles). First South & West Wales.
Visiting: Open all times. Car park - coach parking available. Toilets (9am-5pm), hides, signposted paths. Unsurfaced sandy paths, not suitable for wheelchairs. Flooding possible in winter/spring.
Contact: Kenfig NNR, T: 01656 815 070.

4. LAVERNOCK POINT

The Wildlife Trust of South & West Wales.
Habitats: Sea, coastal calcareous grassland & scrub.
Birds: *Summer:* Chiffchaff, Whitethroat, Lesser Whitethroat, Bullfinch. Important site for migration - Autumn: large flocks of Swallow, thrushes & finches.
Other: Butterflies, wild flowers.
Directions: Sat nav: CF64 5XQ. ST 181 681. Five miles S of Cardiff. Access is from B4267 via Fort Road, signposted Lavernock Point. Limited parking by gate or in public car park at end of Fort Road.
Public Transport: Bus - no.94 Cardiff to Barry stops near turn to Fort Road. Cardiff Bus (T: 02920 666 444).
Visiting: Info boards. Access via a stile, unsuitable for wheelchairs.
Contact: WT of S&W Wales - see site 2.

5. NEWPORT WETLANDS NNR

Natural Resources Wales/ RSPB (Wales HQ)/ Newport City Council.
Habitats: 438 ha, wet meadows, saline lagoons, reedbed, scrub & mudflats on Severn estuary.
Birds: *Spring/summer*: Breeding waders inc. Lapwing & Oystercatcher. Bearded Tit, Cetti's Warbler, Cuckoo & regular migrants on passage. *Autumn*: Large numbers of migrating wildfowl & waders - regulars inc. Curlew, Dunlin, Ringed Plover. Shoveler. *Winter*: Large Starling roost (up to 50,000 birds). Bittern, nationally important numbers of Dunlin, Black-tailed Godwit & Shoveler.
Other: Badger, Wood Mouse, Otter. Great Crested Newt. Orchids in spring, 16 spp. dragonflies, 23 spp. butterflies & ca.200 spp. moths.
Directions: Sat nav: NP18 2BZ. ST 334 834. SW of Newport. From Junc 24 or 28 of M4, take A48 to Spytty Retail Park roundabout, exit on to A4810 Queensway Meadows. At first roundabout take 3rd exit onto Meadow Road - follow brown tourist signs to reserve. Close to Uskmouth Power Station.
Public transport: Bus - no.63 (limited, not Sat/Sun) from Newport city centre to reserve. Newport Bus (T: 01633 670 563).
Visiting: Car park (charge - members free) & visitor Centre open daily (not Dec 25) 9am-5pm. Cafe (10am-4pm), shop, toilets (inc. disabled). Four trails, hide & viewing screens - wheelchair accessible. Dogs only on perimeter footpath.
Contact: Newport Wetlands Reserve (NRW), RSPB Visitor Centre, T: 01633 636 363; E: newport-wetlands@rspb.org.uk

6. OXWICH NNR

Natural Resources Wales (Swansea Office).
Habitats: Freshwater marsh, saltmarsh, foreshore, dunes, woodlands.
Birds: *Summer*: Breeding Reed, Sedge & Cetti's Warblers, Treecreeper, Nuthatch, woodpeckers. *Winter*: Wildfowl.
Directions: Sat nav: SA3 1LS. SS 501 865. From Swansea take A4118 Gower road towards Killay, Parkmill & continue through Nicholaston to Oxwich village.
Public transport: Bus - no.117 (not Sun) Killay to Scurlage, alight Oxwich. New Adventure Travel (T: 02920 442 040).
Visiting: Most of NNR open all times, groups can visit some restricted areas by arrangement. No permit required for access to foreshore, dunes, woodlands & facilities. Private car park (charge) & toilets (Apr-Oct). Marsh boardwalk & lookout.
Contact: NRW, T: 0300 065 3000; E: enquiries@naturalresourceswales.gov.uk

7. PARC SLIP NATURE PARK

The Wildlife Trust of South & West Wales.
Habitats: Restored opencast mining site - wader scrape, lagoons, grassland, woodland.
Birds: *Summer*: Breeding Lapwing, Tufted Duck, Kingfisher, Skylark, Green Woodpecker. Migrant waders (inc. Little Ringed Plover). *Winter*: Wildfowl, Snipe, Water Rail, Bittern.

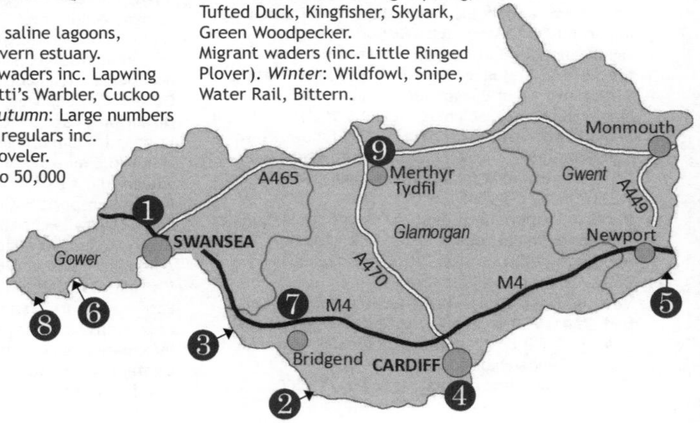

Other: 20 spp. dragonflies, inc. Emperor & Scarce Blue-tailed Damselfly. Great Crested Newt, Harvest Mouse, reptiles. Seven spp. orchid inc. Twayblade & Broad-leaved Helleborine.
Directions: Sat nav: CF32 0EH. SS 880 840. 0.6 mile W of Aberkenfig. From Junc 36 of M4 take A4063 towards Maesteg, then B4281 (signposted Aberkenfig & Pyle) & follow brown signs to visitor centre in Fountain Road.
Public transport: Bus - no.63 Bridgend to Porthcawl stops at Fountain Inn, bottom of Fountain Road. Firstbus South & West Wales.Train - Tondu.
Visiting: Open dawn-dusk. Free car park off Fountain Road, space for coach. Visitor centre/coffee shop open daily (not Mon/Christmas period) 10am-4pm. Five hides, regular events. Good access for wheelchairs.
Contact: WT of S&W Wales - see site 2.

8. PORT EYNON

The Wildlife Trust of South & West Wales.
Habitats: Sea cliff, limestone grassland, heath, scrub, woodland, foreshore/beach.
Birds: *All year*: Common Scoter, Eider, Shag, Peregrine, gulls, Chough, Rock Pipit, Stonechat. *Summer*: Manx Shearwater, Gannet (late-Jul/early Aug). *Passage:* Migrants inc. Whimbrel, Common Sandpiper, Wheatear, Ring Ouzel. *Winter*: Red-throated & Great Northern Divers, Purple Sandpiper.
Other: Intertidal spp., Grey Seal, limestone flora.
Directions: W of Swansea on The Gower. Take 4118 to Port Eynon. Sat Nav: SA3 1NN (SS 467 851 car park). A cluster of Trust sites near Port Eynon: Sedger's Bank (SS 470 844); Port Eynon Point (SS 467 848); Overton Mere (SS 460 850); Overton Cliff & Roydon's Corner (SS 460 848); Long Hole Cliff Overton (SS 455 852).
Public transport: Buses - no.118/119 (not Sun) Swansea to Rhossili stops at Port Eynon. New Adventure Travel (T: 02920 442 040).
Visiting: Open at all times - accessible from coastal footpaths. Sea watching from Point Eynon Point (esp. late-Jul/early Aug). Pay-&-display car park in Port Eynon, facilities in the village.
Contact: WT of S&W Wales - see site 2.

9. TAF FECHAN

The Wildlife Trust of South & West Wales.
Habitats: Ancient broadleaved woodland, calcareous grasslands, river gorge & cliffs.
Birds: Pied Flycatcher (summer), Tawny Owl, Dipper, Kingfisher, Grey Wagtail, Peregrine, Woodcock.
Other: Otter, migrating Salmon.
Directions: Sat nav: CF48 2HH. SO 033 084, SO 037 076 & SO 045 097 (main entrances). Two miles N of Merthyr Tydfil centre. Several entrances along Taff Trail & footpath from Cyfarthfa Park.
Public Transport: Bus - nos.25 (not Sun) Merthyr Tydfil to Tefechan. Stagecoach. Train - Merthyr Tydfil.
Visiting: Open all year. Information boards. Not accessible to wheelchairs due to steep terrain & steps.
Contact: WT of S&W Wales - see site 2.

Carmarthenshire, Ceredigion, Pembrokeshire

Western

Summer boat trips running to the seabird islands of Ramsay & Skomer (daily) & Skokholm (no day trips/ residential only) get you close to the huge Welsh seabird colonies, a must-do outing. In spring & summer, the steep wooded valleys through the area are good for Red Kite, Redstart, Pied Flycatcher & Wood Warbler. The National Wetland Centre (Llanelli) & the Welsh Wildlife Centre (Cardigan) are good for wintering wildfowl & waders.

1. CASTLE WOODS

The Wildlife Trust of South & West Wales.
Habitats: 25ha, old mixed deciduous woodlands overlooking River Tywi, castle.
Birds: Buzzard, Sparrowhawk. 3 spp. woodpecker, Raven. *Summer:* Pied & Spotted Flycatchers, Redstart, Wood Warbler. *Winter:* Teal, Wigeon, Goosander, Shoveler, Tufted Duck, Pochard.
Other: Fallow Deer, Badger, butterflies inc. Silver-washed Fritillary.
Directions: Sat nav: SA19 6RP. SN 623 223. 1.25 miles W of Llandeilo town centre, adjacent to Dinefwr Park (National Trust). Take footpath from Tywi Bridge (Pen Lan Park), Llandeilo or park next to fire station off A40 & walk down Dinefwr Park Drive.
Public transport: Bus - nos.X13 & 103 (not Sun) from Swansea/Ammerford to Llandeilo. First Bus. No.280 (not Sun) from Carmarthen to Llandovery. Morris Travel (T: 01267 235 090). Train - Llandeilo.
Visiting: Open all year - Footpaths, mostly too steep for wheelchairs, hide.
Contact: WT of S&W Wales, T: 01656 724 100; E: info@welshwildlife.org

2. CORS CARON NNR

Natural Resources Wales (Mid Wales Area).
Habitats: Raised bog, river, fen, wet grassland, willow woodland, reedbed.
Birds: *All Year:* Red Kite. *Summer:* Lapwing, Redshank, Curlew, Hobby, Grasshopper Warbler, Whinchat, Redpoll, Reed Bunting. *Winter:* Teal, Wigeon, Whooper Swan, Hen Harrier.
Other: Small Red Damselfly amongst abundant dragonflies. Otter. Adder & Common Lizard.
Directions: Sat nav: SY25 6JF. SN 692 625. Two miles N of Tregaron, Ceredigion, NE of Lampeter. Car park on B4343 (signposted). Also car parking in lay-by just N of Maesllyn Farm.
Public transport: Bus - nos.585 & 588 (not Sun) Lampeter to Aberystwyth stop in Tregaron. Brodyr James T: 0800 084 3596), Lloyds Coaches (T: 01654 702 100) & Mid Wales Travel (T: 01970 828 288).

Visiting: Open access from car park on B4343, space for coaches, toilets & picnic area. Cors Caron walk - boardwalk, accessible, dogs on lead. Riverside Walk, shut at times due to flooding/management requirements - circular walk, no dogs. Old Railway Walk, dogs under control. Hide on boardwalk & hide on Old Railway Walk 1.5 miles from car park. Footpath through reserve part of Ystwyth Trail.
Contact: NRW, T: 0300 065 3000;
E: enquiries@naturalresourceswales.gov.uk

3. GWENFFRWD-DINAS

RSPB (Wales HQ).
Habitats: Hillside oak woods, streams & bracken slopes. Spectacular upland scenery.
Birds: *All year:* Red Kite, Buzzard, Peregrine, Raven, Goosander, Dipper, Grey Wagtail, Marsh Tit & 3 spp. woodpecker. *Summer:* Common Sandpiper, Cuckoo, Pied & Spotted Flycatcher, Wood Warbler, Redstart, Tree Pipit.
Other: Golden-ringed Dragonfly, Purple Hairstreak, Silver-washed Fritillary, Wilson's Filmy Fern.
Directions: Sat nav: SA20 0PG. SN 788 471. N of Llandovery. From A483 take B road signposted to Llyn Brianne Reservoir & then follow signs to reserve, which lies between Cynghordy & Llanwrda.
Public transport: None.
Visiting: Public nature trail at Dinas open dawn-dusk. Car park & information board at start of trail, coach parking can be arranged. Nature trail inc. a boardwalk. Other parts of trail are rugged. Toilets at Llyn Brianne reservoir car park (one mile N).
Contact: RSPB, T: 02920 353 000;
E: gwenffrwd.dinas@rspb.org.uk

4. LLANELLI WETLAND CENTRE

The Wildfowl & Wetlands Trust.
Habitats: Inter-tidal mudflats, reedbeds, pools, marsh, waterfowl collection.
Birds: *Winter*: Up to 50,000 waterbirds, inc. Pintail, Wigeon, Teal. Little Egret, Curlew, Oystercatcher, Redshank. Short-eared & Barn Owls, Peregrine.
Other: Bee & Southern Marsh Orchids, Yellow Bartisa. Dragonflies, Water Vole, Otter.
Directions: Sat nav: SA14 9SH. SS 532 985. Overlooks Burry Inlet near Llanelli on B4304. Leave M4 at Junc 48. Signposted from A484, E of Llanelli.
Public transport: Bus - Llanelli 'Dial a Ride' service operates between Llanelli bus station, railway station & the centre - book with Carmarthanshire County Council T: 01267 228 326 or call centre: T: on T: 0845 634 0661 Mon-Fri 9.30am-12pm up to the day before travel (bookings for Sat & Mon must be made by Fri before).
Visiting: Free car/coach parking. Open daily (not Dec 24/25) 9.30am-5pm grounds open until 6pm in summer). Entrance fee, members free. Visitor centre fully accessible with toilets, hides, restaurant, shop, education facilities. Mobility scooters/ wheelchairs free to hire. Centre has level access & hard-surfaced paths.
Contact: WWT Llanelli Wetland Centre,
T: 01554 741 087; E: info.llanelli@wwt.org.uk

5. PENGELLI FOREST

The Wildlife Trust of South & West Wales.
Habitats: Ancient Oak woodland.
Birds: *All year:* Sparrowhawk, Buzzard, Tawny Owl, common woodland spp. *Summer*: Cuckoo, Redstart, Wood Warbler, Spotted & Pied Flycatchers. *Winter*: Woodcock, winter thrushes, Brambling.
Other: Polecat, Dormouse, 8 spp. Bats, butterflies inc. Silver-washed Fritillary, White-lettered & Purple Hairstreaks, ancient woodland flora.
Directions: Sat nav: SA41 3PU. SN 122 395. Leave A487 Cardigan to Fishguard road just E of Felindre Farchog along unclassified road (CARE - tight turn if approaching from E) - reserve entrance ca. 1.5 miles along narrow lane following foot of hill (around Iron Age mound of Castel Henllys), once across a ford access gate is 0.3 mile, park on road by gate.
Public transport: Bus - no.T5 (not Sun) Cardigan to Fishguard stops at Felindre Farchog (then walk road route to forest). Richard Bros (T: 01239 613 756).
Visiting: Open at all times. Easy walks near entrance but no wheelchair access, paths steeper elsewhere. Can be muddy.
Contact: WT of S&W Wales - see site 1.

6. RAMSEY ISLAND

RSPB (Wales HQ).
Habitats: Acid grassland, maritime heath, sea cliffs.
Birds: *All year:* Peregrine, Raven, Chough. *Spring/ summer:* Cliff-nesting auks (Guillemot, Razorbill), Kittiwake, Fulmar, Shag, Stonechat, Wheatear, Skylark, Linnet, Little Owl. *Passage:* Regular migrants, occasionally scarce or rare spp.
Other: Largest Grey Seal colony in south-west Britain, Red Deer, Harbour Porpoise.
Directions: Sat nav: SA62 6PY. SM 721 249 (mainland). One mile offshore from lifeboat station at St Justinians, two miles west of St Davids, Pembrokeshire.

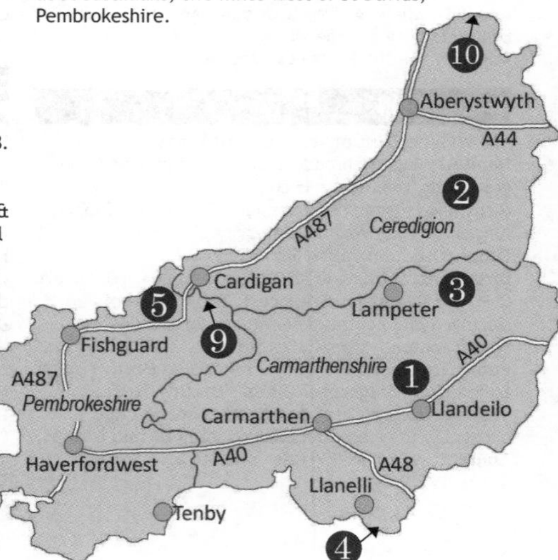

Public transport: Bus - no.T11 (not Sun) from Haverfordwest to St Davids (Richards Bros, T: 01239 613 756) & then no.403 Celtic Coaster St David's to St Justinians, May-Sep (Sarah Bell, T: 07828 940 955). Train - Haverfordwest.
Visiting: Coach & car parking at St Justinians (ask boat company for advice/options). Island open daily 10am-4pm, weather permitting, Apr 1st/Easter if earlier) to Oct. RSPB landing fee for non-members, in addition to boat fare. Small RSPB visitor centre/shop selling snacks & hot/cold drinks. Compost toilets - five minute walk uphill from harbour. 3.5 mile circular trail (or two shorter walks) - rugged in parts. Introduction from resident wardens. Guided walks available. No wheelchair access.
Boat - sails from lifeboat station at 10am & 12pm, returns at 4pm. To book: Thousand Island Expeditions, T: 01437 721 721; E: sales@thousandislands.co.uk
Contact: RSPB, T: 07836 535 733;
E: ramsey.island@rspb.org.uk

7. SKOKHOLM NNR

The Wildlife Trust of South & West Wales.
Habitats: Cliffs, bays & inlets.
Birds: *Spring:* Manx Shearwaters arrive at end of Mar (50,000 pairs). *Summer*: Internationally important colonies of Razorbill, Puffin, Guillemot, Storm Petrel, Lesser Black-backed Gull. *Passage:* Migrants inc. rare species.
Other: Grey Seal, Harbour Porpoise, occasional Common, Bottlenose & Risso's Dolphins, nationally rare moths.
Directions: Sat nav: SA62 3BJ. SM 760 089 (Marloes/Martin's Haven parking). 15 miles SW of Haverfordwest. Take B4327, turn-off for Marloes, continue two miles past village to embarkation point at Martin's Haven (National Trust car park, fee payable).
Public transport: None.
Visiting: No day visitors, residential stays available Apr-Sep (bookings open in autumn for following season). Has Bird Observatory status & welcomes visiting ringers. Self-catering accommodation for up to 20 people, small shop selling basic foodstuffs. Boat fare paid directly to boatman in cash.
Contact: Main Office & Island Bookings (Mon-Fri 9am-5pm), T: 01656 724 100;
E: islands@welshwildlife.org

8. SKOMER

The Wildlife Trust of South & West Wales.
Habitats: Maritime cliff, freshwater ponds.
Birds: *Summer:* World's largest Manx Shearwater colony (300,000+ pairs). Puffin, Guillemot, Razorbill, Kittiwake (until end-Aug), Fulmar, Short-eared Owl, Chough, Peregrine, Buzzard, migrants (inc. rarities).
Directions: See site 7.
Public transport: None.
Visiting: Island open Apr-Sep (Easter if earlier). Information centre, toilets, two hides, booklets, guides, nature trails. Take water/food. Not suitable for infirm (87 steep landing steps/rough ground).
Day visitors: (not Mon, except bank holidays/max 250 tickets per day, on first come first served basis). Island landing fee (members free), payable at Lockley Lodge. Boats leave 10am, 11am & 12pm - returning 3pm. Boat fare paid on boat. T: 01646 636 800 to see if boats running. No dogs.
Overnight visitors: Boat sails at 9am - booking essential (bookings open in autumn for following season)/length of stay conditions apply.
Contact: Main Office & Island Bookings - see site 7.

9. WELSH WILDLIFE CENTRE/TEIFI MARSH NR

The Wildlife Trust of South & West Wales.
Habitats: Wetlands, marsh, swamp, reedbed, open water, creek (tidal), river, saltmarsh, woodland.
Birds: *Summer:* Breeding Kingfisher, gulls, Sand Martin, Great Spotted Woodpecker, Redstart, Cetti's Warbler. *Winter:* Wildfowl inc. Teal, Wigeon & Mallard. Water Rail, Curlew, Snipe, Lapwing & Peregrine. Occasional Bittern & Red Kite.
Other: Otter, Water Shrew, Sika & Red Deer, good variety dragonflies.
Directions: Sat nav: SA43 2TB. SN 188 451. Visitor centre 1.25 miles from Cilgerran, two miles SE of Cardigan. River Teifi is N boundary. Signposted from A478 Cardigan to Fishguard road.
Public transport: Bus - nos.430 (not Sun) Cardigan to Narberth, alight at Cilgerran, then walk to centre. Richards Bros (T: 01239 613 756).
Visiting: Open all year. Free parking for members, charge for non-members. Visitor centre/cafe/shop open 10am-5pm Easter-Oct, 4pm Nov-Mar (not Christmas week), network of four nature trails & seven hides. Binoculars for hire. Disabled access to visitor centre, paths, four hides. Dogs on leads.
Contact: Welsh Wildlife Centre, T: 01239 621 600;
E: wwc@welshwildlife.org

10. YNYS HIR

RSPB (Wales HQ).
Habitats: Estuary, freshwater pools, woodland & wet grassland.
Birds: *All year*: Red Kite, Buzzard, Little Egret, Lapwing, Teal. *Spring/summer*: Redstart, Pied Flycatcher, nine spp. warbler inc. Grasshopper & Wood. *Winter*: Greenland White-fronted & Barnacle Geese, Wigeon, Hen Harrier.
Other: 16 spp. dragonflies inc. Small Red Damselfly & Golden-ringed Dragonfly. Butterflies inc. Dark Green Fritillary, Brimstone & Speckled Wood. Otter (rarely seen), Brown hare.
Directions: Sat nav: SY20 8TA. SN 681 960. Car park is one mile from Eglwys-fach village, off A487, six miles SW of Machynlleth.
Public transport: Bus - no.X28 Machynlleth to Aberystwyth, alight Eglwys-fach. Lloyds Coaches (T. 01654 702 100). Train - Machynlleth.
Visiting: Open daily (dawn-dusk). Coaches welcome, call for parking info. Visitor centre open daily (not Christmas period) 9am-5pm Apr-Oct, 10am-4pm Nov-Mar. Drinks/light refreshments, toilets. Entrance fee for reserve, members free. Three trails, five hides, two viewpoints, some wheelchair access. No dogs.
Contact: RSPB, T: 01654 700 222;
E: ynyshir@rspb.org.uk

INDEX TO RESERVES

INDEX TO RESERVES

INDEX TO RESERVES

Neil Gartshore

It's not all about birds!
Many of the individuals listed in this section offer talks, photos and artwork covering other aspects of natural history such as butterflies.
Dark Green Fritillary *(Speyeria aglaja)* - Martin Down, Hampshire.

DIRECTORY OF WILDLIFE LECTURERS, PHOTOGRAPHERS & ARTISTS

WILDLIFE LECTURERS & PHOTOGRAPHERS

This directory lists a number of individuals who offer lectures covering a wide variety of wildlife related subjects. In addition, a number of them also offer a range of photographic products/services.

Each listing indicates whether the individual offer lectures (L) and/or photographic product/services (P) followed by a short biography.

Under 'Lectures' there is an indication of the talks that are available but bear in mind that this is probably not the full list of what may be available.

Fee: this will vary due to the travel distances involved but will give an idea of charges.

Distance: how far lecturers are willing to travel/any restrictions are noted here.

Time: when lecturers are available/any restrictions are noted here.

If any of the listings offer photographic products/services they are described under 'Photography'.

If you are an organiser of a group looking to book a speaker for your meetings or would like further information about the photographic products/services offered please contact the individuals directly via the details at the end of their listing - please mention *'The Birdwatcher's Yearbook'* when making an enquiry.

Availability of speakers - Covid19 restrictions...

At the time of going to press (Sept 2020) the UK still has a number of restrictions in place with regards to holding social gatherings, including talks. Hopefully over the course of the next few months these will gradually lift and some sort of normality will return.

The speakers are more than happy to take bookings for dates over the coming year (or two!)

Some of the speakers are be able to offer talks by 'Zoom' (or other social media formats) - please ask them if they are able to do so.

Lecturer's Listings

Do you offer talks and / or photographic products & services?

Would you like a listing in this directory?
(A small charge applies)

Contact us for details (see page 6)

WILDLIFE LECTURERS & PHOTOGRAPHERS

ALIBONE, Mike [L]

Northamptonshire-based birder, Optics Editor for Birdwatch magazine, producing equipment reviews and providing buying advice for readers while writing other ad hoc features. Also qualified ecologist and experienced logistician, having undertaken numerous birding trips to the four corners of the Western Palearctic, with Israel as a speciality destination, as well as to Africa, south-east Asia and USA.

Lectures: Birding Israel - north to south, migration and conservation; Birding Northamptonshire - key sites and population dynamics; Birding Optics - how they work, brand overviews and what to look for when buying.

Fee: Standard £85 (negotiable for small groups) plus travel, charged at 15p per mile.
Distance: Any considered. **Time:** Flexible.

Contact:
T: 07950 707 697;
E: alibone.mike@gmail.com;
W: www.northantsbirds.com;
twitter: @bonxie

BOWDEN, Paul [L]

Birdwatcher and nature photographer (4K-Video and DSLR photos of birds and other wildlife) for 30+ years (serious amateur). Founder member and current Treasurer of Glamorgan Wildlife Photographic Club. Member of local and national organisations (Glamorgan Birds, RSPB and WWT). Provide own HD Projector, HD Laptop, amplifier and speakers.

Lectures: Birds of Europe (Austria, Belarus, Bulgaria, Estonia, Finland, Germany, Greece (Lesvos), Hungary, Italy, Portugal & Madeira, Spain & Balearic and Canary Islands, Sweden & UK) and further destinations: Egypt; Libya; Morocco; Oman; Armenia; Azerbaijan; Georgia; India; Hong Kong; Japan; Australia; Panama; Costa Rica; Brazil; USA (nine States: AZ, CA, FL, HI, IL, MO, OR, TX, WA) & Canada. Also Butterflies and Dragonflies from UK, Europe and Overseas. Presentations in HD Video Movie and/or Powerpoint formats.

Fee: £65 plus reasonable travelling expenses (with overnight accommodation for longer trips).
Distance: Any. **Time:** Any by arrangement.

Contact:
4 Patmore Close, Gwaelod-y-Garth,
Cardiff, CF15 9SU;
T: 029 2081 3044 or 07771 664 819;
E: bowden_pe@hotmail.com

BUCKINGHAM, John [L, P]

Long-standing and popular lecturer, worldwide bird and wildlife photographer, tour leader.

Lectures: 60+ titles covering birds, wildlife, botany, ecology and habitats in UK, Europe, Africa, Australia, Indian sub-continent, North-South and Central America. Includes favourites such as How Birds Work; The Natural History of Birds; Wonders of Bird Migration.

Fee: £100 plus expenses. **Distance:** Any. **Time:** Any.

Photography: Huge range of birds, botany and wildlife from UK, Europe, Africa, Americas, Australia, Asia and worldwide. **Products & services:** Digital images available for publication and purchase plus original slides for lectures and personal use.

Contact:
10 Courtlands, Kingsdown Road, Kingsdown,
Walmer, Kent CT14 8BW;
T: 01304 364 231;
E: john.birdtalk@btinternet.com

CLEAVE, Andrew MBE [L]

Wildlife photographer, author, lecturer and tour leader.

Lectures: More than 30 talks (incl. Canadian Rockies; New Zealand seabirds and endemics; Varangerfjord birds and wildlife; India; Southern Sweden; Belarus; Bermuda; Mediterranean birds and wildlife; Isles of Scilly; Lundy; Shetland; Ancient Woodlands; Dormice; Coastal Birds: Life Between the Tides. Full list available.

Fee: £75 plus petrol. **Distance:** Approx. 70 miles without accommodation. **Time:** Afternoons and evenings, not school holidays.

Contact:
31 Petersfield Close, Chineham, Basingstoke,
Hampshire RG24 8WP;
T: 01256 320 050 & 07785 767 263;
E: andrew@bramleyfrith.co.uk;
W: http://andrewcleave.co.uk/

Roller (Spain) - Neil Gartshore

COLLINS, Chris [L]

Wildwings tour leader, Neotropical Bird Club council member & treasurer, experienced lecturer and wildlife photographer.

Lectures: Birds of the Russian Far East/In search of the Spoon-billed Sandpiper; Arctic Russia: Realm of the Ice Bear; Birds of Guyana; Unknown Antarctica: Birds of the Ross Sea and New Zealand Subantarctic Islands; Around the World in 80 minutes; Amazing Birds; Pacific Odyssey: New Zealand to Japan.

Fee: £105 + travel expenses. **Distance:** Four hours from Surrey/London or overnight accommodation. **Time:** Any by prior agreement.

Contact:
9 Pound Close, Long Ditton, Surbiton,
Surrey KT6 5JW;
T: 020 8398 1742;
E: chris@birdsandwildlife.com;
W: www.birdsandwildlife.com/lectures

DAVIES, Alan & MILLER, Ruth [L]

Alan and Ruth both worked for the RSPB before giving up their jobs to travel the world birding for a whole year in 2008. They now run their own birdwatching tour company called BirdwatchingTrips based in North Wales, offering relaxed, small-group birdwatching tours in North Wales, the rest of the UK, Europe and further afield.

Lectures: A wide range of entertaining illustrated talks including: Birdwatching in North Wales- more than just sheep!, Birding in the Land of the Midnight Sun: Finland and Norway; Quetzals and More: Costa Rica; Southern Africa - Birding below the Equator: a fast-paced tour of South Africa, Namibia, Botswana, Zambia and Uganda, packed with colourful birds, wonderful mammals, stunning scenery - and a few hair-raising adventures; Norfolk, where birding began ; South Georgia and Antarctica: a million penguins can't be wrong. We are continuously adding to our range of talks.

Fee: £80 plus the cost of the fuel used on the return trip from Llandudno. This fee usually includes both Alan and Ruth as speakers. **Distance:** Any considered, but overnight accommodation may be required. **Time:** Very flexible all year apart from Mar-Jun and Sep/Oct when we are away guiding. Please e-mail to check availability.

Contact:
12 Ormeside Court, 19 Church Walks, Llandudno,
Clwyd LL30 2HG;
T: 01492 872 407;
E: info@birdwatchingtrips.co.uk;
W: www.birdwatchingtrips.co.uk

FORGHAM, Jonathan [L]

Primary school teacher for 30 years, now running science enhancement company and professional bird guide. Has given over 140 illustrated talks to bird groups in last four years in south east of England and occasionally, further afield. Visited most of Europe and parts of Asia and Australia, too. Life-long birder and all round naturalist, recording all aspects of nature within the parish of Little Hadham, East Hertfordshire. References available, all excellent.

Lectures: The Birds of the North Norfolk Coastal Footpath; The Birds of The Camargue; The Birds of The Algarve and Baixa Alentejo; The Birds of southern Sri Lanka; The Bird Reserves of Kent; The Whole Natural History of an East Hertfordshire Parish; The Walk to Hel (a 50-mile walk around Gdansk Bay, Poland); Moths of Hertfordshire. Lockdown 700. All natural history recorded in my garden during Lockdown as from 23rd March. So far, close to 700 species. (Will provide own laptop, cables, and projector).

Fee: £110 in total for 150 mile round trip. £135 in total for in excess of 150 mile round trip. In excess of 200 mile round trip, fee negotiable. **Distance:** Live in Herts so easy access to motorways, no restrictions under around 200 mile round trip. **Time:** Available evenings, daytime too (if early booking).

Contact:
6 Chapel Lane, Little Hadham, Ware,
Hertfordshire SG11 2AA;
T: 01279 776 112 (eves) or 07805 571 551 (day/texts);
E: jforgham@hotmail.com;
W: http://littlehadhambirding.blogspot.co.uk

GALVIN, Chris [L, P]

A birding photographer with passion for wildlife for more than 30 years.

Lectures: Northwest Year; Around the World in 80 Birds; Bee-eaters & Kingfishers: an intro to the Birds of Goa; Birding by Camera; Birding on the Doorstep; Just Add Water; Kenya - More than just Birds.

Fee: £90 to £150 depending on distance travelled. **Distance:** 150 miles radius from home. **Time:** Any.

Photography: Birds. **Products & services:** Images for publication, prints, mounted prints, commissions considered.

Contact:
17 Henley Rd, Allerton, Liverpool,
Merseyside L18 2DN;
T: 0151 729 0123 or 07802 428 385;
E: chris@chrisgalvinphoto.com;
W: www.chrisgalvin.co.uk

WILDLIFE LECTURERS & PHOTOGRAPHERS

GARNER, Jackie [L]

Professional wildlife artist, author & illustrator of *The Wildlife Artist's Handbook*. Tour leader for Aigas Field Centre and Art Safari Holidays.

Lectures: Birds/Nature in Art; Focus on the Falklands; Wildlife of Ancient Egypt; Lifting the Lid on Lundy; Brief Encounters (the art of field sketching).

Fee: £150 + expenses for almost all groups, though negotiable for venues over 100 miles away.
Distance: Any. **Time: Any.**

Contact:
The Old Cider House Studio, Humphries End, Randwick, Stroud, Gloucestershire GL6 6EW;
T: 01453 847 420 or 07800 804 847;
E: artist@jackiegarner.co.uk;
W: www.jackiegarner.co.uk

GARTSHORE, Neil [L]

Spent 23-years working in the nature conservation field with The National Trust; The Percy FitzPatrick Institute of African Ornithology/Cape Town, South Africa; RSPB. Now a freelance bird surveyor, natural history book seller, tour guide, writer and lecturer. Edits/publishes *'The Birdwatcher's Yearbook' and* author of *'Best Birdwatching Sites in Dorset'*.

Lectures: Dorset's Best Birdwatching Sites; Poole Harbour and its Birds; Japan - birding in the land of the rising sun; Birding in Spain - marshes, mountain and migration; Lesvos - Jewel in the Aegean; The Farne Islands - Northumberland's seabird city; Wildlife Wanderings in South Africa; A Sub-Antarctic Experience: the Prince Edward Islands.
Ask for a list/further details.

Fee: Variable, depending on distance travelled.
Distance: Any considered. **Time:** Flexible - sometimes available at short notice.

Contact:
Moor Edge, 2 Bere Road, Wareham, Dorset BH20 4DD;
T: 01929 552 560 or 07986 434 375;
E: birding@callunabooks.co.uk;
W: www.callunabooks.co.uk

GINNAW, Simon [L]

Birder & naturalist since childhood, worked with the RSPB, as a Country Park Ranger, and Forestry England Woodland Officer in South-east England. Freelance bird surveyor, tour leader & guide, tutor, writer, & lecturer.

Lectures: Kent's Wild Year; A Woodland Year; Birds Beyond The Boughs - Secret Lives Of Our Woodland Birds; Secret Lives Of Our Coastal Birds; Hungary: Birding the heart of Europe; A Year on my Local Patch; Wildlife Tales From The Riverbank; Exploring Britain's Mammals. Ask for a list/details.

Fee: Variable, depending on distance travelled.
Distance: Any considered. **Time:** Evenings preferred, but flexible - sometimes available at short notice.

Contact:
Exploring The Wild, 32 Amsbury Road, Coxheath, Kent ME17 4DP;
T: 07783 354 337;
E: info@simonginnaw.com;
W: www.simonginnaw.com

GLENN, Neil [L]

Author of *Best Birdwatching Sites in Norfolk* and *Best Birdwatching Sites in Yorkshire*; regular contributor to *Bird Watching* magazine; freelance bird tour leader for Avian Adventures. UK Rep for South Texas Nature. Chair of Nottinghamshire Birdwatchers and also a Patron for Birding For All.

Lectures: Wildlife of the Lower Rio Grande Valley, Texas; Birding the Arctic Circle; Moroccan Spice: from The Sahara to the Atlas Mountains; Warbler Wonderland: Spring Migration in Ohio and Michigan; A Year in the Life of a Bird Tour Guide; Bhuthan: In the Land of the Thunder Dragon. More to follow!

Fee: Negotiable. **Distance:** Any. **Time:** Any.

Contact:
13 Gladstone Avenue, Gotham, Nottingham NG11 0HN; T: 07771 934 738;
E: n.glenn@ntlworld.com

Adonis Blue/Dartford Warbler - Joe Mitchell

WILDLIFE LECTURERS & PHOTOGRAPHERS

GROVE, Ashley [L, P]

Professional photographer, wildlife watcher and tour leader, with a specialism in birds. A list of available lectures is below. References on request if required. Recommended speaker by the RSPB, BTO and Royal Horticultural Society.

Lectures: Shetland to Scilly, Birds of the British Isles; Jewels of the Gambia, Kingfishers, Bee-eaters & Rollers; Great British Birds; Lammergeiers of the Spanish Pyrenees; Trinidad & Tobago, Home of the Hummingbird; Wonderful Winter Wildlife, Vibrant Sri Lanka, Blue Magpies, Blue Whales & Blue skies; Crane Spotting..., around Swedens Lake Hornborga; A Beginners Guide to Birdwatching. More talks under construction.

Fee: £85 plus 25p per mile expenses (may be negotiable if you're able to recommend a nearby group to speak to on an adjacent evening). **Distance:** Any within reason. **Time:** Any.

Photography (and Birdwatching Tours) - Ashley's company, 'Experience Nature',run very reasonably priced holidays for wildlife watchers and photographers. Trips to The Gambia, Spain, Sweden, Sri Lanka, Honduras, Scotland and Trinidad & Tobago are run regularly, plus various other foreign and UK destinations. Visit Ashley's website for more information on the holidays and for a selection of images gathered on these trips.

Contact:
16 Lint Meadow, Wythall,
Worcestershire B47 5PH;
T: 07704 189 835;
E: experiencenaturetours@gmail.com;
W: www.experiencenature.co.uk

LOVELL, Stephen [L]

All round naturalist with interests in all aspects of natural history. RSPB and RHS listed speaker and cruise ship speaker for Peel Talent. Guest speaker for the British Wildlife Watching Club in Scotland. Photographer and Adult Education Tutor. Now running Greenspaces which specialises in small group daytrips, short breaks and holidays in the UK. Also organises workshops covering a variety of topics - see website for further details.

Lectures: Available on a wide range of European destinations including Lesvos, Majorca, Menorca, Extremadura. A wide range of talks on various areas of Britain with many covering Scotland. Other talks available on a wide variety of destinations around the world including Costa Rica, Trinidad and Tobago, Cuba, Nepal, Sri Lanka, India, New Zealand, Australia, Tanzania, St Lucia, Borneo, Iceland and whale watching in Mexico. I have a wide variety of talks covering garden related topics such as Encouraging Wildlife into the Garden. There is also a talk on The Miracle of Migration. More talks are constantly being added.

Fee: £70 to £90 + travel (negotiable according to distance travelled). **Distance:** Any considered. **Time:** Any.

Contact:
6 Abingdon Close, Doddington Park,
Lincoln, LN6 3UH;
T: 01522 689 456 or 07957 618 684;
E: stephenlovell58@btinternet.com;
W: www.stevelovellgreenspaces.co.uk

Wheatear - Joe Mitchell

LOWEN, James [L, P]

Multi-award-winning author of 11 nature and travel books making wildlife accessible to the non-specialist: 52 European wildlife weekends: a year of short breaks for nature lovers / 52 wildlife weekends: a year of British wildlife-watching breaks / A summer of British wildlife: 100 great days out watching wildlife / Year round Walks, Norfolk / Antarctic Wildlife / Pantanal Wildlife / The Butterfly Pavilion / Birds of France / Birds of Spain / Spotlight: Hedgehogs / Spotlight: Badgers. Columnist in Bird Watching and The Countryman magazines, and regular feature- and travel-writer for BBC Wildlife and The Telegraph among other publications. Editor, Neotropical Birding magazine. Professional photographer represented by FLPA and Alamy. As well as being a regular on the bird club circuit, James's lectures routinely pack Birdfair marquees each year.

Lectures: Many talks, e.g. Antarctic wildlife; Pantanal wildlife; Europe's best wildlife weekends; A pavilion of butterflies; Gaucho birding in Argentina; Japan - the world's best winter birding?; Much ado about mothing; Norfolk nature; Seeing the best of Britain's summer wildlife; Britain's top wildlife weekends; Britain's dragonflies; Britain's amazing orchids; Wildlife photography made easy; Why moths are magic.

Fee: £80 plus 25p per mile plus £10 per hour travel time over two hours total. **Limits:** Negotiable, overnight accommodation may be needed. **Time:** Any.

Photography: All wildlife, from UK, Argentina, Brazil, Antarctica, Japan, various European countries. **Products & services:** digital images, prints, lectures, commissioned photography.

Contact:
Norwich, Norfolk.
T: 07523 000 490;
E: lowen.james@gmail.com;
W: http://jameslowen.com;
W: www.pbase.com/james_lowen;
Twitter: @JLowenWildlife;
Instagram: @JlowenWildlife

MAYER, Edward [L]

Founder of Swift Conservation advice service, formerly Head of Gallery Management at the Tate Gallery.

Lectures: Swifts, Their Lives and Conservation. Also Biodiversity Awareness and Techniques for the Built Environment - talks and training sessions for enthusiasts, ornithologists, architects, developers, planners, biodiversity and facilities staff. Talks from 30 minutes to two hours, training from one hour to one day.

Fee: From £95, depending on type and length of talk, or collection/donation, plus travel expenses. **Distance:** UK/Europe/North America. **Time:** Any.

Contact:
52 Cholmley Gardens, London NW6 1AH;
T: 020 7794 2098;
E: mail@swift-conservation.org;
W: www.swift-conservation.org

MILES, John [L]

Former warden for RSPB, tour guide [Nature Scotland], consultant, journalist and author of... Best Birdwatching Sites: The Solway; Best Birdwatching Sites: Yorkshire [co-author]; Hadrian's Birds; Exploring Lakeland Wildlife; Pharoah's Birds; Hadrian's Wildlife and a series of children's books [Fifteen titles, growing every year with Chickbooks. Check the web site to see which of these books are now on YouTube].

Lectures: The Solway - the whole of Cumbria and Dumfries & Galloway; Hadrian's Wildlife - History of birds back to Roman times + many present day locations to visit; Death on the Nile - looks at the history of birds from Ancient Egypt to present time birds while cruising the Nile; Mull: Not just Eagles! - year round look at this island; Go Birding - follows John around Britain in search of articles in 'Go Birding' in Bird Watching magazine; British Bee-eaters - Will they ever BEE Every Year!; Caithness - the forgotten part of Scotland!; Islay - Not just Geese!; Yorkshire - Not just a White Rose!

Fee: Prices on request. **Distance:** Anywhere in UK. **Time:** Evenings best.

Contact:
Jockey Shield, Castle Carrock, Carlisle,
Cumbria CA4 9NF;
T: 01228 670 205;
E: john@chickbooks.co.uk;
W: chickbooks.co.uk
Also see:
www.youtube.com/
watch?v=6nokw5m0vgo&feature=youtu.be

WILDLIFE LECTURERS & PHOTOGRAPHERS

OFFORD, Keith L

Raptor specialist. Coordinator of North-east Wales Raptor Study group. Photographer, lecturer, course & workshop tutor, tour leader, conservationist.

Lectures: 16 talks covering raptors (biology and identification), bird flight, British uplands, gardens, migration, woodland wildlife, Texas, Spain, Sri Lanka, Estonia, Morocco, Iceland, Costa Rica, Namibia, Kruger National Park, Western Cape.

Fee: £100 (pro-rota to travel distance per mile after 100 miles) plus travel costs. **Distance:** Any. **Time:** Sept to Apr.

Contact:
Yew Tree Farmhouse, Craignant, Selattyn,
Nr Oswestry, Shropshire SY10 7NP;
T: 01691 718 740;
E: keith@keithofford.co.uk;
W: www.keithofford.co.uk

READ, Mike L, P

Photographer (wildlife/landscapes), tour leader, writer.

Lectures: 12 talks featuring British and foreign subjects (list available on receipt of sae or see website).

Fee: £70 plus travel. **Distance:** 80 miles from Ringwood. **Time:** Available Sept to Mar.

Photography: Birds, mammals, plants, landscapes, and some insects. UK, France, USA, New Zealand, Falkland Isalnds plus many more. Behaviour, action, portraits, artistic pictures available for publication. More than 100,000 images in stock. **Products & services:** Extensive stock photo library. Canvas and giclee prints, greetings cards, books.

Contact:
Claremont, Redwood Close, Ringwood,
Hampshire BH24 1PR;
T: 01425 475 008;
E: mike@mikeread.co.uk;
W: www.mikeread.co.uk

REDMAN, Nigel L

Author, editor and tour leader.

Lectures: Mostly birds, inc. Ethiopia; Somaliland; Eritrea; Kenya; Morocco; Russia (and former Soviet Union); the Caucasus; Antarctica; Arctic (North-west Passage/Svalbard); New Zealand; Mexico.

Fee: Negotiable. **Distance:** Any (but overnight accommodation may be required). **Time:** Any.

Contact:
Hollyhocks, Edgefield Road, Briston,
Norfolk NR24 2HX;
T: 01263 862 866 or 07734 886 515;
E: nigelredman28@hotmail.com

ROTHERHAM, Prof Ian L

Former local authority ecologist, environmental campaigner, researcher, lecturer, writer and broadcaster.

Lectures: Numerous illustrated talks on all aspects of conservation inc.: Rewilding Nature; Rewilding Your Garden; Rewilding the River Don; Wild Deer of the Peak District; the Lost Fens; Yorkshire's Forgotten Fenlands; Shadow Woods - a search for lost landscapes; Wild woods and woodland heritage; Wildlife and history of moors, heaths and bogs; Urban Wildlife; Gardening for Wildlife; Alien and invasive species; Wild Peak District; Eco-history; Wilding Nature; Wilder Visions - re-constructing nature for the 21st century; Eco-fusion - our hybrid future; Loving the aliens?; Understanding the ancient woods; Sherwood Forest - wildlife, history & heritage; Sherwood Forest's Ancient Trees; Wildlife & Heritage - Yorkshire's Viking Coast.

Fee: £85, plus petrol 50p per mile. **Distance:** Prepared to travel if expenses are covered. **Time:** Any by arrangement.

Contact:
42 School Lane, Norton, Sheffield, S8 8BL;
T: 07751 089 499;
E: i.d.rotherham@shu.ac.uk;
W: www.ukeconet.org;
Blog: http://ianswalkonthewildside.wordpress.com/

SCOTT, Ann L

Retired. Formerly Senior Wildlife Adviser for RSPB, lecturer and teacher of ornithology.

Lectures: Various talks on UK & abroad. Latest talk: The Kenyan Coastal Forest and Area - Key Migration Hot-spots. Featuring Mida Creek, Lake Jilore, Dakatcha and Arabuko-Sokoke Forest, all wildlife rich areas. Mentions Bob Scott Memorial Appeal and our work/involvement out there.
Learn more at: http://www.whytsbirds.org or from: www.justgiving.com/ann-scott1/

Fee: £80 plus expenses (negotiable). **Distance:** Normally 2 hours drive from Huntingdon but willing to discuss. **Time:** Available mid-Mar to mid-Nov.

Contact:
17 Springfield Close, Buckden, Huntingdon, Cambridgeshire PE19 5UR;
T: 01480 811 848;
E: abscott@buckdencambs.co.uk

WILDLIFE LECTURERS & PHOTOGRAPHERS

SIMPSON, Rick and Elis [L]

Joint founders of the wader conservation charity Wader Quest. Birders, fundraisers and conservationists. Rick: speaker, artist, writer (Confessions of a Bird Guide (2013); Eury the Spoon-billed Sandpiper (for children 6-11, 2016); An Inspiration of Waders (2018); A Quest for Waders (2020). Elis: team photographer.

Lectures: Wader Quest (stories and facts about waders and their conservation); Confessions of a Bird Guide (guiding in Brazil); many other titles, mainly concerned with the waders of the world... full list on application.

Fee: £110 flat fee. **Distance:** Any considered. **Time:** Any, often available at short notice.

Contact:
20 Windsor Avenue, Newport Pagnell,
Buckinghamshire, MK16 8HA;
T: 07484 186 443;
E: rick@rick-simpson.com;
W: www.waderquest.net

TODD, Ralph [L]

Wildlife photographer and lecturer, former tour leader and course tutor.

Lectures: On the Trail of the Crane - parts 1 and 2; Polar Odyssey; Return of the Osprey; Natural Wonders and Wildlife of Iceland; Birds and People - Travels Through Time; Where Yeehaa meets Ole; Birds in the Land of Disney; Antarctic Adventure.

Fee: £75 plus expenses. **Distance:** Any. **Time:** Any - also short notice.

Contact:
9 Horsham Road, Bexleyheath, Kent DA6 7HU;
T: 01322 528 335;
E: rbtodd@btinternet.com

Portland Bird Obs - Joe Mitchell

van GROUW, Katrina [L]

Katrina van Grouw, author of *The Unfeathered Bird and Unnatural Selection*, inhabits that no-man's land slap bang between art and science. She holds degrees in fine art and natural history illustration, and is a former curator of ornithological collections at a major national museum. She's a self-taught scientist with a passion for evolutionary biology and its history. After a long and varied career on both sides of the art/science divide she now devotes her time exclusively to her books.

Katrina offers two talks about her books:
From Art to Zoology: A story of evolution. An entertaining and inspiring talk on the making of The Unfeathered Bird and the transition from fine artist to science author.

Unnatural Selection: Evolution at the Hand of Man. About Darwin, evolution, and why domesticated animals deserve a second look.

"Katrina is a dazzling speaker. Her talk will enthral anyone interested in birds."

"One of the most interesting and entertaining talks we had heard for a long time. This talk is really not to be missed!"

Fee: £90 local; £100-£150 non-local. **Distance:** Any. **Time:** Flexible - sometimes available at short notice.

Contact:
36 Northern Road, Aylesbury,
Buckinghamshire HP19 9QY;
T: 01296 398 571 & 07503 038 687;
E: katrinavangrouw@aol.co.uk;
W: www.unfeatheredbird.com

WHITE, Mick LRPS [L, P]

Professional wildlife photographer and Lecturer

Lectures: I offer a selection of talks covering a range of wildlife subjects and destinations, along with some practical guidance on taking wildlife Images both in the UK and Abroad. A full list can be found on my web site at mickwhitephotography.com (updated regularly).

Photography: I also offer a range of photographic workshops for small groups and individuals covering a wide range of wildlife subjects, full details of which can be found on my web site along with booking information.

Fee: Lectures: £70 + Travel @ 40p per mile + any accommodation costs incurred. Workshops: max group size 6 is £65pp or Individual tuition is £135 per day. **Distance:** Any. **Time:** Anytime.

Contact:
230 The Glade, Shirley, Croydon, Surrey CR0 7UG;
T: 07765 131 588;
E: mickwhite870@gmail.com;
W: www.mickwhitephotography.com

BTO SPEAKERS

This directory has been compiled to help Bird Clubs and similar organisations in finding speakers from the BTO for indoor meetings. Each entry consists of an individual speaker, a list of talks/lectures available, details of fees and expenses required and travel distance limitations. If you are interested in any of the speakers, please contact Ieuan Evans (ieuan.evans@bto.org). Alternatively, contact the BTO on 01842 750 050.

Austin, Dr Graham (Snr Res Ecol, Wetland & Marine Research)
Subjects: Wetland Bird Survey. **Fee:** £40.
Distance: Travel by agreement.

Baillie, Dr Stephen (Science Director Modelling & Demography)
Subjects: BirdTrack; Population Monitoring. **Fee:** £40.
Distance: Travel by agreement.

Balmer, Dawn (Head of Surveys)
Subjects: Bird Atlas 2007-11; House Martins; BTO Surveys. **Fees:** £40. **Distance:** 100 mile radius of Thetford, further by agreement.

Barimore, Carl (Nest Records Organiser)
Subjects: Nest Records Scheme. **Fee:** £40.
Distance: By agreement.

Blackburn, Jez (Licensing & Sales Manager)
Subjects: Bird Moult (suitable for ringers); Ringing for Conservation; Sule Skerry Seabirds. **Fee:** £40 (£70 for private talks). **Distance:** East Anglia.

Boersch-Supan, Dr Philipp (Ecological Statistician)
Subjects: Southern Ocean Seabirds (penguins, albatrosses); Maths & Models in Ecology & Conservation. **Fee:** Negotiable. **Distance:** Negotiable.

Boothby, Claire (Garden Birdwatch Development Officer)
Subjects: Garden Birds and Wildlife. **Fee:** £40.
Distance: By agreement.

Border, Dr Jennifer (Spatial Ecologist)
Subjects: Population Limitation in Whinchats; The Effect of Planned Housing on Bats. **Fee:** £40.
Distance: Negotiable.

Calbrade, Neil (Wetland Bird Survey National Organiser)
Subjects: BTO/JNCC/RSPB Wetland Bird Survey (WeBS). **Fee:** £40. **Distance:** By agreement.

Conway, Greg (Research Ecologist, Land-use Research)
Subjects: Nightjar Ecology & population change; Nightjar Migration & Tracking Studies; Woodlark Ecology & Population Change; Dartford Warbler Ecology & Population Change; Ecology & Origins of Wintering Warblers in the UK; Firecrests Population Change & Studies in Thetford Forest.
Fee: £40. **Distance:** 100 mile radius of Thetford.

Dadam, Dr Daria (Reseach Ecologist, Demography)
Subjects: Bird Disease; Marsh Tits; House Sparrow Ecology & Decline. **Fees:** £40. **Distance:** By agreement.

Darvill,Ben (Development & Engagement Manager, Scotland)
Subjects: Upland Birds; Ecology, Conservation and How You Can Help; Cuckoos and Other Long-distance Migrants; Birding With Your Eyes Shut; Fascinating Facts About Our Feathered Friends Found Through Technology, Tags and Tracks. **Fee:** Negotiable. **Distance:** Negotiable.

Evans, Ieuan (Director, Engagement)
Subjects: Unravelling the Mysteries of Bird Migration.
Fee: Negotiable. **Distance:** Negotiable.

Franks, Samantha (Research Ecologist, Population Ecology)
Subjects: Bird Migration; North American Waders; Alaska; Wildlife of British Columbia and the Pacific Northwest. **Fee:** Negotiable. **Distance:** Negotiable.

Frost, Dr Teresa (Wetland Bird Survey National Organiser)
Subjects: BTO/JNCC/RSPB Wetland Bird Survey (WeBS). **Fee:** £40. **Distance:** By agreement.

Gillings, Dr Simon (Head of Population Ecology & Modelling)
Subjects: Atlas 2007-11. **Fee:** £40. **Distance:** Negotiable.

Hanmer, Dr Hugh (Terrestrial Res Ecol & Project Owl Coordinator)
Subjects: Urban Birds; Owls; Project Owls. **Fee:** £40.
Distance: By agreement.

Harris, Sarah (Breeding Bird Survey National Organiser)
Subjects: BTO/JNCC/RSPB Breeding Birds Survey; Arctic Skua Tagging Research. **Fee:** £40. **Distance:** By agreement.

Henderson, Dr Ian (Snr Res Ecol, International Research)
Subjects: Arable Farming and Birds; Nightjars. Goshawk. Whinchat. **Fee:** £40. **Distance:** By agreement.

Jones, Kelvin (BTO Cymru Development Officer)
Subjects: Work of the BTO, other subjects via discussion e.g. Hawfinch and Twite in North Wales; Ringing in Aras Turkey. **Fee:** £40. **Distance:** By agreement.

McAvoy, Stephen (BirdTrack Support Officer)
Subjects: Mapping Migration with BirdTrack.
Fee: £40. **Distance:** By agreement.

Moran, Nick (Training Manager)
Subjects: Better Birding; Birding With Your Eyes Shut; Nocmig - Sound-recording Birds at Night; What BirdTrack Can Do For You; Work of the BTO (incl surveys/schemes, tagging); Birds and Birding in Arabia (non-BTO). **Fee:** £40. **Distance:** By agreement.

Musgrove, Dr Andy (Head of Monitoring)
Subjects: Ornithology: How Can Birdwatchers Contribute to Recording Other Wildlife. **Fee:** £40.
Distance: By agreement.

BTO SPEAKERS

Noble, Dr David (Principal Ecologist, Monitoring)
Subjects: Developing Bird Indicators; Population Trends. **Fee:** £40. **Distance:** By agreement.

Pearce-Higgins, Dr James (Director, Science)
Subjects: Birds and Climate Change; Upland Birds; A Year in the Life of a Golden Plover; Where Have All Our Curlews Gone? **Fee:** £40. **Distance:** By agreement.

Risely, Kate (Garden BirdWatch Organiser)
Subjects: Garden Birds and Wildlife. **Fee:** £40. **Distance:** Prefer no overhight stay.

Robinson, Dr Rob (Principle Ecologist, Modelling & Demography)
Subjects: Farming & Birds; Conservation Value of Ringing. **Fee:** £40. **Distance:** By agreement.

Ross-Smith, Dr Viola (Science Communications Manager)
Subjects: Gulls; Seabirds; Tracking Studies (General). **Fee:** £40. **Distance:** By agreement.

Siriwardena, Dr Gavin (Head of Terrestrial Ecology)
Subjects: Farmland Bird Research - Causes of Decline & Potential Solutions; Agri-Environment Schemes; Birds & Ecosystem Sevices. **Fee:** £40. **Distance:** Negotiable.

Stancliffe, Paul (Media Manager)
Subjects: Atlas 2007-11; Homes to Let - Nestboxes; Birds, Birders and the Work of the BTO; Tracking African Migrants. **Fee:** £40. **Distance:** Negotiable.

Toms, Mike (Head of Communications)
Subjects: Are Gardens Good for Birds or Birdwatchers?; Owls and Man - a Cultural History; **Fee:** Negotiable. **Distance:** Negotiable.

Wernham, Dr Chris (Senior Research Ecologist, BTO Scotland)
Subjects: The Work of BTO Scotland; Breeding Bird Survey in Scotland; BirdTrack in Scotland; Working for Scotland's Waders. **Fee:** £40. **Distance:** Travel Scotland and NE England.

Woodward, Ian (Research Officer)
Subjects: House Martins; Heronries Census; London Birds; **Fee:** £40. **Distance:** Negotiable.

WILDLIFE ART

See Dan's illustration in the 'Features' section (page 7)

WILDLIFE ART

There are many talented wildlife artists based in the UK. This section lists a selection of art galleries that regularly display wildlife art and the websites of a number of individual artists. Check them out to see if there is anything you like.

Organisation

SOCIETY OF WILDLIFE ARTISTS (founded 1964)

Registered charity that seeks to generate an appreciation of the natural world through all forms of fine art inspired by wildlife. The Natural Eye exhibition held annually in Oct/Nov at the Mall Galleries, London. Through bursary schemes, the Society has been able to help young artists (16 & over) with awards of up to £750 towards travel, education or the cost of materials.

Contact: The Federation of British Artists,
17 Carlton House Terrace, London SW1Y 5BD.
T: 020 7930 6844;
E: info@mallgalleries.com;
W: www.swla.co.uk

Galleries

BIRDSCAPES GALLERY

Manor Farm Barns, Glandford, Holt, Norfolk NR25 7JP; T: 01263 741 742; E: art@birdscapes.co.uk; W: www.birdscapesgallery.co.uk

Opening times: All year, daily (not wed) 11am to 4pm, may close for part of the day before a new exhibition.

DAVID SHEPHERD WILDLIFE FOUNDATION

7 Kings Road, Shalford, Guildford, Surrey GU4 8JU.
T: 01483 272 323; E: dswf@davidshepherd.org;
W: www.davidshepherd.org

Opening times: Mon - Fri, 9am to 5pm.

CHENG KIM LOKE GALLERY, SLIMBRIDGE

Wildfowl & Wetland Trust, Slimbridge, Gloucestershire GL2 7BT; T: 01453 891 900;
E: info.slimbridge@wwt.org.uk; W: www.wwt.org.uk
Opening times: All year, daily except Dec 25, 9.30am to 5.00pm/last admission at 4.00pm Admission charge for non-WWT members.

GORDALE (host of EXHIBITION OF WILDLIFE ART)

Gordale Garden and Home Centre, Chester High Road, Burton, South Wirral, Cheshire CH64 8TF;
T: 0151 336 2116; E: admin@gordale.co.uk;
W: www.gordale.co.uk & www.ewa-uk.com

Opening times: Stages an annual Exhibition of Wildlife Art in late July. Daily 9.30am to 6pm (11am-5pm Sunday). Free admission.

HOUSE OF BRUAR (includes WILDLIFE ART GALLERY)

By Blair Atholl, Perthshire PH18 5TW;
T: 0345 136 0111; E: mailorder@houseofbruar.com;
W: www.houseofbruar.com/gallery/

Opening times: All year, daily (not Dec 25 & Jan 1). 9.30am to 6pm. Free admission.

MALL GALLERIES

The Mall, London SW1; T: 0207 930 6844;
E: info@mallgalleries.com;
W: www.mallgalleries.org.uk

Opening times: Stages British Wildlife Photography Awards and the Society of Wildlife Artists' annual exhibition around Sep/Oct/Nov (10am to 5pm). Admission charge.

NATURE IN ART

Wallsworth Hall, Main A38, Twigworth, Gloucester GL2 9PA; T: 01452 731 422 (admin); E: via website; W: www.natureinart.org.uk

Opening times: Closed Mondays (exc. Bank Holidays) and Dec 24 to 26 otherwise open daily 10am to 5pm. Admission charge.

PINKFOOT GALLERY

High Street, Cley-next-the-Sea, Norfolk NR25 7RB;
T: 01263 740 947; E: info@pinkfootgallery.co.uk;
W: www.pinkfootgallery.co.uk

Opening times: All year, daily (not Christmas) 10.00am to 5.00pm (Mon to Sat), 11am to 4pm (Sun). Free admission.

WATERSTON HOUSE

Donald Watson Art Gallery, The SOC, Waterston House, Aberlady, East Lothian EH32 0PY; T: 01875 871 330;
E: exhibitions@the-soc.org.uk; W: www.the-soc.org.uk

Opening times: All year, daily (not Dec 25/26 & Jan 1) 10.00am to 4.00pm. Free entry.

THE WILDLIFE ART GALLERY

Online Art Gallery. E: wildlifeartgallery@btinternet.com;
W: www.wildlifeartgallery.com

Artists

AKROYD, Carry

E: via website; W: www.carryakroyd.co.uk

ALLEN, Richard

T: 01206 826 753; E: richardallenart@btinternet.com;
W: www.richardallenillustrator.com

ANGUS, Max

T: 07766 277 915; E: info@maxangus.co.uk;
W: www.maxangus.co.uk

ARTINGSTALL, Nigel

T: 07890 561 329; E: nigel@nigelartingstall.com;
W: www.nigelartingstall.com

BARTLETT, Paul

T: 01382 698 346; E: pauljbartlett@hotmail.com;
W: www.naturalselectiongallery.co.uk

BENNETT, David

E: via website; W: www.davidbennettwildlifeart.com

WILDLIFE ART

BOWLES, Ian
T: 01732 810 637; E: ianbowles.wildlife@btinternet.com;
W: www.ianbowleswildlifeartist.co.uk

BROCKIE, Keith
T: 01887 830 609; E: kbrockie@btinternet.com;
W: www.keithbrockie.co.uk

COOK, Robert
T: 07905 394 099; E: info@robcookart.com;
W: www.robcookart.com

COX, Jackie
T: 07780 877 300; E: jcox953@btinternet.com;
W: www.sindencox-art.co.uk/jackie.html

DALY, David
E: via website; W: www.davedalyartist.com

DAVIS, John
T: 01243 512 351; E: johndavis.wildlife@tiscali.co.uk;
W: www.johndavisartist.co.uk

DAY, Nick
T: 07763 109 020; E: birdmanday@yahoo.com;
W: www.nick-day-wildlife-artist.co.uk

DEMAIN, Michael
E: via website; W: www.michaeldemainwildlifeart.co.uk

DERRY, Nick
E: via website; W: https://nickderry.webs.com/

EDWARDS, Brin
T: 01787 211 162; E: studio@brin-edwards.com;
W: www.brin-edwards.com

FINNEY, David
E: via website; W: www.davidfinney.co.uk

FOKER, John
E: jffoker@googlemail.com; W: www.bearparkartists.co.uk

FORKNER, Andrew
T: 01993 776 322; E: andrew.forkner@gmail.com;
W: www.andrewforkner.co.uk

FULLER, Robert
T: 01759 368 355; E: mail@robertefuller.com;
W: www.robertefuller.com

GALE, John
E: johngaleartist@outlook.com;
W: www.galleryofbirds.co.uk

GARNER, Jackie
T: 01453 847 420; E: artist@jackiegarner.co.uk;
W: www.jackiegarner.co.uk

GREENHALF, Robert
E: via website; W: www.robertgreenhalf.co.uk

GRIFFITHS, Ian
T: 07971 678 464; E: mail@artbygriff.com;
W: www.artbygriff.com

HASLEN, Andrew
E: wildlifeartgallery@btinternet.com;
W: http://andrewhaslen.com/

HESELDEN, Russ
T: 01953 850 145; E: heselden860@btinternet.com;
W: www.russheselden.co.uk

HEWITT, Angela
T: 01983 296 110; E: angela.hewitt@btclick.com;
W: www.angelahewittdesigns.co.uk

HODGES, Gary
T: 01273 047 897; E: gary@garyhodges-wildlife-art.com;
W: www.garyhodges-wildlife-art.com

HOWEY, Paul
E: via website; W: www.paulhowey.co.uk

HUNT, Alan
E: via website; W: www.alanmhunt.com

INGRAM, Alison
T: 01403 263 179; E: alison@alisoningram.co.uk;
W: www.alisoningram.co.uk

JOHNSON, Richard
E: rjohnson.birdart@gmail.com;
W: www.facebook.com/Richard-Johnson-Wildlife-Artist-318774484888727/

JONES, Kitty
E: via website; W: www.kittiejones.com

KEMP, Carolyn
E: via website; W: www.carolynkemp.co.uk

LANGMAN, Mike
T: 07833 178 855; E: via website;
W: www.mikelangman.co.uk

LEWINGTON, Ian
T: 01235 819 792: E: lewbirder@btinternet.com;
W: www.ian-lewington.co.uk

LEWINGTON, Richard
T: 01235 848 451: E: enquiries@richardlewington.co.uk;
W: www.richardlewington.co.uk

LOCKWOOD, Rachel
T: 01263 740 947; E: rachel@rachellockwoodartist.com;
W: www.rachellockwoodartist.co.uk

MACKAY, Andrew
E: via website; W: www.ajm-wildlife-art.co.uk

MANNING, Julia
T: 01458 223 025; E: julia@juliamanning.co.uk;
W: www.juliamanning.co.uk

McCALLUM, James
E: email@jamesmccallum.co.uk;
W: www.jamesmccallum.co.uk

MESSAGE, Steve
T: 07909 585 988;
E: messagewildlifeart@btinternet.com;
W: www.message-wildlife-art.co.uk

MILLER, David
T: 01646 682 907; E: david@davidmillerart.co.uk;
W: www.davidmillerart.co.uk

NEILL, William
E: via website; W: www.william-neill.co.uk

NEWELL, Kerry
T: 07752 325 031; E: kerrynewell1@gmail.com;
W: www.kerrynewell.com

PAIGE, John & Jane
T: 01780 470 247; E: paiges@oldbrewerystudios.co.uk;
W: www.oldbrewerystudios.co.uk

PARRY, David
T: 01672 563 708; E: davidparryart@gmail.com;
W: www.davidparryart.com

PARTINGTON, Peter
T: 07966 579 592;
W: www.facebook.com/PeterPartingtonWildlifeArtist/

PAUL, Jeremy
T: 01624 832 980; E: jpaul@manx.net;
W: www.jeremypaulwildlifeartist.co.uk

PEARSON, Bruce
E: via website; W: www.brucepearson.net

PENDLETON, Chris
T: 07895 058 431; E: chris@pendleton.co.uk;
W: www.pendleton.co.uk

PHILLIPS, Antonia
T: 01308 420 423; E: via website;
W: www.antoniaphillips.co.uk

POMROY, Jonathan
T: 01439 788 014; E: jonathan@pomroy.plus.com;
W: www.jonathanpomroy.co.uk

POLLARD, Nick
E: info@nikpollard.co.uk; W: www.nikpollard.co.uk

POOLE, Greg
E: via website; W: www.gregpoole.co.uk

POWELL, Dan & Rosemary
T: 01329 668 465; E: danpowell11@btinternet.com;
W: www.powellwildlifeart.com

PROUD, Alastair
W: facebook.com/alastair.c.proud/

REES, Darren
T: 01786 870 538;
W: facebook.com/Darren-Rees-Artist-172830002767773/

RIDLEY, Martin
T: 01764 670 695; E: art@martinridley.com;
W: www.martinridley.com

ROSE, Chris
T: 01835 822 547; E: chris@chrisrose-artist.co.uk;
W: www.chrisrose-artist.co.uk

SCOTT, Dafila
E: via website; W: www.dafilascott.co.uk

SINDEN, Chris
T: 01594 829 903; E: chrissinden@btinternet.com;
W: www.sindencox-art.co.uk/chris.html

STOCK, Andrew
E: andrew@andrewstock.co.uk;
W: www.andrewstock.co.uk

THRELFALL, John
T: 01556 630 262; E: john@johnthrelfall.co.uk;
W: www.johnthrelfall.co.uk

TRATT, Richard
E: rtratt@btinternet.com; W: www.richardtratt.co.uk

TRUSS, Jonathan
T: 07765 003 309; E: jon@jonathantruss.com;
W: www.jonathantruss.com

UNDERWOOD, Matthew
E: matt@mattunderwood.info; W: www.mattunderwood.info

WARREN, Michael
E: via website; W: www.mikewarren.co.uk

WATLING, Gareth
T: 01302 880 241; E: garethwatling@yahoo.com;
W: www.garethwatling.com

WHITE, Vicky
E: mail@vicky-white.co.uk; W: www.vicky-white.co.uk

WHITTLESTONE, Richard
T: 01246 582 720; E: art@richardwhittlestone.co.uk;
W: www.richardwhittlestone.co.uk

WILSON, Eric
E: via website; W: www.ericwilsonsart.com

WOOTTON, Tim
T: 01856 831 336; E: tim.wootton@tiscali.co.uk;
http://tim-wootton.blogspot.co.uk

WOODHEAD, Darren
T: 01620 823 213; E: via website;
W: www.darrenwoodheadartist.co.uk

WOOLF, Colin
T: 01852 500 232; E: sales@wildart.co.uk;
W: www.wildlifewatercolourpaintings.co.uk

Neil Gartshore

With the disruptions of 2020, many businesses offering tours for birdwatchers have struggled, along with the local economies that they support. Why not start planning your next trip? Whether you want to stay in the UK or travel overseas, there are plenty of destinations to choose from.

TRADE DIRECTORY

BIRD GARDEN SUPPLIERS

In this section you'll find a comprehensive guide to UK-based companies offering products or services of particular interest to active birdwatchers and wildlife enthusiasts. The aim is to make this directory as up-to-date and comprehensive as possible so if we've overlooked any companies that you feel should be included in future editions, please contact us with the relevant details (see page 6).

If you contact any of these companies please mention *'The Birdwatcher's Yearbook'*.

BIRD GARDEN SUPPLIERS

ARK WILDLIFE LTD
Dog Kennel Farm, Charlton Road, Nr Hitchin, Hertfordshire SG5 2AB; T: 0800 085 4865; E: via website; W: www.arkwildlife.co.uk

BAMFORDS
Globe Mill, Midge Hall, Leyland, Lancashire PR26 6TN; T: 01772 456 300; E: sales@bamfords.co.uk; W: www.bamfords.co.uk

BRINVALE BIRD FOODS
Brinvale Farm, Broughton Lane, Long Clawson, Melton Mowbray, Leicestershire LE14 4NB; T: 01664 823 230; E: info@brinvale.com; W: www.brinvale.com

CJ WILDBIRD FOODS LTD
The Rea, Upton Magna, Shrewsbury, Shropshire SY4 4UR; T: 0800 731 2820; E: sales@birdfood.co.uk; W: www.birdfood.co.uk

EYEBROOK WILD BIRD FEEDS
Rectory Farm, Great Easton, Market Harborough, Leicestershire LE16 8SN; T: 01536 770 771; E: rectoryfarm@eyebrookwildbirdfeeds.co.uk; W: www.eyebrookwildbirdfeeds.co.uk

GARDENATURE
801 Fowler Road, Oakwood Business Park North, Clacton on Sea, Essex CO15 4AA; T: 01255 514 451; E: via website; W: www.gardennature.co.uk

GARDEN WILDLIFE DIRECT
Unit 1 Industrial, Millennium City Park, Millennium Road, Preston, Lancashire PR2 5BL; T: 01772 440 242; E: help@gardenwildlifedirect.co.uk; W: www.gardenwildlifedirect.co.uk

JACOBI JAYNE & CO
Wealden Forest Park, Herne Common, Herne Bay, Kent CT6 7LQ; T: 0800 072 0130; E: enquiries@livingwithbirds.com; W: www.livingwithbirds.com

KENNEDY WILD BIRD FOODS LTD
The Warehouse, 74 Station Rd, Deeping St James, Peterborough, PE6 8RQ; T: 01778 342 665; E: info@kennedywildbirdfood.co.uk; W: www.kennedywildbirdfood.co.uk

NATURE CAMERAS
176 Hungate Street, Aylsham, Norwich, Norfolk NR11 6JZ; T: 07706 427 618; E: sales@stealthbirding.com; W: www.naturecameras.co.uk

NUTBAGS
7 Hampton Close, Blackfield, Southampton, Hampshire SO45 1WQ; T: 02380 894 132; E: via website; W: www.nutbags.co.uk

THE NESTBOX COMPANY
Eastcote House, Barston Lane, Eastcote, Solihull, West Midlands B92 0HS; T: 01675 442 299; E: mail@nestbox.co.uk; W: www.nestbox.co.uk

THE OWL BOX
Tyddyn Waen, Nr Llangaffo, Isle of Anglesey, North Wales LL60 6LP; T: 01248 421 091; E: info@theowlbox.co.uk; W: www.theowlbox.co.uk

SOAR MILL SEEDS
Globe Mill, Midge Hall Lane, Leyland, Lancashire PR26 6TN; T: 01772 456 317; E: sales@soarmillseeds.co.uk; W: www.soarmillseeds.co.uk

VINE HOUSE FARM BIRD FOODS
Vine House Farm, Main Rd, Deeping St Nicholas, Spalding, Lincolnshire PE11 3DG; T: 01775 630 208; E: via website; W: www.vinehousefarm.co.uk

WALTER HARRISON & SONS
Pedigree House, Ambleside, Gamston, Nottingham, NG2 6NQ; T: 0115 982 3900; E: via website; W: www.walterharrisons.com

BIRD & WILDLIFE PUBLICATIONS

BBC WILDLIFE
Subscriptions: BBC Wildlife Magazine, 3 Queensbridge, Northampton, NN4 7BF; T: 03330 162 121; E: via website; W: www.discoverwildlife.com/subscribe/

BIRDWATCH
Subscriptions: The Chocolate Factory, 5 Clarendon Road, London N22 6XJ; T: 01778 392 027; E: birdwatchsubs@warnersgroup.co.uk; W: www.birdguides.com

BIRD WATCHING
Subscriptions: Tower House, Sovereign Park, Market Harborough, Leicestershire LE16 9EF; T: 01858 438 884; E: bauer@subscription.co.uk; W: www.birdwatching.co.uk

BRITISH BIRDS
Subscriptions: 4 Harlequin Gardens, St Leonards-on-Sea, East Sussex TN37 7PF; T: 01424 755 155; E: subscriptions@britishbirds.co.uk; W: www.britishbirds.co.uk

BRITISH WILDLIFE PUBLISHING (part of NHBS Ltd)
Subscriptions: 1-6 The Stables, Ford Road, Totnes, Devon TQ9 5LE; T: 01803 467 166; E: subs@britishwildlife.com; W: www.britishwildlife.com

BOOK PUBLISHERS

BLOOMSBURY PUBLISHING
(inc Helm, Poyser, New Holland)
50 Bedford Square, London WC1B 3DP; T: 0207 631 5600; E: contact@bloomsbury.com; W: www.bloomsbury.com/uk/non-fiction/natural-history/

BRADT TRAVEL GUIDES LTD
31a High Street, Chesham, Bucks HP5 1BW; T: 01753 893 444; E: info@bradtguides.com; W: www.bradtguides.com

BRAMBLEBY BOOKS
15 Lyngford Square, Taunton, Somerset TA2 7ES; T: 01823 259 615; E: info@bramblebybooks.co.uk; W: www.bramblebybooks.co.uk

BUCKINGHAM PRESS LTD
55 Thorpe Park Road, Peterborough PE3 6LJ; T: 01733 561 739; E: buckinghampress@btinternet.com; W: www.buckinghampress.co.uk

HARPER COLLINS PUBLISHERS
103 Westerhill Road, Bishopbriggs, Glasgow, G64 2QT; T: 0141 306 3100; E: enquiries@harpercollins.co.uk; W: www.harpercollins.co.uk

PELAGIC PUBLISHING
E: via website; W: www.pelagicpublishing.com

PRINCETON UNIVERSITY PRESS (inc WILDGUIDES)
6 Oxford Street, Woodstock, Oxfordshire OX20 1TR; T: 01993 814 500; E: sales@press.princeton.edu; W: www.press.princeton.edu/wildguides

THE SOUND APPROACH
Enefco House, 19 The Quay, Poole, Dorset BH15 1NF; T: 01202 641 004; E: enquiries@soundapproach.co.uk; W: www.soundapproach.co.uk

WHITTLES PUBLISHING
Dunbeath Mill, Dunbeath, Caithness, KW6 6EG; T: 01593 731 333; E: info@whittlespublishing.com; W: www.whittlespublishing.com

BOOK SELLERS

ATROPOS BOOKS
The Boat House, Church Cove, Lizard, Nr Helston, Cornwall TR12 7PH; T: 01326 290 287; E: books@atropos.info; W: www.atroposbooks.co.uk

CALLUNA BOOKS
Moor Edge, 2 Bere Road, Wareham, Dorset BH20 4DD; T: 01929 552 560; E: enquiries@callunabooks.co.uk; W: www.callunabooks.co.uk

KEN MULLINS BOOKS
2 Wroxham Close, Upton, Birkenhead, CH49 0UY; T: 07866 479 010; E: kendonago@hotmail.com

NHBS (Natural History Book Service + equipment)
1-6 The Stables, Ford Road, Totnes, Devon TQ9 5XN; T: 01803 865 913; E: customer.service@nhbs.com; W: www.nhbs.com

PANDION BOOKS
23 Wickham Close, Bideford, Devon T: 01237 459 731; E: pandionbks@aol.com

PICTURE BOOK
6 Stanley Street, Leek, Staffs ST13 5HG; T: 01538 399 033; E: info@leekbooks.co.uk; W: www.leekbooks.co.uk

SECOND NATURE
Knapton Bookbarn, Back Lane, Knapton, York, YO26 6QJ; T: 01904 795 489;
E: secondnatureyork@aol.com

STEVE HOLLIDAY (Bird Reports/Journals)
2 Larriston Place, Cramlington, Northumberland NE23 8ER; T: 01670 731 963 (eves/w.ends);
E: birdreports@hotmail.co.uk

WILDSIDE BOOKS
29 Kings Avenue, Eastbourne, East Sussex BN21 2PE; T: 01323 416 211;
E: wildsidebooks@hotmail.com

WILD SOUNDS & BOOKS (+ equipment)
Roses Pightle, Cross Street, Salthouse, Norfolk NR25 7XH; T: 01263 741 100;
E: isales@wildsounds.com;
W: www.wildsounds.com

CLOTHING SUPPLIERS

COUNTRY INNOVATION
The Granary, The Stables Business Park, Rooksbridge, Somerset BS26 2TT; T: 01934 877 333;
E: sales@countryinnovation.com;
W: www.countryinnovation.com

FREET (shoes & boots)
16 High Garth, Richmond, North Yorkshire DL10 4DG; T: 01748 900 421;
E: freet@freet.uk; W: www.freet.uk

PARAMO DIRECTIONAL CLOTHING SYSTEMS
Durgates Industrial Estate, Wadhurst, East Sussex TN5 6DF; T: 01892 786 444; E: via website;
W: www.paramo-clothing.com

ROHAN
30 Maryland Road, Tongwell, Milton Keynes, Bucks MK15 8HN; T: 0800 840 1412;
E: post@rohan.co.uk; W: www.rohan.co.uk

TILLEY ENDURABLES
6 Tresprison Court, Helston, Cornwall TR13 0QD;
T: 01326 574 402; E: via website;
W: www.tilley.com

EQUIPMENT SUPPLIERS

LOWEPRO
Vitec Imaging Distribution UK, Resolution Road, Ashby-de-la-Zouch, Leicestershire LE65 1DW;
T: 01530 566 090; E: via website;
W: www.lowepro.com/uk-en/

(THE) BIRDERS STORE
Unit 4a King Charles Place, St Johns, Worcester, WR2 5AJ; T: 01905 312 877;
E: sales@birders-store.co.uk;
W: www.birders-store.co.uk

(THE) ONE STOP NATURE SHOP
9 Dalegate Market, Burnham Deepdale, Norfolk PE31 8FB; T: 01485 211 223;
E: sales@onestopnature.co.uk;
W: www.onestopnature.co.uk

OUTDOOR PHOTOGRAPHY GEAR
c/o Armadillo Storage, 73 Manchester Road, Warrington, Cheshire WA1 4AE; T: 01925 555 727;
E: sales@outdoorphotographygear.co.uk;
W: www.outdoorphotographygear.co.uk

SCOPAC
T: 07810 560 916; E: enquiries@scopac.co.uk;
W: www.scopac.co.uk

WILDLIFE WATCHING SUPPLIES
The Workshop, Town Living Farmhouse, Puddington, Tiverton, Devon EX16 8LW;
T: 01884 860 692;
E: enquiries@wildlifewatchingsupplies.co.uk;
W: www.wildlifewatchingsupplies.co.uk

HOLIDAY COMPANIES

AIGAS FIELD CENTRE
Beauly, Inverness-shire IV4 7AD; T: 01463 782 443;
E: info@aigas.co.uk; W: www.aigas.co.uk

ART SAFARI
Harbourmaster's Office, Ferry Quay, Woodbridge, Suffolk IP12 1BW; T: 01394 382 235;
E: via website; W: www.artsafari.co.uk

AVIAN ADVENTURES
49 Sandy Road, Norton, Stourbridge, Worcs DY8 3AJ; T: 01384 372 013;
E: avianadventures@btinternet.com;
W: www.avianadventures.co.uk

BIRDFINDERS
Westbank, Cheselbourne, Dorset DT2 7NW;
T: 01258 839 066; E: birdfinders@aol.co.uk;
W: www.birdfinders.co.uk

BIRD HOLIDAYS LTD
10 Ivegate, Yeadon, Leeds, LS19 7RE;
T: 0113 3910 510; E: info@birdholidays.co.uk;
W: www.birdholidays.co.uk

HOLIDAY COMPANIES

(THE) BIRD ID COMPANY
Church Farm House, Church Lane, Hindolveston, Norfolk NR20 5BT;
T: 01263 861 892; E: info@birdtour.co.uk;
W: www.birdtour.co.uk

BIRDWATCHING BREAKS
Cygnus House, Gordon's Mill, Balblair, Ross-shire IV7 8LQ; T: 01381 610 495;
E: via website;
W: www.birdwatchingbreaks.com

BIRD WATCHING & WILDLIFE CLUB
Grant Arms Hotel, 25 The Square, Grantown-on-Spey, Highlands PH26 3HF;
T: 0800 043 8585; E: booking@bwwc.co.uk;
W: www.bwwc.co.uk

BIRDWATCHING TRIPS WITH THE BIGGEST TWITCH
Alan Davies & Ruth Miller, 12 Ormeside Court, 19 Church Walks, Llandudno, LL30 2HG;
T: 01492 872 407;
E: info@birdwatchingtrips.co.uk;
W: www.birdwatchingtrips.co.uk

BIRDQUEST LTD
Two Jays, Kemple End, Stonyhurst, Clitheroe, Lancashire BB7 9QY; T: 01254 826 317;
E: birders@birdquest-tours.com;
W: www.birdquest-tours.com

BRITISH-BULGARIAN SOCIETY
Balkania Travel, Conex House, 148 Field End Road, Eastcote, Middlesex HA5 1RJ; T: 020 7536 9400;
E: ognian@balkaniatravel.com;
W: www.bulgariatours.co.uk

BUTEO WILDLIFE
14 Coolgardie Avenue, London, E4 9HP;
T: n/a; E: info@buteowildlife.co.uk;
W: www.buteowildlife.co.uk

(THE) DORSET BIRDING AND WILDLIFE EXPERIENCE
Moor Edge, 2 Bere Road, Wareham, Dorset BH20 4DD; T: 01929 552 560;
E: birding@callunabooks.co.uk;
W: www.callunabooks.co.uk

DUNGENESS & ROMNEY MARSH BIRD TOURS
Paul Trodd, Plovers, 1 Toby Road, Lydd-on-Sea, Romney Marsh, Kent TN29 9PG;
T: 01797 366 935; E: troddy@plovers.co.uk;
W: www.plovers.co.uk

EXPERIENCE NATURE
T: 07704 189 835;
E: experiencenaturetours@gmail.com;
W: www.experiencenature.co.uk

GLENLOY WILDLIFE
Glenloy Lodge, Banavie, Fort William, Highlands PH33 7PD; T: 01397 712 700;
E: info@glenloywildlife.co.uk;
W: www.glenloywildlife.co.uk

GREENTOURS NATURAL HISTORY HOLIDAYS
8 Eliot Close, Armitage, Rugeley, WS15 4UP;
T: 01298 83563; E: enquiries@greentours.co.uk;
W: www.greentours.co.uk

HEATHERLEA (SCOTLAND) LTD
The Mountview Hotel, Nethy Bridge, Inverness-shire PH25 3EB; T: 01479 821 248;
E: info@heatherlea.co.uk;
W: www.heatherlea.co.uk

LIMOSA HOLIDAYS
West End Farmhouse, Chapelfield, Stalham, Norfolk NR12 9EJ; T: 01692 580 623;
E: info@limosaholidays.co.uk;
W: www.limosaholidays.co.uk

NATURETREK
Mingledown Barn, Wolf's Lane, Chawton, Alton, Hampshire GU34 3HJ; T: 01962 733 051;
E: info@naturetrek.co.uk; W: www.naturetrek.co.uk

NATURES IMAGES
4 Deer Park Drive, Newport, Shropshire TF10 7HB; T: 01952 411 436;
E: mark@natures-images.co.uk;
W: www.natures-images.co.uk

NORTH WEST BIRDS
Mike Robinson, Barn Close, Beetham, Cumbria LA7 7AL; T: 01539 563 191;
E: mike@nwbirds.co.uk; W: www.nwbirds.co.uk

ORCADIAN WILDLIFE
Gerraquoy, St. Margaret's Hope, South Ronaldsay, Orkney KW17 2TH; T: 01856 831 240;
E: enquiries@orcadianwildlife.co.uk;
W: www.orcadianwildlife.co.uk

ORIOLE BIRDING
The Manor House, Great Ryburgh, Norfolk NR21 0DX;
T: 0800 999 3036; E: info@oriolebirding.com;
W: www.oriolebirding.com

ORNITHOLIDAYS
[Managed by SKUA Nature Group, Italy]
T: 0208 144 9814; E: info@ornitholidays.com;
W: www.ornitholidays.com

SARUS BIRD TOURS
12 Walton Drive, Bury, Lancashire BL9 5JU;
T: 0161 761 7279; E: sarus@sarusbirdtours.co.uk;
W: www.sarusbirdtours.co.uk

SHETLAND NATURE
c/o Burkle, Fair Isle, Shetland ZE2 9JU;
T: 01595 760 333; E: info@shetlandnature.net;
W: www.shetlandnature.net

SHETLAND WILDLIFE
Windy Stacks, Quendale, Shetland ZE2 9JD;
T: 01950 460 939; E: info@shetlandwildlife.co.uk;
W: www.shetlandwildlife.co.uk

SPEYSIDE WILDLIFE
Wester Camerorie, Ballieward, Grantown-on-Spey, Highlands PH26 3PR; T: 01479 812 498;
E: enquiries@speysidewildlife.co.uk;
W: www.speysidewildlife.co.uk

SUNBIRD
26B The Market Square, Potton, Sandy, Beds SG19 2NP; T: 01767 262 522;
E: sunbird@sunbirdtours.co.uk;
W: www.sunbirdtours.co.uk

THINK GALAPAGOS
Think Galapagos, 34 Woodlands, Beverley HU17 8BX; T: 01482 887 453;
E: info@thinkgalapagos.com;
W: www.thinkgalapagos.com

(THE) TRAVELLING NATURALIST
Long Barn South, Sutton Manor Farm, Bishop's Sutton, Alresford, Hampshire SO24 0AA;
T: 01305 267 994;
E: sales@thetravellingnaturalist.com;
W: www.naturalist.co.uk

WILD ABOUT TRAVEL
25 Sapley Road, Hartford, Huntingdon, Cambs PE29 1YG; T: 01480 370 593;
E: info@wildabouttravel.co.uk;
W: www.wildabouttravel.co.uk

WILD INSIGHTS
Yew Tree Farmhouse, Craignant, Selattyn, Oswestry, Shropshire SY10 7NP;
T: 01691 718 740; E: keith@keithofford.co.uk;
W: www.wildinsights.co.uk

WILDFOOT TRAVEL
Travel House, 133 Gravel Lane, Wilmslow, Cheshire SK9 6EG; T: 0800 195 3385;
E: info@wildfoottravel.com;
W: www.wildfoottravel.com

WILDLIFE TRAVEL
The Manor House, Broad St, Great Cambourne, Cambridge, CB23 6DH; T: 01954 713 575;
E: wildlifetravel@wildlifebcn.org;
W: www.wildlife-travel.co.uk

WILDLIFE WORLDWIDE
Long Barn South, Sutton Manor Farm, Bishop's Sutton, Alresford, Hampshire SO24 0AA;
T: 01962 302 086;
E: reservations@wildlifeworldwide.com;
W: www.wildlifeworldwide.com

WILDWINGS
Fords Farm, Guildford Road, Pirbright, Woking GU24 0LW; T: 0117 9658 333;
E: tours@wildwings.co.uk;
W: www.wildwings.co.uk

WISE BIRDING HOLIDAYS LTD
3 Moormead, Budleigh Salterton, Devon EX9 6QA; T: 07973 483 227;
E: chris@wisebirding.co.uk;
W: www.wisebirding.co.uk

YORKSHIRE COAST NATURE
Highfield Farm, Southburn, Driffield, East Yorkshire YO25 9AF; T: 01723 865 498;
E: enquiries@yorkshirecoastnature.co.uk;
W: www.yorkshirecoastnature.co.uk

OPTICAL DEALERS

ACE OPTICS
16 Green St, Bath, BA1 2JZ; T: 01225 466 364;
E: via website; W: www.aceoptics.co.uk

BIRDNET OPTICS LTD
5 Trenchard Drive, Harpur Hill, Buxton, Derbyshire SK17 9JY; T: 01298 71844;
E: paulflint@birdnet.co.uk; W: www.birdnet.co.uk

BRESSER UK
Suite 3G, Eden House, Enterprise Way, Edenbridge, Kent TN8 6HF; T: 01342 837 098;
E: sales@bresseruk.com;
W: www.bresseruk.com

CLEY SPY
Manor Farm Barns, Glandford, Holt, Norfolk NR25 7JP; T: 01263 740 088; E: via website;
W: www.cleyspy.co.uk

CLIFTON CAMERAS
28 Parsonage Street, Dursley, Gloucestershire GL11 4AA; T: 01453 548 128;
E: sales@cliftoncameras.co.uk;
W: www.cliftoncameras.co.uk

FOCALPOINT OPTICS
Sevenoaks Saw Mill, Antrobus, Cheshire CW9 6JB;
T: 01925 730 399; E: focalpoint@dial.pipex.com;
W: www.fpoint.co.uk

FOCUS OPTICS
Church Lane, Corley, Coventry, CV7 8BA; T: 01676 540 501; E: enquiries@focusoptics.eu; W: www.focusoptics.eu

H.A.BAKER (LEWES) LTD
44 High Street, Lewes, East Sussex BN7 2DD; T: 01273 476 479; E: sales@habaker.co.uk; W: www.habakerltd.co.uk

IN FOCUS
E: enquiries@infocusoptics.co.uk; T: 01727 827 799; W: www.at-infocus.co.uk

Hertfordshire: Willows Farm, Coursers Road, Colney Heath, Hertfordshire AL4 0PF; T: 01727 827 799

Lancashire: Brockholes, Preston New Road, Samlesbury, Preston, Lancashire PR5 0AG; T: 01704 897 020

Norfolk: Main Street, Titchwell, Nr. King's Lynn, Norfolk PE31 8BB; T: 01485 210 101

Rutland: Anglian Water Birdwatching Centre, Egleton Reserve, Rutland Water, Rutland LE15 8BT; T: 01572 770 656

Somerset: **The Stables Business Park, Bristol Road, Rooks Bridge, BS26 2TT**; T: 01934 750 090

Yorkshire: Westleigh House, Wakefield Road, Denby Dale, West Yorkshire HD8 8QJ; T: 01484 864 729

LONDON CAMERA EXCHANGE
T: 01962 670 007 (online orders); E: shops via website; W: www.lcegroup.co.uk

Bath: 13 Cheap Street, Bath, Avon BA1 1NB; T: 01225 462 234

Bristol (Baldwin Street): 3 Alliance House, Bristol, BS1 1SA; T: 0117 929 1935

Bristol (Broadmead): 53 The Horsefair, Bristol, BS1 3JP; T: 0117 927 6185

Cheltenham: 10-12 The Promenade, Cheltenham, GL50 1LR; T: 01242 519 851

Chester: 9 Bridge Street Row, Chester, CH1 1NW; T: 01244 326 531

Chichester: 17 Eastgate Square, Chichester, PO19 1JL; T: 01243 531 536

Colchester: 12 Eld Lane, Colchester, Essex CO1 1LS; T: 01206 573 444

Derby: 17 Sadler Gate, Derby, Derbyshire DE1 3NH; T: 01332 348 644

Exeter: 174 Fore Street, Exeter, Devon EX4 3AX; T: 01392 279 024

Gloucester: 12 Southgate Street, Gloucester, GL1 2DH; T: 01452 304 513

Guildford: 8/9 Tunsgate, Guildford, Surrey GU1 3QT; T: 01483 504 040

Hereford: 16 Widemarsh Street, Hereford, HR4 9EW; T: 01432 272 655

Leamington: 4C Lunn Poly House, Clarendon Avenue, Royal Leamington Spa, CV32 5PP; T: 01926 886 166

Lincoln: 6 Silver Street, Lincoln, LN2 1DY; T: 01522 514 131

London (Strand): 98 Strand, London WC2R 0EW; T: 0207 379 0200

Manchester: 16 Cross Street, Manchester, M2 7AE; T: 0161 834 7500

Newcastle: 76 High Street, Gosforth, Newcastle Upon Tyne, NE3 1HB; T: 0191 213 0060

Norwich: 12 Timber Hill, Norwich, Norfolk NR1 3LB; T: 01603 612 537

Nottingham: 7 Pelham Street, Nottingham, NG1 2EH; T: 0115 941 7486

Plymouth: 56 Cornwall Street, Plymouth, Devon PL1 1LR; T: 01752 664 894

Portsmouth: Kingswell Path, Cascades Shopping Centre, Portsmouth, PO1 4RR; T: 023 9283 9933

Reading: 7 Station Road, Reading, Berkshire RG1 1LG; T: 0118 959 2149

Southampton (Civic Centre): 11 Civic Centre Road, Southampton, Hants SO14 7FJ; T: 023 8033 1720

Southampton (High Street): 10 High Street, Southampton, Hants SO14 2DH; T: 023 8022 1597

Taunton: 6 North Street, Taunton, Somerset TA1 1LH; T: 01823 259 955

Winchester: 15 The Square, Winchester, Hampshire SO23 9ES; T: 01962 866 203

Worcester: 8 Pump Street, Worcester WR1 2QT; T: 01905 22314

PARK CAMERAS
T: 01444 237 070; E: sales@parkcameras.com; W: www.parkcameras.com

Burgess Hill: York Road, Burgess Hill, West Sussex RH15 9TT

London: 53-54 Rathbone Place, London W1T 1JR

SHERWOODS
The Arden Centre, Little Alne, Wootton Wawen, Henley-in-Arden, Warwickshire B95 6HW;
T: 01789 488 880;
E: sales@sherwoods-photo.com;
W: www.sherwoods-photo.com

SOUTH WEST OPTICS
22 River Street, Truro, Cornwall TR1 2SJ;
T: 01872 263 444; E: internet@swoptics.com;
W: www.swoptics.co.uk

UTTINGS
PO Box 672, Norwich, Norfolk NR3 2ZR;
T: 01603 619 811; E: via website;
W: www.uttings.co.uk

WEX PHOTOGRAPHIC
13 Frensham Road, Sweet Briar Industrial Estate, Norwich, Norfolk NR3 2BT;
T: 01603 486 413; E: via website;
W: www.wexphotographic.com

Belfast: Unit 2 Boucher Plaza,4-6 Boucher Road, Belfast, BT12 6HR; T: 028 9077 7770

Birmingham: Retail Unit 1, 100 Hagley Road, Birmingham, B16 8LT; T: 0121 326 7636

Bristol: Unit 7 Montpelier Central, Station Road, Montpelier, Bristol, BS6 5EE; T: 0117 942 2000

Edinburgh: Bonnington Business Centre, 110 Jane St, Edinburgh, EH6 5HG; T: 0131 553 9979

Glasgow: Block 4, Unit 1 Oakbank Industrial Estate, Off Garscube Road, Glasgow, G20 7LU;
T: 0141 353 0875

London: 37-39 Commercial Road, London, E1 1LF;
T: 020 7380 1144

Manchester: Unit 4, Downing Street Industrial Estate, Charlton Place, Manchester, M12 6HH;
T: 0161 274 4455

Milton Keynes: Unit 14 Lloyds Court, Silbury Boulevard, Milton Keynes, MK9 3EH;
T: 01908 843 000

Norwich: Unit B Frenbury Estate; Drayton High Road, Norwich, NR6 5DP; T: 01603 481 933

WILKINSON CAMERAS
Direct Sales: Unit 25 Charnley Fold, Bamber Bridge, Preston, PR5 6PS; T: 01772 252 188;
E: sales@wilkinson.co.uk; W: www.wilkinson.co.uk

Burnley: 95 James Street, Burnley, Lancs BB11 1PY; T: 01282 424 524

Bury: 61 The Rock, Bury, Greater Manchester, BL9 0NB; T: 0161 764 3402

Carlisle: 13 Grapes Lane, The Lanes Centre, Carlisle, Cumbria CA3 8NH; T: 01228 538 583

Kendal: Unit 19a, The Westmorland Centre, Stricklandgate, Kendal, Cumbria LA9 4LR;
T: 01539 735 055

Lancaster: 6 James Street, Lancaster, Lancs LA1 1UP; T: 01524 380 510

Liverpool: 4 Bold Street, Liverpool, L1 6DS;
T: 0151 255 0345

Preston: 27 Friargate, St George's Centre, Preston, Lancs PR1 2NQ; T: 01772 556 250

Southport: 38 Eastbank Street, Southport, Merseyside PR8 1ET; T: 01704 534 534

Warrington: 10 The Mall, The Golden Square, Warrington, WA1 1QE; T: 01925 638 290

OPTICAL IMPORTERS & MANUFACTURERS

ALPHA OPTICAL DISTRIBUTION LTD (Kite Optics)
Unit 39, Unity Business Centre, 26 Roundhay Road, Leeds, LS7 1AB; E: via website:
www.alphaodl.co.uk; W: www.kiteoptics.com

CANON UK LTD
Canon Support. T: 0207 660 0186;
E: store@cuk.canon.co.uk; W: www.canon.co.uk

CARL ZEISS LTD
ZEISS House, Building 1030, Cambourne Business Park, Cambourne, CB23 6DW;
T: 01223 401 500; E: customercare.uk@zeiss.com;
W: www.zeiss.co.uk

HAWKE
Avocet House, Wilford Bridge Rd, Melton, Woodbridge, Suffolk IP12 1RB;
T: 0345 345 5555; E: uk@hawkeoptics.com;
W: www.hawkeoptics.com

DAVID HINDS LTD (Celestron Optics)
Unit R, Cherrycourt Way, Leighton Buzzard, Bedfordshire LU7 4UH; T: 01525 852 696;
E: contact@dhinds.co.uk;
W: www.celestron.uk.com

INTRO 2020 (Steiner binos, Velbon & Slik tripods & more)
Unit 1, Priors Way, Maidenhead, Berks SL6 2HP;
T: 01628 799 901; E: sales@intro2020.co.uk;
W: www.intro2020.co.uk

KOWA OPTIMED
E: via website; W: www.kowaproducts.com

LEICA CAMERA LTD
64-66 Duke Street, Mayfair, London W1J 6JD; T: 0207 629 1351; E: onlinestore.uk@leica-camera.com; W: www.leica-camera.com

MANFROTTO IMAGE MORE
(inc. Manfrotto & Gitzo Tripods, Bushnell Optics)
Vitec Imaging Distribution, Resolution Rd, Ashby-de-la-Zouch, Leicestershire LE65 1DW; T: 01530 566 090; E: via website; W: www.manfrotto.co.uk

NEWPRO UK LTD (Vortex Optics, PhoneSkope)
3 Radcot Estate, Park Rd, Faringdon, Oxfordshire SN7 7BP; T: 01367 242 411; E: sales@newprouk.co.uk; W: www.newprouk.co.uk

NIKON UK LTD
1 The Crescent, Surbiton, Surrey KT6 4BN; T: 0330 123 0921; E: via website; W: www.nikon.co.uk

OPTICAL VISION LTD (Barr & Stoud, Helios, Acuter Optics)
Unit 3, Woolpit Business Park, Woolpit, Bury St Edmunds, Suffolk IP30 9UP; E: info:opticalvision.co.uk; W: www.opticalvision.co.uk

OPTICRON
Unit 21, Titan Court, Laporte way, Luton, Befordshire LU4 8EF; T: 01582 726 522; E: sales@opticron.co.uk; W: www.opticron.co.uk

SWAROVSKI OPTIK
(Repair service) Tarbot House Unit 11, Perrywood Business Park, Honeycrock Lane, Salfords, Surrey RH1 5JQ; T: 01737 856 812; Customer Service (Austria) T: 00800 3242 5056; E: customerservice@swarovskioptik.com; W: www.swarovskioptik.com

VANGUARD WORLD UK LTD
Unit 73, Basepoint Business Centre, Enterprise Close, Aviation Business Park, Christchurch, Dorset, BH23 6NX; T: 01202 651 281; E: info@vanguardworld.co.uk; W: www.vanguardworld.co.uk

VIKING OPTICAL LTD (Viking & RSPB Optics)
Blyth Road, Halesworth, Suffolk IP19 8EN; T: 01986 875 315; E: sales@vikingoptical.co.uk; W: www.vikingoptical.co.uk

OPTICAL REPAIRS & SERVICING

ACTION OPTICS
18 Butts Ash Gardens, Hythe, Southampton, SO45 3BL; T: 07402 590 740; E: richard@actionoptics.co.uk; W: www.actionoptics.co.uk

FIXATION UK LTD (Nikon/Canon repairs & servicing)
Unit C, 250 Kennington Lane, Lambeth, London SE11 5RD; T: 0207 582 3294; E: admin@fixationuk.com; W: www.fixationuk.com

INTRASIGHTS
4 Wharf Lane, Ilminster, Somerset TA19 0DT; T: 01460 54023; E: intrasights@gmail.com; W: www.intrasights.co.uk

OPTREP OPTICAL REPAIRS
16 Wheatfield Rd, Selsey, W. Sussex PO20 0NY; T: 01243 601 365; E: info@opticalrepairs.com; W: www.opticalrepairs.com

VIKING SERVICE & REPAIR CENTRE
Blyth Road, Halesworth, Suffolk IP19 8EN; T: 01986 875 315; E: repairs@vikingoptical.co.uk; W: www.vikingoptical.co.uk

TECHNOLOGY PRODUCTS

BIRD JOURNAL (Bluebird Technology)
1 Turnbridge Court, Swavesey, Cambridge, CB24 4GH; E: mail@birdjournal.com; W: www.birdjournal.com

BIRDGUIDES LTD
Warners Group Publications, The Chocolate Factory, 5 Clarendon Road, London N22 6XJ; T: 0208 881 0550; E: via website; W: www.birdguides.com

EASYBIRDER DVDS
Dave Gosney, Valley View Cottage, 15 Low Rd, Sheffield, S6 5FY; T: 0114 285 3712; E: dave@easybirder.co.uk; W: www.easybirder.co.uk

ISABELLINE FILMS
Steve Evans, 9 Milverton Close, Halesowen, W.Midlands B63 3QL; E: isabellineart@outlook.co.uk; W: www.isabelline.co.uk

Great Northern Diver *Gavia immer*

Neil Gartshore

Neil Gartshore

Summer visitors to the UK, Sedge *(Acrocephalus schoenobaenus)* - pictured above - & Reed Warblers *(A.scirpaceus)* generally share wetland habitats. The former tend to be more visible as they sing from a perch whilst the latter usually stick to the dense reedbeds, where they're more often heard than seen.

COUNTY DIRECTORY

COUNTY DIRECTORY - EXPLANATION OF HEADINGS

The Information in this directory has been obtained from a number of sources - including the persons listed and the relevant national body. In some cases, where it has not proved possible to verify the details directly, alternative responsible sources have been used. When no satisfactory source was available, previously included entries have sometimes had to be deleted. Readers are requested to advise the editor of any errors, omissions or changes (see page 6).

(*Note:* for completeness, n/a has been used where information is not available or has been withheld)

Bird Atlas/Avifauna
The more recent county publications are listed here. Many of these titles should still be available to buy new but if out of print try the second hand market - check out the booksellers listed in the Trade Directory.

Bird Recorder
The County Bird Recorder is the key point of contact in the area to deal with all aspects of bird records including rarities & rare breeding birds.

Bird Report
The annual county bird report is usually, but not exclusively, published by the county bird club. In some counties, annual reports are also published covering smaller recording areas. The *(date-)* refers to the start of the current title or, in some cases, its predecessor. In the first instance, contact the relevant person/ club for the current report (& back issues). Check out the booksellers listed in the Trade Directory to look for 'out of print' reports.

BTO Regional Representative
Your local BTO Rep is the first point of contact if you wish to help with national bird surveys in your county - get involved, make a difference!

Club
Many counties have their own independent county-wide bird/natural history clubs & some have smaller clubs based on particular areas of the county. Contact details are provided along with information about the indoor meetings.

Get in touch/check out the club website for membership information, to confirm indoor meeting dates/venues & for details about field trips & other club activities.

Ringing Group/Bird Observatory
For more information about becoming a licenced ringer, contact the BTO (see National Directory).

Active groups of ringers are well represented around the counties. The names of the groups are listed under each county - for further details check out their website (if they have one) or contact the BTO to forward your enquiry.

Bird Observatories are a great place to see birds at close quarters, many offer accommodation/events.

If you find a ringed bird, contact the BTO/or other organisation - details will be on the ring.

RSPB Local Group
Groups are active in most counties offering an excellent programme of talks & field trips through the year. Contact details are provided along with information about the indoor meetings.

Get in touch/check out the group website to confirm indoor meeting dates/venues & for details about field trips & other activities the group offers.

Wetland Bird Survey (WeBS) Local Organiser
Get involved with your local monthly wetland bird counts - for details of how to help contact your local organiser or contact the WeBS Office, BTO, The Nunnery, Thetford, Norfolk IP24 2PU. T: 01842 750 050; E: webs@bto.org

Wildlife Trust
Don't forget to check out your local Wildlife Trust who organise/run many talks, walks, events & other activities. The network of 46 independent Wildlife Trusts also manage a wide range of nature reserves providing valuable habitats for birds & other wildlife.

ENGLAND

BEDFORDSHIRE

Bird Atlas/Avifauna
An Atlas of the Breeding Birds of Bedfordshire 1988-92. RA Dazley & P Trodd (Bedfordshire Natural History Society, 1994).

The Birds of Bedfordshire. P Trodd & D Kramer (Castlemead Publications, 1991).

Bird Recorder
Vacant - temporary cover:
Peter Nash, 5 Coopers Close Sandy SG19 1NQ.
T: 07753 411 786; E: recorder@bedsbirdclub.org.uk

Bird Report
BEDFORDSHIRE BIRD REPORT (1946-), from Mary Sheridan, 28 Chestnut Hill, Linslade, Leighton Buzzard, LU7 2TR. T: 01525 378 245; E: membership@bnhs.org.uk

BTO Regional Representative
Roger Hicks. T: 01462 816 028;
E: rogerkhicks@hotmail.com

Judith Knight (Regional Development Officer).
T: n/a; E: judithknight@waitrose.com

Club

BEDFORDSHIRE BIRD CLUB. (1992; 280).
Sheila Alliez (Hon Sec), Flat 61 Adamson Court, Adamson Walk, Kempston, Bedford, MK42 8QZ.
T: 01234 855 227; E: sjalliez12@btinternet.com;
W: www.bedsbirdclub.org.uk
Meetings: 8.00pm, last Tuesday of the month (Sep-Mar). Maulden Village Hall, Maulden, MK45 2DN.

RSPB Local Group
BEDFORD. (1970; 80).
Carolyn Hawkes. T: 01234 768 136;
E: BedfordRSPBlocalgroup@gmail.com;
W: www.rspb.org.uk/groups/bedford
Meetings: 7.30pm, 3rd Thursday of the month (Sep-May). Aircraft Research Association, The Sports & Social Club, Manton Lane, Bedford, MK41 7PF.

Wetland Bird Survey (WeBS) Local Organiser
BEDFORDSHIRE. Richard Bashford.
T: via WeBS Office.
E: richard.bashford@rspb.org.uk

Wildlife Trust. See Cambridgeshire.

BERKSHIRE

Bird Atlas/Avifauna
The Birds of Berkshire. Neil Bucknell, Brian Clews, Renton Righelato & Chris Robinson (Birds of Berkshire Atlas Group, 2nd ed 2013).

Bird Recorder
Marek Walford. Address: n/a. T: n/a;
E: records@berksoc.org.uk

Bird Report
NEWBURY DISTRICT BIRD REPORT: Covers a 10-mile radius from Newbury Museum incl. parts of N Hants, S Oxon *(1960-)*, from Lesley Staves, 39 Priory Avenue, Hungerford, RG17 0BE.
T: 01488 682 301; E: enquiries@newburybirders.co.uk

THE BIRDS OF BERKSHIRE (1974-),
from Sally Wearing, 9 Deans Farm, The Causeway, Reading, RG4 5JZ. E: secretary@berksoc.org.uk

BTO Regional Representative
Sean Murphy. T: n/a; E: s.murphy@cabi.org

Club
BERKSHIRE ORNITHOLOGICAL CLUB. (1947; 300).
Iain Oldcorn (Membership Sec), 28 Huntsman Meadow, Ascot, SL5 7PF. T: 01344 625 883;
E: membership@berksoc.org.uk;
W: www.berksoc.org.uk
Meetings: 8pm, alternate Wednesdays (Sep-Apr). Room 109, Palmer Building, University of Reading, RG6 6UR (usually).

NEWBURY DISTRICT ORNITHOLOGICAL CLUB. (1959; 90). Mrs Lesley Staves (Sec).
Address: n/a; T: 01488 682 301;
E: enquiries@newburybirders.co.uk;
W: www.newburybirders.co.uk
Meetings: 7.30pm, monthly on a Thursday (Oct-Mar). Greenham Church Hall, New Road, Greenham, Newbury, RG19 8RZ.

THEALE AREA BIRD CONSERVATION GROUP. (1988; 75).
Catherine McEwan (Club Sec). Address: n/a.
T: 0118 9415 792; E: tabcgsec@yahoo.com; W: n/a.
Meetings: 8pm, 1st Tuesday of the month (all year). The Fox and Hounds Public House, Deans Copse Road, Reading, RG7 4BE.

Ringing Group/Bird Observatory
BERKSHIRE DOWNS RG.

MIDDLE THAMES RINGING GROUP.
W: https://middlethames.wordpress.com/

NEWBURY RG. W: www.newburyrg.co.uk

RUNNYMEDE RG. W: www.runnymederinging.uk

RSPB Local Group
EAST BERKSHIRE. (1974; 170).
Dave Pearson. T: 01628 639 648;
E: eastberks.rspb@gmail.com;
W: www.eastberksrspb.org.uk
Meetings: 7.30pm, 3rd Thursday of the month (Sep-Jun). Methodist Church Hall, King Street, Maidenhead, SL6 1EA.

READING. (1986; 130).
Carl Feltham. T: 0118 941 1713;
E: info@reading-rspb.org;
W: www.reading-rspb.org
Meetings: 8.00 pm, 2nd Tuesday of the month (Sep-Jun). Pangbourne Village Hall, Station Road, Pangbourne, Reading, RG8 7DY.

WOKINGHAM & BRACKNELL. (1979; 150).
Patrick Crowley. T: 01344 776 473;
E: RSPBwandb@gmail.com;
W: www.rspb.org.uk/groups/wokinghamandbracknell
Meetings: 7.45pm, 2nd Thursday of the month (Sep-Jun). Finchampstead Memorial Hall, The Village, Finchampstead, Wokingham, RG40 4JU.

Wetland Bird Survey (WeBS) Local Organiser
BERKSHIRE. Sean Murphy T: 01344 890 840;
E: seantmurphy8@gmail.com

Wildlife Trust. See Oxfordshire.

BUCKINGHAMSHIRE

Bird Atlas/Avifauna
The Birds of Buckinghamshire. David Ferguson (Buckingham Bird Club, 2nd ed 2012).

Bird Recorder
Mike Wallen, 15 Bennetts Lane, Rowsham, HP22 4QU.
T: 07976 560 040;
E: Recorder@bucksbirdclub.co.uk

Bird Report
BUCKINGHAMSHIRE BIRD REPORT (1980-), from Rob Andrews, 69 Stoke Road, Aylesbury, HP21 8BL. T: 01442 827925; E: r.andrews18@btinternet.com or E: conservation@bucksbirdclub.co.uk

BTO Regional Representative
Phil Tizzard. T: 01280 812 427;
E: phil.tizzard@care4free.net

Club
AMERSHAM BIRDWATCHING CLUB. (n/a; 80).
Eileen Tanner (Sec). Address: n/a. T: n/a;
E: secretary@amershambirdwatchingclub.co.uk;
W: www.amershambirdwatchingclub.co.uk
Meetings: 7.45pm, 3rd Friday of the month (Sep-May). Barn Hall Community Centre, hiltern Avenue, Amersham, HP6 5AH.

BUCKINGHAMSHIRE BIRD CLUB. (1981; 340).
Bill Parker (Sec). Address: n/a; T: n/a;
E: Secretary@bucksbirdclub.co.uk;
W: www.bucksbirdclub.co.uk
Meetings: 7.30pm, 1st Thursday of the month (Oct-Dec/Feb-Apr). St Anne's Hall, Aylesbury Road, Wendover, HP22 6JG.

Ringing Group/Bird Observatory
COLNE VALLEY RG.

HUGHENDEN RG.

RUNNYMEDE RG. W: www.runnymederinging.uk

RSPB Local Group
AYLESBURY. (1981; 80).
Anne Fisher. T: 01844 215 924;
E: anne.fisher50@yahoo.co.uk;
W: www.rspb.org.uk/groups/aylesbury
Meetings: 7.30pm, last Monday of the month (Sep-May). Prebendal Farm Community Centre, Fowler Road, Aylesbury, HP19 7QW.

NORTH BUCKS. (1976; 540).
Jane Grisdale. T: 07999 878 689,;
E: jane.grisdale@googlemail.com;
W: www.rspb.org.uk/groups/northbucks
Meetings: 7.45pm, 2nd Thursday of the month (Sep-May). Cruck Barn, City Discovery Centre, Alston Drive, Bradwell Abbey, Milton Keynes, MK13 9AP.

Wetland Bird Survey (WeBS) Local Organiser
BUCKINGHAMSHIRE (NORTH).
Vacant - contact WeBS Office.

BUCKINGHAMSHIRE (SOUTH).
Vacant - contact WeBS Office.

Wildlife Trust. See Oxfordshire.

CAMBRIDGESHIRE

Bird Atlas/Avifauna
Cambridgeshire Bird Atlas 2007-2011.
Louise Bacon, Alison Cooper & Hugh Venables (Cambridge Bird Club, 2013).

The Birds of Cambridgeshire. PMM Bircham (Cambridge University Press, 1989/pbk ed 2009).

Bird Recorder
Louise Bacon. Address: n/a. T: n/a;
E: recorder@cambridgebirdclub.org.uk

Bird Report
CAMBRIDGESHIRE BIRD REPORT (1927-), from Bruce Martin, 178 Nuns Way, Cambridge, CB4 2NS.
E: brucesmartin@virginmedia.com

BTO Regional Representative
CAMBRIDGESHIRE:
Rob Pople. T: n/a; E: robgpople@hotmail.com

HUNTINGDON & PETERBOROUGH.
Derek Langslow. T: 01733 232 153;
E: drldrl49@outlook.com

Club
CAMBRIDGESHIRE BIRD CLUB. (1925; 350+).
Michael Holdsworth (Sec),
4a Cavendish Ave, Cambridge, CB1 7US.
T: n/a; E: secretary@cambridgebirdclub.org.uk;
W: www.cambridgebirdclub.org.uk
Meetings: 8pm, 2nd Friday of the month (Sep-May). Either at St John's Church Hall, Hills Road, Cambridge CB2 8RN or Cottenham Village College, High Street, Cottenham, Cambridge, CB24 8UA.

PETERBOROUGH BIRD CLUB. (1998; 145).
David Cromack,
55 Thorpe Park Road,
Peterborough, PE3 6LJ.
T: 01733 566 815;
E: cromackd@gmail.com;
W: www.peterboroughbirdclub.com
Meetings: 7.30pm, last Tuesday of the month (Sep-Nov, Jan-Apr). PO Social Club, Bourges Boulevard, Peterborough, PE1 2AU.

Ringing Group/Bird Observatory
UPPER CAM RG.

WICKEN FEN RG.

RSPB Local Group
CAMBRIDGE. (1977; 80).
Andrew Law. T: 01799 501 790;
E: andylaw1954@gmail.com;
W: www.rspb.org.uk/groups/cambridge
Meetings: 7.30pm, 3rd Wednesday of the month (Sep-Nov/Jan-May). Wilkinson Room, St John's the Evangelist, Hills Road, Cambridge, CB2 8RN.

HUNTINGDONSHIRE. (1982; 100).
Mervyn Vickery. T: 01480 492 519;
E: mfvickery52@outlook.com;
W: www.rspb.org.uk/groups/huntingdonshire
Meetings: 7.30pm, last Wednesday of the month (Sep-Apr, Dec may be earlier in month). The Free Church, St Ives, Market Hill, St Ives, PE27 5AL.

Wetland Bird Survey (WeBS) Local Organiser
CAMBRIDGESHIRE (incl. HUNTINGDONSHIRE).
Bruce Martin. T: 01223 700 656;
E: brucemartin@virginmedia.com

NENE WASHES. Charlie Kitchin. T: 01733 205 140;
E: charlie.kitchin@rspb.org.uk

OUSE WASHES. Paul Harrington.
T: 01354 680 212; E: paul.harrington@rspb.org.uk

Wildlife Trust
THE WILDLIFE TRUST FOR BEDFORDSHIRE, CAMBRIDGESHIRE AND NORTHAMPTONSHIRE. (1994; 34,000).
The Manor House, Broad Street, Great Cambourne, Cambridge CB23 6DH.
T: 01954 713 500, (fax) 01954 710 051;
E: cambridgeshire@wildlifebcn.org;
W: www.wildlifebcn.org

CHESHIRE & WIRRAL

Bird Atlas/Avifauna
Rare and Scarce Birds in Cheshire and Wirral. Allan Conlin & Eddie Williams (privately published, 2017).

Birds in Cheshire and Wirral: A Breeding and Wintering Atlas. David Norman (Liverpool University Press, 2008).

Bird Recorder
Hugh Pulsford, 6 Buttermere Drive, Great Warford, Alderley Edge, SK9 7WA. T: 01565 880 171;
E: countyrec@cawos.org [also the Secretary of Association of County Recorders and Editors (ARCE)]

Bird Report
CHESHIRE & WIRRAL BIRD REPORT (1964), from
David Cogger, 71 Parkgate,
Knutsford, WA16 8HF.
T: 01565 228 503;
E: davidcogger@cawos.org

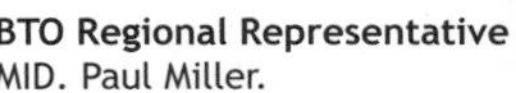

BTO Regional Representative
MID. Paul Miller.
T: 01928 787 535;
E: paulandhilarymiller@live.co.uk

NORTH & EAST. Hugh Pulsford. T: 01565 880 171;
E: ahugh.pulsford@btinternet.com

SOUTH. Hugh Pulsford - see above.

THE WIRRAL. Paul Miller - see above.

Club
CHESHIRE & WIRRAL ORNITHOLOGICAL SOCIETY. (1988; 310). Ted Lock (Sec), 2 Bourne Street, Wilmslow, SK9 5HD. T: 01625 540 466;
E: info@cawos.org; W: www.cawos.org
Meetings: 7.45pm, 1st Friday of the month (Oct-Mar). St Vincent's Church Hall, Tatton Street, Knutsford, WA16 6HR.

KNUTSFORD ORNITHOLOGICAL SOCIETY. (1974; 45).
Derek Pike (Sec). Address: n/a. T: 01565 653 811;
Press Officer/Website - E: tony@10x50.com;
W: www.10x50.com
Meetings: 8pm, 4th Friday of the month (Sept-Apr). Jubilee Hall, Stanley Road, Knutsford, WA16 0GP.

LANCASHIRE & CHESHIRE FAUNA SOCIETY.
See Lancashire.

MID-CHESHIRE ORNITHOLOGICAL SOCIETY. (1962; 60).
Ian Williams (Sec). Address: n/a. T: n/a;
E: secretary@midcheshireos.co.uk;
W: www.midcheshireos.co.uk
Meetings: 7:45pm, 2nd Friday of the month (Oct-Apr). Cuddington and Sandiway Village Hall, Norley Road, Cuddington, CW8 2LB.

NANTWICH NATURAL HISTORY SOCIETY. (1979; 65).
Roger Crow. T: n/a; E: roger.crow@hotmail.co.uk;
W: n/a
Meetings: No indoor meetings but regular social evenings relating to field work and surveys, usually in The Vine Pub, 42 Hospital Street, Nantwich, CW5 5RP.

SOUTH EAST CHESHIRE ORNITHOLOGICAL SOCIETY.
(1964; 120).
Colin Lythgoe (Chairman).
Address: n/a. T: n/a;
E: colin.lythgoe9@uwclub.net;
W: www.secos.org.uk
Meetings: 7.30pm, 2nd Friday of the month (Sep-Apr). Ettiley Heath Church Community Centre, Elton Road, Ettiley Heath, Sandbach, CW11 3NE.

WILMSLOW GUILD BIRDWATCHING GROUP. (1965; 65).
All members of the WGBG are required to be members of the Wilmslow Guild. T: 01625 523 903.
E: via website; W: www.wilmslowguild.org

Brian Dyke (Chairman WGBG). T: 01625 525 936;
W: http://wgbwcopy.wikidot.com/wgbg
Meetings: 7.30pm, usually last Friday of the month - but not always - (Sep-Apr). Wilmslow Guild, 1 Bourne Street, Wilmslow, SK9 5HD.

WIRRAL BIRD CLUB. (1977; 70).
Bill Wonderley. Address: n/a. T: 07795 148 140;
E: wirralbirdclub77@gmail.com;
W: www.wirralbirdclub.com
Meetings: 7.30pm, 4th Thursday of the month (Sep-Nov & Jan-Jul). St Bridget's Church Centre, St Bridget's Lane, West Kirby, CH48 3JT.

Ringing Group/Bird Observatory
CHESHIRE SWAN GROUP.
W: http://cheshireswanstudygroup.wordpress.com

SOUTH MANCHESTER RG.

HILBRE BIRD OBSERVATORY.
Steve Williams. T: 07976 205 574;
E: secretary@hilbrebirdobs.org.uk;
W: http://hilbrebirdobs.blogspot.com

RSPB Local Group
CHESTER. (1988; 140).
Norman Sadler. T: 01244 335 670;
E: rspbchester@googlegroups.com;
W: www.rspb.org.uk/groups/chester
Meetings: 7.30pm, 3rd Wednesday of the month (Sep-Apr). Christleton Parish Hall, Village Road, Christleton, CH3 7AS.

MACCLESFIELD. (1979; 145).
Ray Evans. T: 01625 432 635;
E: Secretary@macclesfieldRSPB.org.uk;
W: www.rspb.org.uk/groups/macclesfield
Meetings: 7.45pm, 2nd Tuesday of the month (Sep-May). Macclesfield Senior Citizens Hall, Duke Street Car Park, Macclesfield, SK11 6UR.

NORTH CHESHIRE. (1976; 80).
Paul Grimmett. T: 01925 268 770;
E: paulwtwitcher@hotmail.com;
W: www.rspb.org.uk/groups/north_cheshire
Meetings: 7.30pm, 3rd Friday of the month (Sep-Nov/Jan-Apr). Appleton Parish Hall, Dudlow Green Road, Appleton, Warrington, WA4 5EQ.

WIRRAL. (1982; 100).
Jeremy Bradshaw. T: 07769 673 018;
E: bradshaws1961@gmail.com;
W: www.rspb.org.uk/groups/wirral
Meetings: 7.30pm, 1st Thursday of the month (Sep-Jun). Bromborough Civic Centre, 2 Allport Lane, Wirral, CH62 7HR.

Wetland Bird Survey (WeBS) Local Organiser
CHESHIRE (NORTH). Phil Hampson. T: 07545 465 069;
E: pjhampers@icloud.com

CHESHIRE (SOUTH). Paul Miller. T: 01928 787 535;
E: paulandhilarymiller@live.co.uk

Wildlife Trust
CHESHIRE WILDLIFE TRUST. (1962; 14,000).
Bickley Hall Farm, Bickley, Malpas, SY14 8EF.
T: 01948 820 728, (fax) 0709 2888 469;
E: info@cheshirewt.org.uk;
W: www.cheshirewildlifetrust.org.uk

CORNWALL & ISLES OF SCILLY

Bird Atlas/Avifauna
The Essential Guide to Birds of The Isles of Scilly. Bob L Flood, N Hudson & B Thomas (privately published, 2007).

The Birds of the Isles of Scilly. Peter Robinson (Christopher Helm, 2003).

The Birds of Cornwall and the Isles of Scilly. RD Penhallurick (Browsers Bookshop, 1978).

Bird Recorder
CORNWALL. Dave Parker, 2 Boslevan, Green Lane, Marizion, TR17 0HQ. T: 07932 354 711; E: recorder@cbwps.org.uk

ISLES OF SCILLY. John Headon, Hivernia, Jackson's Hill, St Mary's, Isles of Scilly TR21 0JZ. T: 01720 423 540; E: recorder@scilly-birding.co.uk

Bird Report
BIRDS IN CORNWALL (1931-), from Phil Taylor (report editor). T: 01736 810 933; E: shimoryu@mac.com or E: birdsincornwall@cwps.org.uk

ISLES OF SCILLY BIRD REPORT and NATURAL HISTORY REVIEW (1969-), from Carole Cilia, Hivemia, Jackson's Hill, St Mary's, Isles of Scilly TR21 0JZ. T: 01720 423 540; E: carole.cilia@btinternet.com

BTO Regional Representative
CORNWALL. Simon Taylor. T: n/a; E: bto_cornwall@yahoo.com

CORNWALL. Sara Booth (Assistant Representative). T: n/a; E: sara28042002@yahoo.co.uk

ISLES OF SCILLY. Will Wagstaff. T: 01720 422 212; E: will@islandwildlifetours.co.uk

Club
CORNWALL BIRD WATCHING & PRESERVATION SOC. (1931; 1100). Phil McVey (Sec), Little Boslymon, Bodmin, PL30 5AP. T: 07740 923 385; E: secretary@cbwps.org.uk; W: www.cbwps.org.uk
Meetings: contact/see website for details.

ISLES OF SCILLY BIRD GROUP. (2000; 375). Carole Cilia, (Membership Sec), Hivemia, Jackson's Hill, St Mary's, Isles of Scilly TR21 0JZ. T: 01720 423 540; E: membership@scilly-birding.co.uk; W: www.scilly-birding.co.uk

Ringing Group/Bird Observatory
DEVON & CORNWALL WADER GROUP. W: www.dcwrg.org.uk/

WEST CORNWALL RG. W: http://cornishringing.blogspot.com/

RSPB Local Group
CORNWALL. (1972; 260). Roger Hooper. T: 01209 820 610; E: rogerwhooper@btinternet.com; W: www.rspb.org.uk/groups/cornwall
Meetings: On a Friday, (Sep-Apr). Chacewater Village Hall, Church Hill, nr Truro, TR4 8PZ - contact/see website for details.

Wetland Bird Survey (WeBS) Local Organiser
CORNWALL (excl. TAMAR COMPLEX). Derek Julian. T: 07725 557 331; E: camelbirder@btinternet.com

TAMAR COMPLEX. Charles Nodder. T: 01752 846 493; E: cnodder@msn.com.

Wildlife Trust
CORNWALL WILDLIFE TRUST. (1962; 18,000). Five Acres, Allet, Truro, TR4 9DJ. T: 01872 273 939, (fax) 01872 225 476; E: info@cornwallwildlifetrust.org.uk; W: www.cornwallwildlifetrust.org.uk

THE ISLES OF SCILLY WILDLIFE TRUST. (1984). Trenoweth, St Marys, Isles of Scilly TR21 0NS. T/fax: 01720 422 153; E: enquiries@ios-wildlifetrust.org.uk; W: www.ios-wildlifetrust.org.uk

CUMBRIA

Bird Atlas/Avifauna
The Breeding Birds of Cumbria: A Tetrad Atlas 1997-2001. M Stott, J Callion, I Kinley, C Raven & J Roberts (Cumbria Bird Club, 2002).

Bird Recorder
Chris Hind, 2 Old School House, Hallbankgate, Brampton, CA8 2NW. T: 01697 746 379; E: chris.m.hind@gmail.com

Regional Recorders
ALLERDALE & COPELAND. Nick Franklin. Address: n/a. T: 01228 810 413; E: nickbirder66@gmail.com

BARROW & SOUTH LAKELAND. Ronnie Irving, 24 Birchwood Close, Vicarage Park, Kendal, LA9 5BJ. T: 01539 727 523; E: ronnieirving2017@gmail.com

CARLISLE & EDEN. Chris Hind - see bird recorder.

Bird Report
BIRDS AND WILDLIFE IN CUMBRIA (1970-), from Dave Piercy, 64 The Headlands, Keswick, CA12 5EJ. T: 01768 773 201; E: info@cumbriabirdclub.org.uk

WALNEY BIRD OBSERVATORY REPORT (1964-), from Keith Parke (Sec), 77 Dalton Lane, Barrow-in-Furness, LA14 4LB. T: 01229 824 219; E: keith.parkes5@btopenworld.com

BTO Regional Representative
Colin Gay. T: 01229 773 820; E: colinathodbarrow@btinternet.com

Club
ARNSIDE & DISTRICT NATURAL HISTORY SOCIETY. (1960's; 200). Gail Armstrong (Sec), 1 Bottoms Lane, Silverdale, LA5 0TN. T: 01524 701 316; E: info@arnsideanddistrictnhs.co.uk; W: www.arnsideanddistrictnhs.co.uk
Meetings: 7.30pm, 2nd Thursday of the month (Sep-Mar). WI Hall, Orchard Rd, Arnside, LA5 0DP.

CUMBRIA BIRD CLUB. (1989; 330). Dave Piercy (Sec), 64 The Headlands, Keswick, CA12 5EJ. T: 01768 773 201; E: info@cumbriabirdclub.org.uk; W: www.cumbriabirdclub.org.uk
Meetings: Various evenings and venues (Oct-Mar) - contact/see website for details.

Ringing Group/Bird Observatory
EDEN RG.

MORECAMBE BAY WADER RG.

Watchtree
NATURE RESERVE

WATCHTREE RG. W: www.watchtree.co.uk

WALNEY BIRD OBSERVATORY. Keith Parkes (Sec), 77 Dalton Lane, Barrow-in-Furness, LA14 4LB. T: 01229 824 219; E: keith.parkes5@btopenworld.com; E (recorder): walneyobs@gmail.com; W: http://walneybo.blogspot.co.uk

RSPB Local Group
NORTH CUMBRIA. (1974; 200). Richard Dixon. T: 07720 067 283; E: sunzeco@hotmail.co.uk; W: www.rspb.org.uk/groups/carlisle
Meetings: 7.30pm, usually 2nd Wednesday (Sep-Mar). Tithe Barn, (Behind Marks & Spencer's), West Walls, Carlisle, CA3 8UF.

WEST CUMBRIA. (1986; 135). Dave Smith. T: 01900 85347; E: smida@talktalk.net; W: www.rspb.org.uk/groups/westcumbria
Meetings: 7.30pm, 1st Tuesday of the month (Sep-Apr). United Reformed Church, Main St, Cockermouth, CA13 9LU.

Wetland Bird Survey (WeBS) Local Organiser
CUMBRIA (excl. ESTUARIES). Dave Shackleton. T: via WeBS Office; E: d.shackleton@btinternet.com

DUDDON ESTUARY. Colin Gay. T: 01229 773 820; E: colinathodbarrow@btinternet.com

IRT/MITE/ESK ESTUARIES. Vacant - contact WeBS Office.

MORECAMBE BAY (NORTH). Mike Douglas. T: 01229 582 018; E: mail@thedouglasfamily.co.uk

SOLWAY ESTUARY (INNER SOUTH). David Blackledge. T: via WeBS Office; E: daveblackledge@rspb.org.uk

SOLWAY ESTUARY (NORTH). See Dumfries & Galloway.

SOLWAY ESTUARY (OUTER SOUTH). Dave Shackleton - see above.

Wildlife Trust
CUMBRIA WILDLIFE TRUST. (1962; 13,000). Plumgarths, Crook Road, Kendal, LA8 8LX. T: 01539 816 300, (fax) 01539 816 301; E: mail@cumbriawildlifetrust.org.uk; W: www.cumbriawildlifetrust.org.uk

DERBYSHIRE

Bird Atlas/Avifauna
The Birds of Derbyshire. RA Frost & Steve Shaw Liverpool University Press, 2014).

Bird Recorder
Joint Recorder. Rodney Key, 3 Farningham Close, Spondon, Derby, DE21 7DZ. T: 01332 678 571 & 07710 770 195; E: r_key@sky.com

Joint Recorder (Annual Report). Anthony Garton. Address: n/a. T: 01283 544 870; E: tonygarton13@sky.com

Rare Breeding Birds Recorder. Roy Frost, 66 St Lawrence Road, North Wingfield, Chesterfield, S42 5LL. T: 01246 850 037; E: frostra66@btinternet.com

Bird Report
CARSINGTON BIRD CLUB ANNUAL REPORT (1992-), from Gary Atkins, 18 Eaton Close, Hulland Ward, Ashbourne, DE6 3EX. E: garyatkins@aol.com

DERBYSHIRE BIRD REPORT (1955-), from Bryan Barnacle, Mays, Malthouse Lane, Froggatt, Hope Valley, S32 3ZA. E: barney@mays1.demon.co.uk

OGSTON BIRD CLUB REPORT (1970-), Mrs J Marshall, 94 Common Road, Huthwaite, Sutton-in-Ashfield, Nottinghamshire NG17 2JT. E: jen.marshall@birdinformation.co.uk

BTO Regional Representative
NORTH. Dave Budworth. T: 01283 215 188; E: dbud01@aol.com

SOUTH. Dave Budworth - see above.

Club
BAKEWELL BIRD STUDY GROUP. (1987; 70).
Brian Shaw (Chairman). Address: n/a.
T: 07768 928 432; E: drgbshaw@gmail.com;
W: www.bakewellbirdstudygroup.org.uk
Meetings: 7.30pm, 2nd Monday of the month (Sep-May). Friends Meeting House, Chapel Lane, Bakewell, DE45 1EL.

BUXTON FIELD CLUB. (1946; 50).
Pat Thompson (Sec), Flat 6, Temple Court, Temple Road, Buxton, SK17 9BA. T: 01298 938 920;
E: 4acrylics9@gmail.com; W: n/a
Meetings: 7.30pm, usually fortnightly on a Saturday (Oct-Mar). Buxton Methodist Church, Chapel Street, Buxton, SK17 6HX.

CARSINGTON BIRD CLUB. (1992; 250).
Roger Carrington (Sec), Address: n/a. T: n/a.
E: rcarrington_matlock@yahoo.co.uk;
W: www.carsingtonbirdclub.co.uk
Meetings: 7.30pm, 3rd Tuesday of the month (Sep-Mar). The Henmore Room, Carsington Water Visitor Centre, Big Lane, Ashbourne, DE6 1ST.

DERBYSHIRE ORNITHOLOGICAL SOCIETY. (1954; 550).
Steve Thorpe. Address: n/a. T: 07815 784 642:
E: derbyshirebirders@gmail.com;
W: www.derbyshireos.org.uk
Meetings: 7.30pm, usually last Friday of the month (Sep-Mar), various venues - contact/see website for details.

OGSTON BIRD CLUB. (1969; 125).
Jenny Marshall (Sec), 94 Common Road, Huthwaite, Sutton-in-Ashfield, Nottinghamshire NG17 2JT.
T: 07533 973 809;
E: jen.marshall@birdinformation.co.uk;
W: www.ogstonbirdclub.co.uk
Meetings: Currently only an AGM is held - contact/see website for details.

Ringing Group/Bird Observatory
SORBY-BRECK RG. See Yorkshire.

SOUDER RG.

RSPB Local Group
CHESTERFIELD. (1987; 275).
Wendy Dyson. T: n/a;
E: wendy2002khan@gmail.com;
W: www.rspb.org.uk/groups/chesterfield
Meetings: 7.15pm, (usually) 1st Monday of the month. St Thomass Centre, Chatsworth Road, Chesterfield, S40 3AW.

DERBY. (1974; 270).
Max Maughan. T: 01332 511 825;
E: RSPBlocalgroupderby@gmail.com;
W: www.rspb.org.uk/groups/derby
Meetings: 7.30pm, 2nd Wednesday of the month (Sep-Apr). The Grange Banqueting Suite, 457 Burton Rd, Littleover, Derby, DE23 6XX.

Wetland Bird Survey (WeBS) Local Organiser
DERBYSHIRE. Vacant - contact WeBS Office.

Wildlife Trust
DERBYSHIRE WILDLIFE TRUST. (1962; 14,000).
Sandy Hill, Main Street, Middleton, Matlock, DE4 4LR.
T: 01773 881 188, (fax) 01773 821 826;
E: enquiries@derbyshirewt.co.uk;
W: www.derbyshirewildlifetrust.org.uk

DEVON

Bird Atlas/Avifauna
Devon Bird Atlas 2007-2013. Stella D Beavan & Mike Lock (Devon Birdwatching & Preservation Society, 2016).

The Birds of Devon. Michael Tyler (Devon Birdwatching & Preservation Society, 2010).

The Birds of Lundy. Tim Davis & Tim Jones (Harpers Mill Publishing, 2007).

Bird Recorder
Kevin Rylands.
Address: n/a. T: n/a;
E: recorder@devonbirds.org

Bird Report
DEVON BIRDS (1929-), from Mike Daniels (Sec), Devon Birds, 16 Erme Drive, Ivybridge, PL21 9BN.
T: 01752 690 278; E: info@devonbirds.org

LUNDY FIELD SOCIETY ANNUAL REPORT (1947-) from Michael Williams (LFS Hon. Sec), 166 Wileman Way, Cambridge CB3 1AR.
E: secretary@lundy.org.uk

BTO Regional Representative
Stella Beavan. T: 07710 879 277;
E: stellabeavan@outlook.com

Club
DEVON BIRDS. (1928; 1200).
Mike Daniels (Sec, Devon Birds), 16 Erme Drive, Ivybridge, PL21 9BN. T: 01752 690 278;
E: secretary@devonbirds.org; W: www.devonbirds.org

Branches
East Devon:
Alex Parsons. T: 01392 669 842;
Meetings: No indoor meetings.

Mid Devon:
Nick Armstrong. T: 01363 866 860;
E: armstrongnick@gmail.com
Meetings: Occasional indoor meetings - contact/ see website for details.

Plymouth:
Liz Harris. T: 01752 789 594;
E: elizmharris@yahoo.com
Meetings: 7.30pm, (Sep-Apr). Spurgeon Hall, Mutley Baptist Church, Mutley Plain, Plymouth, PL4 6LB. For programme see
W: www.devonbirds.org

South Devon:
Mike Goss. T: 01364 72539. E: n/a.
Meetings: 7.30pm, 3rd Monday of the month (Jan-Nov). Church House, Slade Lane, Abbotskerswell, TQ12 5NZ.

Taw & Torridge:
John Towers. T: 01598 710 273.
E: john.towers@devonbirds.org
Meetings: 7.30pm, 2nd Tuesday of the month (Sep-Apr). The Castle Centre, 25 Castle Street, Barnstaple, EX31 1DR.

KINGSBRIDGE NATURAL HISTORY SOCIETY. (1989; 80).
Chris Klee (Chairman), The Old School House, 2 Ebrington Street, Kingsbridge, TQ7 1DF.
T: 01548 288 397; E: jcklee@pobroadband.co.uk;
W: www.knhs.org.uk
Meeting: 7.30pm, 4th Monday of the month (Sep-Apr). West Charleton Village Hall, West Charleton, Kingsbridge, TQ7 2AJ.

LUNDY FIELD SOCIETY. (1946; 525).
Michael Williams (Sec), 166 Wileman Way, Cambridge, CB3 1AR. T: n/a;
E: secretary@lundy.org.uk;
W: www.lundy.org.uk
Meeting: AGM, 2nd Saturday of Mar in Crediton.

TOPSHAM BIRDWATCHING & NATURALISTS' SOCIETY. (1969; 100).
Gordon Davis (Hon Sec). Address: n/a. T: n/a;
E: topshambns@gmail.com;
W: http://topshambns.blogspot.com
Meetings: 7.30pm, 2nd Friday of the month (Sep-Apr). Matthews Hall, Fore Street,Topsham, Exeter, EX3 0HF.

Ringing Group/Bird Observatory
AXE ESTUARY RG.
W: http://axeestuaryringinggroup.blogspot.co.uk

DEVON & CORNWALL WADER GROUP.
W: www.dcwrg.org.uk/

LUNDY FIELD SOCIETY.

SLAPTON BIRD OBSERVATORY RG.

RSPB Local Group
EXETER & DISTRICT. (1974; 220).
Richard Swinbank. T: 01404 813 666;
E: ExeterGroupLeader@RSPB.org.uk;
W: www.rspb.org.uk/groups/exeter
Meetings: 7.30 pm, 1st or 2nd Tuesday of the month, (Sep-Apr). Southernhay Hall, United Reformed Church, Southernhay East, Exeter, EX1 1QD.

PLYMOUTH. (1974; 200).
Vince Bedford. T: n/a; E: via website;
W: www.rspb.org.uk/groups/plymouth
Meetings: 7.30pm, usually on a Wednesday (Sep/Nov/Jan/Mar). Trinity United Reform Church, Tor Lane, Plymouth PL3 5NY - contact/see website for details.

TORBAY & SOUTH DEVON TEAM. (n/a; n/a).
Julie King. T: 01626 351 135;
E: king.julie@hotmail.co.uk;
W: www.rspb.org.uk/groups/torbayandsouthdevon
Meetings: Held at various locations in the area - contact/see website for details.

Wetland Bird Survey (WeBS) Local Organiser
DEVON (OTHER SITES). Peter Reay.
T: 01364 73293; E: peter.p.j.reay@btinternet.com

EXE ESTUARY. Martin Overy. T: via WeBS office;
E: mkovery@gmail.com

TAMAR COMPLEX. See Cornwall

TAW/TORRIDGE. Tim Davis. T: 01271 883 807;
E: tim.davis@djenvironmental.com

Wildlife Trust
DEVON WILDLIFE TRUST. (1962; 32,000).
Cricklepit Mill, Commercial Road, Exeter, EX2 4AB.
T: 01392 279 244, (fax) 01392 433 221;
E: contactus@devonwildlifetrust.org;
W: www.devonwildlifetrust.org

DORSET

Bird Atlas/Avifauna
The Birds of Dorset. George Green (Christopher Helm, 2004)

Bird Recorder
Recorder. Geoff Upton. Address: n/a.
T: n/a; E: sightings@dorsetbirdclub.co.uk

Recorder (Rarities). Ian Stanley. Address: n/a.
T: n/a; E: recorder@dorsetbirds.co.uk

Recorder (Rare Breeding Birds). Shaun Robson.
Address: n/a. T: n/a.
E: shaun.narwhal@btinternet.com

Bird Report
DORSET BIRDS (1977-), from Dorset Bird Club.
E: sales@dorsetbirds.co.uk

PORTLAND BIRD OBSERVATORY REPORT (1963-), from Martin Cade, The Old Lower Light, Portland Bill, DT5 2JT. T: 01305 820 553;
E: obs@btinternet.com

THE BIRDS OF CHRISTCHURCH HARBOUR (1956-), from Ian Southworth, 1 Bodowen Road, Burton, Christchurch, BH23 7JL. E: ianbirder@aol.com

BTO Regional Representative
Jack Winsper. T: n/a;
E: jlwinsper@btopenworld.com

Greg Lambe (Assistant Representative).
T: n/a; E: greg.lambe1@gmail.com

Club
CHRISTCHURCH HARBOUR ORNITHOLOGICAL GROUP. (1956; 440).
Dave Taylor (Gen Sec), Dairy Cottage, Sopley, Hampshire BH23 7AZ. T: 07970 221 549;
E: secretary@chog.org.uk; W: www.chog.org.uk
Meetings: 7.30pm, (usually) 2nd Wednesday of the month (Oct-Mar). St Nicholas Church Hall, The Broadway, Hengistbury Head, Christchurch, BH6 4EP.

DORSET BIRD CLUB. (1987; 450).
Richard Charman (Membership Sec), 20 Stourpaine Road, Poole, BH17 9AT. T: 07391 756 053
E: membership@dorsetbirds.co.uk;
W: www.dorsetbirds.co.uk
Meetings: Irregular indoor meetings/AGM usually in Mar - contact/see website for details.

DORSET NATURAL HISTORY & ARCHAEOLOGICAL SOCIETY. (1845; 2000).
Museum Secretary, The Old Warehouse, 31a Durngate Street, Dorchester, DT1 1JP.
T: 01305 262 735;
E: secretary@dorsetcountymuseum.org;
W: www.dorsetcountymuseum.org

Ringing Group/Bird Observatory
CHRISTCHURCH HARBOUR RS.

RADIPOLE RG.

STOUR RG.

PORTLAND BIRD OBSERVATORY.
Martin Cade (Warden), The Old Lower Light, Portland Bill, DT5 2JT. T: 01305 820 553;
E: obs@btinternet.com;
W: www.portlandbirdobs.com

RSPB Local Group
SOUTH DORSET. (1976; 420).
Michael Neely. T: 01305 262 869;
E: SouthDorsetGroup@RSPB.org.uk;
W: www.rspb.org.uk/groups/southdorset
Meetings: 7.15pm, 4th Tuesday of the month (Sep-Apr, not Dec). Meeting Room 2, County Hall, Colliton Park, Dorchester, DT1 1XJ.

Wetland Bird Survey (WeBS) Local Organiser
DORSET (excl. ESTUARIES). Malcolm Balmer.
T: via WeBS Office; E: malcalmer@gmail.com

POOLE HARBOUR. Paul Morton.
T: via WeBS Office; E: paulolua@yahoo.co.uk

RADIPOLE & LODMOOR. Stephen Hales.
T: 07801 344 024; E: via WeBS Office

THE FLEET & PORTLAND HARBOUR. Stephen Groves.
T: 01305 871 684; E: cygnusolor@yahoo.co.uk

Wildlife Trust
DORSET WILDLIFE TRUST. (1961; 25,000).
Brooklands Farm, Forston, Dorchester, DT2 7AA.
T: 01305 264 620, (fax) 01305 251 120;
E: enquiries@dorsetwildlifetrust.org.uk;
W: www.dorsetwildlifetrust.org.uk

DURHAM

Bird Atlas/Avifauna
The Birds of Durham. Keith Bowey & Mark Newsome (Durham Bird Club, 2012).

Birds of Cleveland. Martin Blick (Tees Valley Wildlife Trust, 2009).

The Breeding Birds of Cleveland: A Tetrad Atlas 1999-2006. Graeme Joynt, James Fairbrother & Ted Parker (Teesmouth Bird Club, 2008).

A Summer Atlas of Breeding Birds of County Durham. Stephen Westerberg & Keith Bowey (Durham Bird Club, 2000).

Bird Recorder
CLEVELAND. Alan Crossley, 32 Sledwick Road, Billingham, Cleveland TS23 3HU. T: 07801 751 952;
E: alancrossley11@outlook.com

DURHAM. Recorder. Andrew Kinghorn. Address: n/a.
T: n/a; E: dbc.records@hotmail.co.uk

Bird Report
CLEVELAND BIRD REPORT (1974-), from John Fletcher, 43 Glaisdale Avenue, Tollesby, Middlesbrough, TS5 7PF. T: 01642 818 825;
E: j.fletcher666@btinternet.com

BIRDS IN DURHAM (1970-), from D Sowerbutts, 9 Prebends Fields, Gilesgate Moor, Durham, DH1 1HH. E: dsowerbutts608@gmail.com

BTO Regional Representative
CLEVELAND. Michael Leakey. T: n/a;
E: mikeaquila@hotmail.com

DURHAM. David Sowerbutts. T: 0191 386 7201;
E: dsowerbutts608@gmail.com

Club

DURHAM BIRD CLUB. (1974; 350). Richard Cowen (Sec), Rose Cottage, Old Quarrington, DH6 5NN. T: 07882 782 833;
E: durhambirdclub@gmail.com;
W: www.durhambirdclub.org.uk
Meetings: Contact/see website for details.

NORTHUMBERLAND & TYNESIDE BIRD CLUB.
NATURAL HISTORY SOCIETY OF NORTHUMBRIA.
- See Northumberland

TEESMOUTH BIRD CLUB. (1960; 475).
Chris Sharp (Sec), 6 Maritime Avenue, Hartlepool, TS24 0XF. T: 01429 865 163;
E: chrisandlucia@ntlworld.com;
W: www.teesmouthbc.com
Meetings: 7.30pm, 1st Monday of the month (Sep-Apr). Stockton Library, Church Road, Stockton, TS18 1TU.

Ringing Group/Bird Observatory
DURHAM DALES RG.

SOUTH CLEVELAND RG.

TEES RG.

WHITBURN RG.

RSPB Local Group
CLEVELAND. (1974; 100).
Jenny Wright. T: n/a;
E: jennyseasonals@gmail.com;
W: www.rspb.org.uk/groups/cleveland
Meetings: 7.30pm, 2nd Monday of the month (Sep-Apr). Middlesbrough Rugby Club, Green Lane, Middlesbrough, TS5 7SL.

DURHAM. (1974; 125).
Richard Cowen. T: 07397 862 833;
E: richard.cowen313@gmail.com;
W: www.rspb.org.uk/groups/durham
Meetings: 7.30pm, 2nd Tuesday of the month (Oct-Apr). Laurel Avenue Community Centre, Laurel Avenue, Durham, DH1 2EY.

Wetland Bird Survey (WeBS) Local Organiser
CLEVELAND (excl. TEES ESTUARY). Chris Sharp.
T: 01429 865 163; E: chrisandlucia@ntlworld.com

DURHAM. Vacant - contact WeBS Office.

TEES ESTUARY. Adam Jones. T: 07872 157 735;
E: adam.jones@rspb.org.uk

Wildlife Trust
DURHAM WILDLIFE TRUST. (1971; 9,000).
Rainton Meadows, Chilton Moor, Houghton-le-Spring, Tyne & Wear DH4 6PU. T: 0191 584 3112,
(fax) 0191 584 3934; E: mail@durhamwt.co.uk;
W: www.durhamwt.com

TEES VALLEY WILDLIFE TRUST. (1979; 5,000).
Margrove Heritage Centre, Margrove Park, Boosbeck, Saltburn, TS12 3BZ. T: 01287 636 382,
(fax) 01287 636 383; E: info@teeswildlife.org;
W: www.teeswildlife.org

ESSEX

Bird Atlas/Avifauna
The Birds of Essex. Simon Wood
(Christopher Helm, 2007).

Tetrad Atlas of the Breeding Birds of Essex.
MK Dennis (Essex Birdwatching Soc, 1996).

Bird Recorder
Michael Tracey, Robins, Hayhouse Rd, Earls Colne, Colchester, CO6 2PD.
T: 07500 866 335;
E: micktrac@aol.com

Bird Report
ESSEX BIRD REPORT (1949/50-), from Peter Dwyer, EBWS, 48 Churchill Avenue, Halstead, CO9 2BE. T: 01787 476 524;
E: info.ebws@gmail.com

BTO Regional Representative
NORTH-EAST. Rod Bleach. T: 07799 547 192;
E: rod.bleach@sesl.eu

NORTH-WEST. Graham Smith. T: 01277 354 034;
E: silaum.silaus@tiscali.co.uk

SOUTH. Vacant - contact Dawn Balmer, BTO.
T: 01842 750 050; E: dawn.balmer@bto.org

Club
ESSEX BIRDWATCHING SOCIETY. (1949; 590).
Peter Dwyer (Membership Sec), 48 Churchill Avenue, Halstead, CO9 2BE. T: 01787 476 524;
E: info.ebws@gmail.com; W: www.ebws.org.uk
Meetings: 8pm, 1st Friday of the month (Sep-Apr). Quaker Meeting House, 82 Rainsford Road, Chelmsford, CM1 2QL.

Ringing Group/Bird Observatory
BRADWELL BIRD OBSERVATORY RG.

NORTH THAMES GULL GROUP. W: www.ntgg.org.uk

SOUTHERN COLOUR RINGING GROUP.
W: www.southern-colour-ringing-group.org.uk

RSPB Local Group
CHELMSFORD & CENTRAL ESSEX. (1975; 360).
Sue McClellan. T: 01245 471 576;
E: suem@idnet.com;
W: www.rspb.org.uk/groups/chelmsford
Meetings: 7.45pm, 2nd Thursday of the month (Sep-Apr). Northumberland Theatre, Writtle University College, Lordship Road, Writtle, CM1 3RP.

COLCHESTER. (1981; 40).
Ron Firmin. T: n/a; E: ron.firmin@btinternet.com;
W: www.rspb.org.uk/groups/colchester
Meetings: 7.45pm (7.30pm Sep) 2nd Thursday of the month (Sep-Apr). Shrub End Social Centre, Shrub End Road, Colchester, CO3 4SA.

SOUTH EAST ESSEX. (1983; 200).
Graham Mee. T: 01702 525 152;
E: grahamm@southendrspb.co.uk;
W: www.southendrspb.co.uk
Meetings: 8.00pm, 1st Wednesday of the month (Sep-May). The EWT Belfairs Woodland Centre, Eastwood Road North, Leigh-on-Sea, SS9 4LR.

Wetland Bird Survey (WeBS) Local Organiser
CROUCH/ROACH ESTUARY and SOUTH DENGIE.
Stephen Spicer. T: 07515 651 736;
E: stephenspicer4@gmail.com

ESSEX (OTHER SITES). Anthony Harbott.
T: 01992 575 213; E: anthonyharbott@gmail.com

HAMFORD WATER. Leon Woodrow.
T: 01255 676 527; E: via WeBS Office

LEE VALLEY. See Hertfordshire.

NORTH BLACKWATER. John Fell.
T: 07785 305 573; E: j.a.fell@protonmail.com

SOUTH BLACKWATER & NORTH DENGIE.
Anthony Harbott - see above.

SWALE, MEDWAY & NORTH KENT MARSHES.
See Kent.

THAMES ESTUARY (FOULNESS). Chris Lewis.
T: via WeBS Office. E: cpm.lewis@gmail.com

Wildlife Trust
ESSEX WILDLIFE TRUST. (1959; 38,000).
Abbotts Hall Farm, Maldon Road,
Great Wigborough, Colchester, CO5 7RZ.
T: 01621 862 960, (fax) 01621 862 990;
E: admin@essexwt.org.uk;
W: www.essexwt.org.uk

GLOUCESTERSHIRE

Bird Atlas/Avifauna
The Birds of Gloucestershire. Gordon Kirk & John Phillips (Liverpool University Press, 2013).

Birds of The Cotswolds: A New Breeding Atlas. Iain Main, Dave Pearce & Tim Hutton (Liverpool University Press 2009).

Bird Recorder
Richard Baatsen. Address: n/a. T: 07879 850 196;
E: richard.baatsen@gmail.com
(excl. S.Gloucs = Avon)

Bird Report
GLOUCESTERSHIRE BIRD REPORT (1948-),from The Membership Secretary (GNS), 50 Kingsmead, Abbymead, Gloucester, GL4 5DY.
E: gnsmembership@btinternet.com

BTO Regional Representative
Gordon Kirk. T: 01452 741 724;
E: GordonKirk@aol.com

Club
CHELTENHAM BIRD CLUB. (1976; 100).
Membership Sec. Address: n/a.
T: 01242 690 660; E: via website;
W: www.cheltenhambirdclub.org.uk
Meetings: 7.15pm, most Mondays (Oct-Mar), Belmont School, Warden Hill Road, Cheltenham, GL51 3AT.

DURSLEY BIRDWATCHING & PRESERVATION SOCIETY. (1953; 240).
Membership Secretary
Address: n/a.
T: 0800 410 1525;
E: membership@dbwps.org.uk;
W: www.dbwps.org.uk
Meetings: 7.45pm, 2nd and last Mondays of the month (Sep-Apr). Dursley Community Centre, Rednock Drive, Dursley, GL11 4BX.

GLOUCESTERSHIRE NATURALISTS' SOCIETY. (1948; 500).
The Membership Secretary, 50 Kingsmead, Abbymead, Gloucester, GL4 5DY. T: 01452 610 085;
E: gnsmembership@btinternet.com;
W: www.glosnats.org
Meetings: 7.30pm, 2nd Friday of the month (Oct-Apr). Normally at Watermoor Church Hall, Watermoor Road, Cirencester, GL7 1JR - some may be held at: Parish Rooms in Gosditch Street, Cirencester, GL7 2AG - contact/check website for details.

Ringing Group/Bird Observatory
COTSWOLD WATER PARK RG.

SEVERN ESTUARY GULL GROUP.

RSPB Local Group
GLOUCESTERSHIRE. (1972; 400).
David Cramp. T: 01242 620 281;
E: djcramp@btinternet.com;
W: www.rspb.org.uk/groups/gloucestershire
Meetings: 7.30pm, 3rd Tuesday of the month (Sep-Nov, Jan-Mar). The Gala Club, Fairmile Gardens, Longford, Gloucester, GL2 9EB.

Wetland Bird Survey (WeBS) Local Organiser
COTSWOLD WATER PARK (GLOUCS/WILTS). Vacant - contact WeBS Office.

GLOUCESTERSHIRE (inc. SEVERN ESTUARY, excl. COTSWOLD WATER PARK). Michael Smart.
T: 01452 421 131; E: smartmike143@gmail.com

Wildlife Trust
GLOUCESTERSHIRE WILDLIFE TRUST. (1961; 28,000).
Conservation Centre, Robinswood Hill Country Park, Reservoir Road, Gloucester, GL4 6SX.
T: 01452 383 333, (fax) 01452 383 334;
E: info@gloucestershirewildlifetrust.co.uk;
W: www.gloucestershirewildlifetrust.co.uk

HAMPSHIRE

Bird Atlas/Avifauna
Hampshire Bird Atlas 2007-2012. John Eyre (Ed). (HOS, 2015).

Birds of Hampshire. JM Clark & JA Eyre (Hampshire Ornithological Society, 1993).

Bird Recorder
Keith Betton, 8 Dukes Close, Folly Hill, Farnham, Surrey GU9 0DR. T: 01252 724 068 or 07809 671 468;
E: keithbetton@hotmail.com

Bird Report
HAMPSHIRE BIRD REPORT (1978-), from Bryan & Sandy Coates, 8 Gardner Way, Chandler's Ford, SO53 1JL.
E: sandyandbryan@tiscali.co.uk

BTO Regional Representative
Glynne Evans. T: 01264 860 697;
E: hantsbto@hotmail.com

Brian Sharkey (Assistant Representative).
T: 01189 814 751; E: briansharkeyuk@yahoo.co.uk

John Shillitoe (Assistant Representative).
T: 01329 833 086; E: jshillitoe.googlemail.com

Club
HAMPSHIRE ORNITHOLOGICAL SOCIETY. (1979; 2000).
John Shillitoe (Sec), 'Westerly', Hundred Acres Road, Wickham, PO17 6HY. T: 01329 833 086;
E: jshillitoe@googlemail.com; W: www.hos.org.uk
Meetings: Members' Day at the end of March - contact/see website for details.

Ringing Group/Bird Observatory
FARLINGTON RG.

ITCHEN RG.

TITCHFIELD HAVEN RG.

RSPB Local Group
BASINGSTOKE. (1979; 65).
Peter E. Hutchins. T: 07895 388 378;
E: RSPBbasingstoke@gmail.com;
W: www.rspb.org.uk/groups/basingstoke
Meetings: 7.45pm, 3rd Wednesday of the month (Sep-May). The Barn, St Michael's Cottage, Church Cottage, St Michael's Church, Church Square, Basingstoke, RG21 7QW.

NEW FOREST. (2000; 150).
Keith Partridge. T: 01425 652 864;
E: NewForestGroup@RSPB.org.uk;
W: www.rspb.org.uk/groups/newforest
Meetings: 7.30pm, 2nd Wednesday of the month (Sep-Jun). Lyndhurst Community Centre, High Street, Lyndhurst, SO43 7NY.

NORTH EAST HANTS. (1976; 150).
Sue Radbourn. T: 01276 29434;
E: NehantsRSPB@gmail.com;
W: www.rspb.org.uk/groups/northeasthants
Meetings: 7.30pm, in halls in Church Crookham and Fleet (Sep-Apr) - contact/see website for details.

PORTSMOUTH. (1974; 210).
Gordon Humby. T: 023 9235 3949;
E: PortsmouthRSPB@gmail.com;
W: www.rspb.org.uk/groups/portsmouth
Meetings: 7.30pm, 4th Saturday of the month (Jan-Nov). St Andrews Church Hall, Havant Road, Farlington, Portsmouth, PO6 1AA.

WINCHESTER & DISTRICT (1974; 80).
Pam Symes. T: 01962 851 821;
E: WinchRSPB1974@gmail.com;
W: www.rspb.org.uk/groups/winchester
Meetings: 7.45pm, 1st Wednesday of the month (not Jan or Aug). Shawford Parish Hall, Pearson Lane, Shawford, Winchester, SO21 2AA.

Wetland Bird Survey (WeBS) Local Organiser
AVON VALLEY. John Clark. T: 01252 623 397;
E: johnclark50@sky.com

HAMPSHIRE (ESTUARIES/COASTAL). John Shillitoe.
T: 01329 833 086; E: jshillitoe.googlemail.com

HAMPSHIRE (INLAND - excl. AVON VALLEY).
Keith Wills. T: via WeBS Office;
E: kwills57@btinternet.com

Wildlife Trust
HAMPSHIRE & ISLE OF WIGHT WILDLIFE TRUST.
(1960; 25,000).
Beechcroft, Vicarage Lane, Curdridge, SO32 2DP.
T: 01489 774 400, (fax) 01489 774 401;
E: feedback@hiwwt.org.uk; W: www.hiwwt.org.uk

HEREFORDSHIRE

Bird Atlas/Avifauna
The Birds of Herefordshire 2007-2012: An Atlas of Their Breeding and Wintering Distributions. Mervyn Davies, Peter Eldridge, Chris Robinson, Nick Smith & Gerald Wells (Liverpool University Press, 2014).

Bird Recorder
Mick Colquhoun,
Old Gore House, Old Gore, Ross on Wye, HR9 7QT.
T: 07587 151 627; E: mickcolquhoun@gmail.com

Bird Report
THE BIRDS OF HEREFORDSHIRE (1951-), from Mervyn Davies, Hunters Moon, Bishopstone, Hereford, HR4 7JE.
E: annualreports@herefordshirebirds.org

BTO Regional Representative
Chris Robinson. T: 01981 510 360;
E: herefordbtorep@btinternet.com

Club
HEREFORDSHIRE ORNITHOLOGICAL CLUB.
(1950; 400+). Martin Winrow (Treasurer),
1 Deer Park Close, Moccas, HR2 9JA. T: n/a;
E: secretary@herefordshirebirds.org;
W: www.herefordshirebirds.org
Meetings: 7.30pm, 2nd Thursday of the month (Sep-Mar), Holmer Parish Centre, Holmer, Hereford, HR4 9RG.

Ringing Group/Bird Observatory
LLANCILLO RG.

Wetland Bird Survey (WeBS) Local Organiser
HEREFORDSHIRE. Chris Robinson. T: 01981 510 360;
E: fredbloggs@btinternet.com

Wildlife Trust
HEREFORDSHIRE NATURE TRUST. (1962; 5,000).
Queenswood Country Park & Arboretum, Dinmore Hill, Nr Leominster, HR6 0PY.
T: 01432 356 872, (fax) 01432 275 489;
E: enquiries@herefordshirewt.co.uk;
W: www.herefordshirewt.org

HERTFORDSHIRE

Bird Atlas/Avifauna
Birds of Hertfordshire. Ken W Smith, Chris W Dee, Jack D Fearnside & Mike Ilett (Herts NHS, 2015).

Bird Recorder
Alan Gardiner, 199 Watford Rd, St Albans AL2 3HH.
T: 01727 863 945; E: birdrecorder@hnhs.org

Bird Report
HERTFORDSHIRE BIRD REPORT (1980-), not for general sale but enquiries to David Utting (Sec).
E: secretary@hnhs.org

BTO Regional Representative
Martin Ketcher. T: n/a;
E: martinketcher@gmail.com

Club
HERTFORDSHIRE BIRD CLUB. (1971) part of HERTFORDSHIRE NATURAL HISTORY SOCIETY.
(1875; 420)
David Utting (Sec), 250 Sandridge Road, St Albans, AL1 4AL. T: n/a; E: secretary@hnhs.org;
W: https://www.hnhs.org/herts-bird-club/home
Meetings: Annual Herts Bird Conference - contact/ see website for details.

Ringing Group/Bird Observatory
MAPLE CROSS RG.

RUNNYMEDE RG. W: www.runnymederinging.uk

RYE MEADS RG. W: www.rmrg.org.uk

SOUTHERN COLOUR RINGING GROUP.
W: southern-colour-ringing-group.org.uk

TRING RG. W: www.tringringinggroup.org.uk
https://tringringinggroup.blogspot.co.uk/

RSPB Local Group
CHORLEYWOOD & DISTRICT. (1976; 90).
Carol Smith. T: 01923 897 885;
E: carolsmithuk@hotmail.com;
W: www.rspb.org.uk/groups/chorleywood
Meetings: 8.00pm, 3rd Thursday of the month (Sep-May). The Florence Brown Hall, Chorleywood Free Church, Hillside Road, Chorleywood, WD3 5AP.

HARPENDEN. (1974; 100).
Geoff Horn. T: 01582 765 443;
E: geoffrhorn@yahoo.co.uk;
W: www.rspb.org.uk/groups/harpenden
Meetings: 8.00pm, 2nd Thursday of the month (Sep-Apr). All Saint's Church Hall, Station Road, Harpenden, AL5 4UU.

HEMEL HEMPSTEAD. (1972; 100).
Ian Wilson. T: 01442 265 022;
E: ian.aeronautics@gmail.com;
W: www.rspb.org.uk/groups/hemelhempstead
Meetings: 8.00pm, 1st Monday of the month (Sep-Jun). The Laureate Academy, Warners End Road, Hemel Hempstead, HP1 3DW.

HITCHIN & LETCHWORTH. (1972; 85).
Martin Johnson. T: 01763 249 459;
E: martinrjspc@hotmail.com;
W: www.rspb.org.uk/groups/hitchinandletchworth
Meetings: 7.30pm, 1st Friday of the month (Sep-May). Letchworth Settlement, 229 Nevells Rd, Letchworth, SG6 4UB.

POTTERS BAR & BARNETS. (1977; 1400/area).
Ian Sharp. T: 01707 662 914;
E: Pbandb.RSPB@gmail.com;
W: www.rspb.org.uk/groups/pottersbarandbarnet
Meetings: 2.00pm, one Wednesday of the month (Sep-Jun). St Johns URC Hall, Mowbray Rd, Barnet, EN5 1RH & 7.45pm, one Friday of the month (Sep-Jun), Tilbury Hall, United Reform Church, Darkes Lane, Potters Bar, EN6 1BZ - contact/see website for details.

SOUTH EAST HERTFORDSHIRE. (1971; 200).
Stan Kitchiner. T: 07821 875 419;
E: Se_herts_RSPB@yahoo.co.uk;
W: www.rspb.org.uk/groups/southeasthertfordshire
Meetings: 8.00pm, last Tuesday of the month (Sep-Jun, Dec = 3rd Tuesday). United Reformed Church, Mill Lane, Broxbourne, EN10 7BQ.

ST ALBANS. (1979; 80).
Colin Rose, T: 01727 767 282;
E: colin.rose20@ntlworld.com;
W: www.rspb.org.uk/groups/stalbans
Meetings: Indoor meetings currently suspended, mainly run outdoor meetings - contact/see website for details.

STEVENAGE. (1982; 50).
Trevor Storey. T: 01438 226 014;
E: trevorstorey54@gmail.com;
W: www.rspb.org.uk/groups/stevenage
Meetings: 7.30pm, 3rd Tuesday of the month (Sep-May). Friends Meeting House, Cutty's Lane, Stevenage, SG1 1UP.

STORT VALLEY. (2009; 40).
Simon Hurwitz. T: 01799 500 996;
E: simon.hurwitz@ntlworld.com;
W: www.rspb.org.uk/groups/stortvalley
Meetings: 7.30pm, 2nd Tuesday of the month (Sep-Jun). Bishops Park Community Centre, 2 Lancaster Way, Bishop's Stortford, SM23 4DA.

WATFORD. (1974; 590).
Janet Reynolds. T: 01923 249 647;
E: WatfordRSPB@gmail.com;
W: www.rspb.org.uk/groups/watford
Meetings: 7.30pm, 2nd Wednesday of the month (Sep-Jun). The Stanborough Centre, 609 St Albans Road, Watford, WD25 9JL.

Wetland Bird Survey (WeBS) Local Organiser
HERTFORDSHIRE (excl. LEE VALLEY). Jim Terry.
T: 0208 905 1461; E: jimjoypaddy@virginmedia.com

LEE VALLEY (GREATER LONDON/ESSEX/HERTFORDSHIRE). Cath Patrick. T: 01992 709 882;
E: cpatrick@leevalleypark.org.uk

Wildlife Trust
HERTFORDSHIRE & MIDDLESEX WILDLIFE TRUST. (1964; 23,000).
Grebe House, St Michael's Street, St Albans, Herts, AL3 4SN. T: 01727 858 901; E: info@hmwt.org;
W: www.hertswildlifetrust.org.uk

ISLE OF MAN

Bird Atlas/Avifauna
Manx Bird Atlas: An Atlas of Breeding and Wintering Birds on the Isle of Man. Chris Sharpe (Liverpool University Press, 2007).

Bird Recorder
Chris Sharpe. Address: n/a. T: 07624 496 519;
E: birdman@manx.net

Bird Report
CALF OF MAN BIRD OBSERVATORY, from Manx National Heritage Shop, Manx Museum, Kingswood Grove, Douglas, IM1 3LY.
T: 01624 648 000; E: enquiries@mnh.gov.im

MANX BIRD REPORT (1972-), from Allen S Moore, 'Lyndale', Derby Road, Peel, IOM IM5 1HH.
E: allen.gobbag@manx.net

BTO Regional Representative
David Kennett. T: n/a; E: dtkennett@manx.net

Janet Thompson (Assistant Representative).
T: n/a; E: jthompson@manx.net

Club
MANX BIRDLIFE.
Laxey & Lanan Commissioners Offices, 35 New Road, Laxey, Isle of Man IM4 7BG. T: 01624 861 130;
E: enquiries@manxbirdlife.im;
W: http://manxbirdlife.im

MANX ORNITHOLOGICAL SOCIETY. (1997; 150). Janet Thompson (Sec), Cott ny Greiney, Beach Road, Port St Mary, IM9 5NF.
T: 01624 835 524; E: jthompson@manx.net;
W: http://manxbirdlife.im/manx-ornithological-society
Meetings: 7.30pm, 1st Tuesday of the month (Oct-Mar). Union Mills Methodist Chapel, Strang Road, Union Mills IM4 4NL.

Ringing Group/Bird Observatory
MANX RG.

CALF OF MAN BIRD OBSERVATORY.
Aron Sapsford (Ornithological Warden).
T: 07624 497 179; E: aron.sapsford@sky.com;
W: www.manxnationalheritage.im/visit/stay-with-us/calf-of-man-bird-observatory/

Accommodation Bookings Officer, Manx National Heritage, Kingswood Grove, Douglas, IOM IM1 3LY.
T: 01624 648 015; E: staywithus@mnh.gov.im

Wetland Bird Survey (WeBS) Local Organiser
ISLE OF MAN. David Kennett. T: 01624 813 298);
E: dtkennett@manx.net

Wildlife Trust
MANX WILDLIFE TRUST. (1973; 1,000).
7-8 Market Place, Peel, Isle of Man IM5 1AB.
T: 01624 844 432, (fax) 01624 842 317;
E: enquiries@manxwt.org.uk;
W: www.manxwt.org.uk

ISLE OF WIGHT

Bird Recorder
Jon Sparshott, Leopards, Main Road, Havenstreet, IoW PO33 4DR. T: 01983 882 549; E: jon1a8@aol.com

Bird Report
ISLE OF WIGHT BIRD REPORT (1996-), from Dave Hunnybun, 40 Church Hill Road, Cowes, IoW PO31 8HH. E: davehunnybun@hotmail.com

BTO Regional Representative
Jim Baldwin. T: 01983 721 137 & 07528 586 683;
E: wightbto@hotmail.com

Club
ISLE OF WIGHT NATURAL HISTORY & ARCHAEOLOGICAL SOCIETY. (1919; 350).
The Secretary, Unit 16, Prospect Business Centre, West Cowes, IoW PO31 7HD.
T: 01983 282 596;
E: iwnhas@iwnhas.org;
W: www.iwnhas.org
Meetings: Contact/see website for details.

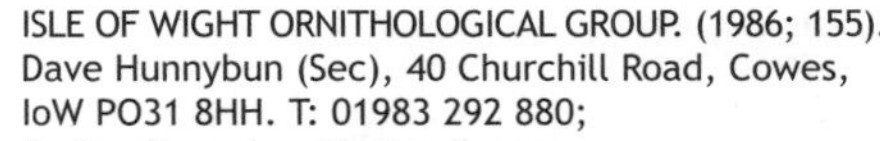

ISLE OF WIGHT ORNITHOLOGICAL GROUP. (1986; 155). Dave Hunnybun (Sec), 40 Churchill Road, Cowes, IoW PO31 8HH. T: 01983 292 880;
E: davehunnybun@hotmail.com;
W: http://iowbirds.awardspace.biz/IWOG.htm
Meetings: Only held occasionally - contact/see website for details.

Ringing Group/ Bird Observatory
ISLE OF WIGHT RG.

Wetland Bird Survey (WeBS) Local Organiser
ISLE OF WIGHT. Jim Baldwin. T: 01983 721 137;
E: wightbto@hotmail.com

Wildlife Trust. See Hampshire.

KENT

Bird Atlas/Avifauna
Kent Breeding Bird Atlas 2008-13. Rob Clements, Murray Orchard, Norman McCanch & Stephen Wood (Kent Ornithological Society, 2015).

The Birds of Kent: A Review of Their Status and Distribution. DW Taylor (Meresborough Books, 2nd ed 1984).

Bird Recorder
Barry Wright, 6 Hatton Close, Northfleet, DA11 8SD.
T: 01474 320 918; E: umbrellabirds66@gmail.com

Bird Report
DUNGENESS BIRD OBSERVATORY REPORT (1989-), from David Walker, Dungeness BO, 11 RNSSS Cottages, Dungeness, Romney Marsh, TN29 9NA.
T: 01797 321 309; E: dungenessobs@vfast.co.uk

KENT BIRD REPORT (1952-), from Chris Roome, Rowland House, Station Road, Staplehurst, TN12 0PY. E: chrisroome105@icloud.com

SANDWICH BAY BIRD OBSERVATORY REPORT (1962-), from SBBOT, Guildford Road, Sandwich Bay, Sandwich, CT13 9PF. T: 01304 617 341;
E: info@sbbot.org.uk

BTO Regional Representative
Mike Roberts. T: n/a. E: mike@miliscer.com

Murray Orchard (Assistant Representative). T: n/a.
E: murray.orchard@live.co.uk

Club
KENT ORNITHOLOGICAL SOCIETY. (1952; 650).
Brendan Ryan (Hon Sec), 18 The Crescent, Canterbury, CT2 7AQ. T: 01227 471 121;
E: brendan.ryan@yahoo.co.uk;
W: www.kentos.org.uk
Meetings: AGM - contact/see website for details.

Ringing Group/Bird Observatory
DARTFORD RG.

EAST KENT WILDLIFE GROUP. W: www.ekwg.org

RECULVER RG.

SWALE WADER GROUP. W: www.swalewaders.co.uk

DUNGENESS BIRD OBSERVATORY.
David Walker (Warden), Dungeness Bird Observatory, 11 RNSSS Cottages, Dungeness, Romney Marsh, TN29 9NA. T: 01797 321 309; E: dungenessobs@vfast.co.uk; W: www.dungenessbirdobs.org.uk

Sandwich Bay Bird Observatory Trust

SANDWICH BAY BIRD OBSERVATORY.
Steffan Walton (Warden), Sandwich Bay Bird Observatory, Guildford Road, Sandwich, CT13 9PF. T: 01304 617 341; E: info@sbbot.org.uk; W: www.sbbot.org.uk

RSPB Local Group
CANTERBURY. (1973; 125).
Babs Golding. T: 01227 470 151; E: babs@squirrels.plus.com; W: www.rspb.org.uk/groups/canterbury
Meetings: 7.30pm 2nd Friday of the month (Sep-Apr). Blean Village Hall, Blean, Nr Canterbury CT2 9JA.

GRAVESEND. (1977; 170).
Paul Yetman. T: 01474 332 417; E: groupleader@RSPBgravesend.org.uk; W: www.rspbgravesend.org.uk
Meetings: 7.30pm, 2nd Thursday of the month (Sep-May). Northfleet School for Girls, Hall Road, Northfleet, Gravesend, DA11 8AQ & 2.00pm, 4th Tuesday of the month (Sep-Nov, Jan-Mar). Masonic Hall, 25 Wrotham Road, Gravesend, DA11 0PA.

MAIDSTONE. (1973; 250).
James Downer. T: 01622 739 475; E: maidstoneRSPB@gmail.com; W: www.rspb.org.uk/groups/maidstone
Meetings: 7.30pm, 3rd Thursday of the month (not Aug). Grove Green Community Hall, Penhurst Close, Grove Green, Bearsted, Maidstone, ME14 5BT.

MEDWAY. (1974; 150).
Warren Mann. T: 01634 234 816; E: medwayrspb-leader@virginmedia.com; W: www.rspb.org.uk/groups/medway
Meetings: 7.30pm, 3rd Tuesday of the month (not Aug). Parkwood Community Centre, Parkwood Green, Gillingham, ME8 9PN.

SEVENOAKS. (1974; 180).
Anne Chapman. T: 01732 456 459; E: anneanddave.chapman@outlook.com; W: www.rspb.org.uk/groups/sevenoaks
Meetings: 7.45pm, 1st Thursday of the month (Sep-May). Otford Memorial Hall, High Street, Otford, Sevenoaks, TN14 5PQ.

THANET. (1975; 165).
Brian Short. T: 07721 452 294; E: theRSPBthanetlocalgroup@talktalk.net; W: www.rspb.org.uk/groups/thanet
Meetings: 7.30pm, 2nd Monday of the month (Jan-Dec). St Peter's Church Hall, Main Hall, Hopeville Avenue, Broadstairs, CT10 2TR.

TONBRIDGE. (1975; no formal membership).
Martin Ellis. T: 01892 521 413; E: rspb.tonbridge@gmail.com; W: www.rspb.org.uk/groups/tonbridge
Meetings: 7.30pm, one Wednesday each month (Sep-Apr). St Philip's Church, Salisbury Road, Tonbridge, TN10 4PA - contact/see website for details.

Wetland Bird Survey (WeBS) Local Organiser
DUNGENESS AREA. David Walker. T: 01797 321 309; E: dungenessobs@vfast.co.uk

KENT (WEST). Vacant - contact WeBS Office.

KENT (EAST). Vacant - contact WeBS Office.

MEDWAY ESTUARY. Robert Knight. T: 07801 449 077; E: rjknight53@gmail.com

PEGWELL BAY. Steffan Walton. T: via WeBS Office; E: via WeBS Office

SWALE ESTUARY. Brian Watmough.
T: 01227 266 746; E: brianrwat@yahoo.co.uk

THAMES ESTUARY (FOULNESS). See Essex.

THAMES ESTUARY (HOO). Murray Orchard.
T: 07788 102 238; murray.orchard@live.co.uk

Wildlife Trust
KENT WILDLIFE TRUST. (1958; 32,000).
Tyland Barn, Sandling, Maidstone, ME14 3BD. T: 01622 662 012, (fax) 01622 671 390; E: info@kentwildlife.org.uk; W: www.kentwildlifetrust.org.uk

LANCASHIRE & NORTH MERSEYSIDE

Bird Atlas/Avifauna

The Birds of Lancashire and North Merseyside. Steve White, Barry McCarthy & Maurice Jones (Hobby Publications, 2008).

Atlas of Breeding Birds of Lancashire and North Merseyside 1997-2000. Robert Pyefinch & Peter Golborn (Hobby Publications, 2001).

Bird Recorder

(Incl. North Merseyside). Steve White, 102 Minster Court, Crown Street, Liverpool, L7 3QD. T: 0151 707 2744; E: stevewhite102@btinternet.com

Bird Report

BIRDS OF LANCASTER & DISTRICT (1959-), from Peter Cook, 21 Threshfield Avenue, Heysham, Morecambe, LA3 2DU. T: 07880 541 798; E: peter.cook33@btinternet.com.

BLACKBURN & DISTRICT BIRD CLUB REPORT (1992-), not for general sale but enquiries to Jonathan Fry, 20 Rhodes Avenue, Blackburn, BB1 8NP. E: blackburnbirdclub@gmail.com

CHORLEY AND DISTRICT NATURAL HISTORY SOCIETY ANNUAL REPORT (1975-), published online. W: www.chorleynats.org.uk

EAST LANCASHIRE ORNITHOLOGISTS' CLUB BIRD REPORT (1982-), from Tony Cooper, 28 Peel Park Ave, Clitheroe, BB7 1ET. E: anthony.cooper34@btinternet.com

FYLDE BIRD REPORT (1983-), from Kinta Beaver, 22 Beach Road, Preesall, Poulton le Fylde, FY6 0HQ. E: kinta.beaver@btinternet.com

LANCASHIRE BIRD REPORT (1914-), from Dave Bickerton, 64 Petre Crescent, Rishton, Blackburn, BB1 4RB. E: sec@lacfs.org.uk

BTO Regional Representative

EAST. Tony Cooper. T: 01200 424 577; E: bto.elancs@btinternet.com

MERSEYSIDE. Vacant - contact Dawn Balmer, BTO. T: 01842 750 050; E: dawn.balmer@bto.org

NORTH-WEST. Jean Roberts. T: n/a; E: jeanrbrts6@aol.com

SOUTH. Vacant - contact Dawn Balmer, BTO. T: 01842 750 050; E: dawn.balmer@bto.org

Club

BLACKBURN BIRD CLUB. (1991; 100). John Collins (Sec). Address: n/a. T: 01254 208 479; E: blackburnbirdclub@gmail.com; W: www.blackburnbirdclub.com
Meetings: 7.30pm, normally 1st Monday of the month (Oct-Apr). Feniscowles Methodist Church, Preston Old Road, Blackburn, BB2 5ER.

CHORLEY & DISTRICT NATURAL HISTORY SOCIETY. (1979; 110). Paul Brennan (Sec). Address: n/a. T: n/a; E: secretary@chorleynats.org.uk; W: www.chorleynats.org.uk
Meetings: 7.30pm, 3rd Thursday of the month (Sep-Apr). St Mary's Parish Centre, West Street, off Devonshire Road, Chorley, PR7 2SR.

EAST LANCASHIRE ORNITHOLOGISTS' CLUB. (1955; 45). David Chew (Sec), Lower Wheathead Barn, Wheathead Lane, Blacko, Nelson, BB9 6PD. T: 01282 695 649; E: via the website; W: www.eastlancsornithologists.org.uk
Meetings: 7.30pm, 1st Tuesday of the month (Sep-May). St Anne's Parish, Wheatley Lane Road, Fence, BB12 9EE.

FYLDE BIRD CLUB. (1982; 180). Paul Ellis (Sec), 22 Beach Road, Preesall, Poulton le Fylde, FY6 0HQ. T: 01253 811 726 (eves); E: paul.ellis24@btopenworld.com; W: www.fyldebirdclub.org
Meetings: 7.45pm, 4th Tuesday of the month (all year). River Wyre Hotel, Breck Road, Poulton le Fylde, FY6 7JZ.

FYLDE NATURALISTS' SOCIETY. (1946; 90). Julie McGough (Sec). Address: n/a. T: n/a; E: secretary@fyldenaturalists.co.uk; W: www.fyldenaturalists.co.uk
Meetings: 7.15pm, 2nd Wednesday of the month (Sep-Mar). Forest Gate Baptist Church Hall, off Whitegate Drive, Blackpool, FY3 9AW (unless otherwise stated in the programme).

LANCASHIRE & CHESHIRE FAUNA SOCIETY. (1914; 200). Dave Bickerton (Sec), 64 Petre Crescent, Rishton, BB1 4RB. T: 01254 886 257; E: sec@lacfs.org.uk; W: www.lacfs.org.uk
Meetings: No indoor meetings held.

LANCASTER & DISTRICT BIRDWATCHING SOCIETY. (1959; 200). Peter Cook (Sec), 21 Threshfield Ave, Heysham, Morecambe, LA3 2DU. T: 01524 851 454 & 07880 541 798; E: peter.cook33@btinternet.com; W: www.lancasterbirdwatching.org.uk
Meetings: 7.30pm, last Monday of the month (Sep-Nov/Jan-Mar) - contact/see website for details.

MERSEYSIDE NATURALISTS' ASSOCIATION. (1938; 140). Sabena Blackbird (Chairman), 18 Ludlow Grove, Bromborough, Wirral CH62 7JH. T: n/a. E: chairman@mnapage.info; W: www.mnapage.info
Meetings: Contact/see website for details.

PRESTON SOCIETY BIRD WATCHING & NATURAL HISTORY. (1876/Preston Scientific Society; 140). Kayleigh Roebuck (Sec). Address: n/a. T: 07565 497 065; E: prestonwildlife@gmail.com; W: www.prestonsociety.co.uk
Meetings: 7.30pm, Monday evenings (Oct-Mar). St. Mary's Church, Church Avenue, Penwortham, PR1 0AH.

ROSSENDALE ORNITHOLOGISTS' CLUB. (1976; 150 online). Ian Brady. T: 01706 222 120; E: n/a; W: http://rocforum.activeboard.com
Meetings: 7.15pm, 3rd Monday of the month (check the forum for details). Weavers Cottage, Bacup Road, Rawtenstall, BB4 7NW.

Ringing Group/Bird Observatory
FYLDE RG.

MERSEYSIDE RG. W: www.merseysiderg.org.uk

NORTH LANCASHIRE RG (inc. North Heysham Bird Obs).

SOUTH WEST LANCS RG.

RSPB Local Group
BOLTON. (1978; 155). Terry Delaney. T: 0161 794 4684. E: terry.delaney@sky.com; W: www.rspb.org.uk/groups/bolton
Meetings: 7.30pm, 2nd Thursday of the month (Sep-Apr). St Catherine's Academy - Sports Centre entrance on Newby Road, Breightmet, Bolton, BL2 4HU.

LANCASTER. (1972; 130). Val Hall. T: 07542 117 064; E: RSPBlancaster@gmail.com; W: www.rspb.org.uk/groups/lancaster
Meetings: 2.30pm, 4th Tuesday of the month (Feb, Mar, Oct, Nov) & 7.30pm, 4th Tuesday of the month (Apr, May, Sep). The United Reformed Church, Sefton Road, Heysham, Morecambe, LA3 1TZ. Sep meeting/AGM held at Leighton Moss.

LIVERPOOL. (1972; 145). Chris Tynan. T: 07831 352 870; E: christtynan@aol.com; W: www.rspb.org.uk/groups/liverpool
Meetings: 7.30pm, 3rd Monday of the month (Sep-Apr, 1st Monday in Dec). Mossley Hill Parish Church Hall, Rose Lane, Liverpool, L18 8DB.

SOUTHPORT. (1974; 200). Kathryn Hall. T: n/a; E: SouthportRSPB@btinternet.com; W: www.rspb.org.uk/groups/southport
Meetings: 7.45pm, 3rd Friday of the month (Sep-May). Lord Street West Church Hall, Duke Street, Southport, PR8 1LS.

WIGAN. (1973; 80). Neil Martin. T: 01695 624 860; E: neimaz07@yahoo.co.uk; W: www.rspb.org.uk/groups/wigan
Meetings: 7.45pm, 2nd Tuesday of the month (Sep-Apr). St Anne's Parish Hall, Church Lane, Shevington, Wigan, WN6 8BD.

Wetland Bird Survey (WeBS) Local Organiser
ALT ESTUARY. Steve White. T: via WeBS Office. E: stevewhite102@btinternet.com

DEE ESTUARY (CLWYD/MERSEYSIDE). Colin Wells. T: via WeBS Office; E: colinewells@outlook.com

EAST LANCASHIRE AND FYLDE. Stephen Dunstan. T: 07985 417 755; E: stephendunstan76@googlemail.com

LANCASHIRE - NORTH (INLAND). Peter Marsh. T: 07532 433 043; E: pmrsh123@aol.com

LANCASHIRE - WEST (INLAND). Phil Hampson. T: 07545 465 069; E: pjhampers@icloud.com

MERSEY ESTUARY. Dermot Smith. T: 01925 602 397; E: dermot.smith71@gmail.com

MERSEYSIDE (INLAND). Phil Hampson - see above.

T: 07545 465 069; E: pjhampers@icloud.com
MORECAMBE BAY (NORTH). See Cumbria.

MORECAMBE BAY (SOUTH). Jean Roberts. T: 01524 770 295; E: jeanrbrts6@aol.com

RIBBLE ESTUARY. Ken Abram. T: via WeBS Office; E: bonkser.ka@gmail.com

RIVER LUNE. Jean Roberts - see above.

Wildlife Trust
THE WILDLIFE TRUST FOR LANCASHIRE, MANCHESTER & NORTH MERSEYSIDE. (1962; 29,000). The Barn, Berkeley Drive, Bamber Bridge, Preston, Lancs PR5 6BY. T: 01772 324 129, (fax) 01772 628 849; E: info@lancswt.org.uk; W: www.lancswt.org.uk

LEICESTERSHIRE & RUTLAND

Bird Atlas/Avifauna
The Birds of Leicestershire and Rutland. Rob Fray, Roger Davies, Dave Gamble, Andrew Harrop & Steve Lister. (Christopher Helm, 2009).

Rutland Breeding Bird Atlas 2008-2011. Terry Mitcham (Spiegl Press, 2013)

Bird Recorder
Carl Baggott, 72 New Street, Earl Shilton, LE9 7FR. T: n/a; E: cdbaggott@gmail.com

Bird Report
LEICESTERSHIRE & RUTLAND BIRD REPORT (1946-), from Mrs S Graham, 5 Lychgate Close, Cropston, LE7 7HU. E: JSGraham83@aol.com

BTO Regional Representative
David Wright. T: 01530 231 102;
E: davewrightbto@gmail.com

Club
BIRSTALL BIRDWATCHING CLUB. (1976; 50).
Jack Wootton. T: 0791 312 9497; E: n/a; W: n/a
Meetings: 7.30pm, 2nd Tuesday of the month (Oct-Apr). Rothley Centre, 12 Mountsorrel Lane, Rothley LE7 7PR.

LEICESTERSHIRE & RUTLAND ORNITHOLOGICAL SOCIETY. (1941; 500).
Peter Williams (Sec), Address: n/a.
T: 0116 236 4704; E: peterwilliams23@btinternet.com;
W: www.lros.org.uk
Meetings: 7.30pm, 1st Friday of the month (Oct-May). The Hall of St. Anne's, Letchworth Road, Leicester LE3 6FN.

RUTLAND NATURAL HISTORY SOCIETY. (1965; 200).
Margaret Conner (Membership Sec), 24 Burrough Road, Somerby, Melton Mowbray, LE14 2PP. T: 01664 454 532;
E: rnhsmembers@gmail.com; W: www.rnhs.org.uk
Meetings: 7.30pm, 1st Tuesday of the month (Oct-Apr). Voluntary Action Rutland, Lands End Way, Oakham, LE15 6RB.

SOUTH LEICESTER BIRDWATCHERS. (2006; 60).
Graham & Marion Turner. Address: n/a.
T: 07852 782 002;
E: graham.turner@btinternet.com;
W: http://southleicesterbirdwatchers.uk/
Meetings: 7.15 pm, 2nd Wednesday of the month (Sep-Jun). All Saints Parish Centre, Wigston Road, Blaby, Leicester, LE8 4FA.

Ringing Group/Bird Observatory
CHARNWOOD RINGING GROUP.
W: http://charnwoodringers.blogspot.com/

RUTLAND WATER RG.

STANFORD RG. W: www.stanfordrg.org.uk

RSPB Local Group
LEICESTER. (1969; 1600/area).
Graham Heninghem. T: 01455 616 098;
E: graham.heninghem@hotmail.co.uk;
W: www.rspb.org.uk/groups/leicester
Meetings: 7.30pm, usually 3rd Friday of the month (Sep-May). Trinity Methodist Hall, Harborough Road, Oadby, Leicester, LE2 4LA.

LOUGHBOROUGH. (1970; 100).
Peter Farnworth. T: n/a;
E: Lboro.RSPBgroup@talktalk.net;
W: www.rspb.org.uk/groups/loughborough
Meetings: 7.45pm, 2nd Friday of the month (Oct-May). Lecture Theatre U020, Brockington Building, Loughborough University, Epinal Way, Loughborough, LE11 3TZ.

Wetland Bird Survey (WeBS) Local Organiser
LEICESTERSHIRE & RUTLAND (excl. RUTLAND WATER). Brian Moore. T: 0116 291 0411 (pm only);
E: b_moore@ntlworld.com

RUTLAND WATER. Tim Appleton.
T: 01572 770 651; E: tappleton@birdfair.org.uk

Wildlife Trust
LEICESTERSHIRE & RUTLAND WILDLIFE TRUST. (1956; 16,000).
The Old Mill, 9 Soar Lane, Leicester, LE3 5DE.
T: 0116 262 9968, (fax) 0116 251 5426;
E: info@lrwt.org.uk; W: www.lrwt.org.uk

LINCOLNSHIRE

Bird Atlas/Avifauna
The Lincolnshire Bird Atlas 1980-1999: an historical perspective. Lincolnshire Bird Club (2020)

The Birds of Lincolnshire & South Humberside. Stephen Lorand & Keith Atkin (Leading Edge Press, 1989).

Bird Recorder
Phil Hyde, The Hawthorns, Legbourne, Louth, LN11 8NH. T: 01507 607 998;
E: recorder_south@lincsbirdclub.co.uk

Bird Report
LINCOLNSHIRE BIRD REPORT (1979-), from Bill Sterling, 'Newlyn', 5 Carlton Avenue, Healing, NE Lincs DN41 7PW. E: sales@lincsbirdclub.co.uk

BTO Regional Representative
EAST. Philip Espin. T: 01507 605 448;
E: pmjespin@gmail.com

NORTH. Chris Gunn. T: 01777 818 742;
E: donandchris@hotmail.co.uk

Iain Turner (Assistant Representative). T: n/a;
E: iainturner80@gmail.co.uk

SOUTH. Vacant - contact Dawn Balmer, BTO.
T: 01842 750 050; E: dawn.balmer@bto.org

WEST. Mike Daly. T: 01522 820 105;
E: Mike.btorrwl@gmail.com;

LINCOLNSHIRE (E,N,S,W): Nicholas Watts (Regional Development Officer). T: n/a;
E: nicholas@vinehousefarm.co.uk

Club
LINCOLNSHIRE BIRD CLUB. (1979; 300).
Jim Wright (Secretary), 33 Parker Street, Cleethorpes, N.E. Lincolnshire DN35 8TH.
T: n/a;
E: secretary@lincsbirdclub.co.uk;
W: www.lincsbirdclub.co.uk
Meetings: Held occasionally - sometimes jointly with other groups such as BTO or Lincolnshire Naturalists' Union. AGM in Mar or Apr with a guest speaker. Contact/see website for details.

LINCOLNSHIRE NATURALISTS' UNION. (1893; n/a) c/o Lincolnshire Wildlife Trust, Banovallum House, Manor House Street, Horncastle, LN9 5HF.
T: 01507 526 667; E: info@lnu.org;
W: https://lnu.org/
Meetings: 2pm, Saturdays (winter) - contact/see website for details. Whisby Education Centre, Whisby Nature Park, Moor Lane, Thorpe on the Hill, Lincoln, LN6 9BW.

Ringing Group/Bird Observatory
MID LINCS RG.

WASH WADER RG. W: www.wwrg.org.uk

GIBRALTAR POINT BIRD OBSERVATORY.
Kevin Wilson (Warden) Gibraltar Point Field Centre, Skegness, PE24 4SU. T: 01754 898 079;
E: kwilson@lincstrust.co.uk;
W: http://gibraltarpointbirdobservatory.blogspot.com

RSPB Local Group
GRIMSBY. (1986; n/a).
Martin Francis. T: 01472 883 436;
E: martin.francis2@ntlworld.com;
W: www.rspb.org.uk/groups/grimsby
Meetings: 7.30pm, 3rd Monday of the month (Sep-Jun). Holy Trinity Parish Hall, 2 Machray Place, Grimsby Road, Cleethorpes, DN35 7LH.

LINCOLN. (1974; 250).
Peter Skelson. T: 01522 695 747;
E: peter.skelson@lincolnRSPB.org.uk;
W: www.lincolnrspb.org.uk
Meetings: 7.30pm, 2nd Thursday of the month (Sep-May). Bishop Grosseteste University, Longdales Road, Lincoln, LN1 3DY.

SOUTH LINCOLNSHIRE SOCIAL GROUP. (1987; n/a).
Robin Dobson. T: 01529 304 370;
E: ro.dobson@btinternet.com;
W: www.rspb.org.uk/groups/southlincolnshire
This is a social group rather than a Local Group - contact/see website for details of activities which include walks & Wash boat trips.

Wetland Bird Survey (WeBS) Local Organiser
HUMBER ESTUARY (INNER SOUTH). Keith Parker.
T: via WeBS Office; E: keithparker69@gmail.com

HUMBER ESTUARY (MID-SOUTH). Barbara Moore.
T: 01484 868 402; E: barbara.moore@rspb.org.uk

HUMBER ESTUARY (NORTH). See Yorkshire.

HUMBER ESTUARY (OUTER SOUTH). John Walker.
T: 01507 338 038; E: johnwalkermbe@gmail.com

NORTH LINCOLNSHIRE (INLAND). Chris Gunn.
T: 01777 818 742; E: donandchris@hotmail.co.uk

SOUTH LINCOLNSHIRE (INLAND INC. PETERBOROUGH). Robert Titman. T: 01733 583 254;
E: bob.titman@gmail.com

THE WASH (LINCOLNSHIRE). Jim Scott.
T: 01485 542 689; E: jim.scott@rspb.org.uk

Wildlife Trust
LINCOLNSHIRE WILDLIFE TRUST. (1948; 28,000).
Banovallum House, Manor House Street, Horncastle, LN9 5HF. T: 01507 526 667, (fax) 01507 525 732; E: info@lincstrust.co.uk;
W: www.lincstrust.org.uk

LONDON (GREATER)

Bird Atlas/Avifauna
The London Bird Atlas. Ian Woodward, Richard Arnold & Neil Smith (John Beaufoy Books, 2017).

The Birds of London. Andrew Self (Christopher Helm, 2014).

Bird Recorder
Roger Payne, 40 Lyndhurst Drive, Harpenden, Herts AL5 5RJ. T: 07930 608005; E: rogerwpayne@gmail.com

Bird Report
LONDON BIRD REPORT: 20-mile radius of St Paul's Cath. (1936-), from Catherine Schmitt, London Natural History Society, 4 Falkland Ave, London N3 1QR. E: catherineschmitt20@gmail.com

BTO Regional Representative
LONDON, NORTH. Vacant - contact Dawn Balmer, BTO. T: 01842 750 050; E: dawn.balmer@bto.org

LONDON, SOUTH. Richard Arnold.
T: 0208 224 1135; E: bto@thomsonecology.com

Club
MARYLEBONE BIRDWATCHING SOCIETY. (1981; 140). Steve Ripley (Chair), 29 Berriman Road, Holloway, London N7 7PN. T: 07929 966 705;
E: birdsmbs@yahoo.com; W: www.birdsmbs.org.uk
Meetings: 7.15pm, usually 3rd Friday of the month (Sep-Apr, not Dec). Gospel Oak Methodist Church, Lisburne Road, London NW3 2NT.

THE LONDON BIRD CLUB (1858; 1000). (Ornithology Section of London NHS). Douglas Bilton (Sec), 75 Walcot Square, London SE11 4UB.
T: 07725 740585;
E: douglas.bilton@yahoo.com;
W: www.lnhs.org.uk/index.php/about-us/london-bird-club
Meetings: 7.00pm, - contact/see website for details. Burgh House, New End Square, Hampstead, London, NW3 1LT.

Ringing Group/Bird Observatory
RUNNYMEDE RG. W: www.runnymederinging.uk

SOUTHERN COLOUR RINGING GROUP.
W: www.southern-colour-ringing-group.org.uk

RSPB Local Group
BEXLEY. (1979; n/a).
Stuart Banks. T: 0208 854 7251;
E: bexleylocalRSPBgroup@gmail.com;
W: www.rspb.org.uk/groups/bexley
Meetings: 7.15pm, 2nd Friday of the month (Sep-May). John Fisher Church Hall, 48 Thanet Road, Bexley, DA5 1AP.

BROMLEY. (1972; 200).
Sandie Wood. T: 07392 790 719;
E: bromleyRSPB@gmail.com;
W: www.rspb.org.uk/groups/bromley
Meetings: 7.00pm, 2nd Wednesday of the month (Sep-Jun). United Reformed Church (Verrall Hall), Widmore Road, Bromley, BR1 1RY.

CENTRAL LONDON. (1974; 250).
Andrew Peel. T: 0208 997 0072;
E: RSPB.centrallondongroup@gmail.com;
W: www.rspb.org.uk/groups/centrallondon
Meetings: 6.45pm, 2nd Thursday of the month (Sep-May). St Columba's Church Hall, Pont St, London SW1X 0BD.

CROYDON. (1973; 500).
John Davis. T: 0208 640 4578;
E: johndaviswine1@gmail.com;
W: www.rspb.org.uk/groups/croydon
Meetings: 2.00pm & 8.00pm, 2nd Monday of the month (not Jun). Whitgift Sports Club, The Clubhouse, Croham Manor Road, South Croydon, CR2 7BG.

NORTH EAST LONDON. (2009; 200).
Ray Watson. T: 07855 140 129;
E: NelondonRSPB@yahoo.co.uk;
W: www.rspb.org.uk/groups/northeastlondon
Meetings: 8.00pm, 2nd Tuesday of the month (Sep-Jun). St Mary's Church - Gwinnell Room, 207 High Road, South Woodford, London E18 2PA.

NORTH WEST LONDON. (1983; n/a).
Bob Husband. T: 0208 441 8742;
E: bobhusband@hotmail.co.uk;
W: www.rspb.org.uk/groups/nwlondon
Meetings: 8pm, usually the last Tuesday of the month (except Nov & Dec). Wilberforce Centre, St Paul's Church, The Ridgeway, London NW7 1QU.

PINNER & DISTRICT. (1972; 300).
Ian Jackson. T: 0208 907 3513;
E: imjpinRSPB@gmail.com;
W: www.rspb.org.uk/groups/pinner
Meetings: 8pm, 2nd Thursday of the month (Sep-May). St John The Baptist Church Hall, Church Lane, Pinner, Middx HA5 3AA.

RICHMOND & TWICKENHAM. (1979; 200).
Clare Million. T: 07794 835 571;
E: richmondRSPB@yahoo.co.uk;
W: www.rspb.org.uk/groups/richmond
Meetings: 7.30pm, usually 1st Wednesday of the month & 2.00pm, on the following Tuesday of the month (Sep-Apr). The Hyde Room, York House, York Street, Twickenham, TW1 3AA.

Wetland Bird Survey (WeBS) Local Organiser
GREATER LONDON (excl. THAMES ESTUARY/see Essex). Andrew Moon. T: 07811 847 732;
E: andrew.moon@talk21.com

LEE VALLEY. See Hertfordshire.

SOUTH WEST LONDON. See Surrey.

Wildlife Trust
LONDON WILDLIFE TRUST. (1981; 8,500).
Dean Bradley House, 52 Horseferry Road, London SW1P 2AF. T: 0207 261 0447, (fax) 0207 633 0811;
E: enquiries@wildlondon.org.uk;
W: www.wildlondon.org.uk

MANCHESTER (GREATER)

Bird Recorder
Ian McKerchar, 42 Green Ave, Astley, Manchester, M29 7EH. T: 01942 701 758 & 07958 687 481; E: ianmckerchar1@gmail.com

Bird Report
BIRDS IN GREATER MANCHESTER (1959-), from the Bird Recorder - see above.

LEIGH ORNITHOLOGICAL SOCIETY BIRD REPORT (1971-), latest report available to members only, then download from website after one year. W: www.leighos.org.uk

BTO Regional Representative
Nick Hilton. T: 07920 494 240; E: nmhilton71@aol.com

Steve Atkins (Assistant Representative). T: 01706 645 097; E: svatkins38@gmail.com

Club
ALTRINCHAM AND DISTRICT NATURAL HISTORY SOCIETY. (1908; 30)
Mike Pettipher (Chairman). Address: n/a. T: n/a; E: info@altnats.org.uk; W: www.altnats.org.uk
Meetings: 7:30pm, 2nd Tuesday of the month (Sep-Apr). Dunham Room, The Jubilee Centre, The Firs, Bowdon, Altrincham, WA14 2TQ.

LEIGH ORNITHOLOGICAL SOCIETY. (1971; 115).
David Shallcross (Chairman), 28 Surrey Avenue, Leigh, WN7 2NN. T: n/a;
E: leighos.chairman@gmail.com;
W: www.leighos.org.uk
LOS Young Birders. W: www.losybc.blogspot.co.uk
Meetings: 7.30pm, usually 1st Friday of the month (ca. 10 talks Sep-May) - contact/see website for details. Derby Room, Leigh Library, Turnpike Centre, Civic Square, Leigh, WN7 1EB.

ROCHDALE FIELD NATURALISTS' SOCIETY. (1874; 100).
Joan Carter (Sec), 57 Plover Close, Bamford, Rochdale, OL11 5PU. T: 07597 838 061;
E: rfnsenquiries@talktalk.net;
W: www.rochdalefieldnaturalists.org.uk
Meetings: 7.30pm, usually 2nd Thursday of the month (Sep-Apr). Cutgate Baptist Church, Edenfield Rd, Rochdale, OL11 5AQ.

STOCKPORT BIRDWATCHING SOCIETY. (1972; 70).
Dave Evans, 36 Tatton Road South, Stockport, SK4 4LU.
T: 0161 432 9513;
E: windhover1972@yahoo.co.uk;
W: http://stockportbirders.blogspot.com/
Meetings: 7.30pm, last Wednesday of the month (Sep-Apr). The Heatons Sports Club, Heaton Moor, Stockport, SK4 2NF.

STOCKPORT BIRDWATCHING SOCIETY

Ringing Group/Bird Observatory
LEIGH RG.

SOUTH MANCHESTER RG.

RSPB Local Group
HIGH PEAK. (1974; 130).
Richard Stephenson. T: 0161 427 4187;
E: stephenson3rj@gmail.com;
W: www.rspb.org.uk/groups/highpeak
Meetings: 7.30pm, 3rd Monday of the month (Sep-May). Marple Senior Citizens Hall, Memorial Park, Marple, Stockport, SK6 6BA.

STOCKPORT. (1979; 140).
Colin Barnes. T: 0161 477 5118;
E: colinbarnes6fg@hotmail.com;
W: www.rspb.org.uk/groups/stockport
Meetings: 7.30pm, 2nd Monday of the month (Sep-Apr). Stockport Masonic Guildhall, 169 Wellington Road South, Stockport, SK1 3UA.

Wetland Bird Survey (WeBS) Local Organiser
GREATER MANCHESTER. Tim Wilcox.
T: via WeBS Office; E: tim.wilcox0@gmail.com

Wildlife Trust. See Lancashire & North Merseyside.

NORFOLK

Bird Atlas/Avifauna
The Norfolk Bird Atlas: Summer and Winter Distributions 1999-2007. Moss Taylor & John H Marchant (BTO 2011).

The Birds of Norfolk. Moss Taylor, Michael Seago, Peter Allard & Don Dorling (Christopher Helm, 1999/rep 2007).

The Birds of Blakeney Point. Andy Stoddart, Steve Joyner & James McCallum (Wren Publishing, 2005).

Bird Recorder
Neil Lawton, Scolt Head Boatshed, Harbour Way, Brancaster Staithe, PE31 8BW. T: n/a;
E: norfolkbirdrecs@gmail.com

Assistant Recorder (Rarities): Kieran Nixon. Address: n/a. T: n/a; E: leicester_cityfc@live.co.uk

Bird Report
NAR VALLEY ORNITHOLOGICAL SOCIETY ANNUAL REPORT (1977-), from Ian Black, Three Chimneys, Tumbler Hill, Swaffham, PE37 7JG.
E: enquiries@narvos.org.uk

NORFOLK BIRD & MAMMAL REPORT (1953-), from Tony Leech, NNNS Publications, 3 Eccles Road, Holt, NR25 6HJ. E: birdreport@nnns.org.uk

NORFOLK ORNITHOLOGISTS' ASSOCIATION ANNUAL REPORT (1962-), from NOA, Broadwater Rd, Holme Next the Sea, Hunstanton, PE36 6LQ.
E: info@noa.org.uk

BTO Regional Representative
NORTH-EAST. Chris Hudson. T: 01603 868 805;
E: chris697@btinternet.com

NORTH-WEST. Vacant - contact Dawn Balmer, BTO.
T: 01842 750 050; E: dawn.balmer@bto.org

Fred Cooke (Assistant Representative)
T: 01553 631 076; E: f.cooke1@btinternet.com

SOUTH-EAST. Rachel Warren. T: 01603 593 912;
E: campephilus@btinternet.com

SOUTH-WEST. Vince Matthews. T: 01953 884 125;
E: norfolksouthwest@gmail.co.uk

Club
CLEY BIRD CLUB. (1986; 620+).
Ann Duff (Chairwoman). Address: n/a. T: n/a;
E: ann.duff.cbc@gmail.com;
W: www.cleybirdclub.org.uk
Meetings: 7.30pm, 2nd Monday of the month (Oct-Mar). Cley Village Hall, The Fairstead, Cley, NR25 7RJ.

NAR VALLEY ORNITHOLOGICAL SOCIETY. (1976; 125).
Ian Black (Chairman), Three Chimneys, Tumbler Hill, Swaffham, PE37 7JG. T: 01760 724 092;
E: enquiries@narvos.org.uk;
W: www.narvos.org.uk
Meetings: 7.30pm, last Tuesday of the month (Jul-Nov & Jan-May). Barn Theatre, Convent of The Sacred Heart, Mangate Street, Swaffham, PE37 7QW.

NORFOLK & NORWICH NATURALISTS' SOCIETY. (1869; 630).
James Emerson (Sec), 108 Sleaford Green, Norwich, NR3 3JT. T: 01603 961939;
E: jamesemerson2007@gmail.com;
W: www.norfolknaturalists.org.uk
Meetings: 7.30pm, 2nd Tuesday of the month (Oct-Mar), St Andrew's Hall, Church Lane, Eaton, NR4 6NW.

NORFOLK ORNITHOLOGISTS' ASSOCIATION. (1970; 1500).
Sophie Barker (Warden/ Secretary), Broadwater Rd, Holme-next-Sea, Hunstanton, PE36 6LQ.
T: 01485 525 406;
E: info@noa.org.uk;
W: www.noa.org.uk
Meetings: AGM held in Sep.

NORTH-EAST NORFOLK BIRD CLUB. (2015; 280).
Colin Blaxill, (Membership Sec), Caitlins, Bernard Close, High Kelling, Holt, NR25 6QY.
T: 01263 711 718; E: info@nenbc.co.uk;
W: www.nenbc.co.uk
Meetings: 7.30pm, last Thursday of the month (Sep-Nov, Jan-Apr, plus a social event in Dec & May). Aylmerton Village Hall, Aylmerton, NR11 8PX.

WENSUM VALLEY BIRDWATCHING SOCIETY. (2003; 130+).
Lin Pateman (Sec). Address: n/a. T: 01263 587 262:
E: wvbs.secretary@gmail.com; W: www.wvbs.co.uk
Meetings: 7.30pm, 3rd Thursday of the month (all year). Great Witchingham (Lenwade) Village Hall, Hubbards Loke, Lenwade, NR9 5AZ.

Ringing Group/Bird Observatory
BTO NUNNERY RG.

EAST ANGLIA GULL GROUP.

EAST NORFOLK RG.
W: http://eastnorfolkringinggroup.blogspot.co.uk/

NORTH NORFOLK RG.

NORTH WEST NORFOLK RG.
W: http://www.nwnrg.co.uk/

SHERINGHAM RG.

SOUTH WEST NORFOLK RG.

THETFORD FOREST RG.

UEA RG. W: http://uearg.blogspot.co.uk/

WASH WADER RG. W: www.wwrg.org.uk

HOLME BIRD OBSERVATORY (NOA RG). See Club - NOA.

RSPB Local Group
NORWICH. (1971; 230).
David Porter. T: 01603 745 310 (day);
E: RSPBnorwichgroup@virginmedia.com;
W: www.rspb.org.uk/groups/norwich
Meetings: 7.30pm, 2nd Monday of the month (Sep-Jun). Hellesdon Community Centre, (off Wood View Road), Middletons Lane, Norwich, NR6 5QB.

Wetland Bird Survey (WeBS) Local Organiser
BREYDON WATER. James Rowe.
T: via WeBS Office; E: via WeBS Office

NORFOLK (excl. ESTUARIES). Tim Strudwick.
T: via WeBS Office; E: tim.strudwick@rspb.org.uk

NORTH NORFOLK COAST. Neil Lawton.
T: via WeBS Office; E: neilscolt@yahoo.com

THE WASH (NORFOLK). See Lincolnshire.

Wildlife Trust
NORFOLK WILDLIFE TRUST. (1926; 36,000).
Bewick House, 22 Thorpe Road, Norwich, NR1 1RY.
T: 01603 625 540, (fax) 01603 598 300;
E: info@norfolkwildlifetrust.org.uk;
W: www.norfolkwildlifetrust.org.uk

NORTHAMPTONSHIRE

Bird Recorder
Jon Cook. Address: n/a. T: n/a;
E: joncooknorthantsbirds@gmail.com

Bird Report
NORTHANTS BIRDS (1969-),
from RW Bullock,
81 Cavendish Drive,
Northampton, NN3 3HL.
E: robertbullock25@hotmail.com

BTO Regional Representative
Barrie Galpin.
T: 01780 444 351;
E: barrie.galpin@zen.co.uk

Club
NORTHAMPTONSHIRE BIRD CLUB. (1973; 50).
Eleanor McMahon (Sec), Oriole House, 5 The Croft, Hanging Houghton, NN6 9HW. T: 01604 880 009;
E: eleanor1960@btinternet.com;
W: https://northantsbirdclub.blogspot.com/
Meetings: 7.30pm, 1st Wednesday of the month (all year). The Lodge, Pitsford Water, 7 Brixworth Road, Holcot, NN6 9SJ.

Ringing Group/Bird Observatory
NORTHANTS RG.

STANFORD RG. W: www.stanfordrg.org.uk

RSPB Local Group
MID NENE. (1975; 280).
Ian Wrisdale. T: 01933 410 566;
E: wrisdale1@tiscali.co.uk;
W: www.rspb.org.uk/groups/midnene
Meetings: 7.30pm, 3rd Thursday of the month (Sep-Mar). The Saxon Hall, Thorpe Street, Raunds, Wellingborough, NN9 6LT.

Wetland Bird Survey (WeBS) Local Organiser
NENE VALLEY. Steve Brayshaw. T: via WeBS Office;
E: via WeBS Office

NORTHAMPTONSHIRE (excl. NENE VALLEY).
Barrie Galpin. T: via WeBS Office;
E: via WeBS Office

Wildlife Trust. See Cambridgeshire.

NORTHUMBERLAND

Bird Atlas/Avifauna
Northumbria Bird Atlas. Tim Dean, Dick Myatt, Muriel Cadwallender, Tom Cadwallender (Northumberland & Tyneside Bird Club, 2015).

Bird Recorder
Tim Dean, 2 Knocklaw Park, Rothbury, NE65 7PW.
T: 01669 621 460; E: t.r.dean@btinternet.com

Bird Report
BIRDS IN NORTHUMBRIA (1970-), from Trevor Blake, 6 Glenside, Ellington, Morpeth, NE61 5LS.
E: trevor.1958@live.co.uk

BIRDS ON THE FARNE ISLANDS: in Northumbrian Naturalist (1971-), from the Natural History Society of Northumbria, Great North Museum, Hancock, Barras Bridge, Newcastle upon Tyne, NE2 4PT. T: 0191 208 2790; E: nhsn@ncl.ac.uk

BTO Regional Representative
Tom Cadwallender. T: 01665 830 884;
E: tomandmurielcadwallender@hotmail.com

Muriel Cadwallender
(Regional Development Officer). T: & E: as above.

Club
NATURAL HISTORY SOCIETY OF NORTHUMBRIA. (1829; 1800).
Natural History Society of Northumbria, Great North Museum: Hancock, Barras Bridge, Newcastle upon Tyne, NE2 4PT. T: 0191 208 2790;
E: nhsn@ncl.ac.uk; W: www.nhsn.ncl.ac.uk
Meetings: 7pm, Fridays (Oct-Mar). Ridley Building Lecture Hall, Claremont Road, Newcastle upon Tyne, NE1 7RU.

NORTH NORTHUMBERLAND BIRD CLUB. (1984; 180).
Glynis Gower (Sec). Address: n/a. T: 01289 330 969;
E: ringouzel@northnorthumberlandbirdclub.co.uk;
W: www.northnorthumberlandbirdclub.co.uk
Meetings: 7.30pm, 2nd Friday of the month (Sep-Jun). Bamburgh Pavilion (corner of green below Bamburgh Castle).

NORTHUMBERLAND & TYNESIDE BIRD CLUB. (1958; 270).
Andrew Brunt (Sec),
South Cottage, West Road,
Longhorsley, Morpeth,
NE65 8UY. T: 01670 788 352;
E: ntbcorg@gmail.com;
W: www.ntbc.org.uk
Meetings: 7.00pm, 2nd Thursday of the month (Sep-Apr). Northern Rugby Club, McCracken Park, Great North Road, Newcastle upon Tyne, NE3 2DT.

Ringing Group/Bird Observatory
NHS OF NORTHUMBRIA.

NORTHUMBRIA RG.
W: https://northumbriaringinggroup.com/

RSPB Local Group
NEWCASTLE UPON TYNE. (1969; 250).
Jeff Mason. T: 0191 289 5058;
E: NewcastleRSPBgroup@gmail.com;
W: www.rspb.org.uk/groups/newcastle
Meetings: 7.00pm, 1st Tuesday of the month (Oct-Mar, not Jan). MEA House, Ellison Place, Newcastle-Upon=Tyne, NE1 8XS.

Wetland Bird Survey (WeBS) Local Organiser
LINDISFARNE. Andrew Craggs. T: 01289 381 470;
E: andrew.craggs@naturalengland.org.uk

NORTHUMBERLAND (COASTAL). Kathy Evans.
T: via WeBS Office; E: via WeBS Office

NORTHUMBERLAND (INLAND). Tim Daley.
T: via WeBS Office; E: timbirdman@gmail.com

Wildlife Trust
NORTHUMBERLAND WILDLIFE TRUST. (1971; 12,000). Garden House, St Nicholas Park, Jubilee Road, Gosforth, Newcastle upon Tyne, NE3 3XT.
T: 0191 284 6884, (fax) 0191 284 6794;
E: mail@northwt.org.uk; W: www.nwt.org.uk

NOTTINGHAMSHIRE

Bird Atlas/Avifauna
Birds of Nottinghamshire. Nick Crouch, Jason Reece, Bernie Ellis, Chris du Feu, David Parkin (Liverpool University Press, 2019).

Bird Recorder - Vacant.

Bird Report
BIRDS OF NOTTINGHAMSHIRE (1943-), from Jenny Swindells, 21 Chaworth Road, West Bridgford, Nottingham, NG2 7AE. T: 0115 9812 432;
E: j.swindells@btinternet.com

BTO Regional Representative
Lynda Milner. T: 01623 862 025;
E: milner.lynda@googlemail.com

Club
LOUND BIRD CLUB. (1990; 60).
Paul Hobson (Chairman). Address: n/a.
T: 07415 671 346; E: hoblong@hotmail.co.uk;
W: facebook - Lound Bird Club
Meetings: 7.30pm, last Wednesday of the month (Sep-Mar, not Dec). Sutton-cum-Lound village hall - see facebook or contact for details.

NETHERFIELD WILDLIFE GROUP. (1999; 130).
NWG, c/o 4 Shellburne Close, Heronridge, Nottingham, NG5 9LL. T: n/a; E: via website;
W: www.gedlingconservationtrust.org/netherfield-lagoons/netherfield-wildlife-group/
Meetings: No indoor meetings held.

NOTTINGHAMSHIRE BIRDWATCHERS. (1935; 290).
Jenny Swindells (Sec),
21 Chaworth Rd, West Bridgford, Nottingham, NG2 7AE.
T: 0115 9812 432;
E: j.swindells@btinternet.com;
W: www.nottsbirders.net
Meetings: Contact/see website for details.

WOLLATON NATURAL HISTORY SOCIETY. (1976; 70).
E: via website;
[Nigel Downes (Bird Group). T: 0115 944 4671]
W: www.spanglefish.com/wollatonnaturalhistory/
Meetings: 7.30pm, 3rd Wednesday of the month (not Aug). St Leonards Community Centre, Bramcote Lane, Wollaton, HG8 2ND.

Ringing Group/Bird Observatory
BIRKLANDS RG.

NORTH NOTTS RG.

SOUTH NOTTS RG.
W: http://southnottsringinggroup.blogspot.co.uk/

TRESWELL WOOD INTEGRATED POPULATION MONITORING GROUP.
W: www.treswellwoodipmg.org

RSPB Local Group
MANSFIELD. (1986; 40).
Diane Bartlam. T: 07305 951 359;
E: dianeashplorers@hotmail.co.uk;
W: www.rspb.org.uk/groups/mansfield
Meetings: 7.30pm, 1st Wednesday of the month (Sep-Jun). The Stanhope Centre, Rock Valley, Mansfield, NG18 1AL.

NOTTINGHAM. (1974; 300).
Doreen Markam. T: 0115 978 2741;
E: RSPBnottmlgmem@gmail.com;
W: www.rspb.org.uk/groups/nottingham
Meetings: 7.30pm, 1st Wednesday of the month (Sep-May). Nottingham Mechanics, 3 North Sherwood Street, Nottingham, NG1 4EZ.

Wetland Bird Survey (WeBS) Local Organiser
NOTTINGHAMSHIRE. David Parkin. T: 0115 932 0090;
E: bluethroat@btinternet.com

Wildlife Trust
NOTTINGHAMSHIRE WILDLIFE TRUST. (1963; 11,000). The Old Ragged School, Brook Street, Nottingham, NG1 1EA. T: 0115 958 8242, (fax) 0115 924 3175;
E: info@nottswt.co.uk;
W: www.nottinghamshirewildlife.org

OXFORDSHIRE

Bird Atlas/Avifauna
Birds of the Heart of England (Banbury area).
TG Easterbrook
(Liverpool University Press, 2013).

Birds of Oxfordshire.
JW Brucker, AG Gosler & AR Heryet
(Pisces Publications, 1992).

Bird Recorder
Ian Lewington, 119 Brasenose Road, Didcot, OX11 7BP. T: 01235 819 792;
E: recorder@oos.org.uk

Bird Report
BIRDS OF OXFORDSHIRE (1915-), from Roy Overall, 30 Hunsdon Road, Iffley, Oxford, OX4 4JE.
E: roy.overall@oos.org.uk

BANBURY ORNITHOLOGICAL SOCIETY ANNUAL REPORT (1966-), from Sandra Bletchly, 11 Orchard Grove, Bloxham, Banbury, Oxon OX15 4NZ. E: sandra.banornsoc@btinternet.com

BTO Regional Representative
NORTH. Frances Buckel. T: 01608 644 425;
E: fran.buckel@btinternet.com

SOUTH. John Melling. T: 01865 820 867;
E: bto-rep@oos.org.uk

Club
BANBURY ORNITHOLOGICAL SOCIETY (incl. parts of Northants/Oxon/Warwick). (1952; 100).
Frances Buckel (Sec), Witts End, Radbones Hill, Over Norton, Chipping Norton, OX7 5RA.
T: 01608 644 425; E: Secretary@banburyos.org;
W: www.banburyornithologicalsociety.org.uk
Meetings: 7.30pm, 2nd Monday of the month (Sep-May). The Banbury Cricket Club, White Post Road, Bodicote, OX15 4BN.

OXFORD ORNITHOLOGICAL SOCIETY. (1921; 330).
Barry Hudson (Sec), Pinfold, 4 Bushey Row, Bampton, Witney, OX18 2JU. T: 01993 200 790 & 07788 496 847;
E: secretary@oos.org.uk;
W: www.oos.org.uk
Meetings: 7.45pm, 2nd Wednesday of the month (Sep-May). Exeter Hall, Oxford Road, Kidlington, OX5 1AB.

RSPB Local Group
OXFORD. (1977; 100).
Roy Grant. T: 01865 774 659;
E: roy.otters@hotmail.co.uk;
W: www.rspb.org.uk/groups/oxford
Meetings: 7.45pm, (usually) 1st Thursday of the month (Sep-May). Sandhills Primary School, Terrett Avenue, Sandhills, Oxford, OX3 8FN.

VALE OF WHITE HORSE. (1977; 100).
Bob Knight. T: 01235 818 072;
E: bob_knight@tiscali.co.uk;
W: www.rspb-vwh.org.uk
Meetings: 7.45pm, 3rd Monday of the month (Sep-May). Didcot Civic Hall, Britwell Road, Didcot, OX11 7JN.

Wetland Bird Survey (WeBS) Local Organiser
OXFORDSHIRE (NORTH). Sandra Bletchly.
T: T: via WeBS Office;
E: sandra.banornsoc@btinternet.com

OXFORDSHIRE (SOUTH). Ben Carpenter.
T: 07814 159 050; E: beniow@yahoo.co.uk

Wildlife Trust
BERKSHIRE, BUCKS. & OXON WILDLIFE TRUST. (1959; 25,000).
The Lodge, 1 Armstrong Road, Littlemore, Oxford, OX4 4XT. T: 01865 775 476, (fax) 01865 711 301;
E: info@bbowt.org.uk; W: www.bbowt.org.uk

SHROPSHIRE

Bird Atlas/Avifauna
The Birds of Shropshire.
Leo Smith (Liverpool University Press, 2019).

Bird Recorder
John Martin, 39 Sandygate Avenue, Shrewsbury, SY2 6TF;
T: 07443 544962;;
E: soscountyrecorder@gmail.com

Bird Report
SHROPSHIRE BIRD REPORT (1956-), from Helen Griffiths (Sec). E: secretary@shropshirebirds.co.uk

BTO Regional Representative
Jonathan Groom. T: n/a;
E: bto.shropshire@gmail.com

Martin George (Assistant Representative). T: n/a;
E: martin@thegreenfuse.net

Club
SHROPSHIRE ORNITHOLOGICAL SOCIETY. (1955; 800).
Helen J Griffiths (Sec).Address: n/a.
T: 01597 811 420;
E: secretary@shropshirebirds.co.uk;
W: www.shropshirebirds.com
Meetings: 7.15pm, 1st Wednesday of the month (Oct-Apr). Bayston Hill Memorial Hall, Lyth Hill Road, Bayston Hill, Shrewsbury, SY3 0DR.

Ringing Group/Bird Observatory
CHELMARSH RG.
W: http://chelmarshrg.blogspot.co.uk/

SHROPSHIRE RG.
W: http://shropshirerg.wordpress.com

WEST MIDLANDS RINGING GROUP.
W: www.westmidlandsringinggroup.co.uk

RSPB Local Group
SHROPSHIRE. (1991; 110).
Nadia Archer. T: 0121 262 6800;
E: ShrewsburyRSPBgroup@gmail.com;
W: www.rspb.org.uk/groups/shropshire
Meetings: 7.30pm, 4th Tuesday of the month (Sep-Apr/2nd Tuesday in Dec). Bayston Hill Memorial Hall, Lyth Hill Rd, Shrewsbury, SY3 0DR.

SOUTH SHROPSHIRE. (2004; 75).
Carol Wood. T: 07807 068 304;
E: carolwood772@outlook.com;
W: www.rspbsouthshropshire.co.uk
Meetings: 7.30pm, 2nd Tuesday of the month (Sep-Apr). Culmington Village Hall, on the B4365, Culmington, SY8 2DA.

Wetland Bird Survey (WeBS) Local Organiser
SHROPSHIRE. Michael Wallace. T: 01743 369 035;
E: michaelwallace47@gmail.com

Wildlife Trust
SHROPSHIRE WILDLIFE TRUST. (1962; 11,000).
193 Abbey Foregate, Shrewsbury, SY2 6AH.
T: 01743 284 280, (fax) 01743 284 281;
E: enquiries@shropshirewildlifetrust.org.uk;
W: www.shropshirewildlifetrust.org.uk

SOMERSET & BRISTOL/AVON

Bird Atlas/Avifauna
The Birds of Exmoor and the Quantocks. David Ballance, Brian Gibbs & Roger Butcher (privately published, 2nd ed 2016).

Somerset Atlas of Breeding and Wintering Birds 2007-2012. David Ballance, Rob Grimmond, Julian Thomas & Eve Tigwell (Somerset OS, 2014).

Avon Atlas 2007-11. Richard L Bland & M Dadds (Bristol Naturalists' Society, 2012).

A History of the Birds of Somerset. DK Ballance (Isabelline Books, 2006).

Bird Recorder
AVON. Rupert Higgins, 28 Egerton Road, Bishopston, Bristol, BS7 8HL. T: n/a;
E: avonbirdrecorder@outlook.com

SOMERSET. Brian Gibbs, 23 Lyngford Road, Taunton, TA2 7EE. T: 01823 274 887;
E: brian.gibbs@somersetbirding.org.uk

Bird Report
AVON BIRD REPORT (1977-), from Harvey Rose, Arncliffe, Coast Road, Walton Bay, Clevedon, BS21 7FW. E: h.e.rose@bris.ac.uk

SOMERSET BIRDS (1912-), from the Somerset Bird Recorder - see above.

BTO Regional Representative
AVON. Gordon Youdale. T: 01454 881 690;
E: gordon.youdale@blueyonder.co.uk

Dave Stoddard (Assistant Representative).
T: 0117 924 698; E: dave.stoddard@tiscali.co.uk

SOMERSET. Eve Tigwell. T: 01373 451 630;
E: eve.tigwell@zen.co.uk

Roger Dickey (Assistant Representative).
T: n/a; E: roger.dickey52@gmail.com

Club
BRISTOL NATURALISTS' SOCIETY. (1862; 500).
Lesley Cox (Ornithology Section Rep). Address: n/a.
T: 07786 437 528; E: secretary@bristolnats.org.uk;
W: www.bristolnats.org.uk
Meetings: 7.30pm, 2nd Wednesday of the month (Oct-Mar). Westbury-on-Trym, Methodist Church, 46 Westbury Hill, Bristol, BS9 3AA.

BRISTOL ORNITHOLOGICAL CLUB. (1967; 560).
Judy Copeland (Membership Sec),
19 St George's Hill, Easton-in-Gordano,
North Somerset BS20 0PS. T: 01275 373 554;
E: bocsecretary@hotmail.com;
W: www.bristolornithologicalclub.co.uk
Meetings: 7.30pm, 3rd Thursday of the month (Sep-Mar). Newman Hall, Grange Court Road, Westbury-on-Trym, BS9 4DR.

EXMOOR NATURAL HISTORY SOCIETY. (1974; 480).
Caroline Giddens (Sec), 12 King George Road, Minehead, TA24 5JD. T: 01643 707 624;
E: carol.enhs@talktalk.net; W: www.enhs.org.uk
Meetings: 7.30pm, 1st Wednesday of the month (Oct-Mar). Methodist Church Hall, The Avenue, Minehead, TA24 5AY - check website for times. 10am, 2nd Tuesday of the month at Luckbarrow, West Luccombe. TA24 8HX.

SOMERSET ORNITHOLOGICAL SOCIETY. (1974; 475).
Dick Best (Membership Sec), Quantock View Farm, Steart, TA5 2PXP. T: 01278 651 063;
E: dick.best@somersetbirding.org.uk;
W: www.somersetbirding.org.uk
Meetings: 7.30pm, 3rd Thursday of the month (Oct-Apr, except Dec). Village Hall, Ruishton, Taunton, TA3 5JD.

Ringing Group/Bird Observatory
CHEW VALLEY RS.
W: www.chewvalleyringingstation.co.uk

GORDANO VALLEY RG.

RSPB Local Group
BATH AND DISTRICT. (1969; 260).
Jean Melksham. T: 01225 404985;
E: jeanmelksham@blueyonder.co.uk;
W: www.rspb.org.uk/groups/bath
Meetings: 7.30pm, 3rd Wednesday of the month (Sep-Apr). St Andrew's Community Church, Hawthorn Grove, Combe Down, Bath, BA2 5QA.

SOUTH SOMERSET. (1979; 200).
Denise Chamings. T: 01460 240 740;
E: denise.chamings@talktalk.net;
W: www.rspb.org.uk/groups/southsomerset
Meetings: 7.30pm, 3rd Thursday of the month (Sep-May). The Millennium Hall, Seavington St. Mary, Ilminster, TA19 0QH.

Wetland Bird Survey (WeBS) Local Organiser
AVON (OTHER SITES). Rupert Higgins.
T: 0117 944 1034; E: rupert@wessexeco.co.uk

SEVERN ESTUARY (SOMERSET & AVON). Harvey Rose.
T: via WeBS Office; E: H.E.Rose@bristol.ac.uk

SOMERSET LEVELS. Eve Tigwell. T: 01373 451 630;
E: eve.tigwell@zen.co.uk

SOMERSET (OTHER SITES). Eve Tigwell - see above.

Wildlife Trust
AVON WILDLIFE TRUST. (1980; 19,000).
32 Jacobs Wells Road, Bristol, BS8 1DR.
T: 0117 917 7270, (fax) 0117 929 7273;
E: mail@avonwildlifetrust.org.uk;
W: www.avonwildlifetrust.org.uk

SOMERSET WILDLIFE TRUST. (1964; 21,000).
34 Wellington Road, Taunton, Somerset TA1 5AW.
T: 01823 652 400, (fax) 01823 652 411;
E: enquiries@somersetwildlife.org;
W: www.somersetwildlife.org

STAFFORDSHIRE

Bird Atlas/Avifauna.
See West Midlands.

Bird Recorder
Nick Pomiankowski,
22 The Villas, West End,
Stoke-on-Trent, ST4 5AQ.
T: 01782 849 682;
E: staffs-recorder
@westmidlandbirdclub.org.uk

Bird Report.
See West Midlands.

BTO Regional Representative
NORTH: Scott Petrek. T: n/a;
E: scott.petrek@gmail.com
Gerald Gittens (Assistant Representative).
T: 01785 815 141;
E: gerald.gittens1@btopenworld.com

SOUTH: Scott Petrek/Gerald Gittens - see above.

WEST: Scott Petrek/Gerald Gittens - see above.

Club
WEST MIDLAND BIRD CLUB (STAFFORD BRANCH).
David Dodd (Chairman). Address: n/a. T: n/a;
E: stafford@westmidlandbirdclub.org.uk;
W: www.westmidlandbirdclub.org.uk/stafford
Meetings: 7.45pm, 1st Tuesday of the month (Nov-Mar). Perkins Engines Sport & Social Club, Tixall Road, Stafford, ST16 3UB.

Ringing Group/Bird Observatory
WEST MIDLANDS RINGING GROUP.
W: www.westmidlandsringinggroup.co.uk

RSPB Local Group
BURTON & SOUTH DERBYSHIRE. (1973; 50).
Dave Lummis. T: 01283 219 902;
E: david.lummis@btinternet.com; W: n/a.
Meetings: 7.30pm, 2nd Wednesday of some months between Sep-May - contact/see website for details. All Saint's Church Hall, Branston Road, Burton-on-Trent, DE14 3BY.

LICHFIELD & DISTRICT. (1977; 1150).
Dennis Muxworthy. T: 0121 353 6886;
E: dennis.muxworthy@btinternet.com;
W: www.rspb.org.uk/groups/lichfield
Meetings: 7.30pm, 2nd Tuesday of the month (Sep-May). Guildhall, Bore Street, Lichfield, WS13 6LU.

NORTH STAFFS. (1982; 200).
Geoff Sales. T: 0121 262 6800;
E: sgeoff31@gmail.com;
W: www.rspb.org.uk/groups/northstaffordshire
Meetings: 7.30pm, 3rd Wednesday of the month (Sep-May). North Staffs Conference Centre (Medical Institute), Hartshill Road, Stoke-on-Trent, ST4 7NY.

SOUTH WEST STAFFORDSHIRE. (1972; 120).
Theresa Dorrance. T: 01902 847 041;
E: tmidorrance@gmail.com;
W: www.rspb.org.uk/groups/southweststaffs
Meetings: 8.00pm, 2nd Tuesday of the month (Sep-May). Codsall Village Hall, Wolverhampton Road, Codsall, WV8 1PW.

Wetland Bird Survey (WeBS) Local Organiser
STAFFORDSHIRE. Scott Petrek. T: 07914 647 755;
E: scott.petrek@gmail.com

Wildlife Trust
STAFFORDSHIRE WILDLIFE TRUST. (1969; 16,000). The Wolseley Centre, Wolseley Bridge, Stafford, ST17 0WT. T: 01889 880 100, (fax) 01889 880 101; E: info@staffs-wildlife.org.uk; W: www.staffs-wildlife.org.uk

SUFFOLK

Bird Atlas/Avifauna
The Birds of Suffolk. Steve Piotrowski (Christopher Helm, 2003).

Bird Recorder
NORTH EAST. Andrew Green, 17 Cherrywood, Harleston, Norfolk IP20 9LP. T: 07766 900 063; E: bird-ne@sns.org.uk

SOUTH EAST. Steve Fryett. Address: n/a. T: n/a; E: bird-se@sns.org.uk

WEST. Colin Jakes, 7 Maltward Avenue, Bury St Edmunds, IP33 3XN. T: 01284 702 215; E: bird-w@sns.org.uk

RECORDER (RARITIES). Craig Fulcher. Address: n/a. T: n/a. E: sorsec@gmail.com

Bird Report
SUFFOLK BIRDS (1950-), from Suffolk Naturalist's Society, c/o The Museum, High St, Ipswich, IP1 3QH. E: enquiries@sns.org.uk

BTO Regional Representative
Mick Wright. T: 01473 721 486; E: kupe1515@sky.com

Club
SUFFOLK BIRD GROUP. (1973; 400). Gi Grieco. Address: n/a. T: 07951 482 547; E: info@suffolkbirdgroup.org; W: www.suffolkbirdgroup.org
Meetings: 7.30pm, last Thursday of the month (Sep-Nov, Jan-Apr). Ipswich Hotel, Old London Road, Copdock, IP8 3JD or The Cedars Hotel, Needham Road, Stowmarket, IP14 2AJ - contact/ check website for details.

WAVENEY BIRD CLUB. (n/a; 185). Rebecca Bedwell (Sec), Garden Cottage, Great Common Lane, Ilketshall St Andrew, NR34 8JB. T: 01986 781 436; E: secretary@waveneybirdclub.com; W: www.waveneybirdclub.com
Meetings: 7.30pm, usually the last Tuesday of the month (Sep-Mar). The Maltings Sports Ground, Pirnhow Street, Ditchingham, NR35 2RU.

Ringing Group/Bird Observatory
DINGLE BIRD CLUB. W: www.dinglebirdclub.org

EAST ANGLIA GULL GROUP.

KESSINGLAND RG.

LACKFORD RG.

LANDGUARD RG.

LITTLE OUSE RG.

WAVENEY RG.

LANDGUARD BIRD OBSERVATORY. Landguard Bird Observatory, View Point Road, Felixstowe, IP11 3TW. T: 01394 673 782; E: langardbo@yahoo.co.uk; W: www.lbo.org.uk

RSPB Local Group
IPSWICH. (1975; 150). Timothy Kenny. T: 01394 809 236; E: IpswichRSPBlocalgroup@yahoo.com; W: www.rspb.org.uk/groups/ipswich
Meetings: 7.30pm, 2nd Thursday of the month (Sep-Apr). St Andrews Church Hall, The Street, Rushmere,Ipswich, IP5 1DH.

LOWESTOFT. (1974; 70). Phil Jackson (Press & Publicity Officer). T: n/a; E: LowestoftRSPBlocalgroup@gmail.com; W: www.rspb.org.uk/groups/lowestoft
Meetings: 7.30pm, 1st Friday of the month (Jan-Dec). St Marks Church Centre, Bridge Road, Oulton Broad, Lowestoft, NR33 9JX.

WOODBRIDGE. (1987; 320). Paul Hetherington. T: 01728 724 504; E: RSPBwoodbridge@paulandgill.com; W: www.rspb.org.uk/groups/woodbridge
Meetings: 7.30pm, 1st Thursday of the month (Oct-May). Woodbridge Community Hall, Station Road,Woodbridge, IP12 4AU.

Wetland Bird Survey (WeBS) Local Organiser
ALDE COMPLEX. Ian Castle. T: 01394 450 188; E: ian@castle-hamlett.co.uk

ALTON WATER. John Glazebrook. T: via WeBS Office; E: johnglazebrook@btopenworld.com

BLYTH ESTUARY (SUFFOLK). Will Russell. T: 07876 796 143; E: will.russell@naturalengland.org.uk

DEBEN ESTUARY. Nick Mason. T: 07876 086 039; E: nick.mason4@btinternet.com

ORWELL ESTUARY. Mick Wright. T: 01473 710 032; E: kupe1515@sky.com

STOUR ESTUARY. Rick Vonk. T: 01206 391 153; E: rick.vonk@rspb.org.uk

SUFFOLK (OTHER SITES). Alan Miller.
T: 01728 833 405;
E: alan.miller@suffolkwildlifetrust.org

Wildlife Trust
SUFFOLK WILDLIFE TRUST. (1961; 28,000).
Brooke House, The Green, Ashbocking, Ipswich, IP6 9JY. T: 01473 890 089, (fax) 01473 890 165;
E: info@suffolkwildlifetrust.org;
W: www.suffolkwildlifetrust.org

SURREY

Bird Atlas/Avifauna
Birds of Surrey Bird Atlas 2007-2012.
Surrey Bird Club (Surrey Bird Club, 2018).

Birds of Surrey. Jeffery J Wheatley
(Surrey Bird Club, 2007).

Bird Recorder
Steve Chastell, 8 Burnet Ave, Guildford, GU1 1YD.
T: 07826 544 221; E: surrey.recorder@btinternet.com

Bird Report
SURBITON AND DISTRICT BIRD WATCHING SOCIETY ANNUAL BIRD REPORT (1970-), from Thelma Caine, 21 More Lane, Esher, KT10 8AJ.
E: thelmacaine512@btinternet.com

SURREY BIRD REPORT (1953-), from Penny Williams, Bournbrook House, Sandpit Hall Lane, Chobham, GU24 8HA. E: membership@surreybirdclub.org.uk

BTO Regional Representative
Penny Williams. T: 01276 857 736;
E: penny@waxwing.plus.com

Andrew Lockett (Assistant Representative).
T: n/a; E: andrew.paul.lockett@gmail.com

Club
SURBITON & DISTRICT BIRDWATCHING SOCIETY. (1954; 130).
Alice Laird (Membership enquiries). Address: n/a.
T: n/a; E: alicesdbws@martinhwatson.co.uk;
W: http://surbitonbirds.org/
Meetings: 8pm, 3rd Tuesday of each month (not Aug). Contact/see website for location.

SURREY BIRD CLUB. (1957; 385).
Penny Williams (Membership Sec),
Bournbrook House,
Sandpit Hall Lane, Chobham,
GU24 8HA. T: 01276 857 736;
E: membership@surreybirdclub.org.uk;
W: www.surreybirdclub.org.uk
Meetings: Contact/see website for details.

Ringing Group/Bird Observatory
HERSHAM RG.

RUNNYMEDE RG. W: www.runnymederinging.uk

RSPB Local Group
DORKING & DISTRICT. (1982; 230).
Roy Theobald. T: 01306 889 976;
E: roytheobald@yahoo.co.uk;
W: www.rspb.org.uk/groups/dorkinganddistrict
Meetings: 8.00pm, 3rd Friday of the month (Sep-Apr). Christian Centre, Church Street, Dorking, RH4 1DW.

EAST SURREY. (1984; 7000+/area).
John Lawrence. T: 01737 553 316;
E: jfjlawrence@gmail.com;
W: www.eastsurreyrspb.co.uk
Meetings: 8.00pm, 2nd Wednesday of the month (not Aug). White Hart Barn, Godstone, RH9 8DT.

GUILDFORD & DISTRICT. (1974; 350).
Margo Scott. T: 01483 767 546;
E: info@RSPBguildford.org.uk;
W: www.rspbguildford.org.uk
Meetings: Generally - 2.00pm, 1st Thursday of the month (Oct-Mar). Shalford Village Hall, Kings Road, Shalford, GU4 8JU & 7.30pm, 4th Wednesday of the month (Sep-May). Onslow Village Hall, The Square, Wilderness Road, Guildford, GU2 7QR.

NORTH WEST SURREY. (1974; 150).
Alan Sharps. T: 01784 244 665;
E: nwsleader@yahoo.co.uk;
W: www.rspb.org.uk/groups/nwsurrey
Meetings: 7.45pm, 4th Thursday of the month (Sep-Nov, Jan-Jun). St Charles Borromeo School, Portmore Way, Weybridge, KT13 8JD.

Wetland Bird Survey (WeBS) Local Organiser
SURREY & SW LONDON. Penny Williams.
T: via WeBS Office; E: penny@waxwing.plus.com

Wildlife Trust
SURREY WILDLIFE TRUST. (1959; 26,000).
School Lane, Pirbright, Woking, GU24 0JN.
T: 01483 795 440, (fax) 01483 486 505;
E: info@surreywt.org.uk;
W: www.surreywildlifetrust.org

SUSSEX

Bird Atlas/Avifauna
The Birds of Sussex. Sussex Ornithological Society/ Adrian LR Thomas (BTO, 2014).

Bird Recorder
Mark Mallalieu, 29 Cobbetts Mead, Haywards Heath, West Sussex RH16 3TQ. T: 01444 441 425
& 07736 788 077; E: recorder@sos.org.uk

Bird Report
SUSSEX BIRD REPORT (1948-), from Val Bentley, Lanacre, Blackgate Lane, Henfield, BN5 9HA.
E: mandpcommittee@sos.org.uk

BTO Regional Representative
Helen Crabtree.
T: 01444 441 687;
E: hcrabtree@gmail.com

Dave Boddington (Assistant Representative).
T: n/a; E: davebodds@yahoo.co.uk

Club
FRIENDS OF RYE HARBOUR NATURE RESERVE. (1973; 2000+).
Friends of Rye Harbour; E: via website;
W: www.rhnrfriends.co.uk
& www.sussexwildlifetrust.org.uk/ryeharbour
Meetings: Special events, including winter talks, held for Friends (info in newsletter).

HENFIELD BIRDWATCH. (1998; 150+).
Mike Russell, Tor-Est-In, Lower Station Road, Henfield, West Sussex BN5 9UG.
T: 01273 649 246; E: mikerussell51@yahoo.co.uk;
W: http://henfieldbirdwatch.co.uk/

SHOREHAM DISTRICT ORNITHOLOGICAL SOCIETY. (1953; 200).
SDOS Hon. Sec, 24 Chancellors Park, Hassocks, West Sussex BN6 8EZ. T: n/a;
E: sdos.memsec@btinternet.com;
W: www.sdos.org
Meetings: 7.30pm, 2nd Tuesday of the month (Oct-Apr). St Peter's Church Hall, West Street, Shoreham-by-Sea, East Sussex BN43 5GZ.

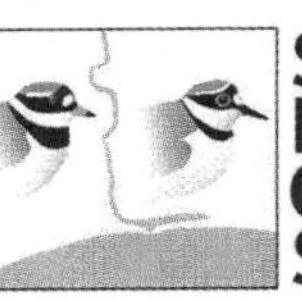

SUSSEX ORNITHOLOGICAL SOCIETY. (1962; 1900+).
Chris Davis (Sec), 27 Salisbury Road, Seaford, East Sussex BN25 2BD. T: 01323 891 267;
E: secretary@sos.org.uk; W: www.sos.org.uk
Meetings: Annual conference (Jan) Haywards Heath. AGM (Apr) - contact/see website for details.

Ringing Group/Bird Observatory
BEACHY HEAD RS.

CUCKMERE RG.

RYE BAY RG.

STEYNING RG.

RSPB Local Group
BRIGHTON & DISTRICT. (1974; 200).
Mark Weston. T: 01903 606 581;
E: mark.weston@RSPB.org.uk;
W: www.rspb.org.uk/groups/brighton
Meetings: 7.30pm, 4th Thursday of the month (Sep-May, for Dec contact/see website). Blatchington Windmill, North Barn, Holmes Avenue, Hove, East Sussex BN3 7LH.

CHICHESTER. (1979; 245).
Rob Yarham. T: 07545 376074;
E: chichesterbirds@gmail.com;
W: www.rspb.org.uk/groups/chichester
Meetings: 7.30pm, 4th Thursday of the month (Sep-May). The Masonic Hall, 7 South Pallant, Chichester, West Sussex PO19 1SY.

CRAWLEY & HORSHAM. (1978; 65).
Andrea Saxton. T: 01403 242 218;
E: andrea.saxton@sky.com;
W: www.rspb.org.uk/groups/crawley
Meetings: 8.00pm, 3rd Wednesday of the month (Sep-Apr). St. Bernadette's Church Hall, Tilgate Way, Crawley, West Sussex RH10 5BS.

EAST GRINSTEAD. (1998; 185).
Shaun Taylor. T: 01342 719 456;
E: eastgrinsteadRSPB@gmail.com;
W: www.rspb.org.uk/groups/egrinstead
Meetings: 8.00pm, last Wednesday of the month (Sep-Jun, not Dec). Main Hall, East Court, College Lane, East Grinstead, West Sussex RH19 3LT.

EASTBOURNE & DISTRICT. (1994; 200).
Tony Vass. T: 01424 844 304;
E: eastbourneRSPB@gmail.com;
W: www.rspb.org.uk/groups/eastbourne
Meetings: 2.15pm & 7.30pm, 1st Wednesday of the month (Sep-Jun). St. Wilfrid's Church Hall, Eastbourne Rd, Pevensey Bay, East Sussex BN24 6HL.

HASTINGS & ST LEONARDS. (1983; 65).
Susan Neighbour. T: 01424 211 140;
E: RSPB.HStL@gmail.com;
W: www.rspb.org.uk/groups/hastings
Meetings: 7.30pm, 3rd Friday of the month. The Taplin Centre, Upper Maze Hill, St Leonards-on-Sea, East Sussex TN38 0LQ.

Wetland Bird Survey (WeBS) Local Organiser
CHICHESTER HARBOUR. Peter Hughes.
T: 01243 510 985;
E: peter.hughes@conservancy.co.uk

SUSSEX (OTHER SITES - COASTAL).
Dave Boddington. T: 07771 758 105;
E: davebodds@yahoo.co.uk

SUSSEX (OTHER SITES - INLAND). Helen Crabtree.
T: 01444 441 687; E: hcrabtree@gmail.com

Wildlife Trust
SUSSEX WILDLIFE TRUST. (1961; 34,000). Woods Mill, Shoreham Road, Henfield, West Sussex BN5 9SD. T: 01273 492 630, (fax) 01273 494 500; E: enquiries@sussexwt.org.uk; W: www.sussexwildlifetrust.org.uk

WARWICKSHIRE

Bird Atlas/Avifauna.
See West Midlands.

Bird Recorder
Chris Hill, 17 Brampton Crescent, Shirley, Solihull, B90 3SY. T: 07900 473 911; E: warks-recorder@westmidlandbirdclub.org.uk

Bird Report.
See West Midlands.

BTO Regional Representative
Annette Jarratt-Knock. T: n/a; E: annettejk@oneuk.com

Club
NUNEATON & DISTRICT BIRDWATCHERS' CLUB (NUNEATON BIRD CLUB). (1950; 30). Address: n/a. T: n/a; E: nuneatonbirdclub@outlook.com; W: http://nuneatonbirdclub.wordpress.com/ **Meetings:** 7.30pm, 3rd Thursday of the month (Sep-May). Hatters Space Community Centre, Upper Abbey Street, Nuneaton, CV11 5DN.

Ringing Group/Bird Observatory
ARDEN RG.

BRANDON RG.

RSPB Local Group
COVENTRY & WARWICKSHIRE. (1969; 120). Peter Worthy. T: 01926 497 967; E: pete@cpworthy.plus.com; W: www.rspb.org.uk/groups/coventryandwarwickshire **Meetings:** 7:30pm, 4th Friday of the month (Sep-May). Baginton Village Hall, Frances Rd, Baginton, Coventry, CV8 3AB.

Wetland Bird Survey (WeBS) Local Organiser
WARWICKSHIRE. Matthew Griffiths. T: via WeBS Office; E: matt_avesmaster@hotmail.com

Wildlife Trust
WARWICKSHIRE WILDLIFE TRUST. (1970; 25,000). Brandon Marsh Nature Centre, Brandon Lane, Coventry, CV3 3GW. T: 02476 302 912, (fax) 02476 639 556; E: enquiries@wkwt.org.uk; W: www.warwickshire-wildlife-trust.org.uk

WEST MIDLANDS

Bird Atlas/Avifauna
The New Birds of the West Midlands. Graham & Janet Harrison - covers Staffordshire, Warwickshire, Worcestershire & the former West Midlands County (West Midland Bird Club, 2005).

Bird Recorder
Peter Forbes. Address: n/a. T: n/a; E: west-mids-recorder@westmidlandbirdclub.org.uk

Bird Report
WEST MIDLAND BIRD REPORT (inc Staffs, Warks, Worcs & West Mids) (1934-), from Focus Optics www.focusopticsltd.co.uk and The Birders Store www.birders-store.co.uk or further info from E: secretary@westmidlandbirdclub.org.uk

BTO Regional Representative
BIRMINGHAM & WEST MIDLANDS. Steve Davies. T: 07782 891 726; E: stevedaviesbtorep@hotmail.co.uk

Club
WEST MIDLAND BIRD CLUB (1929; 1400). (Staffs, Warks, Worcs & the West Midlands.) Mark Rickus (Sec), 27 Ringmere Avenue, Castle Bromwich, Birmingham, B36 9AT. T: 0121 749 5348; E: secretary@westmidlandbirdclub.org.uk; W: www.westmidlandbirdclub.org.uk **Meetings:** Contact/see website for branch details.

Field Trips only:
Liz Palmer. T: 01827 54557 & 07947 456 448; E: Wmbcfieldtrips.liz@westmidlandbirdclub.org.uk

WEST MIDLAND BIRD CLUB (SOLIHULL BRANCH). Richard Harvey (Chairman). Address: n/a. T: 0789 556 125; E: solihull@westmidlandbirdclub.org.uk; W: www.westmidlandbirdclub.org.uk/solihull **Meetings:** 7.30 pm, on a Friday (Oct-Mar). Guild House, 1715 High Street, Knowle, Solihull, B93 0LN.

Ringing Group/ Bird Observatory
BIRMINGHAM UNIVERSITY RG. W: http://www.birmingham.ac.uk/research/activity/ornithology/people/ringing-group/index.aspx

MERCIAN RG.

WEST MIDLANDS RINGING GROUP. W: www.westmidlandsringinggroup.co.uk

RSPB Local Group
SOLIHULL. (1983; 2600).
John Roberts. T: 0121 707 3101;
E: johnbirder@care4free.net;
W: www.rspb.org.uk/groups/solihull
Meetings: 7.30pm, (usually) 1st Thursday of the month (Sep-Apr). Bentley Heath Community Hall, Widney Road, Bentley Heath, Solihull, B93 9BQ.

STOURBRIDGE. (1978; 150).
David Bradford. T: 01384 390 035;
E: djbstourbridge@yahoo.co.uk;
W: www.rspb.org.uk/groups/stourbridge
Meetings: 7.30pm, 2nd Wednesday of the month (Sep-May). St Thomas' Church Hall, Market Street, Stourbridge, DY8 1AQ.

SUTTON COLDFIELD. (1986; 250).
Tony Green. T: 01827 750 633;
E: tonygreen777@hotmail.co.uk;
W: www.rspb.org.uk/groups/suttoncoldfield
Meetings: 7.30pm, 1st Monday of the month (Sep-Jun). Bishop Vesey's Grammer School, Lichfield Road, Sutton Coldfield, B74 2NH.

WALSALL. (1971; n/a).
Michael Pittaway. T: 01922 710 568;
E: michaelpittaway34@gmail.com;
W: www.rspb-walsall.org.uk
Meetings: 7.30pm, 3rd Wednesday of the month (Sep-May). St Marys RC Primary School, Jesson Rd, Walsall, WS1 3AY.

Wetland Bird Survey (WeBS) Local Organiser
WEST MIDLANDS. Nick Lewis. T: 0121 783 0874;
E: nick.r.lewis@virginmedia.com

Wildlife Trust
WILDLIFE TRUST FOR BIRMINGHAM AND THE BLACK COUNTRY. (1980; 8,000).
Centre of the Earth, 42 Norman Street, Winson Green, Birmingham, B18 7EP. T: 0121 523 0094;
E: info@bbcwildlife.org.uk; W: www.bbcwildlife.org.uk

WILTSHIRE

Bird Atlas/Avifauna
Birds of Wiltshire. J Ferguson-Lees, P Castle & P Cranswick (Wiltshire Ornithological Society, 2007).

Bird Recorder
Claire Jones. Address: n/a. T: n/a;
E: recorder@wiltshirebirds.co.uk

Bird Report
WILTSHIRE BIRD REPORT (HOBBY) (1975-), from John Osborne, 4 Fairdown Avenue, Westbury, BA13 3HS. E: josb@talktalk.net

BTO Regional Representative
NORTH: Claire Jones. T: n/a;
E: wiltshirebto@gmail.com

SOUTH: Claire Jones - see above.

Club
SALISBURY & DISTRICT NATURAL HISTORY SOCIETY. (1952; 110).
John Pitman (Ornithology Section). Address: n/a.
T: 01722 327 395; E: jacpitman@btinternet.com;
W: www.salisburynaturalhistory.com
Meetings: 7.30pm, 3rd Thursday of the month (Sep-Apr). The Meeting Room, Salisbury Baptist Church, Brown Street, Salisbury, SP1 2AS.

WILTSHIRE ORNITHOLOGICAL SOCIETY. (1974; 500+).
Matt Prior (Chair).
Address: n/a. T: n/a;
E: chair@wiltshirebirds.co.uk;
W: www.wiltshirebirds.co.uk
Meetings: Contact/see website for details.

Ringing Group/Bird Observatory
COTSWOLD WATERPARK RG.

NORTH WILTS RG.

WEST WILTS RG.

RSPB Local Group
SOUTH WILTSHIRE. (1986; 500).
Tony Goddard. T: 01722 712 713;
E: goddard543@hotmail.com;
W: www.rspb.org.uk/groups/southwiltshire
Meetings: 7.30pm, 2nd Tuesday of the month (Sep-May). Salisbury Arts Centre, Bedwin Street, Salisbury, SP1 3UT.

Wetland Birds Survey Organiser
AVON VALLEY. See Hampshire.

COTSWOLD WATER PARK. See Gloucestershire.

WILTSHIRE. Claire Jones. T: 07921 255 630;
E: wiltshirebto@gmail.com

Wildlife Trust
WILTSHIRE WILDLIFE TRUST. (1962; 20,000).
Elm Tree Court, Long Street, Devizes, SN10 1NJ.
T: 01380 725 670, (fax) 01380 729 017;
E: info@wiltshirewildlife.org;
W: www.wiltshirewildlife.org

WORCESTERSHIRE

Bird Atlas/Avifauna. See West Midlands.

Bird Recorder
Steven Payne, 6 Norbury Close, Redditch, B98 8RP.
T: 01527 60169; E: steven.payne@tiscali.co.uk

Bird Report. See West Midlands.

BTO Regional Representative
Steve Davies. T: 01562 885 789;
E: stevedaviesbtorep@hotmail.co.uk

Harry Green (Assistant Representative).
T: 01386 710 377; E: zen130501@zen.co.uk

Club
WEST MIDLAND BIRD CLUB
(KIDDERMINSTER BRANCH).
Roger Pannell (Chairman), 29 Greensforge Lane, Stourbridge, DY7 5BD. T: n/a;
E: kidderminster@westmidlandbirdclub.org.uk;
W: www.westmidlandbirdclub.org.uk/kidderminster
Meetings: 7.30pm, 4th Wednesday of the month (Sep-Apr). St Oswalds Church Centre, off Broadwaters Drive, Kidderminster, DY10 2RY.

Ringing Group/Bird Observatory
WYCHAVON RG.

RSPB Local Group
WORCESTER & MALVERN. (1980; 150).
Nick Skilbeck. T: 07540 328 945;
E: nickskilbeck@btinternet.com;
W: www.rspb.org.uk/groups/worcester
Meetings: 7.30pm, 2nd Wednesday of the month (Sep-May). Powick Village Hall, on A449, Powick, WR2 4RT.

Wetland Bird Survey (WeBS) Local Organiser
WORCESTERSHIRE. Vacant - contact WeBS Office.

Wildlife Trust
WORCESTERSHIRE WILDLIFE TRUST. (1967; 21,000). Lower Smite Farm, Smite Hill, Hindlip, Worcester, WR3 8SZ. T: 01905 754 919, (fax) 01905 755 868;
E: enquiries@worcestershirewildlifetrust.org;
W: www.worcswildlifetrust.co.uk

YORKSHIRE

Bird Atlas/Avifauna
The Birds of Spurn. *Andy Roadhouse* (Spurn Observatory Trust, 2016).

Breeding Birds of the Sheffield Area including the North-east Peak District. David Wood & Richard Hill (Sheffield Bird Study Group, 2013).

Birds of the Huddersfield Area. Paul & Betty Bray (Huddersfield Birdwatchers Club, 2008).

The Birds of Yorkshire. J Mather (Croom Helm, 1986).

Bird Recorder
YORKSHIRE. Recorder, rarities. Chris Robinson. Address: n/a. T: n/a;
E: YNURCDescriptions@outlook.com

DONCASTER AREA (see D&DOS). Chris Robinson. Address: n/a. T: n/a; E: Sabsgull@hotmail.co.uk

EAST YORKSHIRE. Vacant.

NORTH YORKSHIRE. Ian Court, 2 Burley Mews, Steeton, Keighley, BT20 6TX. T: 01535 658 582;
E: ian.court@mypostoffice.co.uk

SOUTH YORKSHIRE. Martin Wells, 715 Manchester Road, Stocksbridge, Sheffield, S36 1DQ.
T: 0114 288 4211;
E: martinwells@barnsleybsg.plus.com

WEST YORKSHIRE. Ian Court - see above.

Bird Report
BIRDS IN HUDDERSFIELD (1966-), from Helen Sill, Wards End Farm, Marsden, Huddersfield HD7 6NJ;
T: 07854 739 646;
E: hazel.sill@btinternet.com

BIRDS IN THE SHEFFIELD AREA (1973-), from Martin Hodgson, 142 Hangingwater Road, Sheffield, S11 7ET.
W: membership@sbsg.org

BRADFORD ORNITHOLOGICAL GROUP REPORT (1987-), online - download from:
http://www.bradfordbirding.org/reports
or further info: Mr CJ King,
E: bogmembership@live.co.uk

FILEY BIRD REPORT (1976-), from Janet Robinson, 31 Wharfedale, Filey, YO14 0DG. T: 01723 513 991;
E: janetrobinson@yorkshire.net

FLAMBOROUGH HEAD BIRD OBSERVATORY, from Tony Hood. 9 Hartendale Close, Flamborough, East Yorkshire YO15 1PL. E: tonyhood74@gmail.com

HARROGATE & DISTRICT NATURALISTS' SOCIETY BIRD REPORT (1958-), from Stephen Root, 4 Plompton Way, Harrogate, HG2 7DU. E: stephenroot@outlook.com

SCARBOROUGH DISTRICT - download online from www.scarboroughbirding.co.uk

SPURN WILDLIFE (1991-), from Spurn Bird Observatory Trust, Kew Villa, Kilnsea, HU12 0UB.
T: 01964 650 479;
E: friendsofspurn@hotmail.com

YORK ORNITHOLOGICAL CLUB REPORT (1966-), from Jane Chapman, 12 Moorland Road, York, YO10 4HF. T: 01904 633 558;
E: secretary@yorkbirding.org.uk

YORKSHIRE BIRD REPORT (1940-), from Jill Warwick, Sharow Grange, Sharow, Ripon, HG4 5BN. T: 01765 602 832;
E: jill@swland.co.uk

BTO Regional Representative

BRADFORD. Mike Denton. T: 01484 646 990; E: michael@atheta.plus.com

CENTRAL. Mike Brown. T: 01423 567 382; E: mikebtorep@gmail.com

EAST. Brian Walker. T: n/a; E: brianwalker2611@gmail.com

HULL. Brian Walker - see above.

LEEDS & WAKEFIELD. Rachael Dixey. T: n/a; E: rachael.dixey@btopenworld.com

NORTH-EAST. Nicholas Gibbons. T: n/a; E: nicholas.gibbons123@btinternet.com

NORTH-WEST. Alex Gould. T: n/a; E: alexgould2011@hotmail.co.uk

RICHMOND. Mike Gibson. T: 01677 450 542; E: mkgibson@btinternet.com

SOUTH-EAST: Grant Bigg. T: n/a; E: gr_bigg@outlook.com

SOUTH-WEST: Grant Bigg - see above.

YORK. Rob Chapman. T: 01904 633 558; E: robert.chapman@tinyworld.co.uk

Club

BRADFORD ORNITHOLOGICAL GROUP. (1987; 100). Shaun Radcliffe (Chairman), 8 Longwood Avenue, Bingley, Bradford, BD16 2RX. T: 01274 770 960; E: shaun.radcliffe@btinternet.com; W: www.bradfordbirding.org
Meetings: 7.30pm, 1st Tuesday of the month (all year). The Link, 35 Cliffe Avenue, Baildon, Shipley, BD17 6NX.

DONCASTER & DISTRICT ORNITHOLOGICAL SOCIETY. (n/a; 20). Chris Robinson. T: 07534 271 254; E: Sabsgull@hotmail.co.uk; W: www.doncasterbirding.co.uk/wordpress/
Meetings: 7.15pm, last Thursday of the month (Sep-May). Sports & Social Club, Off Wheatley Hall Road, Doncaster DN2 4LT.

FILEY BIRD OBSERVATORY & GROUP. (1977; 165). Chris Blakeley (Membership Sec), Cottage 1, Skipster Hagg Farm, Sinnington, YO62 6SP. T: n/a. E: membership.fbog@gmail.com; W: www.fbog.org.uk

HARROGATE & DISTRICT NATURALISTS' SOCIETY. (1947; 210). Sue Coldwell (Gen Sec), 4 Abbots Way, Knaresborough, HG5 8EU. T: 01423 868 043; E: gensec@hdns.org.uk; W: www.hdns.org.uk
Meetings: 7.30pm, fortnightly, on a Wednesday (Oct-Mar). St. Roberts Centre, 2/3 Robert Street, Harrogate, HG1 1HP.

HUDDERSFIELD BIRDWATCHERS' CLUB. (1966; 80). Chris Abell (Sec), 57 Butterley Lane, New Mill, Holmfirth, HD9 7EZ. T: 01484 681 499; E: cdabell@gmail.com; W: www.huddersfieldbirdwatchersclub.co.uk
Meetings: 7.30pm, Tuesday's fortnightly (Sep-May). The Old Court Room, Town Hall, Ramsden St, Huddersfield, HD1 2TA.

ROTHERHAM & DISTRICT ORNITHOLOGICAL SOCIETY. (1974; 80). RDOS, c/o Galaxy Four, 493 Glossop Road, Sheffield, S10 2QE; T: n/a; E: via website; W: www.rotherhambirds.co.uk
Meetings: 7.30pm, 2nd Friday of the month (Sep-Apr). Herringthorpe United Reform Church Hall, Wickersley Road, Rotherham, S60 4JN.

SCARBOROUGH BIRDERS. (1993; 70). Nick Addey (Chairman). Address: n/a. T: n/a; E: nickaddey@dsl.pipex.com; W: www.scarboroughbirding.co.uk
Meetings: Irregular (7.30pm) - contact/see website for details.

SHEFFIELD BIRD STUDY GROUP. (1972; 350). Richard Hill (Chair), 22 Ansell Road, Sheffield, S11 7PE. T: n/a; E: Secretary@sbsg.org; W: www.sbsg.org
Meetings: 7.15pm, 2nd Wednesday of the month (Sep-May). Diamond Building - Lecture Theatre 2, Sheffield University, 32 Leavygreave Road, Sheffield, S3 7RD. Offers free membership to under-25's.

SK58 BIRDERS. (1992; 50). Paul Tennyson (Chairman), 16/18 Sheffield Road, South Anston, Sheffield, S25 5DT. T: 01909 569 409; E: p.tennyson@sky.com; W: www.sk58birders.com
Meetings: 7.30pm, last Wednesday of the month (Sep-Nov & Jan-May). The Loyal Trooper Inn, Sheffield Road, South Anston, Sheffield, S25 5DT.

SORBY NATURAL HISTORY SOCIETY. (1918; 400). General enquiries: E: secretary@sorby.org.uk; W: www.sorby.org.uk
(Ornithology Group): Secretary - Nigel Hopkins. E: ornithology@sorby.org.uk
Meetings: Regularly held - contact/see website for details.

SWILLINGTON INGS BIRD GROUP. (1989; 230).
Martin Robinson (Sec). Address: n/a; T: n/a;
E: via website; W: http://sibg1.wordpress.com
Meetings: 7.30pm, usually 1st Thursday of the month (Feb, Apr, Jun, Aug, Oct, Dec). Two Pointers, 69 Church Street, Woodlesford, LS26 8RE.

WAKEFIELD NATURALISTS' SOCIETY. (1851; 30).
Address: n/a; T: n/a; E: via website;
W: http://wakefieldnaturalists.org
Meetings: 7.30pm, 2nd Tuesday of the month (Sep-Apr). Quaker Meeting House, Thornhill Street, Wakefield, WF1 1NQ.

YORK ORNITHOLOGICAL CLUB. (1965; 120).
Jane Chapman (Sec), 12 Moorland Road, York YO10 4HF. T: 01904 633 558;
E: secretary@yorkbirding.org.uk;
W: www.yorkbirding.org.uk
Meetings: 7.30pm, 1st Tuesday of the month (Sep-May). St Olaves Church Hall, Marygate Lane, Marygate, York, YO30 7DS.

YORKSHIRE NATURALISTS' UNION (1861; 500).
Becky Bailey (Bird Section - Sec), 38 Birch Drive, Kippax, West Yorkshire LS25 7DU.
T: 07809 461 331; E: beckybailey101@gmail.com;
W: www.ynu.org.uk
Meetings: No indoor meetings held.

Yorkshire Naturalists' Union

Ringing Group/Bird Observatory
BARNSLEY RG.

DONCASTER RG.

EAST DALES RG.
W: https://eastdalesringinggroup.wordpress.com

HUMBER WADER RG.

PICKERING FORESTS RG.

SORBY BRECK RG. W: www.britishringers.co.uk

FILEY BIRD OBSERVATORY. See Club.

FLAMBOROUGH BIRD OBSERVATORY.
Tony Hood, (Sec) 9 Hartendale Close, Flamborough, East Yorkshire YO15 1PL.
T: n/a; E: tonyhood74@gmail.com;
W: http://fbo.org.uk/

SPURN BIRD OBSERVATORY.
Paul Collins (Warden), Spurn Bird Observatory, Easington Road, Kilnsea, Hull, HU12 0UB.
T: 01964 650 479; E: pcnfa@hotmail.com;
W: www.spurnbirdobservatory.co.uk

Acommodation enquiries: T: as above;
E: accommodation.spurnbirdobs@hotmail.com.

RSPB Local Group
AIREDALE & BRADFORD. (1972; 3500/area).
Paul Barrett. T: 01274 582 078;
E: abRSPB@blueyonder.co.uk;
W: www.rspb.org.uk/groups/airedaleandbradford
Meetings: 7.30pm, 2nd Friday of the month (Sep-Apr). The Kirkgate Centre, 39A Kirkgate, Shipley, BD18 3EH.

DONCASTER. (1984; 70).
Steve Pynegar. T: 01302 834 443;
E: steve.pynegar@gmail.com;
W: www.rspbdoncaster.com
Meetings: 7.00pm, 2nd Wednesday of the month (Sep-May). Castle Park Rugby Club, Armthorpe Road, Doncaster, DN2 5QB.

EAST YORKSHIRE. (1986; 120).
Paul Leyland. T: 01723 891 507;
E: EastyorksRSPB@yahoo.co.uk;
W: www.rspb.org.uk/groups/eastyorkshire
Meetings: 7.30pm, 4th Tuesday of the month (Sep-Apr, not Dec). North Bridlington Library, Martongate, Bridlington, YO16 6YD.

HARROGATE DISTRICT. (2005; 100).
Bill Sturman. T: 01423 870 883;
E: billsturman@outlook.com;
W: www.rspb.org.uk/groups/harrogate
Meetings: 7.30pm, 2nd Monday of the month (Sep-Apr). Christ Church Parish Centre, The Stray, Harrogate, HG1 4SW.

HUDDERSFIELD & HALIFAX. (1981; 90).
David Hemingway. T: 01484 301 920;
E: d.hemingway@ntlworld.com;
W: www.rspb.org.uk/groups/huddersfieldandhalifax
Meetings: 7.30pm, 3rd Wednesday of the month (Sep-Jun). New North Road Baptist Church, New North Parade, Huddersfield, HD1 5JU.

HULL & DISTRICT. (1983; 85).
John Hallam. T: 01482 354 595;
E: jobar.hull@hotmail.co.uk;
W: www.rspb.org.uk/groups/hull
Meetings: 7.30pm, 2nd Tuesday of the month (Sep-Apr). Christchurch United Reformed Church, South Ella Way, Kirk Ella, Hull, HU10 7HB.

LEEDS. (1974; 430).
Sue Taylor/Ian Willoughby. T: 0113 258 6555;
E: RSPBleeds@googlemail.com;
W: www.rspb.org.uk/groups/leeds
Meetings: 7.30pm, various Wednesdays (Sep-Apr). Friends Meeting House, 188 Woodhouse Lane, Leeds, LS2 9DX.

RICHMONDSHIRE & HAMBLETON. (2005; n/a).
Ted Cooper. T: 07767 886 358;
E: croftbirder@hotmail.co.uk;
W: www.rspb.org.uk/groups/richmondshireandhambleton
Meeting: Various - contact/see website for details

SHEFFIELD. (1981; 300).
Helen Ensor. T: 07749 932 806;
E: ensorhelen@gmail.com;
W: www.rspb.org.uk/groups/sheffield
Meetings: 7.30pm, 1st Thursday of the month (Sep-May). Central United Reformed Church, Norfolk Street, Sheffield, S1 2JB.

SKIPTON. (1986; 300).
Ewart Dawson. T: 01729 840 601;
E: ewartdawson1@gmail.com;
W: www.rspb.org.uk/groups/skipton
Meetings: 7.30pm, 2nd Wednesday of the month (Sep-Apr). The Church Hall, Skipton Baptist Church, Rectory Lane, Skipton, BD23 1ER.

WAKEFIELD DISTRICT. (1987; 70).
Duncan Stokoe. T: 01924 280 458;
E: duncanstokoe@gmail.com;
W: www.rspb.org.uk/groups/wakefield
Meetings: 7.30pm, 4th Thursday of the month (Sep-Apr). Ossett Community Centre, Prospect Road, Ossett, WF5 8AN.

YORK. (1972; 300).
Peter Reed. T: n/a; E: contact via website;
W: www.rspb.org.uk/groups/york
Meetings: 7.30pm, usually 2nd week of the month on a Tues, Wed or Thurs (Sep-May). Also afternoon meetings, 2.30pm - contact/check website for details. Clements Hall, Nunthorpe Road, York, YO23 1BW.

Wetland Bird Survey (WeBS) Local Organiser
EAST YORKSHIRE & SCARBOROUGH (excl. THE HUMBER). Stephen Morgan. T: 01965 544 947;
E: jimmygpz@hotmail.com

HARROGATE & YORKSHIRE DALES.
Vacant - contact WeBS Office.

HUDDERSFIELD & HALIFAX AREA.
Vacant - contact WeBS Office.

HUMBER ESTUARY (NORTH). Nick Cutts.
T: via WeBS Office; E: via WeBS Office

LEEDS AREA. Paul Morris. T: via WeBS Office;
E: paulr.morris8@outlook.com

SOUTH YORKSHIRE. Grant Bigg. T: 01433 639 631;
E: gr_bigg@tiscali.co.uk

WAKEFIELD AREA. Peter Smith. T: via WeBS Office;
E: via WeBS Office

Wildlife Trust
SHEFFIELD AND ROTHERHAM WILDLIFE TRUST. (1985; 7,000).
37 Stafford Road, Sheffield, S2 2SF.
T: 0114 263 4335, (fax) 0114 263 4345;
E: mail@wildsheffield.com;
W: www.wildsheffield.com

YORKSHIRE WILDLIFE TRUST. (1946; 45,000).
1 St George's Place, Tadcaster Road, York, YO24 1GN. T: 01904 659 570;
E: info@ywt.org.uk; W: www.ywt.org.uk

SCOTLAND

Bird Atlas/Avifauna
The Birds of Scotland. Ron Forrester & Ian Andrews (Scottish Ornithologist's Club, 2007).

Bird Report
SCOTTISH BIRD REPORT
(1968-, data online), from W: www.the-soc.org.uk/about-us/online-scottish-bird-report

Club
SCOTTISH ORNITHOLOGISTS' CLUB.
W: www.the-soc.org.uk See National Directory.

Wildlife Trust
SCOTTISH WILDLIFE TRUST. (1964; 41,000)
W: www.scottishwildlifetrust.org.uk
See National Directory.

ANGUS & DUNDEE

Bird Recorder
Jon Cook, 76 Torridon Road, Broughty Ferry, Dundee, DD5 3JH. T: 01382 738 495;
E: 1301midget@tiscali.co.uk

Bird Report
ANGUS & DUNDEE BIRD REPORT (1985-), from ADBC Secretary, Dorothy Fyffe, 33 Ireland Street, Carnoustie, Angus, DD7 6AS.

BTO Regional Representative
ANGUS. Steve Willis. T: n/a;
E: steve.willis@bto.org

Club
ANGUS & DUNDEE BIRD CLUB. (1997; 200+).
Gus Guthrie. Address: n/a. T: 01575 574 548;
E: gusguthrie@btinternet.com;
W: www.angusbirding.com/html/adbc.html
Meetings: 7.30pm, 3rd Tuesday of the month (Sep-Apr). Panbride Church Hall, 8 Arbroath Road, Carnoustie, Angus DD7 6BL.

SOC TAYSIDE BRANCH. (1960's; 150).
Brian Brocklehurst. Address: n/a.
T: 01382 778 348;
E: brian.brocklehurst1@btinternet.com;
W: www.the-soc.org.uk/local-branches/tayside
Meetings: 7.30pm, 1st Thursday of the month (Sep-Apr, 2nd Thursday in Jan). Methodist Church Halls, 20 Marketgait, Dundee, DD1 1QR.

Ringing Group/Bird Observatory
TAY RG. W: www.tayringinggroup.org/

RSPB Local Group
DUNDEE. (1972; 100).
Darell Berthon. T: 07480 530 963;
E: darell.berthon@icloud.com;
W: www.rspb.org.uk/groups/dundee
Meetings: 7.30 pm, one Wednesday each month (Sep-Nov/Jan-Mar plus AGM Apr & Christmas social Dec). Methodist Church, 20 West Marketgait, Dundee, DD1 1QR - contact/see website for details.

Wetland Bird Survey (WeBS) Local Organiser
ANGUS (excl. MONTROSE BASIN). Jonathan Pattullo.
T: via WeBS Office; E: jon.jpm@tiscali.co.uk

MONTROSE BASIN. Anna Cowie. T: via WeBS Office;
E: acheshier@scottishwildlifetrust.org.uk

ARGYLL

Bird Atlas/Avifauna
Birds of Argyll. Tristan ap Rheinallt, Clive Craik, P Daw, B Furness, S Petty & D Wood (Argyll Bird Club, 2007).

The Birds of Bute: A Bird Atlas and Local Avifauna. Ronald Forrester, Ian Hopkins & Doug Menzies (Buteshire NHS, 2012).

Bird Recorder
Jim Dickson, 11 Pipers Road, Cairnbaan, Lochgilphead, Argyll PA31 8UF. T: 01546 603 967;
E: Argyllbirder@outlook.com

Assistant Recorder. Malcolm Chattwood, 1 The Stances, Kilmichael Glassary, Lochgilphead, Argyll PA31 8QA. T: 01546 603 389;
E: abcrecorder@outlook.com
For submission of all non-rare bird records.

Bird Report
ARGYLL BIRD REPORT (1980/83-), from Peter Hogbin, South Craleckan, Furnace, Inveraray, PA32 8XN.
T: 01499 500 665; E: treasurer@argyllbirdclub.org
Note: Digital only from 2018 - see
W: www.argyllbirdclub.org

ISLE OF MULL BIRD REPORT (2003-), from Alan Spellman, 'Maridon', Lochdon, Isle of Mull, Argyll PA64 6AP. T: 01680 812 448;
E: mullbirds19@gmail.com; W: www.mullbirds.com

BTO Regional Representative
ARGYLL MAINLAND, BUTE & GIGHA. Nigel Scriven.
T: 07901 636 353; E: njscriven@gmail.com.

ARGYLL (MULL, COLL, TIREE & MORVERN).
Ewan Miles. T: n/a; E: ebm.gww@gmail.com

Sue Dewar (Regional Development Officer).
T: n/a; E: suedewar123@btinternet.com

ISLAY, JURA & COLONSAY. David Wood.
T: 01496 300 118; E: david.wood@rspb.org.uk

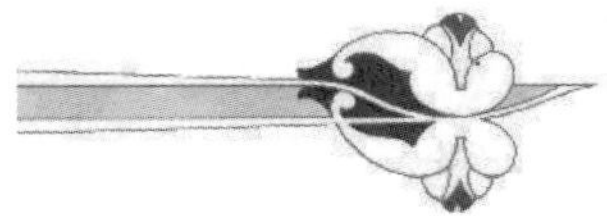

Club
ARGYLL BIRD CLUB. (1985; 270).
Nigel Scriven, 14 Taylor Avenue, Kilbarchan, Johnstone PA10 2LS. T: 01505 706 652;
E: chairman@argyllbirdclub.org;
W: www.argyllbirdclub.org
Meetings: All-day indoor meetings are held on a Saturday in early Mar & early Nov each year - contact/see website for details.

ISLE OF MULL BIRD CLUB. (2001; 150+).
Nancy Somerville (Sec). Address: n/a.
T: 01680 812 527;
E: secretary@mullbirdclub.org.uk;
W: www.mullbirdclub.org.uk
Meetings: 7.30pm, usually 3rd Friday of the month (Sep-Apr). Craignure Village Hall, PA65 6BE. Contact/see website for details.

Ringing Group/Bird Observatory
TRESHNISH ISLES AUK RG.

RSPB Local Group
HELENSBURGH. (1975; 35).
John Clark. T: 01436 821 178;
E: laighfield@gmail.com;
W: www.rspb.org.uk/groups/helensburgh
Meetings: 7.30 pm, 3rd Wednesday of the month (Sep-Apr). The Guide Halls, Lower John Street, Helensburgh, G84 8XL.

Wetland Bird Survey (WeBS) Local Organiser
ARGYLL MAINLAND. Nigel Scriven.
T: 01505 706 652; E: njscriven@gmail.com

BUTE. Ian Hopkins. T: 01700 504 042;
E: hopkins0079@btinternet.com

ISLAY, JURA & COLONSAY. David Wood.
T: 01496 300 118; E: david.wood@rspb.org.uk

MULL. Nigel Scriven - see above.

TIREE & COLL. John Bowler. T: 01879 220 748.
E: john.bowler@rspb.org.uk

AYRSHIRE

Bird Atlas/Avifauna
Arran Bird Atlas 2007-2012: Mapping the breeding and wintering birds of Arran.
Jim Cassels (Arran NHS, 2014).

Bird Recorder
Fraser Simpson, 4 Inchmurrin Drive, Kilmarnock, KA3 2JD;
T: n/a; E: recorder@ayrshire-birding.org.uk

Assistant Recorder. Angus Hogg, 11 Kirkmichael Road, Crosshill, Maybole, KA19 7RJ.
T: 01655 740 317. E: dcgos@globalnet.co.uk

Bird Report
ARRAN BIRD REPORT (1980-), from ANHS c/o Lindsey & Robert Marr, Tiree, Brodick Road, Lamlash, Isle of Arran, KA27 8JU.
E: arrannaturalhistorysociety@gmail.com

AYRSHIRE BIRD REPORT (1976-), from Anne Dick, Rowanmyle House, Tarbolton, Mauchline, KA5 5LU.
E: a_m_dick@hotmail.com

BTO Regional Representative
ARRAN. James Cassels (Assistant Representative).
T: 01770 860 316; E: james.cassels@virgin.net

AYRESHIRE & CUMBRAE. Dave McGarvie. T: n/a;
E: d.mcgarvie@lancaster.ac.uk

Club
SOC AYRSHIRE BRANCH. (1962; 120).
Anne Dick, Rowanmyle House, Tarbolton, Mauchline, KA5 5LU. T: 01292 541 981;
E: a_m_dick@btinternet.com;
W: www.the-soc.org.uk/local-branches/ayrshire
Meetings: 7.30pm, 2nd Tuesday of the month (Sep-Apr). Monkton Community Church, Main Street, Monkton by Prestwick, KA9 2RN.

RSPB Local Group
CENTRAL AYRSHIRE. (1978; 85).
Anne Dick. T: 01292 541 981;
E: a_m_dick@btinternet.com;
W: www.ayrshire-birding.org.uk
Meetings: 7.30pm. 3rd Monday of the month (Sep-Apr). Newton Wallacetown Church Hall, 60 Main Street, Ayr, KA8 8EF.

NORTH AYRSHIRE. (1976; 60).
Hazel Montgomerie. T: 07708 560 512;
E: hazelmo90@hotmail.com;
W: www.narspb.org.uk
Meetings: 7.30pm, normally 2nd Friday of the month (Sep-Apr). Argyle Centre, Donaldson Avenue, Saltcoats, Ayrshire KA21 5AG.

Wetland Bird Survey (WeBS) Local Organiser
ARRAN. Jim Cassels. T: 01770 860 316;
E: jim@arranbirding.co.uk

AYRSHIRE (excl. ISLE OF CUMBRAE). Dave Grant.
T: via WeBS Office; E: daveg466@gmail.com

ISLE OF CUMBRAE. Vacant - contact WeBS Office.

BORDERS

Bird Atlas/Avifauna
Birds in South-east Scotland 2007-2013: A Tetrad Atlas of the Birds of Lothian and Borders. Ray D Murray, Ian J Andrews & Mark Holling (Scottish Ornithologists' Club, 2019).

Bird Recorder
Martin Moncrieff.
Address: n/a; T: 01835 822 398;
E: bordersrecorder@gmail.com

David Parkinson. Address: n/a; T: 07979 365 134;
E: bordersrecorder@gmail.com

Bird Report
BORDERS BIRD REPORT (1979-),
from Malcolm Ross, 24 Netherbank, Galashiels,
TD1 3DH. E: eliseandmalcolm@btinternet.com

BTO Regional Representative
Dave McGarvie. T: n/a; E: 7askja@gmail.com

Club
SOC BORDERS BRANCH. (1980; 150).
Neil Stratton, Heiton Mains, Heiton, Kelson,
TD5 8JR. T: 01573 450 695;
E: neildstratton@btinternet.com;
W: www.the-soc.org.uk/local-branches/borders
Meetings: 7.30pm, 2nd Monday of the month (Sep-Apr, except Jan). The Townhouse Hotel, Market Square, Melrose, TD6 9PQ.

Ringing Group/Bird Observatory
BORDERS RG.

Wetland Bird Survey (WeBS) Local Organiser
SCOTTISH BORDERS. Andrew Bramhall.
T: 01896 755 326; E: andrewtbramhall@gmail.com

CLYDE

Bird Recorder
Recorder. Iain Gibson, 8 Kenmure View, Howwood, Johnstone, Renfrewshire PA9 1DR.
T: 01505 705 874; E: iaingibson.soc@btinternet.com

Assistant Recorder. Val Wilson, Flat 2/1, 12 Rawcliffe Gardens, Langside, Glasgow, G41 3DA. T: n/a; E: val.wilson38@btinternet.com

CLYDE ISLANDS (ARRAN, BUTE & CUMBRAE).
Bernard Zonfrillo, 28 Brodie Road, Glasgow, G21 3SB. T: n/a; E: b.zonfrillo@bio.gla.ac.uk

Bird Report
CLYDE BIRDS (Clyde & Clyde Islands) (1973-),
Val Wilson, Flat 2/1 12 Rawcliffe Gardens, Glasgow, G41 3DA. T: 0141 649 4512;
E: val.wilson38@btinternet.com

BTO Regional Representative
LANARK, RENFREW & DUNBARTON.
Gordon Brady. T: n/a;
E: gordonbrady@outlook.com

David Palmar (Assistant Representative). T: n/a;
E: dpalmar2000@yahoo.co.uk

Club
SOC CLYDE BRANCH. (n/a; 300).
Ian Fulton. Address: n/a. T: n/a;
E: clydesecretary@the-soc.org.uk;
W: www.the-soc.org.uk/local-branches/clyde
Meetings: 7.30pm, 1st Monday of the month (Sep-Apr, except Sep & Jan/2nd Mon). Lecture Theatre 2, Graham Kerr Building, University of Glasgow, G12 8QQ [venue may change - contact/check website for update].

Ringing Group/Bird Observatory
CLYDE RG.

RSPB Local Group
GLASGOW. (1972; 140).
Neil Rankine. T: 07986 580 116;
E: rspbglasgowgroupleader@gmail.com;
W: www.rspb.org.uk/groups/glasgow
Meetings: 7.30pm, 2nd Wednesday of the month (Sep-Apr). Renfield St Stephens Church Centre, 260 Bath Street, Glasgow, G2 4JP.

LANARKSHIRE. (1976; 50).
Jim Lynch. T: 0141 583 1044;
E: contactlanarkshireRSPBgroup@gmail.com;
W: www.rspb.org.uk/groups/lanarkshire
Meetings: 7.30pm, 3rd Thursday of the month (Sep-May). Motherwell South Parish Church, 11 Gavin Street, Motherwell, ML1 2RL.

RENFREWSHIRE. (1986; 70).
Shelley Mellor. T: n/a;
E: shemellor@gmail.com;
W: www.rspb.org.uk/groups/renfrewshire
Meetings: 7.30pm, 1st Friday of the month (Sep-May, 2nd Friday in Jan). The McMaster Centre, 2a Donaldson Drive, Renfrew, PA4 8LX.

Wetland Bird Survey (WeBS) Local Organiser
CLYDE ESTUARY (GLASGOW, RENFREWSHIRE, LANARKSHIRE). John Clark. T: 01436 821 178; E: laighfield@gmail.com

GLASGOW, RENFREWSHIRE, LANARKSHIRE. John Clark - see above.

DUMFRIES & GALLOWAY

Bird Recorder
Paul Collin, 'Gairland', Old Edinburgh Road, Minnigaff, Newton Stewart, DG8 6PL.
T: 01671 402 861;
E: pncollin@live.co.uk

Bird Report
BIRDS IN DUMFRIES & GALLOWAY (1987-), from Peter Swan, 13 Robb Place, Castle Douglas, DG7 1LW.
T: 01556 502 144;
E: pandmswan@btinternet.com

BTO Regional Representative
DUMFRIES. Andy Riches.
T: 07792 142 446 or 07570 915 630;
E: slioch69@aol.com or websdg@aol.com

KIRKCUDBRIGHT. Andrew Bielinski.
T: 01644 430 418; E: redcanoe57@gmail.com

WIGTOWN. Vacant - contact Dawn Balmer, BTO.
T: 01842 750 050; E: dawn.balmer@bto.org

Huw Connick (Assistant Representative). T: n/a;
E: h.connick@me.com

Club
SOC DUMFRIES BRANCH. (1964; 75).
Lesley Creamer, Braeside, Virginhall, Thornhill, DG3 4AD. T: 01848 330 821;
E: dumfriessecretary@the-soc.org.uk;
W: www.the-soc.org.uk/local-branches/dumfries
Meetings: 7.30pm, 2nd Wednesday of the month (Sep-Apr). Dumfries Baptist Church Centre, Gillbrae Rd, Dumfries, DG1 4EJ.

SOC STEWARTRY BRANCH. (1976; 80).
Joan Howie, The Wilderness, High Street, New Galloway, Castle Douglas, DG7 3RL.
T: 01644 420 280;
E: joanospreys1@btinternet.com;
W: www.the-soc.org.uk/local-branches/stewartry
Meetings: 7.30pm, 2nd Thursday of the month (Sep-Mar) except 3rd Thursday in Sep, Mar date will vary depending on Easter. Kells School, New Galloway, DG7 3RU.

SOC WEST GALLOWAY BRANCH. (1975; 35).
Geoff Sheppard, The Roddens, Leswalt, Stranraer, DG9 0QR. T: 01776 870 685;
E: geoff.roddens@btinternet.com;
W: www.the-soc.org.uk/local-branches/west-galloway
Meetings: 7.30pm, usually 1st or 2nd Tuesday of the month (Oct-Apr). Stranraer Library, North Strand Street, Stranraer, DG9 7LD.

Ringing Group/Bird Observatory
NORTH SOLWAY RG.

RSPB Local Group
GALLOWAY. (1985; 120).
David Henshilwood. T: 01566 650 129;
E: david.henshilwood@btinternet.com;
W: www.rspb.org.uk/groups/galloway
Meetings: 7.30pm, irregular Mondays (Sep-Apr). The Gordon Memorial Hall, adjoining St Ninian's Scottish Episcopal Church, Whitepark Road, Castle Douglas, DG7 1EX.

Wetland Bird Survey (WeBS) Local Organiser
AUCHENCAIRN AND ORCHARDTON BAYS.
Euan MacAlpine. T: 01556 640 244;
E: js.eamm@gmail.com

DUMFRIES AND GALLOWAY (OTHER SITES).
Andy Riches. T: 07792 142 446;
E: slioch69@aol.com

FLEET BAY. David Hawker. T: 01557 814 249;
E: davidhawker3@gmail.com

LOCH RYAN. Paul Collin. T: 01671 402 861;
E: pncollin@live.co.uk

ROUGH FIRTH. Andy Riches - see above.

SOLWAY ESTUARY (NORTH). Andy Riches - see above.

WIGTOWN BAY. Paul Collin - see above.

FIFE

Bird Atlas/Avifauna
The Fife Bird Atlas. Norman Elkins, Jim Reid, Allan Brown, Derek Robertson & Anne-Marie Smout. (privately published, 2003).

Bird Recorder
FIFE inc.OFFSHORE ISLANDS (NORTH FORTH) - (excl. Isle of May).
Graham Sparshott, 19 Inverewe Place, Dunfermline, KY11 8FH; T: 07770 225 440;
E: grahamspa@aol.com

ISLE OF MAY. Iain English, 19 Nethan Gate, Chantinghall Road, Hamilton, South Lanarkshire ML3 8NH; T: 01698 891 788;
E: i.english@talk21.com

Bird Report
FIFE BIRD REPORT (1988-), from the 2014 report - only available online, free for members - contact E: chairman@fifebirdclub.org.uk [www.fifebirdclub.org.uk].

ISLE OF MAY BIRD OBSERVATORY REPORT (1985-), from Stuart Rivers, Flat 8 (2F2), 10 Waverley Park, Edinburgh, EH8 8EU.
E: slr.bee-eater@blueyonder.co.uk

BTO Regional Representative
FIFE & KINROSS. Paul Blackburn. T: n/a;
E: p.blackburn89@btinternet.com

ISLE OF MAY. Vacant - contact Dawn Balmer, BTO.
T: 01842 750 050; E: dawn.balmer@bto.org

Club
FIFE BIRD CLUB. (1985; 200).
The Chairman. Address: n/a. T: n/a;
E: chairman@fifebirdclub.org.uk;
W: www.fifebirdclub.org.uk
Meetings: Held regularly through the year - contact/see website for details.
Dean Park Hotel, Kirkcaldy, KY2 6HF.

LOTHIANS AND FIFE SWAN & GOOSE STUDY GROUP. (1978; 12)
Allan & Lyndesay Brown, 61 Watts Gardens, Cupar, Fife KY15 4UG. T: 01334 656 804;
E: swans@allanwbrown.co.uk

SOC FIFE BRANCH. (1950; 170).
Caroline Gordon. Address: n/a. T: 01592 750 230;
E: fifesecretary@the-soc.org.uk;
W: www.the-soc.org.uk/local-branches/fife
Meetings: 7.30pm, 2nd Wednesday of the month (Sep-Apr). St Andrews Town Hall (at corner of South Street & Queen's Gardens), St Andrews, KY16 9TA.

Ringing Group/Bird Observatory
TAY RG. W: www.tayringinggroup.org/

ISLE OF MAY BIRD OBSERVATORY.
Mark Newell (Booking Sec). T: 07909 707971;
E: bookings@isleofmaybirdobs.org;
W: www.isleofmaybirdobs.org

Wetland Bird Survey (WeBS) Local Organiser
FIFE (excl. ESTUARIES). Allan Brown.
T: via WEBS Office; E: swansallan@gmail.com

FORTH ESTUARY (NORTH).
Vacant - contact WeBS Office.

TAY & EDEN ESTUARY. Norman Elkins.
T: 01334 654 348; E: jandnelkins@btinternet.com

FORTH

Bird Atlas/Avifauna
The Birds of Clackmannanshire.
Neil Bielby, Keith Broomfield & John Grainger
(Scottish Ornithologist's Club, 2014).

Bird Recorder
UPPER FORTH. Chris Pendlebury, 23 Ochlochy Park, Dunblane, FK15 0DU.
T: 07798 711 134;
E: chris@upperforthbirds.co.uk

Bird Report
FORTH AREA BIRD REPORT (1975-), published in The Forth Naturalist & Historian, from Roy Sexton, 22 Alexander Drive, Bridge of Allan, Stirling, FK9 4QB. T: n/a;
E: RoyGravedigger@aol.com

BTO Regional Representative
CENTRAL SCOTLAND. Neil Bielby. T: 01786 823 830;
E: neil.bielby@gmail.com

Club
SOC CENTRAL SCOTLAND BRANCH. (1968; 100).
Neil Bielby, 56 Ochiltree, Dunblane, FK15 0DF.
T: 01786 823 830 & 07484 850 959;
E: neil.bielby@gmail.com;
W: www.the-soc.org.uk/local-branches/central-scotland
Meetings: 7.30pm, 1st Thursday of the month (Oct-Mar). The Allan Centre, Fountain Road, Bridge of Allan, FK9 4AT.

RSPB Local Group
FORTH VALLEY. (1995; 50).
Richard Knight. T: 07941 298 688;
E: richard.knight@blueyonder.co.uk;
W: www.rspb.org.uk/groups/forthvalley
Meetings: 7.30pm, 3rd Thursday of the month (Sep-Apr). Hillpark Community Centre, Morrison Drive, Bannockburn, Stirling, FK7 0HZ.

Wetland Bird Survey (WeBS) Local Organiser
CENTRAL SCOTLAND (excl FORTH ESTUARY).
Neil Bielby. T: 01786 823 830;
E: neil.bielby@gmail.com

FORTH ESTUARY (INNER). Michael Bell.
T: via WeBS Office; E: mvbell34@gmail.com

HIGHLAND & CAITHNESS

Bird Atlas/Avifauna

Sutherland Birdlife. Fraser Symonds and Alan Vittery (Independent Publishing Network, 2016).

Birds of Caithness, including The Breeding & Wintering Atlas 2007-2012. P Davey, S Manson,E Maughan, D Omand & J Smith (Caithness SOC, revised ed 2017 - was published as a dvd in 2015).

Birds of Eigg. John Chester (Isle of Eigg Heritage Trust, 2013).

Skye Birds. RL McMillan. (Skye-Birds.com, 2nd ed 2009)

A History of Caithness BIrds 1979 to 2001. Manson Sinclair (Privately published, 2002).

The Birds of Badenoch and Strathspey. Roy Dennis (Colin Baxter Photography Ltd, 1995).

Bird Recorder
CAITHNESS. Sinclair Manson, 7 Duncan Street, Thurso, KW14 7HZ. T: 01847 892 379; E: sinclairmanson@btinternet.com

HIGHLAND [excludes Caithness, covers ROSS-SHIRE, INVERNESS-SHIRE, SUTHERLAND, BADENOCH & STRATHSPEY, LOCHABER, LOCHALSH & SKYE]. John Poyner. Address: n/a. T: 01479 821 357; E: highlandrecorder@yahoo.com

Bird Report
CAITHNESS BIRD REPORT (1983-97), no longer published but the latest report can be downloaded from website
W: www.the-soc.org.uk (local branches link)

HIGHLAND BIRD REPORT (1995-), from Alister Clunas, Ruthven, 12 Academy Street, Fortrose, IV10 8TW. T: 07437 90013; E: alister53@hotmail.co.uk

BTO Regional Representative
CAITHNESS. Donald Omand. T: 01847 811 403; E: achreamie@yahoo.co.uk

INVERNESS (EAST & SPEYSIDE). Hugh Insley. T: 01463 230 652; E: hugh.insley@btinternet.com

INVERNESS (WEST). Hugh Insley - see above.

ROSS-SHIRE. Simon Cohen. T: n/a; E: saraandsimon@hotmail.com

RUM, EIGG, CANNA & MUCK. Bob Swann. T: 01862 894 329; E: robert.swann@homecall.co.uk

SKYE. Carol Hawley. T: n/a; E: bto.skye@gmail.com

SUTHERLAND. Lesley Mitchell. T: 07817 281 352; E: colourflow@btinternet.com

Club
EAST SUTHERLAND BIRD GROUP. (1976; 120). Fraser Symonds, Old Schoolhouse, Balvraid, Dornoch, Sutherland IV25 3JB. T: 01408 633 922; E: esbirdgroup@gmail.com; W: n/a
Meetings: 7.30pm, last Monday of the month (Oct/Nov, Jan-Mar). Golspie Community Centre, Back Rd, Golspie, Highland KW10 6TL.

SOC CAITHNESS BRANCH. (n/a; 50). Nina O'Hanlon. Address: n/a. T: 07810 300 392; E: caithnesssecretary@the-soc.org.uk; W: www.the-soc.org.uk/local-branches/caithness
Meetings: 7.30pm, 1st Wednesday of the month (Sep-Apr not Jan). Castlehill Heritage Centre, Harbour Road, Castletown, Caithness KW14 8TG.

SOC HIGHLAND BRANCH. (1955; 230). Mary Galloway. Address: n/a. T: 01381 621 126 or 07598 320 978; E: highlandsecretary@the-soc.org.uk; W: www.the-soc.org.uk/local-branches/highland; W: www.highlandbirds.scot
Meetings: 7.30pm, 1st or 2nd Tuesday of the month (Sep-Apr). Culloden Library, Keppoch Road, Culloden, IV2 7LL.

Ringing Group/Bird Observatory
HIGHLAND RG.

RSPB Local Group
HIGHLAND. (1987; 110). Maureen MacDonald. T: 01463 220 013; E: macdonald456@btinternet.com; W: www.rspb.org.uk/groups/highland
Meetings: 7.30pm, last Thursday of the month (Sep-Apr). Greyfriars Free Church, Balloan Road, Inverness, IV2 4PP.

Wetland Bird Survey (WeBS) Local Organiser
BADENOCH AND STRATHSPEY. Keith Duncan. T: via WEBS Office; E: via WeBS Office

CAITHNESS. Sinclair Manson. T: 01847 892 387; E: sinclairmanson@btinternet.com

LOCHABER. Calum Ross. T: 07729 128 144; E: funkyhaywood@yahoo.co.uk

SKYE & LOCHALSH. Jonathan Jones. T: 01478 611 328; E: jjonskye@yahoo.co.uk

SUTHERLAND (excl. MORAY BASIN). Vacant - contact WeBS Office.

WEST INVERNESS AND WESTER ROSS. Andy Douse. T: 01463 725 241; E: andyandbronwen@gmail.com

SCOTLAND

LOTHIAN

Bird Atlas/Avifauna. See Borders.

Bird Recorder
Stephen Welch, 25 Douglas Road, Longniddry, EH32 0LQ. T: 01875 852 802 or 07931 524 963; E: lothianrecorder@the-soc.org.uk

Bird Report
LOTHIAN BIRD REPORT (1979-),
from Gillian Herbert, 19 Cammo Grove, Edinburgh, EH4 8EX. E: gillianiherbert@btinternet.com

BTO Regional Representative
Stephen Metcalfe. T:n/a;
E: s.j.metcalfe@outlook.com

Club
LOTHIANS AND FIFE SWAN AND GOOSE STUDY GROUP. See Fife.

SOC LOTHIAN BRANCH. (1936; 800).
Alison Creamer. Address: n/a. T: 07815 037 330;
E: lothiansecretary@the-soc.org.uk;
W: www.the-soc.org.uk/local-branches/lothian
Meetings: 7.30pm, 2nd Tuesday of the month (Sep-Apr). The Cornerston Centre, St Johns Church, Princes Street, Edinburgh, EH2 4BJ.
[Two meetings a year are held at Waterston House, Aberlady.]

Ringing Group/Bird Observatory
LOTHIAN RG.

RSPB Local Group
EDINBURGH. (1974; 480).
Brian Robertson. T: 01875 340 580;
E: brianedinburghrspb@btinternet.com;
W: www.rspb.org.uk/groups/edinburgh
Meetings: 7.30pm, alternating between a Tuesday & a Wednesday each month (Sep-Apr).
Lindsay Stewart Lecture Theatre, Napier University, Craiglockhart Campus, Colinton Road, Edinburgh ED14 1DJ.

Wetland Bird Survey (WeBS) Local Organiser
FORTH ESTUARY (OUTER SOUTH). Duncan Priddle.
T: 01620 827 459; E: duncfala@gmail.com

LOTHIAN (excl ESTUARIES). Allan Brown.
T: via WeBS Office; E: swansallan@gmail.com

TYNINGHAME ESTUARY. Tara Sykes.
T: via WeBS Office; E: tsykes@eastlothian.gov

MORAY & NAIRN

Bird Atlas/Avifauna
The Birds of Moray and Nairn. Martin Cook (Mercat Press, 1992).

Bird Recorder
Martin Cook, Rowanbrae, Clochan, Buckie, Banffshire AB56 5EQ. T: 01542 850 296;
E: martin.cook99@btinternet.com

Bird Report
BIRDS IN MORAY AND NAIRN (1999-), online since 2010), download from website
W: www.birdsinmorayandnairn.org

BTO Regional Representative
MORAY & NAIRN. Melvin Morrison. T: 01542 882 940;
E: wmmorrison@btinternet.com

Club
SOC MORAY BRANCH (Moray Bird Club). (2013; 60).
Alison Richie. Address: n/a. T: 01309 674 379;
E: moraysecretary@the-soc.org.uk;
W: www.the-soc.org.uk/local-branches/moray;
W: www.birdsinmorayandnairn.org
Meetings: 7.30pm, 2nd Thursday of the month (Oct-Feb). Elgin Museum Hall, 1 High Street, Elgin, IV30 1EQ.

Wetland Bird Survey (WeBS) Local Organiser
LOSSIE ESTUARY. Bob Proctor. T: 07976 456 657;
E: bobproctor8246@gmail.com

MORAY & NAIRN (INLAND). David Law.
T: via WeBS Office; E: jdavidlaw@btinternet.com

MORAY BASIN COAST. Bob Swann. T: via WEBS Office;
E: robert.swann@homecall.co.uk

NORTH EAST SCOTLAND

Bird Atlas/Avifauna
The Birds of North-East Scotland Then and Now.
Adam Watson & Ian Francis (Paragon Publishing, 2012).

The Breeding Birds of North-East Scotland.
Ian Francis & Martin Cook (Scottish Ornithologist's Club, 2011).

The Birds of North-East Scotland. ST Buckland, MV Bell & N Picozzi (North-East Scotland Bird Club, 1990).

Bird Recorder
Ian Broadbent, 18 Abbotshall Drive, Cults, Aberdeen, AB15 9JD. T: 07790 562 892;
E: nescotlandrecorder@the-soc.org.uk

SCOTLAND

Bird Report
NORTH-EAST SCOTLAND BIRD REPORT (1974-), from Ian Middleton. T: 07882 411 469; E: balbridie@gmail.com

NORTH SEA BIRD CLUB ANNUAL REPORT (1979-), FINAL report 2018/19 - club now disbanded - from Andrew Thorpe,3 The Red House, Dirleton, North Bewick, EH39 5EP.

BTO Regional Representative
ABERDEEN. Moray Souter. T: 01358 788 828; E: bto_aber_rr@btintrnet.com

KINCARDINE & DEESIDE. Claire Marsden. T: n/a; E: fbears@me.com

Club
SOC NORTH-EAST SCOTLAND BRANCH. (1956; 150). John Wills, Bilbo, Monymusk, Inverurie, Aberdeenshire AB51 7HA. T: 01467 651 296;
E: grampian.secretary@the-soc.org.uk;
W: www.the-soc.org.uk/local-branches/north-east-scotland
Meetings: 7.30pm, 1st Monday of the month (Oct-Apr). Sportsman's Club, 11 Queens Road, Aberdeen, AB15 4YL.

Ringing Group/Bird Observatory
GRAMPIAN RG.
W: http://grampianringing.blogspot.co.uk

RSPB Local Group
ABERDEEN & DISTRICT. (1975; 260).
David Leslie. T: 01651 862 826;
E: davidleslie77@gmail.com;
W: www.rspb.org.uk/groups/aberdeen
Meetings: 7.30pm, 2nd Tuesday of the month (Oct-Apr). Aberdeen University, Main Lecture Theatre, Zoology Building, Tillydrone Ave, Aberdeen, AB24 2TZ.

Wetland Bird Survey (WeBS) Local Organiser
ABERDEENSHIRE. Moray Souter. T: 01358 788 828; E: bto_aber_rr@btinternet.com

ORKNEY

Bird Atlas/Avifauna
The Birds of Orkney. C Booth, M Cuthbert & P Reynolds. (The Orkney Press, 1984).

Bird Recorder
Russ Neave & Emma Neave-Webb, Bressigarth, Sanday, Orkney KW17 2BW. T: 01857 600 289; E: orkbird.recorder@gmail.com

Bird Report
NORTH RONALDSAY BIRD OBSERVATORY BIRD REPORT (2011-), from Alison Duncan, NRBO, Twingness, North Ronaldsay, Orkney KW17 2BE. T: 01857 633 200; E: enquiries@nrbo.org.uk

ORKNEY BIRD REPORT (1974-), from Jim Williams, Fairholm, Finstown, Orkney KW17 2EQ. E: orkneybirdreport@gmail.com

BTO Regional Representative
Colin Corse. T: 01856 874 484; E: ccorse@btinternet.com

Club
SOC ORKNEY BRANCH. (1993; n/a).
Helen Aiton. Address: n/a. T: 01856 751 482;
E: helendavidaiton@hotmail.co.uk;
W: www.the-soc.org.uk/local-branches/orkney
Meetings: 7.30pm, 1st Thursday of the month (Oct & Nov) and 2nd Thursday of the month (Feb & Mar). St Magnus Centre, Kirkwall.

Ringing Group/Bird Observatory
ORKNEY RG.

SULE SKERRY RG.

NORTH RONALDSAY BIRD OBSERVATORY. Alison Duncan (Warden), Twingness, North Ronaldsay, KW17 2BE. T: 01857 633 200; E: enquiries@nrbo.org.uk; W: www.nrbo.org.uk

RSPB Local Group
ORKNEY. (1985; 300/area).
Dick Matson. T: 01856 751 426;
E: P.wilson410@btinternet.com; W: n/a
Meetings: Meetings advertised in newsletter and local press, or phone/e-mail for details.

Wetland Bird Survey (WeBS) Local Organiser
ORKNEY. Sarah Money. T: via WeBS Office; E: via WeBS Office.

OUTER HEBRIDES

Bird Recorder
Yvonne Benting, Suthainn, Askernish, South Uist, HS8 5SY. T: 07501 332 803;
E: recorder@outerhebridesbirds.org.uk;
W: www.outerhebridesbirds.org.uk

Bird Report
OUTER HEBRIDES BIRD REPORT (1997-), from bird recorder - see above.

BTO Regional Representative
BENBECULA & THE UISTS.
Yvonne Benting.
T: 07501 332 803;
E: uistbto@gmail.com

LEWIS & HARRIS. Vacant - contact Dawn Balmer, BTO.
T: 01842 750 050; E: dawn.balmer@bto.org

Ringing Group/Bird Observatory
SHIANTS AUK RG.

Wetland Bird Survey (WeBS) Local Organiser
HARRIS AND LEWIS. Yvonne Benting.
T: 01878 700 849 E: uistbto@gmail.com

UISTS AND BENBECULA. Yvonne Benting - see above.

PERTH & KINROSS

Bird Recorder
Scott Paterson, 12 Ochil View, Kinross, KY13 8TN.
T: 01577 864 248 & 07501 640 518;
E: pkrecorder@the-soc.org.uk

Bird Report
PERTH & KINROSS BIRD REPORT (1974-), digital reports from the Bird Recorder - see above.

BTO Regional Representative
PERTHSHIRE. Michael Bell. T: 01786 822 153;
E: mvbell34@gmail.com

Club
PERTHSHIRE SOCIETY OF NATURAL SCIENCE (1867; Ornithological Section: 25).
Jeanne Freeman,
14 St Mary's Drive, Perth,
PH2 7BY. T: 01738 620 914;
E: birdsatpsns@btinternet.com;
W: www.psns.org.uk
Meetings: 7.30pm, Wednesday - dates vary (Oct-Mar), Sandeman Room, AK Bell Library, 17 York Place, Perth, PH2 8EP - contact/see website for details.

Wetland Bird Survey (WeBS) Local Organiser
LOCH LEVEN. Simon Richie.
E: simon.ritchie@nature-scot.

PERTH AND KINROSS (INLAND). Michael Bell.
T: via WeBS Office; E: mvbell34@gmail.com

TAY & EDEN ESTUARY. See Fife.

SHETLAND

Bird Atlas/Avifauna
The Birds of Shetland. P Harvey, M Pennington, K Osborn, R Riddington, P Ellis, M Huebeck & D Okill (Christopher Helm, 2004).

Bird Recorder
FAIR ISLE. David Parnaby, Fair Isle Bird Observatory, Fair Isle, Shetland, ZE2 9JU.
T: n/a; E: warden@fairislebirdobs.co.uk

SHETLAND. Rob Fray, The Meadows, Bakkasetter, Quendale, Shetland ZE2 9JD. T: 07775 647 463;
E: recorder@shetlandbirdclub.co.uk

Bird Report
FAIR ISLE BIRD OBSERVATORY REPORT (1949-), from Susannah Parnaby, Fair Isle Bird Observatory, Fair Isle, Shetland, ZE2 9JU. T: n/a;
E: warden@fairislebirdobs.co.uk

SHETLAND BIRD REPORT (1969-), from Bird Recorder - see above.

BTO Regional Representative
Dave Okill. T: 01595 880 450;
E: david@auroradesign.plus.com

Club
SHETLAND BIRD CLUB. (1973; 260+).
Helen Moncrieff (Sec), Scholland, Virkie, ZE3 9JL.
T: 01950 460 249;
E: secretary@shetlandbirdclub.co.uk;
W: www.nature-shetland.co.uk
Meetings: Regular evening talks or socials - contact/see website for details.

Ringing Group/ Bird Observatory
SHETLAND RG.

FAIR ISLE BIRD OBSERVATORY.
David Parnaby (Warden), Fair Isle Bird Observatory, Fair Isle, Shetland ZE2 9JU.
T: n/a; E: warden@fairislebirdobs.co.uk;
W: www.fairislebirdobs.co.uk

Due to the fire that destroyed the Observatory in March 2019 accommodation will not be available for the forseeable future, check out the Observatory website for updates/alternative options.

Wetland Bird Survey (WeBS) Local Organiser
SHETLAND. Paul Harvey. T: 01595 694 688;
E: paul@shetlandamenity.org

WALES

Bird Atlas/Avifauna
Birds of Wales/Adar Cymru. Rhion Pritchard, Julian Hughes, Ian M Spence, Bob Haycock, Anne Brenchley, Jon Green & Robin Sandham. (Liverpool University Press, in prep - due 2021).

Report
The WELSH BIRD REPORT is published in 'BIRDS IN WALES', from Alison Noble, Welsh Ornithological Society, E: wosmembership@btinternet.com
Available to members of WOS for downloading
W: www.birdsin.wales/what-we-do/our-journals/

BTO Wales Officer
John Lloyd. T: 01550 750 202;
E: johnvlloyd2000@gmail.com

Club
Welsh Ornithological Society. W: www.birdsin.wales
See National Directory.

EASTERN AREA OF WALES

Bird Atlas/Avifauna
The Birds of Radnorshire. Peter Jennings (Fidedula Books, 2014).

The Birds of Gwent. WA Venables, AD Baker, RM Clarke, C Jones, JMS Lewis & SJ Tyler (Christopher Helm, 2008).

The Birds of Montgomeryshire. B Holt & G Williams (privately published, 2008).

Bird Recorder
BRECONSHIRE. Andrew King, Heddfan, Pennorth, Brecon, Powys LD3 7EX. T: 01874 658 351;
E: andy@breconbirds.wales

GWENT. Darryl Spittle. Address: n/a. T: n/a;
E: countyrecorder@gwentbirds.org.uk

MONTGOMERYSHIRE. Simon Boyes, Bridge Cottage, Middletown, Welshpool, SY21 8DG. T: 01938 570 418;
E: montbird@gmail.com

RADNORSHIRE (VC43). Pete Jennings, The Old Farmhouse, Choulton, Lydbury North, Shropshire SY7 8AH. T: 01588 680 631;
E: radnorshirebirds@hotmail.com

Bird Report
BRECONSHIRE BIRDS (1962-), from Wildlife Trust of South and West Wales, The Nature Centre, Fountain Road, Tondu, Bridgend, Mid-Glamorgan CF32 0EH.
T: 01656 724 100;
E: membership@welshwildlife.org

GWENT BIRD REPORT (1973-), from Andrew Cormack, 29 Chestnut Drive, Abergavenny, Monmouthshire NP7 5JZ.
E: treasurer@gwentbirds.org.uk

MONTGOMERYSHIRE BIRD REPORT (1981/82-), from 2013 report, available as a download from montgomerybirdblog.blogspot.co.uk/p/county-reports.html

BTO Regional Representative
BRECKNOCK. Andrew King. T: 01874 658 351;
E: andy@breconbirds.wales

GWENT. Richard Clarke. T: n/a;
E: chykembro2@aol.com

MONTGOMERY. Jane Kelsall. T: 01970 872 019;
E: janekelsall@phonecoop.coop

RADNOR. Carlton Parry. T: 01597 824 050;
E: cj.parry@tiscali.co.uk

Club
BRECONSHIRE (bird blog)
www.brecknockbirds.co.uk

GWENT ORNITHOLOGICAL SOCIETY. (1961; 420).
Catherine Gregory (Sec). Address: n/a. T: n/a;
E: secretary@gwentbirds.org.uk;
W: www.gwentbirds.org.uk
Meetings: 7.30pm, 1st & 3rd Saturdays of the month (Sep-Apr). Goytre Village Hall, Newtown Road, Penperlleni, Pontypool, NP4 0AW.

MONTGOMERYSHIRE WILDLIFE TRUST BIRD GROUP. (1997; 110).
Sally Davies (Sec). Address: n/a.
T: 01938 580 278; E: montbird@gmail.com;
W: www.montgomerybirdblog.blogspot.co.uk
Meetings: 7.30pm, 3rd Wednesday of the month (Sep-Apr). Welshpool Methodist Hall, 13 High Street, Welshpool, Powys SY21 7JP.

RADNORSHIRE BIRD GROUP. (1988; 75).
Pete Jennings, The Old Farmhouse, Choulton, Lydbury North, Shropshire SY7 8AH.
T: 01588 680 631;
E: radnorshirebirds@hotmail.com; W: n/a
Co-ordinates bird recording and surveys in the county through the Bird Recorder.

Ringing Group/Bird Observatory
GOLDCLIFF RG.

LLANGORSE RG.

MID-WALES RG.

Wetland Bird Survey (WeBS) Local Organiser
BRECONSHIRE. Andrew King. T: via WeBS Office; E: andy@breconbirds.wales

GWENT (excl. SEVERN ESTUARY). Al Venables. T: via WeBS Office; E: via WeBS Office

MONTGOMERYSHIRE. Jane Kelsall. T: 01970 832 625; E: janekelsall@phonecoop.coop

RADNORSHIRE. Pete Jennings. T: 01597 811 522; E: ppjennings@hotmail.co.uk

SEVERN ESTUARY (NORTH (GWENT/GLAMORGAN). Al Venables - see above.

Wildlife Trust
GWENT WILDLIFE TRUST. (1963; 8,000). Seddon House, Dingestow, Monmouth, NP25 4DY. T: 01600 740 600, (fax) 01600 740 299; E: info@gwentwildlife.org; W: www.gwentwildlife.org

MONTGOMERYSHIRE WILDLIFE TRUST. (1982; 3,000). Park Lane House, High Street, Welshpool, Powys, SY21 7JP. T: 01938 555 654, (fax) 01938 556 161; E: info@montwt.co.uk; W: www.montwt.co.uk

RADNORSHIRE WILDLIFE TRUST. (1987; 1,000). Warwick House, High St, Llandrindod Wells, Powys LD1 6AG. T: 01597 823 298, (fax) 01597 823 274; E: info@rwtwales.org; W: www.rwtwales.org

NORTHERN AREA OF WALES

Bird Atlas/Avifauna
Scarce and Rare Birds in North Wales: historic records up to and including 2016. Robin Sandham (privately published, 2018).

Birds of Caernarfonshire. Rhion Pritchard (Cambrian Ornithological Society, 2017).

The Breeding Birds of North Wales. Anne Brenchley, Geoff Gibbs, Rhion Pritchard & Ian M Spence (Liverpool University Press, 2013).

The Birds of Meirionnydd. Rhion Pritchard (Cambrian Ornithological Society, 2012).

The Birds of Anglesey. Peter Hope Jones & P Whalley (Menter Mon, 2004).

Bird Recorder
ANGLESEY. David Wright. Graig Eithin, Mynydd Bodafon, Llanerchymedd, Anglesey LL71 8BG. T: 07973 568 096; E: bodafondavid@yahoo.co.uk

CAERNARFONSHIRE. Rhion Pritchard, Pant Afonig, Hafod Lane, Bangor, Gwynedd LL57 4BU. T: 01248 671 301; E: rhion678pritchard@gmail.com

DENBIGHSHIRE. Ian M Spence, 43 Blackbrook, Sychdyn, Mold, Flintshire CH7 6LT. T: 01352 750118; E: ian.spence@zen.co.uk

FLINTSHIRE. Ian M Spence - see above.

MEIRIONNYDD. Jim Dustow, Afallon, 7 Glan y Don, Rhiwbryfdir, Blaenau Ffestiniog, Gwynedd LL41 3LW. T: 01766 830 976; E: meinirowen@live.co.uk

Bird Report
BARDSEY BIRD AND FIELD OBSERVATORY REPORT (1953-), from Jo Jones, 70 Newmarket Road, Burwell, Cambridgeshire CB25 0AE. E: jojones14@btinternet.com

CAMBRIAN BIRD REPORT (NW Wales) (1953-), from Geoff Gibbs, Fronwen, Llanfairfechan, LL33 0ET. T: 01248 681 936; E: geoffgibbs058@gmail.com

NORTH-EAST WALES BIRD REPORT (2004-), from Ian Spence, 43 Blackbrook, Sychdyn, Mold, Flintshire CH7 6LT. E: ian.spence@zen.co.uk

WREXHAM BIRDWATCHERS' SOCIETY ANNUAL REPORT (1981-), from Marian Williams, 10 Lake View, Gresford, Wrexham, LL12 8PU. T: 01978 854 633

BTO Regional Representative
ANGLESEY. Ian Hawkins. T: 01248 430 590; E: ian.hawkins590@btinternet.com

CAERNARFON. Geoff Gibbs. T: 01248 681 936; E: geoffgibbs058@gmail.com

Rhion Pritchard (Assistant Representative). T: 01248 671 301; E: rhion678pritchard@btinternet.com

CLWYD EAST. Anne Brenchley. T: 01352 750 118; E: annebrenchley@imsab.myzen.co.uk

Jane Hemming (Assistant Representative). T: n/a; E: jane@hemming.myzen.co.uk

CLWYD WEST. Mel ab Owain. T: 01745 826 528; E: melabowain@gmail.com

Glen Heaton (Assistant Representative). T: n/a; E: n/a.

MEIRIONNYDD. Dave Anning. T: n/a; E: davidanning1@btinternet.com

Club
BANGOR BIRD GROUP. (1947; 70).
Ian Wright (Membership Sec). Address: n/a.
T: 01407 860 471; E: bangorbirdgroup@gmail.com;
W: https://birdsin.wales/useful-links/bangor-bird-group/
Meetings: Contact/see website for details.

CAMBRIAN ORNITHOLOGICAL SOCIETY. (1952; 160).
Julian Thompson (Sec), Pensychnant, Sychnant Pass, Conwy, LL32 8BJ. T: 01492 592 595;
E: julian.pensychnant@btinternet.com;
W: www.brnw.cymru/cos
Meetings: 7.30pm, 1st Friday of the month (Sep-May). Pensychnant Centre, Sychnant Pass, Conwy, LL32 8BJ.

CLWYD BIRD RECORDING GROUP (a committee of local birders who produce the North-East Wales Bird Report). Giles Pepler (Sec), Rosedan, Coleshill Fechan, Bagillt, Flintshire CH6 6DH.
T: 01352 732 876; E: gilesp64@gmail.com;
W: www.brnw.cymru/cbrg
Meetings: No indoor meetings held.

CLWYD ORNITHOLOGICAL SOCIETY. (1956; 45).
Angela Ross, 25 Leonard Avenue, Rhyl, LL18 4LN.
T: 01745 338 493; E: angela.ross@talktalk.net; W: n/a.
Meetings: 7.30pm, last Tuesday of the month (Sep-Nov & Jan-Apr). Rhuddlan Community Centre, Parliament Street, Rhuddlan, LL18 5AW.

DEESIDE NATURALISTS' SOCIETY. (1973; 400+).
The Secretary. Address: n/a. T: n/a;
E: secretary@deenats.org.uk;
W: www.deenats.org.uk
Meetings: 7.30pm, 3rd Friday of the month (Sep-Mar). Connah's Quay Community Centre, Tuscan Way, off Chapel Street, Connah's Quay, CH5 4DZ.

WREXHAM BIRDWATCHERS' SOCIETY. (1974; 90).
Kevin Smith. Address: n/a. T: 01978 354 551;
E: kevjsmith3@hotmail.com; W: https://birdsin.wales/useful-links/wrexham-birdwatchers/
Meetings: 7.30pm, 1st Friday of the month (Sep-Apr). Gresford Memorial Hall, High Street, Gresford, Wrexham, LL12 8PS.

Ringing Group/Bird Observatory
CHESHIRE SWAN GROUP.
W: http://cheshireswanstudygroup.wordpress.com

MERSEYSIDE RG. W: www.merseysiderg.org.uk

SCAN RG.

BARDSEY BIRD OBSERVATORY.
Steve Stansfield (Warden), Cristin, Bardsey Island, Pwllheli, Gwynedd LL53 8DE. T: 07855 264 151;
E: warden@bbfo.org.uk; W: www.bbfo.org.uk

Alicia Normand (Booking Sec), 46 Maudlin Drive, Teignmouth, Devon TQ14 8SB. T: 01626 773 908;
E: stay@bbfo.org.uk

RSPB Local Group
NORTH WALES. (1986; n/a).
John Beagan. T: 01492 531 409;
E: colwynbooks@waitrose.com;
W: www.rspb.org.uk/groups/northwales
Meetings: 2.00pm, 3rd Friday of the month (Sep-Apr). St Davids Church Hall, Penrhyn Bay, Llandudno, Conwy, LL30 3NT.

Wetland Bird Survey (WeBS) Local Organiser
ANGLESEY. Ian Sims. T: 01248 421 100;
E: ian.sims@rspb.org.uk

CAERNARFONSHIRE.
Rhion Pritchard. T: via WeBS Office;
E: rhion678pritchard@gmail.com

CLWYD (COASTAL). Henry Cook. T: 07976 377 215;
E: henerz1@yahoo.co.uk

CLWYD (INLAND). Vacant - contact WeBS Office.

DEE ESTUARY. Mr CE Wells - see Lancashire.

FORYD BAY. Simon Hugheston-Roberts.
T: 01248 385 500; E: sm.roberts@ccw.gov.uk

MEIRIONNYDD (ESTUARIES). Jim Dustow.
T: 01766 830 976; E: meinirowen@live.co.uk

MEIRIONNYDD (OTHER SITES). Jim Dustow - see above.

Wildlife Trust
NORTH WALES WILDLIFE TRUST. (1963; 6,000).
Llys Garth, Garth Road, Bangor, Gwynedd LL57 2RT.
T: 01248 351 541, (fax) 01248 353 192;
E: nwwt@wildlifetrustswales.org;
W: www.northwaleswildlifetrust.org.uk

SOUTHERN AREA OF WALES

Bird Atlas/Avifauna
Birds of Glamorgan. Clive Hurford & Peter Lansdown (Privately Published, 1995).

An Atlas of Breeding Birds in West Glamorgan. DK Thomas (Gower Ornithological Society, 1992).

Bird Recorder
EAST GLAMORGAN. Phil Bristow, 2 Forest Oak Close, Cyncoed, Cardiff CF23 6QN. T: 07769 973 890;
E: phlbrstw@gmail.com

WEST GLAMORGAN. Robert Taylor. Address: n/a.
T: n/a. E: gowerbirdrecorder@gmail.com

WALES

Bird Report
EAST GLAMORGAN BIRD REPORT (1985-), from John Wilson, 122 Westbourne Road, Penarth, Vale of Glamorgan, CF64 3HH. E: johndw1948@gmail.com

GOWER BIRDS (1968-), from Jeremy Douglas-Jones, 14 Alder Way, West Cross, Swansea, SA3 5PD. T: 01792 551 331; E: jeremy@douglas-jones.biz

BTO Regional Representative
GLAMORGAN (MID). Wayne Morris.
T: 01443 430 284; E: eastglambto@gmail.com

Daniel Jenkins-Jones (Assistant Representative).
T: 01292 062 1394; E: jenkinsjones@btinternet.com

GLAMORGAN (SOUTH). Wayne Morris/
Daniel Jenkins-Jones - see above.

GLAMORGAN (WEST). Lyndon Jeffery.
T: 01792 874 337; E: norma.jeffery@virginmedia.com

Rob Jones (Assistant Representative). T: n/a;
E: rob.jones27@outlook.com

Club
CARDIFF NATURALISTS' SOCIETY. (1867; 150).
Mike Dean (Sec), 36 Rowan Way, Lisvane, Cardiff, CF14 0TD. T: 029 2075 6869;
E: secretary@cardiffnaturalists.org.uk;
W: www.cardiffnaturalists.org.uk
Meetings: 7.30pm, various evenings (Sep-May). Lecture Theatre, Room D.106 on 1st floor of the UWIC Llandaff Campus on Western Avenue, Cardiff, CF5 2YB.

GLAMORGAN BIRD CLUB. (1990; 400).
Alan Rosney (Membership Sec), 10 Parc-y-Nant, Nantgarw, RCT, CF15 7TJ.
T: 01443 841 555
& 07906 558 489;
E: alanrosney@gmail.com;
W: www.glamorganbirds.org.uk
Meetings: 7.45pm, generally 1st Tuesday of the month (Oct-Apr). The Miners Welfare Hall, 51-53 Heol-Y-Groes, Pencoed, Bridgend CF35 5PE.

GOWER ORNITHOLOGICAL SOCIETY. (1956; 100).
Jeremy Douglas-Jones (Sec), 14 Alder Way, West Cross, Swansea, SA3 5PD. T: 01792 551 331;
E: jeremy@douglas-jones.biz;
W: www.gowerbirds.org.uk
Meetings: 7.15pm, usually held the 4th Friday of the month (Sep-Mar, not Dec). The Environment Centre, Pier Street, Swansea, SA1 1RY. Contact/see website for details.

Ringing Group/Bird Observatory
FLAT HOLM RG.

GOWER RG.
W: www.gowerbirds.org.uk/category/gower-ringing-group/

KENFIG RG. W: http://kenfigrg.blogspot.co.uk

RSPB Local Group
CARDIFF & DISTRICT. (1973; n/a).
Huw Moody-Jones. T: 01446 760 757;
E: huwmoodyjones@hotmail.com;
W: www.RSPB.org.uk/groups/cardiff
Meetings: 7.30pm, 2nd Friday of the month (Sep-May). Llandaff Parish Hall, (next car park off) High St, Llandaff, Cardiff, CF5 2DX.

WEST GLAMORGAN. (1985; 130).
Maggie Cornelius. T: 01792 229 244;
E: rspbwglamgrp@gmail.com;
W: www.rspb.org.uk/groups/westglamorgan
Meetings: Contact/see website for details. Environment Centre, Pier Street, Swansea, SA1 1RY.

Wetland Bird Survey (WeBS) Local Organiser
BURRY INLET (NORTH). Lyndon Jeffery.
T: 01792 874 337;
E: norma.jeffery@virginmedia.com

EAST GLAMORGAN. Daniel Jenkins-Jones.
T: 02920 621 394; E: eastglamwebs@gmail.com

SEVERN ESTUARY (NORTH (GWENT/GLAMORGAN). See Eastern Area.

WEST GLAMORGAN. Lyndon Jeffery - see above.

Wildlife Trust
WILDLIFE TRUST OF SOUTH AND WEST WALES. (2002; 11,000).
The Nature Centre, Fountain Road, Tondu, Bridgend, Mid-Glamorgan CF32 0EH.
T: 01656 724 100, fax 01656 726 980;
E: info@welshwildlife.org;
W: www.welshwildlife.org

WESTERN AREA OF WALES

Bird Atlas/Avifauna
Birds of Ceredigion. Hywel Roderick & Peter Davis (Wildlife Trust, S & SW Wales, 2010).

Atlas of Breeding Birds in Pembrokeshire 2003-07. Annie Haycock et al (Pembrokeshire Bird Group, 2009).

Birds of Pembrokeshire. Jack Donovan & Graham Rees (Dyfed Wildlife Trust, 1994).

Bird Recorder
CARMARTHENSHIRE. Gary Harper, Maesteg, Capel Seion, Drefach, Llanelli, SA14 7BS. T: 01269 831 496 & 07748 970 124; E: gary.harper3@gmail.com

CEREDIGION. Russell Jones, Bron y Gan, Talybont, Ceredigion SY24 5ER. T: 07753 774 891; E: russell.jones@rspb.org.uk

PEMBROKESHIRE. Joint Recorder (Rarities). Jon Green, Crud Yr Awel, Bowls Road, Blaenporth, Ceredigion SA43 2AR. T: 01239 811 561; E: jonrg@tiscali.co.uk

PEMBROKESHIRE. Joint Recorder. Stephen Berry, The Old Mill, Llanychaer, Pembrokeshire SA65 9TB. T: 01348 875 604; E: stepheneb@icloud.com

Bird Report
CARMARTHENSHIRE BIRDS (1982-), from Wendell Thomas, 48 Glebe Road, Loughhor, Swansea, SA4 6QD. E: wendellthomas57@gmail.com

CEREDIGION BIRD REPORT (1982/85), from RSPB Ynys-hir, Teifi Marshes Welsh Wildlife Centre and Ystwyth Bookshop (Aberystwyth) - online from WTS&WW www.welshwildlife.org/shop/
or by post from John Davis, Pant Llidiart, Trisant, Aberystwyth SY23 4RQ.

PEMBROKESHIRE BIRD REPORT (1981-), download from website - http://pembrokeshirebirdgroup.blogspot.com/p/reports.html

SKOKHOLM BIRD REPORT (1981-), download from website - www.welshwildlife.org/reports/

BTO Regional Representative
CARDIGAN. Naomi Davis. T: n/a; E: naomi.davis25@gmail.com

CARMARTHEN. Paul Aubrey. T: n/a; E: paulnwrg@outlook.com

PEMBROKESHIRE. Bob Haycock. T: 01834 891 667; E: bob.haycock@btinternet.com

Annie Haycock (Assistant Representative). T: n/a; E: n/a

Club
CARMARTHENSHIRE BIRD CLUB. (2003; 140+). Sian Rees-Harper (Sec), Maesteg, Capel Seion, Drefach, Llanelli, SA14 7BS. T: 01269 831 496; E: gary.harper3@gmail.com;
W: www.carmarthenshirebird.club
Meetings: 7.30pm, on a Wednesday (Oct-Mar). Llanelli Cricket Club, Stradey Park, Llanelli, SA15 4BT. Contact/see website for details.

PEMBROKESHIRE BIRD GROUP. (1983; 60). Peter Royle (Sec), Orlandon Kilns, St. Brides, Haverfordwest, SA62 3AP. T: 01646 636 970; E: pdroyle@orlandon.co.uk;
W: http://pembrokeshirebirdgroup.blogspot.co.uk/
Meetings: No indoor meetings held.

Ringing Group/Bird Observatory
SKOKHOLM RG.

PEMBROKESHIRE RG.
W: http://birdringingpembrokeshire.blogspot.com/

TEIFI RG. W: www.teifimarshbirds.blogspot.co.uk

SKOKHOLM BIRD OBSERVATORY. Richard Brown/Giselle Eagle (Wardens), The Welsh Wildlife Centre, Cilgerran, Cardigan SA43 2TB; T: 01239 621 212 (wardens: 07971 114 303); E: skokholmwarden@gmail.com;
W: http://skokholm.blogspot.co.uk

Accommodation: T: 01656 724 100; E: islands@welshwildlife.org
W: www.welshwildlife.org/staying-on-skokholm/

Wetland Bird Survey (WeBS) Local Organiser
CARMARTHENSHIRE. Alan Seago. T: 01792 369 247; E: alan.seago47@btinternet.com

CEREDIGION (incl DYFI ESTUARY). Russell Jones. T: via WeBS Office; E: via WeBS Office

PEMBROKESHIRE. Annie Haycock. T: via WeBS Office; E: annie@rushmoorphotos.co.uk

Wildlife Trust
WILDLIFE TRUST OF SOUTH AND WEST WALES. See Southern Area of Wales.

CHANNEL ISLANDS

ALDERNEY

Atlas/Avifauna
The Birds of Alderney. Jeremy G Sanders. (Privately Published, 2007).

Bird Recorder
John Horton, c/o Alderney Bird Observatory - see below.

BTO Regional Representative
Chris Mourant. T: n/a;
E: chris.mourant@yahoo.co.uk

Ringing Group/BIrd Observatory
ALDERNEY BIRD OBSERVATORY.
The Warden, Alderney Bird Observatory, The Nunnery, Longis Road, Alderney, GY9 3YB.
T: 01481 822 954 or 07815 549 191;
E: abo.warden@outlook.com;
W: www.alderneybirdobservatory.org

Wetland Bird Survey (WeBS) Local Organiser
Alderney Wildlife Trust RAMSAR Officer.
T: 07781 423 635; E: ramsar@alderneywildlife.org

Wildlife Trust
ALDERNEY WILDLIFE TRUST. (2002)
Slades, 48 Victoria Street, St Anne, Alderney GY9 3TA. T/fax: 01481 822 935;
E: info@alderneywildlife.org;
W: www.alderneywildlife.org

GUERNSEY

Bird Atlas/Avifauna
Birds of the Bailiwick: Guernsey, Alderney, Sark and Herm. Duncan Spencer & Paul Hillion (Jill Vaudin Publishing 2011).

Bird Recorder
Mark Lawlor, St Etienne, Les Effards, St Sampsons, Guernsey GY2 4YN. T: 07781 122 313;
E: mplawlor@cwgsy.net

Bird Report
GUERNSEY BIRD REPORT (1992-), download from website: W: www.guernseybirds.org.gg

BTO Regional Representative
Chris Mourant. T: n/a;
E: chris.mourant@yahoo.co.uk

Club

La Société
For nature, history and science in Guernsey

LA SOCIÉTÉ GUERNESIAISE. (1882).
Secretary, La Société Guernesiaise, Candie Gardens, St Peter Port, Guernsey GY1 1UG.
T: 01481 725 093; E: societe@cwgsy.net;
W: www.societe.org.gg

Chris Mourant (Sec, Ornithology Section).
Address: n/a. T: 07911 130 415;
E: info@guernseybirds.org.gg;
W: www.guernseybirds.org.gg
Meetings: (Ornithology Section). 7.30pm, 1st Thursday of the month. Frossard Theatre, Candie - address, as above.

RSPB Local Group
GUERNSEY BAILIWICK. (1975; 200+).
Anne Seebeck. T: 01481 241 401;
E: anneseebeck@cwgsy.net;
W: www.rspbguernsey.co.uk
Meetings: Several during the year - contact/ see website for details. La Villette Hotel, St Martins, Guernsey GY4 6QG.

Wetland Bird Survey (WeBS) Local Organiser
GUERNSEY COAST. Mary Simmons.
T: 01481 256 016; E: msim@cwgsy.net

JERSEY

Bird Recorder
Tony Paintin, 1 Ficquet House, La Verte Rue, St Brelade, Jersey JE3 8EL. T: 01534 741 928;
E: cavokjersey@hotmail.com

Bird Report
JERSEY BIRD REPORT (1991-), from Ornithology Section, La Société Jersiaise - see below.

BTO Regional Representative
Tony Paintin. T: 01534 741 928;
E: cavokjersey@hotmail.com

Club
SOCIÉTIÉ JERSIAISE. (1873).
La Société Jersiaise, 7 Pier Road, St Helier, Jersey JE2 4XW. T: 01534 758 314;
E: info@societe-jersiaise.org;
W: www.societe-jersiaise.org

Roger Noel (Sec, Ornithology Section).
Address: n/a. T: n/a;
E: rogernoel1@googlemail.com
Meetings: (Ornithology Section). 8pm, 1st & 3rd Thursdays of the month. Arthur Mourant Room - address as above.

Wetland Bird Survey (WeBS) Local Organiser
JERSEY COAST. Roger Noel. T: 01534 481 409;
E: rogernoel1@googlemail.com

JERSEY INLAND. Vacant - contact WeBS Office.

NORTHERN IRELAND

Bird Recorder
George Gordon, 2 Brooklyn Avenue, Bangor, Co Down BT20 5RB. T: 028 9145 5763; E: nimbus10111947@gmail.com

Bird Report
IRISH BIRD REPORT (1953-), included in Irish Birds, see BirdWatch Ireland in Republic of Ireland.

COPELAND BIRD OBSERVATORY REPORT, from David Galbraith, Bookings Sec. T: 028 9338 2539 & 07934 416 668; E: davidgalbraith903@btinternet.com

BTO Regional Representative
BTO IRELAND OFFICER. Stephen Hewitt. T: n/a; E: stephen.hewitt@bto.org

ANTRIM & BELFAST. Adam McClure. T: 028 9346 2562 & 07793 038 211; E: adamdmcclure@yahoo.co.uk

ARMAGH. Stephen Hewitt. T: n/a; E: sjameshewitt@hotmail.com

DOWN. Kerri-Ann Armstrong. T: n/a; E: kestrelsni@gmail.com

FERMANAGH. Michael Stinson. T: 07890 358 239; E: mick.stinson@hotmail.com

LONDONDERRY. John Clarke. T: 028 7032 7675; E: jclarke48@gmail.com

TYRONE. Michael Stinson - see above.

Club
NORTHERN IRELAND BIRDWATCHERS' ASSOCIATION. See National Directory. W: http://nibirds.blogspot.co.uk/

NORTHERN IRELAND ORNITHOLOGISTS' CLUB. See National Directory. W: nioc.co.uk

Ringing Group/Bird Observatory
BELFAST AND DOWN RG. W: https://www.facebook.com/BogMeadowsCes

COPELAND BIRD OBSERVATORY. David Galbraith (Booking Secretary). T: 028 9338 2539 or 07934 416 668; E: davidgalbraith903@btinternet.com; W: www.thecbo.org.uk

RSPB Local Group
ANTRIM. (1977; 25). Brenda Campbell. T: 028 9332 3657; E: brendacampbell961@gmail.com; W: www.rspb.org.uk/groups/antrim
Meetings: 7.30pm, 2nd Monday of the month (Sep-May). College of Agriculture Food & Rural Enterprise, 22 Greenmount Road, Antrim, BT41 4PU.

BELFAST. (1970; 50). Eleanor Brennan. T: 028 9064 7571; E: eleanor.brennan@btinternet.com; W: www.rspb.org.uk/groups/belfast
Meetings: 7.30pm, 1st Monday of the month (Sep-Apr). Cooke Centenary Church Hall, Park Road, Belfast, BT7 2FW.

COLERAINE. (1978; 45). Jim McDowell. T: 028 7034 2747; E: jdmcdowell12@talktalk.net; W: n/a
Meetings: 7.30pm, 3rd Monday of the month (Sep-Nov, Jan-Apr). Ballysally Youth and Community Centre, Ballysally Road, Coleraine, BT52 2QA.

FERMANAGH. (1977; 30). Rozy McConkey. T: 028 6632 0794; E: harry_mcconkey@yahoo.co.uk; W: www.rspb.org.uk/groups/Fermanagh
Meetings: 8pm, 4th Tuesday of the month (Sep-Apr, not Dec). St Macartins Cathedral Hall, Halls Lane, Enniskillen, BT74 7DR.

LARNE. (1974; 35). Jimmy Christie. T: 028 2858 3223; E: jameschristie310@gmail.com; W: n/a
Meetings: 7.30pm, 1st Wednesday of the month (Sep-Mar). Larne Grammar School, 4-6 Lower Cairncastle Rd, Larne, BT40 1PQ.

LISBURN. (1978; 30). Richard Crothers. T: 028 9262 1866; E: Richardcrothers@btinternet.com; W: www.rspb.org.uk/groups/lisburn
Meetings: 7.30pm, 4th Monday of the month (Sep-May). Harmony Hill Presbyterian Church, Moss Road, Lambeg, Lisburn, BT27 4NW.

Wetland Bird Survey (WeBS) Local Organiser
ANTRIM (OTHER SITES). Adam McClure. T: 028 2827 1875; E: adamdmcclure@yahoo.co.uk

ARMAGH (excl. LOUGHS NEAGH & BEG). Stephen Hewitt. T: 07784 546 403; E: stephen.hewitt@bto.org

BELFAST LOUGH. Shane Wolsey. T: 07831 697 371; E: shane.wolsey@bto.org

CARLINGFORD LOUGH. Jennifer Lynch.
T: via WeBS Office; E: jenny.lynch9@gmail.com

DUNDRUM BAY. Patrick Lynch. T: 028 4375 1467;
E: patrick.Lynch@nationaltrust.org.uk

FERMANAGH. Michael Stinson.
T: 07890 358 239; E: mick.stinson@hotmail.com

LARNE LOUGH. Doreen Hilditch.
T: via WeBS Office; E: mail18brae@btinternet.com

LONDONDERRY (OTHER SITES) - Stephen Hewitt - see above.

LOUGH FOYLE. Matthew Tickner.
T: 028 9049 1547; E: matthew.tickner@rspb.org.uk

LOUGHS NEAGH AND BEG. Claire MacNamara.
E: claire.macnamara@deara-ni.gov.uk

OUTER ARDS. Claire MacNamara - see above.

STRANGFORD LOUGH. Kerry Mackie.
T: 07719 537 275; E: kerrymackie9@gmail.com

TYRONE (excl. LOUGHS NEAGH AND BEG). Stephen Hewitt - see above

Vacant sites - contact WeBS Office:
BANN ESTUARY (LONDONDERRY).
DOWN (OTHER SITES).
SOUTH DOWN COAST.

Wildlife Trust
ULSTER WILDLIFE. (1978; 13,000).
McClelland House, 10 Heron Road, Belfast, BT3 9LE.
T: 028 9045 4094; E: info@ulsterwildlife.org;
W: www.ulsterwildlife.org

REPUBLIC OF IRELAND

BirdWatch Ireland
Unit 20, Block D
Bullford Business Campus
Kilcoole, Greystones
Co. Wicklow, A63 RW83,
Eire.
T: +353 (0)1 281 9878;
E: info@birdwatchireland.ie;
W: www.birdwatchireland.ie

Bird Recorder
IRELAND (all non-rarities): BirdWatch Ireland, P.O.Box 12, Greystones, Co. Wicklow.
E: info@birdwatchireland.ie

CLARE. John Murphy. E: murphyjohn@gmail.com

CORK. Mark Shorten. E: mshorten@gmail.com

DONEGAL. Ralph Sheppard. E: rsheppard@eircom.net

DUBLIN, LOUTH, MEATH & WICKLOW.
Dick Coombes. E: rcoombes@birdwatchireland.ie

GALWAY. Chris Peppiatt. E: chris.peppiatt@iol.ie

KERRY. Michael O'Clery & Jill Crosher.
E: moclery@tinet.ie

LIMERICK. Tony Mee, Ballyorgan, Kilfinane, Co. Limerick.

MAYO. National Parks and Wildlife, Lagduff More, Ballycroy, Westport.

MID-SHANNON. Stephen Heery. E: sheery@eircom.net

MONAGHAN. Joe Shannon. E: joeshan@eircom.net

WATERFORD. Paul Walsh, 16 Castlepoint, Crosshaven, Co. Cork.
E: pmwalsh@waterfordbirds.com

WEXFORD. Tony Murray, Wexford Wildfowl Reserve, North Slob. E: murraytony@hotmail.com

Bird Report
IRISH BIRD REPORT (1977),
contact BirdWatch Ireland.

BirdWatch Ireland Branches
There is a network of local branches around the country who organise events including field trips and talks - they can be contacted via BirdWatch Ireland.

Ringing Group/Bird Observatory
GREAT SALTEE RS.

IRISH MIDLANDS RG.

MUNSTER RG.

CAPE CLEAR BIRD OBSERVATORY.
Birdwatch Ireland - see above.
E: info@birdwatchireland.ie;
W: https://birdwatchireland.ie/our-work/cape-clear-bird-observatory/

WILDLIFE WELFARE

A number of organisations work towards the care and rehabilitation of injured, sick and abandoned birds/wildlife across the UK, and individual wildlife hospitals carry out the same role on a local basis - some of these are listed below. The RSPCA (England & Wales), SSPCA (Scotland) and USPCA (Northern Ireland) are the national charities that help and advise on injured wildlife (NOT the RSPB). You can also find an independent local rescue centre on www.helpwildlife.co.uk

ORGANISATIONS

BRITISH WILDLIFE REHABILITATION COUNCIL (1987)

Promoting the care and rehabilitation of wildlife casualties through the exchange of information between people such as rehabilitators, zoologists and veterinary surgeons who are active in this field. Organises symposiums and regional workshops. Periodically issues a newsletter, *The Rehabilitator*. Website includes a list of rehabilitators.
Contact: BWRC, PO Box 8686, Grantham, Lincolnshire NG31 0AG; E: admin@bwrc.org.uk; W: www.bwrc.org.uk

HELPWILDLIFE.CO.UK (2005)

HelpWildlife.co.uk is maintained by a very small team of people involved in British wildlife rehabilitation to fully utilise the internet to help with wildlife issues. The site aims to provide informed, unbiased advice about caring for sick or injured birds and animals. Volunteers trawl the internet for details of those who might be able to help so that assistance can be offered quickly in an emergency. Visitors to the site are invited to provide feedback on listings published to ensure they are kept as up to date as possible.
Contact: for general enquiries NOT for a specific wildlife rescue - E: enquiries@helpwildlife.co.uk; W: www.helpwildlife.co.uk

INTERNATIONAL CENTRE FOR BIRDS OF PREY (1967)

The ICBP works for the conservation of birds of prey and their habitats through public education, captive breeding, treatment and rehabilitation of wild injured birds of prey. Education is on-going to visitors and specific groups and parties, from first schools to universities. The Centre continues its captive breeding aims; to research species; maintain the collection and provide birds for demonstrations. The Centre also works with many other groups and facilities to continue to support worldwide field research projects and international conservation programmes. It accepts, treats and rehabilitates injured wild birds of prey. Membership available. The Centre is open from Feb-Nov, 10.30am-5.30pm (4.30pm Feb/early Mar & Nov) and closed in Dec/Jan.
Contact: ICBP, Boulsdon House, Newent, Gloucs GL18 1JJ. T: 01531 820 286; E: info@icbp.org; W: www.icbp.org

PEOPLE'S DISPENSARY FOR SICK ANIMALS (1917)

Provides free veterinary treatment for sick/injured animals whose owners qualify for this charitable service and promotes responsible pet ownership.
Contact: PDSA, Whitechapel Way, Priorslee, Telford, Shropshire TF2 9PQ. T: 0800 917 2509; W: www.pdsa.org.uk

RAPTOR FOUNDATION (1989)

RAPTOR FOUNDATION

Provides mediacl care for injured raptors and returns rehabilitated birds back to the wild or provides a sanctuary for un-releasable birds. Researches into environmental and conservation matters. A full 24-hour rescue service is available for injured raptors and owls and the centre assists in breed-and-release schemes to rebuild populations across Europe. Centre is open daily, 10am-5pm (4pm mid Oct-mid-Feb), closed Jan 1 & Dec 25/26.
Contact: The Raptor Foundation, The Heath, St Ives Road, Woodhurst, Cambs PE28 3BT. T: 01487 741 140; E: via website; W: www.raptorfoundation.org.uk

RAPTOR RESCUE (1978)

Raptor Rescue has evolved into one of the UK's foremost organisations dedicated to ensuring all sick and injured birds of prey are cared for by suitably qualified people, and wherever possible, released back into the wild.
Contact: Raptor Rescue. T: 0870 241 0609; E: secretary@raptorrescue.org.uk; W: www.raptorrescue.org.uk

ROYAL SOCIETY FOR THE PREVENTION OF CRUELTY TO ANIMALS (1824): RSPCA

The oldest welfare charity looking out for the needs of animals on farms, in research labs, in the wild in paddocks and in our homes. The RSPCA also operate four wildilfe centres providing specialist care for the rehabilitation of wildlife throughout England and Wales (see wildlife hospitals below). In cases of animal cruelty, inspectors are contacted through their National Communication Centre, which can be reached via the Society's 24-hour national cruelty and advice line: T: 0300 1234 999.
Contact: RSPCA Headquarters, Willberforce Way, Southwater, Horsham, West Sussex RH13 9RS. W: www.rspca.org.uk

SCOTTISH SOCIETY FOR THE PREVENTION OF CRUELTY TO ANIMALS (1839): SCOTTISH SPCA
Represents animal welfare interests to Government, local authorities and others. Educates young people to realise their responsibilities. Maintains an inspectorate to patrol and investigate and to advise owners about the welfare of animals and birds in their care. Maintains a National Wildlife Rescue Centre. Bird species, including birds of prey, are rehabilitated and where possible released back into the wild.
Contact: Scottish SPCA, Kingseat Road, Halbeath, Dunfermline, Fife KY11 8RY.
T: 03000 999 999 (animal helpline 7am-9pm);
E: via website; W: www.scottishspca.org

SWAN SANCTUARY (1980s)
Founded by Dorothy Beeson, this registered charity is the largest and only completely self-contained swan hospital in the UK. It has several nursing ponds and rehabilitation lakes. 24-hr rescue service, with volunteers on hand to recover swans (and other animals).
Contact: The Swan Sanctuary, Felix Lane, Shepperton, Middlesex TW17 8NN.
T: 01932 240 790 (emergency); E: via website;
W: www.theswansanctuary.org.uk

ULSTER SOCIETY FOR THE PREVENTION OF CRUELTY TO ANIMALS (1836): USPCA
Represents animal welfare in Northern Ireland with the purpose of preventing cruelty and revlieve suffering to all animals, both pets and wildlife.
Contact: UPSCA, Unit 6, Carnbane Industrial Estate (East), Newry, Co Down BT35 6HQ.
T: 028 3025 1000; E: enquiries@uspca.co.uk;
W: www.uspca.co.uk

WILDLIFE HOSPITALS

England

SWAN LIFELINE
Swan Rescue HQ & Treatment Centre, Cuckoo Weir Island, South Meadow Lane, Eton, BERKSHIRE SL4 6SS.
T: 01753 859 397 (24hr emergency line);
E: enquiries@swanlifeline.org.uk (non-emergency);
W: www.swanlifeline.org.uk
Thames Valley 24-hour swan rescue & treatment service. Veterinary support & hospital unit. Membership available.

TIGGYWINKLES, THE WILDLIFE HOSPITAL TRUST
Tiggywinkles, Aston Road, Haddenham, Aylesbury, BUCKINGHAMSHIRE HP17 8AF.
T: 01844 292 292 (24hr helpline);
E: mail@tiggywinkles.org (non-emergency);
W: www.sttiggywinkles.org.uk
All British species. Veterinary referrals & helpline for vets & others on wild bird treatments. Full veterinary unit & staff. Membership available.

RSPCA WILDLIFE CENTRES (not 24-hours)
EAST WINCH, Gayton Rd, East Winch, NORFOLK PE32 1LG. T: 0300 123 0709 (9am-4pm, Mon-Fri).

MALLYDAMS WOOD, Peter James Lane, Hastings, EAST SUSSEX TN35 4AH. T: 0300 123 0723 (8am-8pm Apr-Sep, 9am-5pm Oct-Mar).

STAPELEY GRANGE, London Road, Stapeley, Nantwich, CHESHIRE CW5 7JW. T: 0300 123 0722 (8am-9pm May-Oct, 8am-8pm Nov-Apr).

WEST HATCH, Cold Road,Taunton SOMERSET TA3 5RT. 0300 123 0721 (8am-9pm daily).

T: 0300 1234 999 (24-hr national cruelty line);
W: www.rspca.org.uk/whatwedo/care/wildlifecentres & www.rspca.org.uk/whatwedo/yourlocal

SWAN RESCUE SANCTUARY
The Widgeons, Crooked Withies, Holt, Wimborne, DORSET BH21 7LB. T: 01202 828 166;
W: www.swan-rescue.co.uk
Rescue service for swans. Large sanctuary of ponds/lakes. Hospital and intensive care. Veterinary support. Free advice and help line. Rescue water craft for emergencies. Viewing by appointment only.

VALE WILDLIFE HOSPITAL & REHABILITATION CENTRE.
Station Road, Beckford, Tewkesbury, GLOUCESTERSHIRE GL20 7AN. T: 01386 882 288;
E: info@valewildlife.org.uk;
W: www.valewildlife.org.uk
All wildlife. Intensive care. Veterinary support.

HAWK CONSERVANCY TRUST
Visitor Centre, Sarson Lane, Weyhill, Andover, HAMPSHIRE SP11 8DY. T: 01264 773 850;
E: info@hawkconservancy.org;
W: www.hawk-conservancy.org
The HCT is an important centre for receiving injured birds of prey and has one of the only specialist birds of prey hospitals in the UK.

RAPTOR CENTRE
c/o Hobbledown, Horton Lane, Epsom, SURREY KT19 8PT. T: 01372 848 990; E: via website; W: www.raptorcentre.co.uk
Birds of prey. Veterinary support. Rescue service for sick and injured birds of prey that covers the South-East. Flying displays and demonstrations.

BERWICK SWAN & WILDLIFE TRUST
Windmill Way East, Ramparts Business Park, Berwick-upon-Tweed, NORTHUMBERLAND TD15 1TU. T: 01289 302 882;
E: swan-trust@hotmail.co.uk;
W: www.swan-trust.org
All categories of wildlife. Pools for swans, other waterfowl. Veterinary support. Membership available.

BRITISH WILDLIFE RESCUE CENTRE
Wildlife Barn, London Road, Weston, STAFFORDSHIRE ST18 0JS. T: 01889 271 308;
E: admin@thebwrc.com; W: www.thebwrc.com
All species, including imprints and permanently injured. Hospital, large aviaries and caging. Veterinary support.

GENTLESHAW BIRD OF PREY & WILDLIFE CENTRE
Fletcher's Country Garden Centre, Stone Road, Eccleshall, STAFFORDSHIRE ST21 6JY.
T: 01785 850 379; E: gentleshaw1@btconnect.com;
W: www.gentleshawwildlife.co.uk
All birds of prey (incl. owls). Hospital cages and aviaries; release sites. Veterinary support. Open to the public.

THE WILDLIFE AID FOUNDATION
Randalls Farm House, Randalls Road, Leatherhead, SURREY KT22 0AL. 24-hr Wildlife Help & Enquiries line: 09061 800 132 (50p/min);
E: via website; W: www.wildlifeaid.org.uk
Wildlife hospital and rehabilitation centre helping all native British species. Special housing for birds of prey. Membership scheme and fund raising activities. Veterinary support.

BRENT LODGE BIRD & WILDLIFE TRUST
Cow Lane, Sidlesham, Chichester, WEST SUSSEX PO20 7LN. T: 01243 641 672 (emergency number);
E: enquiries@brentlodge.org; W: www.brentlodge.org
All species of wild birds and small mammals.

ANIMAL HOUSE BIRDS OF PREY
58 Dale Edge, Eastfield, Scarborough, NORTH YORKSHIRE YO11 3EP.
T: 07807 038 553; E: via website;
W: www.animalhousewildlifewelfare.com
Specialises in the rescue and rehabilitation of birds of prey.

Scotland

HESSILHEAD WILDLIFE RESCUE CENTRE
Gateside, Beith, AYRSHIRE KA15 1HT.
T: 01505 502 415;
E: info@hessilhead.org.uk;
W: www.hessilhead.org.uk
All species. Releasing aviaries. Veterinary support. Visits on open days. Membership available.

NATIONAL WILDLIFE RESCUE CENTRE
Scottish SPCA, National Wildlife Rescue Centre, Fishcross, CLACKMANNANSHIRE FK10 3AN.
T: 03000 999 999 (7am-9pm); E: via website;
W: www.scottishspca.org/our-work/our-centres
Ten centres around the country - no visiting, but casualties accepted at any time.

Wales

GOWER BIRD HOSPITAL
Sandy Lane, Pennard, SWANSEA, SA3 2EW.
T: 01792 371 630;
E: info@gowerbirdhospital.org.uk;
W: www.gowerbirdhospital.org.uk
All species of wild birds, also small mammals. Cares for sick, injured and orphaned wild birds and animals with the sole intention of returning them to the wild.

Channel Islands

GUERNSEY.
GSPCA ANIMAL SHELTER, Les Fiers Moutons, St Andrews, GUERNSEY GY6 8UD.
T: 01481 257 261; (T: 07781 104 082 emergency);
E: admin@gspca.org.gg; W: www.gspca.org.gg
All species. 24-hour emergency service. Veterinary support.

JERSEY
JSPCA ANIMALS' SHELTER, 89 St Saviour's Road, St Helier, JERSEY JE2 4GJ. T: 01534 724 331;
(T: 07797 720 331 emergency);
E: via website; W: www.jspca.org.je
All species. 24-hour emergency service. Veterinary support. Educational Centre.

~~~~~

In an emergency, DO NOT send an e-mail, use the emergency phone numbers.

All of the organisations and wildlife hospitals that look after the health and welfare of our wildlife rely on funding from memberships and/or donations.
~~~~~

BIRD INFORMATION SERVICES & BIRDLINE NUMBERS

Bird Forum
Free to join, online forum. W: www.birdforum.net

BirdGuides
Offers subscription bird news services online and via e-mail, text message and apps for Apple and Android devices. T: 01778 392 027;
E: via website; W: www.birdguides.com

Flightline
Northern Ireland's daily bird news service.
T: 028 91467408; E: nibirds@live.co.uk;
http://nibirds.blogspot.co.uk

Rare Bird Alert
Offers subscription instant bird news service - available online, by pager or phone app.
T: 01603 457 016; E: admin@rarebirdalert.co.uk;
W: www.rarebirdalert.co.uk

Birdline

Scotland 09068 700 234
W: https://www.the-soc.org.uk/content/bird-recording/birdline-scotland

South East closed

South West closed

East Anglia 09068 700 245
W: www.birdlineeastanglia.co.uk

North East 09068 700 246

Midlands 09068 700 247

Wales closed

North West closed

Note:
The 09068 Birdline numbers are charged at premium line rates (65p per minute from landline or mobile + any connection charges your mobile provider may charge).

FOUND A DEAD BIRD OF PREY?

Our Research monitors pollutants in birds of prey

WE NEED YOUR HELP

If you find a dead bird of prey, collect it and call the (PBMS) **Predatory Bird Monitoring Scheme** on 01524 595 830

Email: PBMS@ceh.ac.uk

Twitter: @PBMSatCEH

Facebook: www.facebook.com/COLLECTRAPTORS

Website: http://pbms.ceh.ac.uk

Photo -©fotogenix.www.fotosearch.co.uk

Neil Gartshore

The world's six species of Spoonbills are spread across every continent except Antarctica - our own, the Eurasian Spoonbill *(Platalea leucorodia)* is the most widespread. Now established (& increasing) as a breeding/wintering species in the UK, their numbers/distribution are tracked by Birdtrack, RBBP and WeBs.

DIRECTORY OF ORGANISATIONS

UK/UK-BASED ORGANISATIONS

Many bird organisations operate across, or are based in, the UK. Some cater for specialist groups of people/interests, others are open to a wider audience. The majority are membership-based - contact them directly for more information about their work and subscription rates. A selection of other organisations and governmental departments are also listed in this directory. Have a browse.

AFRICAN BIRD CLUB (1994)

Provides a worldwide focus for African Ornithology and raises funds to support conservation projects through its Conservation Fund. Liaises and promotes the work of existing regional societies. Holds an annual meeting in London, publishes a colour bulletin twice yearly.
Contact: c/o BirdLife International, The David Attenborough Building, Pembroke Street, Cambridge, CB2 3QZ. T: n/a. E: info@africanbirdclub.org; E (membership): membership@africanbirdclub.org; W: www.africanbirdclub.org

AMPHIBIAN & REPTILE CONSERVATION TRUST (2009)

amphibian and reptile conservation

Formed out of The Herpetological Conservation Trust (1989) to widen its role. ARC conserves amphibians and reptiles and their habitats, including a number of reserves.
Contact: ARC, 744 Christchurch Rd, Boscombe, Bournemouth BH7 6BZ. T: 01202 391 319; E: enquiries@arc-trust.org; W: www.arc-trust.org

ARMY ORNITHOLOGICAL SOCIETY (1960)

Open to any serving and ex-Army personnel, other Services and their families, MOD civil servants and members of the Commonwealth Forces who have an interest in bird life, either on a casual basis or in more depth. Activities include field meetings, expeditions, assistance with bird surveys and ringing projects, and a long term survey of seabirds on Ascension Island. AOS newsletter & annual journal *Adjutant*.
Contact: The Army Ornithological Society, Prince Consort's Library, Knollys Road, South Camp, Aldershot, Hampshire GU11 1PS. E: via website; W: www.armybirding.org.uk

ASSOCIATION FOR THE PROTECTION OF RURAL SCOTLAND (1926)

Works to protect Scotland's world renown landscape and the amenity of the countryside from unnecessary or inappropriate development. APRS recognise the needs of those who live and work in rural Scotland and the necessity of reconciling these needs with the sometimes competing requirements of industry and recreation. Members have access to specialist advice, newsletters and regular e-bulletins.
Contact: Association for the Protection Rural Scotland, Dolphin House, 4 Hunter Square, Edinburgh EH1 1QW. T: 0131 225 7012; E: info@aprs.scot; W: http://aprs.scot/

ASSOCIATION OF COUNTY RECORDERS & EDITORS (1993)

ACRE's basic aim is to promote best practice in the work of County Recorders, providing a forum for discussions on producing county bird reports and in problems arising in assessing records, managing county databases systems and archives. Also provides a discussion medium for interactions of the County Recorders and report Editors with British Birds Rarities Committee (BBRC), Rare Breeding Bird Panel (RBBP) and the British Trust for Ornithology (BTO).
Contact: Hugh Pulsford (Secretary). T: 01565 880 171; E: countyrec@cawos.org

BARN OWL TRUST (1988)

A registered charity dedicated to conserving the Barn Owl and its environment - it is the main source of Barn Owl information in the UK. The Trust, and its members, erect nestboxes and are closely involved in habitat creation both on its own land and through farm visits. Also offers practical guidance to developers and planners - advising on Barn Owl mitigation measures, undertakes research and provides care for injured owls. Produces a number of publications inc. 'The Barn Owl Conservation Handbook'. Events held.
Contact: Barn Owl Trust, Waterleat, Ashburton, Devon TQ13 7HU. T: 01364 653 026; E: info@barnowltrust.org.uk; W: www.barnowltrust.org.uk

BAT CONSERVATION TRUST (1991)

Supports local bat groups across the UK. Their vision includes: learning more about bats and how they use the landscape; taking action to protect bats and to enhance the landscapes they rely on; and inspiring people about bats and their environment.
Contact: Bat Conservation Trust, 5th floor, Quadrant House, 250 Kennington Lane, London SE11 5RD. T: Bat Helpline 0345 1300 228 (9.30am-4.30pm Mon-Fri & up to 10.30pm daily May-Sep for emergencies only); E: enquiries@bats.org.uk; W: www.bats.org.uk

BIRD OBSERVATORIES COUNCIL (1946)

The BOC co-ordinates and promotes the work of bird observatories at a national level. All accredited bird observatories (20 at present) affiliated to the Council undertake a ringing programme and provide a ringing experience to those interested. Most are also able to provide accommodation for visiting birdwatchers.
Contact: Alison Duncan, The Secretary BOC, North Ronaldsay Bird Observatory, Twingness, North Ronaldsay, Orkney KW17 2BE. T: 01857 633200; E: info@birdobscouncil.org.uk; W: www.birdobscouncil.org.uk

BIRD STAMP SOCIETY (1986)

Quarterly magazine *Flight* contains philatelic and ornithological articles. Lists all new issues and identifies species. Runs a quarterly Postal Auction (between 500-700 lots per auction, depending on stock levels).
Contact: Graham Horsman (Mem Sec), 23A East Main Street, Blackburn, West Lothian EH47 7QR. T: 01506 651 029; E: membership@birdstampsociety.org.uk; W: www.birdstampsociety.org

UK/UK-BASED ORGANISATIONS

BIRDING FOR ALL (2000)

Formally known as The Disabled Birder's Association, Birding For All (2010) is a registered charity and international movement, which aims to promote access to reserves and other birding places and to a range of services, so that people with different needs can follow the birding obsession as freely as able-bodied people. Membership is currently free (donations welcomed) and is open to everyone - new members are needed to help send a stronger message to those who own and manage nature reserves to improve access when they are planning and improving facilities. BFA also seeks to influence those who provide birdwatching services and equipment.

Contact: Bo Beolens (Chairman), Birding For All, 18 St Mildreds Road, Cliftonville, Margate, Kent CT9 2LT. E: fatbirder@gmail.com; W: www.birdingforall.com

BIRDLIFE INTERNATIONAL (1993)

Formally ICBP - International Committee for Bird Preservation (1922). See page 306.

BIRDWATCH IRELAND (1968, network of 21 branches)

The largest independent conservation organisation in Ireland with over 15,000 members. Its primary objective is the protection of wild birds and their habitats in Ireland through the efforts of its staff, members and volunteers alike. It carries out extensive research and survey work, operates applied conservation projects and manages a network of reserves nationwide. It publishes *Wings* (quarterly magazine), e*Wings* (electronic) magazine, *Irish Birds* (annual journal) and *Bird Detectives* (children's magazine, twice yearly).

Contact: BirdWatch Ireland, Unit 20, Block D, Bullford Business Campus, Kilcoole, Greystones, Co. Wicklow, A63 RW83 Ireland. T: +353 (0)1 2819 878; Fax: +353 (0)1 281 0997; E: info@birdwatchireland.ie; W: www.birdwatchireland.ie

BRITISH BIRDS RARITIES COMMITTEE (1959)

The Committee (with 10 experts who vote) adjudicate records of species of rare occurrence in Britain (these are marked 'R' in the Checklists, P.55) and publishes its annual report in B*ritish Birds*. The BBRC also assesses records from the Channel Islands. In the case of rarities trapped for ringing, records should be sent to the Ringing Office of the British Trust for Ornithology, who will in turn forward them to the BBRC.

Contact: Chas Holt (Secretary), British Birds Rarities Committee, 307 St John's Way, Thetford, Norfolk IP24 3PA. E: secretary@bbrc.org.uk; W: www.bbrc.org.uk

BRITISH DECOY & WILDFOWL CARVERS ASSOCIATION (1990)

The Association is a non-profitmaking organisation, run by carvers to promote all aspects of their art. It produces *Wingspan* magazine 3x p.a.; keeps members in touch with the art; promotes regional groups; generates local interest; holds competitions and exhibitions; and cares for the interests of bird carvers. Each Sept the BDWCA stages the 'Festival of Bird Art' in Bakewell, in the Peak District, and includes the National Bird Carving Championships.

Contact: E: bdwcaenquiries@bdwca.org.uk; W: www.bdwca.org.uk

BRITISH DRAGONFLY SOCIETY (1983)

The BDS aims to promote the recording and the conservation of dragonflies. Members receive two issues of *Dragonfly News* and *BDS Journal* each year and *Hawker*, a monthly e-newsletter. Dragonfly recorders also receive *Darter*, an annual magazine. There are countrywide field trips, an annual members' day, and training is available on aspects of dragonfly identification and ecology.

Contact: Carolyn Cooksey (Sec), British Dragonfly Society, Ashcroft, Brington Road, Old Weston, Huntingdon, PE28 5LP. E: secretary@british-dragonflies.org.uk; W: www.british-dragonflies.org.uk

BRITISH ENTOMOLOGICAL & NATURAL HISTORY SOCIETY (1872)

The Society promotes and advances research in entomology. Holds a number of indoor and outdoor meetings, publishes a journal (4 p.a.) and makes small grants. Its HQ has a library and reference collections.

Contact: The Secretary, c/o The Pelham-Clinton Building, Dinton Pastures Country Park, Davis Street, Hurst, Reading, Berkshire RG10 0TH. T: n/a; E: enquiries@benhs.org.uk; W: www.benhs.org.uk

BRITISH FALCONERS' CLUB (1927)

The BFC is the oldest and largest falconry club in Europe and has 13 regional branches in the UK. Its aim is to encourage responsible falconers and conserve birds of prey by breeding, holding educational meetings and providing facilities, guidance and advice to those wishing to take up the sport. Publishes *The Falconer* and a newsletter.

Contact: British Falconers' Club, Westfield Meeting Hill, Worstead, North Walsham, Norfolk NR28 9LS. T: 01692 404 057; E: admin@britishfalconersclub.co.uk; W: www.britishfalconersclub.co.uk

BRITISH LIBRARY SOUND ARCHIVE - WILDLIFE SOUNDS (1969)

The most comprehensive collection of bird sound recordings in existence. Consists of 240,000+ wildlife recordings inc. 10,000+ species (birds, mammals, amphibians, reptiles, fish & insects) from around the world, many accessible for free listening. Copies or sonograms of most recordings can be supplied for private study or research and, subject to copyright clearance, for commercial uses. Contribution of new material and enquiries on all aspects of wildlife sounds and recording techniques are welcome. Publishes a number of magazines and periodicals, CD guides to bird songs and other wildlife, inc. ambience titles. Catalogue available on-line at http://cadensa.bl.uk/uhtbin/cgisirsi/x/x/0/49/

Contact: Cheryl Tipp, Curator, Wildlife & Environmental Sounds, The British Library, 96 Euston Road, London NW1 2DB. T: 020 7412 7403; E: wildlifesound@bl.uk; W: www.bl.uk/collection-guides/wildlife-and-environmental-sounds

BRITISH NATURALISTS' ASSOCIATION (1905)

The association was founded to promote the interests of nature lovers and bring them together. It encourages and supports schemes and legislation for the protection of the country's natural resources. It organises meetings, field weeks, lectures and exhibitions to help popularise the study of nature. BNA publishes two magazines, *Country-Side* and *British Naturalist* and has nine local branches. **Contact:** General Sec, British Naturalists' Association, 27 Old Gloucester Street, London WC1N 3AX. T: 0844 892 1817; E: info@bna-naturalists.org; W: www.bna-naturalists.org/

BRITISH ORNITHOLOGISTS' CLUB (1892)

The Club's objects are 'the promotion of scientific discussion between members and others interested in ornithology, and to facilitate the publication of scientific information in connection with ornithology'. The Club maintains a special interest in avian systematics, taxonomy and distribution and publishes the B*ulletin of the British Ornithologists' Club* quarterly (online only), as well as a continuing series of publications. It also holds a number of evening meetings each year (see website for details). **Contact:** BOC, c/o Natural History Museum at Tring, Akeman Street, Tring, Herts HP23 6AP. T: 0220 8876 4728 & 07919 174 898; E: info@boc-online.org; W: www.boc-online.org

BRITISH ORNITHOLOGISTS' UNION (1858)

The BOU is one of the world's oldest and most respected ornithological societies. It aims to promote ornithology within the scientific and birdwatching communities, in Britain and around the world - this is largely achieved by the publication of its quarterly international journal, *Ibis*, featuring work at the cutting edge of our understanding of the world's birdlife. It also runs an active programme of meetings, seminars and conferences covering ornithological topics and issues of the day - the proceedings are published free on the BOU website. Via social media (see website for links) the BOU acts as a global ornithological hub providing details of newly published research articles, conferences, PhD opportunities, jobs and more. Work being undertaken around the world can include research projects that have received financial assistance from the BOU's on-going programme of Small Research Grants and Career Development Bursaries (for ornithological students).

The BOU's Records Committee (see below) maintains the official British List. It has also published a series of country/island group 'checklists'. **Contact:** British Ornithologists' Union, P.O. Box 417, Peterborough, PE7 3FX. E: via website; W: www.bou.org.uk

BRITISH ORNITHOLOGISTS' UNION RECORDS COMMITTEE

A standing committee of the BOU, the BOURC's function is to maintain the British List, the official list of birds recorded in Great Britain (the up-to-date list can be viewed on the BOU website). The British List follows the International Ornithological Union's (IOU) IOC World Bird List. Where vagrants are involved it is concerned only with those which relate to potential additions to the British List (i.e. first records) - in this it differs from the British Birds Rarities Committee. It also examines, where necessary, important pre-1950 records, monitors introduced species for possible admission to, or deletion from, the List. BOURC reports are published in Ibis and are also available via the BOU website. **Contact:** as above (BOU).

BRITISH TRUST FOR ORNITHOLOGY (1933)

The BTO is an independent charitable research institute that combines professional and citizen science aimed at using evidence of change in wildlife populations, particularly birds, to inform the public, opinion-formers and environmental policy/decision makers. Through the fieldwork of 60,000 volunteer birdwatchers, in partnership with professional research scientists, the BTO collects high quality monitoring data on birds and other wildlife. Surveys include the National Ringing Scheme, the Nest Record Scheme, the Breeding Bird Survey (in collaboration with JNCC/RSPB), the Wetland Bird Survey, in particular Low Tide Counts (in collaboration with WWT/RSPB/JNCC) which all contribute to an integrated programme of population monitoring. The BirdTrack recording system is an important resource for recording bird data and all birdwatchers are encouraged to use it to log their bird sightings.
The Trust has a network of voluntary regional representatives (see County Directory) who organise fieldworkers for the BTO's programme of national surveys in which members participate. The results of these co-operative efforts are communicated to government departments, local authorities, industry and conservation bodies for effective action. For details of current activities see National Projects. Members receive *BTO News* regularly throughout the year and have the option of subscribing to *Bird Study* (four times yearly) and *Ringing & Migration* (twice yearly). Local meetings are held in conjunction with bird clubs and societies, there are regional and national birdwatchers' conferences, and specialist courses in bird identification and modern censusing techniques. Grants are made for research, and members have the use of a lending and reference library at Thetford. **Contact:** British Trust for Ornithology, The Nunnery, Thetford, Norfolk IP24 2PU. T: 01842 750 050; Fax: 01842 750 030; E: info@bto.org; W: www.bto.org

BTO IRELAND

The role of the Northern Ireland team is to develop the BTO presence in the country, particularly to assist the voluntary reps to find enough volunteers to undertake key bird monitoring surveys.
Contact:
W: www.bto.org/about-bto/national-offices/ireland

UK/UK-BASED ORGANISATIONS

BTO SCOTLAND

BTO Scotland's main functions are to promote the work of the Trust and develop wider coverage for surveys in Scotland, by encouraging greater participation in survey work. With a landscape and wildlife so different from the rest of the UK, BTO Scotland ensure that the Trust's work is not just related to the priorities of the UK as a whole but is also focused on the priorities of Scotland.
Contact: BTO Scotland, Unit 15, Beta Centre, Stirling University Innovation Park, Stirling, FK9 4NF.
T: 01786 458 021; E: scot.info@bto.org;
W: www.bto.org/about-bto/national-offices/scotland

BTO WALES/CYMRU

An office is located in Bangor University to provide more support to provide a Welsh voice for the BTO and to focus on Welsh priorities.
Contact: BTO Wales, Thoday Building, Deiniol Rd, Bangor, Gwynedd LL57 2UW. T: 01248 383 285;
W: www.bto.org/about-bto/national-offices/wales

BRITISH WATERFOWL ASSOCIATION

The BWA is an association of enthusiasts interested in keeping, breeding and conserving all types of waterfowl, inc. wildfowl and domestic ducks and geese. It is a registered charity, without trade affiliations, dedicated to educating the public about waterfowl and the need for conservation as well as to raising the standards of keeping and breeding ducks, geese and swans in captivity. Publishes *Waterfowl* members magazine three times a year.
Contact: BWA Secretary, 81 Browning Road, Ledbury, Herts HR8 2GA. T: 01531 671 250;
E: info@waterfowl.org.uk; W: www.waterfowl.org.uk

BUGLIFE (2000)

The only organisation in Europe devoted to the conservation of all invertebrates, actively engaged in halting the extinction of Britain's rarest slugs, snails, bees, wasps, ants, spiders, beetles and many more. It works to achieve this through practical conservation projects; promoting the environmental importance of invertebrates and raising awareness about the challenges to their survival; assisting in the development of helpful legislation and policy; developing and disseminating knowledge about how to conserve invertebrates; and encouraging and supporting invertebrate conservation initiatives by other organisations in the UK, Europe and worldwide.
Contact: Buglife, Age UK, The Lindens, 86 Lincoln Road, Peterborough, PE1 2SN. T: 01733 201 210;
E: info@buglife.org.uk; W: www.buglife.org.uk

BUTTERFLY CONSERVATION (1968)

One of the largest insect conservation organisations in the world. Their core aims: to recover threatened butterflies and moths; to increase numbers of widespread species; to promote international conservation actions; and to inspire people to understand and deliver species conservation. Runs 36 nature reserves and are involved in 73 landscape-scale projects to conserve habitats. There are 32 volunteer-run branches through the British Isles.

Contact: Head Office, Manor Yard, East Lulworth, Wareham, Dorset, BH20 5QP. T: 01929 400 209 ;
E: info@butterfly-conservation.org;
W: www.butterfly-conservation.org

Northern Ireland: Ned's Place, 66 Dublin Road, Kilcoo, Newry, BT34 5JG. T: 028 4377 1497;
E: northernireland@butterflyconservation.org

Scotland: Balallan House, Allan Park, Stirling, FK8 2QG.
T: 01786 447 753; E: scotland@butterfly-conservation.org

Wales: 4D Cwm Road, Hafod, Swansea, SA1 2AY.
T: 01792 642 972; E: wales@butterfly-conservation.org

CAMPAIGN FOR THE PROTECTION OF RURAL WALES (1928)

Its aims are to help the conservation and enhancement of the landscape, environment and amenities of the countryside, towns and villages of rural Wales and to form and educate opinion to ensure the promotion of its objectives. It gives advice and information upon matters affecting protection, conservation and improvement of the visual environment. Publishes *Rural Wales* (2 p.a.).
Contact: Tŷ Gwyn, 31 High Street, Welshpool, Powys SY21 7YD. T: 01938 552 525; E: info@cprwmail.org.uk;
W: www.cprw.org.uk

CENTRE FOR ECOLOGY & HYDROLOGY (CEH)

The work of the CEH, a component body of the Natural Environment Research Council, includes a range of ornithological research, covering population studies, habitat management and work on the effects of pollution. The CEH has a long-term programme to monitor pesticide and pollutant residues in the corpses of predatory birds sent in by birdwatchers, and carries out detailed studies on affected species. The Biological Records Centre (BRC), which is part of the CEH, is responsible for the national biological data bank on plant and animal distributions (except birds) - see BRC website, www.brc.ac.uk
Contact: Centre for Ecology & Hydrology, Maclean Building, Benson Lane, Crowmarsh Gifford, Wallingford, Oxfordshire OX10 8BB. T: 01491 838 800;
E: via website; W: www.ceh.ac.uk

CLA (Country Land & Business Association) (1907)

The CLA is at the heart of rural life and is the voice of the countryside for England and Wales, campaigning on issues which directly affect those who live and work in rural communities. Anyone who owns rural land or runs a rural business will benefit from joining the CLA and its members range from some of the largest landowners, with interests in forest, moorland, water and farming, to some with little more than a paddock or garden.
Contact: Country Land and Business Association Ltd, 16 Belgrave Square, London SW1X 8PQ. T: 020 7235 0511;
E: mail@cla.org.uk; W: www.cla.org.uk

CONSERVATION FOUNDATION (1982)
Created by David Bellamy and David Shreeve, it provides a means for people in public, private and not-for-profit sectors to collaborate on environmental causes. Over the years its programme has included award schemes, conferences, promotions, special events, field studies, school programmes, media work, seminars and workshops etc. The Conservation Foundation has created and managed environmental award schemes of all kinds. For information about how to apply for current award schemes visit the website.
Contact: Conservation Foundation, 1 Kensington Gore, London SW7 2AR. T: 020 7591 3111;
E: info@conservationfoundation.co.uk;
W: www.conservationfoundation.co.uk

CPRE (Campaign to Protect Rural England) (1926)
CPRE campaigns at all levels for a beautiful and living countryside by working to protect, promote and enhance our towns and countryside to make them better places to live, work and enjoy, and to ensure the countryside is protected for now and future generations.
Contact: Campaign to Protect Rural England, 5-11 Lavington Street, London SE1 0NZ.
T: 020 7981 2800; E: info@cpre.org.uk;
W: www.cpre.org.uk

EARTHWATCH INSTITUTE (1971)
Earthwatch developed the innovative idea of engaging the general public into the scientific process by bringing together individual volunteers and scientists on field research projects, thereby providing an alternative means of funding, as well as a dedicated labour force for field scientists. Earthwatch have invested in nearly 1400 conservation research projects in more than 120 countries.
Contact: Earthwatch (Europe), Mayfield House, 256 Banbury Road, Oxford, OX2 7DE. T: 01865 318 838;
E: hello@earthwatch.org.uk; W: www.earthwatch.org.uk

EDWARD GREY INSTITUTE OF FIELD ORNITHOLOGY (1937)
The EGI takes its name from Edward Grey, first Viscount Grey of Fallodon, a life-long lover of birds and former Chancellor of the University of Oxford. The Institute now has a permanent (research) staff of research students, senior visitors and post-doctoral research workers. The Institute houses the Alexander Library of Ornithology, one of the largest collections of 20th Century material on birds in the world, which is supported by the British Ornithologists' Union who provide much of the material. It also houses the British Falconers Club library. The Library is open for reference use only to all holders of a university card or valid Bodleian Library card. External visitors are welcome on a one-off day pass by arrangement by contacting: Sophie Wilcox, Alexander (and Sherardian) Library, South Parks Road, Oxford OX1 3RB; T: 01865 275 025;
E: sophie.wilcocx@bodleian.ox.ac.uk
Contact: Lynne Bradley, PA to Prof. Ben Sheldon, The EGI, Department of Zoology, University of Oxford, The John Krebs Field Station, Wytham, Oxford, OX2 8QJ;
T: 01865 271 234; E: ben.sheldon.pa@zoo.ox.ac.uk;
W: www.zoo.ox.ac.uk/egi/

ENVIRONMENT AGENCY (1996)
A non-departmental body which aims to protect and improve the environment and to contribute towards the delivery of sustainable development through the integrated management of air, land and water. Functions include pollution prevention and control, waste minimisation, management of water resources, flood defence, improvement of salmon and freshwater fisheries, conservation of aquatic species, navigation and use of inland and coastal waters for recreation.
Contact: Environment Agency, National Customer Contact Centre, PO Box 544, Rotherham, S60 1BY.
General enquiries T: 03708 506 506 (Mon-Fri, 8am-6pm)
Environment incident hotline (24hrs) T: 0800 80 70 60;
Floodline (24 hrs) T: 0345 988 1188;
E: enquiries@environment-agency.gov.uk;
W: www.gov.uk/government/organisations/environment-agency

EURING (European Union for Bird Ringing) (1963)
EURING co-ordinates bird-ringing schemes throughout Europe. It aims to promote and encourage: Scientific and administrative co-operation between national ringing schemes; development and maintenance of high standards in bird ringing; scientific studies of birds, in particular those based on marked individuals; and the use of data from bird ringing for the management and conservation of birds. These objectives are achieved mainly through co-operative projects, the organisation of meetings and the collection of data in the EURING Data Bank.
Contact: E: enquiries@euring.org;
W: www.euring.org

EUROPEAN COLOUR-RING BIRDING
This is a platform enabling field observers to find out who the project leaders are if they find a colour-ringed bird.
Contact: W: www.cr-birding.org

FAUNA & FLORA INTERNATIONAL (1903)
Their mission is to conserve threatened species and ecosystems worldwide by finding sustainable solutions based on sound science and taking human needs into account. They work in over 40 countries, supporting over 320 partners. Members receive a regular newsletter update and *Flora & Fauna (magazine)*. Also publishes *Oryx (journal)*.
Contact: The David Attenborough Building, Pembroke Street, Cambridge CB2 3QZ. T: 01223 571 000;
E: info@fauna-flora.org;
W: www.fauna-flora.org

FIELD STUDIES COUNCIL (1943)
Manages a UK wide network of centres where students from schools, universities and colleges, as well as individuals of all ages, can stay to study various aspects of the environment under expert guidance. Courses include many bird related themes. Research workers and naturalists wishing to use the records and resources are welcome. There are centres in England, Scotland, Wales and Northern Ireland - see website for contacts/courses available. Publishes identification charts, guides and handbooks.
Contact: Field Studies Council, Preston Montford, Montford Bridge, Shrewsbury, SY4 1HW.
T: 01743 852 100; E: enquiries@field-studies-council.org;
T (FSC publications): 01952 208 910;
E: publications@field-studies-council.org;
W: www.field-studies-council.org

FORESTRY COMMISSION (1919)
Supports the delivery of English forestry operations inc. grants for forestry activities and felling licences.
Contact: National Office, 620 Bristol Business Park, Coldharbour Lane, Bristol, BS16 1EJ. T: 0300 067 4000;
E: nationalenquiries@forestrycommission.gov.uk;
W: www.gov.uk/government/organisations/forestry-commission

FORESTRY ENGLAND (2019)
Looks after England's public forests by carrying out management for people, wildlife and the economy.
Contact: National Office, 620 Bristol Business Park, Coldharbour Lane, Bristol, BS16 1EJ. T: 0300 067 4000;
E: info@forestryengland.uk;
W: www.forestryengland.uk

FORESTRY & LAND SCOTLAND (2019)
Looks after national forests and land to enhance biodiversity, support tourism and increase access to the green spaces that will help improve Scotland's physical and mental health and well-being.
Contact: Head Office, 1 Highlander Way, Inverness Business Park, Inverness, IV2 7GB. T: 0300 067 6000;
E: enquiries@forestryandland.gov.scot;
W: www.forestryandland.gov.scot

SCOTTISH FORESTRY (2019)
Supports the delivery of sustainable Scottish forestry operations including grants for forestry activities and felling permissions.
Contact: Silvan House, 231 Corstorphine Road, Edinburgh EH12 7AT. T: 0131 370 5250;
E: Scottish.Forestry@forestry.gov.scot;
W: www.forestry.gov.scot

FORESTRY - Wales
See under listing for Natural Resources Wales.

FRESHWATER HABITATS TRUST (1988)
Formally Pond Conservation, Freshwater Habitats Trust aim is to protect freshwater life in ponds, streams, rivers and lakes through research, surveys and practical conservation work. Practical projects are targeted on the places that will bring the greatest benefits for freshwater life at regional and UK scale.
Contact: Freshwater Habitats Trust, Bury Knowle House, North Place, Headington, Oxford, OX3 9HY.
T: 01865 595 505; E: info@freshwaterhabitats.org.uk;
W: www.freshwaterhabitats.org.uk

FRIENDS OF THE EARTH (1971)
The largest international network of environmental groups in the world, represented in over 75 countries. In the UK it has a unique network of campaigning local groups, working in communities in England, Wales, Northern Ireland and Scotland. It is largely funded by supporters with more than 90% of income coming from individual donations, the rest from special fundraising events, grants and trading.

Contact: Friends of the Earth, The Printworks, 139 Clapham Road, London SW9 0HP.
T: 020 7490 1555; W: www.foe.co.uk

Friends of the Earth Cymru
33 Castle Arcade Balcony, Cardiff, CF10 1BY.
T: 029 2022 9577; E: cymru@foe.co.uk;
W: www.foe.cymru

Friends of the Earth Northern Ireland
W: www.friendsoftheearth.uk/northern-ireland

Friends of the Earth Scotland
Thorn House, 5 Rose Street, Edinburgh EH2 2PR.
T: 0131 243 2700; E: via website; W: https://foe.scot/

FWAG ASSOCIATION (2011)
The FWAG Association succeeded the Farming & Wildlife Advisory Group (FWAG - established in the 1960's) to represent local Farming & Wildlife Advisory Groups across the UK. FWAG's provide trusted, independent environmental advice to farmers helping them to understand the environmental value of their land and make the most of the agri-environment options available.
Contact: FWAG Association. E: info@fwag.org.uk;
W: www.fwag.org.uk

Local FWAG Groups:
Chris Seabridge & Associates Limited (West Midlands)
T: 01785 710 564; E: info@chrisseabridge.co.uk;
W: www.chrisseabridge.co.uk

East Midlands FWAG (Derbys, Notts, Leics, Rutland, Northants, Lincs)
E: info@eastmidlandsfwag.co.uk;
W: www.eastmidlandsfwag.co.uk

ELM Associates (Cheshire and the North West)
E: info@elmassocuiates.co.uk;
W: https://elmassociates.co.uk

FWAG Cymru
T: 01341 421 456; E: fwagcymru@btconnect.com

FWAG East (Cambs, Herts, Essex, Beds)
T: 01223 841 507; E: hello@fwageast.org.uk;
W: www.fwageast.org.uk

FWAG South East (Kent, Sussex, Surrey, Hants, IoW, Oxon)
T: 01483 810 887 & 07713 333 182;
E: shaun.page@fwagsoutheast.co.uk;
W: www.fwagadvice.co.uk

FWAG South West (Glous, Somerset, Dorset, Wilts, Devon, Cornwall)
T: 01823 660 684; E: info@fwagsw.org.uk;
W: www.fwagsw.org.uk

Norfolk FWAG
T: 01603 814 869; E: advice@norfolkfwag.co.uk;
W: www.norfolkfwag.co.uk

Suffolk FWAG
T: 01728 748 030; E: tim.schofield@suffolkfwag.co.uk;
W: www.suffolkfwag.co.uk

GAME & WILDLIFE CONSERVATION TRUST (1931)

A registered charity which uses science to promote game and wildlife management as an essential part of nature conservation and support best practice for field sports that contribute to improving the biodiversity of the countryside. 100+ staff, inc. many scientists, run over 60 research projects. The results are used to advise government, landowners, farmers and conservationists on practical management techniques which will benefit game species, their habitats and other wildlife. In June the *Annual Review* lists papers published in the peer-reviewed scientific press. Members receive *Gamewise* magazine three times a year.
Contact: Game & Wildlife Conservation Trust, Burgate Manor, Fordingbridge, Hampshire SP6 1EF.
T: 01425 652 381; Fax: 01425 655 848;
E: info@gwct.org.uk; W: www.gwct.org.uk

GAY BIRDERS CLUB (1994)

A voluntary society for gay, lesbian, bisexual or transgender birdwatchers, their friends and supporters, over the age of consent, in the UK and worldwide. The club has a network of regional contacts and organises (up to 100 p.a.) day trips, weekends and longer events at notable birding locations in the UK and abroad. Members receive a quarterly newsletter *Out Birding* with details of all events. There is a 'Grand Get Together' every two years.
Contact: E: contact@gbc-online.org.uk;
W: www.gbc-online.org.uk

HAWK & OWL TRUST (1969)

A registered charity dedicated to the conservation and appreciation of wild birds of prey and their habitats. Publishes a members' magazine, *Peregrine* and educational materials for all ages. The Trust achieves its major aim of creating and enhancing nesting, roosting and feeding habitats for birds of prey through projects which involve practical research, creative conservation and education, both on its own reserves and in partnership with landowners, farmers and others. Members are invited to take part in fieldwork, population studies, surveys, etc.

The Trust manages two reserves: Sculthorpe Moor in Norfolk and Shapwick Moor on the Somerset Levels.
Contact: Hawk and Owl Trust, Turf Moor Road, Sculthorpe, Fakenham, Norfolk NR21 9GN.
T: 01328 856 788; E: enquiries@hawkandowl.org;
W: http://hawkandowl.org

INTERNATIONAL WADER STUDY GROUP (1970)

An association of wader enthusiasts, both amateur and professional, from all parts of the world, the Group aims to maintain contact between them, help organise co-operative studies, and provide a vehicle for the exchange of information. Publishes *Wader Study* three times a year and holds annual meetings throughout Europe.
Contact: E: membership@waderstudygroup.org;
W: www.waderstudygroup.org

IRISH RARE BREEDING BIRDS PANEL

The (UK) RBBP is responsible for collating data on rare breeding species that are found within the whole of the UK including those which breed/attempt to breed in Northern Ireland, but they do not cover the Republic of Ireland. The IRBBP operates across the whole of Ireland.
Contact: E: secretary.irbbp@gmail.com;
W: www.irbbp.org

IRISH RARE BIRDS COMMITTEE (1985)

Assesses records of species of rare occurrence in the Republic of Ireland. Details of records accepted and rejected have been published annually since 2004 in the *Irish Rare Bird Report* and previously (1953-2003) in the *Irish Bird Report*, published annually in *Irish Birds*. The Committee operates under the auspices of BirdWatch Ireland and also works closely with the Northern Ireland Birdwatchers' Association Rarities Committee to maintain a comprehensive record of birds found on the island of Ireland.
Contact: E: secretary@irbc.ie;
W: www.irbc.ie

JOINT NATURE CONSERVATION COMMITTEE (1990)

A committee with members from Natural Resources Wales, Northern Ireland's Council for Nature Conservation and the Countryside, Natural England and Scottish Natural Heritage as well as the Northern Ireland Environment Agency and independent members. Their role is to provide evidence, information and advice so that decisions are made to protect natural resources and systems, specifically to work on nature conservation issues the UK as a whole and internationally. The committee is the UK Government's nature conservation advisor in European and global fora, taking issues forward from the four home countries to inform policy development and then provide support to ensure that European and international requirements are met.
Contact: Joint Nature Conservation Committee, Monkstone House, City Road, Peterborough, PE1 1JY.
T: 01733 562 626; E: via website;
W: www.jncc.defra.gov.uk

UK/UK-BASED ORGANISATIONS

LINNEAN SOCIETY OF LONDON (1788)
Named after Carl Linnaeus, the 18th Century Swedish biologist, who created the modern system of scientific biological nomenclature, the Society promotes all aspects of pure and applied biology. It houses Linnaeus' collection of plants, insects and fishes, library and correspondence. The Society has a major reference library consisting of books, journals and archives. Publishes the *Biological*, *Botanical* and *Zoological* Journals, and the *Synopsis of the British Fauna* series.
Contact: Linnean Society of London, Burlington House, Piccadilly, London W1J 0BF. T: 020 7434 4479 (ext. 210); E: info@linnean.org; W: www.linnean.org

LIPU-UK (1989)
(Italian League for the Protection of Birds)
A voluntary organisation that supports the work of LIPU in Italy by raising funds to carry out projects in the country. Members receive *Ali (Wings)* four times a year.
Contact: David Lingard, Fernwood, Doddington Road, Whisby, Lincs LN6 9BX. T: 01522 689 030; E: mail@lipu-uk.org; W: www.lipu-uk.org

MAMMAL SOCIETY (1954)
The Mammal Society is the only organisation solely dedicated to the study and conservation of all British mammals. It seeks to raise awareness of mammal ecology and conservation needs, to survey British mammals and their habitats to identify the threats they face, and to promote mammal studies in the UK.
Contact: The Mammal Society, Black Horse Cottage, 33 Milton Abbas, Blandford Forum, Dorset, DT11 0BL. T: 0238 001 0981; E: info@themammalsociety.org; W: www.mammal.org.uk

MARINE CONSERVATION SOCIETY (1983)
MCS is the UK charity that campaigns for clean seas and beaches around the British coastline, sustainable fisheries, and protection for all marine life. MCS is consulted on a wide range of marine issues and provides advice primarily to government, but also to industry, on topics ranging from offshore wind, oil and gas, to marine strategies and fisheries reform. It provides advice to ensure that further action is taken to conserve our seas and reduce the effect of marine activities on marine habitats and species. It has an extensive programme for volunteers, ranging from fund-raising and an annual clean-up of UK beaches, to surveys of species such as basking shark.

Contact: Marine Conservation Society, Overross House, Ross Park, Ross-on-Wye, HR9 7US. T: 01989 566 017; E: info@mcsuk.org; W: www.mcsuk.org

NATIONAL TRUST (1895)
The charity works for the preservation of places of historic interest or natural beauty in England, Wales and Northern Ireland. It has a membership of over five million and over 65,000 volunteers (contributing nearly five million hours of work). Over 25 million visits are made to the pay-for-entry sites and it is estimated that 200 million visits are made to the open air properties. The Trust protects over 250,000ha of land, 780 miles of coastline and over 500 historic houses, castles, ancient monuments, gardens and parks and nature reserves (many of the latter SSSIs/ASSIs, NNRs, Ramsar sites and SPAs).

Contact: The National Trust (Membership), PO Box 574, Manvers, Rotherham, S63 3FH. T: 0344 800 1895; E: enquiries@nationaltrust.org.uk; W: www.nationaltrust.org.uk

NATIONAL TRUST FOR SCOTLAND (1931)
The charity protects and promotes Scotland's natural and cultural heritage for present and future generations to enjoy. Amongst its responsibilities it looks after 271 listed buildings, 38 gardens and designed landscapes, 76,000ha of countryside - inc. eight National Nature Reserves and 46 Munro mountains.
Contact: The National Trust for Scotland, Hermiston Quay, 5 Cultins Rd, Edinburgh EH11 4DF. T: 0131 458 0200; E: via website; W: www.nts.org.uk

NATURAL ENGLAND
Natural England is the government's adviser for the natural environment in England, helping to protect England's nature and landscape for people to enjoy and for the services they provide. Responsibilities include helping land managers and farmers to protect wildlife and landscapes; improving public access to the coastline; managing about two thirds of the 224 National Nature Reserves; managing programmes that help restore and create wildlife habitats; and providing evidence to help make decisions affecting the natural environment. There are 12 area teams.
Contact: Natural England (Enquiries), County Hall, Spetchley Road, Worcester, WR5 2NP. T: 0300 060 3900 (enquiries); E: enquiries@naturalengland.org.uk; W: www.gov.uk/government/organisations/natural-england

NATURAL HISTORY MUSEUM AT TRING (1937)
Founded by Lord Rothschild, the museum has 80 million specimens inc. many rarities and extinct species, only a tiny fraction ever go on display. The galleries are open daily 10am-5pm (2pm-5pm on Sun) except Dec 24-26. Bird Group: the Museum at Tring looks after one of the largest ornithological collections in the world - with over a million skins, skeletons, nests, sets of eggs and specimens preserved in spirit, and there is an extensive ornithological library with 75,000 works. The Bird Group collection and library are not open to the public but can be visited by researchers (enquire by E: via website).
Contact: The Walter Rothschild Building, Akeman Street, Tring, Herts HP23 6AP. T: 020 7942 5000; W: www.nhm.ac.uk/visit/tring.html

NATURAL RESOURCES WALES (2013)

Natural Resources Wales brought together the work of the Countryside Council for Wales, Environment Agency Wales and Forestry Commission Wales, as well as some functions of Welsh Government. Its purpose is to ensure that the natural resources of Wales are sustainably maintained, enhanced and used, now and in the future.
Contact: Natural Resources Wales, c/o Customer Care Centre, Tŷ Cambria, 29 Newport Road, Cardiff CF24 0TP. T: 0300 065 3000 (Mon-Fri, 9am-5pm); to report an environmental incident - T: 0300 065 3000 (1 for Welsh, 2 for English then option1 (24 hrs); to check flood warnings - Floodline - T: 0345 988 1188 (24 hrs); E: enquiries@naturalresourceswales.gov.uk; W: https://naturalresources.wales/

NATURESCOT (2020)

Formally Scottish Natural Heritage (1991), now NatureScot. Funded by the Scottish Government. Its purpose is to promote and care for Scotland's natural heritage; to enable people to enjoy the outdoors; and to support those who manage it.
Contact: NatureScot HQ, Great Glen House, Leachkin Road, Inverness, IV3 8NW. T: 01463 725 000; E: enquiries@nature.scot; W: www.nature.scot

NEOTROPICAL BIRD CLUB (1994)

(Middle & South America and the Caribbean)
An international organisation for those interested in birds of the Neotropics, the NBC aims to foster an interest in the region and to increase awareness of the importance of support for conservation there. Publishes *Neotropical Birding* and *Cotinga*.
Contact: Neotropical Bird Club, c/o The Lodge, Sandy, Bedfordshire SG19 2DL. T: 01255 821 083; E: secretary@neotropicalbirdclub.org; W: www.neotropicalbirdclub.org

NORTHERN IRELAND BIRDWATCHERS' ASSOCIATION (1991)

NIBA publishes the Northern Ireland Bird Report and is responsible for Flightline, a local rate telephone hotline for rare bird sightings. The NIBA Records Committee assesses the records in N Ireland.
Contact: NIBA. T: 028 9146 7408 (Flightline); E: nibirds@live.co.uk; W: http://nibirds.blogspot.com

NORTHERN IRELAND ORNITHOLOGISTS' CLUB (1965)

Formed to focus the interests of active birdwatchers in Northern Ireland. There is a regular programme of lectures (Oct-Apr) and field trips for members and the Club organises an annual photographic competition.
Contact: Carol Gillespie (Hon Sec), NIOC, 4 Demesne Gate, Saintfield, Co. Down BT24 7BE. T: 028 9751 9371; E: carolgillespie@btinternet.com; W: www.nioc.co.uk

NORTHERN IRELAND RARE BIRDS COMMITTEE (1997)

NIRBC manages the records of rare birds in Northern Ireland and maintains the Northern Ireland Bird List.
Contact: NIRBC. E: NIRBComm@gmail.com; W: https://nirbc.blogspot.co.uk

ORIENTAL BIRD CLUB (1984)

Membership is open to anyone who has an interest in birds of the Oriental region and their conservation. This interest in encouraged; the work of regional bird and nature societies is promoted; and information on Oriental birds is collated and published. Publishes *Forktail* and *BirdingASIA*.
Contact: Oriental Bird Club, P.O.Box 324, Bedford, MK42 0WG. E: mail@orientalbirdclub.org; W: www.orientalbirdclub.org

ORNITHOLOGICAL SOCIETY OF THE MIDDLE EAST, THE CAUCASUS & CENTRAL ASIA (OSME) (1978)

Encourages birdwatchers to visit the region; to participate in surveys; and to work with others involved there. A conservation and research fund offers small grants. Publishes *Sandgrouse*.
Contact: OSME, c/o The Lodge, Sandy, Bedfordshire SG19 2DL. E: via website; W: www.osme.org

PLANTLIFE (1989)

Works nationally and internationally to save threatened wild flowers, plants and fungi - this includes working with others to protect rare flora and to ensure familiar flowers and plants continue to thrive; managing 23 nature reserves; and identifying 165 IPA's (Important Plant Areas) across the UK.
Contact: Plantlife, Brewery House, 36 Milford Street, Salisbury, Wiltshire SP1 2AP. T: 01722 342 730; E: enquiries@plantlife.org.uk; W: www.plantlife.org.uk/uk

RARE BREEDING BIRDS PANEL (1972)

With a representative from BTO, JNCC, RSPB, three independent members and a Secretary, the RBBP collects all information on rare breeding birds in the UK, so that changes in status can be monitored as an aid to conservation and is stored for posterity. Bespoke recording forms are used (obtainable from the website). Records should be submitted via county and regional recorders. RBBP also monitor breeding by scarcer non-native species and seek records of these in the same way. An Annual report is published in *British Birds*. For details of species covered by RBBP see 'Checklists' section (P.57).
Contact: Mark Eaton, Secretary Rare Breeding Birds Panel, 21 Chapel Lands, Alnwick, Northumberland, NE66 1EL. E: secretary@rbbp.org.uk; W: www.rbbp.org.uk

UK/UK-BASED ORGANISATIONS

ROYAL AIR FORCE ORNITHOLOGICAL SOCIETY (1965)

Open to any serving and ex-RAF personnel, other Services, MOD civil servants and their families. Organises field meetings and expeditions at home and abroad and undertakes surveys and ringing operations. Publishes a newsletter and a journal.
Contact: Jan Knight (Gen Sec).
E: rafos_secretary@hotmail.com;
W: www.rafornithology.org.uk

ROYAL ENTOMOLOGICAL SOCIETY (1833)

The RES promotes and develops entomological science and supports international collaboration, research and publication - demonstrating the importance of studying insects to everyone.
Contact: Royal Entomological Society, The Mansion House, Chiswell Green Lane, St Albans, AL2 3NS.
T: 01727 899 387; E: info@royensoc.co.uk;
W: www.royensoc.co.uk

ROYAL NAVAL BIRDWATCHING SOCIETY (1946)

RNBWS is open to anyone with a common interest in birds at sea. Maintains an extensive seabird database with records received from most sea areas of the world. Publishes a newsletter four times a year and an annual report - *The Sea Swallow*. The RNBWS administers a fund left by the late Cpt David Simpson with small grants available for scientific seabird studies.
Contact: Warrant Officer Steve Copsey RN (Memb. Sec).
E: secretary@rnbws.org.uk; W: www.rnbws.org.uk

ROYAL PIGEON RACING ASSOCIATION (1897)

Promotes the sport of pigeon racing and controls pigeon racing within the Association. Organises liberation sites, issues rings, calculates distances between liberation sites and home lofts, and assists in the return of strays. May be able to assist in identifying owners of ringed birds found.
Contact: The Royal Pigeon Racing Association, The Reddings, Cheltenham, GL51 6RN.
T: 01452 713 529; E: via website; W: www.rpra.org

ROYAL SOCIETY FOR THE PROTECTION OF BIRDS (1889)

The RSPB is the UK Partner of BirdLife International. With over 1.2 million members (inc. 200,000+ youth members - see RSPB Phoenix/RSPB Wildlife Explorers), it is Europe's largest voluntary wildlife conservation body. As a registered charity, it is governed by an elected body. Its work in the conservation of wild birds and habitats covers a range of areas including: acquisition and management of nature reserves; research and surveys; monitoring; responding to development proposals, land use practices and pollution which threaten wild birds and biodiversity; and the provision of an advisory service on wildlife law enforcement.

The RSPB currently manages over 200 nature reserves in the UK, covering ca.130,000ha and home to 80% of Britain's rarest or most threatened bird species. The aim is to conserve a countrywide network of reserves with all examples of the main bird communities and with due regard to the conservation of plants and other animals.
There is an active network of 139 local groups (see County Directory) which hold regular indoor and outdoor meetings. Over 12,000 people volunteer in a wide range of capacities, inc. working on the RSPB's nature reserves. The RSPB's International Dept works closely with Birdlife International and its partners in other countries and is involved with numerous projects overseas, especially in Europe and Asia.

Contact: RSPB, The Lodge, Potton Road, Sandy, Bedfordshire SG19 2DL. T: 01767 680 551; E: individual members of staff (firstname.surname)@rspb.org.uk;

Membership enquiries: T: 01767 693 680 (9am-5.15pm, Mon-Fri); E: membership@rspb.org.uk

Wildlife enquiries: T: 01767 693 690 (9.30am-4.30pm, Mon-Fri); E: wildlife@rspb.org.uk

W: www.rspb.org.uk

Regional Offices:

ENGLAND

Eastern England: Stalham House, 65 Thorpe Road, Norwich, NR1 1UD. T: 01603 660 066.
Covers: Bedfordshire, Cambridgeshire, Essex, Hertfordshire, Lincolnshire, Norfolk, Suffolk.

London Office: 5th Floor, 50 Southwark Street, London SE1 1UN. T: 0207 940 3050.

Midlands: 1st Floor, One Cornwall Street, Birmingham, B3 2JN. T: 01767 693 777.

Covers: Buckinghamshire, Derbyshire, Herefordshire, Leicestershire, Northamptonshire, Nottinghamshire, Oxfordshire, Rutland, Shropshire, Staffordshire, Warwickshire, West Midlands, Worcestershire.

Northern England:
Denby Dale Office, Westleigh Mews, Wakefield Road, Denby Dale, Huddersfield, HD8 8QD. T: 0300 7772 676.

Newcastle Office, 1 Sirius House, Amethyst Road, Newcastle Business Park, Newcastle-upon-Tyne, NE4 7YL. T: 0300 7772 676.

Lancaster Office, 7.3.1 Cameron House, White Cross Estate, Lancaster, LA1 4XF. T: 0300 7772 676.

Covers: Cheshire, Cleveland, County Durham, Cumbria, East Riding of Yorkshire, Greater Manchester, Lancashire, Merseyside, Middlesbrough, North Yorkshire, North East Lincolnshire, North Lincolnshire, Northumberland, South Yorkshire, Tyne & Wear, West Yorkshire.

South East: 1st Floor, Pavilion View, 19 New Road, Brighton, BN1 1UF. T: 01273 775 333.

Covers: East Sussex, Hampshire, Isle of Wight, Kent, Surrey, Berkshire, West Sussex.

South West: 4th Floor (North Block), Broadwalk House, Southernhay West, Exeter, EX1 1TS. T: 01392 432 691.

Covers: Bristol, Cornwall, Devon, Dorset, Gloucestershire, Somerset, Wiltshire.

NORTHERN IRELAND
Northern Ireland Headquarters: Belvoir Park Forest, Belfast, BT8 7QT. T: 028 9049 1547.

Covers: Co. Antrim, Co. Armagh, Co. Down, Co. Fermanagh, Co. Londonderry, Co. Tyrone.

SCOTLAND
Scotland Headquarters: 2 Lochside View, Edinburgh Park, Edinburgh EH12 9DH. T: 0131 317 4100. E: RSPB.Scotland@rspb.org.uk

East Scotland: 10 Albyn Terrace, Aberdeen, Aberdeenshire AB10 1YP. E: esro@rspb.org.uk; T: 01224 624 824.

Covers: Aberdeen, Aberdeenshire, Angus, Dundee, Fife, Moray, Orkney, Perth and Kinross, Shetland.

North Scotland: Etive House, Beechwood Park, Inverness, IV2 3BW. T: 01463 715 000; E: nsro@rspb.org.uk

Covers: Eilean Siar, Highland.

South and West Scotland: 10 Park Quadrant, Glasgow, G3 6BS. T: 0141 331 0993; E: glasgow@rspb.org.uk

Covers: Argyll and Bute, Clackmannanshire, Dumfries and Galloway, East Ayrshire, East Lothian, East Dunbartonshire, East Renfrewshire, Edinburgh, Falkirk, Glasgow, Interclyde, Midlothian, North Ayrshire, North Lanarkshire, Renfrewshire, Scottish Borders, South Ayrshire, South Lanarkshire, Stirling, West Dunbartonshire, West Lothian.

WALES
Wales Headquarters: Castlebridge 3, 5-19 Cowbridge Road East, Cardiff CF11 9AB. T: 029 2035. 3000; E: cymru@rspb.org.uk

Covers: Blaenau Gwent, Bridgend, Caerphilly, Cardiff, Carmarthenshire, Ceredigion, Merthyr Tydfil, Monmouthshire, Neath Port Talbot, Newport, Pembrokeshire, Powys, Rhondda Cynon Taff, Swansea, Torfaen, Vale of Glamorgan.

North Wales Office: Uned 14, Llys Castan, Ffordd Y Parc, Parc Menai, Bangor, Gwynedd LL57 4FD. T: 01248 672 850.

Covers: Conwy, Denbighshire, Flintshire, Gwynedd, Isle of Anglesey, Wrexham.

RSPB WILDLIFE EXPLORERS (4-19) / RSPB PHOENIX (13+)
Junior section of the RSPB (formally the YOC), with a local network of around 80 youth groups. Activities include projects, holidays, roadshows, competitions, and local events for children, families and teenagers. All members receive a magazine tailored to their age group 4 or 6 times a year (*Wild Times, Wild Explorer or Wingbeat*).
Contact: RSPB - as above.
W: www.rspb.org.uk/fun-and-learning/for-kids

SCOTTISH BIRDS RECORDS COMMITTEE (1984)
Set up by the Scottish Ornithologists' Club to ensure that records of species not deemed rare enough to be considered by the British Birds Rarities Committee, but which are rare in Scotland, are fully assessed; also maintains the official list of Scottish birds.
Contact: Chris McInerny (Sec), SBRC, 10 Athole Gardens, Glasgow, G12 9AZ E: chris.mcinerny@glasgow.ac.uk; W: www.the-soc.org.uk/bird-recording/about-sbrc

SCOTTISH ORNITHOLOGISTS' CLUB (1936)
The SOC promotes the study, enjoyment and conservation of wild birds and their habitats across Scotland. The Club has 15 local branches (see County Directory), each with a programme of indoor meetings and field trips. The SOC organises an annual weekend conference in the autumn and a joint SOC/BTO one-day birdwatchers' conference in spring. *Scottish Birds* is published quarterly. The SOC is based in a large resource centre offering panoramic views of Aberlady Bay and houses the George Waterston Library.
Contact: The SOC, Waterston House, Aberlady, East Lothian EH32 0PY. T: 01875 871 330;
E: via website; W: www.the-soc.org.uk

SCOTTISH WILDLIFE TRUST (1964)
A member of The Wildlife Trusts partnership. The Trust's vision is for 'healthy, resilient ecosystems across Scotland's land and seas.' Its main activities focus on managing 120 wildlife reserves, and four visitor centres, undertaking practical conservation tasks; influencing and campaigning for better wildlife-related policy and action; inspiring people to enjoy and find out more about wildlife - offering a network of 19 local groups.
Contact: Scottish Wildlife Trust, Harbourside House, 110 Commercial Street, Edinburgh, EH6 6NF.
T: 0131 312 7765, () 0131 312 8705;
E: enquiries@scottishwildlifetrust.org.uk;
W: www.scottishwildlifetrust.org.uk

SEABIRD GROUP (1966)
The group promotes and helps to coordinate the study and conservation of seabirds. It maintains close links with other national and international ornithological bodies and organises regular conferences on seabird biology and conservation topics. Small grants available to assist with research/survey work on seabirds. Publishes regular newsletters and the journal '*Seabird*'.
Contact: Annette Fayet (Secretary).
E: secretary@seabirdgroup.org.uk;
W: www.seabirdgroup.org.uk

SWIFT CONSERVATION (2009)
An advice service aiming to reverse the decline in the UK's Swifts. Swift Conservation runs a website providing extensive information on Swifts, and on how to both preserve existing and set up new Swift nest sites. Swift Conservation also runs a lecture and training service, providing guidance for the general public, planners, developers and architects. It supplies advice and help both directly and via volunteers, and has links to similar assistance across Europe, the Middle East, Central Asia and North America. It campaigns for better protection of Swifts and other birds that rely on nest places in or on buildings.
Contact: E: mail@swift-conservation.org;
W: www.swift-conservation.org

THE CONSERVATION VOLUNTEERS (formerly BTCV) (1959)
The Conservation Volunteers helps thousands of people each year to reclaim local green spaces. Through their own environmental projects and through a network of community groups people are enabled to take responsibility for their local environments. TCV has published a series of practical handbooks (digital format/subscribe online).
Contact: TCV, Sedum House, Mallard Way, Potteric Carr, Doncaster, DN4 8DB. T: 01302 388 883;
E: information@tcv.org.uk; W: www.tcv.org.uk

TRAFFIC International (1976)
(the wildlife trade monitoring network)
Works globally on trade in wild animals and plants in the context of biodiversity conservation and sustainable development, ensuring that this trade is not a threat to the conservation of nature. Publishes *The TRAFFIC Bulletin*.
Contact: Traffic Global Office, The David Attenborough Building, Pembroke Street, Cambridge CB2 3QZ.
T: 01223 277 427; E: traffic@traffic.org;
W: www.traffic.org

WADER QUEST (2012)
A voluntary charity dedicated to supporting wader conservation through fundraising and increasing awareness about the acute problems facing wader populations around the world. Specialises in supporting community wader conservation projects by purchasing equipment and materials from the charity's Grants Fund. Members (Friends of Wader Quest & Sponsors) receive a quarterly e-newsletter. Talks and events are undertaken throughout the year in partnership with other organisations.
Contact: Rick and Elis Simpson, Wader Quest, 20 Windsor Avenue, Newport Pagnell, Bucks, MK16 8HA.
T: 07484 186 443; E: info@waderquest.net;
W: www.waderquest.net

WELSH ORNITHOLOGICAL SOCIETY (1988)
Promotes the study, conservation and enjoyment of birds throughout Wales. Runs the Welsh Records Panel which maintains then Welsh bird list and produces an annual report of accepted rare birds in Wales. Publishes the journal *Birds In Wales* twice a year and organises an annual conference.
Contact: E: web@birdsin.wales; W: www.birdsin.wales

WEST AFRICAN ORNITHOLOGICAL SOCIETY (1964)
Grew out of the Nigerian Ornithologists' Society. The Society's aim is to promote scientific interest in the birds of West Africa (28 countries) and to further the region's ornithology, mainly through its journal, *Malimbus*.
Contact: Tim Dodman (Membership Secretary), Hundland, Papa Westray, Orkney KW17 2BU.
E: tim@timdodman.co.uk; W: www.malimbus.org

for **EAST AFRICA NATURAL HISTORY SOCIETY (1909)**
(see Kenya/Nature Kenya under BirdLife Africa, P306)

WILDFOWL & WETLANDS TRUST (1946)
Founded by Sir Peter Scott to conserve wetlands and their biodiversity, WWT has 10 wetland centres (see below). The centres are nationally, or internationally, important for wintering wildfowl. Walks, talks and events are available for visitors, and resources and programmes are provided for school groups. Most of the centres have collections of wildfowl from around the world, inc. many endangered species. The Trust's conservation programmes focus on a variety of aspects inc. science and processes that underpin conservation action, threats to wetlands and their wildlife and threatened species. WWT Consulting undertakes commercial contracts and Wetland Link International promotes the role of wetland centres for education and public awareness. Publishes the journal *Wildfowl*.
Contact: Wildfowl and Wetlands Trust, Slimbridge, Gloucestershire GL2 7BT. T: 01453 891 900;
E: enquiries@wwt.org.uk; W: www.wwt.org.uk

WWT Wetland Centres:

Arundel, Mill Road, Arundel, Sussex BN18 9PB.
T: 01903 883 355; E: info.arundel@wwt.org.uk

Caerlaverock, Eastpark Farm, Caerlaverock, Dumfriesshire DG1 4RS. T: 01387 770 200;
E: info.caerlaverock@wwt.org.uk

Castle Espie, 78 Ballydrain Road, Comber, Co Down, N Ireland BT23 6EA. T: 028 9187 4146;
E: info.castleespie@wwt.org.uk

London, Queen Elizabeth's Walk, Barnes, London SW13 9WT. T: 020 8409 4400; E: info.london@wwt.org.uk

Llanelli Wetland Centre, Llwynhendy, Llanelli, Carmarthenshire SA14 9SH. T: 01554 741 087;
E: info.llanelli@wwt.org.uk

Martin Mere, Fish Lane, Burscough, Lancashire L40 0TA. T: 01704 895 181;
E: info.martinmere@wwt.org.uk

Slimbridge, Bowditch, Slimbridge, Gloucestershire GL2 7BT. T: 01453 891 900;
E: info.slimbridge@wwt.org.uk

Steart Marshes, Steart, Somerset, TA5 2PU.
T: 01278 651 090; E: info.steart@wwt.org.uk

Washington, Pattinson, Washington, Tyne & Wear NE38 8LE. T: 0191 416 5454;
E: info.washington@wwt.org.uk

Welney, Hundred Foot Bank, Welney, Nr. Wisbech, Cambridgeshire PE14 9TN. T: 01353 860 711;
E: info.welney@wwt.org.uk

UK/UK-BASED ORGANISATIONS

WILDLIFE SOUND RECORDING SOCIETY (1968)

Works closely with the Wildlife Section, British Library Sound Archive. Members carry out recording work for scientific purposes as well as for pleasure. A field weekend is held each spring, and members organise meetings locally. Four CD sound magazines of members' recordings are produced for members each year, and a journal, *Wildlife Sound*, is published twice a year.
Contact: David Mellor (Hon Membership Secretary), WSRS, Fuchsia Cottage, Helperthorpe, Nr Malton, North Yorkshire YO17 8TQ;
E: membership@wildlife-sound.org;
W: www.wildlife-sound.org

WILDLIFE TRUSTS (1995)

Founded in 1912 and now the largest UK charity dedicated to conserving all habitats and species, with a membership of 850,000+ in 46 individual county trusts (see County Directory). Collectively, they manage over 2,300 nature reserves covering 98,500 ha. The Trusts also lobby for better protection of the UK's natural heritage and are dedicated to protecting wildlife for the future. Members receive their local Trust magazine which includes a UK News section.
Contact: The Wildlife Trusts, The Kiln, Waterside, Mather Road, Newark, NG24 1WT. T: 01636 677 711; Fax: 01636 670 001; E: enquiry@wildlifetrusts.org;
W: www.wildlifetrusts.org

WILDLIFE WATCH (1977)

Junior branch of the Wildlife Trusts with 150,000 members. There are ca.300 Wildlife Watch groups across the UK where children can join in a wide range of activities. Membership is through a local Trust as a junior member.
Contact: Wildlife Watch - address as above.
T: 01636 677 711; E: watch@wildlifetrusts.org;
W: www.wildlifewatch.org.uk

WOODLAND TRUST (1972)

The UK's largest woodland conservation charity works to protect, and campaign on behalf of, the country's woods inc. creating new native woodlands and restoring ancient woodland for the benefit of wildlife and people. Manages over 1000 sites.

Contact:
E: enquiries@woodlandtrust.org.uk (general enquiries);
W: www.woodlandtrust.org.uk

England: Kempton Way, Grantham, Lincolnshire NG31 6LL.
T: 0330 333 3300; E: england@woodlandtrust.org.uk

Northern Ireland: 1 Dufferin Court, Bangor, Co. Down BT20 3BX. T: 028 9127 5787;
E: northernireland@woodlandtrust.org.uk

Scotland: South Inch Business Centre, Perth, PH2 8BW.
T: 01738 635 544; E: scotland@woodlandtrust.org.uk

Wales: Castle Court, 6 Cathedral Road, Cardiff, CF11 9LJ.
T: 029 2002 7732; E: wales@woodlandtrust.org.uk

WORLD OWL TRUST

Works on owl conservation nationally and internationally. Their conservation programmes protect populations of endangered owls until their habitat has been restored. A new World Owl Centre is under construction to house its owl collection.
Contact: World Owl Trust, Millstones, Bootle, Cumbria LA19 5TJ. T: 01229 718 080; E: jen@owls.org;
W: www.owls.org

WORLD PHEASANT ASSOCIATION (1975)

WPA is committed to the conservation of *Galliformes* and their habitats which they do by: promoting the conservation of those species that are rare or in danger of extinction; advancing the education of the public and the knowledge of such species; and conducting research and studying captive and wild species. Publishes *WPA News*.
Contact: Barbara Ingman (administrator), WPA, Middle, Nimebanks, Hexham, Northumberland NE47 8DL.
T: 01434 345 526; E: office@pheasant.org.uk;
W: www.pheasant.org.uk

WWF-UK (1961)

WWF is the world's largest independent conservation organisation, working in more than 100 countries. It works to conserve habitats and species, protect endangered spaces, and address global threats to nature by seeking long-term solutions with people in government and industry, education and civil society. Members receive *Action* magazine three times a year.
Contact: WWF-UK, The Living Planet Centre, Rufford House, Brewery Road, Woking, Surrey GU21 4LL.
T: 01483 426 444; E: supportercare@wwf.org.uk;
W: www.wwf.org.uk & W: www.panda.org

WWF Cymru, Churchill House, 17 Churchill Way, Cardiff, CF10 2HH. T: 029 2045 4970; E: wales@wwf.org.uk

WWF Scotland, The Tun, 4 Jackson's Entry, Holyrood Road, Edinburgh, EH8 8PJ. T: 0131 659 9100;
E: scotland@wwf.org.uk

ZOOLOGICAL PHOTOGRAPHIC CLUB (1899)

The Club allows wildlife photographers to view and comment on each others' work on a regular basis and to provide a forum for the discussion of photographic locations, equipment and techniques. Membership is strictly limited to 28 - applications to join can be made.
Contact: John Tinning (Hon. Secretary).
E: john.tinning@btinternet.com;
W: www.zpc-naturefolio.org.uk

ZOOLOGICAL SOCIETY OF LONDON (1826)

Carries out research, organises symposia and holds scientific meetings. Manages the Zoological Gardens in Regent's Park (first opened in 1828) and Whipsnade Wild Animal Park near Dunstable, Beds, each with extensive collections of birds. The Society's library has a large collection of ornithological books and journals. Publications include *Journal of Zoology* and *The International Zoo Yearbook*.
Contact: Zoological Society of London, Regent's Park, London NW1 4RY. T: 0344 225 1826;
E: generalenquiries@zsl.org; W: www.zsl.org

NATIONAL PROJECTS

National ornithological projects depend for their success on the active participation of amateur birdwatchers. In return they provide birdwatchers with an excellent opportunity to contribute in a positive and worthwhile way to the scientific study of birds and their habitats, which is the vital basis of all conservation programmes. The following entries provide a description of a number of ongoing projects and who to contact for further information.

BIG GARDEN BIRDWATCH

RSPB

The Big Garden Birdwatch, first launched in 1979, has grown into fun for all the family. The long-term trends of birds coming into gardens can be monitored. All you need to do is count the birds in your garden, or a local park, for one hour during (usually) the last weekend of January. In 2020 nearly half a million people counted a total of almost 8 million birds, with House Sparrow, Starling and Blue Tit in 1st, 2nd and 3rd places.
Contact: RSPB.

BIRDTRACK

Project Partners: BTO, RSPB, BirdWatch Ireland, SOC, WOS & BirdLife International

BirdTrack is a free, online bird recording system for birdwatchers to store and manage bird records from anywhere in Britain and Ireland. The idea is simple: make a note of the birds that you see/hear at any time and then enter your observations on an easy-to-use web page. Visit: https://www.bto.org/our-science/projects/birdtrack/taking-part/birdtrack-apps Registration is required - complete lists are preferred but casual records and incomplete lists can also be entered.There's also a free App for Android and iPhone smartphones through which you can log your sightings whilst you're in the field and upload them at the click of a button.

Exciting real-time outputs are generated by BirdTrack, including species reporting-rate graphs and animated maps of sightings, all freely-available online. The data collected are used by researchers to investigate migration movements and the distribution of scarce birds, and to support species conservation at local, national and international scales.
Contact: BTO. E: birdtrack@bto.org

BREEDING BIRD SURVEY (BBS)

Project Partners: BTO, JNCC & RSPB

First started in 1994, the BBS is the main scheme for monitoring population changes of the UK's common breeding birds and provides an indicator of the health of the countryside. It is dependent on volunteer birdwatchers throughout the country. A pre-visit recce then two visits (early-Apr/mid-May and mid-May/late-Jun) of about five hours in total, are made to survey the breeding birds in a 1x1km square. Survey squares are picked at random by computer to ensure that all habitats and regions are covered. BBS trends are produced annually for nearly 120 species.

Since its inception, BBS has been a tremendous success - now nearly 3000 volunteers cover nearly 4000 squares recording more than 200 species annually.
Contact: BTO. E: bbs@bto.org or your local BTO Regional Representative (see County Directory).

BTO GARDEN BIRDWATCH (GBW)

BTO

Started in January 1995, this project is a year-round survey that monitors the use that birds and other species groups of wildlife make of gardens. Participants from all over the UK and Ireland keep a weekly log of species using their gardens. The data collected are used to monitor regional, seasonal and year-to-year changes in the garden populations of our commoner birds, mammals, butterflies, reptiles and amphibians. The project is funded through an annual subscription, participants receive a magazine four times a year.
Contact: BTO. E: gbw@bto.org

In conjunction with GBW, GBFS (below) is limited to about 250 gardens each year with gardens chosen from GBW participants).

GARDEN BIRD FEEDING SURVEY (GBFS)

BTO

Starting in 1970/71, the Garden Bird Feeding Survey is the longest-running study of garden birds in Britain. Each year, a network of householders record the numbers and variety of birds using the different food supplements, feeders and water that they have provided in their garden - the results examine the effects on birds using these resources. Observations are made on a weekly basis from October to March inclusive, with two recording periods (Oct/Dec & Jan/Mar). Gardens are selected by region and by type - from city flats to suburban semis, rural houses to outlying farms - to give a good spread of sites. The project is funded through an annual subscription.
Contact: BTO. E: gwb@bto.org

GARDEN WILDLIFE HEALTH

Project Partners: BTO, Zoological Society of London, RSPB & Froglife

This project aims to monitor the health of, and identify disease threats to, British garden wildlife. The particular focus is on garden birds, amphibians, reptiles and hedgehogs. Members of the public are asked to submit reports of sick or dead wildlife and may be to submit samples for analysis (contact first).
Contact: Garden Wildlife Health
E: report sick/dead wildlife via a website link;
other enquiries E: GWH@zsl.org
W: www.gardenwildlifehealth.org

NATIONAL PROJECTS

GOOSE AND SWAN MONITORING PROGRAMME (GSMP)

Project Partners: WWT, JNCC & Scottish National Heritage

WWT Waterbird monitoring

Geese and swans are a cornerstone of the Wildfowl and Wetland Trust's conservation work. The UK supports 14 native goose and migratory swan populations, 13 are monitored through the GSMP network. During winter, geese and swans from Canada to central Russia undertake arduous migrations to reach their wintering grounds in the UK. In order to safeguard them WWT tracks how many individuals are in each population, where they are found, and the overall trend of the population (increasing, decreasing or remaining stable). Other demographic measures - most importantly productivity (how many young are born each year) and survival (or mortality) rates - help to understand the reasons behind any increases or decreases. To gather the information the WWT use a number of techniques and tools, including counts and capture/marking. A large amount of this work is carried out by volunteer birdwatchers who give their time to assist with the data collection.

Contact: WWT. E: via website;
W: http://monitoring.wwt.org.uk/our-work/

HERONRIES CENSUS

BTO

This survey, started in 1928, has been carried out under the auspices of the BTO since 1934 and represents the longest continuous series of population data for any European breeding bird (Grey Heron). Counts of apparently occupied nests are made at as many UK heronries as possible each year to provide an index of current population levels.

Data from Scotland and Wales is relatively scant, and more contributions from these countries are especially welcomed, as are notifications of new colonies elsewhere. Herons may be hit hard during periods of severe weather and are vulnerable to pesticides and pollution. Little Egret and other incoming species of colonial waterbird (i.e. Cattle Egret) are included, whether nesting with Grey Herons, or on their own. Counts of Cormorant nests at heronries are also encouraged. Heronries Surveys are periodically undertaken and the data added to the Heronries Census database. The 2018 Survey was the most complete survey ever recorded in one year, giving an estimate of 10,000+ Grey Herons and 1,000+ Little Egrets (a.o nests).

Contact: BTO. E: herons@bto.org

IRISH WETLAND BIRD SURVEY (I-WeBS)

A joint project of BirdWatch Ireland, the National Parks & Wildlife Service and the Dept of Arts, Culture & the Gaeltacht

The Irish Wetland Bird Survey (I-WeBS) is the scheme that monitors wintering waterbirds in the Republic of Ireland. The survey runs from September to March each winter. Wetlands of all types and sizes are monitored, including estuaries, coastlines, bays, rivers, turloughs, lakes, streams and flooded fields.

Each winter, more than 400 people take part counting waterbirds at over 250 wetlands throughout the country. The counts are undertaken once a month on predefined count days by skilled volunteers, as well as by professional staff of the National Parks and Wildlife Service and BirdWatch Ireland.

New counters welcomed!

Contact: I-WeBS Office, BirdWatch Ireland.
T: 353 (0)1 281 9878; E: iwebs@birdwatchireland.ie

NATIONAL BEACHED BIRD SURVEY

RSPB

In its current format the NBBS has been running since 1971. The results of the annual survey (in February) are used in conjunction with those from other European countries and aim to contribute to international monitoring efforts to document trends in chronic marine oil pollution and to promote adequate methods of controlling illegal oil discharge to help reduce seabird mortality.

Contact: RSPB.

NEST RECORD SCHEME

Project Partners: BTO and JNCC

The scheme monitors changes in the nesting success and the timing of breeding of Britain's bird species by gathering information on nests found anywhere in the country, from a Blackbird in a garden to an Oystercatcher on a Scottish loch. Participants locate nests and monitor their progress over several visits, making counts of the number of eggs and/or chicks on each occasion and recording whether they are successful.

Information from NRS complements demographic information collected by other BTO surveys and feeds into the BTO's Integrated Population Monitoring, highlighting the causes of changes in bird populations. Since the scheme started in 1939, 1.25 million nest record histories have been collected from 232 species. Now more than 30,000 nest records (of 160-170 species) are submitted each year by over 600 volunteer surveyors. The results are updated annually and published online as part of the BirdTrends Report. Guidance on how to become a BTO nest recorder, including best practice guidelines on minimising disturbance while visiting nests, is available online. Free starter pack available on request.

Contact: BTO. E: nrs@bto.org

NESTING NEIGHBOURS

BTO

NBC is an on-line survey which aims to monitor the breeding success of birds in Britain's green spaces. Participants are asked to register one or more nests, or nest boxes, in their garden or local green space, monitoring their progress via regular nest inspections and recording the number of eggs and/or chicks present at each visit. Records of unused boxes are also valuable as they can be used to determine next box occupancy rates. Anyone who has a nest box or nest in their garden or local park can take part.

Contact: BTO.

NATIONAL PROJECTS

RINGING:

RINGING SCHEME

Project Partners: BTO, JNCC, The National Parks & Wildlife Service (Ireland) & ringers

Marking birds with individually numbered metal rings allows us to study survival, productivity and movements of British and Irish birds. Over 2,600 trained and licensed ringers operate in Britain and Ireland, marking nearly a million birds annually. Training to be a ringer takes at least a year, but more often two or more years, depending on the aptitude of the trainee and the amount of ringing they do. A restricted permit can usually be obtained more quickly (around 6 months). To find a trainer visit: www.bto.org/our-science/projects/ringing/taking-part/learn-ring or email: ringing.licensing@bto.org

Anyone can contribute to the scheme by reporting ringed or colour-marked birds seen or found - W: http://blx1.bto.org/euring/main/index.jsp or contact BTO HQ. Anyone finding a ringed bird should note the ring number, species, when and where found and, if possible, what happened to it. If the bird is dead, it may also be possible to remove the ring, which should be kept in case there is a query. Anyone reporting a ringed bird will be sent details of where and when the bird was originally ringed.

Check out the 'Demog Blog' for up to date news and stories: http://btoringing.blogspot.co.uk

Contact: BTO. E: ringing@bto.org

CONSTANT EFFORT SITES (CES) SCHEME

Project Partners: BTO, JNCC, The National Parks & Wildlife Service (Ireland) & ringers

The CES scheme, run since 1983, coordinates standardised mist-netting at over 130 sites across Britain and Ireland (12 visits between May-Aug). The scheme allows the BTO to monitor trends on abundance of adults and juveniles, productivity and adult survival rates for 24 species of common songbirds.

Information from CES complements demographic information collected by other BTO surveys and feeds into the BTO's Integrated Population Monitoring programme which highlights the causes of changes in bird populations. Results are updated annually and published on-line as part of the BirdTrends Report.

Contact: BTO. E: ces@bto.org

RETRAPPING ADULTS FOR SURVIVAL (RAS) SCHEME

Project Partners: BTO, JNCC & ringers

Under the RAS scheme, started in 1999, ringers aim to catch or re-sight at least 50 adult birds of a single species in a study area in the breeding season. This data allows the BTO to monitor survival rates in adult birds and is particularly useful for those species not widely covered by CES scheme. and forms part of the BTO's Integrated Population Monitoring framework.

Contact: BTO. E: ras@bto.org

WATERWAYS BREEDING BIRD SURVEY

Project partners: BTO, JNCC & RSPB

WBBS

WBBS uses transect methods of surveying, like those of the Breeding Bird Survey, to record bird populations along more than 500 randomly chosen stretches of rivers and canals throughout the UK. Just three survey visits are needed during April-June (a recce and two morning visits), all birds seen or heard are recorded. WBBS began in 2008 taking over from the Waterways Bird Survey (which started in 1974) as the main monitoring scheme for birds in this habitat.

Contact: BTO Regional Representative to enquire if any local stretches require coverage (see County Directory), otherwise BTO HQ. E: wbbs@bto.org

WETLAND BIRD SURVEY (WeBS)

Project Partners: BTO, RSPB, JNCC and in association with WWT

The Wetland Bird Survey (WeBS) is the monitoring scheme for non-breeding waterbirds in the UK. The principal aims of the scheme are:

1. To identify population sizes of waterbirds.
2. To determine trends in numbers and distribution.
3. To identify important sites for waterbirds.

WeBS Core Counts are made annually at around 2,800 wetland sites of all habitats, although estuaries and large still waters predominate. Monthly coordinated counts are made mostly by over 3,000 volunteers (making over 40,000 visits), principally between September and March, with fewer summer counts. Estuaries in the UK provide an important habitat for non-breeding waterbirds. Low Tide Counts are made on about 20 of them each winter to identify important feeding areas (Core Counts tend to quantify birds present at high tide roosts).

Counts are relatively straightforward and can take from a few minutes up to a few hours, depending on the size of the site - numbers of all target species in the count area are recorded.

The WeBS data is used to designate important waterbird sites and protect them against adverse development, for research into the causes of declines, for establishing conservation priorities and strategies, and to formulate management plans for wetland sites and waterbirds. WeBS participants receive an annual newsletter and a comprehensive annual report. New counters are always welcome - contact the local WeBS Organiser (see County Directory).

Contact: Gillian Birtles (General WeBS enquiries), WeBS Office, BTO. E: webs@bto.org

In addition to these projects, many others (such as individual species surveys) are active over short time periods. The BTO website is a good source of information to find out more: www.bto.org/our-science/projects

As an alternative, why not contact your local nature reserve - surveys and projects often rely on volunteer help. It is a great way of getting to know your local patch!

INTERNATIONAL/BIRDLIFE ORGANISATIONS

The BirdLife Partnership: www.birdlife.org
BirdLife is a Partnership of non-governmental organisations (NGOs) with a special focus on nature and people. Each NGO Partner represents a unique geographic territory/country. Publishes *World Birdwatch*.

The BirdLife Network explained:

Secretariat: The co-ordinating and servicing body of BirdLife International.

Partners: Membership-based NGOs who represent BirdLife in their own territory. Vote holders and key implementing bodies for BirdLife's Strategy and Regional Programmes in their own territories.

Partners Designate: Membership-based NGOs who represent BirdLife in their own territory, in a transition stage to becoming full Partners. Non-vote holders.

Affiliates: Usually NGOs, but also individuals, foundations or governmental institutions when appropriate. Act as a BirdLife contact with the aim of developing into, or recruiting, a BirdLife Partner in their territory.

SECRETARIAT ADDRESSES

BirdLife Global Office
The David Attenborough Building
1st Floor, Pembroke Street
Cambridge CB2 3QZ, UK
T: 01223 277 318
Fax: 01223 281 441
E: birdlife@birdlife.org

Birdlife Africa Regional Office
Westcom Point Building 6th Floor
Mahiga Mairu Ave, off Waiyaki Way
Westlands
Kenya

Postal Address
PO Box 3502 - 00100 GPO
Nairobi, Kenya
T: +254 020 247 3259
T: +254 020 806 8314
Fax: +254 020 806 8315
E: birdlife-africa@birdlife.org

Birdlife West Africa Sub-Regional Office
35A Sam Nujoma Rd
North Ridge
Accra, Ghana

Postal Address
PO Box GP 22521
Accra, Ghana
T: +233 (0) 302 255 015
T: +233 (0) 261 737 101

BirdLife Americas Regional Office
Av. Julio Zaldumbide N25-82 y
Valladolid
2do Piso
La Floresta 170109, Ecuador

Postal address
BirdLife International
Casilla 17-17-717
Quito, Ecuador
T: +593 2 2255 361
Fax +593 2 2233 086
E: americas@birdlife.org

BirdLife Asia Regional Office [Japan]
Unizo Kakigara-cho Kitajima Bldg
1F, 1-13-1 Nihonbashi Kakigara-cho,
Chuo-ku, Tokyo 103-0014, Japan
T: +81 (3) 6206 2941
Fax.+81 (3) 6206 2942
E: info@birdlife-asia.org

[Singapore]
354 Tanglin Road
#01-16/17
Tanglin International Centre
Singapore 247672
T: +65 6479 3089
Fax: +65 6479 3090
E: singapore.office@birdlife.org

BirdLife Europe
Avenue de la Toison d'Or 67
(2nd floor)
B-1060 Brussels, Belgium
T: +32 2280 08 30
Fax +32 2230 38 02
E: europe@birdlife.org

BirdLife Middle East Regional Office
Khalda
Salameh El-Ma'aaytah Street
Building No 6.
Amman, Jordan

Postal address
PO Box 2295
Amman 11953, Jordan
T: +962 6 554 8173
Fax: +962 6 554 8172
E: me@birdlife.org

BirdLife Pacific Regional Office
10 MacGregor Road
Suva, Fuji

Postal address
GPO Box 18332
Suva, Fuji
T: +679 331 3492
Fax: +679 331 9658
E: suva.office@birdlife.org

AFRICA

PARTNERS

Burkina Faso
NATURAMA 01 B.P. 6133, 01, Ouagadougou.
E: info@naturama.bf; W: www.naturama.bf

Ethiopia
Ethiopian Wildlife and Natural History Society EWNHS), PO Box 13303, Addis Ababa. E: ewnhs.ble@gmail.com; W: www.ewnhs.org.et; Pub: *Agazen (school magazine); Ethiopian Wildlife & Nat. Hist. Soc. (quarterly newsletter); Walia (semi-scientific journal)*

NatureKenya
The East Africa Natural History Society

Ghana
Ghana Wildlife Society (GWS), PO Box 13252, Accra.
E: info@ghanawildlifesociety.org;
W: www.ghanawildlifesociety.org; Pub: *NKO (magazine)*

Kenya
NatureKenya, PO Box 44486, 00100 GPO, Nairobi. E: office@naturekenya.org; W: www.naturekenya.org; Pub: *Nature Net (newsletter); Kenya Birding (magazine); Journal of East African Natural History (scientific); Scopus (scientific)*

Mauritania
Nature Mauritania, 6th district, Ilot 70. BP: 2647, Nouakchott.
E: nature.mauritanie@laposte.net;
W: www.natmau.org/en/

Nigeria
Nigerian Conservation Foundation (NCF), PO Box 74638, Victoria Island, Lagos. E: info@ncf-nigeria.org;
W: www.ncfnigeria.org/

Seychelles
Nature Seychelles, Roche Caiman, Box 1310, Victoria, Mahe.
E: nature@seychelles.net; W: www.natureseychelles.org;
W: www.cousinisland.net; Pub: *Zwazo (magazine)*

Sierra Leone
Conservation Society of Sierra Leone (CSSL), 86 Main Road, Congo Town, Freetown. E: cssl_03@yahoo.com

South Africa
BirdLife South Africa (BLSA), Private Bag X5000, Gauteng, ZA, 2121. E: info@birdlife.org.za;
W: www.birdlife.org.za; Pub: *e-newsletter; African BirdLife (magazine); Ostrich (scientific)*

Tunisia
Association Les Amis des Oiseaux (AAO), Bureau No 4 au 2eme etage, 14 Rue Ibn El Heni, 2080 Ariana.
E: aao.org@gmail.com; W: www.aao.org.tn; Pub: *(newsletter)*

Uganda
NatureUganda (NU), The EANHS, PO Box 27034, Kampala.
E: nature@natureuganda.org; W: www.natureuganda.org;
Pub: *The Naturalist (newsletter)*

Zimbabwe
BirdLife Zimbabwe (BLZ), PO Box RVL 100, Runiville, Harare. E: birds@zol.co.zw; W: www.birdlifezimbabwe.org;
Pub: *The Babbler (newsletter); Honeyguide (scientific)*

PARTNERS DESIGNATE

Botswana
BirdLife Botswana (BLB),
Kgale Siding, Plot K1069,
Unit B1, Gaborone.
E: blb@birdlifebotswana.org.bw;
W: www.birdlifebotswana.org.bw;
Pub: *The Babbler (scientific); Familiar Chat (newsletter); Birds and People (conservation newsletter)*

Burundi
Association Burundaise pour la Protection de la Nature (ABN), PO Box 7069, Bujumbura.
E: info@aboconservation.org; W: http://www.abn.bi

Madagascar
Asity Madagascar, Lot IIN 83DM Analamahitsy, Antananarivio. E: contact@asity-madagascar.org;
W: www.asity-madagascar.org

Zambia
BirdWatch Zambia, Box 33944, Lusaka 10101.
E: birdwatch.zambia@gmail.com;
W: www.birdwatchzambia.org;
Pub: *BirdWatch Zambia (newsletter)*

AFFILIATES

Egypt
Nature Conservation Egypt, 56A Mahrousa St, Aguouza, 1st Floor, Apt 20, Giza. E: info@natureegypt.org;
W: www.natureegypt.org; Pub: *(newsletter)*

Ivory Coast
SOS-FORETS (SF), 22 BP 918, Abidjan 22.
E: sosforets@hotmail.com; W: www.sosforets.ci

Liberia
Society for Conservation of Nature in Liberia (SCNL), Monrovia, PO Box 2628, Monrovia, LR, 1000.
E: scnlliberia@yahoo.com; W: www.scnlliberia.org

Malawi
Wildlife & Environmental Society of Malawi (WESM), Private Bag 578, Limbe. E: wesmhq@wesm.mw;
W: www.wildlifemalawi.org; Pub: *WESM News (newsletter)*

Mauritius
Mauritian Wildlife Foundation, Grannum Road, Vacoas.
E: executive@mauritian-wildlife.org;
W: www.mauritian-wildlife.org

Morocco
GREPOM, Scientific Institutre Av Ibn Battota, BP 703, Agdal, 10090, Rabat. E: grepom@grepom.org;
W: www.grepom.org

AMERICAS

PARTNERS

Argentina
Aves Argentina (AOP), Matheu 1246/8 (C1249AAB), Buenos Aires. E: info@avesargentinas.org.ar;
W: www.avesargentinas.org.ar; Pub: *Aves Argentinas (magazine); Nuestras Aves (magazine); The Hornero (scientific)*

Bahamas
Bahamas National Trust (BNT), PO Box 4105, Nassau.
E: bnt@bnt.bs; W: www.bnt.bs; Pub: *Trust Notes (newsletter)*

Belize
Belize Audubon Society (BAS), PO Box 1001, 12 Fort St, Belize City. E: base@btl.net; W: www.belizeaudubon.org;
Pub: *Belize Audubon Society (newsletter)*

Bolivia
Asociacion Armonia, Avenidad Lomas de Arena 400, Casilla 3566, Santa Cruz.
E: armonia@armonia-bo.org;
W: www.armoniabolivia.org

Canada
Birds Canada, PO Box 160, 115 Front Street, Port Rowan, Ontario N0E 1M0. E: generalinfo@bsc-eoc.org; W: www.birdscanada.org; Pub: *Bird Studies Canada (annual report); Birdwatch Canada (magazine)*

Canada
Nature Canada, 85 Albert Street, Suite 900, Ottawa, K1P 6A4. E: info@naturecanada.ca;
W: www.naturecanada.ca; Pub: *(annual report)*

INTERNATIONAL/BIRDLIFE ORGANISATIONS

Colombia
Asociación Calidris, Cra. 24 #420, Cali, Valle del Cauca. E: calidris@calidris.org.co; W: www.calidris.org.co

Ecuador
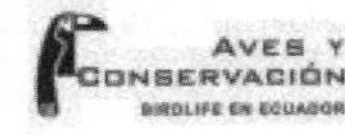

Aves y Conservación, Calle Mariana de Jesús E7-69 y La Pradera (2do piso), Quito.
E: aves_direccion@avesconservacion.org;
W: www.avesconservacion.org

Falkland Islands
Falklands Conservation, 41 Ross Road, Jubilee Villas, Stanley, FIQQ 1ZZ. E: info@falklandsconservation.com; W: www.falklandsconservation.com; Pub: *Falklands Conservation (newsletter); Wildlife Conservation (magazine)*

Panama
Panama Audubon Society (PAS), Apartado 0843-03076, Panama City. E: info@panamaaudubon.org;
W: www.audubonpanama.org; Pub: *Toucan (newsletter)*

Paraguay
Guyra, Av. Cnel. Carlos Bóveda, Parque Ecológico Capital Verde, Viñas Cué, Asunción, CC 1132.
E: guyra.paraguay@guyra.org.py; W: www.guyra.org.py; Pub: *Memoria Anual (annual report)*

United States
American Bird Conservancy, P.O. Box 249, 4249 Loudoun Ave, The Plains, VA 20198-2237. E: via website;
W: www.abcbirds.org; Pub: *Bird Conservation (magazine)*

Audubon, 225 Varick Street, 7th Floor New York, NY, 10004.
E: international@audubon.org;
W: www.audubon.org; Pub: *Audubon (magazine)*

AFFILIATES

Brazil
SAVE Brasil, Rua Fernão Dias, 219 conj 2 Pinheiros, São Paulo SP, 05427-010. E: aves@savebrasil.org.br;
W: www.savebrasil.org.br; Pub: *(annual report); (newsletter)*

Chile
Comité Nacional Pro Defensa de la Flora y Fauna (CODEFF), Ernesto Reyes 035, Providencia, Santiago.
E: administra@codeff.cl; W: www.codeff.cl; Pub: *Ecos Codeff (newsletter)*

Cuba
Centro Nacional de Áreas Protegidas (CNAP), Calle 18a, No 1441, 41 y 47, Playa, Havana.
E: cnap@snap.cu;
W: www.snap.cu

Dominican Republic
Grupo Jaragua (GJI), Calle El Vergel No 33, Ensanche, El Vergel, Santo Domingo.
E: jaragua@tricom.net;
W: www.grupojaragua.org.do

El Salvador
SalvaNATURA (SN), Finca Vista Alegre Km 3½, Planes de Randeros, San Salvador. E: info@salvanatura.org;
W: www.salvanatura.org

Mexico
Pronatura, 1 Calle Pedro Moreno esq. Benito Juárez, Barrio Santa Lucia, San Cristobal de las Casas, Chiapas, 29200.
E: pronatura@pronatura.org.mx;
W: www.pronatura.org.mx; Pub: *(annual report)*

Puerto Rico (to USA)
Sociedad Ornitológica Puertorriqueña, Inc. (SOPI), PO Box 195166, San Juan, 00919-5166.
E: directivasopi@yahoo.com; W: www.sopipr.org;
Pub: *El Bien-Te-Veo (magazine)*

Uruguay
Aves Uruguay (GUPECA), Canelones 1164, Montevideo.
E: info@avesuruguay.org.uy; W: www.avesuruguay.org.uy;
Pub: *Achara (magazine)*

ASIA

PARTNERS

Bhutan
Royal Society for the Protection of Nature, PO Box 325, Building #25, Lhado Lam Kawajangsa, Thimphu-11001.
E: rspn@rspnbhutan.org; W: www.rspnbhutan.org;
Pub: *Rangzhin (newsletter); (annual report)*

(China) Hong Kong
Hong Kong Birdwatching Society, (HKBS) 7C, V Ga Building, 532 Castle Peak Road, Lai Chi Kok, Kowloon.
E: hkbws@hkbws.org.uk;
W: www.hkbws.org.hk;
Pub: *Hong Kong Bird Report; HKBWS (bulletin)*. HKBWS currently operates BirdLife's Direct Action Programme in China.

India
Bombay Natural History Society (BNHS), Hornbill House, Shaheed Bhagat Singh Road, Mumbai, 400 001.
E: director@bnhs.org; W: www.bnhs.org;
Pub: *Hornbill (magazine); Journal of BNHS (scientific)*

Japan
Wild Bird Society of Japan (WBSJ), Maruw Bldg, 3-9-23, Nishi-Gotanda, Shinagawa-ku, Tokyo 141-0031.
E: hogo@wbsj.org; W: www.wbsj.org; Pub: *Wild Bird (magazine); Toriino (magazine); Strix (scientific)*

Malaysia
Malaysian Nature Society (MNS), PO Box 10750, Kuala Lumpur 50724. E: mns@mns.org.my; W: www.mns.my;
Pub: *Pencinta Alam (newsletter); Malaysian Naturalist (magazine); Malayan Nature Journal (scientific)*

Myanmar
Biodiversity and Nature Conservation Association (BANCA), No.943, Second Floor (right), Kyeikwine Pagoda Road, Ward (3), Mayangone Township, Yangon.
E: bancamayanmar@gmail.com;
W: www.banca-env.org

Nepal

Bird Conservation Nepal (BCN), PO Box 12465, Uttardhoka,Lazimpat, Kathmandu.
E: bcn@birdlifenepal.org;
W: www.birdlifenepal.org

Philippines
Haribon Foundation, 2/F, Santos and Sons Building, 973 Aurora Blvd, Cubao, Quezon CIty 1109.
E: act@haribon.org.ph; W: www.haribon.org.ph

Singapore
Nature Society (Singapore) (NSS), 510 Geylang Road, #02-05, The Sunflower, 398466. E: contact@nss.org.sg; W: www.nss.org.sg; Pub: *Nature News (newsletter); Nature Watch (magazine)*

Taiwan
Chinese Wild Bird Federation CWBF), 1F, No. 3, Lane 36 Jing-Long St., 116 Taipei. E: mail@bird.org.tw; W: www.bird.org.tw; Pub: *Flying Feather (newsletter)*

Thailand
Bird Conservation Society of Thailand (BCST), 221 Moo 2, Soi Ngamwongwan 2, Tambol Bangkhen, Ampur Meung, Nontaburi 11000.
E: bcst@bcst.or.th;
W: www.bcst.or.th; Pub: *BCST (bulletin)*

AFFILIATES

Indonesia
Burung Indonesia, Jl. Dadali 32, Bogor 16161.
E: birdlife@burung.org; W: www.burung.org

Sri Lanka
Field Ornithology Group of Sri Lanka (FOGSL), Dept of Zoology, Univ of Colombo, Colombo 03. E: fogsl@cmb.ac.lk; W: http://fogsl.cmb.ac.lk

BIRDLIFE DIRECT ACTION PROGRAMMES

Cambodia
BirdLife International Cambodia Programme, House #32A, Street 494, Sangkat Phsar Daeum Thkov, Chamkarmon, Phnom Penh. E: admin@birdlifecambodia.org

Vietnam
BirdLife International in Vietnam, Viet Nature Conservation Centre, PO Box 89, 6 Dinh Le, Hanoi.
E: birdlife@birdlife.org.vn

EUROPE & CENTRAL ASIA

PARTNERS

Austria
BirdLife Austria, Museumplatz 1/10/8, AT-1070 Wien.
E: office@birdlife.at; W: www.birdlife.at; Pub: *VogelSchutz in Osterreich (magazine); Egretta (scientific)*

Belarus
BirdLife Belarus (APB), PO Box 306, Minsk, 220050.
E: info@ptushki.org; W: www.ptushki.org; Pub: *Homeland Security birds (newsletter); Birds and We (magazine); Subbuteo (scientific)*

Belgium
(Flanders) Natuurpunt, Coxiestraat 11, Mechelen, BE-2800.
E: info@natuurpunt.be;
W: www.natuurpunt.be;
Pub: *(newsletters); Natuur.blad (magazine)*

(Wallonia) Natagora, Rue Nanon 98, Namur, BE-5000.
E: info@natagora.be; W: www.natagora.be;
Pub: *(newsletter); Natagora (magazine)*

Bulgaria
Bulgarian Society for the Protection of Birds (BSPB), PO Box 50, Sofia, BG-Sofia 1111. E: bspb_hq@bspb.org; W: www.bspb.org; Pub: *(magazine)*

Croatia
Association BIOM, Cazmanska 2, Zagreb, HR, 1000.
E: info@biom.hr; W: www.biom.hr; Pub: *Pogled U Divljinu (magazine)*

BirdLife Cyprus, PO Box 12026, Nicosia, CY-2340.
E: birdlifecyprus@birdlifecyprus.org.cy;
W: www.birdlifecyprus.org; Pub: *Annual Bird Report; (newsletter)*

Czech Republic
Czech Society for Ornithology (CSO), Na Belidle 252/34, Prague, CZ-150 00 Praha 5. E: cso@birdlife.cz;
W: www.birdlife.cz; Pub: *Spolkové Zprávy (information journal); Ptaci Svet (magazine); Sylvia (scientific)*

Denmark
Dansk Ornitologisk Forening (DOF), Vesterbrogade 140, Copenhagen , DK-1620 Copenhagen V. E: dof@dof.dk;
W: www.dof.dk; Pub: *Fuglearet (bird report); Fugle & Natur (magazine); Dansk Ornitologisk Forenings Tidsskrift (scientific)*

Estonia
Estonian Ornithological Society (EOS), Veski 4, Tartu, EE-51005.
E: eoy@eoy.ee; W: www.eoy.ee;
Pub: *Tiiutajat (newsletter); Hirundo (scientific)*

Finland
BirdLife Suomi, Annankatu 29 A 16, Helsinki, FI-00101.
E: toimisto@birdlife.fi; W: www.birdlife.fi; Pub: *Tiira (newsletter); Linnut (magazine & yearbook); Ornis Fennica (scientific)*

France
Ligue pour la Protection des Oiseaux (LPO), Fonderies Royale, 8 rue de Docteur Pujos, BP 90263, FR-17305.
E: lpo@lpo.fr; W: www.lpo.fr; Pub: *Ornithos (journal); L'Oiseau Magazine (magazine); L'Oiseau Mag junior (magazine for juniors); Rapaces de France (magazine)*

Georgia
Society for Nature Conservation (SABUKO), 11/13 Navtlughi Street, 0190 Tbilisi. E: office@sabuko.ge;
W: www.sabuko.ge; Pub: *(newsletter)*

Germany
Nature and Biodiversity Conservation Union (NABU), Charitestr. 3, Berlin, D-10117. E: nabu@nabu.de;
W: www.nabu.de; Pub: *Naturschutz Heute (magazine)*

Gibraltar
Gibraltar Ornithological & Natural History Society (GONHS), The Gibraltar Natural History Field Centre, Jew's Gate, Upper Rock Nature Reserve, PO Box 843, Gibraltar.
E: info@gonhs.org; W: www.gonhs.org; Pub: *Gibraltar Bird Report; Gibraltar Nature News (magazine)*

INTERNATIONAL/BIRDLIFE ORGANISATIONS

Greece
Hellenic Ornithological Society (HOS), Themistokleous 80, Athens, GR-10861. E: info@ornithologiki.gr; W: www.ornithologiki.gr; Pub: *(newsletter)*

Hungary
Magyar Madártani és Természetvédelmi Egyesület (MME), Kolto u. 21, Budapest, H-1121. E: mme@mme.hu; W: www.mme.hu; Pub: *(newsletter); Madártávlat (magazine); Ornis Hungarica (scientific)*

Ireland
BirdWatch Ireland, Unit 20, Block D, Bullford Business Campus, Kilcoole, Co Wicklow. E: info@birdwatchireland.org; W: www.birdwatchireland.ie; Pub: *eWings (newsletter); Wings (magazine); Bird Detectives (children's magazine); Irish Birds (scientific)*

Israel
Society for the Protection of Nature in Israel (SPNI), Hanagev 2, Tel-Aviv 66186. E: ioc@inter.net.il; W: www.natureisrael.org; Pub: *(newsletter)*

Italy
Lega Italiana Protezione Uccelli (LIPU), Via Udine 3/a, Parma, IT-43100. E: info@lipu.it; W: www.lipu.it; Pub: *(newsletter); Ali & Ali Junior (magazines)*

Kazakhstan
Association for the Conservation of Biodiversity of Kazakhstan (ACBK), Beibitshilik 18, Astana, 020000. E: acbk@acbk.kz; W: www.acbk.kz; Pub: *Saiga News (newsletter); Remez (newsletter); Selevinia (scientific)*

Latvia
Latvian Ornithological Society (LOB), A.k. 105, Riga, LV-1046. E: putni@lob.lv; W: www.lob.lv; Pub: *Putni Daba (magazine)*

Luxembourg
Natur&ëmwelt, Kräizhaff, 5 Route de Luxembourg, Kockelscheuer, L-1899. E: secretariat@naturewelt.lu; W: www.naturemwelt.lu; Pub: *(newsletter); Regulus (magazine)*

Malta
BirdLife Malta, 57 /28, Triq Abate Rigord, Ta' Xbiex, XBX 1120. E: info@birdlifemalta.org; W: www.birdlifemalta.org; Pub: *Bird's Eye View (magazine); Il-Huttafa (children's magazine); Il-Merill (scientific)*

Netherlands
Society for the Protection of Birds (VBN), PO Box 925, NL-3700 AX. E: info@vogelbescherming.nl; W: www.vogelbescherming.nl; Pub: *(newsletter); Vogels (magazine); Vogels Junior (children's magazine)*

Norway
Norwegian Ornithological Society (NOF), Sandgata, Trondheim, N-7012. E: nof@birdlife.no; W: www.birdlife.no; Pub: *Var Fuglefauna (magazine); Fuglevennen (magazine); Ornis Norvegica (scientific)*

Poland
Polish Society for the Protection of Birds (OTOP), ul. Odrowaza 24, Marki 05-270. E: office@otop.org.pl; W: www.otop.org.pl; Pub: *(newsletter); Ptaki (magazine)*

Portugal
Portuguese Society for the Study of Birds (SPEA), Avenida Columbano Bordalo Pinheiro, 87, 3.° Andar, 11070-062, Lisboa. E: spea@spea.pt; W: www.spea.pt; Pub: *(newsletters); Pardela (magazine); AIRO (scientific)*

Romania
Romanian Ornithological Society (SOR)/BirdLife Romania, Bd. Hristo Botev, nr. 3, ap 6, Bucuresti, 030231. E: office@sor.ro; W: www.sor.ro; Pub: *(newsletter)*

Slovakia
SOS/BirdLife, Zelinarska 4, Bratislava, SK-821 08. E: vtaky@vtaky.sk; W: www.birdlife.sk; Pub: *Vtáky (magazine); Tichodroma (scientific)*

Slovenia
BirdLife Slovenia (DOPPS), Tržaška 2, p.p. 2990, Ljubljana, SI-1001. E: dopps@dopps.si; W: www.ptice.si; Pub: *Svet Ptic (magazine); Acrocephalus (scientific)*

Spain
SEO/BirdLife, Melquiades Biencinto 34, Madrid, ES-28053. E: seo@seo.org; W: www.seo.org; Pub: *Aves y Naturaleza (magazine); Ardeola (scientific)*

Sweden
Swedish Ornithological Society (SOF), Stenhusa Gard, Morbylanga, SE-380 62. E: info@birdlife.se; W: www.birdlife.se; Pub: *Vår Flågelvärld (magazine); Ornis Svecica (scientific)*

Switzerland
SVS/BirdLife Switzerland, PO Box Wiedingstrasse 78, Zurich, CH-8036. E: svs@birdlife.ch; W: www.birdlife.ch; Pub: *(newsletters); Ornis/Ornis Junior (magazines); Info BirdLife Suisse/Schweiz (magazines)*

Ukraine
Ukrainian Society for the Protection of Birds (USBP), PO Box 33, Kyivv, 01003. E: uspb@birdlife.org.ua; W: www.birdlife.org.ua; Pub: *'Bird' (magazine)*

United Kingdom (see National listing)
Royal Society for the Protection of Birds (RSPB), The Lodge, Sandy, Bedfordshire, SG19 2DL. W: www.rspb.org.uk

PARTNERS DESIGNATE

Azerbaijan
Azerbaijan Ornithological Society (AOS), M. Mushbig Street 4B, Ap. 60, Baku, AZ1021. E: info@aos.az; W: www.aos.az

Iceland
Fuglavernd - BirdLife Iceland (ISPB), Hverfisgata 105, 101 Reykjavík, IS, IS-101. E: fuglavernd@fuglavernd.is; W: www.fuglavernd.is; Pub: *Fuglar (magazine)*

Turkey
Doğa Derneği (DD), Orhanlı Mahallesi, 7102 sokak No:1, Seferihisar/İzmir. E: doga@dogadernegi.org; W: www.dogadernegi.org; Pub: *(newsletter); Kuş Sesi (magazine)*

AFFILIATES

Faroe Islands
Faroese Orginithological Society (FOS), Postboks 1230, FO-110 Torshavn. E: ffff@kallnet.fo; W: www.faroenature.net

Liechtenstein
Botanish-Zoologische Gesellschaft (BZG), St.Markusgasse 19, FL-9490 Vaduz. E: bzg@bzg.li or renat@renat.li; W: www.bzg.li

Lithuania
Lithuanian Ornithological Society (LOD), Naugarduko St. 47-3, Vilnius, LT-03208. E: lod@birdlife.lt; W: www.birdlife.lt; Pub: *Paukščiai (magazine)*

Montenegro
Center for Protection & Research of Birds of Montenegro (CZIP), Veliše Mugoše bb, Podgorica, 81 000. E: czip@czip.me; W: www.czip.me

North Macedonia
Macedonian Ecological Society (MES), Bul. Boris Trajkovski ul.7 br.9A, 1000 Skopje. E: contact@mes.org.mk; W: www.mes.org.mk

Serbia
Bird Protection and Study Society of Serbia, Radnička 20a, Novi Sad, 21000. E: sekretar@pticesrbije.rs; W: www.pticesrbije.rs; Pub: *Detlić (magazine); Ciconia (scientific)*

Uzbekistan
Uzbekistan Society for the Protection of Birds (UzSPB), Off. 501, Institute of Gene Pool of Plants & Animals of Academy of Science, 32-Durmon-yuki Street, Tashkent 100125. E: roman.kashkarov@iba.uz; W: www.uzspb.uz; Pub: *(newsletter)*

MIDDLE EAST

PARTNERS

Jordan
Royal Society of the Conservation of Nature (RSCN), PO Box 6354, Jubeiha-Abu-Nusseir Circle 11183, Amman. E: adminrscn@rscn.org.jo; W: www.rscn.org.jo

Lebanon
Society for the Protection of Nature in Lebanon (SPNL), Awad Bldg, 6th Floor Abdel Aziz Street, PO Box: 11-5665, Beirut. E: spnlorg@cyberia.net.lb; W: www.spnl.org; Pub: *Wings & Waves (newsletter)*

Palestine
Palestine Wildlife Society (PWLS), PO Box 89, Beit Sahour, Palestine. E: pwls@wildlife-pal.org; W: www.wildlife-pal.org

AFFILIATES

Iraq
Nature Iraq, House 29, Street 77, Qtr 104 Ashti, Sulaymaniyah. E: info@natureiraq.org; W: www.natureiraq.org; Pub: *(newsletter)*

Kuwait
Kuwait Environment Protection Society (KEPS), PO Box 1896, Safat 13019. E: info@keps.org.kw; W: www.keps.org.kw

Saudi Arabia
Saudi Wildlife Authority (SWA), Riyadh. E: ncwcd@zajil.net; W: www.swa.gov.sa

Syria
Syrian Society for Conservation of Wildlife (SSCW), Al-Mazza- Al-Sheikh Saad, Shabaan Building No. 20 - 1st Floor, Damascus. E: sscw.syria@gmail.com

PACIFIC

PARTNERS

Australia
BirdLife Australia, Suite 2-05, 60 Leicester Street, Carlton, VIC 3053. E: info@birdlife.org.au; W: www.birdlife.org.au; Pub: *BirdLife (e-news); Australian BirdLife (magazine); Australian Field Ornithology (scientific); Emu - Austral Ornithology (scientific)*

Cook Islands
Te Ipukarea Society (TIS), PO Box 649, Rarotonga. E: 2tis@oyster.net.ck or info@tiscookislands.org; W: www.tiscookislands.org; Pub: *(Te Manu newsletter)*

Fiji
Nature Fiji, 14 Hamilton-Beattie Street, Suva. E: support@naturefiji.org; W: www.naturefiji.org; Pub: *(newsletter)*

French Polynesia
Société d'Ornithologie de Polynésie (MANU), Residence du plateau Mitirapa, Lot 48, Impasse Des Acacias B.P. 7023, Taravao, 98719, Tahiti. E: sop@manu.pf; W: www.manu.pf; Pub: *Te Manu (bulletin)*

New Zealand
Forest & Bird, 90 Ghunzee Street, Wellington 6140. E: office@forestandbird.org.nz; W: www.forestandbird.org.nz; Pub: *(newsletters); Forest & Bird (magazine); Wild Things (magazine for children)*

Palau
Palau Conservation Society (PSC), PO Box 1811, Koror, 96940. E: pcs@palaunet.com; W: www.palauconservation.org; Pub: *(newsletter)*

PARTNERS DESIGNATE

New Caledonia (to France)
Société Calédonienne d'Ornithologie (SCO); 41 rue du 18 juin, Nouméa. E: president@sco.asso.nc; W: www.sco.nc; http://sco.over-blog.org

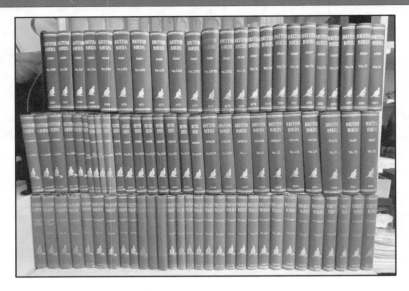

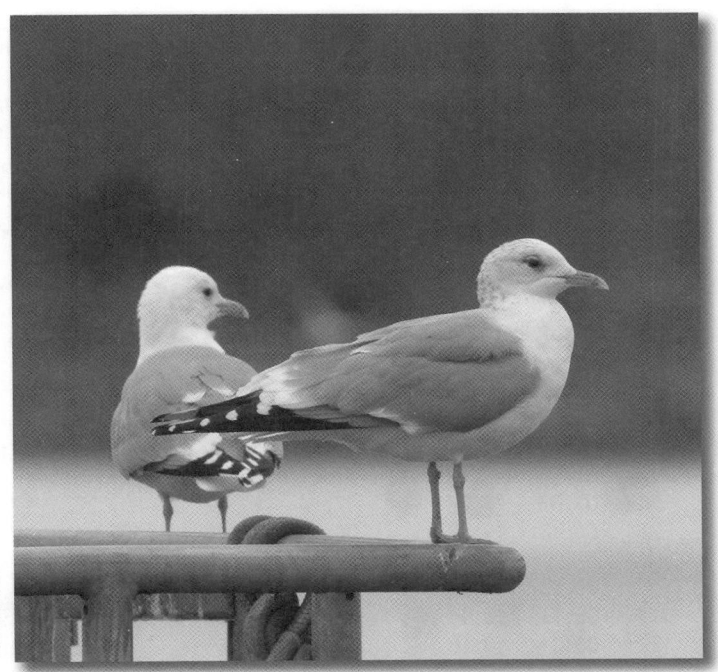

Neil Gartshore

Although widely seen during the winter, the Common Gull *(Larus canus canus)* makes it on to the UK's 'yellow list' of the Birds of Conservation Concern (BOCC4) because of its international importance as a non-breeding species. The UK holds at least 20% of the European wintering population.

QUICK REFERENCE SECTION

SUNRISE & SUNSET TIMES FOR 2021

Predictions are given for the times of sunrise and sunset on every SUNDAY throughout the year. For places on the same latitude as the following, add FOUR minutes for each degree of longitude west (subtract if east).

These times are in Greenwich Mean Time (GMT), except between 01:00 on Mar 28th and 01:00 on Oct 31st, when the times are in British Summer Time (one hour in advance of GMT).

		London		Manchester		Edinburgh	
		Rise	Set	Rise	Set	Rise	Set
January	3	08:06	16:05	08:25	16:03	08:43	15:52
	10	08:03	16:14	08:21	16:13	08:39	16:03
	17	07:58	16:25	08:15	16:24	08:31	16:15
	24	07:50	16:36	08:06	16:37	08:21	16:29
	31	07:40	16:49	07:55	16:50	08:09	16:44
February	7	07:29	17:01	07:43	17:04	07:55	17:00
	14	07:16	17:14	07:29	17:18	07:40	17:15
	21	07:02	17:27	07:14	17:32	07:23	17:30
	28	06:48	17:39	06:59	17:45	07:06	17:45
March	7	06:32	17:52	06:42	17:58	06.49	18:00
	14	06:17	18:04	06:26	18:12	06:30	18:15
	21	06:01	18:16	06:09	18:25	06:12	18:29
	28	06:45	19:28	06:52	19:37	06:54	18:43
April	4	06:29	19:39	06:35	19:50	06:35	19:58
	11	06:13	19:51	06:18	20:03	06:17	20:12
	18	05:58	20:03	06:02	20:16	06:00	20:26
	25	05:44	20:14	05:47	20:28	05:43	20:40
May	2	05:30	20:26	05:32	20:41	05:27	20:54
	9	05:18	20:37	05:19	20:53	05:12	21:08
	16	05:07	20:48	05:07	21:05	04:58	21:22
	23	04:58	20:58	04:57	21:16	04:47	21:34
	30	04:51	21:06	04:48	21:25	04:37	21:45
June	6	04:46	21:13	04:43	21:33	04:31	21:53
	13	04:43	21:19	04:40	21:39	04:27	22:00
	20	04:43	21:21	04:39	21:42	04:26	22:03
	27	04:45	21:22	04:42	21:42	04:29	22:03

SUNRISE & SUNSET TIMES FOR 2021

		London		Manchester		Edinburgh	
		Rise	Set	Rise	Set	Rise	Set
July	4	04:50	21:20	04:47	21:39	04:34	22:00
	11	04:57	21:15	04:54	21:34	04:43	21:53
	18	05:05	21:08	05:03	21:26	04:53	21:44
	25	05:14	20:59	05:14	21:16	05:05	21:33
August	1	05:25	20:48	05:25	21:05	05:17	21:20
	8	05:35	20:36	05:37	20:51	05:31	21:05
	15	05:46	20:23	05:49	20:37	05:44	20:49
	22	05:57	20:08	06:01	20:22	05:58	20:32
	29	06:09	19:53	06:13	20:05	06:12	20:14
September	5	06:20	19:38	06:25	19:49	06:25	19:56
	12	06:31	19:22	06:37	19:32	06:39	19:38
	19	06:42	19:06	06:50	19:15	06:52	19:19
	26	06:53	18:49	07:02	18:57	07:06	19:01
October	3	07:05	18:33	07:14	18:40	07:20	18:42
	10	07:16	18:18	07:27	18:24	07:34	18:24
	17	07:28	18:03	07:40	18:08	07:48	18:07
	24	07:40	17:48	07:53	17:52	08:03	17:50
	31	06:53	16:35	07:06	16:38	07:18	16:34
November	7	07:05	16:23	07:20	16:25	07:33	16:20
	14	07:17	16:12	07:33	16:13	07:47	16:07
	21	07:29	16:04	07:46	16:03	08:01	15:55
	28	07:40	15:57	07:58	15:56	08:14	15:47
December	5	07:49	15:53	08:08	15:51	08:26	15:41
	12	07:57	15:51	08:16	15:49	08:35	15:38
	19	08:03	15:53	08:22	15:50	08:41	15:39
	26	08:06	15:57	08:25	15:54	08:44	15:43

TIDE TABLES FOR January 2021-April 2022

The tide tables on pages 318-321 are for DOVER (location 1 on the map opposite) and cover the period January 2021 to April 2022. All times are shown on the 24-hour clock and relate to GREENWICH MEAN TIME (GMT). An adjustment (add one hour) should be made to the times during BRITISH SUMMER TIME (BST) - in 2021, BST applies from 01:00 on March 28th to 01:00 on October 31st.

The times of high tides at locations 2 to 45 (table below/map opposite) may be obtained by adding or subtracting their 'tidal difference', using the table below (subtractions are indicated by a minus sign). This height (in metres) only applies to the high water level at Dover and will be different in other areas around the country. Note: Care should be taken when making calculations at the beginning and the end of British Summer Time. See worked examples:

Example 1
To calculate the time of high water at Blakeney on November 24th, 2021:
1. Look up the time at Dover (13:21) = 1:21 pm
2. Subtract the tidal difference for Blakeney = minus 4 hours, 07 minutes
3. Therefore the time of high water at Blakeney = 9:14 am

Example 2
To calculate the time of high water at Holy Island on 5th May, 2021:
1. Look up the time at Dover (06:04) = 6:04 am
2. Add 1 hour for British Summer Time = 7:04 am
3. Add the tidal difference for Holy Island = plus 3 hours, 58 minutes
4. Therefore the time of high water at Holy Island = 11:02 am

TIDAL DIFFERENCES

No.	Location	Hours	Minutes
1	Dover	See pp 318-321	
2	Dungeness	-0	12
3	Selsey Bill	0	09
4	Swanage (lst H.W.Springs)	-2	36
5	Portland	-4	23
6	Exmouth (Approaches)	-4	48
7	Salcombe	-5	23
8	Newlyn (Penzance)	5	59
9	Padstow	-5	47
10	Bideford	-5	17
11	Bridgwater	-4	23
12	Sharpness Dock	-3	19
13	Cardiff (Penarth)	-4	16
14	Swansea	-4	52
15	Skomer Island	-5	00
16	Fishguard	-3	48
17	Barmouth	-2	45
18	Bardsey Island	-3	07
19	Caernarvon	-1	07
20	Amlwch	-0	22
21	Connahs Quay	0	20
22	Hilbre Island (Hoylake/West Kirby)	-0	05
23	Morecambe	0	20
24	Silloth	0	51
25	Girvan	0	54
26	Lossiemouth	0	48
27	Fraserburgh	1	20
28	Aberdeen	2	30
29	Montrose	3	30
30	Dunbar	3	42
31	Holy Island	3	58
32	Sunderland	4	38
33	Whitby	5	12
34	Bridlington	5	53
35	Grimsby	-5	20
36	Skegness	-5	00
37	Blakeney	-4	07
38	Gorleston	-2	08
39	Aldeburgh	-0	13
40	Bradwell Waterside	1	11
41	Herne Bay	1	28
42	Sullom Voe	-1	34
43	Lerwick	0	01
44	Kirkwall	-0	26
45	Widewall Bay	-1	30

TIDE TABLES FOR January 2021-April 2022

Tidal predictions for Dover have been computed by the National Oceanographic Centre.

Shetland 42, 43
Orkney 44, 45

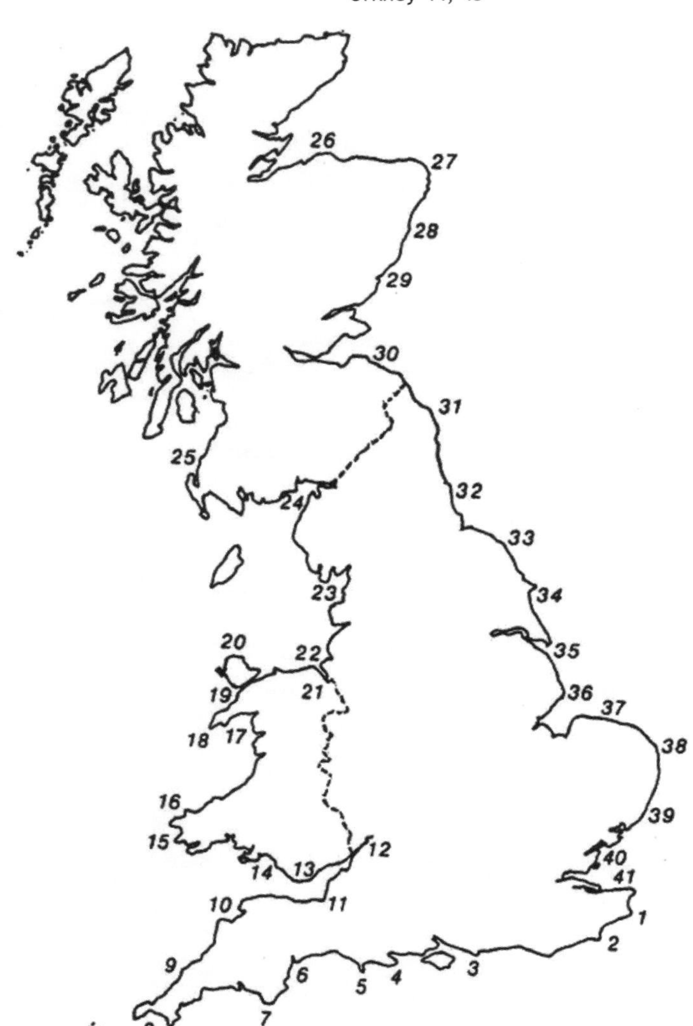

Map showing locations for which tidal differences are given on facing page.

TIDE TABLES JANUARY-APRIL 2021

Time Zone:UT(GMT)

Tidal Predictions : HIGH WATERS 2021

Datum of Predictions = Chart Datum : 3.67 metres below Ordnance Datum (Newlyn)

British Summer Time Dates for 2021 : 28th March to 31st October (data not adjusted)

Units: METRES

DOVER – January

Day		Morning time	m	Afternoon time	m
1 F		00:06	6.47	12:15	6.39
2 Sa		00:45	6.50	12:55	6.37
3 Su		01:26	6.47	13:39	6.28
4 M		02:09	6.38	14:26	6.16
5 Tu		02:56	6.27	15:19	6.01
6 W	D	03:48	6.16	16:19	5.88
7 Th		04:48	6.05	17:24	5.79
8 F		05:54	6.00	18:32	5.77
9 Sa		07:02	6.03	19:41	5.86
10 Su		08:09	6.15	20:47	6.05
11 M		09:10	6.31	21:46	6.27
12 Tu		10:07	6.47	22:38	6.47
13 W	A	10:58	6.57	23:24	6.61
14 Th		11:45	6.60		
15 F		00:06	6.67	12:28	6.54
16 Sa		00:46	6.66	13:09	6.42
17 Su		01:25	6.59	13:48	6.26
18 M		02:04	6.46	14:28	6.06
19 Tu		02:45	6.27	15:12	5.81
20 W	B	03:27	6.01	16:00	5.54
21 Th		04:17	5.71	16:57	5.28
22 F		05:17	5.43	18:07	5.12
23 Sa		06:29	5.28	19:21	5.15
24 Su		07:40	5.32	20:25	5.35
25 M		08:39	5.51	21:16	5.62
26 Tu		09:27	5.75	21:58	5.91
27 W		10:07	5.98	22:35	6.17
28 Th	C	10:44	6.21	23:12	6.40
29 F		11:22	6.40	23:50	6.59
30 Sa				12:02	6.54
31 Su		00:30	6.71	12:44	6.60

DOVER – February

Day		Morning time	m	Afternoon time	m
1 M		01:12	6.75	13:27	6.56
2 Tu		01:54	6.71	14:11	6.45
3 W		02:36	6.60	14:57	6.28
4 Th	D	03:21	6.44	15:48	6.06
5 F		04:15	6.21	16:48	5.81
6 Sa		05:19	5.95	17:59	5.60
7 Su		06:35	5.76	19:22	5.55
8 M		07:57	5.78	20:42	5.75
9 Tu		09:09	5.98	21:43	6.04
10 W		10:08	6.20	22:32	6.32
11 Th	A	10:55	6.37	23:13	6.52
12 F		11:36	6.47	23:51	6.65
13 Sa				12:13	6.49
14 Su		00:27	6.70	12:48	6.45
15 M		01:02	6.68	13:23	6.36
16 Tu		01:36	6.58	13:56	6.21
17 W		02:09	6.42	14:29	6.00
18 Th		02:42	6.17	15:03	5.74
19 F	B	03:18	5.86	15:45	5.43
20 Sa		04:04	5.49	16:43	5.12
21 Su		05:12	5.15	18:09	4.94
22 M		06:43	5.02	19:39	5.06
23 Tu		08:03	5.21	20:44	5.40
24 W		09:00	5.55	21:31	5.80
25 Th		09:44	5.91	22:11	6.16
26 F		10:23	6.25	22:49	6.48
27 Sa	C	11:01	6.52	23:28	6.74
28 Su		11:42	6.72		

DOVER – March

Day		Morning time	m	Afternoon time	m
1 M		00:09	6.91	12:24	6.81
2 Tu		00:50	6.98	13:06	6.78
3 W		01:30	6.94	13:49	6.65
4 Th		02:11	6.79	14:33	6.44
5 F		02:56	6.55	15:22	6.14
6 Sa	D	03:49	6.20	16:22	5.78
7 Su		04:56	5.79	17:37	5.44
8 M		06:22	5.49	19:14	5.36
9 Tu		07:58	5.54	20:37	5.62
10 W		09:12	5.81	21:34	5.97
11 Th		10:05	6.08	22:18	6.26
12 F		10:45	6.28	22:55	6.48
13 Sa	A	11:19	6.40	23:30	6.62
14 Su		11:52	6.47		
15 M		00:03	6.69	12:24	6.47
16 Tu		00:36	6.68	12:54	6.41
17 W		01:06	6.59	13:22	6.29
18 Th		01:32	6.43	13:48	6.12
19 F		01:57	6.22	14:15	5.91
20 Sa		02:27	5.95	14:51	5.63
21 Su	B	03:07	5.59	15:42	5.29
22 M		04:10	5.18	17:04	4.98
23 Tu		05:51	4.94	18:50	4.99
24 W		07:26	5.11	20:06	5.34
25 Th		08:30	5.52	20:59	5.80
26 F		09:16	5.95	21:42	6.22
27 Sa		09:57	6.34	22:21	6.59
28 Su	C	10:36	6.64	23:00	6.87
29 M		11:17	6.85	23:42	7.04
30 Tu		11:59	6.93		
31 W		00:23	7.10	12:42	6.89

DOVER – April

Day		Morning time	m	Afternoon time	m
1 Th		01:05	7.03	13:27	6.73
2 F		01:48	6.82	14:12	6.48
3 Sa		02:36	6.50	15:03	6.15
4 Su	D	03:33	6.08	16:04	5.75
5 M		04:43	5.62	17:22	5.40
6 Tu		06:18	5.36	19:01	5.35
7 W		07:54	5.49	20:19	5.62
8 Th		09:00	5.77	21:13	5.95
9 F		09:48	6.03	21:54	6.22
10 Sa		10:24	6.21	22:30	6.42
11 Su		10:55	6.34	23:03	6.55
12 M	A	11:26	6.42	23:36	6.61
13 Tu		11:57	6.44		
14 W		00:08	6.59	12:27	6.40
15 Th		00:36	6.49	12:51	6.30
16 F		00:58	6.35	13:15	6.17
17 Sa		01:22	6.18	13:42	6.00
18 Su		01:51	5.96	14:17	5.78
19 M		02:32	5.65	15:07	5.47
20 Tu	B	03:36	5.28	16:28	5.18
21 W		05:15	5.06	18:05	5.15
22 Th		06:47	5.22	19:24	5.44
23 F		07:54	5.61	20:21	5.88
24 Sa		08:43	6.03	21:08	6.30
25 Su		09:27	6.41	21:50	6.66
26 M		10:08	6.69	22:31	6.92
27 Tu	C	10:51	6.87	23:13	7.07
28 W		11:35	6.93	23:57	7.08
29 Th				12:21	6.87
30 F		00:44	6.96	13:09	6.72

National Oceanography Centre (www.noc.ac.uk)

Time Zone:UT(GMT)

Tidal Predictions : HIGH WATERS 2021

Units: METRES

Datum of Predictions = Chart Datum : 3.67 metres below Ordnance Datum (Newlyn)

British Summer Time Dates for 2021 : 28th March to 31st October (data not adjusted)

DOVER

January

		Morning		Afternoon	
		time	m	time	m
1 F		00:06	6.47	12:15	6.39
2 Sa		00:45	6.50	12:55	6.37
3 Su		01:26	6.47	13:39	6.28
4 M		02:09	6.38	14:26	6.16
5 Tu		02:56	6.27	15:19	6.01
6 W	D	03:48	6.16	16:19	5.88
7 Th		04:48	6.05	17:24	5.79
8 F		05:54	6.00	18:32	5.77
9 Sa		07:02	6.03	19:41	5.86
10 Su		08:09	6.15	20:47	6.05
11 M		09:10	6.31	21:46	6.27
12 Tu		10:07	6.47	22:38	6.47
13 W	A	10:58	6.57	23:24	6.61
14 Th		11:45	6.60		
15 F		00:06	6.67	12:28	6.54
16 Sa		00:46	6.66	13:09	6.42
17 Su		01:25	6.59	13:48	6.26
18 M		02:04	6.46	14:28	6.06
19 Tu		02:45	6.27	15:12	5.81
20 W	B	03:27	6.01	16:00	5.54
21 Th		04:17	5.71	16:57	5.28
22 F		05:17	5.43	18:07	5.12
23 Sa		06:29	5.28	19:21	5.15
24 Su		07:40	5.32	20:25	5.35
25 M		08:39	5.51	21:16	5.62
26 Tu		09:27	5.75	21:58	5.91
27 W		10:07	5.98	22:35	6.17
28 Th	C	10:44	6.21	23:12	6.40
29 F		11:22	6.40	23:50	6.59
30 Sa				12:02	6.54
31 Su		00:30	6.71	12:44	6.60

DOVER

February

		Morning		Afternoon	
		time	m	time	m
1 M		01:12	6.75	13:27	6.56
2 Tu		01:54	6.71	14:11	6.45
3 W		02:36	6.60	14:57	6.28
4 Th	D	03:21	6.44	15:48	6.06
5 F		04:15	6.21	16:48	5.81
6 Sa		05:19	5.95	17:59	5.60
7 Su		06:35	5.76	19:22	5.55
8 M		07:57	5.78	20:42	5.75
9 Tu		09:09	5.98	21:43	6.04
10 W		10:08	6.20	22:32	6.32
11 Th	A	10:55	6.37	23:13	6.52
12 F		11:36	6.47	23:51	6.65
13 Sa				12:13	6.49
14 Su		00:27	6.70	12:48	6.45
15 M		01:02	6.68	13:23	6.36
16 Tu		01:36	6.58	13:56	6.21
17 W		02:09	6.42	14:29	6.00
18 Th		02:42	6.17	15:03	5.74
19 F	B	03:18	5.86	15:45	5.43
20 Sa		04:04	5.49	16:43	5.12
21 Su		05:12	5.15	18:09	4.94
22 M		06:43	5.02	19:39	5.06
23 Tu		08:03	5.21	20:44	5.40
24 W		09:00	5.55	21:31	5.80
25 Th		09:44	5.91	22:11	6.16
26 F		10:23	6.25	22:49	6.48
27 Sa	C	11:01	6.52	23:28	6.74
28 Su		11:42	6.72		

DOVER

March

		Morning		Afternoon	
		time	m	time	m
1 M		00:09	6.91	12:24	6.81
2 Tu		00:50	6.98	13:06	6.78
3 W		01:30	6.94	13:49	6.65
4 Th		02:11	6.79	14:33	6.44
5 F		02:56	6.55	15:22	6.14
6 Sa	D	03:49	6.20	16:22	5.78
7 Su		04:56	5.79	17:37	5.44
8 M		06:22	5.49	19:14	5.36
9 Tu		07:58	5.54	20:37	5.62
10 W		09:12	5.81	21:34	5.97
11 Th		10:05	6.08	22:18	6.26
12 F		10:45	6.28	22:55	6.48
13 Sa	A	11:19	6.40	23:30	6.62
14 Su		11:52	6.47		
15 M		00:03	6.69	12:24	6.47
16 Tu		00:36	6.68	12:54	6.41
17 W		01:06	6.59	13:22	6.29
18 Th		01:32	6.43	13:48	6.12
19 F		01:57	6.22	14:15	5.91
20 Sa		02:27	5.95	14:51	5.63
21 Su	B	03:07	5.59	15:42	5.29
22 M		04:10	5.18	17:04	4.98
23 Tu		05:51	4.94	18:50	4.99
24 W		07:26	5.11	20:06	5.34
25 Th		08:30	5.52	20:59	5.80
26 F		09:16	5.95	21:42	6.22
27 Sa		09:57	6.34	22:21	6.59
28 Su	C	10:36	6.64	23:00	6.87
29 M		11:17	6.85	23:42	7.04
30 Tu		11:59	6.93		
31 W		00:23	7.10	12:42	6.89

DOVER

April

		Morning		Afternoon	
		time	m	time	m
1 Th		01:05	7.03	13:27	6.73
2 F		01:48	6.82	14:12	6.48
3 Sa		02:36	6.50	15:03	6.15
4 Su	D	03:33	6.08	16:04	5.75
5 M		04:43	5.62	17:22	5.40
6 Tu		06:18	5.36	19:01	5.35
7 W		07:54	5.49	20:19	5.62
8 Th		09:00	5.77	21:13	5.95
9 F		09:48	6.03	21:54	6.22
10 Sa		10:24	6.21	22:30	6.42
11 Su		10:55	6.34	23:03	6.55
12 M	A	11:26	6.42	23:36	6.61
13 Tu		11:57	6.44		
14 W		00:08	6.59	12:27	6.40
15 Th		00:36	6.49	12:51	6.30
16 F		00:58	6.35	13:15	6.17
17 Sa		01:22	6.18	13:42	6.00
18 Su		01:51	5.96	14:17	5.78
19 M		02:32	5.65	15:07	5.47
20 Tu	B	03:36	5.28	16:28	5.18
21 W		05:15	5.06	18:05	5.15
22 Th		06:47	5.22	19:24	5.44
23 F		07:54	5.61	20:21	5.88
24 Sa		08:43	6.03	21:08	6.30
25 Su		09:27	6.41	21:50	6.66
26 M		10:08	6.69	22:31	6.92
27 Tu	C	10:51	6.87	23:13	7.07
28 W		11:35	6.93	23:57	7.08
29 Th				12:21	6.87
30 F		00:44	6.96	13:09	6.72

National Oceanography Centre (www.noc.ac.uk)

Time Zone:UT(GMT)

Tidal Predictions : HIGH WATERS 2021

Datum of Predictions = Chart Datum : 3.67 metres below Ordnance Datum (Newlyn)

British Summer Time Dates for 2021 : 28th March to 31st October (data not adjusted)

Units: METRES

DOVER — January

Day		Morning time	m	Afternoon time	m
1 F		00:06	6.47	12:15	6.39
2 Sa		00:45	6.50	12:55	6.37
3 Su		01:26	6.47	13:39	6.28
4 M		02:09	6.38	14:26	6.16
5 Tu		02:56	6.27	15:19	6.01
6 W	D	03:48	6.16	16:19	5.88
7 Th		04:48	6.05	17:24	5.79
8 F		05:54	6.00	18:32	5.77
9 Sa		07:02	6.03	19:41	5.86
10 Su		08:09	6.15	20:47	6.05
11 M		09:10	6.31	21:46	6.27
12 Tu		10:07	6.47	22:38	6.47
13 W	A	10:58	6.57	23:24	6.61
14 Th		11:45	6.60		
15 F		00:06	6.67	12:28	6.54
16 Sa		00:46	6.66	13:09	6.42
17 Su		01:25	6.59	13:48	6.26
18 M		02:04	6.46	14:28	6.06
19 Tu		02:45	6.27	15:12	5.81
20 W	B	03:27	6.01	16:00	5.54
21 Th		04:17	5.71	16:57	5.28
22 F		05:17	5.43	18:07	5.12
23 Sa		06:29	5.28	19:21	5.15
24 Su		07:40	5.32	20:25	5.35
25 M		08:39	5.51	21:16	5.62
26 Tu		09:27	5.75	21:58	5.91
27 W		10:07	5.98	22:35	6.17
28 Th	C	10:44	6.21	23:12	6.40
29 F		11:22	6.40	23:50	6.59
30 Sa				12:02	6.54
31 Su		00:30	6.71	12:44	6.60

DOVER — February

Day		Morning time	m	Afternoon time	m
1 M		01:12	6.75	13:27	6.56
2 Tu		01:54	6.71	14:11	6.45
3 W		02:36	6.60	14:57	6.28
4 Th	D	03:21	6.44	15:48	6.06
5 F		04:15	6.21	16:48	5.81
6 Sa		05:19	5.95	17:59	5.60
7 Su		06:35	5.76	19:22	5.55
8 M		07:57	5.78	20:42	5.75
9 Tu		09:09	5.98	21:43	6.04
10 W		10:08	6.20	22:32	6.32
11 Th	A	10:55	6.37	23:13	6.52
12 F		11:36	6.47	23:51	6.65
13 Sa				12:13	6.49
14 Su		00:27	6.70	12:48	6.45
15 M		01:02	6.68	13:23	6.36
16 Tu		01:36	6.58	13:56	6.21
17 W		02:09	6.42	14:29	6.00
18 Th		02:42	6.17	15:03	5.74
19 F	B	03:18	5.86	15:45	5.43
20 Sa		04:04	5.49	16:43	5.12
21 Su		05:12	5.15	18:09	4.94
22 M		06:43	5.02	19:39	5.06
23 Tu		08:03	5.21	20:44	5.40
24 W		09:00	5.55	21:31	5.80
25 Th		09:44	5.91	22:11	6.16
26 F		10:23	6.25	22:49	6.48
27 Sa	C	11:01	6.52	23:28	6.74
28 Su		11:42	6.72		

DOVER — March

Day		Morning time	m	Afternoon time	m
1 M		00:09	6.91	12:24	6.81
2 Tu		00:50	6.98	13:06	6.78
3 W		01:30	6.94	13:49	6.65
4 Th		02:11	6.79	14:33	6.44
5 F		02:56	6.55	15:22	6.14
6 Sa	D	03:49	6.20	16:22	5.78
7 Su		04:56	5.79	17:37	5.44
8 M		06:22	5.49	19:14	5.36
9 Tu		07:58	5.54	20:37	5.62
10 W		09:12	5.81	21:34	5.97
11 Th		10:05	6.08	22:18	6.26
12 F		10:45	6.28	22:55	6.48
13 Sa	A	11:19	6.40	23:30	6.62
14 Su		11:52	6.47		
15 M		00:03	6.69	12:24	6.47
16 Tu		00:36	6.68	12:54	6.41
17 W		01:06	6.59	13:22	6.29
18 Th		01:32	6.43	13:48	6.12
19 F		01:57	6.22	14:15	5.91
20 Sa		02:27	5.95	14:51	5.63
21 Su	B	03:07	5.59	15:42	5.29
22 M		04:10	5.18	17:04	4.98
23 Tu		05:51	4.94	18:50	4.99
24 W		07:26	5.11	20:06	5.34
25 Th		08:30	5.52	20:59	5.80
26 F		09:16	5.95	21:42	6.22
27 Sa		09:57	6.34	22:21	6.59
28 Su	C	10:36	6.64	23:00	6.87
29 M		11:17	6.85	23:42	7.04
30 Tu		11:59	6.93		
31 W		00:23	7.10	12:42	6.89

DOVER — April

Day		Morning time	m	Afternoon time	m
1 Th		01:05	7.03	13:27	6.73
2 F		01:48	6.82	14:12	6.48
3 Sa		02:36	6.50	15:03	6.15
4 Su	D	03:33	6.08	16:04	5.75
5 M		04:43	5.62	17:22	5.40
6 Tu		06:18	5.36	19:01	5.35
7 W		07:54	5.49	20:19	5.62
8 Th		09:00	5.77	21:13	5.95
9 F		09:48	6.03	21:54	6.22
10 Sa		10:24	6.21	22:30	6.42
11 Su		10:55	6.34	23:03	6.55
12 M	A	11:26	6.42	23:36	6.61
13 Tu		11:57	6.44		
14 W		00:08	6.59	12:27	6.40
15 Th		00:36	6.49	12:51	6.30
16 F		00:58	6.35	13:15	6.17
17 Sa		01:22	6.18	13:42	6.00
18 Su		01:51	5.96	14:17	5.78
19 M		02:32	5.65	15:07	5.47
20 Tu	B	03:36	5.28	16:28	5.18
21 W		05:15	5.06	18:05	5.15
22 Th		06:47	5.22	19:24	5.44
23 F		07:54	5.61	20:21	5.88
24 Sa		08:43	6.03	21:08	6.30
25 Su		09:27	6.41	21:50	6.66
26 M		10:08	6.69	22:31	6.92
27 Tu	C	10:51	6.87	23:13	7.07
28 W		11:35	6.93	23:57	7.08
29 Th				12:21	6.87
30 F		00:44	6.96	13:09	6.72

National Oceanography Centre (www.noc.ac.uk)

Time Zone:UT(GMT) — Tidal Predictions : HIGH WATERS 2021 — Units: METRES

Datum of Predictions = Chart Datum : 3.67 metres below Ordnance Datum (Newlyn)

British Summer Time Dates for 2021 : 28th March to 31st October (data not adjusted)

DOVER — January

Day		Morning time	m	Afternoon time	m
1 F		00:06	6.47	12:15	6.39
2 Sa		00:45	6.50	12:55	6.37
3 Su		01:26	6.47	13:39	6.28
4 M		02:09	6.38	14:26	6.16
5 Tu		02:56	6.27	15:19	6.01
6 W	D	03:48	6.16	16:19	5.88
7 Th		04:48	6.05	17:24	5.79
8 F		05:54	6.00	18:32	5.77
9 Sa		07:02	6.03	19:41	5.86
10 Su		08:09	6.15	20:47	6.05
11 M		09:10	6.31	21:46	6.27
12 Tu		10:07	6.47	22:38	6.47
13 W	A	10:58	6.57	23:24	6.61
14 Th		11:45	6.60		
15 F		00:06	6.67	12:28	6.54
16 Sa		00:46	6.66	13:09	6.42
17 Su		01:25	6.59	13:48	6.26
18 M		02:04	6.46	14:28	6.06
19 Tu		02:45	6.27	15:12	5.81
20 W	B	03:27	6.01	16:00	5.54
21 Th		04:17	5.71	16:57	5.28
22 F		05:17	5.43	18:07	5.12
23 Sa		06:29	5.28	19:21	5.15
24 Su		07:40	5.32	20:25	5.35
25 M		08:39	5.51	21:16	5.62
26 Tu		09:27	5.75	21:58	5.91
27 W		10:07	5.98	22:35	6.17
28 Th	C	10:44	6.21	23:12	6.40
29 F		11:22	6.40	23:50	6.59
30 Sa				12:02	6.54
31 Su		00:30	6.71	12:44	6.60

DOVER — February

Day		Morning time	m	Afternoon time	m
1 M		01:12	6.75	13:27	6.56
2 Tu		01:54	6.71	14:11	6.45
3 W		02:36	6.60	14:57	6.28
4 Th	D	03:21	6.44	15:48	6.06
5 F		04:15	6.21	16:48	5.81
6 Sa		05:19	5.95	17:59	5.60
7 Su		06:35	5.76	19:22	5.55
8 M		07:57	5.78	20:42	5.75
9 Tu		09:09	5.98	21:43	6.04
10 W		10:08	6.20	22:32	6.32
11 Th	A	10:55	6.37	23:13	6.52
12 F		11:36	6.47	23:51	6.65
13 Sa				12:13	6.49
14 Su		00:27	6.70	12:48	6.45
15 M		01:02	6.68	13:23	6.36
16 Tu		01:36	6.58	13:56	6.21
17 W		02:09	6.42	14:29	6.00
18 Th		02:42	6.17	15:03	5.74
19 F	B	03:18	5.86	15:45	5.43
20 Sa		04:04	5.49	16:43	5.12
21 Su		05:12	5.15	18:09	4.94
22 M		06:43	5.02	19:39	5.06
23 Tu		08:03	5.21	20:44	5.40
24 W		09:00	5.55	21:31	5.80
25 Th		09:44	5.91	22:11	6.16
26 F		10:23	6.25	22:49	6.48
27 Sa	C	11:01	6.52	23:28	6.74
28 Su		11:42	6.72		

DOVER — March

Day		Morning time	m	Afternoon time	m
1 M		00:09	6.91	12:24	6.81
2 Tu		00:50	6.98	13:06	6.78
3 W		01:30	6.94	13:49	6.65
4 Th		02:11	6.79	14:33	6.44
5 F		02:56	6.55	15:22	6.14
6 Sa	D	03:49	6.20	16:22	5.78
7 Su		04:56	5.79	17:37	5.44
8 M		06:22	5.49	19:14	5.36
9 Tu		07:58	5.54	20:37	5.62
10 W		09:12	5.81	21:34	5.97
11 Th		10:05	6.08	22:18	6.26
12 F		10:45	6.28	22:55	6.48
13 Sa	A	11:19	6.40	23:30	6.62
14 Su		11:52	6.47		
15 M		00:03	6.69	12:24	6.47
16 Tu		00:36	6.68	12:54	6.41
17 W		01:06	6.59	13:22	6.29
18 Th		01:32	6.43	13:48	6.12
19 F		01:57	6.22	14:15	5.91
20 Sa		02:27	5.95	14:51	5.63
21 Su	B	03:07	5.59	15:42	5.29
22 M		04:10	5.18	17:04	4.98
23 Tu		05:51	4.94	18:50	4.99
24 W		07:26	5.11	20:06	5.34
25 Th		08:30	5.52	20:59	5.80
26 F		09:16	5.95	21:42	6.22
27 Sa		09:57	6.34	22:21	6.59
28 Su	C	10:36	6.64	23:00	6.87
29 M		11:17	6.85	23:42	7.04
30 Tu		11:59	6.93		
31 W		00:23	7.10	12:42	6.89

DOVER — April

Day		Morning time	m	Afternoon time	m
1 Th		01:05	7.03	13:27	6.73
2 F		01:48	6.82	14:12	6.48
3 Sa		02:36	6.50	15:03	6.15
4 Su	D	03:33	6.08	16:04	5.75
5 M		04:43	5.62	17:22	5.40
6 Tu		06:18	5.36	19:01	5.35
7 W		07:54	5.49	20:19	5.62
8 Th		09:00	5.77	21:13	5.95
9 F		09:48	6.03	21:54	6.22
10 Sa		10:24	6.21	22:30	6.42
11 Su		10:55	6.34	23:03	6.55
12 M	A	11:26	6.42	23:36	6.61
13 Tu		11:57	6.44		
14 W		00:08	6.59	12:27	6.40
15 Th		00:36	6.49	12:51	6.30
16 F		00:58	6.35	13:15	6.17
17 Sa		01:22	6.18	13:42	6.00
18 Su		01:51	5.96	14:17	5.78
19 M		02:32	5.65	15:07	5.47
20 Tu	B	03:36	5.28	16:28	5.18
21 W		05:15	5.06	18:05	5.15
22 Th		06:47	5.22	19:24	5.44
23 F		07:54	5.61	20:21	5.88
24 Sa		08:43	6.03	21:08	6.30
25 Su		09:27	6.41	21:50	6.66
26 M		10:08	6.69	22:31	6.92
27 Tu	C	10:51	6.87	23:13	7.07
28 W		11:35	6.93	23:57	7.08
29 Th				12:21	6.87
30 F		00:44	6.96	13:09	6.72

National Oceanography Centre (www.noc.ac.uk)

MAP OF SEA AREAS

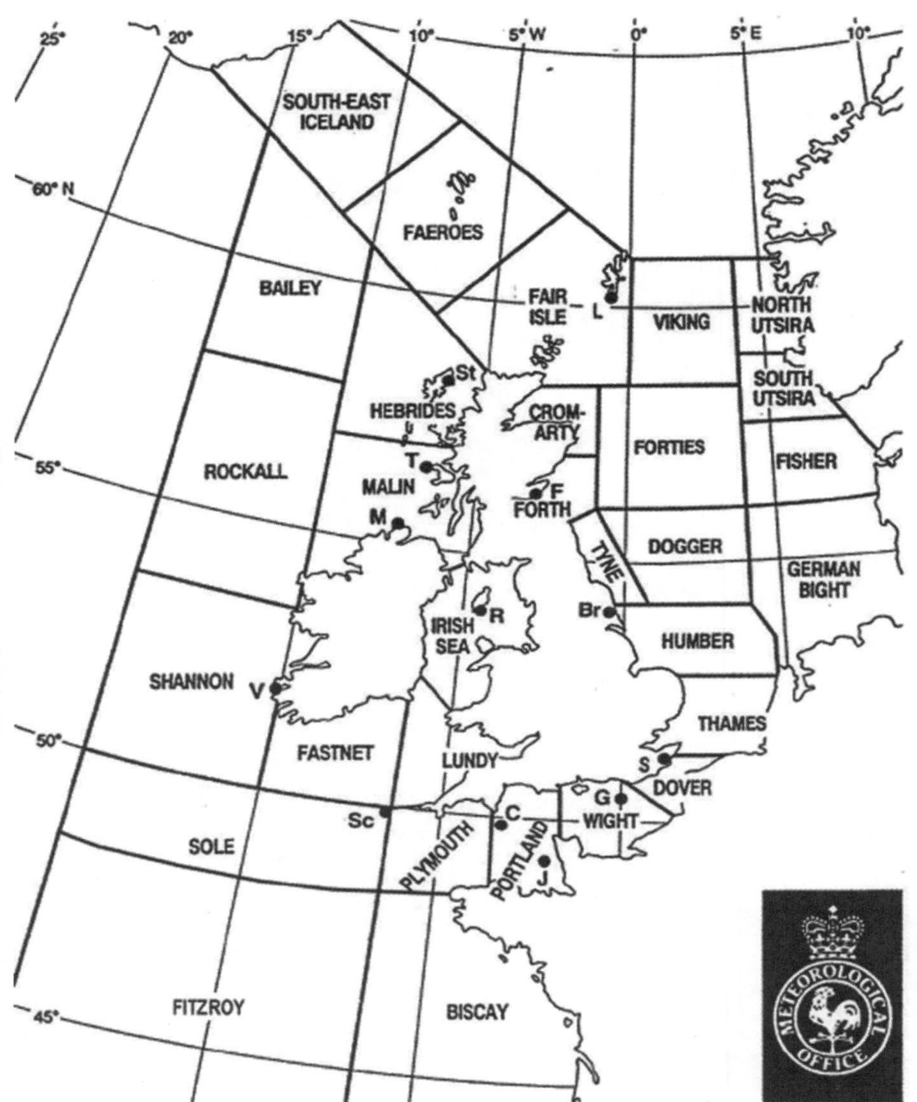

STATIONS WHOSE LATEST REPORTS ARE BROADCAST IN THE 5-MINUTE FORECASTS

Br Bridlington; C Channel Light-Vessel Automatic; F Fife Ness; G Greenwich Light-Vessel Automatic; J Jersey; L Lerwick; M Malin Head; R Ronaldsway; S Sandettie Light-Vessel Automatic; Sc Scilly Automatic; St Stornoway; T Tiree; V Valentia.

BEAUFORT WIND SCALE (Sea)

Scale	Description	MPH	Knots	State of the Sea
0	Calm	<1	<1	Sea surface smooth and mirror-like.
1	Light Air	1-3	1-3	Scaly ripples/no crests.
2	Light Breeze	4-7	4-6	Small wavelets, crests glassy - no breaking.
3	Gentle Breeze	8-12	7-10	Large wavelets, crests begin to break, scattered whitecaps
4	Moderate Breeze	13-18	11-16	Moderate waves taking longer form, many whitecaps, some spray.
5	Fresh Breeze	19-24	17-21	Small waves - becoming longer, fairly frequent whitecaps.
6	Strong Breeze	25-31	22-27	Large waves, whitecap common, more spray.
7	Near Gale	32-38	28-33	Sea heaps up & white foam streaks off breaking waves.
8	Gale	39-46	34-40	Moderately high waves of greater length, edges of crests begin to break into spindrift, foam blown in streaks.
9	Strong Gale	47-54	41-47	High waves, dense streaks of foam, sea begins to roll, spray may reduce visibility.
10	Storm	55-63	48-55	Very high waves with overhanging crest, sea white with densely blown foam, heavy rolling, lowered visibility.
11	Violent Storm	64-72	56-63	Exceptionally high waves, foam patches cover sea, visibility more reduced.
12	Hurricane	73+	64+	Air filled with foam, waves over 45ft, sea completely white with driving spray, visibility greatly reduced.

THE COUNTRYSIDE CODE

Launched on 12 July 2004, this Code for England has been produced through a partnership between the Countryside Agency and Countryside Council for Wales.

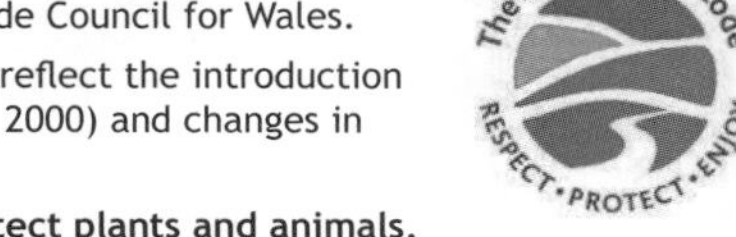

The Countryside Code has been revised and re-launched to reflect the introduction of new open access rights (Countryside & Rights of Way Act 2000) and changes in society over the last 20 years.

• Be safe - plan ahead
Follow any signs, even when going out locally, it's best to get the latest information about where and when you can go; for example, your rights to go onto some areas of open land may be restricted while work is carried out, for safety reasons or during breeding seasons. Follow advice and local signs, and be prepared for the unexpected.

• Leave gates and property as you find them
Please respect the working life of the countryside, as our actions can affect people's livelihoods, our heritage, and the safety and welfare of animals and ourselves.

• Protect plants and animals, and take your litter home
We have a responsibility to protect our countryside now and for future generations, so make sure you don't harm animals, birds, plants, or trees.

• Keep dogs under close control
The countryside is a great place to exercise dogs, but it's every owner's duty to make sure their dog is not a danger or nuisance to farm animals, wildlife or other people.

• Consider other people
Showing consideration and respect for other people makes the countryside a pleasant Environment for everyone - at home, at work and at leisure.

BIRDS OF CONSERVATION CONCERN (BOCC) 4

The 4th list of the BOCC was published in December 2015 - the species under the 'Red', 'Yellow' and 'Green' categories are listed below. The full details of the assessment was published in *British Birds* 108, 708-746:

Eaton MA, Aebischer NJ, Brown AF, Hearn RD, Lock L, Musgrove AJ, Noble DG, Stroud DA and Gregory RD (2015). Birds of Conservation Concern 4: the population status of birds in the United Kingdom, Channel Islands and Isle of Man.

RED LIST
White-fronted Goose
Pochard
Scaup
Long-tailed Duck
Common Scoter
Velvet Scoter
Black Grouse
Capercaillie
Grey Partridge
Balearic Shearwater
Shag
Red-necked Grebe
Slavonian Grebe
White-tailed Eagle
Hen Harrier
Corncrake
Lapwing
Ringed Plover
Dotterel
Whimbrel
Curlew
Black-tailed Godwit
Ruff
Red-necked Phalarope
Woodcock
Arctic Skua
Puffin
Roseate Tern
Kittiwake
Herring Gull
Turtle Dove
Cuckoo
Lesser Spotted Woodpecker
Merlin
Golden Oriole
Red-backed Shrike
Willow Tit
Marsh Tit
Skylark
Wood Warbler
Grasshopper Warbler
Savi's Warbler
Aquatic Warbler
Marsh Warbler
Starling
Ring Ouzel
Fieldfare
Song Thrush
Redwing
Mistle Thrush
Spotted Flycatcher
Nightingale
Pied Flycatcher
Black Redstart
Whinchat
House Sparrow
Tree Sparrow
Yellow Wagtail
Grey Wagtail
Tree Pipit
Hawfinch
Linnet
Twite
Lesser Redpoll
Yellowhammer
Cirl Bunting
Corn Bunting

YELLOW LIST
Mute Swan
Bewick's Swan
Whooper Swan
Bean Goose
Pink-footed Goose
Greylag Goose
Barnacle Goose
Brent Goose
Shelduck
Wigeon
Gadwall
Teal
Mallard
Pintail
Garganey
Shoveler
Eider
Goldeneye
Smew
Quail
Red Grouse
Black-throated Diver
Great northern Diver
Fulmar
Manx Shearwater
Storm Petrel
Leach's Petrel
Gannet
Bittern
Spoonbill
Black-necked Grebe
Honey Buzzard
Marsh Harrier
Montagu's Harrier
Osprey
Spotted Crake
Crane
Stone Curlew
Avocet
Oystercatcher
Grey Plover
Bar-tailed Godwit
Turnstone
Knot
Curlew Sandpiper
Sanderling
Dunlin
Purple Sandpiper
Common Sandpiper
Green Sandpiper
Spotted Redshank
Greenshank
Wood Sandpiper
Redshank
Snipe
Great Skua
Black Guillemot
Razorbill
Guillemot
Little Tern
Sandwich Tern
Common Tern
Arctic Tern
Black-headed Gull
Mediterranean Gull
Common Gull
Lesser black-backed Gull
Yellow-legged Gull
Caspian Gull
Iceland Gull
Glaucous Gull
Great black-backed Gull
Stock Dove
Tawny Owl
Short-eared Owl
Nightjar
Swift
Kingfisher
Kestrel
Shorelark
House Martin
Willow Warbler
Dartford Warbler
Short-toed Treecreeper
Dipper
Redstart
Dunnock
Meadow Pipit
Water Pipit
Bullfinch
Mealy Redpoll
Scottish Crossbill
Parrot Crossbill
Snow Bunting
Lapland Bunting
Reed Bunting

BIRDS OF CONSERVATION CONCERN (BOCC) 4

GREEN LIST
Tufted Duck
Red-breasted Merganser
Goosander
Ptarmigan
Red-throated Diver
Great Shearwater
Sooty Shearwater
Great Cormorant
Little Egret
Grey Heron
Little Grebe
Great Crested Grebe
Red Kite
Goshawk
Sparrowhawk
Buzzard
Golden Eagle
Water Rail
Moorhen
Coot
Golden Plover
Little Ringed Plover
Little Stint
Jack Snipe
Pomarine Skua
Long-tailed Skua
Little Auk
Black Tern
Little Gull
Rock Dove
Wood Pigeon
Collared Dove
Barn Owl
Long-eared Owl
Green Woodpecker
Great Spotted Woodpecker
Hobby
Peregrine
Chough
Magpie
Jay
Jackdaw
Rook
Carrion Crow
Hooded Crow
Raven
Goldcrest
Firecrest
Blue Tit
Great Tit
Crested Tit
Coal Tit
Bearded Tit
Woodlark
Sand Martin
Swallow
Cetti's Warbler
Long-tailed Tit
Chiffchaff
Blackcap
Garden Warbler
Lesser Whitethroat
Whitethroat
Sedge Warbler
Reed Warbler
Waxwing
Nuthatch
Treecreeper
Wren
Blackbird
Robin
Stonechat
Wheatear
Pied Wagtail
Rock Pipit
Brambling
Chaffinch
Greenfinch
Crossbill
Goldfinch
Siskin

SCHEDULE 1 SPECIES

Under the provisions of the Wildlife and Countryside Act 1981 the following bird species (listed in Schedule 1 - Part I of the Act) are protected by special penalties at all times.

Avocet
Bee-eater
Bittern
Bittern, Little
Bluethroat
Brambling
Bunting, Cirl
Bunting, Lapland
Bunting, Snow
Buzzard, Honey
Chough
Corncrake
Crake, Spotted
Crossbills (all species)
Divers (all species)
Dotterel
Duck, Long-tailed
Eagle, Golden
Eagle, White-tailed
Falcon, Gyr
Fieldfare
Firecrest
Garganey
Godwit, Black-tailed
Goshawk
Grebe, Black-necked
Grebe, Slavonian
Greenshank
Gull, Little
Gull, Mediterranean
Harriers (all species)
Heron, Purple
Hobby
Hoopoe
Kingfisher
Kite, Red
Merlin
Oriole, Golden
Osprey
Owl, Barn
Owl, Snowy
Peregrine
Petrel, Leach's
Phalarope, Red-necked
Plover, Kentish
Plover, Little Ringed
Quail, Common
Redstart, Black
Redwing
Rosefinch, Scarlet
Ruff
Sandpiper, Green
Sandpiper, Purple
Sandpiper, Wood
Scaup
Scoter, Common
Scoter, Velvet
Serin
Shorelark
Shrike, Red-backed
Spoonbill
Stilt, Black-winged
Stint, Temminck's
Stone-curlew
Swan, Bewick's
Swan, Whooper
Tern, Black
Tern, Little
Tern, Roseate
Tit, Bearded
Tit, Crested
Treecreeper, Short-toed
Warbler, Cetti's
Warbler, Dartford
Warbler, Marsh
Warbler, Savi's
Whimbrel
Woodlark
Wryneck

The following birds and their eggs (listed in Schedule 1 - Part II of the Act) are protected by special penalties during the close season, which is Feb 1 to Aug 31 (Feb 21 to Aug 31 below high water mark), but may be killed outside this period - Goldeneye, Greylag Goose (in Outer Hebrides, Caithness, Sutherland, and Wester Ross only), Pintail.

BIRD REPORTS

Looking for a local Bird Report?

Check out the 'County Directory' for details of where to get the latest copies for each county.

To find those reports that are long out of print, contact:

STEVE HOLLIDAY
(Birds Reports/Journals)

2 Larriston Place, Cramlington,
Northumberland NE23 8ER
T: 01670 731 963 (eves/w.ends)
E: birdreports@hotmail.co.uk

Or check out Steve's latest list on the Calluna Books website:

www.callunabooks.co.uk/
sales_and_wanted.html
(and follow the link)

'BEST BIRDWATCHING SITES' GUIDES

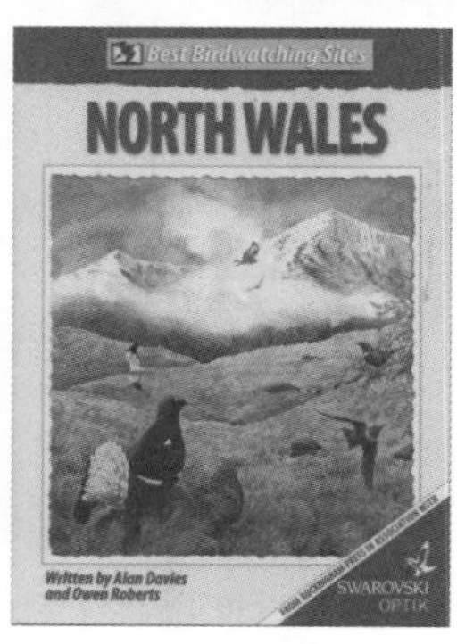

The UK's leading site guides are available for:

Cornwall & Scilly
Dorset
Norfolk (3rd ed)
North Wales (revised ed)
North-east England
Sussex (out of print)
The Scottish Highlands (2nd ed)
The Solway
Yorkshire

Accurate information • Detailed Maps • Helpful Advice • Terrific Value

To place an order, contact Buckingham Press
online - www.buckinghampress.co.uk
or by phone - 01733 561 739